Revisiting the Contracts Scholarship of Stewart Macaulay

On the Empirical and the Lyrical

Edited by

Jean Braucher
John Kidwell
and
William C Whitford

·HART·
PUBLISHING
OXFORD AND PORTLAND, OREGON
2013

Published in the United Kingdom by Hart Publishing Ltd
16C Worcester Place, Oxford, OX1 2JW
Telephone: +44 (0)1865 517530
Fax: +44 (0)1865 510710
E-mail: mail@hartpub.co.uk
Website: http://www.hartpub.co.uk

Published in North America (US and Canada) by
Hart Publishing
c/o International Specialized Book Services
920 NE 58th Avenue, Suite 300
Portland, OR 97213-3786
USA
Tel: +1 503 287 3093 or toll-free: (1) 800 944 6190
Fax: +1 503 280 8832
E-mail: orders@isbs.com
Website: http://www.isbs.com

British Library Cataloguing in Publication Data
Data Available

ISBN: 978-1-84946-301-0

Typeset by Hope Services (Abingdon) Ltd
Printed and bound in Great Britain by
MPG Books Ltd

International Studies in the Theory of Private Law

This series of books edited by a distinguished international team of legal scholars aims to investigate the normative and theoretical foundations of the law governing relations between citizens. The context for such investigations of private law systems is set by important modern tendencies in systems of governance. The advent of the regulatory state marks the withdrawal of the state from direct control and management of social and economic activity, and the adoption instead of procedural regulation and co-regulatory strategies that promote the use of private law techniques of ordering and self-regulation in social and economic interactions between citizens. The tendency known as globalisation and the corresponding increases in cross-border trade produce the responses of transnational regulation of commerce and private governance regimes, and these new systems of governance challenge the hegemony of traditional national private law systems. Furthermore, these tendencies towards transnational governance regimes compel an interaction between different national legal traditions, with their differences in culture and philosophy as well as their differences based upon variations in market systems, which provokes questions not only about competing policy frameworks but also about the nature and adequacy of different kinds of legal reasoning.

The series encompasses a diverse range of theoretical approaches in the examination of these issues including approaches using socio-legal methods, economics, critical theory, systems theory, regulation theory, and moral and political theory. With the aim of stimulating an international discussion of these issues, volumes will be published in Germany, France and the United Kingdom in one of the three languages.

Volumes published with Hart Publishing, Oxford

1. David Campbell, Hugh Collins and John Wightman (eds), *Implicit Dimensions of Contract: Discrete, Relational and Network Contracts* (2003)
2. Christian Joerges, Inger-Johanne Sand and Gunther Teubner (eds), *Transnational Governance and Constitutionalism* (2004)
3. Oren Perez, *Ecological Sensitivity and Global Legal Pluralism: Rethinking the Trade and Environment Debate* (2004)
4. Harm Schepel, *The Constitution of Private Governance* (2004)
5. Nili Cohen and Ewan McKendrick, *Comparative Remedies for Breach of Contract* (2005)
6. Marc Amstutz and Gunther Teubner (eds), *Networks: Legal Issues of Multilateral Co-operation* (2010)

7. Gunther Teubner (edited and with an Introduction by Hugh Collins), *Networks as Connected Contracts* (2010)
8. Christian Joerges and Josef Falke (eds), *Karl Polanyi, Globalisation and the Potential of Law in Transnational Markets* (2011)
9. Poul F Kjaer, Gunther Teubner and Alberto Febbrajo (eds), *The Financial Crisis in Constitutional Perspective: The Dark Side of Functional Differentiation* (2011)

Volumes published in German by Nomos Verlagsgesellschaft, Baden-Baden

1. Peer Zumbansen, *Ordnungsmuster im modern Wohlfahrtsstaat: Lernerfahrungen zwischen Staat, Geseelschaft und Vertrag* (2000)
2. Dan Wielsch, *Freiheit und Funktion: Zur Struktur- und Theoriegeschichte des Rechts der Wirtschaftsgesellschaft* (2001)
3. Marc Amstutz, *Evolutorisches Wirtschaftsrecht: Vorstudien zum Recht und seiner Methode in den Diskurskollisionen der Marktgesellschaft* (2001)
4. Christian Joerges and Gunther Teubner, Gunther (eds), *Rechtsverfassungsrecht: Recht-Fertigungen zwischen Sozialtheorie und Privatrechtsdogmatik* (2003)
5. Gunther Teubner, *Netzwerk als Vertragsverbund: Virtuelle Unternehmen, Franchising, Just in Time in sozialwissenschaftlicher und juristischer Sicht* (2004)
6. Daniel Dédeyan, *Macht durch Zeichen: Rechtsprobleme der Kennzeichnung und Zertifikation* (2004)
7. Dietrich Claus Becker, *Von Namen und Nummern: Kollisionen unverträglicher Rechtsmassen im Interent* (2005)
8. Vagias Karavas, *Digitale Grundrechte: Elemente einer Verfassung des Informationsflusses im Intenet* (2007)
9. Cordula Heldt, *Baukooperation und Franchising als multilaterale Sonderverbindung. Vertragsnetzwerke – Parallelschuldverhältnisse – Personengesellschaften* (2010)
10. Peter Korth, *Dritthaftung von Ratingagenturen* (2009)
11. *Jan Lüsing, Die Pflichten aus culpa in contrahendo und positiver Vertragsverletzung* (§ 241 II BGB): *Über den hybriden Charakter der Schutzpflichten und zur Selbstbindung ohne Vertrag* (2010)
12. Moritz Renner, *Zwingendes transnationales Recht: Elemente einer Wirtschaftsverfassung jenseits des Staates* (2010)

Preface

Overview

Stewart Macaulay began his extremely productive academic career at the Wisconsin Law School in 1957. He was assigned to teach Contracts as his first course. The pre-eminent scholar at the Law School at that time was Professor Willard Hurst, a man who had pioneered interdisciplinary scholarship in law schools. Hurst was renowned for how generous he was in giving time and assistance to his younger colleagues.[1] Not long before, Macaulay had begun a very successful marriage and intellectual collaboration with Jacqueline Ramsey.[2] Jacqueline's father, John R (Jack) Ramsey, had been general manager of SC Johnson & Sons, a worldwide manufacturing company with headquarters in Racine, Wisconsin. Conversations with his father-in-law led Macaulay to conduct an extensive empirical study of business practices and then write the paper that became his most famous article, 'Non-Contractual Relations in Business – A Preliminary Study'.[3] Hurst was very interested in this paper and connected Macaulay to some prominent sociologists of the day, leading to its publication in the *American Sociological Review*.[4] Hurst thus helped to launch Macaulay in a direction that has resulted in his recognition as a leading scholar in both contracts and the interdisciplinary study of law.

Throughout the 1960s, both before and after the publication of this most famous paper, Macaulay published other articles that, though not as well known, nonetheless broke new paths in contracts scholarship and have

[1] S Macaulay, 'In Memoriam: Willard's Law School?', (1997) 1997 *Wisconsin Law Review* 1163, 1170 (describing the ways in which Hurst was an 'ideal mentor').

[2] Macaulay credits his late wife with making his career possible, not the least because until her death she edited all his publications: 'A Jackie edit was thorough and challenging. She had to understand every sentence and see why it was where it was in the manuscript.' S Macaulay, 'Crime and Custom in Business Society', (1995) 22 *Journal of Law and Society* 248–58.

[3] In addition to Jack Ramsey's influence on 'Non-Contractual Relations in Business', his correspondence with Frank Lloyd Wright concerning the Johnson building in Racine inspired a later article. S Macaulay, 'Organic Transactions: Contract, Frank Lloyd Wright and the Johnson Building,' (1996) 1996 *Wisconsin Law Review* 75, fn a (noting that Jacqueline Macaulay found her father's correspondence with Frank Lloyd Wright).

[4] For fuller accounts of the circumstances surrounding the preparation and publication of Macaulay's most famous article, see Macaulay, 'In Memoriam' (n 1) 1170; Macaulay, 'Crime and Custom' (n 2) 248–58. The article has been included in an anthology of the 20 most important works of American legal thought. D Kennedy and W Fisher, *The Canon of American Legal Thought* (Princeton, Princeton University Press, 2006) 445–59.

proved highly influential. Macaulay became, along with his good friend, Ian Macneil, one of the two legal theorists to participate in the founding of what has become known as relational contract theory. Sparked by Macaulay's formal retirement (though he continues to teach and write), the Wisconsin Law School decided to host a conference revisiting his early scholarship and reflecting on its impact on subsequent contracts scholarship. Sixteen well-known contracts scholars from the UK and the USA were invited to present papers and all responded affirmatively. The conference was held in Madison on 21–22 October 2011. Fifteen of the papers were later revised and are included in this volume.

This volume begins with a reproduction of Macaulay's most famous article. It also provides excerpts from another article from the 1960s, 'Private Legislation and the Duty To Read – Business Run by IBM Machine, the Law of Contracts and Credit Cards',[5] and from a more contemporary Macaulay article that is much commented upon, 'The Real and the Paper Deal: Empirical Pictures of Relationships, Complexity and the Urge for Transparent Simple Rules'.[6] Preceding these excerpts there is a bibliography of all of Macaulay's major publications.

We have divided the 15 conference papers into four sections, as shown in the Table of Contents. Such categorisations are inevitably oversimplifications, and perhaps even misleading. There are cross-currents in many of the papers that could have led to placement in a different section. What is common to all the papers is that they refer to one or more of Macaulay's early contracts articles, reflecting on their influence on subsequent scholarship by others and their relevance to current developments.

In the first section there are four papers that discuss the relationship of Macaulay's work to contract and legal theory. Robert W Gordon, in 'Is the World of Contracting Relations One of Spontaneous Order or Pervasive State Action? Stewart Macaulay Scrambles the Public–Private Distinction', describes how Macaulay's work makes it difficult to maintain that there is a strong public/private dichotomy, despite the importance of that distinction to so many of the most influential works on contract theory. Edward Rubin, in 'Empiricism's Crucial Question and the Transformation of the Legal System', relates Macaulay's commitment to empirical studies to theories about how equilibriums in social and legal theory and practice get dislodged and readjusted. Rubin draws on the important work of Niklas Luhman and Gunther Teubner. Robert Scott, in 'The Promise and the Peril of Relational Contract Theory', identifies two schools of thought in American relational contract theory – one identified with the law and economics tradition and the other with the law and society tradition. Scott

[5] S Macaulay, 'Private Legislation and the Duty To Read – Business Run by IBM Machine, the Law of Contracts and Credit Cards' (1966) 19 *Vanderbilt Law Review* 1051.

[6] S Macaulay, 'The Real and the Paper Deal: Empirical Pictures of Relationships, Complexity and the Urge for Transparent Simple Rules' (2003) 66 *Modern Law Review* 44.

calls for the two schools to respect each other's traditions and to draw together, in order not to become overwhelmed by contract theorists who pay no attention to empirical studies on contracting behaviour. Jay Feinman, in 'Ambition and Humility in Contract Law', explores the rich theoretical organisation of contract and legal system policies developed in Macaulay's early article, 'Private Legislation and the Duty to Read'.[7] Feinman concludes that Macaulay's theoretical construct continues to be powerful both as description and as a tool for critical evaluation of contract law in action.

The second section also contains four papers, all dealing in various ways with contractual practices between businesses. David Campbell, in 'What Do We Mean By the Non-Use of Contract?', defends the relevance of legal rules to contracts between businesses, but argues that our traditional legal theory – classical contract law – needs to be discarded, in favour of a theory that understands that co-operation, not adversarialness, is the core principle reflected in both contractual behaviour and, as properly understood, contract law. Li-Wen Lin and Josh Whitford, in 'Conflict and Collaboration in Business Organisation: A Preliminary Study', present empirical findings in their quantitative study of the dynamics between co-operation and conflict in inter-organisational networks; they argue that not only dyads but also triads of allied businesses need to be examined to understand these dynamics. Their paper also traces how Macaulay's 'Non-Contractual Relations in Business – A Preliminary Study' anticipated and influenced many of the themes in contemporary economic sociology. Claire A Hill, in 'What Mistakes Do Lawyers Make in Complex Business Contracts, And What Can and Should be Done About Them?', offers a typology of mistakes lawyers make in written contracts created in complex business deals and speculates why these mistakes persist. Because of the limited (though not negligible) impact of the content of written contracts on how businesspeople behave in contract performance, she concludes that the mistakes do little harm and perhaps even some good. Brian Bix, in 'The Role of Contract: Stewart Macaulay's Lessons from Practice', emphasises Macaulay's critique of formalism in both legal education and scholarship, as well as Macaulay's teaching that the true subject of contract law is the actual practices and promises of business people and other parties engaged in transactions.

Our third section contains papers concerning contractual relations where at least one party is an individual, acting in a consumer or other non-business capacity. Ethan Leib, in 'What is the Relational Theory of Consumer Form Contract?', argues that the doctrine of 'reasonable expectations' offers the best judicial tool for policing consumer deals and that

[7] Macaulay, 'Private Legislation' (n 5).

the key question is what counts as a reasonable expectation, a question that he believes should be empirically evaluated. Carol Sanger, in 'Acquiring Children Contractually: Relational Contracts at Work at Home', addresses use of contracts to provide for post-adoption visitation rights. She draws upon the relational approach to contracts generally and also on an article published by Jacqueline and Stewart Macaulay in 1978, 'Adoption for Black Children: A Case Study of Expert Discretion'.[8] Charles Knapp, in 'Is There a "Duty to Read"?', examines recent case law concerning this sometimes asserted duty and develops a suggested judicial methodology for deciding whether to hold parties to a signed writing. He argues that reading should not be conceived of as a duty and that assent in these circumstances should be no more than a rebuttable presumption.

The final section contains four papers using relational contract theory to critique various contract doctrines. William J Woodward Jr, in 'Restitution Without Context: An Examination of the Losing Contract Problem in the *Restatement (Third) of Restitution*', builds upon Macaulay's 1959 article, 'Restitution in Context'.[9] Woodward examines the Restatement's complex compromise approach to the losing contract problem, which is to use the 'contract rate' to set recovery, and questions both its normative premises and predicted effects. John Wightman, in 'Contract in a Pre-Realist world: Professor Macaulay, Lord Hoffmann and the Rise of Context in the English Law of Contract', explores a number of opinions by Lord Hoffmann in English House of Lords (now the Supreme Court) decisions, and argues that these decisions have allowed prevailing business practices, of the type effectively studied and exposed by Macaulay, to influence the application of historic doctrines of neoclassical contract law, particularly with respect to the availability of consequential damages. Deborah Post, in 'The Deregulatory Effects of Seventh Circuit Jurisprudence', critiques several contract law opinions by Judges Richard Posner and Frank Easterbrook of the Seventh Circuit Court of Appeals (in the USA), arguing that they fail to use Macaulay's commitment to understanding what is actually happening in a transaction to help reach a result that is fair and just. Gordon Smith, in 'Doctrines of Last Resort', offers a view about why such contract law doctrines as good faith, fiduciary duty and unjust enrichment play an important role in controlling opportunistic party behaviour. Such behaviour is mostly deterred by informal social sanctions, as Macaulay has observed, but in Smith's view these 'doctrines of last resort' play an important supportive role precisely when informal sanctions prove inadequate.

[8] J Macaulay and S Macaulay, 'Adoption for Black Children: A Case Study of Expert Discretion' in R Simon (ed), *Research in Law and Sociology: An Annual Compilation of Research* (Greenwich, JAI Press, 1978) 265–318.

[9] S Macaulay, 'Restitution in Context' (1959) 107 *University of Pennsylvania Law Review* 1133.

MACAULAY'S TEACHING MATERIALS

No accounting of Stewart Macaulay's impact on the world of the academic study of contract law and behaviour would be complete without some discussion of the contracts teaching materials that bear his (and our) names.[10] Since no paper describes these materials, we provide a brief account here. These materials express a distinct point of view, closely associated with Macaulay's early contracts scholarship. They use the term 'Law in Action' to describe their perspective, which emphasises how legal doctrine influences or fails to influence the behaviour of contracting parties (and others). The materials include several in-depth contextual discussions of contractual interactions, why litigation occurred, and how the litigation affected the relationship.[11] They stress that law is not free and that the haves often come out ahead. The approach is challenging for both teachers and students, a point acknowledged in an introductory chapter:

> One major theme of the course is that things are not as they seem. But debunking can be upsetting. It can lead to a resigned cynicism that undercuts any effort toward bettering the world. It is true that naïve idealism may seriously mislead those whose goal is to effect change . . . We think good lawyers are skeptical idealists, aware of how the system works but unwilling to retreat into an easy cynicism.[12]

These materials have their origin in Macaulay's early teaching career. When Macaulay began teaching at Wisconsin in 1957 and was assigned Contracts as a class, he adopted a casebook co-authored by Malcolm Sharp, one of his mentors as a Bigelow Fellow at the University of Chicago Law School.[13] That casebook emphasised competing themes of autonomy and a minimal state as opposed to regulation as a way of achieving social justice. Macaulay immediately began to supplement the casebook with materials emphasising the law in action. Later his long-time colleagues and casebook co-editors, Whitford and Kidwell, joined the Wisconsin law faculty, and both used and contributed to the growing set of supplementary materials. When the other great relational contract legal theorist of the era, Ian Macneil, produced his first casebook in 1971, Macaulay and his Wisconsin contracts colleagues adopted it.[14] It was not many years

[10] S Macaulay and others (eds), *Contracts: Law in Action*, 3rd edn (New Providence, LexisNexis, 2010).

[11] The materials were significantly influenced by Richard Danzig's important book, *The Capability Problem in Contract Law*, first published in 1978 (Mineola, Foundation Press) and intended as a supplement to a traditional Contracts casebook. Macaulay and his colleagues contributed importantly to Danzig's initial book.

[12] Macaulay and others, *Contracts: Law in Action* (n 10) 26–27.

[13] F Kessler and M Sharp, *Contracts: Cases and Materials* (New York, Prentice-Hall, 1953).

[14] I Macneil, *Cases and Materials on Contracts: Exchange Transactions and Relationships* (Mineola, Foundation Press, 1971). The Wisconsin contracts teachers actually used a prepublication draft of these materials and offered feedback to Macneil before publication.

later, however, when a Wisconsin supplement to the Macneil casebook began growing. Within the decade the supplement had become so voluminous that the Wisconsin contracts group abandoned the Macneil casebook and began teaching from their own materials that were produced annually by the very efficient 'Copy Shop' at the Wisconsin Law School. For the next decade and more the materials received annual revisions, contributed to by all of Macaulay's colleagues at Wisconsin who were teaching Contracts. The materials were finally stabilised and published, initially in 1993.[15] For the current third edition, published in 2010, Jean Braucher of the University of Arizona College of Law joined the group of editors.[16] The casebook is now adopted in approximately 15 law schools.

DEBTS OF GRATITUDE

Our greatest debt of gratitude goes to the authors of the papers that make up this volume. We also are indebted to many other academics who served as discussants at the conference or who attended and participated in the debate.[17] The conference itself was hosted by the Wisconsin Law School, through the auspices of its Institute for Legal Studies.[18] We are grateful for institutional support provided by the Institute and the Law School. We are especially indebted to the Institute's Associate Director, Pamela Hollenhorst. Her skill and experience in running conferences are extraordinary. Without Pam's able efforts and wise guidance, the conference would never have happened.

This book would not have come to fruition without the able assistance of Natalie Hoeper, JD, 2012, University of Wisconsin Law School. Natalie served both as a copyeditor and as overall administrative assistant in the task of converting conference papers into book chapters. Natalie's dedication to her job, her promptness in completing her tasks, and her knowledge of the Hart Style manual are all of the highest order. Natalie also helped out with the conference. We have every confidence that Natalie is headed to a highly successful legal career.

[15] The first edition was initially published, in 1993, by the Institute for Legal Studies at Wisconsin Law School. This edition was commercially published in 1995 by Michie Company. Marc Galanter joined Macaulay, Kidwell and Whitford as a co-editor of the first edition.

[16] The Michie Company was acquired by LexisNexis, the publisher of the second and third editions. The second edition appeared in 2003.

[17] The website for the conference is: www.law.wisc.edu/ils/2011contractsconf/homepage.html. The following persons served as discussants for the panels held at the conference: Professors Lisa Alexander (Wisconsin), Jean Braucher (Arizona), Alan Hyde (Rutgers-Newark), Jonathan Lipson (Wisconsin), Keith Rowley (Nevada-Las Vegas), Daniel Schwarcz (Minnesota), William Whitford (Wisconsin) and Jason Yackee (Wisconsin).

[18] The conference was funded by the Contracts Enrichment Fund at Wisconsin Law School. This Fund receives the royalties from contracts casebook described above.

John Kidwell, one of our co-editors, passed away in February 2012. Before his untimely death, John fully participated in the planning for the conference, and he performed the substantive edits on some of the chapters in this volume. We miss John more than we can describe, and we are deeply indebted to him for all his contributions over many years to the Wisconsin contracts team. We know that Stewart shares these sentiments.

Jean Braucher
William Whitford
May, 2012

Table of Contents

List of Contributors

Brian H Bix, Frederick W Thomas Professor for the Interdisciplinary Study of Law and Language at the University of Minnesota Law School.

Jean Braucher, Roger C Henderson Professor of Law at the University of Arizona's James E Rogers College of Law.

David Campbell, Professor of International Business Law at School of Law, University of Leeds.

Jay M Feinman, Distinguished Professor of Law at Rutgers School of Law, Camden.

Robert W Gordon, Professor of Law at Stanford Law School and Chancellor Kent Professor of Law and Legal History Emeritus at Yale Law School.

Claire A Hill, Professor of Law and James L Krusemark Chair in Law and Director, Institute for Law and Rationality at the University of Minnesota Law School.

John Kidwell, Professor of Law Emeritus at the University of Wisconsin Law School (died 10 March 2012).

Charles L Knapp, Joseph W Cotchett Distinguished Professor of Law at the University of California's Hastings College of Law.

Ethan J Leib, Professor of Law at Fordham University School of Law.

Li-Wen Lin, PhD student in sociology at Columbia University.

Stewart Macaulay, Malcolm Pitman Sharp Professor and Theodore W Brazeau Professor of Law at the University of Wisconsin Law School.

Deborah Waire Post, Professor of Law at Touro College, Jacob D Fuchsberg Law Center.

Edward Rubin, University Professor of Law and Political Science at Vanderbilt University.

Carol Sanger, Barbara Aronstein Black Professor of Law at Columbia Law School.

Robert E Scott, Alfred McCormack Professor of Law and the Director of the Center for Contract and Economic Organization at Columbia Law School.

D Gordon Smith, Associate Dean and Glen L Farr Professor of Law, J Reuben Clark Law School, Brigham Young University.

Josh Whitford, Associate Professor of Sociology at Columbia University.

William Whitford, Professor of Law Emeritus at the University of Wisconsin Law School.

John Wightman, Dean of the Faculty of Social Sciences at Kent University and a Senior Lecturer at the United Kingdom's Kent Law School.

William J Woodward, Jr, Senior Fellow, Santa Clara University, and Professor of Law Emeritus at Temple University.

Bibliography of Publications by Stewart Macaulay

Macaulay, S and Manne, H, 'A Low-Cost Legal Writing Program – The Wisconsin Experience' (1958–59) 11 *Journal of Legal Education* 387.

Macaulay, S, 'Restitution in Context' (1959) 107 *University of Pennsylvania Law Review* 1133.

Macaulay, S, 'Justice Traynor and the Law of Contracts' (1961) 13 *Stanford Law Review* 812.

Macaulay, S, 'Non-Contractual Relations in Business: A Preliminary Study' (1963) 28 *American Sociological Review* 55.

Macaulay, S, 'The Use and Non-Use of Contracts in the Manufacturing Industry' (1963) 9 *Practical Lawyer* 13.

Macaulay, S, 'Changing a Continuing Relationship Between a Large Corporation and Those Who Deal With It: Automobile Manufacturers, Their Dealers, and the Legal System' (1965) 1965 *Wisconsin Law Review* 483.

Finman, T and Macaulay, S, 'Freedom to Dissent: The Vietnam Protests and the Words of Public Officials' (1966) 1966 *Wisconsin Law Review* 632.

Macaulay, S, *Law and the Balance of Power – The Automobile Manufacturers and Their Dealers* (New York, Russell Sage Foundation, 1966).

Macaulay, S, 'Private Legislation and the Duty to Read – Business Run by IBM Machine, the Law of Contracts and Credit Cards' (1966) 19 *Vanderbilt Law Review* 1051.

Friedman, L and Macaulay, S, 'Contract Law and Contract Teaching: Past, Present, and Future' (1967) 1967 *Wisconsin Law Review* 805.

Macaulay, S, 'Law Schools and the World Outside Their Doors: Notes on the Margins of 'Professional Training in the Public Interest' (1968) 54 *Virginia Law Review* 617.

Friedman, L and Macaulay, S, *Law and the Behavioral Sciences* (Indianapolis, Bobbs-Merrill, 1969).

Macaulay, S and Walster, E, 'Legal Structures and Restoring Equity' (1971) 27 *Journal of Social Issues* 173 (1971) (translated as 'Las Estructuras Legales y El Restablecimiento de la Equidad' (1972) 15 *Boletin del Onstituto de Docencia e Investigacion Juridicas* 89–107).

Macaulay, S, 'El Derecho y Las Ciencias Conductuales: Algunas Reflexiones (Some Reflections on Law and the Social Sciences)' (1972) 134 *Boletin del Onstituto de Docencia e Investigacion Juridica* 19–34.

Macaulay, S, 'The Standardized Contracts of United States Automobile Manufacturers' in vol 7 *International Encyclopedia of Comparative Law* (Leiden, Koninklijke Brill NV, 1973) ch 3.

Macaulay, S, *Access to the Legal Systems of the Americas: Informal Processes* (Madison, Center for Law and Behavioral Science, 1976).

Friedman, L and Macaulay, S, *Law and the Behavioral Sciences*, 2nd edn (Indianapolis, Bobbs-Merrill, 1977).

Macaulay, S, 'Elegant Models, Empirical Pictures, and the Complexities of Contract' (1977) 11 *Law & Society Review* 507.

Macaulay, J and Macaulay, S, 'Adoption for Black Children: A Case Study of Expert Discretion' in R Simon (ed), *Research in Law and Sociology: An Annual Compilation of Research* (Greenwich, JAI Press, 1978) 265–318.

Macaulay, S, 'Lawyers and Consumer Protection Laws: An Empirical Study' (1979) 14 *Law & Society Review* 115.

Macaulay, S, 'Professional Competence and the Law' (1981) Dalhousie Continuing Legal Education Series No 21.

Macaulay, S, *Law and Social Change in Mediterranean Europe and Latin America: A Handbook of Legal And Social Indicators for Comparative Study* by John Henry Merryman, David S Clark and Lawrence M Friedman. Stanford: Stanford Law School, 179, 618, (1981) 29 *American Journal of Comparative Law* 542 (book review).

Macaulay, S, 'Law Schools and the World Outside Their Doors II: Some Notes on Two Recent Studies of the Chicago Bar' (1982) 32 *Journal of Legal Education* 506.

Macaulay, S, 'Law and the Behavioral Sciences: Is There Any There There?' (1984) 6 *Law & Policy* 149.

Macaulay, S, 'An Empirical View of Contract' (1985) 1985 *Wisconsin Law Review* 465.

Macaulay, S, *Lawyer Advertising: "yes, But . . ."* (Madison, Institute for Legal Studies, University of Wisconsin-Madison Law School, 1985).

Macaulay, S, 'Control, Influence, and Attitudes: A Comment on Nelson' (1985) 37 *Stanford Law Review* 553.

Macaulay, S, 'Law, Private Governance and Continuing Relationships: An Empirical View of Contract' (1985) 1985 *Wisconsin Law Review* 465.

Macaulay, S, 'Private Government' in L Lipson and S Wheeler (eds), *Law and Social Science* (New York, Russell Sage Foundation, 1986) 445–518.

Macaulay, S, 'The Judge as Mentor: A Personal Memoir' (1986) 36 *Journal of Legal Education* 144.

Macaulay, S, 'Images of Law in Everyday Life: The Lessons of School, Entertainment, and Spectator Sports' (1987) 21 *Law & Society Review* 185.

Macaulay, S, 'Popular Legal Culture: An Introduction' (1989) 98 *Yale Law Journal* 1545.

Macaulay, S, 'Bambi Meets Godzilla: Reflections on Contract Scholarship and Teaching vs. State Unfair and Deceptive Trade Practices and Consumer Protection Statutes' (1989) 26 *Houston Law Review* 575.

Macaulay, S, 'Long-Term Continuing Relations: The American Experience Regulating Dealerships and Franchises' in C Joerges (ed), *Franchising and the Law: Theoretical and Comparative Approaches in Europe and the United States* (Baden Baden, Nomos Verlagsgesellschaft, 1991) 179–237.

Macaulay, S, 'The Reliance Interest and the World Outside the Law Schools' Doors' (1991) 1991 *Wisconsin Law Review* 247.

Macaulay, S, 'Frank Remington: Defining the Law Professor's Job' (1992) 1992 *Wisconsin Law Review* 553.

Macaulay, S, 'On Rattling Cages: Joel Handler Goes to Philadelphia and Gives a Presidential Address' (1992) *Law & Society Review* 825.

Macaulay, S, 'Business Adaptation to Regulation: What Do We Know and What Do We Need to Know?' (1993) 15 *Law & Policy Quarterly* 259.
Macaulay, S, 'The Future of American Lawyers' (1993) 20 *Sociologia del Diritto* 51.
Macaulay, S, 'Wisconsin's Legal Tradition' (1994) 24 *Gargoyle* 6.
Macaulay, S, 'The Impact of Contract Law on the Economy: Less Than Meets the Eye?' (Conference on Law and Modernization, Lima, Peru, July 1994).
Macaulay, S, 'The Last Word' (1995) 22 *Journal of Law & Society* 149.
Macaulay, S, 'Crime and Custom in Business Society' (1995) 22 *Journal of Law & Society* 248.
Macaulay, S, Friedman, L and Stookey, J, *Law & Society: Readings on the Social Study of Law* (New York, WW Norton & Co, 1995).
Macaulay, S, 'Organic Transactions: Contract, Frank Lloyd Wright and the Johnson Building' (1996) 1996 *Wisconsin Law Review* 75.
Kenworthy, L, Macaulay, S and Rogers, J, 'The More Things Change: Business Litigation and Governance in the American Automobile Industry' (1996) 21 *Law & Social Inquiry* 631 (1996).
Macaulay, S, 'Willard's Law School?' (1997) 1997 *Wisconsin Law Review* 1163.
Grossman, J, Kritzer, H and Macaulay, S, 'Do the "Haves" Still Come Out Ahead?' (1999) 33 *Law & Society Review* 803.
Macaulay, S, Relational Contracts Floating on a Sea of Custom? Thoughts about the Ideas of Ian Macneil and Lisa Bernstein, 94 *Northwestern University Law Review* 775 (2000).
Macaulay, S, 'Almost Everything That I Did Want to Know About Contract Litigation: A Comment on Galanter' (2001) 2001 *Wisconsin Law Review* 629.
Macaulay, S, 'The Real and the Paper Deal: Empirical Pictures of Relationships, Complexity and the Urge for Transparent Simple Rules' (2003) 66 *Modern Law Review* 44 (also included in D Campbell, H Collins and J Wightman (eds), *Implicit Dimensions of Contract: Discrete, Relational & Network Contracts* (Oxford, Hart Publishing, 2003)).
Macaulay, S, 'Freedom From Contract: Solutions in Search of a Problem?' (2004) 2004 *Wisconsin Law Review* 777.
Macaulay, S, 'The New Versus The Old Legal Realism: "Things Ain't What They Used to Be"' (2005) 2005 *Wisconsin Law Review* 367.
Macaulay, S, 'Klein and the Contradictions of Corporations Law' (2005) 2 *Berkeley Business Law Journal* 119.
Macaulay, S, 'Contracts, New Legal Realism, and Improving the Navigation of the Yellow Submarine' (2006) 80 *Tulane Law Review* 1161.
Macaulay, S, Friedman, L and Mertz, E, *Law in Action: A Socio-Legal Reader* (New York, Foundation Press, 2007).
Macaulay, S, 'Renegotiations and Settlements: Dr Pangloss's Notes on the Margins of David Campbell's Papers' (2007) 29 *Cardozo Law Review* 261.
Macaulay, S and others, 'Transcript of Panel Discussion – Transactional Economics: Victor Goldberg's Framing Contract Law' (2007–2008) 49 *South Texas Law Review* 469.
Krishnan, J and Macaulay, S, 'Toward the Next Generation of Galanter-Influence Scholars: The Influential Reach of a Law-and-Society Founder' (2008) 71 *Law & Contemporary Problems* i.

Whitford, W and Macaulay, S, '*Hoffman v. Red Owl Stores*: The Rest of the Story' (2009–2010) 61 *Hastings Law Journal* 801.
Macaulay, S and others, *Contracts: Law in Action*, 3rd edn (New Providence, LexisNexis, 2011).
Macaulay, S, 'Dodos, Unicorns and Sleeping Rattlesnakes' (Foreword) in L Friedman, *Contract Law in America* (New Orleans, Quid Pro Books, 2011).
Macaulay, S, 'The Death of Contract: Dodos and Unicorns or Sleeping Rattlesnakes' in R Gordon and M Horwitz (eds), *Law, Society and History* (Cambridge, Cambridge University Press, 2011).
Macaulay, S, 'Notes on the Margins of Lawyering, in Three and a Half Minutes' (2011) 40 *Hofstra Law Review* 25.
Macaulay, S, 'Dodging the Worst of the Thorns on the Bramble Bush' in K Llewellyn, *The Bramble Bush* (New Orleans, Quid Pro Books, 2011 Oxford, Oxford University Press, 2012).
Macaulay, S, 'A New Legal Realism: Elegant Models and Messy Law in Action' in S Macaulay and others (eds), *New Legal Realism* (Cambridge, Cambridge University Press, forthcoming) vol 1.

Non-Contractual Relations in Business: A Preliminary Study[*]

STEWART MACAULAY
Law School, University of Wisconsin

Preliminary findings indicate that businessmen often fail to plan exchange relationships completely, and seldom use legal sanctions to adjust these relationships or to settle disputes. Planning and legal sanctions are often unnecessary and may have undesirable consequences. Transactions are planned and legal sanctions are used when the gains are thought to outweigh the costs. The power to decide whether the gains from using contract outweigh the costs will be held by individuals having different occupational roles. The occupational role influences the decision that is made.

WHAT GOOD IS contract law? who uses it? when and how? Complete answers would require an investigation of almost every type of transaction between individuals and oganizations. In this report, research has been confined to exchanges between businesses, and primarily to manufacturers.[1] Furthermore, this report will be limited to a presentation of the findings concerning when contract is and is not used and to a tentative explanation of these findings.[2]

* Revision of a paper read at the annual meeting of the American Sociological Association, August, 1962. An earlier version of the paper was read at the annual meeting of the Midwest Sociological Society, April, 1962. The research has been supported by a Law and Policy Research Grant to the University of Wisconsin Law School from the Ford Foundation. I am grateful for the help generously given by a number of sociologists including Robert K. Merton, Harry V. Ball, Jerome Carlin and William Evan.

[1] The reasons for this limitation are that (a) these transactions are important from an economic standpoint, (b) they are frequently said in theoretical discussions to represent a high degree of rational planning, and (c) manufacturing personnel are sufficiently public-relations-minded to cooperate with a law professor who wants to ask a seemingly endless number of questions. Future research will deal with the building construction industry and other areas.

[2] For the present purposes, the what-difference-does-it-make issue is important primarily as it makes a case for an empirical study by a law teacher of the use and nonuse of contract by businessmen. First, law teachers have a professional concern with what the law ought to be. This involves evaluation of the consequences of the existing situation and of the possible alternatives. Thus, it is most relevant to examine business practices concerning contract if one is

This research is only the first phase in a scientific study.[3] The primary research technique involved interviewing 68 businessmen and lawyers representing 43 companies and six law firms. The interviews ranged from a 30-minute brush-off where not all questions could be asked of a busy and uninterested sales manager to a six-hour discussion with the general counsel of a large corporation. Detailed notes of the interviews were taken and a complete report of each interview was dictated, usually no later than the evening after the interview. All but two of the companies had plants in Wisconsin; 17 were manufacturers of machinery but none made such items as food products, scientific instruments, textiles or petroleum products. Thus the likelihood of error because of sampling bias may be considerable.[4] However, to a great extent, existing knowledge has been inadequate to permit more rigorous procedures – as yet one cannot formulate many precise questions to be asked a systematically selected sample of "right people." Much time has been spent fishing for relevant questions or answers, or both.

Reciprocity, exchange or contract has long been of interest to sociologists, economists and lawyers. Yet each discipline has an incomplete view of this kind of conduct. This study represents the effort of a law teacher to draw on sociological ideas and empirical investigation. It stresses, among other things, the functions and dysfunctions of using contract to solve exchange problems and the influence of occupational roles on how one assesses whether the benefits of using contract outweigh the costs.

To discuss when contract is and is not used, the term "contract" must be specified. This term will be used here to refer to devices for conducting exchanges. Contract is not treated as synonymous with an exchange itself,

interested in what commercial law ought to be. Second, law teachers are supposed to teach law students something relevant to becoming lawyers. These business practices are facts that are relevant to the skills which law students will need when, as lawyers, they are called upon to create exchange relationships and to solve problems arising out of these relationships.

[3] The following things have been done. The literature in law, business, economics, psychology, and sociology has been surveyed. The formal systems related to exchange transactions have been examined. Standard form contracts and the standard terms and conditions that are found on such business documents as catalogues, quotation forms, purchase orders, and acknowledgment-of-order forms from 850 firms that are based in or do business in Wisconsin have been collected. The citations of all reported court cases during a period of 15 years involving the largest 500 manufacturing corporations in the United States have been obtained and are being analyzed to determine why the use of contract legal sanctions was thought necessary and whether or not any patterns of "problem situations" can be delineated. In addition, the informal systems related to exchange transactions have been examined. Letters of inquiry concerning practices in certain situations have been answered by approximately 125 businessmen. Interviews, as described in the text, have been conducted. Moreover, six of my students have interviewed 21 other businessmen, bankers and lawyers. Their findings are consistent with those reported in the text.

[4] However, the cases have not been selected because they *did* use contract. There is as much interest in, and effort to obtain, cases of nonuse as of use of contract. Thus, one variety of bias has been minimized.

which may or may not be characterized as contractual. Nor is contract used to refer to a writing recording an agreement. Contract, as I use the term here, involves two distinct elements: (a) Rational planning of the transaction with careful provision for as many future contingencies as can be foreseen, and (b) the existence or use of actual or potential legal sanctions to induce performance of the exchange or to compensate for non-performance.

These devices for conducting exchanges may be used or may exist in greater or lesser degree, so that transactions can be described relatively as involving a more contractual or a less contractual manner (a) of creating an exchange relationship or (b) of solving problems arising during the course of such a relationship. For example, General Motors might agree to buy all of the Buick Division's requirements of aluminum for ten years from Reynolds Aluminum. Here the two large corporations probably would plan their relationship carefully. The plan probably would include a complex pricing formula designed to meet market fluctuations, an agreement on what would happen if either party suffered a strike or a fire, a definition of Reynolds' responsibility for quality control and for losses caused by defective quality, and many other provisions. As the term contract is used here, this is a more contractual method of creating an exchange relationship than is a home-owner's casual agreement with a real estate broker giving the broker the exclusive right to sell the owner's house which fails to include provisions for the consequences of many easily foreseeable (and perhaps even highly probable) contingencies. In both instances, legally enforceable contracts may or may not have been created, but it must be recognized that the existence of a legal sanction has no necessary relationship to the degree of rational planning by the parties, beyond certain minimal legal requirements of certainty of obligation. General Motors and Reynolds might never sue or even refer to the written record of their agreement to answer questions which come up during their ten-year relationship, while the real estate broker might sue, or at least threaten to sue, the owner of the house. The broker's method of *dispute settlement* then would be more contractual than that of General Motors and Reynolds, thus reversing the relationship that existed in regard to the "contractualness" of the creation of the exchange relationships.

TENTATIVE FINDINGS

It is difficult to generalize about the use and nonuse of contract by manufacturing industry. However, a number of observations can be made with reasonable accuracy at this time. The use and nonuse of contract in creating exchange relations and in dispute settling will be taken up in turn.

The creation of exchange relationships. In creating exchange relationships, businessmen may plan to a greater or lesser degree in relation to several types of issues. Before reporting the findings as to practices in creating such relationships, it is necessary to describe what one can plan about in a bargain and the degrees of planning which are possible.

People negotiating a contract can make plans concerning several types of issues: (1) They can plan what each is to do or refrain from doing; e.g., S might agree to deliver ten 1963 Studebaker four-door sedan automobiles to B on a certain date in exchange for a specified amount of money. (2) They can plan what effect certain contingencies are to have on their duties; e.g., what is to happen to S and B's obligations if S cannot deliver the cars because of a strike at the Studebaker factory? (3) They can plan what is to happen if either of them fails to perform; e.g., what is to happen if S delivers nine of the cars two weeks late? (4) They can plan their agreement so that it is a legally enforceable contract – that is, so that a legal sanction would be available to provide compensation for injury suffered by B as a result of S's failure to deliver the cars on time.

As to each of these issues, there may be a different degree of planning by the parties. (1) They may carefully and explicitly plan; e.g., S may agree to deliver ten 1963 Studebaker four-door sedans which have six cylinder engines, automatic transmissions and other specified items of optional equipment and which will perform to a specified standard for a certain time. (2) They may have a mutual but tacit understanding about an issue; e.g., although the subject was never mentioned in their negotiations, both S and B may assume that B may cancel his order for the cars before they are delivered if B's taxi-cab business is so curtailed that B can no longer use ten additional cabs. (3) They may have two inconsistent unexpressed assumptions about an issue; e.g., S may assume that if any of the cabs fails to perform to the specified standard for a certain time, all S must do is repair or replace it. B may assume S must also compensate B for the profits B would have made if the cab had been in operation. (4) They may never have thought of the issue; e.g., neither S nor B planned their agreement so that it would be a legally enforceable contract. Of course, the first and fourth degrees of planning listed are the extreme cases and the second and third are intermediate points. Clearly other intermediate points are possible; e.g., S and B neglect to specify whether the cabs should have automatic or conventional transmissions. Their planning is not as careful and explicit as that in the example previously given.

The following diagram represents the dimensions of creating an exchange relationship just discussed with "X's" representing the example of S and B's contract for ten taxi-cabs.

	Definition of Performances	Effect of Contingencies	Effect of Defective Performances	Legal Sanctions
Explicit and careful	X			
Tacit agreement		X		
Unilateral assumptions			X	
Unawareness of the issue				X

Most larger companies, and many smaller ones, attempt to plan carefully and completely. Important transactions not in the ordinary course of business are handled by a detailed contract. For example, recently the Empire State Building was sold for $65 million. More than 100 attorneys, representing 34 parties, produced a 400 page contract. Another example is found in the agreement of a major rubber company in the United States to give technical assistance to a Japanese firm. Several million dollars were involved and the contract consisted of 88 provisions on 17 pages. The 12 house counsel – lawyers who work for one corporation rather than many clients – interviewed said that all but the smallest businesses carefully planned most transactions of any significance. Corporations have procedures so that particular types of exchanges will be reviewed by their legal and financial departments.

More routine transactions commonly are handled by what can be called standardized planning. A firm will have a set of terms and conditions for purchases, sales, or both printed on the business documents used in these exchanges. Thus the things to be sold and the price may be planned particularly for each transaction, but standard provisions will further elaborate the performances and cover the other subjects of planning. Typically, these terms and conditions are lengthy and printed in small type on the back of the forms. For example, 24 paragraphs in eight point type are printed on the back of the purchase order form used by the Allis Chalmers Manufacturing Company. The provisions: (1) describe, in part, the performance required, e.g., "DO NOT WELD CASTINGS WITHOUT OUR CONSENT"; (2) plan for the effect of contingencies, e.g., ". . . in the event the Seller suffers delay in performance due to an act of God, war, act of the Government, priorities or allocations, act of the Buyer, fire, flood, strike, sabotage, or other causes beyond Seller's control, the time of completion shall be extended a period of time equal to the period of such delay if the Seller gives the Buyer notice in writing of the cause of any such delay within a reasonable time after the beginning thereof"; (3) plan for the effect of defective performances, e.g., "The buyer, without waiving any other legal rights, reserves the right to cancel without charge or to postpone deliveries of any of the articles covered by this order which are not shipped in time reasonably to meet said agreed dates"; (4) plan for a legal sanction, e.g., the clause "without waiving any other legal rights," in the example just given.

In larger firms such "boiler plate" provisions are drafted by the house counsel or the firm's outside lawyer. In smaller firms such provisions may be drafted by the industry trade association, may be copied from a competitor, or may be found on forms purchased from a printer. In any event, salesmen and purchasing agents, the operating personnel, typically are unaware of what is said in the fine print on the back of the forms they use. Yet often the normal business patterns will give effect to this standardized planning. For example, purchasing agents may have to use a purchase order form so that all transactions receive a number under the firm's accounting system. Thus, the required accounting record will carry the necessary planning of the exchange relationship printed on its reverse side. If the seller does not object to this planning and accepts the order, the buyer's "fine print" will control. If the seller does object, differences can be settled by negotiation.

This type of standardized planning is very common. Requests for copies of the business documents used in buying and selling were sent to approximately 6,000 manufacturing firms which do business in Wisconsin. Approximately 1,200 replies were received and 850 companies used some type of standardized planning. With only a few exceptions, the firms that did not reply and the 350 that indicated they did not use standardized planning were very small manufacturers such as local bakeries, soft drink bottlers and sausage makers.

While businessmen can and often do carefully and completely plan, it is clear that not all exchanges are neatly rationalized. Although most businessmen think that a clear description of both the seller's and buyer's performances is obvious common sense, they do not always live up to this ideal. The house counsel and the purchasing agent of a medium size manufacturer of automobile parts reported that several times their engineers had committed the company to buy expensive machines without adequate specifications. The engineers had drawn careful specifications as to the type of machine and how it was to be made but had neglected to require that the machine produce specified results. An attorney and an auditor both stated that most contract disputes arise because of ambiguity in the specifications.

Businessmen often prefer to rely on "a man's word" in a brief letter, a handshake, or "common honesty and decency" – even when the transaction involves exposure to serious risks. Seven lawyers from law firms with business practices were interviewed. Five thought that businessmen often entered contracts with only a minimal degree of advance planning.

They complained that businessmen desire to "keep it simple and avoid red tape" even where large amounts of money and significant risks are involved. One stated that he was "sick of being told, 'We can trust old Max,' when the problem is not one of honesty but one of reaching an agreement that both sides understand." Another said that businessmen when bargaining often talk only in pleasant generalities, think they have a contract, but fail to reach agreement on any of the hard, unpleasant questions until forced to do so by a lawyer. Two outside lawyers had different views. One thought that large firms usually planned important exchanges, although he conceded that occasionally matters might be left in a fairly vague state. The other dissenter represents a large utility that commonly buys heavy equipment and buildings. The supplier's employees come on the utility's property to install the equipment or construct the buildings, and they may be injured while there. The utility has been sued by such employees so often that it carefully plans purchases with the assistance of a lawyer so that suppliers take this burden.

Moreover, standardized planning can break down. In the example of such planning previously given, it was assumed that the purchasing agent would use his company's form with its 24 paragraphs printed on the back and that the seller would accept this or object to any provisions he did not like. However, the seller may fail to read the buyer's 24 paragraphs of fine print and may accept the buyer's order on the seller's own acknowledgment-of-order form. Typically this form will have ten to 50 paragraphs favoring the seller, and these provisions are likely to be different from or inconsistent with the buyer's provisions. The seller's acknowledgment form may be received by the buyer and checked by a clerk. She will read the face of the acknowledgment but not the fine print on the back of it because she has neither the time nor ability to analyze the small print on the 100 to 500 forms she must review each day. The face of the acknowledgment – where the goods and the price are specified – is likely to correspond with the face of the purchase order. If it does, the two forms are filed away. At this point, both buyer and seller are likely to assume they have planned an exchange and made a contract. Yet they have done neither, as they are in disagreement about all that appears on the back of their forms. This practice is common enough to have a name. Law teachers call it "the battle of the forms."

Ten of the 12 purchasing agents interviewed said that frequently the provisions on the back of their purchase order and those on the back of a supplier's acknowledgment would differ or be inconsistent. Yet they would assume that the purchase was complete without further action unless one of the supplier's provisions was really objectionable. Moreover, only occasionally would they bother to read the fine print on the back of suppliers' forms. On the other hand, one purchasing agent insists that agreement be reached on the fine print provisions, but he represents the utility whose lawyer reported that it exercises great care in planning. The other purchasing agent who said that his company did not face a battle of the forms problem, works for a division of one of the largest manufacturing corporations in the United States. Yet the company may have such a problem without recognizing it. The purchasing agent regularly sends a supplier both a purchase order and another form which the supplier is asked to sign and return. The second form states that the supplier accepts the buyer's terms and conditions. The company has sufficient bargaining power to force suppliers to sign and return the form, and the purchasing agent must show one of his firm's auditors such a signed form for every purchase order issued. Yet suppliers frequently return this buyer's form *plus* their own acknowledgment form which has conflicting provisions. The purchasing agent throws away the supplier's form and files his own. Of course, in such a case the supplier has not acquiesced to the buyer's provisions. There is no agreement and no contract.

Sixteen sales managers were asked about the battle of the forms. Nine said that frequently no agreement was reached on which set of fine print was to govern, while seven said that there was no problem. Four of the seven worked for companies whose major customers are the large automobile companies or the large manufacturers of paper products. These customers demand that their terms and conditions govern any purchase, are careful generally to see that suppliers acquiesce, and have the bargaining power to have their way. The other three of the seven sales managers who have no battle of the forms problem, work for manufacturers of special industrial machines. Their firms are careful to reach complete agreement with their customers. Two of these men stressed that they could take no chances because such a large part of their firm's capital is tied up in making any one machine. The other sales manager had been influenced by a law suit against one of his competitors for over a half million dollars. The suit was brought by a customer when the competitor had been unable to deliver a machine and put it in operation on time. The sales manager interviewed said his firm could not guarantee that its machines would work perfectly by a specified time because they are designed to fit the customer's requirements, which may present difficult engineering problems. As a result, contracts are carefully negotiated.

A large manufacturer of packaging materials audited its records to determine how often it had failed to agree on terms and conditions with its customers or had failed to create legally binding contracts. Such failures cause a risk of loss to this firm since the packaging is printed with the customer's design and cannot be salvaged once this is done. The orders for five days in four different years were reviewed. The percentages of orders where no agreement on terms and conditions was reached or no contract was formed were as follows:

1953	75.0%
1954	69.4%
1955	71.5%
1956	59.5%

It is likely that businessmen pay more attention to describing the performances in an exchange than to planning for contingencies or defective performances or to obtaining legal enforceability of their contracts. Even when a purchase order and acknowledgment have conflicting provisions printed on the back, almost always the buyer and seller will be in agreement on what is to be sold and how much is to be paid for it. The lawyers who said businessmen often commit their firms to significant exchanges too casually, stated that the performances would be defined in the brief letter or telephone call; the lawyers objected that nothing else would be covered. Moreover, it is likely that businessmen are least concerned about planning their transactions so that they are legally enforceable contracts.[5] For example, in Wisconsin requirements contracts – contracts to supply a firm's requirements of an item rather than a definite quantity – probably are not legally enforceable. Seven people interviewed reported that their firms regularly used requirements contracts in dealings in Wisconsin. None thought that the lack of legal sanction made any difference. Three of these people were house counsel who knew the Wisconsin law before being interviewed. Another example of a lack of desire for legal sanctions is found in the relationship between automobile manufacturers and their suppliers of parts. The manufacturers draft a carefully planned agreement, but one which is so designed that the supplier will have only minimal, if any, legal rights against the manufacturers. The standard contract used by manufacturers of paper to sell to magazine publishers has a pricing clause which is probably sufficiently vague to make the contract legally unenforceable. The house counsel of one of the largest paper producers said that everyone in the industry is aware of this because of a leading New York case concerning the contract, but that no one cares. Finally, it seems likely that planning for contingencies and defective performances are in-between cases – more likely to occur than planning for a legal sanction, but less likely than a description of performance.

Thus one can conclude that (1) many business exchanges reflect a high degree of planning about the four categories – description, contingencies, defective performances and legal sanction – but (2) many, if not most, exchanges reflect no planning, or only a minimal amount of it, especially concerning legal sanctions and the effect of defective performances. As a

[5] Compare the findings of an empirical study of Connecticut business practices in Comment, "The Statute of Frauds and the Business Community: A Re-Appraisal in Light of Prevailing Practices," *Yale Law Journal*, 66 (1957), pp. 1038–1071.

result, the opportunity for good faith disputes during the life of the exchange relationship often is present.

The adjustment of exchange relationships and the settling of disputes. While a significant amount of creating business exchanges is done on a fairly non-contractual basis, the creation of exchanges usually is far more contractual than the adjustment of such relationships and the settlement of disputes. Exchanges are adjusted when the obligations of one or both parties are modified by agreement during the life of the relationship. For example, the buyer may be allowed to cancel all or part of the goods he has ordered because he no longer needs them; the seller may be paid more than the contract price by the buyer because of unusual changed circumstances. Dispute settlement involves determining whether or not a party has performed as agreed and, if he has not, doing something about it. For example, a court may have to interpret the meaning of a contract, determine what the alleged defaulting party has done and determine what, if any, remedy the aggrieved party is entitled to. Or one party may assert that the other is in default, refuse to proceed with performing the contract and refuse to deal ever again with the alleged defaulter. If the alleged defaulter, who in fact may not be in default, takes no action, the dispute is then "settled."

Business exchanges in non-speculative areas are usually adjusted without dispute. Under the law of contracts, if B orders 1,000 widgets from S at $1.00 each, B must take all 1,000 widgets or be in breach of contract and liable to pay S his expenses up to the time of the breach plus his lost anticipated profit. Yet all ten of the purchasing agents asked about cancellation of orders once placed indicated that they expected to be able to cancel orders freely subject to only an obligation to pay for the seller's major expenses such as scrapped steel.[6] All 17 sales personnel asked reported that they often had to accept cancellation. One said, "You can't ask a man to eat paper [the firm's product] when he has no use for it." A lawyer with many large industrial clients said,

> Often businessmen do not feel they have "a contract" – rather they have "an order." They speak of "cancelling the order" rather than "breaching our contract." When I began practice I referred to order cancellations as breaches of contract, but my clients objected since they do not think of cancellation as wrong. Most clients, in heavy industry at least, believe that there is a right to cancel as part of the buyer-seller relationship. There is a widespread attitude that one can back out of any deal within some very vague limits. Lawyers are often surprised by this attitude.

Disputes are frequently settled without reference to the contract or potential or actual legal sanctions. There is a hesitancy to speak of legal rights or to threaten to sue in these negotiations. Even where the parties

[6] See the case studies on cancellation of contracts in *Harvard Business Review*, 2 (1923–24), pages 238–40, 367–70, 496–502.

have a detailed and carefully planned agreement which indicates what is to happen if, say, the seller fails to deliver on time, often they will never refer to the agreement but will negotiate a solution when the problem arises apparently as if there had never been any original contract. One purchasing agent expressed a common business attitude when he said,

> if something comes up, you get the other man on the telephone and deal with the problem. You don't read legalistic contract clauses at each other if you ever want to do business again. One doesn't run to lawyers if he wants to stay in business because one must behave decently.

Or as one businessman put it, "You can settle any dispute if you keep the lawyers and accountants out of it. They just do not understand the give-and-take needed in business." All of the house counsel interviewed indicated that they are called into the dispute settlement process only after the businessmen have failed to settle matters in their own way. Two indicated that after being called in house counsel at first will only advise the purchasing agent, sales manager or other official involved; not even the house counsel's letterhead is used on communications with the other side until all hope for a peaceful resolution is gone.

Law suits for breach of contract appear to be rare. Only five of the 12 purchasing agents had ever been involved in even a negotiation concerning a contract dispute where both sides were represented by lawyers; only two of ten sales managers had ever gone this far. None had been involved in a case that went through trial. A law firm with more than 40 lawyers and a large commercial practice handles in a year only about six trials concerned with contract problems. Less than 10 per cent of the time of this office is devoted to any type of work related to contracts disputes. Corporations big enough to do business in more than one state tend to sue and be sued in the federal courts. Yet only 2,779 out of 58,293 civil actions filed in the United States District Courts in fiscal year 1961 involved private contracts.[7] During the same period only 3,447 of the 61,138 civil cases filed in the principal trial courts of New York State involved private contracts.[8] The same picture emerges from a review of appellate cases.[9] Mentschikoff has suggested that commercial cases are not brought to the courts either in periods of business prosperity (because buyers unjustifiably reject goods only when prices drop and they can get similar goods

[7] *Annual Report of the Director of the Administrative Office of the United States Courts*, 1961, p. 238.

[8] State of New York, The Judicial Conference, Sixth Annual Report, 1961, pp. 209-11.

[9] My colleague Lawrence M. Friedman has studied the work of the Supreme Court of Wisconsin in contracts cases. He has found that contracts cases reaching that court tend to involve economically-marginal-business and family-economic disputes rather than important commercial transactions. This has been the situation since about the turn of the century. Only during the Civil War period did the court deal with significant numbers of important contracts cases, but this happened against the background of a much simpler and different economic system.

elsewhere at less than the contract price) or in periods of deep depression (because people are unable to come to court or have insufficient assets to satisfy any judgment that might be obtained). Apparently, she adds, it is necessary to have "a kind of middle-sized depression" to bring large numbers of commercial cases to the courts. However, there is little evidence that in even "a kind of middle-sized depression" today's businessmen would use the courts to settle disputes.[10]

At times relatively contractual methods are used to make adjustments in ongoing transactions and to settle disputes. Demands of one side which are deemed unreasonable by the other occasionally are blocked by reference to the terms of the agreement between the parties. The legal position of the parties can influence negotiations even though legal rights or litigation are never mentioned in their discussions; it makes a difference if one is demanding what both concede to be a right or begging for a favor. Now and then a firm may threaten to turn matters over to its attorneys, threaten to sue, commence a suit or even litigate and carry an appeal to the highest court which will hear the matter. Thus, legal sanctions, while not an everyday affair, are not unknown in business.

One can conclude that while detailed planning and legal sanctions play a significant role in some exchanges between businesses, in many business exchanges their role is small.

TENTATIVE EXPLANATIONS

Two questions need to be answered: (A) How can business successfully operate exchange relationships with relatively so little attention to detailed planning or to legal sanctions, and (B) Why does business ever use contract in light of its success without it?

Why are relatively non-contractual practices so common? In most situations contract is not needed.[11] Often its functions are served by other devices. Most problems are avoided without resort to detailed planning or legal sanctions because usually there is little room for honest misunderstandings or good faith differences of opinion about the nature and quality of a seller's performance. Although the parties fail to cover all foreseeable contingencies, they will exercise care to see that both understand the primary obligation on each side. Either products are standardized with an accepted description or specifications are written calling for production to

[10] New York Law Revision Commission, *Hearings on the Uniform Code Commercial Code*, 2 (1954), p. 1391.

[11] The explanation that follows emphasizes a *considered* choice not to plan in detail for all contingencies. However, at times it is clear that businessmen fail to plan because of a lack of sophistication; they simply do not appreciate the risk they are running or they merely follow patterns established in their firm years ago without reexamining these practices in light of current conditions.

certain tolerances or results. Those who write and read specifications are experienced professionals who will know the customs of their industry and those of the industries with which they deal. Consequently, these customs can fill gaps in the express agreements of the parties. Finally, most products can be tested to see if they are what was ordered; typically in manufacturing industry we are not dealing with questions of taste or judgment where people can differ in good faith.

When defaults occur they are not likely to be disastrous because of techniques of risk avoidance or risk spreading. One can deal with firms of good reputation or he may be able to get some form of security to guarantee performance. One can insure against many breaches of contract where the risks justify the costs. Sellers set up reserves for bad debts on their books and can sell some of their accounts receivable. Buyers can place orders with two or more suppliers of the same item so that a default by one will not stop the buyer's assembly lines.

Moreover, contract and contract law are often thought unnecessary because there are many effective non-legal sanctions. Two norms are widely accepted. (1) Commitments are to be honored in almost all situations; one does not welsh on a deal. (2) One ought to produce a good product and stand behind it. Then, too, business units are organized to perform commitments, and internal sanctions will induce performance. For example, sales personnel must face angry customers when there has been a late or defective performance. The salesmen do not enjoy this and will put pressure on the production personnel responsible for the default. If the production personnel default too often, they will be fired. At all levels of the two business units personal relationships across the boundaries of the two organizations exert pressures for conformity to expectations. Salesmen often know purchasing agents well. The same two individuals occupying these roles may have dealt with each other from five to 25 years. Each has something to give the other. Salesmen have gossip about competitors, shortages and price increases to give purchasing agents who treat them well. Salesmen take purchasing agents to dinner, and they give purchasing agents Christmas gifts hoping to improve the chances of making sale. The buyer's engineering staff may work with the seller's engineering staff to solve problems jointly. The seller's engineers may render great assistance, and the buyer's engineers may desire to return the favor by drafting specifications which only the seller can meet. The top executives of the two firms may know each other. They may sit together on government or trade committees. They may know each other socially and even belong to the same country club. The interrelationships may be more formal. Sellers may hold stock in corporations which are important customers; buyers may hold stock in important suppliers. Both buyer and seller may share common directors on their boards. They may share a common financial institution which has financed both units.

The final type of non-legal sanction is the most obvious. Both business units involved in the exchange desire to continue successfully in business and will avoid conduct which might interfere with attaining this goal. One is concerned with both the reaction of the other party in the particular exchange and with his own general business reputation. Obviously, the buyer gains sanctions insofar as the seller wants the particular exchange to be completed. Buyers can withhold part or all of their payments until sellers have performed to their satisfaction. If a seller has a great deal of money tied up in his performance which he must recover quickly, he will go a long way to please the buyer in order to be paid. Moreover, buyers who are dissatisfied may cancel and cause sellers to lose the cost of what they have done up to cancellation. Furthermore, sellers hope for repeat orders, and one gets few of these from unhappy customers. Some industrial buyers go so far as to formalize this sanction by issuing "report cards" rating the performance of each supplier. The supplier rating goes to the top management of the seller organization, and these men can apply internal sanctions to salesmen, production supervisors or product designers if there are too many "D's" or "F's" on the report card.

While it is generally assumed that the customer is always right, the seller may have some counterbalancing sanctions against the buyer. The seller may have obtained a large downpayment from the buyer which he will want to protect. The seller may have an exclusive process which the buyer needs. The seller may be one of the few firms which has the skill to make the item to the tolerances set by the buyer's engineers and within the time available. There are costs and delays involved in turning from a supplier one has dealt with in the past to a new supplier. Then, too, market conditions can change so that a buyer is faced with shortages of critical items. The most extreme example is the post World War II gray market conditions when sellers were rationing goods rather than selling them. Buyers must build up some reserve of good will with suppliers if they face the risk of such shortage and desire good treatment when they occur. Finally, there is reciprocity in buying and selling. A buyer cannot push a supplier too far if that supplier also buys significant quantities of the product made by the buyer.

Not only do the particular business units in a given exchange want to deal with each other again, they also want to deal with other business units in the future. And the way one behaves in a particular transaction, or a series of transactions, will color his general business reputation. Blacklisting can be formal or informal. Buyers who fail to pay their bills on time risk a bad report in credit rating services such as Dun and Bradstreet. Sellers who do not satisfy their customers become the subject of discussion in the gossip exchanged by purchasing agents and salesmen, at meetings of purchasing agents' associations and trade associations, or even at country clubs or social gatherings where members of top management meet. The American male's habit of debating the merits of new cars carries over to industrial items. Obviously, a poor reputation does not help a firm make sales and may force it to offer great price discounts or added services to remain in business. Furthermore, the habits of unusually demanding buyers become known, and they tend to get no more than they can coerce out of suppliers who choose to deal with them. Thus often contract is not needed as there are alternatives.

Not only are contract and contract law not needed in many situations, their use may have, or may be thought to have, undesirable consequences. Detailed negotiated contracts can get in the way of creating good exchange relationships between business units. If one side insists on a detailed plan, there will be delay while letters are exchanged as the parties try to agree on what should happen if a remote and unlikely contingency occurs. In some cases they may not be able to agree at all on such matters and as a result a sale may be lost to the seller and the buyer may have to search elsewhere for an acceptable supplier. Many businessmen would react by thinking that had no one raised the series of remote and unlikely contingencies all this wasted effort could have been avoided. Even where agreement can be reached at the negotiation stage, carefully planned arrangements may create undesirable exchange relationships between business units. Some businessmen object that in such a carefully worked out relationship one gets performance only to the letter of the contract. Such planning indicates a lack of trust and blunts the demands of friendship, turning a cooperative venture into an antagonistic horse trade. Yet the greater danger perceived by some businessmen is that one would have to perform his side of the bargain to its letter and thus lose what is called "flexibility." Businessmen may welcome a measure of vagueness in the obligations they assume so that they may negotiate matters in light of the actual circumstances.

Adjustment of exchange relationships and dispute settlement by litigation or the threat of it also has many costs. The gain anticipated from using this form of coercion often fails to outweigh these costs, which are both monetary and non-monetary. Threatening to turn matters over to an attorney may cost no more money than postage or a telephone call; yet few are so skilled in making such a threat that it will not cost some deterioration of the relationship between the firms. One businessman said that customers had better not rely on legal rights or threaten to bring a breach of contract law suit against him since he "would not be treated like a criminal" and would fight back with every means available. Clearly actual litigation is even more costly than making threats. Lawyers demand substantial fees from larger business units. A firm's executives often will have to be transported and maintained in another city during the proceedings if, as often is the case, the trial must be held away from the home office. Top management does not travel by Greyhound and stay at the Y.M.C.A. Moreover, there will be the cost of diverting top management, engineers, and others in the organization from their normal activities. The firm may lose many days work from several key people. The non-monetary costs may be large too. A breach of contract law suit may settle a particular dispute, but such an action often results in a "divorce" ending the "marriage" between the two businesses, since a contract action is likely to carry charges with at least overtones of bad faith. Many executives, moreover, dislike the prospect of being cross-examined in public. Some executives may dislike losing control of a situation by turning the decision-making power over to lawyers. Finally, the law of contract damages may not provide an adequate remedy even if the firm wins the suit; one may get vindication but not much money.

Why do relatively contractual practices ever exist? Although contract is not needed and actually may have negative consequences, businessmen do make some carefully planned contracts, negotiate settlements influenced by their legal rights and commence and defend some breach of contract law suits or arbitration proceedings. In view of the findings and explanation presented to this point, one may ask why. Exchanges are carefully planned when it is thought that planning and a potential legal sanction will have more advantages than disadvantages. Such a judgment may be reached when contract planning serves the internal needs of an organization involved in a business exchange. For example, a fairly detailed contract can serve as a communication device within a large corporation. While the corporation's sales manager and house counsel may work out all the provisions with the customer, its production manager will have to make the product. He must be told what to do and how to handle at least the most obvious contingencies. Moreover, the sales manager may want to remove certain issues from future negotiation by his subordinates. If he puts the matter in the written contract, he may be able to keep his salesmen from making concessions to the customer without first consulting the sales manager. Then the sales manager may be aided in his battles with his firm's financial or engineering departments if the contract calls for certain practices which the sales manager advocates but which the other departments resist. Now the corporation is obligated to a customer to do what the sales manager wants to do; how can the financial or engineering departments insist on anything else?

Also one tends to find a judgment that the gains of contract outweigh the costs where there is a likelihood that significant problems will arise.[12] One factor leading to this conclusion is complexity of the agreed performance over a long period. Another factor is whether or not the degree of injury in case of default is thought to be potentially great. This factor cuts

[12] Even where there is little chance that problems will arise, some businessmen insist that their lawyer review or draft an agreement as a delaying tactic. This gives the businessman time to think about making a commitment if he has doubts about the matter or to look elsewhere for a better deal while still keeping the particular negotiations alive.

two ways. First, a buyer may want to commit a seller to a detailed and legally binding contract, where the consequences of a default by the seller would seriously injure the buyer. For example, the airlines are subject to law suits from the survivors of passengers and to great adverse publicity as a result of crashes. One would expect the airlines to bargain for carefully defined and legally enforceable obligations on the part of the airframe manufacturers when they purchase aircraft. Second, a seller may want to limit his liability for a buyer's damages by a provision in their contract. For example, a manufacturer of air conditioning may deal with motels in the South and Southwest. If this equipment fails in the hot summer months, a motel may lose a great deal of business. The manufacturer may wish to avoid any liability for this type of injury to his customers and may want a contract with a clear disclaimer clause.

Similarly, one uses or threatens to use legal sanctions to settle disputes when other devices will not work and when the gains are thought to outweigh the costs. For example, perhaps the most common type of business contracts case fought all the way through to the appellate courts today is an action for an alleged wrongful termination of a dealer's franchise by a manufacturer. Since the franchise has been terminated, factors such as personal relationships and the desire for future business will have little effect; the cancellation of the franchise indicates they have already failed to maintain the relationship. Nor will a complaining dealer worry about creating a hostile relationship between himself and the manufacturer. Often the dealer has suffered a great financial loss both as to his investment in building and equipment and as to his anticipated future profits. A cancelled automobile dealer's lease on his showroom and shop will continue to run, and his tools for servicing, say, Plymouths cannot be used to service other makes of cars. Moreover, he will have no more new Plymouths to sell. Today there is some chance of winning a law suit for terminating a franchise in bad faith in many states and in the federal courts. Thus, often the dealer chooses to risk the cost of a lawyer's fee because of the chance that he may recover some compensation for his losses.

An "irrational" factor may exert some influence on the decision to use legal sanctions. The man who controls a firm may feel that he or his organization has been made to appear foolish or has been the victim of fraud or bad faith. The law suit may be seen as a vehicle "to get even" although the potential gains, as viewed by an objective observer, are outweighed by the potential costs.

The decision whether or not to use contract – whether the gain exceeds the costs – will be made by the person within the business unit with the power to make it, and it tends to make a difference who he is. People in a sales department oppose contract. Contractual negotiations are just one more hurdle in the way of a sale. Holding a customer to the letter of a contract is bad for "customer relations." Suing a customer who is not bankrupt and might order again is poor strategy. Purchasing agents and their buyers are less hostile to contracts but regard attention devoted to such matters as a waste of time. In contrast, the financial control department – the treasurer, controller or auditor – leans toward more contractual dealings. Contract is viewed by these people as an organizing tool to control operations in a large organization. It tends to define precisely and to minimize the risks to which the firm is exposed. Outside lawyers – those with many clients – may share this enthusiasm for a more contractual method of dealing. These lawyers are concerned with preventive law – avoiding any possible legal difficulty. They see many unstable and unsuccessful exchange transactions, and so they are aware of, and perhaps overly concerned with, all of the things which can go wrong. Moreover, their job of settling disputes with legal sanctions is much easier if their client has not been overly casual about transaction planning. The inside lawyer, or house counsel, is harder to classify. He is likely to have some sympathy with a more contractual method of dealing. He shares the outside lawyer's "craft urge" to see exchange transactions neat and tidy from a legal standpoint. Since he is more concerned with avoiding and settling disputes than selling goods, he is likely to be less willing to rely on a man's word as the sole sanction than is a salesman. Yet the house counsel is more a part of the organization and more aware of its goals and subject to its internal sanctions. If the potential risks are not too great, he may hesitate to suggest a more contractual procedure to the sales department. He must sell his services to the operating departments, and he must hoard what power he has, expending it on only what he sees as significant issues.

The power to decide that a more contractual method of creating relationships and settling disputes shall be used will be held by different people at different times in different organizations. In most firms the sales department and the purchasing department have a great deal of power to resist contractual procedures or to ignore them if they are formally adopted and to handle disputes their own way. Yet in larger organizations the treasurer and the controller have increasing power to demand both systems and compliance. Occasionally, the house counsel must arbitrate the conflicting positions of these departments; in giving "legal advice" he may make the business judgment necessary regarding the use of contract. At times he may ask for an opinion from an outside law firm to reinforce his own position with the outside firm's prestige.

Obviously, there are other significant variables which influence the degree that contract is used. One is the relative bargaining power or skill of the two business units. Even if the controller of a small supplier succeeds within the firm and creates a contractual system of dealing, there will be no contract if the firm's large customer prefers not to be bound to anything. Firms that supply General Motors deal as General Motors wants to do business, for the most part. Yet bargaining power is not size or share of the market alone. Even a General Motors may need a particular supplier, at least temporarily. Furthermore, bargaining power may shift as an exchange relationship is first created and then continues. Even a giant firm can find itself bound to a small supplier once production of an essential item begins for there may not be time to turn to another supplier. Also, all of the factors discussed in this paper can be viewed as *components* of bargaining power – for example, the personal relationship between the presidents of the buyer and the seller firms may give a sales manager great power over a purchasing agent who has been instructed to give the seller "every consideration." Another variable relevant to the use of contract is the influence of third parties. The federal government, or a lender of money, may insist that a contract be made in a particular transaction or may influence the decision to assert one's legal rights under a contract.

Contract, then, often plays an important role in business, but other factors are significant. To understand the functions of contract the whole system of conducting exchanges must be explored fully. More types of business communities must be studied, contract litigation must be analyzed to see why the nonlegal sanctions fail to prevent the use of legal sanctions and all of the variables suggested in this paper must be classified more systematically.

Private Legislation and the Duty To Read – Business Run by IBM Machine, the Law of Contracts and Credit Cards

STEWART MACAULAY*

INTRODUCTION

'IT WILL NOT do for a man to enter into a contract, and, when called upon to abide by its conditions, say that he did not read it when he signed it, or did not know what it contained.'[1] This rallying cry often is sounded in contracts and restitution opinions. Sometimes it makes such good sense that it is axiomatic. Yet in common with all grand slogans, there are situations where it just doesn't fit. For example, where the one who signs cannot read and has reason to trust another who tricks him by misreading the document, most courts have thought that the limits of the duty to read and understand have been reached.[2] Undoubtedly courts would find other boundaries to the principle, if asked to do so. For example, a company that manufactures paper uses a purchase order form printed on gray paper. On the back are a number of terms and conditions printed in such light gray ink that they can be seen only by holding the paper at an angle to the light.[3] Clearly, if a court were ever to enforce any of these terms and conditions, it would be marching to some other ideology than 'choice', even 'choice' in one of its more extreme definitions.

* Professor of Law, University of Wisconsin; Fellow, Center for Advanced Study in the Behavioral Sciences, 1966–67. AB, 1952, LLB, 1954, Stanford University. [Eds Note: See S Macaulay, 'Klein and the Contradictions of Corporations Law' (2005) 2 *Berkeley Business Law Journal* 119, 121–26, revisiting the argument in this article concerning contradictions in the goals of contract law.]

[1] *Sanger v Dun*, 47 Wis. 615, 620 (1879).

[2] See, eg *Bixler v Wright*, 116 Me 133 (1917).

[3] I obtained this purchase order in my survey of business practices related to contracts problems. See S Macaulay, 'Non-Contractual Relations in Business: A Preliminary Study' (1963) 28 *American Sociological Review* 55 (1963).

More difficult are the cases where the words are there in a form more easily read and understood but where the probabilities are very great that only the most suspicious will discover and translate them correctly. This is often true of printed form 'contracts' and procedures for using them which are produced by large corporations to govern what to them are routine transactions.[4] As we know, often these organizations attempt to use contract ideology to legislate privately; sometimes successfully, sometimes not. How then should we decide that one does or does not have a duty to read and understand? . . .

[Eds Note: Part II is omitted; it discusses several examples of the duty to read in the case law, particularly of Wisconsin.]

III. THE UNDERLYING FACTORS

A. General Considerations

It is fairly easy to spin out examples of where the duty to read and understand does and does not take hold. Moreover, some of the relevant dimensions seem obvious. Assuming an arms-length bargain between businessmen who are experienced risk-takers, one of them should not be able to disappoint the other's expectations and likely or actual reliance by asserting, 'Oh, but I didn't read the contract.' The signed document is too useful a form for signaling the closing of a deal to allow such a defense without very strong reasons for upsetting the transaction. Moreover, the magic of the act of signing is well-known; and usually there is reason to assume that the deal was set as written since typically the one does not know of the other's failure to read and understand. On the other hand, at some point there seems good reason to ignore a written contract procured by trickery. Rational planning and risk assumption would not be served by enforcing the part of a contract written in lemon juice which could only be read over the heat of a candle when the one signing had not been informed of the secret. Some business forms and the ways they are used are almost this bad. There is some danger that a judge, temporarily bereft of his common sense, could apply the duty-to-read slogan to what really is close to an invisible ink case and enforce the document as written. It is easy to be swept up in the moralistic attitude of self-reliance in situations where this is demanding conduct more properly classified as paranoid.

[4] See generally 'Note' (1950) 63 *Harvard Law Review* 494.

B. An Organization of Substantive Contract and Legal System Policies

1. *The Dimensions of the Substantive Policies.*

While it is hard to disagree with this quick explanation of the duty to read and understand, I think much more is involved in the kinds of cases that were offered as examples. The first step toward judgments about the proper results in these cases is to make explicit the major policy considerations necessarily involved. An analytical scheme I find helpful calls for first separating out the substantive policies that contract and restitution may serve and then identifying at least some of the goals related to the proper or efficient operation of the legal system.[5] For example, we might want our legal system to aid the operation of the insurance industry in order to minimize premium costs (a substantive policy), but we also might want our legal system, insofar as reasonably possible, to reflect the policy choices of a community consensus or those made by an elected legislature rather than those of an appointed judge (a system policy).

Substantive policies primarily can be classified on two dimensions. The first concerns a choice of a market or non-market orientation, in which contract law and restitution can either (a) be tools to facilitate the operation of a market economy – focusing on the needs of those exchanging goods, services, labor and capital or (b) serve to blunt the impact of the unregulated market by refusing to recognize some socially undesirable business practices or by giving aid to people or groups seeking to get out

[5] [original fn 18] These classifications were first worked out in S Macaulay, 'Restitution in Context' (1959) 107 *University of Pennsylvania Law Review* 1133; S Macaulay, 'Justice Traynor and the Law of Contracts' (1961) 13 *Stanford Law Review* 812. Recently my colleague John Hetherington refined these classifications in his article, 'Trends in Enterprise Liability: Law and the Unauthorized Agent', which is to appear in the *Stanford Law Review*. I learned much from his article.

My colleague Lawrence M Friedman has dealt with the problem of more or less generalized rules in L Friedman, *Contract Law in America* (Madison, University of Wisconsin Press, 1965), and in L Friedman, 'Law, Rules, and the Interpretation of Written Documents' (1965) 59 *Northwestern University Law Review* 751. In *Contract Law in America,* he describes a continuing trend from abstract rules toward standards that allow the judges to look at the nuances of each case. In my terms, this progression is from rigorous market functioning rules to either transactional or relief-of-hardship approaches. In 'Law, Rules, and the Interpretation of Written Documents', he discusses 'mandatory' and 'discretionary' rules which is one of the dimensions of my classification. Both of the Friedman pieces are of major importance. Both of us owe a good deal to Max Weber.

Social planning policy tends to be carried out by legislation removing a whole area from the domain of contract law-areas 'spin off' for special treatment such as labor law or occupational licensing. This process is the major theme of the Friedman book, and one that is developed brilliantly. For my comments on the possible relevance of contracts ideas after an area has been removed and given special treatment, see S Macaulay, 'Changing a Continuing Relationship Between a Large Corporation and Those Who Deal With It: Automobile Manufacturers, Their Dealers, and the Legal System Part II' (1965) 1965 *Wisconsin Law Review* 740, 848–50.

from under onerous contracts. The second dimension concerns the approaches by which contract law and restitution can proceed, tending toward either (a) relatively precise general rules or (b) a case-by-case approach.[6] This classification yields four primary categories which must be explained in some detail. The categories, and their somewhat arbitrary names, can be represented as follows:

	market goals	**other than market goals**
Generalizing approach ("rules")	market functioning policy	social (or economic) planning policy
Particularistic approach ('Case-by-case')	transactional policy	relief-of-hardship policy

a. *Market functioning policy* calls for rules of general application in relatively specific terms which minimize (but never eliminate) the creative role of judge and jury or administrators. Predictable law is to be preferred to results that satisfy in particular cases. Thus the parties can consider the impact of contract law both in planning their bargains and in settling disputes. Legal results will not turn on vague abstractions such as 'good faith' but on specific conduct such as signing a contract. In addition to certainty, the rules should tend to reward rational assessment of risks in the market and penalize unbusiness-like conduct. One can usefully identify at least three products of market functioning policy: increased self-reliance, rewards to the crafty, and advantages to the operation of bureaucratic organizations.

The duty to read in a fairly strict form carries out the substantive goal. The legal system should enforce contracts 'as written' and ignore pleas that one party did not read or understand, that the parties agreed that some of the written terms would not apply or that additional ones which were never reduced to writing would apply, and that the words used should be read in some unusual fashion, or in light of some general abstraction such as 'reasonableness'. On the basis of common sense but not much evidence, some have assumed that this tack will promote

[6] [original fn 19] Of course, my transactional and market functioning categories differ from the orthodox learning about the meeting of the minds (subjective theory) and the objective theory of contracts. I would view a meeting of the minds approach as entirely a non-market approach; it usually operates as a rationalization for relief-of-hardship. Moreover, there are many kinds of objective theories which fall on the scale that ranges from transactional to market functioning. At one extreme, an objective theory can mean that a contract neither party intended but both appear to have made will be enforced. At the other extreme, transactional policy can call for imposing liability on one who has, without using due care, misled another by his language and conduct, even though the careless person did not "intend" to make a contract. As is apparent from this discussion, my categories are not dichotomies but extreme points on a range: a given rule or standard is *more or less*, say, transactional or market functional, or *more or less*, say, transactional or based on relief-of-hardship.

self-reliance. If one knows he will be legally bound to what he signs, he will take care to protect himself (or so it is said). And this would be a good thing. People will recognize risks, allocate them in their bargains and plan to deal with them rationally. As a result, more bargains will approach the economists' ideal where both leave the bargaining table in a better position than when the negotiations began. Moreover, disputes during the life of the transaction should tend to be minimized since the process of reading and understanding should make clear who is to do what and who is to take what loss if a particular risk occurs. Also where the legal result is clearly that documents will mean what they say, there is less chance that in settlement negotiations one party's rights must be discounted because of the risk of what a jury might do or because of delay.

Such rules reward those who plan and are careful. In one view those who can drive the best bargains, short of gross fraud, are entitled to their winnings. Perhaps one who can slip into a contract with terms highly favorable to himself which are undetected by the other party, is to be praised for his skill rather than censured. This is just good salesmanship. In this view, a bargain is not an exchange of mutual advantage but a game where each party is to maximize his own gains at the expense of the other. Some may feel that the ability to do well in this game is a skill to be rewarded. A strict duty-to-read rule often will help supply this reward.

Another product of market functioning policy – advantages to the operation of bureaucratic organizations – often derives from people being treated as if they had read and understood a written contract even when it is probable they have not done so. Large economic organizations frequently promulgate rules to govern their exchanges with other organizations and individuals. Typically these rules are cast, or can be cast, in the form of a contract. The other unit's representative or the other individual signs a printed form document or accepts a contractual symbol (say, delivery of a document or goods) although he has little chance or incentive to read, understand, bargain to change the rules or do any or all of these things. Larger firms operate this way for a number of reasons. They must deal through a corps of agents in a myriad of transactions. As a result, there is a need to standardize and formalize procedures. On one hand, the large organization must control its agents who deal with the outside world and limit their power to 'give the company away'. These agents are under many pressures to treat their customers as individuals and tailor the particular deal to suit their customers' needs; most obvious is the pressure to make sales to earn commissions or promotions. Also, 'the customer is always right' in the salesman's world. A rigid form contract which the customer must sign without alteration often is thought to be an efficient way to exercise control over salesmen. The customer is 'on notice' of the salesman's limited authority, and the firm wants to avoid being legally bound to expectations its salesman has created by his conduct that are inconsistent with company policy. On the other hand, the written document signed by the customer becomes the obligation within the larger organization because of the problems of internal communication. It specifies what must be produced or shipped, and it indicates the full extent of future payments to be received and contingent obligations assumed. If a salesman has made a promise inconsistent with the formal written contract which is highly standardized, it is difficult to communicate this to those who must perform and to those who must make plans based on cash flow and risk assumption. Even if the inconsistent promise is communicated, it poses a problem for a rational bureaucratic organization which tends to thrive on routine. Large organizations are helped if they can control and plan their exposure to risks; if they can do so, their accounting and pricing will be more accurate, and they will not have to set up large reserves to cover a host of unpredictable contingencies. Arguably, this kind of certainty will foster their activities in the market which in turn should yield more jobs and more products at lower prices. A rather strict duty to read, rather than attacking the balance of economic power in the society, supports the operations of large organizations that have this power. This tends to promote rational business affairs, whatever the impact on the individual who assumed he could rely on what he was told rather than what he signed. . . .

Usually these bureaucratic considerations are coupled with the self-reliance idea – the large organization can deal through standardized forms and the prudent individual will protect himself by reading and taking appropriate action – although at times the likelihood of self protection is slim indeed. Occasionally, bureaucratic policy is coupled with a requirement designed to help self-reliance. For example, a Virginia statute demands that a written contract be set in a certain size type to be legally enforceable,[7] the *Uniform Commercial Code* requires some warranty disclaimers to be conspicuous to be effective.[8]

b. *Transactional policy*, the second policy category, also seeks to aid the operation of the market, but with a case-by-case strategy rather than by rules that ignore particular circumstances. The courts ought to take steps to carry out the particular transaction brought before them – they should discover the bargain-in-fact and enforce it with appropriate remedies cut to fit the facts of the case. If this discovery is not possible, the court should work out a result involving the least disruption of plans and causing the least amount of reliance loss in light of the situation at the time of the dispute. In short, courts should seek to implement the 'sense of the transaction', and thus solve the problem in the particular case in market terms – assumption of the risk, reasonable reliance, and so on.

[7] [original fn 20] Virginia Code Annotated § 11-4 (1950).

[8] [original fn 21] *Uniform Commercial Code* § 2-316(2).

Transactional policy calls for a duty to read and understand only where the one who has failed to do this is responsible for misleading the other into believing that the document has been read and approved or that the careless one is willing to sign and assume the risk of whatever might be found in the document. Suppose seller sends buyer an offer quoting a price in a letter which also very clearly spells out a number of conditions the seller says are most important to him. The buyer reads the first few sentences of the letter and the price quoted but not the seller's important conditions. The buyer writes on the bottom margin of the seller's letter, 'We accept your offer', and signs it; he then mails this back to the seller who begins production of the items in question. The buyer later wants to back out and asserts he did not read the seller's conditions and would not have agreed to them if he had. The buyer has been negligent in conveying his agreement, resulting in disappointed plans and at least the probability of a good deal of reliance loss. A court following a transactional approach would treat the buyer as if he had read and understood the seller's letter. But the decision would turn on the rather extreme facts of the case – the buyer's communication was careless and caused either very probable or actual injury.

Perhaps more often transactional policy will call for overturning or modifying a written document (by reforming or construing it) in the light of the bargain-in-fact of the parties.[9] While a case can be made for self-reliance, part of decent social and business conduct is trust. In many negotiation situations all of the pressures push for friendly gestures rather than a suspicious line-by-line analysis of the writing. The buyer of home siding can believe the president of the home remodeling company when he says his siding will not rust or crack; the buyer does not have to parse the text of the lengthy and technical printed form and spot the integration clause at his peril. In cases such as this, the writing was drafted to run counter to the likely agreement-in-fact. If a court is seeking the actual sense of the transaction, it will not let such a writing get in its way.

It seems to me that the growing English doctrine of fundamental breach[10] is an expression of transactional policy. There, judicial enforcement of clauses limiting liability is denied when enforcement would be inconsistent with the 'core' or primary purposes and obligations of the contract. For example, a seller cannot agree in the typed part of a contract to deliver a machine which will produce so many units a minute to a certain tolerance and then successfully disclaim all liability for the failure of his machine to

[9] [original fn 22] Comment 1 to *Uniform Commercial Code* § 2-302 states, 'The principle is one of the prevention of oppression and unfair surprise ... not of disturbance of allocation of risks because of superior bargaining power.' This clearly pushes for a transactional approach in applying the concept 'unconscionable contract or clause'. It is highly ambiguous as to whether or not it contemplates also a relief-of-hardship approach. The 'superior bargaining power' reference indicates that it does not, but then what is the meaning of 'oppression'?

[10] [original fn 23] See Meyer, *Contracts of Adhesion and the Doctrine of Fundamental Breach*, 50 VA. L. REV. 1178 (1964).

perform by printing boiler-plate clauses on the back of a form he uses. From the standpoint of the particular transaction, assertion of the disclaimer clause is little more than trickery. In this kind of case, market functioning policy would call for enforcing the contract as written; transactional policy demands enforcement of the contract-in-fact so that the buyer's reasonable expectations are honored.

c. *Social planning policies* can be reflected in contracts and restitution, as well. In one sense, rather than enforcing the bargain that was made, in this third type of policy the courts will enforce the bargain which the parties should have made. Conversely, the courts may refuse to take any action when the actual bargain is found offensive. This policy is something of a catchall, as social planning can call for a variety of things ranging from wealth redistribution to the regulation, or even promotion, of particular types of people, industries or transactions. The most obvious examples involve a change in the market context by removing certain types of bargains from the kinds that will be enforced by the legal system or by requiring or prohibiting particular terms in some bargains. Again, this is a generalizing approach stressing specific rules, so it parallels market functioning policy in strategy – but the goals of the two are very different since social planning policies, by definition, seek to blunt the impact of the market.

A social planning rule relevant to our topic would be one that said certain classes of people could not be held to contracts they signed or accepted, despite their careless failure to read and protect themselves. One could conceive of a rule protecting such people as consumers, illiterates, those of limited mental ability or minors. In effect, the power of a minor to disaffirm even contracts that he has read and understood is such a rule.[11] Since, in theory, the minor cannot guard his own interests, the legal system protects him from his own carelessness and improvident bargains. Consumers may get some of the same treatment under *Uniform Commercial Code* section 2-719's provisions on limiting remedies for breach of warranty; perhaps consumers need not read and protect themselves since limitations of liability for personal injury caused by a breach of warranty are prima facie unconscionable. It is difficult to offer many examples of this kind of social planning rule since the legal system has preferred a more case-by-case (relief of hardship) approach, rather than letting a whole class of people out of certain kinds of contracts. On the other hand, social planning goals often enter as the price for following the bureaucratic type of market functioning policy. For example, the standard fire insurance policy is set by statute in many states.[12] One side of the coin involves the setting of terms deemed fair to the consumer by the legislature – removing the

[11] [original fn 24] See, e.g., RESTATEMENT (SECOND), CONTRACTS §§ 18, 18B (Tent. Draft No. 1, 1964).

[12] original fn 25] See, e.g., WIS. STAT. § 203.01 (1963).

insurance contract from the area of self-reliance and the exercise of market power. The other side of the coin, however, involves telling insurance companies that if they follow the statute, certain practices have been validated. An insurance company can know where it stands, and this certainty may be extremely important to it. The insurers get certainty at the cost of following fair terms imposed by the legal system.

d. *Relief-of-hardship* is the fourth policy. It calls for the legal system to let one party out of his bargain in exceptional cases where enforcement would be unduly harsh, or, where the content of the bargain is in doubt, to place the burden on the party best able to spread the loss or absorb it. This case-by-case approach is based not upon considerations of market functioning or protecting actual expectations but upon ethical ideals and emotional reactions to the plight of the underdog, to pressing an advantage too far, to making too much profit, or to inequality of resources. To a great extent, this is the policy that is not expressed openly in contract doctrine, but courts can construe language and stretch the innocent misrepresentation or mistake doctrines to help out when the facts are particularly appealing. When done with a deft hand, a relief-of-hardship approach will leave little trace of a precedent to embarrass the court in the next case, where the facts are not quite so appealing.

It is hard to offer a pure example of this policy in operation, but it can be suggested that a good deal of it lurks in the insurance release cases where a duty to read and understand sometimes is and sometimes is not applied.[13] Also the Supreme Court of Wisconsin in several cases has stressed the lack of education of the person seeking to be relieved from a written contract he signed or accepted.[14] On one hand, this factor tracks with transactional policy and the degree of care one could expect from a particular individual. Arguably, an illiterate is not responsible for misleading one who knows the illiterate cannot read the document he signed. But on the other hand, the party seeking to uphold the contract, especially the home office of a corporation that deals through salesmen in the field, may have no way accurately to gauge the education and literacy of the man who signed the printed form. Its expectations and potential reliance remain despite the literacy of the man it dealt with. Still the factor may lead to the overthrow of the written treaty. We can speculate that the inability to read and understand is correlated with a generally low socio-economic status, and such people may be the best candidates for relief-of-hardship in the eyes of many.

[13] [original fn 26] One of my favorite notes in any casebook is Dawson and Palmer's historical survey of the Minnesota insurance release cases. In Minnesota, as in other states, sometimes insurance releases stick, but often they do not. See DAWSON & PALMER, CASES ON RESTITUTION 686-88 (1958). See also Ricketts v. Pennsylvania R.R., 153 F.2d 757 (2d Cir. 1946).

[14] [original fn 27] See, *e.g.*, Engel v. Van Den Boogart, 255 Wis. 81, 37 N.W.2d 852 (1949); Lefebvre v Nickolai, 205 Wis. 115, 236 N.W. 684 (1931). *But see* Institute of Commercial Art v. Maurice, 272 Wis. 499, 76 N.W.2d 332 (1956).

e. *Overlaps and Interrelationships.* Of course, a great deal of overlap among these policies is possible because they refer to tendencies rather than pure categories. A particular decision may be justified by reference to several different policies, both market and non market in orientation. For example, in *Miller v Stanich,*[15] a tenant had a right to renew his lease for five years. He wanted to renew it for that term, and, in addition, get a right to renew for another five years after the first renewal term had expired. The landlord's agent told the tenant that the landlord was unlikely to agree to an additional renewal term. The tenant, following the adage that 'there is no harm in asking', sent two lease forms to the landlord. One called for the five-year term to which the tenant was entitled; the other called for that five years plus an option to renew for an additional five years. The landlord, who could read only German, took both leases to his lawyer since they were written in English. The landlord, as predicted, did not want to give the tenant an option to renew for an additional five years after the next five year term expired. However, by oversight, the landlord's lawyer filled in the date on the lease form that contained the option to renew. The landlord took the forms home, signed the dated lease and sent it to the tenant. Undoubtedly, the tenant was delighted at his good fortune, but his joy was short-lived. The landlord discovered his error and demanded that it be corrected. If we were to apply a strict self-reliance duty to read approach consistent with functional policy, the result would be clear – the landlord would be bound. And indeed, this was the view of three Justices of the Supreme Court of Wisconsin. But four Justices joined in an opinion reforming the lease to strip it of the additional option for a five-year term,[16] arguing that the tenant had not 'taken any steps whatever in reliance upon the provision for a five-year extension'.[17] On one hand, transactional policy claims are weak because of the unusually low risk of reliance; it seems unlikely that the tenant could not have found good alternative premises for a term to begin five years in the future. On the other hand, the balance of hardship and fault favors the landlord. The majority thought the facts called for relief, despite the landlord's failure to read and understand.

Even though these policies are interrelated and overlap, the classification suggested here has proved useful. It serves to clarify the issues and separates distinct arguments so that they reinforce each other rather than confuse matters. The classification also serves as a checklist to lessen the chance that a relevant argument will be neglected.

[15] [original fn 28] 202 Wis. 539, 230 N.W. 47, *rev'd on rehearing,* 233 N.W. 753 (1930).

[16] [original fn 29] *Miller v Stanich,* 202 Wis. 539, 233 N.W. 753 (1930). The court granted rescission on the condition that the landlord execute and file a lease in the form and terms of the lease he intended to deliver.

[17] [original fn 30] *Miller v. Stanich,* supra note 15 [original fn 28], at 545, 230 N.W. at 49 (dissent).

2. The Dimensions of Some Legal System Policies.

In addition to these substantive goals of contract and restitution, there are also a number of goals related to one's view of the proper or efficient functioning of the legal system.

a. *Pressure on the Docket.* The simplest example is the goal of preventing the dockets from becoming overcrowded. To the extent that a person could easily reopen an insurance release, for example, because he did not read or understand it, and try his claim, an already crowded personal injury docket could be increased. This would obviously produce problems: the courts would be faced with even more personal injury cases – a type that in many cities is not handled well or quickly. More personnel might be required to prevent the courts from falling even further behind. Moreover, the condition of the court dockets is a key ploy in the settlement process. Those that can afford to wait have great advantages in cities where there are great delays. A claimant's legal rights are less valuable if he does not have sufficient assets to await trial or cannot borrow. Obviously, it does not make sense to incur costs of this sort unless the gains in terms of substantive policies are thought to be great.

b. *Accurate Fact Finding.* Another legal system policy clearly wrapped up in the duty to read and understand is the goal of accurate fact-finding. Often when a court announces a sweeping duty to read and confines counter-rules narrowly, one senses that the court is concerned with the likelihood of perjury and the difficulties of adjudicating facts. It is easy to make up a story about one's assumptions that are contradicted by a written contract. Moreover, appellate judges might be concerned about jury sympathy playing a role which would undercut substantive policies calling for the enforcement of written contracts. For example, several of the Wisconsin duty-to-read cases involve a buyer who spoke or read only German, seeking to overturn a contract written in English before a jury that probably was composed of his neighbors and friends. The seller was an outsider to the community. One can seldom prove that the risk of jury bias was influential in a court's decision, but one can be suspicious.[18]

[18] [original fn 31] In a number of cases decided between the 1870's and the early 1900's, the Supreme Court of Wisconsin dealt harshly with the defense that the party who wanted to avoid a written contract spoke or read only German and not English, the language in which the contract was written. See Deering v. Hoeft, 111 Wis. 339, 87 N.W. 298 (1901); Dowagiac Mfg. Co. v. Schroeder, 108 Wis. 109, 84 N.W. 14 (1900); German Bank v. Muth, 96 Wis. 342, 71 N.W. 361 (1897); Albrecht v. Milwaukee & S. Ry., 87 Wis. 105, 58 N.W. 72 (1894); Fuller v. Madison Mut. Ins. Co., 36 Wis. 599 (1875). *But see* Walker v. Ebert, 29 Wis. 194 (1871). On one hand, these seem rigorous market functioning policy opinions, but it is likely that there is a good deal of social planning too. The rule was that the German population of Wisconsin during that period could not escape written contracts they signed by testifying before a jury composed of fellow German speaking neighbors that the oral deal was different. This served the social policy of integration-the cases were one more incentive for the German immigrants to learn English and become 'Americanized'. By 1930, things were different. See the discussion of *Miller v Stanich* in the text at notes 15–17 [original fns 28-30] *supra*.

A prominent Wisconsin lawyer from a smaller city told me that he feels he can break most printed-form contracts by inviting the national organization seeking to enforce one to come to his city and face a local jury. As we move from relatively general rules to case-by-case standards involving particulars, we may increase this jury factor and promote bargaining at the settlement stage based on jury risk. Some might think this undesirable. On the other hand, a duty to read coupled with exceptions largely in the court's control can be useful in allowing the court to deal with perjury without being forced to label it as such. But while this tactic may be useful, it carries the costs of most case-by-case approaches–a loss of predictability and an increased risk of arbitrariness.

c. *Efficacy and Efficiency: What Can Be Done and at What Costs?* On another level, the four substantive policies place differing demands upon the capacity of the legal system to gain information about the nature of particular problems with which it must deal-the 'input' stage–and the consequences of the existing legal situation and possible alternative courses of action-the 'feedback' stage. First, the problem of inputs of information: a case-by-case approach increases the demands on the fact-finding process. *Transactional policy* calls for a careful assessment of expectations created by the entire exchange situation and of possible reliance losses from opportunities that might have been taken had the contract in question not been made. Often one would have to work with tacit assumptions and implicit understandings based on practices in particular industries. This is not easy, and there is a great risk of error. Rather than take this chance, a judge can follow the safety of the written word and preach about the duty to make it correspond with the bargain in fact. *Relief-of-hardship* policy calls for a careful weighing of such factors as who can best bear the loss, decisions loaded with implicit value judgments as well as factual issues. From the feedback stand-point a case-by-case approach can be administered to have a relatively less serious impact than a 'rules' approach. Each decision need go no further than handling the dispute between the particular parties. However, the chance of winning in a decision system based on particular nuances can influence the settlement negotiation process, and all 'legal rights' then have to be discounted by this factor. Insofar as there are types of business transactions where the legal enforceability of contracts is important, uncertainty is increased and claims with some plausibility become worth more. Of course, it is most difficult for either courts or administrative agencies to assess the impact of their actions on private dispute settlement. There is little, if any, systematically obtained knowledge about such matters, and it would not be easy to study this process if one set out to do so.

An approach based upon rules of relatively specific content makes a different set of demands on the legal system. One can adopt *market functioning policy* as the primary strategy and assume that once the rules are known it matters little what they are; if the consequences of their application are substantively offensive to some, the relations between people and organizations can be arranged by the parties to avoid the situations covered by the rule or an appeal to the legislature can be made to carve out a special area to protect a deserving class of people. Thus, a court could routinely hold a man to a written contract he signed, overturning only the most extreme forms of deception. Of course, sometimes one can prompt a heated political discussion by exploring the assumptions involved in this line of argument. Perhaps some people need protection or relief of hardship. On the other hand, if the legal system is going to do some *social planning*, several most difficult, and fairly obvious, input and feedback problems are presented. Case-finding often is accidental; a court lacks the chance to legislate about problems not brought before it, and even a legislature is hampered in discovering some social problems because of pressure of major issues such as taxation and budgets. (An administrative agency sometimes can do better if it is not blocked by political pressure or limited resources.) Moreover, even when a problem is presented for solution, the entire legal system, and particularly a court, lacks tools to produce data about both the likely consequences of proposals for change as well as the community consensus on the right mix of values relevant to the problem. Moreover, both courts and legislatures often have no way of discovering the full range of consequences of their past actions; if a result is sufficiently bad, someone may bring up a new case to the court or may appear before the legislature. But some attempts at planning can have impacts that are hard to see or impacts on those not able to use the legal system effectively. It is difficult to know exactly what will happen if people need not read certain contracts or if they must read others as far as the legal system is concerned. Sometimes the impact would be great; sometimes no one would care.

d. *Democratic Ideals as Related to Who Makes Policy and How.* Furthermore, the ideal of a democratic government poses some restraint on how free courts or agencies are or should be to decide cases based upon reaction to particular circumstances or to create rules based upon social policies not enacted by legislatures and not endorsed by a wide public consensus. Of course, the practical problem is not one of the right to base decisions on whim or the duty to apply hard and fast rules that allow no 'leeways'. The problem is one of proportion – few if any people call for a judge to decide by taking bribes or flipping coins ('discretion' doesn't mean this), or for judges to apply mechanically set doctrines of fixed content where the rule just does not fit. (We also can deny that any such mechanically pure rules exist. It seems doubtful that the duty to read, unless there is a good excuse, is such a rule.)

Judges are more removed from the electorate than legislators, and judges have some obligation to remember this before they undertake social reform through case law. However, given the need to decide cases, the very nature of law forces the decision-maker to choose between one policy and another in many situations. Our traditions impose some limits on the frame from which a judge may choose – for example, he is not to reward his friends and punish his enemies. Yet these limitations often are not decisive. Within the area of acceptable decisions there are judgments to be made.This is particularly true of the duty to read and understand situations. Within the common law tradition one can hold a man to precisely what he signed or turn in the other direction and talk of his actual expectations and construe a duty of good faith into the contractual language. Moreover, there is no manifest, strongly-held public consensus on such questions. Nonetheless, the allocation of functions within the United States legal system counsels those officials whose policy choices are more removed from approval or disapproval by an electorate to remember the nature of their place in the system. Perhaps this calls for making judgments, other things being equal, so that the burden of getting them changed by another unit of government rests on the one practically best able to present his case there. For example, organized interest groups usually can take care of themselves before a legislature; individuals often cannot.

When, then, should there be a duty to read? The problem is one of balancing the capabilities of and the values we hold about the legal system against our substantive goals. *The Uniform Commercial Code* suggests that it may be helpful to make a rather crude division into contracts between merchants and all others. It is true that one's judgement about a duty to read and understand *may* differ in various kinds of cases involving various kinds of people. An exchange of written documents between parties advised by lawyers perhaps calls for different treatment than a printed form used by a large corporation and accepted by a consumer under circumstances where he is unlikely to read and understand. One can subdivide the categories even further. Perhaps the documents involved in multi-party financing transactions should be given far more deference than the conflicting purchase order and acknowledgement forms so typical of the sale of 'shelf' goods by one manufacturer to another. Perhaps a printed form used in dealing with relatively high socio-economic status consumers which reflects a reasonable or customary allocation of risks should be treated differently from a printed form designed to aid in the exploitation of the poor. On the other hand, while such a case-type approach has immediate appeal to most law teachers who cut their teeth on realistic jurisprudence, it does have real costs if we assume that the legal enforceability of any large number of contracts really makes a difference to anyone. Instead of supporting the existing allocation of power in the society, courts, in some if not all of the examples given, are being asked to protect individuals from the exercise of that power. Moreover, courts are being asked to plan without much more than common sense and hunches about the nature of the problem they are confronting or the likely consequences of their decisions. And a court's choice may be what we think is the wrong policy in an area where it has the last word because the doors to the legislature are closed as a result of the balance of economic and political power in the situation. No solution is cost free; the best that can be asked is that our judges and legislators proceed with caution to avoid any unnecessary costs.

[*Eds Note: A final section of the article, Part IV, examines the question of cardholder liability for use of a lost or stolen credit card and the response of the courts, focusing on their use of the idea of a duty to read and understand. A few years later, Congress adopted the federal Truth In Lending Act of 1968, which capped consumer liability in these situations at $50 and eliminated it entirely if, inter alia, the consumer gave notice of the loss or theft before the unauthorized use. 15 USC § 1643.*]

V. CONCLUSION

The example of the kinds of things I see in the concept of a duty to read indicates what a complex problem is inherent in a simple slogan. I suspect that an equally lengthy essay would result if one were to look to the operation of the whole cluster of duty to read rules as they apply to the sale of residential real estate, insurance releases, personal injury disclaimers found in instruction manuals to consumer items, and the other areas where documents and actual understanding is alleged to conflict. I think it is clear that it will help to ask in each area to what extent standardization is valuable. Do we care about the actual or likely expectations of the one trying to avoid the written document or are we content if he had a fighting chance to protect himself? Do we want to aid those who promulgate form documents so much that notice is a minor value? The substantive contract policy scheme suggested – transactional, market functioning, relief-of-hardship, and social planning – helps focus attention on these crucial questions. Then we cannot forget the demands of our kind of legal system. Finally, we need data about the likely consequences of proposals and the actual consequences of legal action. If we lack this, we have to consider the risks of shooting in the dark. Sometimes this is the only sensible course open; often it is not. If it must be done, the risk can be minimized by adopting approaches that particularize rather than approaches that work like a shotgun.

The Real and the Paper Deal: Empirical Pictures of Relationships, Complexity and the Urge for Transparent Simple Rules

STEWART MACAULAY*

ASSUME THAT CONTRACT law matters, at least in some subset of all the situations where people consider making or do make contracts. Also assume that contract law should rest to a large extent on choice or responsibility for misleading others about one's choices. Making these assumptions, we must be concerned with how the legal system deals with the expectations of the parties. One approach is formal. Judges can limit themselves to dealing with only the formal expressions of the parties – the paper deal. They need ask only whether the parties signed or accepted a document, and if they did, what is the 'plain meaning' of the words they used. Sometimes, writings labeled 'contract' do capture many if not most of the expectations of those who sign them.

Often, however, the paper deal will not reflect the real deal: a writing can be inconsistent with the actual expectations of the parties. Courts frequently have sought to protect such actual expectations despite the presence of a writing that does not mention them or even one that is inconsistent with them. However, establishing real expectations often is very difficult. Courts face what Richard Danzig has called 'the capability problem.'[1] Some expectations, for example, are only tacit assumptions – what I would have said if I had thought about a question that I did not think about. Even if the parties did have real expectations that they did not express in their written

* Malcolm Pitman Sharp Hilldale Professor, Theodore W. Brazeau Bascom Professor of Law, The University of Wisconsin Law School. I have discussed the issues considered in this article with my Wisconsin colleagues, John Kidwell and William Whitford, and I have learned much from them. David Campbell commented on a draft of this article, and it is much better as a result. All mistakes are mine; I did not take all the good advice offered. An earlier draft of this paper was presented at a seminar, 'Implicit Dimensions of Contracts', held at the LSE on 26 November 2001 and funded by the MLR Annual Seminar Competition.

[1] R. Danzig, The Capability Problem in Contract Law (Mineola, NY: Foundation Press, Inc., 1978).

document, we must worry that today's testimony about them will be self-serving and fabricated to make the case come out the right way. Also, proving the real deal often will be very costly. The parties must convey a commercial context to a judge or to jurors. They may come to the task with little, if any, knowledge of the part of the business world in question. Experts can inform them, but experts are not free.

If we want our courts to carry out the expectations of the parties to contracts, both those that they express in writing and those that are left unrecorded or even unspoken, we must accept a contract law that rests on standards rather than on clear, quantitative rules. Contract law then will talk of 'good faith', 'duties of cooperation', or 'within limits set by commercial reasonableness.'[2] Others have written much about what standards are most appropriate.[3]

However, there are objections to writing contract law in the qualitative fashion that seems necessary that are so well known that we can call them classic. Furthermore, there are also classic responses to these objections.[4] In this paper I will ask whether we can do more than just reprise these old songs and hear one group of scholars, judges and lawyers sing one song while another group whistles the other. We can clarify our choices by examining each from a law and society perspective – that is, by asking how the law in action appears from the point of view of business people and their lawyers. Moreover, we can gain a little ground in at least one limited subset of contract cases if we focus on judges in such disputes serving as agents of settlement. With all of its flaws, such coerced cooperation may be the least bad solution in many situations.

I will review briefly some of the reasons that the paper deal often does not reflect the real deal or the implicit dimension of contract. . . . My conclusion is not startling: we cannot have our cake and eat it too. There are

[2] See, eg, Uniform Commercial Code §2-311(1): 'An agreement for sale which is otherwise sufficiently definite . . . to be a contract is not made invalid by the fact that it leaves particulars of performance to be specified by one of the parties. Any such specification must be made in good faith and within the limits set by commercial reasonableness.'

[3] D. Campbell, 'Reflexivity and Welfarism in the Modem Law of Contract' (2000) 20 *Oxford Journal of Legal Studies* 477, 497, notes that much American writing on contracts, except that of Ian Macneil, criticises classical contract law but fails to set out a rival theory. I have said: 'people should not attempt to write about contracts until they have studied Macneil.' S. Macaulay, 'Relational Contracts Floating on a Sea of Custom? Thoughts About the Ideas of Ian Macneil and Lisa Bernstein' (2000) 94 *Northwestern University Law Review* 775, 776. Nonetheless, I am skeptical about whether anyone can create a complete rival theory applicable to all kinds of contracts without a good deal of oversimplification. I also doubt that any such grand rival theory could be sold to the judges and lawyers who would have to put it into practice. See J. M. Feinman, 'Relational Contract Theory in Context' (2000) 94 *Northwestern University Law Review* 737. I would be pleased to be proven wrong. My contribution, if any, will be only to look at proposals and arguments advocating positions and to ask whether they seem compatible with business practices about which I know something. Pointing out over generalisations and questionable assumptions is still valuable work.

[4] The best discussion of these classic pro and con arguments is D. Kennedy, 'Form and Substance in Private Law Adjudication' (1976) 89 *Harvard Law Review* 1685.

costs and benefits flowing from focusing on the paper deal and from focusing on the real deal. The twentieth century history of American contract law and scholarship reflects cycles of privileging one judgment about those costs and benefits and then rejecting it and adopting another. Finally, I will suggest that in a limited subset of all contract cases, we should be content with almost any approach that leads to settlements that give expression, more or less, to relational norms and values.

THE GAP BETWEEN THE REAL DEAL AND THE PAPER DEAL

Things are easier for some parties and courts if the legal system focuses entirely on any written document that the parties have signed or accepted. If legal agencies do this consistently, corporate lawyers, for example, need worry less about what their client's sales people say or do. However, this approach requires courts to close their eyes to real expectations resting in the implicit dimensions of contract and significant reliance on them. Contracts are always more than the contract document. We have long known the many reasons for this: Words do not have a fixed meaning that every speaker of the language will translate the same way. We create the meaning of written language by bringing to the words some measure of context, background assumptions, our experiences, and, too often, our bias, ignorance and stupidities.[5]

Also, it is very hard to bring the future to the present and provide that X will happen if event Y takes place.[6] Our ability to predict the future is limited, and even careful business people often leave gaps in written contracts. The world changes and surprises us: wars break out in places where we do not expect them; or our contract may have dealt with a war but left open what happens when the indirect effect of a major terrorist attack makes performance much more costly; OPEC drives up energy costs unexpectedly; new technologies, often involving computers, change things so that an older contract no longer makes sense.

[5] See Professor Linzer's discussion of *Shore* v *Motorola*, in P. Linzer, 'Rough Justice: A Theory of Restitution and Reliance, Contracts and Torts' (2001) *Wisconsin Law Review* 695, 764–772. The price of the position I take in this article is that I have to accept that sometimes judges will use their discretion to reach results that I think are outrageous. *Shore* v *Motorola* was for me an unhappy example.

[6] By the 'real deal' I mean both those actual expectations that exist in and out of a written contract and the generalized expectation that a trading partner will behave reasonably in solving problems as they arise. My experience talking with business people suggest that reading written contracts clauses to one another seldom would be seen as a reasonable way to solve problems. There may be situations where applying the letter of a written document would be a reasonable way to cope with a contract problem, but I suspect that these situations are a very limited group of all contract problems. Also, there are situations where parties do not expect the other to act reasonably for the mutual benefit of the relationship. Again, I would expect this to be a very limited group of cases because some trust is needed before most people will make contracts.

Even when we can foresee that it is possible that something might happen, there are limits on the time that we can or should spend on trying to provide for all contingencies in our contracts. In most instances, it would not pay to hire enough people with the skill needed to review what is printed in fine print on the back of various sellers' forms such as proposals, acknowledgment of orders and invoices. A firm that is filling thousands of purchase orders every week could not afford to take the time to negotiate all the details of every transaction. Moreover, as Tom Palay notes: 'looking beyond the [written] contract is important because parties who have, or anticipate, strong relational ties with their contracting opposites are not particularly worried about initial terms of agreement.'[7] In many situations careful contract negotiation signals distrust when the situation calls for a business marriage.

Furthermore, we must remember that business corporations are collections of people and their activities are seldom tightly coordinated. Those who negotiate the deal often are not the people who draft the written document recording it. Still others must perform the contract. This opens the possibility that, for example, a firm's lawyers may have different assumptions and expectations than its purchasing agents, sales people, and engineers.

Strategy may be involved too. If I want a clause that says if event X takes place, then consequence Y will follow, you may demand something in exchange that I do not want to give you. When I anticipate this, it may be better to avoid raising the issue in negotiations and hope that the matter can be resolved if event X ever takes place.

Lawyers deal with many of these problems by fabricating detailed standard form contracts that typically are written in legal or technical language that 'is not meant to be read, still less to be understood.'[8] The written document, however, may be seen by purchasing agents, sales personnel and engineers as a formality created only to please the whims of the lawyers. It is also possible that parties will write or accept a flat, unqualified contract clause but assume that there are exceptions or qualifications that are not worth the effort to spell out in advance. In short, there are many reasons that the paper deal will fail to capture the real deal. As a matter of fact, there is a 'text between the lines.'

The performance of contractual obligations often will be prolonged in time and require the active cooperation of both parties. Situations may change during the time that one or both parties are attempting to perform or it may become clear that the written language is an inadequate guide to performance. While parties can modify their written contract, often they do not engage in an explicit renegotiation. Rather, they make adjustments

[7] T. M. Palay, 'A Contract Does Not a Contract Make' (1985) *Wisconsin Law Review* 561, 562.

[8] The phrase is Lord Justice Devlin's. See *McCutcheon* v *David MacBrayne, Inc* [1964] 1 WLR 125.

as they attempt to cope with the demands of the original agreement and the new situation. Sometimes we can say that when the parties signed a written agreement, they intended their contract to be adjusted in light of continually changing circumstances. In some kinds of contracts, cancellation for convenience or broad impossibility/frustration clauses are common. Sometimes the written contract provides that if event X happens, 'the contract shall be equitably adjusted.' Often, however, we can suspect that those who signed the written document never thought about the possibility of changes beyond a general tacit assumption that both sides would proceed in good faith.

AMERICAN LAW: RULE AND COUNTER-RULE, CORE AND PERIPHERY

The law: something less than certainty and perfect predictability

How does or should contract law respond to any gap between the paper deal and the real deal? Let me briefly sketch some of the approaches taken by American courts or advocated by American writers.[9] I offer American law and writing only as an example which I know. I do not presume that they should be a model for the rest of the world.

People can respond to a problem by denying that it exists. We could point to many judicial opinions that talk about the plain meaning of a written contract without ever considering how they know that this is what the parties meant. This is the strongest version of the parol evidence rule.[10] There is an old American expression that tells us that 'if it looks like a duck, waddles like a duck and quacks like a duck, it is a duck!' Sometimes an objective theory of contracts gives us, essentially, the duck test. If I signed a writing, you are entitled to rely on my agreement to the plain meaning of the words written, typed or printed. Sometimes this position is reinforced by a tort-like duty to read and understand which can transform contract law's claim to rest on choice into pure magic. Also, there is an assumption, often unstated, that all the parties' rights and duties must be traced back to the specific provisions of their written agreement. Courts say that they will not make a contract for the parties. However, when judges want to impose contractual liability, implied conditions and strange readings of contract language rationalize the enforcement of what

[9] See J.M. Feinman, 'The Significance of Contract Theory (1990) 58 *Cincinnati Law Review* 1283.

[10] See J.D. Calamari and J. M. Perillo, 'A Plea for a Uniform Parol Evidence Rule and Principles of Contract Interpretation' (1967) 42 *Indiana Law Journal* 333; W. C. Whitford, 'The Role of the Jury (and the Fact/Law Distinction) in the Interpretation of Written Contracts' (2001) *Wisconsin Law Review* 931.

judges think parties ought to have done. Sometimes, of course, implied conditions and strange readings rationalize a judge's refusal to enforce the bargain that the parties made.

Lawrence Friedman pointed out that American contract law in the late Nineteenth and early Twentieth Centuries was grounded in abstraction; it offered rules assumed to be applicable whether the parties were rich or poor and without regard to the subject matter of the transaction. The rules purported to be unchanging over time. However, when faced with the demands of a developing economy, American courts used tools such as waiver and estoppel and construction of language to bend specific rules into conforming with standards of higher generality.[11] Often careful study would reveal that contract law featured a rule opposed by a counter rule with no principled way of knowing when one or the other would apply. American law, for example, tells us that it is not duress to threaten to do what you have a legal right to do.[12] Yet a wrongful although not illegal threat can be duress.[13] These two statements of the law do not live together happily.

The legal realists had a fine time dropping bombs on ideas about plain meaning and abstraction. The more you know about language, the less comfortable you are with ideas that any collection of words has but one complete and clear meaning apart from context. Recognising this, Professor Corbin would reduce doctrines such as the parol evidence rule to a possibility that seldom would apply. Parol evidence is to be excluded when the parties intended their writing to be the final expression of their agreement. Corbin, however, argued that such an intention about finality was a fact to be proved by any relevant evidence that was credible. He thought that judges should not blind themselves to everything but the text of a writing. Justice Roger Traynor of the Supreme Court of California wrote this form of realism into the law of his state, at least for a time.[14] A California judge was not to look for the plain meaning. He or she could look to evidence of intention other than the text of a written contract even when the words did not seem to be ambiguous.

To a great extent, legal realism was written into American law when Professor Karl Llewellyn became the Reporter for Article 2 of our Uniform

[11] L.M. Friedman, *Contract Law in America: a Social and Economic Case Study* (Madison, WI: Univ Wisconsin Press, 1965).

[12] See eg, *Wurtz* v *Fleischman* 97 Wis.2d 100, 293 N.W.2d 155 (1980).

[13] Restatement (2d) Contracts §176(2)(c) tells us that a threat is 'improper if the resulting exchange is not on fair terms, and . . . what is threatened is otherwise a use of a power for illegitimate ends.' See C. Dalton, 'An Essay in the Deconstruction of Contract Doctrine' (1985) 94 *Yale Law Journal* 997, 1035–36, for a criticism of this approach. Dalton sees the Restatement as evading the real but difficult questions about what are 'illegitimate ends' for the use of power.

[14] See eg, *Masterson* v *Sine* 68 Cal.2d 222, 436 P.2d 561 (1968); *Pacific Gas & Elect Co* v *GW Thomas Drayage & Rigging Co* 69 Cal.2d 33, 442 P.2d 641 (1968).

Commercial Code. Article 2 became the law in almost all American states by 1965. In Llewellyn's Code, much turns on the concept of 'agreement.' Section 1-201(3) defines this concept as 'the bargain of the parties in fact as found in their language or by implication from other circumstances . . .' The phrase 'bargain of the parties in fact' would seem to call for enforcing the real deal rather than holding people to any asserted plain meaning of the documents which they signed or accepted. The Code also attempts to cut back the idea that contracts must be defined with certainty.[15] Llewellyn celebrated what he called the grand style of common law judging.[16] Judges working in the grand style did not apply rules mindlessly. Rather, drawing on their situation sense, rules served only as guides to judgment.[17]

However, the Code is not pure Llewellyn but a compromise between the legal realism of the academics who produced the first drafts and the traditional views of the commercial lawyers who forced revisions.[18] Llewellyn was not free to innovate at will. He had to obtain the blessing of the American Law Institute and the National Conference of Commissions on Uniform State Law. Moreover, the Code had to be passed by state legislatures, most of which had many members who were lawyers trained in the conventional wisdom. Article 2 has, for example, a parol evidence rule and a Statute of Frauds. In the hands of a judge holding traditional views, there are ways to read the Code that can serve as a road back to the

[15] Section 2-204(1) says '[a] contract for sale of goods may be made in any manner sufficient to show agreement, including conduct by both parties which recognises the existence of a contract.' We can have an enforceable contract although the price is uncertain, quantity is defined only as 'requirements,' and nothing is said about the date for performance.

[16] See K. N. Llewellyn, *The Common Law Tradition: Deciding Appeals* (Boston, MA: Little, Brown and Co., 1960) 64–72; W. Twining, *Karl Llewellyn and the Realist Movement* (Norman, OK: Univ Oklahoma Press, 1973) 210–245.

[17] For example, Section l-102(1), Official Comment 1, says: 'The Act should be construed in accordance with its underlying purposes and policies. The text of each section should be read in the light of the purpose and policy of the rule or principle in question, as also of the Act as a whole, and the application of the language should be construed narrowly or broadly, as the case maybe, in conformity with the purposes and policies involved.' Section 1-205, Official Comment 1, says: 'The measure and background for interpretation are set by the commercial context, which may explain and supplement even the language of a formal or final writing.'

[18] See A. R. Kamp, 'Downtown Code: A History of the Uniform Commercial Code 1949–1954' (2001) 49 *Buffalo Law Review* 359 ('[1lhe present Code is a product of two conflicting visions of what commercial law should be – one, a regulatory system based on self-regulation by the trade, judicial supervision according to commercial norms, and legislative dictate, as opposed to one based on an autonomous business world operating under a regime of unregulated contract.') *Ibid* 361. 'Llewellyn's views and his original program for the Code grew out of the matrix of the collectivist mentality of the 1930s . . . Llewellyn was once part of an academic avant guard, a supporter of FDR [President Roosevelt] in his court-packing plan, a folk dancer, a student of Boas' anthropology, part of a 1930s radical, collectivist milieu.' *Ibid* 392.) See also, A. R. Kamp, 'Between-The-Wars Social Thought: Karl Llewellyn, Legal Realism, and the Uniform Commercial Code in Contex' (1995) 59 *Albany Law Review* 325; A. R. Kamp, 'Uptown Act: A History of the Uniform Commercial Code: 1940–1949' (1998) 51 SMU Law Review 275; A. R. Kamp, 'Increasing Complexity in Commercial Law: The Failure of the Uniform Commercial Code' (1991) 10 *Corporate Counsel Review* 59.

familiar territory of the common law of contracts. In making this move, it helps to ignore the definitional sections of the statute. As a result, Article 2 often preserves aspects of the classic common law approaches but seeks to change the common law enough to deal with modern conditions. It can be considered an example of 'neoclassical contract.'[19] In short, many of the tools needed to seek the implicit dimensions of contract are in Article 2,[20] but even judges who read statutes carefully do not have to use these tools. . .

[Eds Note: In omitted sections of the article, Macaulay discusses scholarly challenges to the relational approach as well as international perspectives on it and acknowledges the need to trust courts to be able to implement it.]

A limited trace of optimism: the real deal resting on relational norms can be supported by courts inducing settlements rather than announcing judgments.

Perhaps we should not conclude too quickly that the moral of my story is damned if you do and damned if you don't. While there is more to law than just legal rules, doctrine can matter. I applaud the efforts of those attempting to give us better conceptual tools. We will, however, do better if we attempt to fashion doctrines more or less suited for specific types of contracts rather than trying to fabricate one grand contract law. Nonetheless, doctrine rests on assumptions about the society and its proper organisation. Brownsword tells us:

> There are two plausible ethics for contract law, individualism and cooperativism . . . It is not easy for contract doctrine (whether through notions of good faith, unconscionability, reasonableness, loyalty, legitimate expectation, or whatever) to hold strictly to either of these ethics in their most robust form. Doctrinal adherence to individualism will often seem out of touch with business practice (where compromise, adjustment, and partnering and the like govern dealings); but, equally, doctrinal adherence to cooperativism can put too great a strain on the idea of a common enterprise (at any rate, in the sense of an identity of interest).[21]

But Americans always want to eat their cake and have it too: We want both individualism and cooperativism at the same time. We bounce back and forth through cycles where we emphasize one and then the other. Yet

[19] In the right hands, however, Article 2 offers an opportunity for an application of a relational theory of contract to specific problems. See I. R. Macneil, 'Restatement (2d) of Contracts and Presentation' (1974) 60 *Virginia Law Review* 589; Richard E. Speidel, 'Article 2 and Relational Sales Contracts' (1993) 26 *Loyola of Los Angeles Law Review* 789.

[20] See A. H. Kastely, 'Stock Equipment for the Bargain in Fact: Trade Usage, "Express Terms," and Consistency Under Section 1-205 of the Uniform Commercial Code' (1986) 64 *North Carolina Law Review* 777.

[21] [original fn 74] R. Brownsword, 'Individualism, Cooperativism and an Ethic for European Contract Law' (2001) 64 *Modem Law Review* 628, 630.

it is a question of emphasis: words rationalising individualism are still there when our legal culture accepts more cooperativism. The one safe statement about American contract law in action is that it is messy.

In some situations, there is no reason to think that courts will not be able to do as well in a contract case as they do in any other type of case. If we impose duties of cooperation or tell a court to give a remedy 'if injustice can be avoided only by enforcement of the promise',[22] our legal system often will reach at least acceptable results. Assuming that cost barriers permit, lawyers may be able to show judges what would be fair in a particular commercial context. The judges and the lawyers involved might never define 'fair' in a precise fashion that would satisfy a critic or offer answers to judges and lawyers in future cases. Nonetheless, all involved might accept that the results seemed to fall within an intuited zone of fairness. This process, however, might be very costly because it could require an exploration of the full commercial context. Of course, there is a risk that the judges might get it wrong, and cost barriers to proving the full context of a transaction would likely increase that risk. However, there is no reason to presume that the process always will be unduly costly or judges will always get it wrong. Perhaps if we conclude that there is a problem in a type of case such as those involving consumers, we should advocate flat rules for those kinds of situations. . . .

Macneil has pointed out that there are situations where it is in the interest of the parties, and even perhaps of the economy as a whole, where the law should treat parties as if their relationship was discrete and entirely contained within the borders of a written document. The task is to identify such situations. One approach is to submit such documents to a regulatory agency for approval, such as is often done with insurance policies. This seems to be a sensible solution as long as we are confident that the regulatory agency will not be captured by trade associations that make campaign contributions. We have long distinguished consumer transactions from those between merchants. Yet even this leaves me uneasy; it seems too crude. Some transactions between businesses have many elements of a consumer transaction. Often a franchise agreement is one-sided and written by the more powerful party. Often these agreements or amendments to them are hard to read and understand. Perhaps courts can approach documents such as franchises as if the relationships involved were discrete. They may be able to do this because those involved can gain legislation that calls for a more relational approach to the legal rights of the parties. Courts can avoid the difficulties involved in a relational approach unless a legislature determines that it is worth the costs of attempting to reinforce the norms of cooperation. Yet, here too, we would

[22] [original fn 75] Contracts scholars will recognise that the quoted phrase is a key passage in the American Restatement (2d) Contracts §90.

be more comfortable if we had more faith in our American legislatures as something other than places where law is sold to the highest bidder.[23]

Whatever our success in identifying places for treating relationships as if they were discrete, we must remember that it is not just a question of legal doctrine. Doctrine does not have little legs so that it can hop down from law books and enforce itself. Doctrine is delivered in an extremely expensive system for which someone must pay. Often the reason that a transaction broke down is that one side lost the ability to perform because it ran out of money. A claim in bankruptcy often is not worth the effort. Even when there is little risk of bankruptcy, suing someone usually destroys relationships and invites retaliation.

We might be happier if we took a lawyer's perspective and saw the game as one involving acceptable, if not ideal, settlements. While not all cases can be nor should be settled, more often than not the 'least bad' solution is a compromise fashioned in light of the situation facing the parties at the time of the dispute. Many, if not most, settlements fall beneath the radar screen of contract scholars. Publishers do not deliver reports of these cases to our door or to our computer. The parties often want their settlement to be secret. However, parties do invoke the legal system as part of a strategy to produce settlements. When cooperative approaches fail, letters can be written on an attorney's letterhead in order to make an implicit threat. Complaints may be filed in court, and negotiations may be commenced if summary judgment is not granted. Sometimes, however, cases involving large sums of money may proceed far down the path to a final judgment affirmed on appeal and still be settled. Furthermore, sometimes the settlement provokes the parties to resume their relationship, although often with a modified balance of power. This may be a way, if not the most common way, that the ideas of relational contract are implemented in the American legal system.

What appears to be a final judgment at the trial level may be only a step toward settlement. The judgment may affect the balance of power between the parties, but often it will not go into effect as written. . . .

Often efforts at settlement cannot begin until the summary judgment hurdle has been cleared. American conditions and culture allow one party before summary judgment motions have been decided to run up the costs of litigation in order to discourage the other. Settlement should be easier when both parties are wealthy, so that one party will not have an incen-

[23] [original fn 80] Special interest pressure has even moved from the public legislative arena to the National Conference of Commissioners on Uniform Laws, the group that proposes revisions to the Uniform Commercial Code. See R. E. Speidel, 'Introduction to Symposium on Proposed Revised Article 2' (2001) 54 SMU Law Review 787; R. E. Speidel, 'Revising UCC Article 2: A View from the Trenches' (2001) 52 *Hastings Law Review* 607; A. Schwartz and R. E. Scott, 'The Political Economy of Private Legislatures' (1995) 143 *University of Pennsylvania Law Review* 595.

tive to try to induce the other to quit the litigation because of continuing court costs.

Sometimes litigation is a pure salvage operation. The parties are not interested in continuing their relationship. Settlement then becomes a question of costs and benefits. By settling, the parties reduce or eliminate uncertainty and contain costs. Things are in their control rather than in the control of judges and jurors. It may make more sense to litigate and take one's chances that any judgment recovered could be satisfied. Having conceded this, still we cannot forget that settlements also can produce compromises that keep relationships alive. The effort to settle can force the parties to cooperate and seek common interests.

We should notice how similar this coercive mediation approach is to what takes place in bankruptcy in the United States. To a great extent, in bankruptcy the parties are pushed to accept some sort of compromise to remedy the debtor's inability to perform many contracts. We get little predictability if we move from contract to bankruptcy, and the original contract controls then only if one party took a secured interest in the right form and recorded it. Those who write about contracts often fail to consider this remedy – bankruptcy – for multiple breaches of contract. Yet the most formal approach to relational contracts will have limited impact if firms facing difficulty often use bankruptcy. Any theory about the role of contract law must include the functions of bankruptcy or it will be seriously incomplete. . . .

[S]ometimes legal uncertainty could be a factor provoking parties to spend more effort seeking a settlement. Litigation usually is expensive and unpleasant. Business people must turn over a large measure of control to lawyers, and many resist this. Even the threat of having a lawyer for the other side take a deposition, might be enough to deter some business people from taking the legal route; few business people would enjoy being cross examined at trial. My judgment is that in all but unusual situations, flexible doctrine will provoke settlements. The only way to determine how the doctrine applies to the particular facts of the case would be to litigate until some court provides an answer. While lawyers may be able to predict what courts will do, they cannot guarantee that their clients will win. Even if they win, lawyers cannot guarantee that the legal rules dealing with contracts damages and an inability to satisfy a judgment will not leave a plaintiff with but a Pyrrhic victory. Settlements are under the control of business people and their lawyers. Unless money is no object and there is a point of principle, rational business people will salvage what they can by settlement and avoid throwing good money after bad in the litigation game.

Moreover, . . . litigation can produce settlements. A judge . . . who rewrites a contract based on his own view of what is demanded by relational norms may provoke the parties to rededicate their efforts to find a compromise that is more compatible with their needs. A judge . . . who participates actively in settlement negotiations may be able to act as a mediator backed up by his power as a judge to discipline lawyers and even the parties.

CONCLUSION

Clearly, contract documents often fail to capture the real deal between the parties. There are many arguments rationalising treating documents in such situations as if they were the complete expressions of the contracts made by the bargainers. This may avoid giving courts discretion so that we reduce the risk of arbitrary action by judges. This may even reduce the risk of decisions based on bribery. This may avoid sending courts on missions that often they cannot carry out because of the very real capability problem. Taking this approach to writings may cut the costs of goods and services so that we may have computers, airplanes, compact disks, machine tools and microwave ovens at lower prices. In some, but not all, situations these arguments have merit. Nonetheless, all of them assume that it is worth running the real risk of defeating actual reasonable expectations of bargainers in the service of some more important end.

We might at least focus the issues if we were to accept that there is a text between the lines in most contracts, and if we do not attempt to implement this implicit text, we are denying reasonable expectations. If we are willing to take an as if approach, we then must ask whether reputational sanctions are enough to support most ongoing transactions. Sometimes a formal approach that treats a contract as if it were a discrete transaction may be justified, but we must be sure that we consider all the costs of this approach. We might decide that there is a high cost in legitimacy if the legal system comes to symbolise that contract rests on manipulations of forms and courts reject the substance of the real deal of the parties. At the very least, if our courts allow those who draft written contracts to impose terms inconsistent with expectations and the implicit dimensions of contract, we can expect reformers to demand that the law police those bits of private legislation that masquerade as contracts so that they are fair.

Part I

Relational Contracts and Theory

1

Is the World of Contracting Relations One of Spontaneous Order or Pervasive State Action? Stewart Macaulay Scrambles the Public–Private Distinction

ROBERT W GORDON

> [Ian] Macneil . . . sees consumers [whose deals are governed by form contracts] as 'bureaucrats' participating in large-scale transactions characterized by standardized planning. I prefer to see such 'consumers' as citizens of a private government.[1]

INTRODUCTION

THIS PAPER BRIEFLY summarises some old and recurring debates in political, social and legal theory about the relationship of the 'public' realm of law and the state to the 'private' realms of social life and markets, and more specifically, about the relationship of contract law to contracting behaviour; and then looks at the work of Stewart Macaulay as an intervention in those debates.

I. THE BASIC ARGUMENT

One side of this debate, which (correctly or not) we often associate with Adam Smith and FA Hayek, asserts the *priority of private ordering*. It posits the existence of a largely self-sustaining autonomous sphere of privately-ordered social relations. In this sphere people generally engage in

[1] S Macaulay, 'Relational Contracts Floating on a Sea of Custom? Thoughts about the Ideas of Ian Macneil and Lisa Bernstein' (2000) 94 *Northwestern University Law Review* 775, 780.

co-operative relationships without being coerced by any kind of state-backed authority. Hayek's nice phrase for this social sphere is 'spontaneous order'.[2] One type of private ordering that we could call 'thick' social ordering is sustained by custom, networks of kinship or ethnic solidarity, or ongoing relations of exchange, which generate trust and expectations of reciprocity that people in those relations come to internalise as norms. Another – and very different – kind of ordering, the one that Hayek himself had primarily in mind, is the 'thin' economic ordering of markets, in which self-interested people who don't know each other use price signals (the 'invisible hand') to co-ordinate their self-interested behaviour for mutual benefit.

Most theorists who tend to this set of views concede a small, but important and perhaps even essential, role for law and government in sustaining private ordering. In the classical–liberal view that came to dominance in the late nineteenth century, the law is the ultimate last-resort guarantor of property and contract enforcement, stepping in where private sanctions fail to deter force and fraud, rogues, free riders, and would-be monopolists; preserving law and order against criminals and rebels; and repairing (rare) instances of systemic market failure. Private sanctions will suffice to deter most contract-breaching between parties who know one another through prior dealings or membership in common trading cultures or ethnic groups or institutional networks, but the threat of legal sanctions for breach may be needed to provide security for dealings across distances and cultural and national communities.

Yet in the classical view this public role is both normatively and necessarily strictly limited. The best thing government can do is to remove unnecessary public interventions into the private sphere, keeping them and the taxes needed to support them to a minimum. Such interventions are almost invariably ineffective or inefficient. Law that tries to supplant or work against the grain of the rules and norms of customary networks and associations of ongoing social relations is likely to be resisted, ignored or worked around. If it does have an effect, that effect is likely to be perverse, hurting the intended beneficiaries by raising their costs or limiting their freedom. Since public laws are usually the result of state capture by rent-seeking private interests, their redistributive effects are – and are likely to be perceived as – unjust.

Within this school there are large differences of opinion on the need for and proper scope of government provision of public goods such as common defence against – and productive diplomatic and commercial relations with – foreign powers, and of economic infrastructure such as roads, bridges, transportation and power networks. What is essential

[2] See FA Hayek, *Law, Legislation and Liberty: Rules and Order*, vol 1 (Chicago, University of Chicago Press, 1973) 38–54.

public provision is naturally greatly disputed, even within libertarian circles: some maintaining that private groups can substitute for almost all state functions, including public goods such as roads and lighthouses,[3] and maintaining law and order; others allowing for a more ample scope to correct market failures such as property-rights holdouts, negative externalities of market choices, and so forth.

Classical thinkers who recommend only a minimal role for law, tend to prefer that such law as there is be formal. Hayek believes that the 'constitution of liberty' is one of a few general rules applicable to everyone, regardless of peculiarities of parties or contexts.[4] Modern neo-formalists call for a contract law that enforces the terms of deals – at least deals between business firms – by a strictly textual reading of their paper terms, rather than by trying to reconstruct the actual expectations of parties or to police against opportunistic advantage-taking or substantive unfairness.

This general picture of a vast primary sphere of spontaneous ordering surrounded by a narrow periphery of public lawmaking is sometimes complicated by a move that takes certain kinds of law out of the public sphere and folds them back into the private sphere. For Hayek, as for nineteenth-century legal evolutionists and some modern efficiency-of-the-common-law theorists, the common law itself is a form of spontaneous order,[5] much like the market in that its thousands of decentralised decisions lead – without any judges' intending them to do so – to results supportive of market institutions, such as results mimicking the market outcomes which would have occurred if they had not been impeded by transaction costs. Common law, a part of the naturalised realm of private order, is thus distinguished from legislation and administrative regulation, and alien and artificial interventions into private order.

On the public side, much fewer in number, are those who think that all social activity, including the most 'private' activity such as family life and market dealings between equals, is pervasively permeated and regulated, and often effectively produced, by state action, including legal action. State policy and state coercion are everywhere. There is no difference between common law and legislation/administration. This line of thought – that the legal is pervasively manifested in the social – also draws heavily on various strands of Legal Realism. One strand, for which the customary cites are to Karl Polanyi, Robert Hale and Morris Cohen, observes the

[3] For some reason lighthouses figure prominently in debates over what are necessary public goods. See R Coase, 'The Lighthouse in Economics' (1974) 17 *Journal of Law and Economics* 57. Coase pointed out that early English lighthouses were private enterprises financed by user fees. They were, however, operated as government-granted monopolies and the state made payment of the fees compulsory.

[4] FA Hayek, *The Constitution of Liberty* (Chicago, University of Chicago Press, 1960) 148–61.

[5] Hayek, *Rules and Order* (n 2) 118–22.

pervasive structuration of social relations by regimes of legal rules.[6] The state regulates 'private' conduct though common law as much as it regulates through legislation and administration: the rules of property, tort and contract delegate and distribute the powers to coerce and to organise; property gives the authority to subject others to the holder's rule; grants of legal immunities empower the grantees to inflict harm on others without penalty. A corporation or business owner regulates those subject to its control under delegation or license from the state; backed up with the civil and criminal trespass or enforcement-of-contract sanctions. Measures that purport to 'privatise' state functions simply redistribute state authority to other delegates.[7]

Using (some versions of) this view social relationships are naturally rife with conflict. The state (Hobbes's sovereign) is the necessary enforcer of the basic terms of the social contract. It may tolerate by silence and omissions or explicit or implicit delegations many subaltern lawmakers such as corporations or associations, or regulated commons, or even legally permitted free-for-all zones in which people are allowed to engage in wars of all-against-all for control of territory or scarce resources or dominance within the family or group; but all these operate under its sufferance, which is revocable when public convenience or necessity requires. Its most basic mandate is to secure social peace and order. But – and this is particularly relevant to the law's role in contract enforcement – in a society of plural communities and ideologies, where interpretations of agreements are likely to proliferate wildly, the state is also the master definer and interpreter of disputes about the meanings of terms, both public and private.

Caveat. This summary of the basic argument simplifies and caricatures complicated positions. Some prominent interpreters of Smith, including Lionel Robbins, believe that Smith conceived of the market sphere he described in *The Wealth of Nations* as almost entirely an artifact of state policy, which in this typology would locate him on the Hobbes/Hale side of the divide.[8] It is clearly correct that for Smith the establishment of

[6] See, eg K Polanyi, *The Great Transformation* (New York, Farrar & Rinehart, 1944); R Hale, 'Coercion and Distribution in a Supposedly Non-coercive State' (1923) 38 *Political Science Quarterly* 470; M Cohen, 'Property as Sovereignty' (1927) 13 *Cornell Law Review* 8. The best modern expositions and analysis of the structuration of market conduct by legal rules is B Fried, *The Progressive Assault on Laissez Faire: Robert Hale and the First Law and Economics Movement* (Cambridge, First Harvard University Press, 1998); see also B Harcourt, *The Illusion of Free Markets: Punishment and the Myth of Natural Order* (Cambridge, Harvard University Press, 2011).

[7] For an up-to-date survey, see G Metzger, 'Privatization as Delegation' (2003) 103 *Columbia Law Review* 1367.

[8] 'The invisible hand which guides men to promote ends which were no part of their intention . . . is the hand of the lawgiver, the hand which withdraws from the sphere of the pursuit of self-interest those possibilities which do not harmonize with the public good.' L Robbins, *The Theory of Economic Policy in English Classical Political Economy* (London, Macmillan Press, 1952) 56.

public institutions capable of securing 'justice' (the effectual protection of people and property from injury) are preconditions to civilised society.[9]

II. COMPETING VIEWS OF HISTORY

These basic positions generate further debates over theory and history, especially over the role of law and the state in promoting capitalist development.

We have to distinguish here between: (1) theoretical arguments over how much state power, bureaucratic capacity and legal legitimacy are *necessary* to development – arguments particularly vigorous inside libertarian and neo-liberal circles, and often influential in the design of law-and-development schemes for foreign export; and (2) empirical–historical arguments about how much states actually were and are active and important promoters – or impeders – of capitalist development. My focus here is mostly on the second type of argument. Are private regulatory and enforcement mechanisms – such as self-regulated commons, traders' networks, extended-family-or-kinship-groups networks and associations, self-help enforcement of rules through private sanctions or associational sanctions – formed prior to the state, and only later (some of them) taken over by the state? Do some of them flourish just by borrowing the barest minimum of state power – for example, FW Maitland's example of the trust device for creating and perpetuating self-regulating associations such as mutual-insurance associations, stock exchanges, Jockey clubs, charitable endowments and churches, and the like?[10] The counter perspective is that much of what we credit to spontaneous self-generating activities are actually sponsored and promoted by states for their own purposes, such as commercial expansion, imperial conquest and war, and extraction of taxes to finance these, trading corporations, patent and copyright monopolies, consolidation of property rights as with enclosures of common fields, and construction of (or legal support for) markets like capital markets.

A version of these debates has been reproduced in arguments over the role of the state and law in specifically American capitalist development. An extreme version of this argument holds that American success was predicated on the adoption of the policy of relative laissez-faire attributed to Smith; indeed to *constitutional* protections of a private sphere of property rights and free market activity from legislative interference.[11] This imagined

[9] See D Lieberman, 'Contract Before "Freedom of Contract"' in H Scheiber (ed), *The State and Freedom of Contract* (Stanford, Stanford University Press, 1998) 89, 96–101.

[10] FW Maitland, 'Trust and Corporation' in HD Hazeltine, G Lapsley and PH Winfield (eds), *Maitland: Selected Essays* (Manchester, Ayer Co Publishing, 1936) 141, 189–222.

[11] See, eg B Siegan, *Economic Liberties and the Constitution* (Chicago, University of Chicago Press, 2006).

history is often used as a basis for promoting Rule of Law projects in transitional societies, which try to limit governance to courts that stick to enforcing property rights and contracts and restricting the sphere of further state action.

This very libertarian account, however, vastly understates the role of law and government in underwriting capitalist development in the USA. With respect to the nineteenth century, it leaves out: high tariff barriers promoting domestic manufacturing; a national bank promoting a stable currency; the constitutional protection of slavery and the vast body of state police regulations defining slave status and slaveowners' rights over their human chattels, restricting emancipation and repressing rebellion and movements for abolition; federal government help in acquiring and colonising territory, giving incentives to settlers to occupy and gradually dispossess native inhabitants from western lands, and in evicting and then deploying military force to clear out Indian tribes; myriad forms of public support for infrastructure, especially land grants for railroads and land grant colleges, eminent domain powers and immunity from tort suits for public service corporations; a free universal public education system; an extensive national postal delivery system; grants of patent monopolies; judicially supervised management of bankrupt railroads; and frequent deployment of court injunctions, the police and military force to suppress labour organisations. (This was a set of policies often promoting creative destruction, rather than protection, of existing property rights.) With respect to the twentieth century, it leaves out: highways, bridges, dams, irrigation projects, scientific research on basic science, technology, medicine, pharmaceuticals; public lands management and resource conservation; foreign policy and a far-flung network of navies and military bases promoting markets for products overseas and protecting foreign direct investment; colonial and post World War II occupation of and imposition of law and government on entire countries; reconstruction of war-devastated economies; promoting imports of low-wage labour; and direct taxpayer investment in industry, especially defence procurement; not to mention enormous subsidies in the form of tax expenditures for favoured industries such as agribusiness, petroleum and housing construction.[12] The many foreign interventions in particular showed no hesitation in intervening, often brutally, in organic systems of ongoing social relations: it was those systems that the intervention was designed to smash – sometimes, to be

[12] The literatures on public policies designed to promote capitalism and economic growth in the USA are now vast. Exceptionally useful and concise summaries of public policies and their economic effects are in the three-volume work by S Engerman and R Gallman (eds), *The Cambridge Economic History of the United States* (Cambridge, Cambridge University Press, 2000).

sure, in the hope of rebuilding them in the utopian designs of the neo-liberal public–private models.[13]

Moreover, the notion that the early Constitutions were meant to protect laissez-faire markets from encroaching government action is completely ahistorical, with limited exceptions such as the federal Contracts Clause which sought to prohibit state legislatures from interfering with debt collection or diluting the value of obligations. The governors and legislatures of the early states energetically pursued projects of 'improvement' – local economic development – such as construction of turnpikes, canals, railroads, ports and bridges, and state-backed public finance to support these ventures; deployed their plenary police power to regulate new industries and markets in the furtherance of 'public welfare'; and asserted 'public rights', enforced in derogation of private property claims, in rivers and streams, beaches, wharves and natural resources.[14] The federal Constitution came into being not to limit government, but to promote its capacity to deal with foreign nations and Indian tribes, overcome obstructions to interstate commerce, and stabilise the currency; and soon after its formation the new federal government would mobilise its formidable latent regulatory authority to administer large-scale national programmes, among them the Embargo and tariff enforcement and the distribution of public lands.[15]

The society and economy of America in 1800 are a wonderful menagerie of hybrid (as we have since come to distinguish them) public and private elements: state-sponsored and heavily regulated markets (including wages and prices of staple commodities); family households consisting of regulated servants with regulatory authority shared between masters and magistrates; supervised work relations of paupers and indentured servants; legally established churches with powers to coerce tax support from parishioners; and corporations, including towns and cities and churches and business ventures and banks and insurance companies, conceived of as state-created entities designed to carry out public purposes. Almost every aspect of social relations might become the object of local justice: in the magistrates' and county courts, law and justice were

[13] The most recent of such projects to build a free-market utopia on foreign soil was launched in US-occupied Iraq, with farcical results. See R Chandrasekeran, *Imperial Life in the Emerald City: Inside Iraq's Green Zone* (New York, Knopf, 2006).

[14] O Handlin and M Handlin, *Commonwealth: A Study of the Role of Government in the American Economy: Massachusetts, 1774–1861*, 2nd edn (Cambridge, Harvard University Press, 1969); L Hartz, *Economic Policy and Democratic Thought: Pennsylvania, 1776–1860* (Cambridge, Harvard University Press, 1948); H Scheiber, *Ohio Canal Era: A Case Study of Government and the Economy, 1820–1861* (Athens, Ohio University Press, 1969); W Novak, *The Peoples' Welfare: Law and Regulation in Nineteenth Century America* (Chapel Hill, University of North Carolina Press, 1996).

[15] See M Edling, *A Revolution in Favor of Government* (Oxford, Oxford University Press, 2008); J Mashaw, *Creating the Administrative Constitution: The Lost One Hundred Years of American Administrative Law* (New Haven, Yale University Press, 2012).

not some kind of add-on or supplement to private ordering but completely embedded in private ordering, an instrument for promoting community norms, maintaining and resolving competing claims to rights and privileges, local social hierarchies and customs.[16]

The public–private distinction as we have come to understand it is the product of several different developments, intellectual and political. At the time of the founding of the USA, the concept of the private sphere of the autonomous self-regulating economy – a naturalised 'market', to be distinguished and insulated from the public realm of undue state intervention – existed at the time only as an intellectuals' theory. This self-regulating 'market' was an invention of eighteenth-century political economists, which later public policies, including legal policies, eventually contrived to convert into a reality.

The other side of the equation – society constituted by emanations of state power – was given a big boost by absolutist rulers. Indeed, the consolidation of state power in Europe, as in America, is in part a response to the emergence of new classes of hired labourers, 'masterless men', not pre-appertaining to a household, but drifting around towns and cities, threatening masses of vagabonds. Centralised state power was wielded against 'feudal' vestiges to liberate free contracting individuals from ascriptive hierarchies and to eviscerate the role of intermediate hybrid institutions (the French Revolution went as far as anyone by abolishing all corporations) without damaging the world of 'commerce'. The liberal project was to break up the old hierarchies – and contain threatening new collectives of masterless men – but also to limit the reach of the centralising process.[17] Even in England, the legal doctrine of 'freedom of contract' in employment – the freedom of parties to set the terms of their own bargain – actually originates in coercive statutes (the Combination Acts of 1799 and 1800). The Acts abolish the old regimes mandating the specific terms – wages, lengths, performance – of many different kinds of contracts. They leave the parties 'free' to set their own terms. But at the same time they criminalise another kind of contracting, agreements among labourers to act collectively.[18]

The US never went as far as France – indeed they saw the Jacobins as an object lesson in going much too far – but public and legal policy worked either to deprive associations of public powers altogether (for example, churches), or to subject them to strict state controls (for example, corporations and cities). Eventually business corporations, originally on the

[16] See L Edwards, *The People and Their Peace: Legal Culture and the Transformation of Inequality in the Post-Revolutionary South* (Chapel Hill, University of North Carolina Press, 2009).

[17] See D Grewal, *The Invention of the Economy: A History of Economic Thought* (Cambridge, Harvard University Press, forthcoming 2012).

[18] See J Orth, 'Contract and the Common Law' in H Scheiber (ed), *The State and Freedom of Contract* (Stanford, Stanford University Press, 1998) 44–65.

public side of the emerging divide, jumped the divide altogether, becoming like 'individuals' – with the law counting on competition and antitrust laws to control them.[19] And the emancipation of slaves, at least formally, transformed slaves from heavily regulated chattels to free labour. Collective labour actions were partially decriminalised – by the 1840s it was no longer illegal simply to associate for common purposes – but remained under the heavy supervisory hand of the legal system. Family relations were increasingly – though never wholly – theorised and were treated in law as private-contracts-in-which-the-state-has-an-interest rather than as mini-states with husbands-as-rulers.

While privatising many intermediate associations, US jurisdictions expanded the reach and capacity of state governments. The new republic gradually brought state functions previously performed by private actors in-house, functions were turned over to salaried officials rather than bounty hunters, informers, or private contractors and tax collectors.[20] The governments abolished private property in public offices. They used public power to restrain private excess, and indeed theorised all property as being subject to reasonable restrictions by the police power to secure the public welfare with regulations such as factory regulations and anti-trust laws to preserve competition. They built huge new agencies and institutions of social control: police forces, prisons and asylums. At the same time, they expanded the powers and capacities of some government agencies – the courts – to restrain other government agencies – legislatures and administrative agencies.[21]

The public–private distinction reaches its apogee in the law of the late nineteenth century, just as it is becoming visibly absurd as an actual description of social relations. That is the high age of articulation within the legal system of a theory of the private realm and market as a naturalised sphere of free voluntary action, the paradigmatic exercise of freedom being seen – rather strangely, given the degree of arbitrary command and hierarchy inherent in that relation – as the employment contract. The private sphere is theorised as voluntary – contract law enforces the will of the parties; tort law repairs harms that could have been avoided by voluntary action; constitutional law protects the private law regime for governance of the private sphere from undue revision by rent-seeking interests seeking redistributive advantage through 'class legislation'.[22] But of

[19] See J Hurst, *The Legitimacy of the Business Corporation in the Law of the United States* (Charlottesville, University Press of Virginia, 1970); H Hartog, *Public Property and Private Power* (Chapel Hill, University of North Carolina Press, 1989).

[20] See generally N Parrillo, *Against the Profit Motive: The Salary Revolution in American Government, 1780–1940* (New Haven, Yale University Press, forthcoming 2013).

[21] See Novak, *Peoples' Welfare* (n 14); D Rothman, *The Discovery of the Asylum* (Boston, Little Brown, 1971).

[22] See generally D Kennedy, *The Rise and Fall of Classical Legal Thought* (Washington DC, Beard Books, 2006).

course, the legal system of 1880–1920 is anything but laissez-faire: it is also a period of expanding and multiplying public powers and functions, an outpouring of repressive and socially-controlling paternalist legislation, meant to protect society from threats to social order: anarchy and sedition, predatory combinations of labour and capital, vagrancy, alien hordes of immigrants, dissolute families, crime, urban disorder and vice, alcohol, and polygamy. Constitutional courts' growing insistence that the private sphere be protected against excessive regulation is matched by vast expansion – almost all of it approved by the same Constitutional courts – of the sphere, reach and responsibilities of the coercive state, both at home and in the administration of empire (and, eventually, in waging wars).[23] These developments make one appreciate the force of Bernard Harcourt's arresting paradox, in *The Illusion of Free Markets*, that conceptualising markets as 'free' goes hand in hand with the increasing power and range of the carceral state.[24]

Meanwhile, the strong public–private distinction was becoming more questionable as a description of reality with the proliferation of new 'private governments' (as Macaulay calls them) – self-governing professions, universities, trade associations, labour unions, marketing co-operatives; and especially large business corporations, some of them private governments larger than any state, employing more lawyers, and forming the real shadow governments, occupying and directing the operations of the public sphere. The Progressive movements and New Deal sought to reassert public control of these hybrid associations, most dramatically in the corporatist National Recovery Administration, and, even after the demise of the NRA, in the 'little NRAs', the semi-captured regulatory agencies, and the associations that succeeded it. Legal theorists of the Realist school took note of these developments to critique the classical public–private distinction: corporations and professional associations exercised dominion as much as – and often more than – public governments, regulating the lives of and extracting taxes and tribute from those subject to their control.[25]

Yet despite the evident and unavoidable reality of the mixed economy or mutually dependent, mutually constituted, and interdependent public and private spheres, the old distinctions between autonomous markets and intervening states have not gone away.

[23] For a summary overview of this new archipelago of coercive measures, see R Gordon, 'The Constitution of Liberal Order at the Troubled Beginnings of the Modern State' (2004) 58 *University of Miami Law Review* 373.

[24] Harcourt, *Illusion of Free Markets* (n 6) 208–20.

[25] See, eg T Arnold, *The Folklore of Capitalism* (New Haven, Yale University Press, 1937); L Jaffe, 'Lawmaking by Private Groups' (1937) 51 *Harvard Law Review* 201.

III. ENTER STEWART MACAULAY

Stewart Macaulay's first major contribution to this debate – somewhat ironically as we shall see – is with an article that has become a poster child for the Smith–Hayek side of the great debate. This famous article has often been cited (1,007 times at least) usually as an example of what Robert Ellickson, in his own classic study of Shasta Country ranchers settling their disputes through private norms and sanctions and paying no attention to the rules and processes of the official legal system, calls 'order without law'.[26] The article is, of course, 'Non-Contractual Relations in Business',[27] which, after a pretty long time lag, inaugurated what is now a fairly well-populated field, the study of relational contracting as a relatively autonomous zone of self-regulation. For Macaulay, of course, self-regulating networks and social fields and 'private governments' are facts, not norms. This classic article deals with horizontal relations among approximate equals. It had two big points to make. One was to describe the norms of mutual obligation generated by businesses in continuing relations and the sanctions such firms brought to bear against violators of such norms. Famously, Macaulay found that repeated business dealings create expectations of trust and reciprocity, such that parties do not hold one another to literal performance of written contract terms, but make allowances for shortfalls in performance such as late deliveries or payments or imperfect goods, and are flexible in adjusting contract terms to meet changing business needs or economic conditions. Even if disappointed with a contract partner's performance, firms rarely sue, instead threatening refusal to deal in the future, and in the last resort making good on that threat. The other point was that even though such business parties did, on rare occasions, sue one another, the formal law of contract played almost no role in structuring their transactions or mutual planning. For sociologists, the great contribution of the piece was its discovery of the world of relational contracting and its governing norms and sanctions. For lawyers, its – most unwelcome, and for 25 years after its publication mostly ignored – main implication seemed to be that contract law was very nearly irrelevant to a good deal of actual business contracting.

Macaulay's next big project was the study of vertical relations (or what one might call industrial feudalism) – relations between big auto manufacturers and their dealers.[28] His basic story: dealers complain to courts

[26] R Ellickson, *Order Without Law: How Neighbors Settle Disputes* (Cambridge, Harvard University Press, 1991).

[27] S Macaulay, 'Non-Contractual Relations in Business: A Preliminary Study' (1963) 28 *American Sociological Review* 55.

[28] S Macaulay, *Law and the Balance of Power: The Automobile Manufacturers and Their Dealers* (New York, Russell Sage Foundation, 1966).

about one-sided terms and powers in their contracts with manufacturers, and get some doctrines limiting manufacturing discretion to terminate contracts; manufacturers then change the contracts to include checklists of explicit reasons to terminate. The dealers then go to legislatures; get some sympathy there as independent small-business entrepreneurs being reduced to dependent vassals of big business; and generate lots of bad publicity for manufacturing managers. In response to legislation, manufacturers change contracts allowing for more consultation, due process and softer terms. But manufacturers have plenty of resources to invest hoping to gain favourable interpretations, through litigation in courts and more legislative lobbying. (He could now add: through campaign contributions designed to buy sympathetic judges in state judicial elections.) Ultimately, of course, manufacturers retain the market power to dictate (within some limits set by dealer resistance and public regulation) the terms on which they will deal.

Since he is mostly concerned with economic transactions, Macaulay sees much regulatory intervention in this sphere as relatively benign attempts to level the playing field. Yet he agrees with much of the conservative critique of legal intervention as futile, perverse and counterproductive – for example, he believes that regulation of contracts by means of unconscionability doctrine is largely symbolic, giving weaker parties rights to bring extremely expensive lawsuits to obtain results potentially valid for only one case – because it is so easily deflected or resisted by powerful private groups with entrenched interests and customs. However, he generally deplores that set of consequences: he is not a romantic about spontaneous order or private government and perceives very clearly that stronger parties can use the cloak of 'freedom' to oppress or exploit weaker ones. He's a depressed liberal, not a libertarian.

Take for example, his pioneering article on 'Lawyers and Consumer Protection Laws'.[29] The formal legal system gives consumer debtors many defences against creditors' enforcement of their contracts. But these legal defences rarely function to protect debtors. The debtors have to fight against the dominant norm that debtors should pay their debts, and, more practically, the fact that most lawyers in town will not take their cases, because the lawyers need and want repeat business from businesses creditors. The enforcement agents of the legal system, the private bar, are embedded in local society and economy; like lawyers in the Jim Crow South, they can't buck the power structure without losing their paying clients (and perhaps being subject to other social sanctions). In a similar vein see Macaulay's sceptical view of the judicial regulation of 'unconscionable' contracts: regulation may drive up the price of credit; whether

[29] S Macaulay, 'Lawyers and Consumer Protection Laws' (1979) 14 *Law & Society Review* 115.

or not that happens, judicial regulation tends to be completely ineffectual because repeat players can overwhelm the enforcement resources of consumer litigants and simply ignore results of case-by-case litigation.[30]

His views of the interactions between fields of largely self-regulated activity and the official legal system also emerge in his studies of when parties litigate and the role that the official law of contract plays in business affairs. The official story, of course, is that, through contract law, the state underwrites party agreements (private lawmaking) with coercive force. A general abstract law of contracts says that the state will enforce your contract (except if obtained by force or fraud), whatever it is; and this provides a generally secure and predictable framework for market transactions. 'Non-Contractual Relations in Business' raised doubts about the extent to which, if at all, commercial parties relied on the framework or even paid any attention to it. Macaulay's study of the contract forms that car manufacturers used with their suppliers nicely illustrated a theme that runs through all his work. The contracts are probably unenforceable as requirements contracts because they give the manufacturers unlimited discretion to unilaterally revise their terms, but neither the manufacturers nor the suppliers are troubled by this – the carmakers want the flexibility, the suppliers want the business, so legal enforcement is far from their minds.[31] Even in cases where contracting parties would like to assert rights apparently agreed to by contract or conferred by regulation, they may have no practical means to enforce them, since cost barriers to litigation create a 'freedom from contract'.

Macaulay, building on the foundational historical work of Lawrence Friedman,[32] looked at developments within contract law that called into question its official role. One was that the most important and contentious fields of contract relations (insurance, labour, consumer credit, and so on) have been split off from the general field into areas of specialised statutory and administrative action. Also, the growth of non-state regulatory mechanisms – relational contract (networks with private sanctions), semi-autonomous social fields and private governments (such as trade associations) – has taken over much of the work of supplying default terms and settling disputes. Thus contract-law-as-taught-in-law-schools, does not function as a general supporter-definer-regulator of markets: since litigated cases are almost all oddities, contract courts find themselves as dispensers of particularised ad hoc ex post justice. They don't need to worry about crafting general predictable rules, or general market-supporting

[30] See S Macaulay, 'Bambi Meets Godzilla' (1989) 26 *Houston Law Review* 525; S Macaulay, 'Freedom from Contract' (2007) *Wisconsin Law Review* 777.

[31] S Macaulay, 'The Standardized Contracts of United States Automobile Manufacturers' in *International Encyclopedia of Comparative Law*, vol 7, (Leiden, Koninklijke Brill NV, 1974) ch 3, S3–21/29.

[32] L Friedman, *Contract Law in America* (Madison, University of Wisconsin Press, 1965).

policies (though some judges and more law professors do nonetheless), because most of the time nobody looks to courts for that.[33]

This story seems to undermine both sides of the basic argument that opens this paper. It undermines the Hayek spontaneous-order side, which wants to present the state and law as essentially-but-minimally involved in private ordering as the mechanical enforcer of party-made agreements. That was the aim of the classical abstract law of contract, but that system's day is certainly over and probably never existed. But the story also undermines the side that sees the state as pervasively regulating everything. Yes, modern contract law sometimes regulates and equitably distributes, instead of merely formally ratifying party-made agreements. But it does so in a piecemeal fashion, case-by-case, without affecting most transactions.

Thus the role of contract law as such is largely peripheral, just as the theorists of self-sustaining social relations would assume. Still, Macaulay makes clear that the periphery can sometimes suddenly move into the centre. In some moments – as when big unanticipated external shocks are delivered to ongoing contract relations, commercial parties turn to the courts. Examples of this include periods of sharp and sudden price changes; occasions such as the closing of the Suez Canal and the Arab oil embargo; and the sudden shift from de facto tenure on the job in the long boom of the postwar economy (1945–68) to a new insecurity of employment. Indeed, whenever circumstances make performance very costly for one party, that party may be tempted to use litigation to: (a) force the other party into a more favourable settlement by exploiting delays and costs of process; and (b) try to get rulings that will shift the balance of power between parties to ongoing relations. In other words, even relational contract doesn't always preclude resort to courts: if parties perceive the relationship as being asymmetric or oppressive, or as suddenly disadvantageous because of economic change, they turn to courts to gain bargaining advantages and to shift balance of power.[34]

IV. PRIVATE GOVERNMENTS

Macaulay's most extended reflections and theoretical treatment of the public–private distinction is in his pioneering 1986 article on 'Private Government'.[35] So far as I've been able to find out, this brilliant article – which had the misfortune of appearing as an essay in an edited collection

[33] See especially S Macaulay, 'Private Legislation and the Duty to Read – Business Run by IBM Machine, the Law of Contracts and Credit Cards' (1966) 19 *Vanderbilt Law Review* 1051.

[34] S Macaulay, 'Elegant Models, Empirical Pictures, and the Complexities of Contract' (1977) 11 *Law & Society Review* 507.

[35] S Macaulay, 'Private Government' in L Lipson and S Wheeler (eds), *Law and Social Science* (New York, Russell Sage Foundation, 1986) 445.

– has only been cited four times in social science and legal periodicals, but it deserves to be much better known. In this essay he gives us both extensive examples of public–private interactions and connections and reflections on various theories of law–society relations.

His starting point is complete acceptance of the post-Legal-Realist picture and evident social reality of mongrel hybridisation of public and private spheres. One of his main objects is to identify many of the different ways in which non-state actors and institutions are partly constituted by and dependent upon state power, sponsorship and facilitation; and when and how they seek to draw upon resources of the state, for example for financing, coercion, authorisation of privileges or organisational advantages, capacity to inflict costs or delays through legal proceedings, or legislation changing rules in their favour. Another objective is to examine non-state institutions and relationships as a thick 'filter' of autonomous fields through which official law must strive to make effective state policies and goals.

He paints a richly variegated landscape of 'interpenetrated rather than distinct entities', a variety – in ascending order of degree of formal organisation – of networks, 'semi-autonomous social fields',[36] and private governments; all of them lawmakers in the sense of generating norms and rules and imposing sanctions on those subject to them, creating a de facto society of 'legal pluralism'.[37] Some of these lawmaking realms deliberately mimic procedures and methods of the official state and legal system (like administrative rule-making within industry trade associations). As the private realm is infused with public-like norms and behaviours, the public is infiltrated or taken over by the private: industry groups may capture administrative agencies, and may do much of the drafting of legislation supposedly designed to regulate them, or be given state authority to act as delegates (as with professional self-regulation). Private groups assume law-enforcement functions (security, counter-espionage and so on), dealing with employee theft or misbehaviour with private sanctions, forming a 'second criminal justice system' that is more efficient but also has fewer procedural safeguards. Such informal sanctions work best within communities that are hard to leave. Sometimes public law tries to solve problems of clubby cartel-like behaviour of private groups such as trade associations or professional organisations (or oppressive families) by intervening in their internal affairs.

So Macaulay's is a view that asserts a determining importance of government in the structuring of social relations – but of many governments, not necessarily of 'the state' or central 'legal system'. His is a picture of

[36] S Moore, 'Law and Social Change: The Semi-Autonomous Social Field as an Appropriate Object of Study' (1973) 7 *Law & Society Review* 719.

[37] M Galanter, 'Justice in Many Rooms: Courts, Private Ordering, and Indigenous Law' (1981) 19 *Journal of Legal Pluralism & Unofficial Law* 1.

legal pluralism, not legal centrism. Some private governments act under authority delegated by the legal system, such as the authority to control what happens on one's property. Often, Macaulay points out, legal pluralism is a tool of colonial imposition, as the imperium makes use of existing groups to legitimate and extend the reach of its own rule. But plural de facto sovereigns may be created out of resistance to such imposition. Some groups have practical immunity from enforcement of general norms, and use it to act contrary to official policy. Public policies and laws bring into existence networks of new private actors settling disputes in the shadow of law, such as the system of insurance adjusters spawned by the legal regulation of car accidents;[38] and the web of relations of prosecutors, defence lawyers, court clerks, judges, linked in networks of reciprocal favours and sanctions.

Macaulay's treatment of 'limits of effective legal action' starts with problems identified by Diane Vaughan and Jack Coffee.[39] Corporate internal incentives and culture often work against compliance with public goals of the central legal system; and it's hard to make the official sanctions effective because the organisation can resist. Corporations accept deviance as the way things are done. Coffee points out that decentralised organisation structure – top management pressing for results – produces middle managers ready to cut corners and break rules. Macaulay adds that scofflaws also often include top managers. In Latin America, for example, top managements pursue their own foreign policies to promote coups, support client governments, or sell arms through subsidiaries to favoured political factions.

Another example Macaulay gives of private-government 'filters' is that of the history of affirmative action in universities for women. In this field (at least as of 1986, when 'Private Government' was published) the law imposes many requirements but there is little compliance. Academics believe they hire on pure merit and resist what they perceive as arbitrary mandates to favour status-based criteria. State enforcement efforts were weakened as affirmative action lost legitimacy, and they were in any case difficult because principles of faculty governance and academic freedom decentralised hiring decisions. Internal affirmative action officers who were put in charge of compliance actually served to deflect or delay compliance efforts. There was no effective threat of sanctions because the ultimate sanction – cutting off funds – was not realistic.

[38] See, eg HL Ross, *Settled Out of Court: The Social Process of Insurance Claims Adjustment* (New York, Aldine Publishing Co, 1980).

[39] D Vaughan, *Controlling Unlawful Organizational Behavior: Social Structure and Corporate Misconduct* (Chicago, University of Chicago Press, 1983); J Coffee Jr, 'No Soul to Damn, No Body to Kick: An Unscandalized Inquiry into the Problem of Corporate Punishment' (1981) 79 *Michigan Law Review* 386.

As we have seen, Macaulay does not buy into the Hayek/Smith view of 'private' social life as dominated by the co-operative interactions arising out of '*doux commerce*', the institutions and norms of sociability, trust and reciprocity generated by the mutual pursuit of self-interest. Such benign relations – like the famous 'Non-Contractual Relations in Business' – can and do arise. But many ongoing business relations are formed as much by conflict as by co-operation – such as those between manufacturers and franchised dealers, and employers and employees. Norms of trust, decency and fair treatment of others may sometimes prevail even outside contexts where parties have specific self-interested motives for co-operation. But without the restraints of self-interested co-operation, business can behave brutally, especially in their foreign operations.

I would venture that Macaulay on the whole has a more Hobbesian than Smithian view of social life as riven with conflicts and rivalries for advantage, power and status. But he lacks Hobbes's confidence in sovereign authority to resolve such conflicts. The web of social networks, autonomous social fields and private governments filters out many such resolutions. Official state actions which cut against entrenched social norms are likely to be weakened or nullified through evasion or resistance. Moreover, endorsement by 'law' does not necessarily add any legitimacy to despised or disrespected state action. Macaulay is very sceptical of Marxisant sociologists' claims that law adds much persuasive force to power, except perhaps in the minds of the middle classes: neither the poor, who experience law as hostile imposition, nor the rich, who see how easy it is to manipulate, are much 'mystified' by legal enactment.

V. LEGAL FORMALISM AND THE ENFORCEMENT OF CONTRACTS

Some of the most influential scholars of modern contract law have accepted and built on Macaulay's and Ian Macneil's studies of relational contracting but have reintegrated those studies into a neoclassical formalist view of the proper role of contract law. Most business firms, they acknowledge, settle disputes with regard to informal norms of solidarity and reciprocity and a desire for advantageous continuing relations, and these norms do not much resemble those of formal contract law. Nonetheless, if informal norms and sanctions do not work, firms may wish to seek contract enforcement through the courts. If they do so, according to these scholars, the firms prefer predictable enforcement relying on strict textual interpretations of their paper deal – however little resemblance the written contract may have come to share with their actual expectations as they have evolved over the course of the contract. Formalist adjudication is the most efficient regime for such 'end-game' litigation (in Lisa Bernstein's phrase[40]) because it is cheap and predictable, as compared to the prescription of Karl Llewellyn and other Legal Realists, which is built into the *Uniform Commercial Code*,[41] for deep contextual inquiry into the parties' informal expressions of their agreement, course of performance, prior dealings and trade usage. Over time, these scholars suggest, court-standardised interpretations of contract terms will teach parties how to use contract language to express their actual intentions. Courts are not likely to be competent at reconstructing parties' actual expectations and accurately observing when they have been breached.[42] Moreover, if courts try to incorporate relational norms of reciprocity and fair dealing into adjudication, they may actually damage the delicate ecology of trust relations: the threat of coercive enforcement may crowd out informal sanctions, reduce co-operation, and encourage parties to turn back into self-interested income maximisers.[43]

The contemporary neo-formalists thus arrive at the same destination as the classical-liberals about how courts should decide cases, favouring formal rules and formal interpretive methods over informal standards, substantive regulation of contracts for fairness and equity, and interpretation aimed at reconstructing the purposes and intentions-in-context of contracting parties. But their rationale for formalism is efficiency rather than liberty. And most important for present purposes, unlike their classical forbears, the neo-formalists do not ignore or deny the empirical realities of contracting behaviour. They are immersed in those realities, having built on and substantially added to Macaulay's pioneering work. In his illuminating essay for this symposium, Robert Scott generously and sympathetically notes the basic kinship between law-and-economics and law-and-society scholars' treatment of relational contracting. He proposes a sort of Peace of Augsburg, in which the theories and methods of each school would predominate in the study of different domains of contracting: law-and-economics (Protestants, to pursue the metaphor) over contracts between firms, where the main task for law and lawyers is helping

[40] See, eg L Bernstein, 'Merchant Law in a Merchant Court: Rethinking the Code's Search for Immanent Business Norms' (1996) 144 *University of Pennsylvania Law Review* 176.

[41] See, eg, UCC 1-303, 2-202, 2-208.

[42] ibid; A Schwartz and R Scott, 'Contract Theory and the Limits of Contract Law' (2003) 113 *Yale Law Journal* 541; A Schwartz and R Scott, 'Contract Interpretation Redux' (2010) 119 *Yale Law Journal* 926.

[43] eg R Scott, 'The Death of Contract Law' (2004) 54 *University of Toronto Law Journal* 369, 386–89. In more recent and extremely interesting work, Scott and others have studied complex contracting arrangements between business firms 'contracting for innovation'. These firms intertwine or 'braid' formal and informal contracting mechanisms: they use formal contracting to establish 'processes that make behavior observable enough to support informal contracting over the substance of the innovation'. See, eg R Gilson, C Sabel and R Scott, 'Braiding: The Interaction of Formal and Informal Contracting in Theory, Practice and Doctrine' (2010) 110 *Columbia Law Review* 1377, 1402.

the parties realise their joint goals; law-and-society (Catholics) over contracts between firms and unequal partners like consumers and employees, where the law has to worry about abuses of superior power and knowledge. His key point is that both schools are committed to the study of law in action, as it affects – or fails to affect – people in real social relationships; and that basic post-Realist commitment should make them allies in a world of contract scholarship that seems perversely tending to revert to treating contract law as a body of very abstract rules and principles.[44]

Although Macaulay would surely sign this treaty with enthusiasm, he remains something of a sceptic about the law-and-economics preference for formal adjudication, while, admitting the validity of the point about cost barriers to litigation. He does not believe that contract adjudication can hope to rely entirely on rules rather than standards, since so much contract law – such as doctrines of 'substantial performance' or 'waiver' or a view of whether a victim of breach has taken 'reasonable' steps to cover or avoid consequential loss or contract performance should be excused because of the failure of a basic condition on which the contract was based – inevitably requires inquiry into contextual particulars. (To this point the neo-formalists would probably respond that sophisticated parties would substite rules for default standards such as the substantial performance doctrine.) He believes that strict enforcement of a 'hard' parol evidence rule, allowing the terms of a paper contract to exclude proof of the 'real deal' negotiated by the parties' agents, is a licence to the party controlling the forms to cheat and lie.[45] And being a product of a legal realist legal education, he doubts that many (most?) judges would uphold such results even if doctrine told them they should; they would find some way around a result they perceived to be arbitrary or unjust.

Thus – interestingly – the scholar who has done more than any other to point out the marginality of courts to actual contracting behaviour, the advantages that litigation costs confer upon stronger parties, and the ineffectuality of most contract doctrines to remedy structural inequalities, retains a residual faith in the capacity of courts to understand the real stakes and to do substantial justice in litigated contract cases. Other work of his makes clear, however, that the contribution courts can make is less likely to take the form of 'correct' decisions than of the compromises that effective managerial judges can produce by knocking the parties' heads together and threatening adverse rulings if they do not co-operate.[46]

[44] R Scott, 'The Promise and the Peril of Relational Contract Theory' (ch 3 in this volume).

[45] See Macaulay, 'Relational Contracts' (n 1) 775–804; S Macaulay, 'The Real and the Paper Deal: Empirical Pictures of Relationships, Complexity and the Urge for Transparent Simple Rules' (2003) 66 *Modern Law Review* 44.

[46] See, eg Macaulay, 'Elegant Models' (n 34).

CONCLUSION

We began with an extreme contrast of positions in social theory: visions of social life as (private) spontaneous orders only marginally affected by the actions of laws and governments versus visions of social life as pervasively structured by and permeated with (public) government-derived rules and actions. Almost nobody (so far as I know) adopts the pure version of either position, as either a factual account of social reality or as a norm to be aspired to. Most people – I would guess – agree that the reality is, and the ideal would be, some mixture of both. The classical view of the relation of contract law to contracting behaviour is that contracting behaviour is largely private ordering (through ongoing continuing relations or party-made contract forms), but that contract law plays a minor though essential role in sustaining this ordering by providing coercive enforcement against breachers who cannot be deterred by private sanctions. Maybe the most common view is that contracting behaviour did once largely conform to the model of largely self-sustaining private ordering with a minimum of legal support, but that, over the last century, it has been snowed under by a thick blanket of statutory, administrative and judicial public regulation. This is the story of the 'rise and fall of freedom of contract' (Atiyah), or the 'death of contract' (Gilmore).[47] Some think this story is one of progress, others that it is one of decay, a set of mistakes that should be reversed, but they agree on the story of a sphere of private ordering gradually being interpenetrated with state action.

Macaulay's intervention in this argument continues a post-Realist tradition of scrambling the public–private distinction. Especially in 'Private Government', he sees many 'private' institutions such as business corporations, universities and other associations as exercising delegated public powers of governance: policing and regulating people under their control. (If the consumers Macaulay describes, in the quote that opens this piece, are like 'citizens' of a private government, they are citizens without much of a franchise.) But he also sees such subdelegates of public power, like feudal baronies or proprietors of commons, as generators of their own norms and customs and procedures and sanctions so as enable them to operate independently of public authority and even in defiance of it – drawing on the state for enforcement when they want it, but filtering out and neutralising legal enactments when they don't like them. Yet Leviathan turns out to be a bit of a wimp. Official legal remedies are generally too expensive, uncertain and disruptive of co-operative relations for practical use: thus 'freedom of contract' – the notional right to enforce

[47] PS Atiyah, *The Rise and Fall of Freedom of Contract* (Oxford, Clarendon Press, 1979); G Gilmore, *The Death of Contract* (Columbus, Ohio State University Press, 1974).

agreed-upon or state-imposed terms – often becomes 'freedom from contract', an immunity from legal compulsion. The immunity is far from absolute – there are circumstances in which parties faced with what they perceive to be an intolerable bind will file lawsuits or seek legislative remedies. Sometimes, like the auto dealers chafing under the despotic yoke of manufacturers, or uranium sellers locked into fixed-price contracts in a steeply rising market, they can use formal law to leverage favourable settlements. But for the most part contracting parties can and do ignore contract law.

Macaulay's vision is, however, far from a claim that contracting behaviour takes place in a sphere unaffected by law generally, a sort of anarchist utopia. In fact, contracting parties live in a social milieu saturated by law. Contract law may not be an important piece of this milieu, but lots of other kinds of law are. And what kinds of law are those? A serious treatment of the question would open up vast territories of knowledge for exploration: I offer here only a few almost-random examples. Some of these investigations would surely reveal many more-or-less spontaneous orders, trading or favour-or-gift-exchanging communities operating with little or no law or state compulsion in the background except as constraints to be deftly worked around. After all, contracting communities in many Asian societies seem to have achieved quite a lot of commercial success without the help of law; as have traders in the Chinese and Jewish diasporas, often faced with active popular and state hostility, and even illegal squatters such as *favela* slum-dwellers who, disqualified from participation in the formal legal system by a lack of legal title, construct their own norms and sanctions. Avner Greif has given us some memorable case studies of 'private-order contract enforcement institutions', such as the mechanisms evolved by coalitions of medieval Mahgribi merchants in the Middle Ages for collective sanctions against faithless agents.[48] Examples like these create considerable doubt about whether any specific set of legal arrangements is actually functionally necessary, much less indispensable, to supporting contracting relations.

Whether necessary or not, however, state and legal action affecting contracting have in fact been pervasive. Greif gives us many examples of merchant communities seeking state guarantees of protection of their property; and – just as or more important – forming merchants guilds to exert political and economic pressure (for example, refusals to deal or lend, boycotts and so on) against rulers who try to confiscate instead of protecting merchants' property.[49] Traders must have something to trade and find ways of keeping their gains from the hands of greedy predators

[48] A Greif, *Institutions and the Path to the Modern Economy* (Cambridge, Cambridge University Press, 2006) 58–90.

[49] ibid 91–123.

and overlords: in many times and places, the chief service the legal system can perform for traders is not so much to enforce their contracts as to help them secure their persons against robbery and extortion; though, of course, it is always helpful to create legal institutions capable of routine debt-collection and enforcement of secured-credit liens. Emily Kadens, looking at the history of the medieval law merchant – often instanced as an example of non-state private-trader-made international customary law – discovers that the 'law merchant' is not one but many different bodies of law, each deriving much of its content and enforcement sanctions from what we would call public sources, the laws and edicts of states and cities.[50] Merchant traders have almost always had to rely on states and their diplomatic accords to protect them from the predations of pirates and rival states and clans.[51] Law does not only create and protect tradeable property, it also creates the very capacity to trade. As Durkheim pointed out, the capacity to make and keep promises is the creation of status law, especially family law[52] (and this is no relic of primitive law – American married women couldn't even legally sign cheques or retain their earnings from work until late in the nineteenth century). Law incorporates cultural codes defining what may be traded, what only given away or received as gift, what is inalienable altogether. As the histories cited earlier in this paper of government actions affecting commercial transactions demonstrate, non-state lawmaking and enforcement by commercial communities has to be seen against a vast backdrop of state activity – building of transportation, banking and innovation infrastructure, protection and expansion of commercial markets through war and empire, and much, much more. Looked at against this backdrop, private custom and private markets no longer appear as the basic fabric of society, with law and the state relegated largely to the (useful and sometimes indispensable) periphery of formal contract enforcement and the (invasive and often inefficient) periphery of state regulation, but as one pattern in the weave of a larger tapestry. Or, to vary the image, contracting parties seem like Brecht's Mother Courage, the peddler who buys and sells her wares while weaving between and behind the lines of opposing armies in the Thirty Years War. Commercial life goes on, in the spaces between artillery fire. The trade supplies the war, and the war supplies the trade: private and public, perpetually interlinked.

[50] E Kadens, 'Order Within Law, Variety Within Custom: The Character of Medieval Merchant Law' (2004) 5 *Chicago Journal of International Law* 67.

[51] See, eg M Greene, *Catholic Pirates and Greek Merchants: A Maritime History of the Mediterranean* (Princeton, Princeton University Press, 2010).

[52] E Durkheim, C Brookfield (trans), *Professional Ethics and Civic Morals* (London, Routledge, 1992) 179–87.

BIBLIOGRAPHY

Arnold, T, *The Folklore of Capitalism* (New Haven, Yale University Press, 1937).

Atiyah, PS, *The Rise and Fall of Freedom of Contract* (Oxford, Clarendon Press, 1979).

Bernstein, L, 'Merchant Law in a Merchant Court: Rethinking the Code's Search for Immanent Business Norms' (1996) 144 *University of Pennsylvania Law Review* 176.

Chandrasekeran, R, *Imperial Life in the Emerald City: Inside Iraq's Green Zone* (New York, Knopf, 2006).

Coase, R, 'The Lighthouse in Economics' (1974) 17 *Journal of Law and Economics* 57.

Coffee, Jr, J, 'No Soul to Damn, No Body to Kick: An Unscandalized Inquiry into the Problem of Corporate Punishment' (1981) 79 *Michigan Law Review* 386.

Cohen, M, 'Property as Sovereignty' (1927) 13 *Cornell Law Review* 8.

Durkheim, E, C Brookfield (trans), *Professional Ethics and Civic Morals* (London, Routledge, 1992).

Edling, M, *A Revolution in Favor of Government* (Oxford, Oxford University Press, 2008).

Edwards, L, *The People and Their Peace: Legal Culture and the Transformation of Inequality in the Post-Revolutionary South* (Chapel Hill, University of North Carolina Press, 2009).

Ellickson, R, *Order Without Law: How Neighbors Settle Disputes* (Cambridge, Harvard University Press, 1991).

Engerman, S and Gallman, R (eds), *The Cambridge Economic History of the United States* (Cambridge, Cambridge University Press, 2000).

Fried, B, *The Progressive Assault on Laissez Faire: Robert Hale and the First Law and Economics Movement* (Cambridge, First Harvard University Press, 1998).

Friedman, L, *Contract Law in America* (Madison, University of Wisconsin Press, 1965).

Galanter, M, 'Justice in Many Rooms: Courts, Private Ordering, and Indigenous Law' (1981) 19 *Journal of Legal Pluralism & Unofficial Law* 1.

Gilmore, G, *The Death of Contract* (Columbus, Ohio State University Press, 1974).

Gilson, R, Sabel, C and Scott, R, 'Braiding: The Interaction of Formal and Informal Contracting in Theory, Practice and Doctrine' (2010) 110 *Columbia Law Review* 1377.

Gordon, R, 'The Constitution of Liberal Order at the Troubled Beginnings of the Modern State' (2004) 58 *University of Miami Law Review* 373.

Greene, M, *Catholic Pirates and Greek Merchants: A Maritime History of the Mediterranean* (Princeton, Princeton University Press, 2010).

Greif, A, *Institutions and the Path to the Modern Economy* (Cambridge, Cambridge University Press, 2006).

Grewal, D, *The Invention of the Economy: A History of Economic Thought* (Cambridge, Harvard University Press, forthcoming 2012).

Hale, R, 'Coercion and Distribution in a Supposedly Non-coercive State' (1923) 38 *Political Science Quarterly* 470.

Handlin, O and Handlin, M, *Commonwealth: A Study of the Role of Government in the American Economy: Massachusetts, 1774–1861*, 2nd edn (Cambridge, Harvard University Press, 1969).

Harcourt, B, *The Illusion of Free Markets: Punishment and the Myth of Natural Order* (Cambridge, Harvard University Press, 2011).
Hartog, H, *Public Property and Private Power* (Chapel Hill, University of North Carolina Press, 1989).
Hartz, L, *Economic Policy and Democratic Thought: Pennsylvania, 1776–1860* (Cambridge, Harvard University Press, 1948).
Hayek, FA, *Law, Legislation and Liberty: Rules and Order*, vol 1 (Chicago, University of Chicago Press, 1973).
——, *The Constitution of Liberty* (Chicago, University of Chicago Press, 1960).
Hurst, J, *The Legitimacy of the Business Corporation in the Law of the United States* (Charlottesville, University Press of Virginia, 1970).
Jaffe, L, 'Lawmaking by Private Groups' (1937) 51 *Harvard Law Review* 201.
Kadens, E, 'Order Within Law, Variety Within Custom: The Character of Medieval Merchant Law' (2004) 5 *Chicago Journal of International Law* 67.
Kennedy, D, *The Rise and Fall of Classical Legal Thought* (Washington DC, Beard Books, 2006).
Lieberman, D, 'Contract Before "Freedom of Contract"' in H Scheiber (ed), *The State and Freedom of Contract* (Stanford, Stanford University Press, 1998).
Macaulay, S, 'Freedom from Contract: Solutions in Search of a Problem?' (2007) *Wisconsin Law Review* 777.
——, 'The Real and the Paper Deal: Empirical Pictures of Relationships, Complexity and the Urge for Transparent Simple Rules' (2003) 66 *Modern Law Review* 44.
——, 'Relational Contracts Floating on a Sea of Custom? Thoughts about the Ideas of Ian Macneil and Lisa Bernstein' (2000) 94 *Northwestern University Law Review* 775.
——, 'Bambi Meets Godzilla: Reflections on Contract Scholarship and Teaching vs. State Unfair and Deceptive Trade Practices and Consumer Protection Statutes' (1989) 26 *Houston Law Review* 525.
——, 'Private Government' in L Lipson and S Wheeler (eds), *Law and Social Science* (New York, Russell Sage Foundation, 1986).
——, 'Lawyers and Consumer Protection Laws' (1979) 14 *Law & Society Review* 115.
——, 'Elegant Models, Empirical Pictures, and the Complexities of Contract' (1977) 11 *Law & Society Review* 507.
——, 'The Standardized Contracts of United States Automobile Manufacturers' in *International Encyclopedia of Comparative Law*, vol 7, ch 3 (Leiden, Koninklijke Brill NV, 1974).
——, *Law and the Balance of Power: The Automobile Manufacturers and Their Dealers* (New York, Russell Sage Foundation, 1966).
——, 'Private Legislation and the Duty to Read – Business Run by IBM Machine, the Law of Contracts and Credit Cards' (1966) 19 *Vanderbilt Law Review* 1051.
——, 'Non-Contractual Relations in Business: A Preliminary Study' (1963) 28 *American Sociological Review* 55.
Maitland, FW, 'Trust and Corporation' in HD Hazeltine, G Lapsley and PH Winfield (eds), *Maitland: Selected Essays* (Manchester, Ayer Co Publishing, 1936).
Mashaw, J, *Creating the Administrative Constitution: The Lost One Hundred Years of American Administrative Law* (New Haven, Yale University Press, 2012).
Metzger, G, 'Privatization as Delegation' (2003) 103 *Columbia Law Review* 1367.

Moore, S, 'Law and Social Change: The Semi-Autonomous Social Field as an Appropriate Object of Study' (1973) 7 *Law & Society Review* 719.
Novak, W, *The Peoples' Welfare: Law and Regulation in Nineteenth Century America* (Chapel Hill, University of North Carolina Press, 1996).
Orth, J, 'Contract and the Common Law' in H Scheiber (ed), *The State and Freedom of Contract* (Stanford, Stanford University Press, 1998).
Parrillo, N, *Against the Profit Motive: The Salary Revolution in American Government, 1780–1940* (New Haven, Yale University Press, forthcoming 2013).
Polanyi, K, *The Great Transformation* (New York, Farrar & Rinehart, 1944).
Robbins, L, *The Theory of Economic Policy in English Classical Political Economy* (London, Macmillan Press, 1952).
Ross, HL, *Settled Out of Court: The Social Process of Insurance Claims Adjustment* (New York, Aldine Publishing Co, 1980).
Rothman, D, *The Discovery of the Asylum* (Boston, Little Brown, 1971).
Scheiber, H, *Ohio Canal Era: A Case Study of Government and the Economy, 1820–1861* (Athens, Ohio University Press, 1969).
Schwartz, A and Scott, R, 'Contract Interpretation Redux' (2010) 119 *Yale Law Journal* 926.
——, 'Contract Theory and the Limits of Contract Law' (2003) 113 *Yale Law Journal* 541.
Scott, R, 'The Death of Contract Law' (2004) 54 *University of Toronto Law Journal* 369.
Siegan, B, *Economic Liberties and the Constitution* (Chicago, University of Chicago Press, 2006).
Vaughan, D, *Controlling Unlawful Organizational Behavior: Social Structure and Corporate Misconduct* (Chicago, University of Chicago Press, 1983).

2

Empiricism's Crucial Question and the Transformation of the Legal System

EDWARD RUBIN

INTRODUCTION

STEWART MACAULAY IS one of the founders of empirical legal studies. This is, at present, an important approach to the study of law, and all indications suggest that it will become increasingly important as time goes on. In order to understand the nature of its importance, and of Professor Macaulay's achievement, however, it seems necessary to explain what this approach involves and how it differs from others. We sometimes refer to empirical legal studies as reflecting a 'law and society' orientation, but no one has ever seriously asserted that law was isolated from society. The first part of this article specifies the way in which modern empirical legal studies, such as Professor Macaulay's study of contracting practices among Wisconsin manufacturing firms,[1] is distinctive. The second part then discusses the potential importance of empirical legal studies. It argues that this approach to law, because of its distinctive features, has the potential to transform the legal system in a direction that is more consistent with the goals and practices of the modern administrative state in which it is now embedded.

The last section of the article discusses the methodology of empirical legal studies. Although Professor Macaulay is one of the founders of this field, it seems to be headed in a somewhat different direction from the one he initiated. Professor Macaulay's pioneering work did not involve surveys, nor did it contain very much statistical analysis. Instead, he talked to people and reported what they told him. At present, surveys and statistical analysis are very much the rage in empirical legal studies and much of the methodological debate focuses on whether they are being done

[1] S Macaulay, 'Non-Contractual Relations in Business: A Preliminary Study' (1963) 28 *American Sociological Review* 55.

well, not whether they should be done at all.[2] Does this mean that Professor's Macaulay's approach to the field he helped initiate is no longer relevant, or do the current practitioners have something to learn from what might seem to be a more intuitive, and thus perhaps less sophisticated methodology?

I. WHY MODERN EMPIRICAL LEGAL SCHOLARSHIP IS DIFFERENT FROM PRIOR SCHOLARSHIP

Any study of a particular society's legal system is in fact an empirical inquiry, namely, an inquiry into a specific component of that society. No one has asserted that the rules of a society's legal system could be derived from abstract principles. Moreover, no one has denied that the description of a legal system includes the way that legal rules diverge from their theoretical justifications and doctrinal formulations. The extent to which this is true is of course a matter on which legal scholars differ, but not as much as might appear. Many scholars have approached law as a largely autonomous and doctrinal discipline, but that does not necessarily mean that they are denying the interaction of law and society; their position, rather, is that the legal system is significant in its own right, that it merits sustained attention, and that their particular expertise lies in that area.

Given the essentially empirical character that the study of law has possessed since its inception, it is necessary to determine what makes empirical legal studies, in its modern form, distinctive. There is a tendency to answer this question by referring to techniques, such as the systematic use of survey data and statistical analysis, or methodologies, such as social science.[3] To this might be added the laboratory studies that constitute an essential methodology of behavioural economics.[4] These explanations should certainly not be dismissed; survey techniques and social science methodology have transformed our approach to our society and ourselves over the course

[2] See, eg L Epstein, A Martin and M Schneider, 'On the Effective Communication of the Results of Empirical Studies, Parts I & II' (2006) 59 *Vanderbilt Law Review* 1811, (2007) 60 *Vanderbilt Law Review* 801; L Epstein and G King, 'The Rules of Inference' (2002) 69 *University of Chicago Law Review* 1.

[3] See, eg M Heise, 'The Past, Present and Future of Empirical Legal Scholarship: Judicial Decision Making and the New Empiricism' (2002) 2002 *Illinois Law Review* 819, 821 ('when I speak of empirical legal scholarship, I refer only to the subset of empirical legal scholarship that uses statistical techniques and analyses'); T George, 'An Empirical Study of Empirical Legal Scholarship: The Top Law Schools' (2006) 81 *Indiana Law Journal* 141, 141 ('ELS, as the term is generally used in law schools, refers to a specific type of empirical research: a model-based approach coupled with a quantitative method.').

[4] See, eg D Kahneman, P Slovic and A Tversky, *Judgment Under Uncertainty: Heurisitics and Biases* (Cambridge, Cambridge University Press, 1982); A Tversky and D Kahneman, 'The Framing of Decisions and the Psychology of Choice' (1981) 211 *Science* 453.

of the past two hundred years.[5] But, as David Trubek has suggested,[6] there is a more conceptual distinction. It asserts that empirical legal studies represents a new approach to the legal system itself, rather than merely being new methodology for studying that system. From this perspective, empirical legal study is different from the empiricism of the past and represents a truly transformative insight for legal scholarship and the legal system.

Transformative insights often begin with deceptively simple and apparently obvious questions. The question that Stewart Macaulay and several other initiators of empirical legal studies asked is whether people will obey the law.[7] The answer that seems obvious is that sometimes they do and sometimes they don't. Under normal circumstances, most people will obey the law because they accept its legitimacy and understand its purpose, and because it carries criminal or civil sanctions that they want to avoid. But, as Madison famously declared: 'What is government itself, but the greatest of all reflections on human nature? If men were angels, no government would be necessary.'[8] The highly secular Madison's[9] reference to angels connects this statement to a long tradition that regards government as a necessary response to people's fallen nature.[10] In our modern, secular society, where Adam Smith has replaced Scripture, this same thought is formulated as the assertion that people act in their individual self-interest. Thus, they will disobey the law if such disobedience is to their advantage; this tendency, while universal, will vary in strength from one person to another depending on their imagination, opportunism and level of risk aversion.

The obvious fact that some people will disobey the law in many circumstances, and perhaps that everyone will disobey the law in a few, leads both government lawmakers and jurisprudentialists to emphasise the role of sanctions in their descriptions of legal systems. Most laws contain enforcement provisions of one sort or another, often the most elaborate

[5] See S Igo, *The Averaged American: Surveys, Citizens, and the Making of the Mass Public* (Cambridge, Harvard University Press, 2007).

[6] D Trubek, 'Where the Action Is: Critical Legal Studies and Empiricism' (1984) 36 *Stanford Law Review* 575, 579–88. See also D Trubek and J Esser, 'Critical Empiricism in American Legal Studies: Paradox, Program or Pandora's Box' (1989) 14 *Law & Social Inquiry* 1.

[7] For other early and influential works along these lines, see, eg G Calabresi, *The Cost of Accidents: A Legal and Economic Analysis* (New Haven, Yale University Press, 1970); HL Ross, *Settled Out of Court: The Social Process of Insurance Claims Adjustment*, rev 2nd edn (New York, Aldine Publishing, 1980).

[8] J Madison, 'The Same Subject Continued With the Same View and Concluded' (Federalist No 51) in J Madison, A Hamilton and J Jay, *The Federalist Papers* (London, Penguin, 1987; first published 1788) 318–19.

[9] See B Allen, *Moral Minority: Our Skeptical Founding Fathers* (Chicago, Ivan R Dee, 2007) 103–21. In 'Federalist 51', Madison refers to the religious pluralism of the United States as a 'multiplicity of sects'. Madison, 'Same Subject' (n 8) 321.

[10] T Aquinas, *Summa Theologica*, Fathers of the English Dominican Province trans (New York, Benziger Bros, 1948) 944–62 (I–II, Qs 79–83); Saint Augustine, Marcus Dods (trans), *The City of God* (New York, Modern Library, 1993) 412–77 (Bks XIII-XIV).

and carefully crafted provisions in modern legislation. Many legal scholars regard the presence of such provisions as essential in determining whether some government promulgation or customary rule is in fact a law. When positivists identify the formal criteria for law, they refer to sanctions and often, like Hans Kelsen, declare this to be the law's defining feature.[11] Hart modifies this approach by arguing that most people obey the law out of a sense of obligation, but he retains the element of sanctions as a basic feature of primary rules, while recognising power-conferring or secondary rules as a partial exception.[12] Although natural law theorists insist that additional criterion beyond the formal ones be recognised as necessary for a custom or promulgation to be counted as a law, they generally have no argument with this emphasis on sanctions.

Building on this view that sanctions are central to the concept of law, legal scholars often regard the law-breaker as performing an essential function in the legal system. It is when the law is violated, they argue, that its contours and boundaries are defined.[13] Vague norms or commands are crystallised in the enforcement process, establishing precedents that serve as guides to the obedient and threats to the refractory. This does not mean that any of these scholars are adopting an ironic position that wrongdoers benefit society. It would be better, in nearly everyone's view, 'if men were angels', but of course they are not. The point, rather, is that violation of prevailing rules is inevitable, and so legal authorities can, and generally should, use these inevitable violations to clarify the meaning of their strictures.

The crucial insight that Professor Macaulay and other founders of modern empirical legal studies advanced is that disobedience is much more than an opportunity to clarify the law's extent. Rather, they have realised, the purpose of law is generally to produce some effect in the real world, and the question is always whether the law has produced that effect, as opposed to producing no effect, or producing some different and unintended effect. Professor Macaulay asked this question in 1963.[14] As Mitu Gulati and Laura Beth Nielsen write with respect to discrimination law, the analysis of judicial opinions 'sheds light on but one aspect of what discrimination is, how organizations define it, and how the law does (or does not) effectively redress the phenomenon. A fuller understanding . . . requires that we examine . . . how discrimination operates as a function – of individual perceptions, market structures and institutional dynamics.'[15]

[11] H Kelsen, *General Theory of Law and the State* (Cambridge, Harvard University Press, 1945); H Kelsen, *Pure Theory of Law* (Berkeley, University of California Press, 1967).

[12] HLA Hart, *The Concept of Law* (New York, Oxford University Press, 1961) 77–96.

[13] See K Llewellyn, *The Common Law Tradition: Deciding Appeals* (Buffalo, William S Hein & Co, 1960); L Fuller, 'The Forms and Limits of Adjudication' (1978) 92 *Harvard Law Review* 353.

[14] Macaulay, 'Non-Contractual Relations' (n 1). The fact that this article was published in a sociology journal is itself significant. See Part II below.

[15] M Gulati and LB Nielsen, 'Introduction: A New Legal Realist Perspective on Employment Discrimination' (2006) 31 *Law & Social Inquiry* 797, 798.

In other words, the question is not merely whether we should impose sanctions on those who disobey the law, but how to determine the full range of responses that define the law's effect.

This perspective was not an entirely new inquiry in American legal scholarship. Most notably, some of the legal realists of the previous generation had taken the same approach.[16] But, as John Henry Schlegel has documented, their efforts had little traction in the field and produced few results, in part because they were not trained social scientists, in part because their efforts to conceal their lack of training produced a relatively opaque and inaccessible body of work.[17] Modern empiricists are fully trained; in fact, it has become common for aspiring legal academics to have a PhD in some social science field such as economics, political science, sociology or anthropology in addition to a law degree. When this process began, some of these highly qualified young faculty were so entranced with their credentials – 'teched up' in the argot of the academy – that their work was as opaque as the former Realists, although motivated by the desire for display rather than concealment.[18] As time has gone on, however, and dual credentials have become more common, these scholars have added clarity and accessibility to their technical competence. Their work has then begun to merge with a more broadly interdisciplinary movement that sees itself as a lineal descendant of the Legal Realists, and thus describes itself as New Legal Realism.[19]

The law that Professor Macaulay chose to study was not some new enactment that might have triggered such an investigation by virtue of its novelty. Rather, it was the common law of contracts, a body of rules that had been around, in the same essential form, for more than a hundred years, that was a standard first year course in every American law school, and that was, in fact, the course in which the venerable Langdell initiated the case book and the case law method that formed – and still forms – the basic approach of virtually every law school.[20] Moreover, Macaulay did not focus on consumers in this article, although he did so in subsequent

[16] eg WU Moore and C Callahan, 'Law and Learning Theory: A Study of Legal Control' (1943) 53 *Yale Law Journal* 1. See L Kalman, *Legal Realism at Yale: 1927–1960* (Chapel Hill, University of North Carolina Press, 1986).

[17] J Schlegel, *American Legal Realism and Empirical Social Science* (Chapel Hill, University of North Carolina Press, 1995).

[18] I am not going to cite anyone to illustrate this proposition.

[19] See, eg 'Symposium, New Legal Realism' (2006) 31 *Law & Social Inquiry* 797; S Macaulay, 'Contracts, New Legal Realism, and Improving the Navigation of *The Yellow Submarine*' (2006) 80 *Tulane Law Review* 1161; T Miles and C Sunstein, 'The New Legal Realism' (2008) 75 *University of Chicago Law Review* 831. For an illuminating discussion of the relationship between the empirical legal studies movement and New Legal Realism, see M Suchman and E Mertz, 'Toward a New Legal Empiricism: Empirical Legal Studies and New Legal Realism' (2010) 6 *Annual Review of Law and Social Science* 555.

[20] L Friedman, *A History of American Law*, 3rd edn (New York, Touchstone, 2005) 466–72; W Chase, 'The Birth of the Modern Law School' (1979) 23 *American Journal of Legal History* 329.

and similar studies.[21] This earlier article concerned the behaviour of business executives in Wisconsin manufacturing firms and the attorneys who represented those firms. In other words, Macaulay's question was whether a group of standard, well-established legal rules were being followed by a group of standard, well-established professional people to whom those rules unquestionably and unproblematically applied.

As soon as the question is phrased in this manner, it becomes apparent that the law's effectiveness does not simply depend on the obvious and relatively uninteresting observation that 'men are not angels', but also on the particular features of the law itself and its relation to the society to which the law applies. With that shift in focus, an enormous terrain of inquiry opens out to the legal researcher. What sorts of laws elicit obedience and what sorts of laws are ignored or resisted? What are the types of enforcement provisions that will induce obedience? If the law is in fact followed, will it produce the desired effects? If not, will any social harm result, and if so, what kind and how much? What social factors will influence or determine the answers to each of these inquiries? This is the terrain that Richard Abel identified as scholarship about law, as opposed to legal scholarship.[22]

In his Wisconsin study, Macaulay found some rather surprising answers. Although the business people and attorneys whose behaviour he studied did not question the legitimacy of contract law, they did not pay much attention to it. Instead, they developed their own rules governing commercial agreements, rules that differed dramatically from the established law. Contrary to the law, for example, parties to commercial exchanges did not agree to a single set of contractual terms before proceeding with the deal, they treated a cancellation constituting legal breach as standard practice, and they either ignored violations of legally binding terms or addressed these violations by compromise and renegotiation, rather than by asserting contract rights in court. Little harm seemed to result from this cavalier approach to the legal rules for contracts because these businesses dealt with each other on a regular basis and developed their own mechanisms for defining their agreements and resolving their disputes. The standard idea that judicially enforced remedies for breach of contract are necessary to avoid resort to violence[23] turned out to appear absurd in the world revealed by Macaulay's study. Indeed, one major

[21] eg S Macaulay, 'Lawyers and Consumer Protection Laws' (1979) 14 *Law & Society Review* 115.

[22] R Abel, 'Law Books and Books About Law' (1973) 26 *Stanford Law Review* 175 (reviewing M Rheinstein, *Marriage Stability, Divorce, and the Law* (Chicago, University of Chicago Press, 1972)).

[23] See J Grogger, 'An Economic Model of Recent Trends in Violence' in A Blumstein and J Wallman, *The Recent Crime Drop in America*, (Cambridge, Cambridge University Press, 2006) 266; A Resignato, 'Violent Crime: A Function of Drug Use or Drug Enforcement' (2000) 32 *Applied Economics* 681.

reason Wisconsin business people avoided contract law is that its use would have been far more conflictual than the irenic dispute resolution practices that they developed on their own.

As Abel points out, scholarship about law (as opposed to legal scholarship) regularly noted the 'gap' between law and behaviour, or, to use the familiar formulation, between law on the books and 'law in action'.[24] This could be regarded as an invitation to ignore legal doctrine – a reassuringly welcome conclusion for non-lawyers – and focus on sociological explanations of behaviour. Macaulay's article, and many of the empirical legal studies that follow it, adopts a more sophisticated and penetrating stance. The question is not whether law provides a complete explanation of behaviour or no explanation at all, but rather how the law affects behaviour. The complexity inherent in this stance is that it must explain behaviour on sociological, rather than legal, grounds because it necessarily problematises the impact of law; that is, no matter how much impact the law has, it must be viewed from an external perspective in order to place that impact in context and explore its extent. At the same time, as Victoria Nourse and Gregory Shaffer observe, empirical legal scholarship must be able to relate that explanation to the law itself if it is to count as legal studies at all, that is, if it is to participate in legal scholarship's normative enterprise of framing criticisms of enacted or decided law, and making recommendations for its improvement.[25] 'Like the original Realists, who also sought to use social science in service of advancing legal knowledge, new legal realist scholars bring together legal theory and empirical research to build a stronger foundation for understanding law and formulating legal policy.'[26]

Given the scholarly traditions we have inherited, these varied goals are not easy to reconcile or unite. One framework that can be proposed for accomplishing this daunting task is Niklas Luhmann's reinterpretation of general systems theory. While it is probably incorrect, and certainly imprecise, to describe the legal system as autonomous, Luhmann proposes that it can be usefully described as autopoietic.[27] The term, like much of systems theory, comes originally from biology, but it differs from

[24] Abel, 'Law Books' (n 22) 184–89.

[25] V Nourse and G Shaffer, 'Varieties of New Legal Realism: Can a New World Order Prompt a New Legal Theory?' (2009) 95 *Cornell Law Review* 61. For my own views on legal scholarship's mission, see E Rubin, 'What Does Prescriptive Legal Scholarship Say and Who Is Listening to It: A Response to Professor Dan-Cohen' (1992) 63 *University of Colorado Law Review* 731; E Rubin, 'The Practice and Discourse of Legal Scholarship' (1988) 86 *Michigan Law Review* 1835.

[26] H Erlanger and others, 'Is It Time for a New Legal Realism?' (2005) 2005 *Wisconsin Law Review* 335, 337.

[27] N Luhmann, K Ziegert (trans), *Law as a Social System* (Oxford, Oxford University Press, 2004) 76–88, 232–34, 423–90. Gunther Teubner has also made important contributions to this theory. See G Teubner, 'Evolution of Autopoietic Law' in G Teubner (ed), *Autopoietic Law: A New Approach to Law and Society* (Berlin, Walter de Gruyter, 1988).

biology, and from standard system theory, because it focuses on discourse and meaning, rather than structure. In other words, it represents a 'linguistic turn' in systems theory.[28] That is the sense in which it merges behaviourist social science to which the original form of systems theory belonged, with the interpretive or hermeneutic perspective.

An autopoietic system, according to Luhmann, is a system that is bounded by virtue of being self-referential – that is, it is an organised structure that constructs or defines its elements. The function or meaning of these elements is then derived from their connectivity to other elements within the structure, and anything that this process creates is part of the structure.[29] For this reason, an autopoietic system can be considered closed, following the conventional systems theory notion that systems are either open to the environment or are closed to it and self-contained.[30] This does not mean, however, that an autopoietic system is isolated from its environment and does not react to it. Such a system would not survive very long. Rather, it means that the system reacts to the environment by constructing elements within the system, not by directly absorbing external elements.[31] As the system reproduces itself it becomes complex; that is, its elements are all connected to each other, but often indirectly through intermediate pathways that create challenging questions of internal co-ordination.[32]

The stock market provides a simple example.[33] Stock markets are exquisitely sensitive to certain types of external signals, such as earning projections by a listed company, changes in government monetary policy, or worldwide shortages of a critical resource. But the market does not describe the status of the company, the nature of the policy or the availability of the

[28] See, eg HG Gadamer, G Barden and J Cumming (trans), *Truth and Method*, 2nd edn (London, Continuum, 1988); J Habermas, T McCarthy (trans), *The Theory of Communicative Action, vol 1: Reason and the Rationalization of Society*, (Boston, Beacon Press, 1984); M Heidegger, J Macquarrie and E Robinson (trans), *Being and Time* (Malden, Blackwell Publishing, 1962); L Wittgenstein, GEM Anscombe (trans), *Philosophical Investigations*, 3rd edn (Oxford, Blackwell Publishing, 1958).

[29] Luhmann, *Law as a Social System* (n 27) 76–88, 232–34, 423–90. See generally N Luhmann, J Bednarz (trans), *Social Systems* (Stanford, Stanford University Press, 1995). For a related approach, see W Buckley, *Sociology and Modern Systems Theory* (Englewood Cliffs, Prentice Hall, 1967).

[30] See L von Bertalanffy, *General Systems Theory: Foundations, Development, Applications* (New York, George Braziller, 1968) 39–41, 120–60; WR Scott, *Organizations: Rational, Natural, and Open Systems*, 5th edn (Englewood Cliffs, Prentice Hall, 2002).

[31] G Teubner, 'How Law Thinks' (1989) 23 *Law & Society Review* 727, 731 (observing that autopoiesis seeks to 'replace the autonomous individual, not with supra-individual entities, but with communicative processes').

[32] Luhmann defines complexity as follows: '[W]e will call an interconnected system "complex" when, because of immanent constraints in the elements' connective capacity, it is no longer possible at any moment to connect every element with every other element.' Luhmann, *Social Systems* (n 29) 24; see generally ibid 23–28.

[33] See W Powell, 'Expanding the Scope of Institutional Analysis' in W Powell and P DiMaggio (eds), *The New Institutionalism in Organizational Analysis* (Chicago, University of Chicago Press, 1991) 183.

resource. Instead, it translates all these events into stock prices, the element of its internal functioning that it designs through its interconnected processes. The result is internal complexity, the response of one price to another within the system itself. This internal process not only replaces the image of the system as immersed in an otherwise undefined environment, but also replaces the well-known feedback loop that plays such a central role in general systems theory.[34] In the feedback model, the system samples its output and feeds that signal back into the system as an input, so that it can determine what it is doing to the environment and co-ordinate its further actions. This, of course, is not what a stock market does. Its operation is more effectively described by the autopoietic idea that the system reproduces itself, that it elaborates its internally defined prices as time goes on. The fact that its prices affect the economy, that they determine the level of investment in particular companies or particular industries, does not exercise a direct effect over the manner is which prices within the market are set.

To explain how an autopoietic system interacts with forces outside its boundary, Luhmann employs the idea of interpenetration.[35] Rather than viewing the forces that act on the system as part of a generalised and, in terms of the theory, unspecified surrounding space, he regards them as behaviours by other systems.

> We speak of 'penetration', if a system makes its own complexity . . . available for constructing another system. Accordingly, interpenetration exists when this occurs reciprocally, that is, when both systems enable each other by introducing their already-constituted complexity into each other.[36]

For example, Luhmann regards both society and each individual within each society as autopoietic systems; the concept of interpenetration, therefore, serves as his solution to the micro–macro problem, that is, the problem of providing a sociological explanation for the relationship between the individual and the society.[37] More generally, the concept enables Luhmann to account for the way in which external forces act upon a system while providing a systems theory explanation for these forces. By doing so, he is able to eliminate the implication of inevitability that seems to accompany the depiction of external forces as part of the system's environment. Whether two systems interpenetrate, and to what extent this occurs,

[34] See Bertalanffy, *General Systems Theory* (n 30) 41–44, 160–63; D Meadows, *Thinking in Systems: A Primer* (White River Junction, Chelsea Green Publishing, 2008); G Richardson, *Feedback Thought in Social Science and Systems Theory* (Philadelphia, University of Philadelphia Press, 1999).

[35] Luhmann, *Law as a Social System* (n 27) 210–54.

[36] ibid 213.

[37] See J Alexander and others, *The Micro-Macro Link* (Berkeley, University of California Press, 1987); R Collins, 'On the Micro-Foundations of Macro-Sociology' (1981) 86 *American Journal of Sociology* 984; K Knorr-Cetina and A Cicourel (eds), *Advances in Social Theory and Methodology: Toward an Integration of Micro- and Macro- Sociology* (Boston, Routledge & Kegan Paul, 1981).

depends on the particular features of each system as well as their relationship with each other. If the systems are complex, moreover, their internal processes will not necessarily be fully co-ordinated, which will lead to additional variations of the interpenetration process.

If we regard law as an autopoietic system, we can see that the empiricism of traditional legal scholarship is limited. When traditional scholars argue that particular cases were wrongly decided, they phrase their arguments in terms of the legal system's internal norms for judicial decision making, such as precedent, dictum and distinguishing, or in reference to specific concepts such as agreement, negligence and foreseeability.[38] Social policy is often taken into consideration, but it is translated into legal terms, such as the law's need to maintain consistency or address new issues presented by the cases. The same is true of social morality. Both natural law theorists and positivists acknowledge morality's importance. Natural law theorists deploy it to determine what qualifies as law and why some enactments that meet the formal criteria for law should nonetheless be excluded from its ambit. Positivists reject this use of morality, but agree that morality can be invoked to determine whether something that is undoubtedly a law is desirable or undesirable. Thus, law and morality are treated as interpenetrating systems, with moral precepts appearing in the legal system for the purpose of distinguishing law from non-law, or good law from bad law. This may seem obvious; why would a legal scholar discuss moral issues unless they related to the legal system? But it indicates that the autopoietic character of a functioning system is often maintained by constructing concepts of scope and relevance. The general rules for scholarly excellence, reinforced by the institutional rules for tenure, promotion and academic prizes, can thus be regarded as mechanisms for validating these concepts of relevance that police the boundaries of a closed, albeit complex and interpenetrated, legal system.

Professor Macaulay's empiricism, and the empiricism of the scholarly movement that he played an important role in initiating, was distinctly different. The behaviours that he explored in his Wisconsin business study were outside the legal system. That was the basic point of the study. Although the firms he studied were engaged in practices that the legal system was attempting, and indeed claiming to regulate, they were not being regulated by the legal system. They were certainly affected by that system, but it was the social system that was regulating them. This included both general social norms and the kinds of community-specific norms that social systems almost invariably generate as part of their own complexity and self-reproduction process. In autopoietic terms, the legal

[38] See G Fletcher, 'Two Modes of Legal Thought' (1981) 90 *Yale Law Journal* 970; Rubin, 'The Practice and Discourse of Legal Scholarship' (n 25) 1835; P Schlag, 'Normative and Nowhere to Go' (1990) 43 *Stanford Law Review* 167; M Tushnet, 'Legal Scholarship: Its Causes and Cure' (1981) 90 *Yale Law Journal* 1205.

system interpenetrated with this system, but the supposedly legal behaviours of the business people belong to the social system, not the legal one.

It is in this sense that modern empirical legal studies are different from other forms of legal scholarship. It answers the standard legal question about whether people obey the law in sociological or non-legal terms. Rather than being content with the only answer that the internal structure of the legal system provides – sometimes they do and sometimes they don't because people are basically sinful or selfish – empirical legal studies answers this question in sociological terms. Doing so places the answer outside the legal system which, lacking any internal structures to incorporate these behaviours, defines them as non-legal. One way to say this is that the answers simply escape from the available categories of legal analysis, and thus must be formulated in different terms. An alternative approach, suggested by systems theory, is that the answers involve behaviours that belong to the social system rather than the legal system and that the legal system had no way to respond to the social system's complexity in this area.

The terrain that Macaulay and other pioneers of empirical legal studies opened up, therefore, has to be explored in sociological, or, more generally, in social science terms. The doctrinal analysis that had been established to describe the law, analyse its relationship to social morality and explain its origins, cannot account for the behaviours that reflect people's response to the law. This is true even when people follow the law, that is, even when they do not behave like the Wisconsin firms which Macaulay studied. The conceptual resources internal to the legal system, and the study of the legal system, can describe their behaviour because, by hypothesis, their behaviour follows the rules internal to the system. But it cannot explain why they are following the rules.[39] There is, of course, one legal system explanation, which is that the rules impose sanctions or various kinds of punishments for disobedience. But as soon as empirical studies are conducted, it turns out that even rules that carry the most serious sanctions, namely criminal rules, are often disobeyed. It also turns out that a lot can be said about that disobedience beyond the good man–bad man model.[40]

[39] Contrast this with a modern empirical study devoted to this precise issue, T Tyler, *Why People Obey the Law* (Princeton, Princeton University Press, 2006).

[40] For literature reviews, see R Weisberg, 'The Death Penalty Meets Social Science: Deterrence and Jury Behavior Under New Scrutiny' (2005) 1 *Annual Review of Law & Social Sciences* 151; F Zimring, *The Great American Crime Decline* (Oxford, Oxford University Press, 2008) 45–106.

II. HOW EMPIRICAL LEGAL STUDIES CAN TRANSFORM THE LEGAL SYSTEM

In order to count as legal scholarship, however, empirical legal studies, no matter how sociological its explanation of law's impact, must do more than merely explain if it is to count as legal scholarship. In addition, it must speak to legal actors, and address ways in which the legal system can be altered and improved. In conjunction with other events, empirical legal studies may well serve as a means for the transformation of the legal system. The legal system has already been transformed, during the past two centuries, by the process often described as the advent of bureaucratic government or the administrative state.[41] The promise of empirical legal studies is that it can induce changes in the legal system that support this basic transformation and thus represent the continued self-reproduction of that system's complexity. The result, which is perhaps ironic, would be that empirical legal studies would thereby counteract its prior distinctiveness and join the scholarship describing law and explaining its origins as part of the autopoietic legal system.

Prior to the administrative state, the main purpose of government was to conduct foreign policy, both defensive and aggressive, and to maintain civil order within the area of its jurisdiction. Law was seen as a process of stating norms of behaviour, norms that would be proper in themselves and would secure civil order. But the administrative state represents a qualitatively different mode of governance. For the most part, civil order is generally not a problem for modern states, in part because people identify with the state and accept its control, in part because of well-established and effective police forces. Instead, the state's tasks are to manage the economic and social system of the society. This is demanded, and is in large part necessary, because urbanisation and industrialisation have generated a much more massive and complicated society, while simultaneously undermining traditional institutions such as the village and the parish church. Thus, people need housing and electricity, education, public health services, welfare, unemployment, old age and disability benefits. Only the state can provide these services in a consistent and comprehensive manner. In other words, the modern state is responsible for managing society and this responsibility requires it to assume its

[41] The classic statement is from Max Weber; M Weber, G Roth and C Wittich (eds), *Economy and Society* (Berkeley, University of California Press, 1978) 956–1005. For more recent discussions, see, eg M Albrow, *Bureaucracy* (New York, Praeger Publishers, 1970); W Mommsen, *The Age of Bureaucracy* (Oxford, Blackwell Publishers, 1974). My own contribution is E Rubin, *Beyond Camelot: Rethinking Politics and Law for the Modern State* (Princeton, Princeton University Press, 2005).

administrative form.[42] To put the matter in its simplest terms, people in traditional society can get their water from a well; people in a modern city will all die in a few days if the public water supply fails.

Law serves as an instrument of this managerial mode of governance; it is a mechanism by which the legislature, executive and administrative agencies carry out many of their tasks. Its role in stating norms of conduct continues, but in much reduced form. Thus, the modern transformation of law is that it shifts its emphasis from stating the proper norm to achieving the politically desired result. As a result, society becomes less concerned about whether the law possesses the formal qualities we associate with a coherent set of norms. Instead, the concern is that it operates effectively in the crucial task of governmental management, of providing the control, services and benefits that people need to survive and flourish in an urbanised, industrial society.[43]

The question that defines empirical legal studies becomes crucially important in this context. If law is primarily an instrument of management, rather than a statement of norms, then what we want to know is whether it is achieving its desired results. Do people obey the law? Under what circumstances, and to what extent do they do so? When do they ignore or consciously disobey it, and why do they do so? And are the policy objectives of law compromised by disobedience? These are all matters that we need to determine in order to use law effectively in its modern instrumental role. And, as discussed above, they are precisely the questions that empirical legal studies attempt to answer. Professor Macaulay discovered that contract law has relatively little effect on the business practices of Wisconsin firms, that the general concept of a contract shapes their transactions with each other but that particular provisions are largely ignored. Other empirical legal scholarship has investigated whether criminal law deters people from committing crimes, whether people actually avail themselves of public benefits, whether firms comply with environmental laws or civil rights laws or occupational health and safety laws, and so forth.[44]

Given that these are crucial questions for the kinds of laws that are being enacted in the modern state and, more generally, for the way that the modern states uses law, the conclusion that empirical legal studies lies outside the autopoietic legal system is somewhat disconcerting. It means that there is no established discourse, and no institutional structure, for determining whether modern laws are in fact achieving the effects they

[42] See A Giddens, *The Consequences of Modernity* (Stanford, Stanford University Press, 1990).

[43] Habermas, *Theory of Communicative Action* (n 28) 243–72.

[44] One aspect of this shift in focus is the development of implementation studies. See, eg I Ayres and J Braithwaite, *Responsive Regulation: Transcending the Deregulation Debate* (Oxford, Oxford University Press, 1992); E Bardach, *The Implementation Game: What Happens After a Bill Becomes a Law* (Cambridge, MA, MIT Press, 1977).

are intended to achieve, and that generally constitute the rationale for their enactment. But this is in fact the situation. Consider first the legislature, the most important source of law in the administrative state. The legislative process, at both the federal and state level, generally begins when a member of the legislature introduces a draft of the bill. That bill is then referred to a committee. If it is an important matter, the committee will hold hearings, which typically consist of lobbyists or other interested parties verbally explaining why the bill is good or bad, and then being examined and cross-examined by the committee members. The committee members then revise, or mark up the bill, on the basis of the testimony or their own political predilections, and send it to the floor of the chamber, where it may be further debated and revised.[45] Empirical data may seep into this process at various points. The author of the bill may use it to design particular provisions in the draft, one of the witnesses may introduce it, either verbally or by submission of a document, a legislative staff member may look up some previously published study, or a member of the legislature may invoke it during the floor debate. At no point in the process, however, is empirical data about the possible effects of the bills systematically incorporated. At no point is such data regarded as part of the legal system, that is, a required element of the procedure by which the legal system reproduces itself through the creation of new legislation.

We can contrast this absence of empirical data with the goal of achieving internal consistency. The decision to assign a bill to a particular committee is generally based on the committee's jurisdiction as defined by the existing codification. Staff members on the committee are specifically assigned to determine whether the bill will conflict with or overturn some other legislation, and clauses specifically addressing this issue are a standard feature of any bill where they are relevant. A well-established discourse, with agreed-upon terms, is available to the legislators in discussing these clauses. Most bills are also reviewed by legislative counsel, a body of non-partisan specialists whose role is to determine possible conflicts between new bills and existing legislation. If the bill is enacted into law, it is generally referred back to legislative counsel for codification, that is, incorporation into the existing code, at which point any remaining uncertainties about the law's effect on other laws can be clarified, or at least identified. This process can be regarded as part of the legal system's complexity, that is, the way it reproduces itself through functions that are interconnected with certain other functions, although not with every other aspect of the system. No such statement can be made about the incorporation of empirical data, however.

[45] See generally A Black, *From Inspiration to Legislation: How an Idea Becomes a Bill* (Upper Saddle River, NJ, Prentice Hall, 2006); C Deering and S Smith, *Committees in Congress* (Washington DC, CQ Press, 1997).

Now consider judicial decision-making. In some cases, the judge sees her role, and observers see her role, as applying an existing law, whose meaning is clear, to a particular individual or entity. This depends on factual or empirical data in the general sense, but that data is not gathered by empirical or social science methods. Rather it is introduced by the advocates and assessed according to the rules of evidence, that is, the law's self-defined process for incorporating factual information into its autopoietic system. This process is well established and generally agreed upon, and the features of courts, as institutions, are designed to implement it. There are many instances, however, where the judge must make new law in order to decide the case. If this falls within the ambit of the common law, there is once again an established procedure; after the factual material has been gathered and incorporated, the judge will look to other judicial decisions and use well-established rules of analogising and distinguishing to generate the new rule for the case.[46] Again, this process fits comfortably within the autopoietic structure of the system.

But suppose the judge feels that she must articulate a new legal rule that goes beyond the limits of analogy to prior cases. Although social scientists who study law recognise this as a frequent occurrence, many legal scholars, perhaps because they feel compelled to keep judicial decisions within the autopoietic limits of the legal system, have denied that it occurs. Ronald Dworkin, for example, has gone to great and implausible lengths, to attempt to make this argument.[47] Whether judicial rule-making truly creates a democratic legitimacy problem is a much-debated question; for present purposes, the relevant point is that judges unquestionably make new rules in certain circumstances but have no established way to obtain or deploy the factual data that would be relevant to wise rule-making, as they do for obtaining and incorporating the factual data relevant to the process of applying established law to particular persons. The relevant data is empirical in the empirical legal studies sense; it consists of information about the effect that the judge's rule will have on those to whom it applies. Because this data lies outside the legal system, no judicial staff members in the judiciary are assigned to gather it, no process within the judiciary is established to evaluate it, and few sitting judges are trained to employ it. Mansfield's commercial jury might have evolved into such an institution, but failed to do so.[48] Sometimes a particularly sophisticated advocate will

[46] For descriptions of the common law method that judges use to interpret cases and deal with new situations, see M Eisenberg, *The Nature of the Common Law* (Cambridge, Harvard University Press, 1988); C Sunstein, *Legal Reasoning and Political Conflict* (New York, Oxford University Press, 1996).

[47] R Dworkin, 'Hard Cases' in *Taking Rights Seriously* (Cambridge, Harvard University Press, 1978); R Dworkin, *Law's Empire* (Cambridge, Harvard University Press, 1986).

[48] See C Fifoot, *Lord Mansfield* (Oxford, Oxford University Press, 1936) 104–15; D Lieberman, *The Province of Legislation Determined* (Cambridge, Cambridge University Press, 1989) 106–20; E Rubin, 'Learning from Lord Mansfield: Toward a Transferability Law for Modern Commercial Practice' (1995) 31 *Idaho Law Review* 775.

introduce social science data into evidence, as Louis Brandeis famously did in *Mueller v Oregon*,[49] and sometimes the judge will root around and find something on his or her own. The only standard that exists within our autopoietic legal system for assessing such judicial initiatives is the obviously inadequate concept of judicial notice. As Peggy Davis has observed, the result of this lacuna is that judges rely, in a casual or cavalier manner, on information that comes to their attention because it has attracted general attention or because of their own idiosyncratic interests.[50]

Even expert bodies that are established to modernise the legal system remain constrained by the existing boundaries of the autopoietic legal system. One of the issues that Professor Macaulay discusses in his Wisconsin contracting study involves the so-called battle of the forms. In a typical case, the buyer sends an order to the seller on its standard purchasing form, which includes a litany of standardised terms favourable to the buyer.[51] The seller responds by sending its standard acceptance form, with a litany of different standardised terms that are, of course, favourable to the seller. Common law had established the mirror image rule, which held that there was no contract until the parties agreed to the same terms. This was, in effect, the enactment of a norm, contract being viewed as a form of agreement. It could have the unfortunate effect of putting the seller at a disadvantage, since it was then shipping goods to the buyer as a volunteer, without the buyer having undertaken any legal obligation to pay. The drafter of *Uniform Commercial Code* (UCC) Article 2, Karl Llewellyn, recognised that modern contracting often involves a battle of forms. His solution was Section 2-207, which provides that if the forms do not match, a contract is still created, and the seller's additional terms become part of the contract unless they 'materially' alter the contract or the buyer objects. This is better, but it may still hurt the buyer, who may now be bound by the seller's terms.

Even though the UCC is sponsored by the American Law Institute (ALI) and the National Conference of Commissioners on Uniform State Laws (NCCUSL), two ongoing and fairly well-funded organisations with a legally sophisticated membership that could draw on further financial resources from the affected industries, it did not occur to Llewellyn to commission empirical studies of contracting practices.[52] Neither did it

[49] *Mueller v Oregon*, 208 US 412 (1908). See M Urofsky, *Louis D Brandeis, A Life* (New York, Pantheon Books, 2009) 212–27; M Doro, 'The Brandeis Brief' (1958) 11 *Vanderbilt Law Review* 783.

[50] P Davis, '"There Is a Book Out . . .": An Analysis of Judicial Absorption of Legislative Facts' (1987) 100 *Harvard Law Review* 1539.

[51] The roles could be reversed, with the buyer sending out the first form.

[52] This is particularly striking since Llewellyn was a founder of the law and society approach, having co-authored a book about Native American customary law with an anthropologist. K Llewellyn and EA Hoebel, *The Cheyenne Way: Conflict and Case Law in Primitive Jurisprudence* (Norman, University of Oklahoma Press, 1941).

occur to any of the drafters of the other articles, which covered bank collection practices, bank relations with consumers, and secured transactions. Had it occurred to Llewellyn, he might have discovered what Professor Macaulay discovered – that the two conflicting forms are simply filed away after the basic deal terms have been checked by a low-level employee. Macaulay's survey of one firm found that between 60 per cent and 75 per cent of their transactions over a five-year period were covered by agreements that were unenforceable under the common law mirror image law.[53] These would have been enforceable under the UCC, but to the possible disadvantage of one or the other party, since neither had paid any attention to the agreement. The ALI and NCCUSL, though conceived as modernising law reform organisations, simply failed to see that obtaining empirical data about a legal provision's effect on people should be a basic part of the process by which such a provision is designed.

The reason why both legislative and judicial rulemaking, and even conscious law reform by independent organisations, has failed to incorporate relevant empirical information into their decision-making processes is that these processes developed in the pre-administrative era and have not been re-thought and reformed in the modern one. They are still designed to declare norms, that is, proper rules of behaviour. The criteria for evaluating them still relate to values such as clarity, internal consistency and propriety that are relevant to norm formation. The legislature knows how to ensure that its enacted statutes do not inadvertently conflict with other laws; the judiciary knows how to ensure that its decisions are consistent with prior ones. The legislature knows how to determine that it is amending or replacing an earlier statute; judges know how to overrule earlier cases and what arguments they need to make in doing so. Both institutions know how to promulgate their decisions so that they can be recognised and incorporated in the legal system's complexity. But neither institution has an established discourse or established mechanisms, for obtaining the information needed to manage the economic and social systems of an advanced industrial society, and thus achieving the principle value or goal of the modern administrative state.

That information and those values are the ones to which empirical legal scholarship is addressed. This is the reason, of course, why this scholarship is qualitatively different from prior forms of scholarship, and why it lies outside the legal system. The question that arises is whether this scholarship can change the legal system, whether it can induce that system to reproduce itself in the direction of incorporating the empirical information and modes of analysis that it needs in order to carry out its lawmaking tasks in a modern administrative state. This may seem like a tall order, but the structural conditions for achieving it seem to be in place.

[53] Macaulay, 'Non-Contractual Relations' (n 1) 62.

The faculty members who conduct this research are often members of the same institutions that carry out traditional legal research, and are sometimes even the same individuals. They are thus the teachers of the future legislators, judges and advocates who populate the legal system. The academic journals where this work is published are increasingly the same journals that publish legal research that falls within the present discourse of the legal system. This interpenetration of systems satisfies a precondition for one system's transformation, particularly when that system is obviously and deleteriously out of date.

It is probably too much to expect that empirical legal scholarship will generate the institutional structures within the legislature and judiciary that are needed to collect and make use of empirical data on the effect of their enactments or decisions. It seems possible, however, that this scholarship will create a discourse in the legal system that will make the absence of such data appear undesirable, and ultimately unacceptable. What may ultimately be persuasive is not the fact that scholars who study the effects of legal rules often find that these effects are different from those that the sponsors or authors of those rules intended. Such findings may well elicit a defensive hostility and besides, people are often adept at making excuses for themselves. Rather, the most persuasive thing that scholars can do is simply to reveal the sort of information that it is possible to know about the effects of legal rules. This is the sort of information, it says to legal decision-makers, that you ought to know about the possible effects of the rule you are considering before you deploy the enormous power of the modern state to establish and enforce that rule. At some point, the rule-makers may realise that they ought to know this information, that they ought to have some mechanism for taking advantage of the social science experience that is available in this society. Empirical legal scholarship may thus be most persuasive by serving as a demonstration, rather than a condemnation.

Not surprisingly, the institution that is in the best position to respond to, and ultimately institutionalise, this truly empirical perspective is the administrative agency, a product of the administrative state and the primary implementer of administrative law. Agencies often have sufficient social science expertise on staff to carry out empirical research, and their budgets give them access to additional expertise. The process by which they design and promulgate their regulations is conceived as being neither political nor judicial, and is subject to very few procedural constraints, so it should certainly permit the use of that research. But in actual fact, the use of empirical data by administrative agencies can be described as spotty. There is no clearly defined set of standards about the level of empirical knowledge that is expected before major regulations are adopted; very often, the agency seems to be balancing interest groups against each other, rather than engaging in a systematic effort to evaluate its proposals in empirical terms. A number of commentators have noted the triumph of the interest group model over the expertise model.[54] This process can certainly be attributed to the waning of the New Deal and the loss of its accompanying enthusiasm. But that only reflects the more basic problem that the need for empirical data has not become incorporated into the discourse of the legal system in a way that renders it too secure for passing political attitudes to dislodge.

Efforts to reform the regulatory process have been disappointing. The 1980s saw two major efforts at the federal level, negotiated rule-making and cost-benefit analysis. Negotiated rule-making, developed as an experiment by several agencies and ultimately codified by Congress, indicated the triumph of the interest group model.[55] While it added one defined instrumentality to the crucial period before the agency's first draft of a regulation was publicised for comment, this instrumentality was a co-ordinated meeting of interest group representatives. One could thus regard it as a reassertion of the legal system's pre-modern boundary, its exclusion of empirical data from the concept of legal relevance in favour of normative debate.[56]

The other effort was to subject all major regulations to cost-benefit review.[57] This incorporates economics, the one social science that the legal system has partially absorbed, into the procedures and institutional structure of the regulatory process. It was conceived, however, as a deregulatory device, that is, as a means of cutting back on the extent of regulation, and only secondarily as a means of improving the quality of regulation and aiding it in achieving its intended effects. It has survived through four subsequent administrations because it is now seen as a means by which the President can control the sprawling administrative apparatus[58] – not an unworthy goal, but one that is more closely related to a concep-

[54] T Lowi, *The End of LIberalisim: The Second Republic of the United States*, 2nd edn (New York, WW Norton & Co, 1979); T Sargentich, 'The Reform of American Administrative Law: The Contemporary Debate' (1984) 1984 *Wisconsin Law Review* 385; R Stewart, 'The Reformation of American Administrative Law' (1975) 88 *Harvard Law Review* 1667.

[55] Negotiated Rulemaking Act of 1990, 5 USC § 563(b).

[56] See C Coglianese, 'Assessing Consensus: The Promise and Performance of Negotiated Rulemaking' (1997) 46 *Duke Law Journal* 1255; J Rossi, 'Participation Run Amok: The Costs of Mass Participation for Deliberative Agency Decisionmaking' (1997) 92 *Northwestern University Law Review* 173. For a more favourable view, see J Freeman and L Langbein, 'Regulatory Negotiation and the Legitimacy Benefit' (2000) 9 *New York University Environmental Law Journal* 60.

[57] Instituted by executive order under Ronald Reagan, see Executive Order 12, 291 (1981), and renewed with revisions by each subsequent President. See Executive Order 12,866 (W Clinton, 1993), 3 CFR Sec 63, reprinted in 5 USC Sec 601, revised by Executive Order 13,563 (B Obama, 2011).

[58] See N Bagley and R Revesz, 'Centralized Oversight of the Regulatory State' (2006) 106 *Columbia Law Review* 1260; S Croley, 'White House Review of Agency Rulemaking: An Empirical Investigation' (2003) 70 *University of Chicago Law Review* 821; E Kagan, 'Presidential Administration' (2001) 114 *Harvard Law Review* 2245.

tion of government as clashing interests, rather than as a means of managing a complex society. For this reason, federal agencies tend to regard the Office of Management and Budget (OMB), the institution that reviews their cost–benefit analyses, as an adversary rather than a source of valued expertise.[59] In any event, cost–benefit analysis is a distinctly limited mechanism, and one whose artificial precision renders it counter-productive in the opinion of many observers.[60]

In short, the promise of empirical legal scholarship is to alter the boundaries of the autopoietic legal system. On its own, scholarship is unlikely to induce the legal system to create new institutions. But it can succeed in changing the discourse, the mode of thought that is as important as institutions in establishing the self-reproducing process of an autopoietic system. If that occurs, the institutional changes will follow, as will further changes in discourse and conceptualisation. One such change, ironically, will be to end the distinctiveness of empirical legal studies. If the discourse should change, this field could no longer be defined by its position outside the boundary of the legal system. It would become a component of that system, and thus allied to current descriptive scholarship about the content and origin of legal actions. That loss of distinctiveness, of course, will be an indication of its success, not failure. By changing the discourse of the legal system so that it is included within its boundaries, the field that Professor Macaulay did so much to create will bring the legal system into conformity with the administrative state in which it is now ineluctably embedded.

III. HOW THE CURRENT METHODOLOGY OF EMPIRICAL LEGAL STUDIES CAN BE IMPROVED

The argument thus far is that the essence of empirical legal studies is not a technique, such as quantitatively analysed surveys, nor even a methodology, like social science, but rather a concept that the effect of legal rules merits systematic exploration. The potentially transformative capacity of empirical legal studies stems from this conceptual orientation. Neither a technique nor a methodology could transform an autopoietic system because the system would either ignore their findings or translate those findings into its own internal discourse, as the legal system transforms facts into evidence. Only a new conceptual orientation, a new way of looking at the system's subject matter, could produce such an effect. And only the interpenetration of the legal system with another complex system, in this

[59] See L Bressman and M Vandenberg, 'Inside the Administrative State: A Critical Look at the Process of Presidential Control' (2006) 105 *Michigan Law Review* 47.

[60] See, eg F Ackerman and L Heinzerling, 'Pricing the Priceless: Cost-Benefit Analysis of Environmental Protection' (2002) 150 *University of Pennsylvania Law Review* 1553.

case the social system and the theory by which we understand that system, could produce a new conceptual orientation. If empirical legal studies is to change the discourse of the legal system by being absorbed into its autopoietic structure, then it will be through a process of that sort.

Although the definition of empirical legal studies and its potential effect on the legal system is conceptual, it is worth considering how the techniques and methodologies of empirical legal studies will be altered if they transform the legal system by becoming part of it. Another way of asking essentially the same question is whether there are currently technical or methodological impediments that keep empirical legal studies at the interpenetration level with respect to legal scholarship, rather than allowing the field to be fully absorbed into the legal system. The question has normative force because of the effects of discourse on legal institutions. The extent to which law schools hire faculty members trained in social science, or with joint degrees, may not seem like an earth-shaking issue. But, as discussed above, it is emblematic of legal decision makers' ability to assess the real-world effects of their actions, and to develop institutions that make those effects an integral part of the decision-making process. Given the scope and responsibilities of the modern administrative state, that ability is crucial to the effectiveness of modern government.

The question of methodology has already been addressed. Empirical legal studies, as defined above, uses the approach to knowledge that we identify as social science. This is, of course, a basic feature of modernity, and represents modern society's essential mechanism of self-understanding. It is hardly accidental that the dawn and development of social science parallels the advent of the administrative state, as well as the advance of industrialisation. An administrative state is characteristically devoted to the conscious management of its society, just as industrialisation is characterised by the conscious management of production processes. The failure to deploy this methodology to assess the effects of state policy thus represents a serious lacuna in our approach to governance, an atavism resulting from the autopoietic isolation of the legal system. Empirical legal studies has the potential to transform law precisely because it can end this isolation by merging law and social science.

A remaining question, however, involves the techniques that are characteristic of social science as currently practiced, and particularly as it is practiced by empirical legal scholars. As noted at the outset, the seminal study by Professor Macaulay consisted of in-depth interviews with a limited number of individuals and the examination of some business records whose relevance was suggested by the interviews. At present, empirical legal studies relies heavily on survey data that is then interpreted by statistical analysis. For many observers this is the defining feature of empirical legal studies. The social science trained faculty members who are currently being hired by law schools, whether they also have a law degree or not, are often fairly heavily 'teched up'. That is, they are well-trained in statistics and survey techniques, and use these techniques as an essential element in their research.

This statistical turn in empirical legal studies appears to create a problem for the absorption of empirical legal studies into the legal system. While surveys are a familiar and relatively accessible feature of modern discourse,[61] statistical analysis tends to be opaque to people without training in this technique, a category that includes most law professors, judges, legislators and administrators. This is probably one of the reasons that the empirical research conducted during the legal realist period proved to be a false start.[62] The problem is not insoluble, however; rudimentary training in statistical analysis, sufficient to make someone a consumer if not a producer of contemporary social science research, could be readily included in the law school curriculum. Moreover, in a system that meets Luhmann's definition of complexity, not everyone needs to be able to interpret statistics, as long as some people who can do so are connected to the system as a whole. It thus seems clear that training in statistical analysis should be much more prevalent in law school and much more important for legal decision-makers. Before concluding that this additional training will remove the major impediment to transforming law through empirical legal studies, or deciding the extent of the resources that should be invested in the effort, it is worthy asking whether the statistical turn has been entirely beneficial. Does it represent a more systematic and sophisticated phase of empirical legal studies that has outgrown the field's simpler, less sophisticated origins, or does the field still have something to learn from Professor Macaulay?

To explore this question, we might consider a recent social science study that received widespread attention and seems to have major implications for social policy – Robert Putnam's *Bowling Alone*.[63] Putnam's basic argument is that social capital in the US has declined disastrously during the past half-century or so, but he does not define the term 'social capital' in a rigorous way. He describes it at one point as a combination of reciprocity and trust among groups of people, and at another point as a form of social networking consisting of exclusive relationships which he calls bonding, and inclusive relationships which he calls bridging.[64] Acknowledging that it is difficult to measure something of this sort, and still more difficult to trace its increase or decrease over time, he assures the reader that he has 'sought as diverse a range of evidence as possible'.[65] It consists of

[61] See Igo, *The Averaged American* (n 5).

[62] See p 78 above.

[63] R Putnam, *Bowling Alone: The Collapse and Revival of American Community* (New York, Simon & Schuster, 2000).

[64] ibid 19–25.

[65] ibid 26.

membership data from a large number of organisations, plus voluminous surveys of social attitudes conducted by professional survey organisations.[66]

Putnam concedes that these surveys are imperfect measurements of social trends due to problems of comparability, continuity, comprehensiveness and timeliness. To counteract these problems, he tells us, '[n]early every major generalisation here rests on more than more than one body of independent evidence'.[67] And he adds: '*Virtually every generalisation in this book has been subjected to detailed statistical analysis . . . controlling simultaneously for age (or year of birth), gender, education, income, race, marital status, parental status, job status (working full-time, part-time, or not at all), and size of community of residence.*'[68] Based on all this data, Putnam not only concludes that social capital has declined in the US, but also that this decline has brought a variety of misfortunes in its wake. Distinguishing among the social capital levels of the 50 states, he concludes that the states with lower social capital have lower levels of child welfare, worse schools, more crime, less friendly people, worse adult health, higher levels of tax evasion and less income equality. This conclusion has enormous consequences for social policy; if legal decision-makers were willing to use social science data, they might decide that improvements in all these important social indicators could be achieved by enacting laws designed to increase social capital.

Unfortunately, for all his italicised efforts to control for social variables, Putnam has overlooked the need to control for his own attitudes. As Richard Abel observed in his discussion of scholarship about law, 'an author's values influence his inquiry at many points, including his decisions about what is worth studying, how to study it – the definition of the problem, the kind of explanation or understanding to seek, the concepts to use, the facts to examine for potential explanations – and what policy recommendations to make'.[69] This is not in itself a criticism, as Abel notes, since there is probably no such thing as value-free observation, but it becomes a criticism if the author is unaware of those values and asserts or implies that his conclusions are value-neutral. That is what Putnam does. Social capital, as he uses the term, is not quite what he declares it to be at the beginning of the book, but rather a reflection of a set of old-fashioned, idiosyncratic preferences that he has used to select his data. One immediate indication of this is his map that colours each of the 50 states according to a 'social capital index' that he has constructed on the basis of 14 meas-

[66] ibid 415–24. These pages constitute a detailed methodological appendix, in small print. In addition, there is a nine-page list of the sources for all the charts that appear in the book, ibid 426–35, plus nearly 60 pages of notes in even smaller print, ibid 445–504.

[67] ibid 26.

[68] ibid 419 (italics in original).

[69] Abel, 'Law Books' (n 22) 177.

ured factors such as serving on the committee of a local organisation, attending public meetings 'on town or school affairs', working on community projects and believing that most people can be trusted.[70] According to his map, all the lowest social capital states are in the South, with the exceptions of Nevada and West Virginia. Putnam acknowledges that this might be a residual effect of slavery and Jim Crow legislation.[71] What he fails to note is that his high social capital states – the ones where life is best according to his social indicators – are almost exclusively small, rural states with overwhelmingly white, non-Hispanic populations. His top eight social capital states, North Dakota, South Dakota, Vermont, Minnesota, Montana, Nebraska, Iowa and New Hampshire, have the following national rankings for proportion of non-Hispanic whites: 2, 3, 5, 6, 7, 10, 11 and 14.[72] All except Minnesota are predominantly rural. The only large metropolitan area in all of his top eight states is Minneapolis, the sixteenth largest in the nation; the next largest metropolitan area is Omaha, which ranks fifty-ninth.[73]

Putnam seems unaware that his criteria for social capital may in fact embed a preference for small town, predominantly white communities. People who live in small towns are likely to attend town or school meetings, in part because they are politically identified with their locality, in part because small town meetings are readily accessible, and in part because attending such a meeting may be the most exciting thing going on in North Dakota. They may be particularly inclined to do so when there is little racial diversity and they can feel comfortable going to the meetings. People in large cities may be more likely to attend spectator sports, visit a museum, stroll on the street, shop in a mall, work out at the gym or become involved in national organisations. Putnam does take account of organisational membership in a separate section, which offers charts showing changes in membership over the course of the twentieth century for some 40 organisations. Most of them show declines, which he regards as a major indication of decreasing social capital, but his selection of organisations is equally small-town oriented, and concomitantly old-fashioned. It includes, in addition to the American Bowling Congress, a variety of antiquated organisations that flourished in small-town America such as the Grange, Elks, Kiwanis, Lions, Odd Fellows, Masons, and Woman's Christian Temperance Union.[74] On the first page of the book, he bemoans the demise of organisations such as the Charity League of Dallas, where people met 'every Friday morning for fifty-seven years to sew, knit

[70] Putnam, *Bowling Alone* (n 63) 291, 293.
[71] ibid 294.
[72] Social Science Data Analysis Network, 'Percent Non-Hispanic White, 2000' (*CensusScope*, 2000) www.censusscope.org/us/rank_race_nonhispaniclatino_white.html. As it happens, the available census data is from the same year as the publication of Putnam's book.
[73] US Census Bureau, *Metropolitan Statistical Areas of the United States* (2009).
[74] Putnam, *Bowling Alone* (n 63) 440–44.

and visit' before it closed its doors in 1999.[75] He acknowledges the meteoric membership increases in environmental organisations and other social movements, but fails to include them in his charts.

What seems to have happened is that Putnam's faith in his 'detailed statistical analysis' has given him licence to let his personal attitudes run unchecked in the selection and evaluation of his data. Attendance at sports events has risen dramatically, but he characterises this as watching rather than doing, and so does not count as an experience of social solidarity.[76] The same is true for museum attendance, which he apparently regards as equally passive.[77] Shopping does not count because of its changed character: 'Rather than at the grocery store or the five-and-dime on Main Street, where the faces were familiar, today's suburbanites shop in large, impersonal malls.'[78] Once one makes such judgments, of course, rural areas that have no spectator sports, no museums and no suburban malls are quite likely to come up higher on the social capital index than New York, Illinois or California. Putnam does not count membership of national organisations as evidence of social capital because such membership is often passive, a point that he argues at considerable length.[79] But people in cities tend to be more connected with national and world events. Similarly, Putnam correlates his high social capital states with virtues such as better health, less crime and more friendly people. But he does not try to measure people's knowledge of national or world events, their cultural sophistication, their creativity, or their range of interests and he misreads his chart regarding tolerance of diversity.

Putnam is not thoughtless – he anticipates and tries to respond to some of these fairly obvious questions – nor is he prejudiced. What he seems to be, to use a technical term, is a fuddy-duddy. He has taken his personal preference for small towns, community meetings, conventional social organisations and the five and dime store and used it to select and interpret all the survey data he so assiduously canvassed. What he failed to do is what Professor Macaulay did, which is talk to people. Had he carried out some in-depth interviews, he might have discovered that many modern people, and particularly younger people (that is, below the age of 75 or so) would regard attendance at the local charity club on Friday morning to sew, knit and visit as the equivalent of hell, rather than as a sustaining experience of social solidarity. This might have alerted him to the peculiarity of his own attitudes, and suggested different ways of interpreting the decline of early twentieth century fraternal organisations.

[75] ibid 15.
[76] ibid 113–14.
[77] ibid 114.
[78] ibid 211.
[79] ibid 152–66.

Putnam's work suffers from the lack of what Max Weber called *verstehen*, an interpretive understanding of human beings as conscious entities.[80] Insects or asteroids can be studied as objects, by statistical methods, but because humans construct meaning for themselves through an internal or phenomenological process, purely statistical studies will generally be incomplete, and will frequently run off the rails. Such studies are valuable, but they must be balanced by, or combined with, a willingness to speak directly to people to find out how they process the world. If one does not do so, one will ask the wrong questions or ignore the right ones, and obtain answers that reproduce one's own beliefs. No level of statistical sophistication can overcome this problem because the data that is being crunched by the statistics will be incorrect or incomplete.[81] Perhaps people in Putnam's high social capital states enjoy better health, and perhaps this is causally related to their willingness to attend town meetings and believe that most people are trustworthy. But their health may also have something to do with the facts that his high capital states have very few minorities, that minorities continue to suffer from sub-standard healthcare, and that they are justifiably distrustful of the society that continues to subject them to these and other inequalities. Even more seriously, statistics will rarely guide the researchers to find correlations between variables that did not occur to them. For example, Putnam never considers the creativity of the people in the different states, the amount of music, art and literature that they produce. Without being excessively Nietzschean about this, one can note that many people find such creativity highly fulfilling,[82] and the results of such creative efforts probably enrich many people's lives rather more than would their attendance at the Elks and the Kiwanis.

In-depth interviewing has obvious defects as well. In his Wisconsin study, Macaulay concedes that the number of people he interviewed was relatively small, 68 in all, and that nearly all of them were located in a single state. The solution to this defect is obvious – interview 68 people from each state or, better still, 680 people from each state. Because in-depth interviews are considerably more time-consuming than sending out a survey form, the practicality of this solution is limited, however. With adequate funding, a team of interviewers can be established, but then problems of standardisation and comparability would arise, particularly if the interviewers are trying to understand how the subject perceives the

[80] Weber, *Economy and Society* (n 41) 8–11 ('For a science that is concerned with the subjective meaning of action, explanation requires a grasp of the complex of meaning in which an actual course of understandable action thus interpreted belongs.'). See F Ringer, *Max Weber's Methodology: The Unification of the Cultural and Social Sciences* (Cambridge, Harvard University Press, 1997) 100–10.

[81] Compare D Stone, *Policy Paradox: The Art of Political Decision Making*, rev edn (New York, WW Norton & Co, 2002) (arguing that policy analysis rests on normatively contested concepts).

[82] See E Weiner, *The Geography of Bliss* (New York, Twelve, 2008) 141–84.

world, rather than simply administer an oral survey. The point is not that interviews are better than statistically analysed surveys, but rather that each method can assist and inform the other. Surveys can certainly help confirm or invalidate less formal observations derived from in-depth interviews, but interviews can guide the collection and analysis of survey data so that it provides comprehensive insights into its subject matter, rather than being a map of the researcher's subconscious.

CONCLUSION

The development of empirical legal studies, as a distinctly separate discipline, has focused attention on an issue that is absolutely crucial to the effectiveness of modern administrative governance – the actual effect of law on human behaviour. Because modern society uses law as an instrument for managing a highly advanced economic and social system, it can no longer treat law as merely declaring norms of behaviour, nor treat disobedience as a moral lapse to be met with individualised punishment. Rather, it needs to design law so that it achieves its intended effects. Doing so demands not only a conceptual shift, but also the development of new institutions and procedures by which consideration of a proposed law's potential effects can be integrated into the process by which the law is designed. In order for empirical legal studies to serve this crucial role, it needs to be both accurate and comprehensible to law-trained public decision-makers. The increasing sophistication of social science survey techniques and statistical analysis is certainly promising. In order to achieve higher levels of accuracy and comprehensibility, however, it must combine and modify its approach with a deeper understanding of the people whose behaviour it is assessing. This requires the sort of interpretive understanding that can only result from listening carefully to people, and appreciating their perception of the world. In other words, empirical legal studies has a promising and beneficial future, but it still has a lot to learn from Stewart Macaulay.

BIBLIOGRAPHY

Abel, R, 'Law Books and Books About Law' (1973) 26 *Stanford Law Review* 175.

Ackerman, F and Heinzerling, L, 'Pricing the Priceless: Cost–Benefit Analysis of Environmental Protection' (2002) 150 *University of Pennsylvania Law Review* 1553.

Albrow, M, *Bureaucracy* (New York, Praeger Publishers, 1970).

Alexander, J and others, *The Micro-Macro Link* (Berkeley, University of California Press, 1987).

Allen, B, *Moral Minority: Our Skeptical Founding Fathers* (Chicago, Ivan R Dee, 2007).

Aquinas, T, *Summa Theologica*, Fathers of the English Dominican Province trans (New York, Benziger Bros, 1948).
Ayres, I and Braithwaite, J, *Responsive Regulation: Transcending the Deregulation Debate* (Oxford, Oxford University Press, 1992).
Bagley, N and Revesz, R, 'Centralized Oversight of the Regulatory State' (2006) 106 *Columbia Law Review* 1260.
Bardach, E, *The Implementation Game: What Happens After a Bill Becomes a Law* (Cambridge, MA, MIT Press,1977).
von Bertalanffy, L, *General Systems Theory: Foundations, Development, Applications* (New York, George Braziller, 1968).
Black, A, *From Inspiration to Legislation: How an Idea Becomes a Bill* (Upper Saddle River, NJ, Prentice Hall,2006).
Bressman, L and Vandenberg, M, 'Inside the Administrative State: A Critical Look at the Process of Presidential Control' (2006) 105 *Michigan Law Review* 47.
Buckley, W, *Sociology and Modern Systems Theory* (Englewood Cliffs, Prentice Hall, 1967).
Calabresi, G, *The Cost of Accidents: A Legal and Economic Analysis* (New Haven, Yale University Press, 1970.
Chase, W, 'The Birth of the Modern Law School' (1979) 23 *American Journal of Legal History* 329.
Coglianese, C, 'Assessing Consensus: The Promise and Performance of Negotiated Rulemaking' (1997) 46 *Duke Law Journal* 1255.
Collins, R, 'On the Micro-Foundations of Macro-Sociology' (1981) 86 *American Journal of Sociology* 984.
Croley, S, 'White House Review of Agency Rulemaking: An Empirical Investigation' (2003) 70 *University of Chicago Law Review* 821.
Davis, P, '"There Is a Book Out . . .": An Analysis of Judicial Absorption of Legislative Facts' (1987) 100 *Harvard Law Review* 1539.
Deering, C and Smith, S, *Committees in Congress* (Washington DC, CQ Press, 1997).
Doro, M, 'The Brandeis Brief' (1958) 11 *Vanderbilt Law Review* 783.
Dworkin, R, *Law's Empire* (Cambridge, Harvard University Press, 1986).
——, 'Hard Cases' in *Taking Rights Seriously* (Cambridge, Harvard University Press, 1978).
Eisenberg, M, *The Nature of the Common Law* (Cambridge, Harvard University Press, 1988).
Epstein, L, Martin, A and Schneider, M, 'On the Effective Communication of the Results of Empirical Studies, Parts I & II' (2006) 59 *Vanderbilt Law Review* 1811, (2007) 60 *Vanderbilt Law Review* 801.
Epstein, L and King, G, 'The Rules of Inference' (2002) 69 *University of Chicago Law Review* 1.
Erlanger, H and others, 'Is It Time for a New Legal Realism?' (2005) 2005 *Wisconsin Law Review* 335.
Fifoot, C, *Lord Mansfield* (Oxford, Oxford University Press, 1936).
Fletcher, G, 'Two Modes of Legal Thought' (1981) 90 *Yale Law Journal* 970.
Freeman, J and Langbein, L, 'Regulatory Negotiation and the Legitimacy Benefit' (2000) 9 *New York University Environmental Law Journal* 60.
Friedman, L, *A History of American Law*, 3rd edn (New York, Touchstone, 2005).

Fuller, L, 'The Forms and Limits of Adjudication' (1978) 92 *Harvard Law Review* 353.
Gadamer, HG, GBarden and J Cumming (trans), *Truth and Method*, 2nd edn (London, Continuum, 1988).
George, T, 'An Empirical Study of Empirical Legal Scholarship: The Top Law Schools' (2006) 81 *Indiana Law Journal* 141.
Giddens, A, *The Consequences of Modernity* (Stanford, Stanford University Press, 1990).
Grogger, J, 'An Economic Model of Recent Trends in Violence' in A Blumstein and J Wallman, *The Recent Crime Drop in America*, (Cambridge, Cambridge University Press, 2006).
Gulati, M and Nielsen, LB, 'Introduction: A New Legal Realist Perspective on Employment Discrimination' (2006) 31 *Law & Social Inquiry* 797.
Habermas, J, T McCarthy (trans), *The Theory of Communicative Action, vol 1: Reason and the Rationalization of Society*, (Boston, Beacon Press, 1984).
Hart, HLA, *The Concept of Law* (New York, Oxford University Press, 1961).
Heidegger, M, J Macquarrie and E Robinson (trans), *Being and Time* (Malden, Blackwell Publishing, 1962).
Heise, M, 'The Past, Present and Future of Empirical Legal Scholarship: Judicial Decision Making and the New Empiricism' (2002) 2002 *Illinois Law Review* 819.
Igo, S, *The Averaged American: Surveys, Citizens, and the Making of the Mass Public* (Cambridge, Harvard University Press, 2007).
Kagan, E, 'Presidential Administration' (2001) 114 *Harvard Law Review* 2245.
Kahneman, D, P. Slovic and Tversky, A, *Judgment Under Uncertainty: Heurisitics and Biases* (Cambridge, Eng., Cambridge University Press, 1982).
Kalman, L, *Legal Realism at Yale: 1927–1960* (Chapel Hill, University of North Carolina Press, 1986).
Kelsen, H, *Pure Theory of Law* (Berkeley, University of California Press, 1967).
——, *General Theory of Law and the State* (Cambridge, Harvard University Press, 1945).
Knorr-Cetina, K and Cicourel, A (eds), *Advances in Social Theory and Methodology: Toward an Integration of Micro- and Macro- Sociology* (Boston, Routledge & Kegan Paul, 1981).
Lieberman, D, *The Province of Legislation Determined* (Cambridge, Cambridge University Press, 1989).
Llewellyn, K and Hoebel, EA, *The Cheyenne Way: Conflict and Case Law in Primitive Jurisprudence* (Norman, University of Oklahoma Press, 1941).
Llewellyn, K, *The Common Law Tradition: Deciding Appeals* (Buffalo, William S Hein & Co, 1960).
Lowi, T, *The End of Liberalisim: The Second Republic of the United States*, 2nd edn (New York, WW Norton & Co, 1979).
Luhmann, N, K Ziegert (trans), *Law as a Social System* (Oxford, Oxford University Press, 2004).
Luhmann, N, J Bednarz (trans), *Social Systems* (Stanford, Stanford University Press, 1995).
Macaulay, S, 'Contracts, New Legal Realism, and Improving the Navigation of *The Yellow Submarine*' (2006) 80 *Tulane Law Review* 1161.
——, 'Lawyers and Consumer Protection Laws: An Empirical Study' (1979) 14 *Law & Society Review* 115.

——, 'Non-Contractual Relations in Business: A Preliminary Study' (1963) 28 *American Sociological Review* 55.
Madison, J, 'The Same Subject Continued With the Same View and Concluded' (Federalist No 51) in J Madison, A Hamilton and J Jay, *The Federalist Papers* (London, Penguin, 1987; first published 1788).
Meadows, D, *Thinking in Systems: A Primer* (White River Junction, Chelsea Green Publishing, 2008).
Miles, T and Sunstein, C, 'The New Legal Realism' (2008) 75 *University of Chicago Law Review* 831.
Mommsen, W, *The Age of Bureaucracy* (Oxford, Blackwell Publishers, 1974).
Moore, WU and Callahan, C, 'Law and Learning Theory: A Study of Legal Control' (1943) 53 *Yale Law Journal* 1.
Nourse, V and Shaffer, G, 'Varieties of New Legal Realism: Can a New World Order Prompt a New Legal Theory?' (2009) 95 *Cornell Law Review* 61.
Powell, W, 'Expanding the Scope of Institutional Analysis' in W Powell and P DiMaggio (eds), *The New Institutionalism in Organizational Analysis* (Chicago, University of Chicago Press, 1991).
Putnam, R, *Bowling Alone: The Collapse and Revival of American Community* (New York, Simon & Schuster, 2000).
Resignato, A, 'Violent Crime: A Function of Drug Use or Drug Enforcement' (2000) 32 *Applied Economics* 681.
Richardson, G, *Feedback Thought in Social Science and Systems Theory* (Philadelphia, University of Philadelphia Press, 1999).
Ringer, F, *Max Weber's Methodology: The Unification of the Cultural and Social Sciences* (Cambridge, Harvard University Press, 1997).
Ross, HL, *Settled Out of Court: The Social Process of Insurance Claims Adjustment*, rev 2nd edn (New York, Aldine Publishing, 1980).
Rossi, J, 'Participation Run Amok: The Costs of Mass Participation for Deliberative Agency Decisionmaking' (1997) 92 *Northwestern University Law Review* 173.
Rubin, E, *Beyond Camelot: Rethinking Politics and Law for the Modern State* (Princeton, Princeton University Press, 2005).
——, 'Learning from Lord Mansfield: Toward a Transferability Law for Modern Commercial Practice' (1995) 31 *Idaho Law Review* 775.
——, 'What Does Prescriptive Legal Scholarship Say and Who Is Listening to It: A Response to Professor Dan-Cohen' (1992) 63 *University of Colorado Law Review* 731.
——, 'The Practice and Discourse of Legal Scholarship' (1988) 86 *Michigan Law Review* 1835.
Saint Augustine, Marcus Dods (trans), *The City of God* (New York, Modern Library, 1993).
Sargentich, T, 'The Reform of American Administrative Law: The Contemporary Debate' (1984) 1984 *Wisconsin Law Review* 385.
Schlag, P, 'Normative and Nowhere to Go' (1990) 43 *Stanford Law Review* 167.
Schlegel, J, *American Legal Realism and Empirical Social Science* (Chapel Hill, University of North Carolina Press, 1995).
Scott, WR, *Organizations: Rational, Natural, and Open Systems*, 5th edn (Englewood Cliffs, Prentice Hall, 2002).

Social Science Data Analysis Network, 'Percent Non-Hispanic White, 2000' (*CensusScope*, 2000).
Stewart, R, 'The Reformation of American Administrative Law' (1975) 88 *Harvard Law Review* 1667.
Stone, D, *Policy Paradox: The Art of Political Decision Making*, rev edn (New York, WW Norton & Co, 2002).
Suchman, M and Mertz, E, 'Toward a New Legal Empiricism: Empirical Legal Studies and New Legal Realism' (2010) 6 *Annual Review of Law and Social Science* 555.
Sunstein, C, *Legal Reasoning and Political Conflict* (New York, Oxford University Press, 1996).
'Symposium, New Legal Realism' (2006) 31 *Law & Social Inquiry* 797.
Teubner, G, 'How Law Thinks' (1989) 23 *Law & Society Review* 727.
——, 'Evolution of Autopoietic Law' in G Teubner (ed), *Autopoietic Law: A New Approach to Law and Society* (Berlin, Walter de Gruyter, 1988).
Trubek, D and Esser, J, 'Critical Empiricism in American Legal Studies: Paradox, Program or Pandora's Box' (1989) 14 *Law & Social Inquiry* 1.
Trubek, D, 'Where the Action Is: Critical Legal Studies and Empiricism' (1984) 36 *Stanford Law Review* 575.
Tushnet, M, 'Legal Scholarship: Its Causes and Cure' (1981) 90 *Yale Law Journal* 1205.
Tversky, A and Kahneman, D, 'The Framing of Decisions and the Psychology of Choice' (1981) 211 *Science* 453.
Tyler, T, *Why People Obey the Law* (Princeton, Princeton University Press, 2006).
Urofsky, M, *Louis D Brandeis, A Life* (New York, Pantheon Books, 2009).
US Census Bureau, *Metropolitan Statistical Areas of the United States* (2009).
Weber, M, Roth, G and Wittich, C (eds), *Economy and Society* (Berkeley, University of California Press, 1978).
Weiner, E, *The Geography of Bliss* (New York, Twelve, 2008).
Weisberg, R, 'The Death Penalty Meets Social Science: Deterrence and Jury Behavior Under New Scrutiny' (2005) 1 *Annual Review of Law & Social Sciences* 151.
Wittgenstein, L, GEM Anscombe (trans), *Philosophical Investigations*, 3rd edn (Oxford, Blackwell Publishing, 1958).
Zimring, F, *The Great American Crime Decline* (Oxford, Oxford University Press, 2008).

3

The Promise and the Peril of Relational Contract Theory

ROBERT E SCOTT

INTRODUCTION

IN 1963, STEWART Macaulay published a paper that became the foundation of what is now known as relational contract theory.[1] The paper is justly famous: it is the most widely cited paper on contract law of the past 50 years.[2] Forty years later, Macaulay published an equally remarkable paper, one that is less widely known, in which he assessed what had become of relational contract scholarship in the intervening years.[3] In this chapter, I draw on both papers as well as some of his intervening work to trace the intellectual history of relational contract scholarship from its early promise as reflected in the 1963 paper to the peril that Macaulay so vividly understood in 2003.

But first, we must address a few definitional difficulties. Relational contract scholarship has evolved in two separate, and often opposing, intellectual traditions during this period. One camp consists of scholars who are typically associated with the 'law and economics' movement; in the other camp are scholars who more readily identify with the 'law and society' tradition. These labels are imperfect for any number of reasons, but in the absence of any other sensible classification, I will use them throughout my discussion. Within each camp are scholars who see themselves, in Mary Anne Case's pungent classification, as 'fundamentalists'.[4] According to Case, a fundamentalist approach is one in which no compromise to

[1] S Macaulay, 'Non-Contractual Relations in Business: A Preliminary Study' (1963) 28 *American Sociological Review* 55.

[2] F Shapiro, 'The Most-Cited Law Review Articles Revisited' (1996) 71 *Chicago-Kent Law Review* 751.

[3] S Macaulay, 'The Real and the Paper Deal: Empirical Pictures of Relationships, Complexity and the Urge for Transparent Simple Rules' (2003) 66 *Modern Law Review* 44.

[4] MA Case, 'Perfectionism and Fundamentalism in the Application of the German Abortion Laws' in S Williams (ed), *Constituting Equality: Gender Equality and Comparative Constitutional Law* (Cambridge, Cambridge University Press, 2009).

principle is acceptable, but the fundamentalist does not necessarily insist on imposing his or her principles on others. Case contrasts the fundamentalist approach with the 'perfectionist'. A perfectionist has as her goal wide acceptance of all the principles, but the perfectionist is willing to compromise in order to come closer to achieving this goal. Stewart Macaulay is, by this definition, a perfectionist. This habit of mind comes from his primary allegiance to empiricism: in his view, first principles always give way to the evidence. As one who regards himself as a true disciple of Macaulay (and that is not to say that Macaulay sees me in the same light), I, too, adhere to that goal, albeit perhaps not with the same unmatched intellectual rigor that Macaulay gives to that effort. And so, to put the matter bluntly, my argument in this chapter will be that the promise of relational contract theory lies with the perfectionists and the peril is a product of fundamentalism.

To illustrate the point, I return to the definitional problem alluded to above. Neither of the opposing camps that identify themselves as relational contract theorists are prepared to acknowledge that the other is entitled to the same designation. Fundamentalist economic relationalists scoff at the notion that any of those who have worked in the law and society tradition, including Ian Macneil – who coined the term relational contract theory – deserve to be called 'theorists'. Theory, they argue, requires a rigorous formulation of hypotheses based on formal modes of analysis that can be tested through equally rigorous empirical observations.[5] They accuse 'socio-relationalists' of drawing unwarranted conclusions from casual empiricism that lacks rigor and thus lacks the grounds for any generalising claims. Fundamentalist socio-relationalists, for their part, deny that economic relationalists have any right to call themselves 'relationalists'.[6] They argue that relationalists must subscribe to a form of legal centrism, one in which key relational norms are incorporated into formal doctrine and deployed by courts to require relational solutions when parties are unable to achieve co-operative outcomes on their own. They are particularly appalled by the normative claim that sophisticated parties should be allowed to have their written agreements interpreted according to formal rules of interpretation; rules that thus acontextualise formal resolution of disputes between such relational contractors.[7]

[5] The flavour of this criticism can be found in A Schwartz, 'Law and Economics Next?' (2011) 105 *Illinois Law Review* 1531, 1537 ('To teach "Contracts" while remaining ignorant of [theory] is like teaching basic human anatomy without knowing where the major organs are.').

[6] See, eg R Speidel, 'The Characteristics and Challenges of Relational Contracts' (2000) 94 *Northwestern University Law Review* 823, 845 ('Scott now states that "we are all relationalists" . . . Nonsense. Those arguing the virulent strain of the new formalists are neither realists nor relationalists and the sooner we say so the better.'); W Whitford, 'Relational Contracts and the New Formalism' (2004) 2004 *Wisconsin Law Review* 631, 634 ('In his recent work developing what I have called the new formalism, [Scott] has strayed from relational contract theory in a critically important way.').

[7] ibid.

The peril in this internecine struggle (one that is all too common among academics who insist on their own orthodoxies) is that the sharp disagreements on fundamentalist premises that divide these two groups will accelerate the decline of relational theory in the academy. The irony, of course, is that these analysts have much more in common with each other than with the majority of contract scholars who continue to focus both their teaching and their writing exclusively on traditional contract doctrine as embodied in a few celebrated 'chestnuts' of the common law as up-dated by the *Restatement of Contracts*. Relationalists of all stripes believe that the institution of contract can only be understood by observing the law 'in action', and, in particular, by exploring the interaction between the threat of legal coercion and the array of informal norms that also regulate the relationship in important ways. To be sure, there are key points of contention that divide relationalists, but nevertheless both groups understand the world in much the same terms (albeit with somewhat different vocabularies).

Moreover, I fear that the relationalist revival which has dominated contracts scholarship for almost half a century, may be on the wane. The younger cohort of law and economics scholars, armed with impressive technical skills, have abandoned relational questions in favour of projects that are capable of being analysed through formal models or sophisticated empirical techniques.[8] Many of the other bright stars in contract are formally trained in analytic philosophy and focus their energies on classical contract doctrine and the extent to which it adheres to deontological principles grounded in Kantian notions of autonomy.[9]

This pessimistic view of the legacy of relational scholarship is tempered, however, by the promise of a perfectionist accommodation. Macaulay pointed the way to this accommodation in his 2003 paper: different legal mechanisms, some judicial and some regulatory, are required if the goal is to match the appropriate legal response to the particular needs of highly diverse relationships.[10] This accommodation thus rejects the classical 'unitary' theory of contract in which a single set of common law rules (and governing policies) applies to all enforceable promises regardless of the status of the contracting parties. The traditional view requires a court to treat contracts between sophisticated parties who negotiate multi-million dollar agreements with the aid of competent counsel in precisely the same way as it treats 'click-wrap' agreements between individual consumers and merchant sellers over the purchase of $50 of products on the internet. Equally difficult is the task of applying this unitary set of doctrines to informal

[8] See nn 33–36, 82–84 below and accompanying text.

[9] See, eg J Kraus, 'The Correspondence of Contract and Promise' (2009) 109 *Columbia Law Review* 1603; S Shiffrin, 'The Divergence of Contract and Promise' (2007) 120 *Harvard Law Review* 708.

[10] Macaulay, 'The Real and the Paper Deal' (n 3) 73–77.

agreements between small businesspersons; or to ongoing supply chain relationships in which some transactions, but not all, are conducted within well-defined trade norms; or to collaborative agreements to share private technological information under conditions of great uncertainty. All relationalists should be able to agree that a unitary contract law appropriate to all these environments is a hopeless fiction.

The chapter proceeds as follows. In Part I, I identify the major claims of Macaulay's classic 1963 paper and show how those claims laid the foundation less than a decade later for the emergence of two disparate traditions in relational contract theory. The economic relationalist school developed directly from Macaulay in 1963, but the socio-relationalists departed from that tradition, influenced in large part by the work of Ian Macneil. Part II focuses on the methodological divide among relationalists and on three points of disagreement that are the primary result of that divide. I show that the disagreements rest largely on the fact that each group grounds its principles on very different contracting paradigms that reflect the poles of the contracting landscape. Part III then argues that the peril facing relational theory can be overcome by recognising the disunity of contract. Widely diverse contracting environments require very different legal responses and the commitment to cabin those responses within their separate domains offers the best hope for advancing the shared interests of all relationalists.

I. THE EMERGENCE OF RELATIONAL CONTRACT THEORY

A. Macaulay's Foundational Claims

The foundational principles of relational contract theory were laid in 1963 when Stewart Macaulay published a relatively short article, 'Non-Contractual Relations in Business: A Preliminary Study' (hereafter 'Non-Contractual Relations').[11] The article reported the results of an empirical study of the prevalence of formal contract law in exchange relations between business firms. Although the paper has been cited over 1,500 times, to date few scholars have reflected carefully on the totality of its claims. That is a great pity because careful reading yields great fruit. Among other observations, Macaulay made six key claims on the basis of his research:

— 'Most larger firms, and many smaller ones, attempt to plan carefully and completely.'[12]

[11] Macaulay, 'Non-Contractual Relations' (n 1).
[12] ibid 57.

— 'Transactions are planned and legal sanctions are used when the gains are thought to outweigh the costs.'[13]
— [However,] 'Legal sanctions are often unnecessary and may have undesirable consequences.'[14]
— Legal enforcement 'indicates a lack of trust and blunts the demands of friendship, turning a cooperative venture into an antagonistic horse trade [in which] . . . one gets performance only to the letter of the contract'.[15]
— [Thus,] 'Businessmen . . . seldom use legal sanctions to adjust [their] relationship.'[16] [Rather,] 'Business exchanges are usually adjusted informally, without disputes.'[17]
— [In sum,] 'Businessmen often prefer to rely on a man's word in a brief letter, a handshake or common honesty and decency even when the transaction involves exposure to serious risks.'[18] [Indeed,] 'Firms regularly use [unenforceable] contracts . . . None thought that the lack of legal sanction made a difference.'[19]

These six claims led Macaulay to pose two central questions as the key issues for future research. First, 'Why are relatively non-contractual practices so common?' And, second, 'Why does business ever use contract in light of its success without it?'[20]

Macaulay offered answers to both questions even as he called for further research. He explained the ubiquity of non-contractual practices by highlighting the potency of self-enforcing mechanisms. In particular, he noted that: 'In most situations, [formal] contract is not needed. Often its functions are served by other devices.'[21] Among the other devices, he emphasised the potency of reputation,[22] the discipline of future relations,[23] and trust and reciprocity.[24]

[13] ibid 55.
[14] ibid 55.
[15] ibid 64. The loss of reciprocity and trust that formal enforcement can stimulate led Macaulay to conclude that 'the gain from [legal] coercion often fails to outweigh its costs'. ibid 64. This observation foreshadows the 'crowding out' literature in law, social psychology and economics of a generation later. See, eg D Houser and others, 'When Punishment Fails: Research on Sanctions, Intentions and Non-Cooperation' (2008) 62 *Games and Economic Behavior* 509; see also additional sources cited in n 36 below.
[16] Macaulay, 'Non-Contractual Relations' (n 1) 55.
[17] ibid 61.
[18] ibid 58.
[19] ibid 60. Macaulay emphasised the frequency with which parties used indefinite agreements: '[The standard supply chain] contract is probably sufficiently vague to make the contract legally unenforceable.' ibid.
[20] Macaulay, 'Non-Contractual Relations' (n 1) 62.
[21] ibid 62.
[22] ibid 63.
[23] ibid 63.
[24] ibid 63.

The second question follows logically from the first. If informal enforcement of exchange agreements is so successful, then why do parties ever turn to formal, legally enforceable contract? Here the data suggested several answers. Legally enforceable contracting was advisable when the interactions were complex, as complexity leads to formality. In addition, legal enforcement was used when the relationship had broken down, for example, in the case of franchise terminations that were followed by franchisee lawsuits.[25] But more subtly, Macaulay pointed to a further consideration, one that has become known in law and economics circles as the 'hold-up problem'.[26] He stated: 'Bargaining power is not size or market share alone. Even a giant firm can find itself bound to a small supplier once production of an essential item begins for there may not be time to turn to another supplier.' Thus, he concluded: 'To understand the functions of contract the whole business of conducting exchanges must be explored fully.'[27]

B. The Disparate Influences of Macaulay and Macneil

i. Macaulay and the Rise of Relational Law and Economics

'Non-Contractual Relations' was an astonishingly prescient paper; it foreshadowed the next 40 years of economically-focused relational contract scholarship. Starting in the early 1970s, economists such as Victor Goldberg and Oliver Williamson who were interested in law began to use Macaulay's framework to focus on the economics of long-term contractual relations and the choice of organisational form to govern those relations. Of particular note here is the emphasis of this work on business-to-business relationships and how the parties dealt with the asymmetries in bargaining power that arise during the different stages of the relationship. Rather than talking in terms of power, solidarity and exploitation, these economic relationalists described the problem in economic terms as a product of asymmetric specific investments in the relationship by one party or the other. Dubbed 'the hold-up problem' by Goldberg,[28] it became a major focus of the economic relationalists for the next 35 years.

[25] See generally S Macaulay, 'Changing a Continuing Relationship Between a Large Corporation and Those who Deal with It: Automobile Manufacturers, Their Dealers, and the Legal System, Law and Society' (1965) Summer 1965 *Wisconsin Law Review* 483–575, Fall 1965 *Wisconsin Law Review* 740–858.

[26] See text accompanying n 29 below.

[27] Macaulay, 'Non-Contractual Relations' (n 1) 67.

[28] V Goldberg, 'Regulation and Administered Contracts' (1976) 7 *Bell Journal of Economics* 426, 439.

Goldberg's particular focus, followed subsequently by Charles Goetz and Robert Scott,[29] was to examine salient contractual relationships and analyse how parties to those relationships were motivated to solve holdup problems through a combination of ex ante contract and reliance on strategies of adjustment *ex post*.[30] Williamson, in turn, used the holdup problem to analyse the conditions under which firms would choose between market exchange, contract and vertical integration to organise their transactions.[31] The important point, however, is that all of this work, both in its premises and in its focus, followed directly from the way 'Non-Contractual Relations' explained how business firms solved relational problems without the *ex post* intervention of courts.

As the economic relationalist tradition matured, scholars increasingly focused attention on the two key questions raised in 'Non-Contractual Relations'. First, how do formal legal obligations to abide by the terms of a contract interact with informal norms based on trust, reciprocity and a desire to maintain a reputation as a co-operator? In responding to this question, economic relationalists focused on a growing body of experimental evidence from behavioural investigators. That research yielded several key findings. Initially, substantial experimental evidence showed that approximately half of the tested subjects did not behave opportunistically even when it was in their economic interest to do so and they were not under threat of sanction or retaliation.[32] Similarly, the evidence also indicated a widespread, but not universal, taste for reciprocity – an inclination to reward co-operators and punish opportunists even when the subjects derived no direct and particular benefits from doing so.[33] A preference for reciprocity thus provides one explanation for how (and why) informal sanctioning works. Moreover, this research also suggested that the relationship between formal contract and informal norms was antagonistic: the

[29] See generally C Goetz and R Scott, 'Principles of Relational Contracts' (1981) 67 *Virginia Law Review* 1089; C Goetz and R Scott, 'The Mitigation Principle: Toward a General Theory of Contractual Obligation' (1983) 69 *Virginia Law Review* 967.

[30] Goldberg, 'Regulation and Administered Contracts' (n 28); V Goldberg, 'The Law and Economics of Vertical Restrictions: A Relational Perspective' (1979) 58 *Texas Law Review* 91; V Goldberg, 'Relational Exchange: Economic and Complex Contracts' (1980) 23 *American Behavioral Scientist* 337.

[31] O Williamson, 'Transaction Costs Economics: The Governance of Contractual Relations' (1978) 22 *Journal of Law and Economics* 223; O Williamson, *Markets and Hierarchies: Analysis and Antitrust Implications* (New York, Free Press, 1975); O Williamson, *The Economic Institutions of Capitalism* (New York, Free Press, 1985).

[32] For a review of the literature, see E Fehr and K Schmidt, 'Theories of Fairness and Reciprocity – Evidence and Economic Applications' (2001) Institute for Empirical Research in Economics, University of Zurich Working Paper No 75, 2–3 (available at ideas.repec.org/p/zur/iewwpx/075.html).

[33] See E Fehr, S Gachter, and G Kirchsteiger, 'Reciprocity as a Contract Enforcement Device: Experimental Evidence' (1997) 65 *Econometrica* 833, 850 (finding roughly half of subjects punishing shirkers, and roughly half rewarding non-shirkers).

introduction of formal contract and its 'high-powered' sanctions[34] may 'crowd out' the otherwise powerful informal forces that 'Non-Contractual Relations' had found were the primary mechanisms for on-going adjustment in relational contracts.[35]

To the economic relationalists, the evidence of crowding out argued for a leaner and more modest contract law; one that worked in tandem with, rather than undermined, the informal norms supporting the adjustment process.[36] This, in turn, led to the second question posed initially by 'Non-Contractual Relations': given these two means of inducing co-operation and adjustment in relational contract, what kinds of contract law rules would sophisticated business parties prefer? The responses to that question led to the development of what has come to be known as the 'new formalism' in contract theory. The new formalists argued that, notwithstanding the importance of adjustment over time, both the theory and available evidence[37] showed that most sophisticated parties to relational contracts preferred clear, transparent ('formal') contract law rules.[38] This included the claim that business firms preferred a textualist interpretive regime, one that authorised a court to exclude extrinsic evidence of the commercial context whenever the parties signaled their intent to rely extensively on the written contract.[39]

The questions that 'Non-Contractual Relations' posed are still regarded as the central issues for any scholar seeking to understand the role played by contract law in business-to-business economic activity. Indeed, as I will describe in more detail below, one cannot overstate the importance of Macaulay's paper to the development of the law and economics branch of relational theory. Curiously, perhaps, Macaulay's paper has been signific-

[34] High-powered enforcement consists in the imposition of standard breach of contract remedies for a failure to perform specified contractual obligations.

[35] Compare D Houser and others, 'When Punishment Fails' (n 15); I Bohnet, B Frey, and S Huck, 'More Order with Less Law: On Contract Enforcement, Trust and Crowding' (2001) 95 *American Political Science Review* 131 (all finding evidence of crowding out) with S Lazzarini, G Miller, and T Zenger, 'Order with Some Law: Complementarity versus Substitution of Formal and Informal Arrangements' (2004) 20 *Journal of Law, Economics, and Organization* 261; and M Rigdon, 'Trust and Reciprocity in Incentive Contracting' (2009) 70 *Journal of Economic Behavior and Organization* 93 (all finding complementarity).

[36] D Charny, 'Non-Legal Sanctions in Commercial Relationships' (1990) 104 *Harvard Law Review* 373; R Scott, 'A Theory of Self-Enforcing Indefinite Agreements' (2003) 103 *Columbia Law Review* 1641. See also R Gilson, C Sabel, and R Scott, 'Braiding: The Interaction of Formal and Informal Contracting in Theory, Practice, and Doctrine' (2010) 110 *Columbia Law Review* 1377.

[37] G Miller, 'Bargaining on the Red-Eye: New Light on Contract Theory' (2008) New York University Law and Economics, Working Paper No 131, lsr.nellco.org/nyu/lewp/papers/131.

[38] L Bernstein, 'Merchant Law in a Merchant Court: Rethinking the Code's Search for Immanent Business Norms' (1996) 144 *University of Pennsylvania Law Review* 1765; see L Bernstein, 'Private Commercial Law in the Cotton Industry: Creating Cooperation Through Rules, Norms, and Institutions' (2001) 99 *Michigan Law Review* 1724, 1745–54, 1762–87.

[39] A Schwartz and R Scott, 'Contract Theory and the Limits of Contract Law' (2003) 113 *Yale Law Journal* 541, 601–605; A Schwartz and R Scott, 'Contract Interpretation Redux' (2010) 119 *Yale Law Journal* 926.

antly less influential in framing the debates for the law and society relational scholars. While they continue to cite this paper (and revere Macaulay the scholar), they focus only on the most general claim in the paper that contractual relationships are complex, require adjustment over time, and rely on norms of reciprocity and co-operation.

ii. Ian Macneil and the Rise of Sociological Relationalism

The lesser influence of 'Non-Contractual Relations' on the rise of sociological or 'socio-relationalism' is, in part, due to Macaulay himself. As noted above, Macaulay views himself as an empiricist rather than a theorist. Thus, in the intervening years, his scholarship (as well as that of his long-time colleague, Bill Whitford)[40] has ranged over a much wider terrain, moving beyond inter-firm contracting to a study of franchise relationships, standard form adhesion contracts, and many other specific contexts far removed from the pure business environment.[41] Until recently, he was content to describe what he discovered without seeking to generalise over the entire domain of contract.[42] Macaulay took the opportunity to offer his own reflections on the 1963 paper in a symposium marking the twenty-first anniversary of its publication,[43] and in so doing he revealed a significant shift in emphasis that appeared to be a product of his explorations of franchise relations and adhesion contract environments. In these contexts, he argued that, 'power, exploitation and dependence are also significant factors [and] continuing relationships are not necessarily nice'.[44]

The focus on contracting environments characterised by power disparities naturally led many socio-relationalist scholars to turn from studying pure business environments toward analyses of consumer transactions and the imperfections in markets dominated by adhesion contracts. Law and society relationalists published important theoretical and empirical papers on consumer product warranties,[45] consumer credit,[46] consumer

[40] See text accompanying nn 46–51 below.

[41] See generally Macaulay, 'Automobile Manufacturers' (n 25); S Macaulay, 'Private Legislation and the Duty to Read – Business Run by IBM Machine, the Law of Contracts and Credit Cards' (1966) 19 *Vanderbilt Law Review* 1051; S Macaulay, 'Lawyers and Consumer Protection Laws' (1979) 14 *Law & Society Review* 115.

[42] Generalisations have come only in the last decade. See, eg S Macaulay, 'Relational Contracts Floating on a Sea of Custom? Thoughts About the Ideas of Ian Macneil and Lisa Bernstein' (2000) 94 *Northwestern University Law Review* 775; Macaulay, 'The Real and the Paper Deal' (n 3); S Macaulay, 'Freedom from Contract: Solutions in Search of a Problem?' (2004) 2004 *Wisconsin Law Review* 777.

[43] S Macaulay, 'An Empirical View of Contract' (1985) 1985 *Wisconsin Law Review* 465.

[44] ibid 469.

[45] See, eg W Whitford, 'Law and the Consumer Transaction: A Case Study of the Automobile Warranty' (1968) 1968 *Wisconsin Law Review* 1006; J Braucher, 'An Informal Resolution Model of Consumer Product Warranty Law' (1985) 1985 *Wisconsin Law Review* 1405.

[46] See, eg W Whitford, 'A Critique of the Consumer Credit Collection System' (1979) 1979 *Wisconsin Law Review* 1047; W Whitford, 'The Appropriate Role of Security Interests in

mortgage transactions,[47] and the protection in bankruptcy of unsecured creditors[48] and consumers.[49] These papers pointed to an asymmetry in long-term relations between business and consumer interests and to the deficiencies of common law contract in dealing with the consequences of market failure.[50]

The more important reason for the move by law and society scholars away from 'Non-Contractual Relations', however, was the pervasive influence of the work of Ian Macneil. Beginning in the early 1970s,[51] and continuing for 25 years thereafter,[52] Macneil developed a socio-cultural account of contractual relations that he described as 'relational contract theory'.[53] Macneil's work appealed to the socio-relationalists, and, conversely, not to the economic relationalists, precisely because of his central claim that exchange relations, even the sort that Macaulay had studied, could only be understood within a wider social, cultural and political context.[54]

The differing influence of these two giants of contracts scholarship is explicable in terms of the different methodological commitments of the two relational camps. The economic relationalists were drawn to 'Non-Contractual Relations' because Macaulay's framework enabled them to isolate salient factors and distill them from the complex phenomena of

Consumer Transactions' (1986) 7 *Cardozo Law Review* 959; J Braucher, 'Defining Unfairness: Empathy and Economic Analysis at the Federal Trade Commission' (1988) 68 *Boston University Law Review* 349.

[47] E Warren and O Bar-Gill, 'Making Credit Safer' (2008) 157 *University of Pennsylvania Law Review* 1.

[48] See, eg E Warren, 'Making Policy with Imperfect Information: The Article 9 Full Priority Debates' (1998) 82 *Cornell Law Review* 101; L LoPucki, 'The Unsecured Creditors Bargain' (1994) 80 *Virginia Law Review* 1887.

[49] See, eg T Sullivan, E Warren, and J Westbrook, *As We Forgive Our Debtors: Consumer Credit and Bankruptcy in America* (Oxford, Oxford University Press, 1989); W Whitford, 'Consumer Protection in Consumer Bankruptcy' (1994) 68 *American Bankruptcy Law Journal* 397; E Warren, 'A Principled Approach to Consumer Bankruptcy' (1997) 71 *American Bankruptcy Law Journal* 483.

[50] W Whitford, 'Structuring Consumer Protection Legislation to Maximize Effectiveness' (1981) 1981 *Wisconsin Law Review* 1018; J Braucher, 'Politics and Principle in the Drafting of UCC Consumer Protection Provisions' (1996) 29 *Uniform Commercial Code Law Journal* 68.

[51] I Macneil, 'The Many Futures of Contracts' (1974) 47 *Southern California Law Review* 1018; I Macneil, 'Restatement (Second) of Contracts and Presentation' (1974) 60 *Virginia Law Review* 589; I Macneil, 'Contracts: Adjustment of Long-Term Economic Relations Under Classical, Neoclassical, and Relational Contract Law' (1978) 72 *Northwestern University Law Review* 85.

[52] See generally I Macneil, 'Economic Analysis of Contractual Relations: Its Shortfall and the Need for a "Rich Classificatory Apparatus"' (1981) 75 *Northwestern University Law Review* 1018; I Macneil, 'Values in Contract: Internal and External' (1983) 78 *Northwestern University Law Review* 340.

[53] I Macneil, *The New Social Contract* (New Haven, Yale University Press, 1980). Macneil was not a theorist in the sense of offering an explanation of empirical phenomena, described in such a way that any scholar in the field could verify or challenge. Rather, he used the tools of thick description to classify the full universe of contractual relations. See I Macneil, 'Relational Contract Theory: Challenges and Queries' (2000) 94 *Northwestern University Law Review* 877.

[54] See generally Macneil, 'Many Futures' (n 51).

which they were a part so as to make their theory tractable. The socio-relationalists were drawn to Macneil because he self-consciously embedded these same factors within a more complex socio-cultural framework thus increasing the richness of the description of particular contractual contexts. Of particular importance to the sociological perspective were two key features of Macneil's theory. The first was the claim that these exchange relationships had important social and psychological purposes in addition to the goal of maximising the economic surplus from the contract.[55] Secondly, and equally significant, was the shift in focus from how these relationships succeeded to the ways in which they might fail. Macneil's focus on power disparities and the threat of exploitation was an important ingredient in his normative views on the role of contract law in regulating and facilitating these relationships.[56]

The salience of power and politics led Macneil to emphasise modern labour relations as paradigmatic examples of relational contract to which the classical (or even neoclassical) common law of contract with its focus on ex ante planning and risk allocation was ill-suited. Macneil saw business-to-business contracting as a part of the whole, one that fits naturally within the classical, discrete paradigm, but which should not be given centre stage. Instead, when he ventured his normative views on what a relational contract law should look like, the labour paradigm provided the answer: a regulatory regime with an on-going administrative apparatus could mediate disputes and reach fair and just outcomes while preserving the relationship over time.[57]

As Macneil would subsequently concede, his primary mission was to teach scholars how to understand contractual relationships rather than to offer normative arguments about the proper shape of relational contract law.[58] His views on the role of common law courts in creating a 'relational contract law' were tentative at best and, at worst, opaque.[59] In particular, he never addressed the key question that was central to 'Non-Contractual Relations': What is the role of informal norms and sanctions in maintaining

[55] ibid 723–25. For a discussion of the influence of this claim, see W Whitford, 'Ian Macneil's Contribution to Contracts Scholarship' (1985) 1985 *Wisconsin Law Review* 545.

[56] See, eg Macneil, 'Economic Analysis' (n 52). While 'coercion and domination' were entirely absent from 'Non-Contractual Relations', these concerns were part of Macaulay's 1985 retrospective and are reflected more inferentially in his classic study of automobile franchise relationships. See Macaulay, 'Empirical View' (n 43) 469; Macaulay, 'Automobile Manufacturers' (n 25).

[57] Macneil, 'Contracts: Adjustment' (n 51). Macneil's own examples of relational contract law are of regulatory and administrative solutions to problems in employment relations. Macneil, 'Challenges' (n 53) 897.

[58] Macneil, 'Challenges' (n 53) 899 ('I challenge to a duel anyone who . . . persists in converting my descriptions of relational contract into prescriptions of what the law should be, particularly prescription of some universal application of relational contract law.').

[59] Indeed, when pushed to identify a 'relational contract law', Macneil adverted entirely to regulatory limitations on the common law such as 'EISA, OSHA, other workplace regulations, wage and hours legislation'. Macneil, 'Challenges' (n 53) 897.

contractual relationships and what kind of contract law would be most compatible with the normative structure of those relationships? This omission was not a rejection of 'Non-Contractual Relations'; rather, it reflected Macneil's own lack of interest in whether contract law should impose relational duties if the normative constraints that hold the parties together should happen to break down under stress.

But the socio-relationalists who followed Macneil's lead were not so reticent about the proper shape of the common law of contract. Richard Speidel and Robert Hillman, in particular, took up the baton and, in a series of papers, articulated the view that relational contracts between commercial parties require a relational 'common law'.[60] They argued that relational duties arise from the reasonable expectations that each party has regarding what the other party will do when a particular contingency arises. These relational duties direct the court to impose fair outcomes when disputes arise and the parties cannot agree. Such outcomes might include, for example, a redistribution of burdens through loss sharing or new pricing mechanisms that are perceived by the court as fair *ex post*.[61]

Implicit in the claim that relational contract law should mirror the complexity of relational contracts were three key premises that departed sharply from the economic relationalist work that followed from 'Non-Contractual Relations'. First, a court charged with finding and then imposing legally enforceable relational duties would necessarily have to consider evidence of the contextual factors that Macneil showed were essential to understand the relationship.[62] Thus, even a formal written agreement with a merger clause is open to the question of whether the parties actually agreed that disputes were to be governed by the terms in the agreement and no other terms.[63] Second, the requirement for ex post review of the contractual context would not create costly uncertainty for future parties.[64] While parties might not be able to predict and plan ex ante the outcomes that would result if particular contractual risks materialised, they would know that the courts, employing their informational advantage ex post, would reach an equitable solution as viewed from that vantage point. Third, informal sanctions imposed by counterparties punishing non-co-operative actions in various ways are sometimes inadequate to maintain relationships. When disputes arise, additional legal

[60] R Speidel, 'Court-Imposed Price Adjustments Under Long-Term Supply Contracts' (1983) 76 *Northwestern University Law Review* 369; R Hillman, 'Court Adjustment of Long-Term Contracts: An Analysis Under Modern Contract Law' (1987) *Duke Law Journal* 1; R Speidel, 'The New Spirit of Contract' (1982) 2 *Journal of Law and Commerce* 193; E Leib, 'Contracts and Friendship' (2010) 59 *Emory Law Journal* 649.

[61] L Trakman, 'Winner Take Some: Loss Sharing and Commercial Impracticability' (1985) 69 *Minnesota Law Review* 471.

[62] See generally T Palay, 'A Contract Does not a Contract Make' (1985) 1985 *Wisconsin Law Review* 561, 562.

[63] See A Corbin, *Contracts* vol 3 paras 581, 582.

[64] Whitford, 'Relational Contracts' (n 6) 636–37.

intervention is required to prevent exploitation. Presumably, such intervention would complement rather than undermine those mechanisms.[65]

In the following Part, I trace in more detail how these two traditions diverged and how the resulting clash of viewpoints threatens the survival of relational theory. Part IIA examines the methodological commitments of relationalists of both stripes. These commitments explain the fidelity of the economic relationalists to the business-to-business frame of 'Non-Contractual Relations' and the shift by law and society relationalists to environments that are vulnerable to exploitation of the weak by the powerful. In Part IIB, I discuss the three major points of contention that currently divide fundamentalist scholars of both camps. Part IIC describes the peril facing relational theory unless these contentious issues can somehow be resolved.

II. THE RELATIONALIST DIVIDE

A. The Methodological Divide between Relationalists

The two quite different paths taken by economic and socio-relational scholars have led them to move farther and farther away from their shared origins. Currently, much of the scholarship on relational theory consists of criticisms directed at scholars working in the other tradition. As I suggested above, one consequence of this growing separation has been the hardening of methodological commitments on each side and a consequent rejection of the work done by those across the methodological divide. This trend can be understood, in part, as the triumph (in Mary Anne Case's terms) of fundamentalists over perfectionists. As a generalisation, scholars who are committed to empiricism are perfectionists – they believe that the search for truth provides principles that all can share. These principles are not the product of a priori claims but rather the product of theory as informed by facts. Fundamentalists are committed to principles that derive from a priori methodological commitments. They reject claims that are inconsistent with those principles. The relationalist divide is attributable to differences in these pre-existing methodological commitments. The shorthand for those differences is expressed as the gulf between law and society, and law and economics. These two analytic traditions rest on fundamentally different conceptions of the role of law and the relative power of context versus theory.[66]

[65] ibid 640–41.

[66] I have previously discussed this divide in the context of the relationship between law and social norms. The following discussion draws on that analysis. See R Scott, 'The Limits of Behavioral Theories of Law and Social Norms' (2000) 86 *Virginia Law Review* 1603.

Analysing the influence of legal rules on contracting behaviour has been a fruitful source of inquiry for analysts using the techniques of law and economics. By imposing sanctions or granting subsidies, the law gives parties incentives for desirable behaviour. Analysing the incentive effects of legal rules thus provides a useful tool both to explain the legal rules we see and to support a normative critique of those rules that are thought to have undesirable effects. Economic theory, especially the theory of rational choice, is well suited to analysing the effects of both formal and informal sanctions on the behaviour of sophisticated commercial parties. In this setting, contract law rules share space with powerful informal sanctions that encourage performance and penalise breach. These informal influences include the fear of losing expected future dealings with the counterparty, the threat of loss of reputation with the resulting reduction in future business with other potential counterparties, and an individual taste for reciprocity. The law and economics approach thus rests on the assumption that the behaviour of contracting parties during the life of their relationship is affected either by the threat of legal sanctions or by the anticipation of social sanctions associated with that behaviour.[67]

Law and society scholars tend to adopt a bottom-up rather than a top-down approach to understanding the law. If the goal of the analyst is to examine the behaviour of parties in particular contexts and to eschew abstraction, prediction and generalisation, then the tools of social theory and sociological description offer a rich story of the human experience. From sociology we learn about the existence of social norms, an alternative, complex regime of social control that interacts with law in many different ways. From psychology, we learn something about the relationship between external law and internal values and emotions. We know that external, material incentives are not the only forces that govern behaviour. Rather, behaviour is stimulated by complex psychological reward mechanisms. Moreover, evolutionary psychology teaches us that there is long-term advantage in moral behaviour. Salient emotional reactions – such as guilt, anger or empathy – mark one as a 'co-operator' who is able to make credible commitments concerning her future actions.[68]

The focus on values other than surplus maximisation leads the law and society analyst to turn away from transactions between sophisticated

[67] R Scott and P Stephan, *The Limits of Leviathan: Contract Theory and the Enforcement of International Law* (Cambridge, Cambridge University Press, 2006); R Gilson, C Sabel, and R Scott, 'Contracting for Innovation: Vertical Disintegration and Interfirm Collaboration' (2009) 109 *Columbia Law Review* 431.

[68] Robert Frank argues that moral behaviour has its source in the emotions rather than in 'rationality' and reason. R Frank, *Passions Within Reasons: The Strategic Role of the Emotions* (New York, Norton, 1988) 11–12. Cognitive and social psychology teaches us that there are systematic 'errors' in human judgment and decision-making. See D Kahneman, P Slovic, and A Tversky (eds), *Judgment Under Uncertainty: Heuristics and Biases* (Cambridge, Cambridge University Press, 1982).

commercial parties toward settings in which disparities in power may lead to exploitation. In these environments, rational choice theory is impoverished and legal intervention to protect the weak against the powerful is more compelling. A danger, however, is that the law and society analyst may be guided more by the strength of her a priori beliefs in the efficacy of judicial intervention than by the evidence that generalist courts may lack the tools to address fundamental social problems of which the case at hand is only a symptom.

In sum, economic relationalists critique the ad hoc empiricism and lack of theoretical rigor of the law and society school, while the socio-relationalists reject the law and economics project as, at best, naive and unduly narrow and, at worst, as undermining the entire relational enterprise. This methodological divide, aggravated by fundamentalists on both sides, has provoked profound disagreement on three major issues central to relational theory. Any hope of rescuing relational contract theory from its current peril requires some accommodation on each of these points of contention.

B. Three Points of Contention

i. Textualist v Contextualist Interpretation

Legal enforcement of relational contracts necessarily requires the state to interpret the terms the contracting parties use to allocate contractual risks. Interpretation disputes are the largest single source of commercial contract litigation.[69] Nonetheless, contract interpretation is the least settled question in relational contract scholarship. Instead, relational scholars vigorously debate the relative merits of two polar approaches to the interpretation of contracts.

Economic relationalists defend the traditional common law approach to interpretation, an approach that a large majority of common law courts continue to follow.[70] This interpretive approach privileges integrated written contracts over context evidence that purports to show that the agreement contained additional or different terms. In addition, it bars context evidence designed to show that parties intended clear and unambiguous

[69] D Dilts, 'Of Words and Contracts: Arbitration and Lexicology' (May–July 2005) *Dispute Resolution Journal* 40, 41–43; J Tomaszewski, 'The Pandora's Box of Cyberspace: State Regulation of Digital Signatures and the Dormant Commerce Clause' (1997–1998) 33 *Gonzaga Law Review* 417, 432.

[70] A strong majority of US courts continue to follow the traditional, textualist or 'formalist', approach to contract interpretation. A state-by-state survey of recent court decisions shows that 38 states follow the textualist approach to interpretation. Nine states, joined by the *Uniform Commercial Code*'s Article 2 on Sales (hereinafter UCC) and the *Restatement (Second) of Contracts*, have adopted a contextualist or anti-formalist interpretive regime. The remaining states' doctrines are indeterminate.

language to be understood in non-standard ways. Textualist courts, such as New York, use a hard parol evidence rule that gives presumptively conclusive effect to merger clauses, and, in the absence of such a clause, determines whether the written agreement is fully integrated by applying a 'four corners' presumption that the contract is fully integrated if it appears final and complete on its face.[71] The scholars who defend textualist arguments ground their analysis on a particular contracting paradigm: the negotiated contract between sophisticated commercial parties.[72] Textualist arguments thus focus on the importance of contract design and the insight that for these parties context is endogenous; the parties can embed as much or as little context into an agreement as they wish. In this way, sophisticated parties can economise on contracting costs by shifting costs between the front end (or drafting stage) and the back end (or enforcement stage) of the contracting process.[73]

At the other pole is the contextualist approach to interpretation. Socio-relationalist commentators are reluctant to endorse formal rules for determining either the terms of a contract or the presumed meaning of those terms once they have been identified.[74] They argue that formal interpretive rules that exclude certain categories of extrinsic evidence necessarily deprive the fact finder of potentially relevant information and thus distort the court's assessment of what the parties meant by their agreement. Contextualist courts, such as California, thus favour a soft parol evidence rule. Here the test for integration admits extrinsic evidence notwithstanding an unambiguous merger clause or, absent such a clause, notwithstanding the fact that the writing otherwise appears final and complete on its face.[75] These courts regard a merger clause as raising only a rebuttable presumption of integration, one that is subject to being overridden by extrinsic evidence that the parties lacked such intent. The contextualist approach is framed by a very different paradigm from the one that justifies textualism: here the argument focuses on contracts between parties to

[71] See, eg *Morgan Stanley High Yield Sec, Inc v Seven Circle Gaming Corp*, 269 F Supp 2d 206 (SDNY 2003); *Tempo Shain Corp v Bertek Inc*, 120 F3d 16, 21 (2d Cir 1997).

[72] See Schwartz and Scott, 'Contract Theory' (n 39); Schwartz and Scott, 'Contract Interpretation Redux' (n 39).

[73] For a discussion of how contracting parties can economise on total contracting costs by shifting costs between the drafting or front end of the contracting process and the adjudication or back end of the process, see R Scott and G Triantis, 'Anticipating Litigation in Contract Design' (2006) 115 *Yale Law Journal* 814.

[74] Contextualist interpretive principles are exemplified by the *Uniform Commercial Code* and the *Restatement (Second) of Contracts*. California is the most significant contextualist jurisdiction.

[75] *Pac Gas & Elec Co v GW Thomas Drayage & Rigging Co*, 442 P2d 641, 645 (CA 1968) ('[R]ational interpretation requires at least a preliminary consideration of all credible evidence offered to proved the intention of the parties.'); see also *Int'l Milling Co v Hachmeister, Inc*, 110 A 2d 186 (PA 1955) (extrinsic evidence of negotiations and antecedent agreements admissible to show buyer had not assented to the contract as a complete integration of the contract despite the presence of an express merger clause).

standardised, non-negotiated transactions (the consumer context) or contracts embedded in customary norms and terms of trade (the sales context). Both of these transactional prototypes undermine the assumptions of individualised contract design that animates the textualist view.

This description of the two approaches and their key assumptions exposes a deep puzzle: since different central paradigms support the two competing approaches to interpretation, why do they engage in debate at all, much less struggle for supremacy? The answer lies in their shared presumption of the unitary and mandatory nature of contract law and doctrine. For both sides in the interpretation debate, when a court (or legislature) chooses either a textualist or a contextualist approach to interpretation, that choice applies to all transactional prototypes, and particular parties cannot choose ex ante to have their contract interpreted according to the disfavoured approach. Thus, the on-going interpretation debate is binary – either text or context – and in any particular 'jurisdiction' victory is total for one approach or the other.

ii. Ex ante v Ex Post Perspective

The preceding discussion focused on the debate over text versus context that separates scholars working in law and economics from those in law and society. In this part, I turn to a second area where the focus of the two disciplines diverges: the tension between the ex ante and the ex post.[76] Socio-relationalists generally take an ex post perspective in adjudication. They view adjudication as an occasion for identifying and vindicating the pre-existing rights of the litigants. In contrast, economic relationalists generally take an ex ante, and therefore consequentialist, perspective on common law adjudication. These theorists view adjudication primarily as a mechanism for creating rules and rights that will provide incentives for individuals in the future. Judicial decisions are then evaluated according to whether or not these prospective effects are socially desirable. Economic analysis asks, for example, how legal enforcement of relational duties when informal norms have broken down is likely to affect the behaviour of contracting parties in the future.[77]

This tension between the ex ante and the ex post is more sharply illustrated by what I have elsewhere called the justice paradox.[78] The focus on the litigation at hand is a natural point of reference for a lawyer concerned with whether justice was done. To appreciate the justice paradox, however, we must accept that common law cases have both distributive and

[76] The discussion that follows draws on R Scott, '*Hoffman v. Red Owl Stores* and the Limits of the Legal Method' (2010) 61 *Hastings Law Journal* 859.

[77] For discussion, see Schwartz and Scott, 'Contract Theory' (n 39).

[78] For discussion of the justice paradox and its implications for legal scholarship, see R Scott, 'Chaos Theory and the Justice Paradox' (1993) 35 *William and Mary Law Review* 329.

behavioural effects. Contract rules not only redistribute wealth and entitlements between the immediate parties to a dispute, but also influence the behaviour of future parties who may find themselves similarly situated. The justice of all legal outcomes under our common law system should therefore be evaluated from two distinct perspectives: Does the law accomplish justice between the parties to any particular dispute? And, does the law appropriately regulate the conduct of other parties likely to have similar disputes in the future?

The paradox arises from two propositions. First, *both* criteria must be satisfied in order to achieve a just outcome. Second, these two criteria of justice are frequently in opposition. Simply put, sometimes you cannot have it both ways. We aspire to a just society that satisfies both of the essential conditions of justice, and yet we live in a world that often requires us to choose one or the other. Viewed this way, the tension between the law and economics and law and society relationalists is both understandable and inevitable: the two perspectives seem committed to incompatible assumptions about the role and effects of adjudication.

iii. Formal versus Informal Enforcement: The 'Crowding Out' Problem

Economic relational theory has focused much attention in recent years on the relationship between formal and informal enforcement that was first identified by 'Non-Contractual Relations'. As noted above, the effects of formal enforcement on informal enforcement was ignored by Macneil and has since received little attention by socio-relationalists. The reason for this sharp difference can best be explained in terms of the divide between the ex ante and ex post perspectives. The ex ante perspective naturally asks whether the two separate regimes are compatible because both are likely to be an important influence on the relationship looking forward from the time of contracting. But viewed ex post, once the relationship has fractured and the parties are in litigation, the informal norms are no longer relevant – clearly they failed to hold the relationship together. Thus, from an ex post perspective, the choice is either to let the losses lie where they fall or to advocate for legal intervention that imposes fairer outcomes. This approach is even more compelling when the dispute concerns disadvantaged or unsophisticated parties in unbalanced power relationships. But the success of such a strategy – as 'Non-Contractual Relations' points out – ultimately turns on whether formal and informal enforcement mechanisms are *complements*, and therefore a mixed strategy is feasible, or are *substitutes*, such that recourse to formal enforcement when the informal norms have failed 'crowds out' the operation of informal contracting in future transactions.

The existing theory and evidence offer limited guidance in answering this key question. Experimental research has demonstrated that, in many instances, formal enforcement tends to undermine the informal mechanisms.[79] Studies indicate that when offered a contract whose performance is based only on trust, a substantial number of individuals will extend greater efforts to perform than narrow self-interest would dictate. But when offered the same contract *plus* the possibility of having a third party impose a monetary sanction if the promisor fails to perform as promised, the average effort made declines significantly. The introduction of the formal enforcement option causes shirking to increase and trust vanishes almost completely.[80] In effect, the introduction of a formal sanction that governs all of the parties' actions under the contract results in a 'cognitive shift that crowds out norm-based social behaviour'.[81]

Economic relationalists have argued that the crowding out effect results when the presence of a formal contract and the potential for high-powered legal sanctions *degrade* the information about the nature of the counterparties and the nature of their interactions.[82] This occurs, these scholars suggest, because of the effects of two interrelated factors: (a) formal enforcement changes the way a party *perceives* the observed behaviour of the counterparty; and (b) formal enforcement reduces the frequency, and thereby the number of observations, of the very behaviour that signals an intention to co-operate.[83]

Socio-relationalists have declined to engage in the crowding out debate. To be sure, these experimental results may not mirror real world interactions and so some scepticism may be justified. Nevertheless, the position of ignoring the question entirely, rather than seeking to test it further, smacks more of fundamentalism than of the scepticism of the dedicated empiricist.

C. The Peril of Relational Theory

An outsider to this debate might be forgiven for responding: 'So what?' It is hardly news that theorists quarrel. Indeed, in other disciplines, especially in the humanities where theory is rarely subject to empirical testing, fights among fundamentalists are legion. The problem here is that the divide is eroding the influence of the shared conception of contract as a

[79] See sources cited in nn 33–36 above.

[80] E Fehr and S Gachter, 'Do Incentive Contracts Crowd Out Voluntary Cooperation?' (2002) Institute for Empirical Research in Economics, University of Zurich Working Paper No 34 (available at ssrn.com/abstract=313028). A similar result is reported by D Houser and others, 'When Punishment Fails' (n 15).

[81] Houser and others, 'When Punishment Fails' (n 15) 21.

[82] Gilson, Sabel, and Scott, 'Braiding' (n 36).

[83] An extensive literature in social psychology also considers the crowding out of intrinsic motivations. See E Deci, R Koestner, and R Ryan, 'A Meta-Analytic Review of Experiments Examining the Effects of Extrinsic Rewards on Intrinsic Motivations' (1999) 125 *Psychological Bulletin* 627.

complex relationship that must be studied in all its dimensions. In short, to return to Macaulay's famous formulation, the very conception of 'law in action' is currently at risk.

The signs of a return to the study of discrete contract law and doctrine are everywhere. Few young scholars today have joined either of the relationalist camps. The dominant academic discipline among young contract scholars is analytic philosophy. This deontological approach requires a commitment to the analysis of 'pure' contract doctrine – and of the moral language courts use in deciding cases – from a Kantian perspective.[84] There is nothing pernicious in a commitment to autonomy values as the sole justification for the legal enforcement of contract. The problem is that the autonomy enterprise focuses solely on what the court says when it decides a contract case. This court-centred approach renders the study of relational contract irrelevant.

A similar turn to abstract concepts grounded in the technical skills of another discipline characterises the work of many of the young contract scholars working in the law and economics tradition. At its best, this scholarship is analytically elegant and generates counter-intuitive insights. But its analytical rigor requires strong simplifying assumptions in order to sustain tractable formal models. As a consequence, the bulk of this work is a far remove from the complex environment of relational contracting.[85]

Moreover, a careful review of the contracts listserv – a vantage point that provides the best window into the concerns of contract teachers across the US – reveals a continuing and, to a relationalist, distressing preoccupation with familiar cases as reported in judicial opinions and with correspondingly little concern for understanding the transaction between the parties and the context in which it arose. In short, if all relationalists believe in 'law in action', there is little evidence that it is a focus of either emerging scholarly trends or classroom experiences.

But there are some reasons to be hopeful. As I noted at the outset, there are two important papers by Macaulay that bear analysis. 'Non-Contractual Relations' is justly famous. It was the impetus for relational contract theory. But equally important for insights into how to escape our current dilemma is a paper Macaulay published 40 years later in 2003 (hereafter 'The Real

[84] For a representative sampling of this literature, see, eg Kraus, 'The Correspondence of Contract' (n 9); S Shiffrin, 'Divergence' (n 9); M Pratt, 'Contract: Not Promise' (2008) 35 *Florida State University Law Review* 801; D Kimel, *From Promise to Contract: Toward a Liberal Theory of Contract* (Oxford, Hart Publishing, 2003) 89; G Klass, 'Three Pictures of Contract: Duty, Power and Compound Rule' (2008) 83 *New York University Law Review* 1726.

[85] For a representative sampling of the best of this new law and economics of contract scholarship, see A Choi and G Triantis, 'Completing Contracts in the Shadow of Costly Verification' (2008) 37 *Journal of Legal Studies* 503; O Bar-Gill and L Bebchuk, 'Consent and Exchange' (2010) 39 *Journal of Legal Studies* 375; O Bar-Gill and OB Shahar, 'The Law of Duress and the Economics of Credible Threats' (2004) 33 *Journal of Legal Studies* 391; R Brooks and A Stremitzer, 'Remedies On and Off Contract' (2011) 120 *Yale Law Journal* 690.

and the Paper Deal').[86] In this article, Macaulay, the committed empiricist, carefully examined the claims of the economic relationalists with his customary generosity. Placing the socio-relationalist commitment to understanding the complexity of the 'real deal' beside the economic relationalist claim that too much law can be counterproductive, he asked the key question: Should courts be responsible for uncovering the 'real deal'? While Macaulay did not attempt to disguise his own views, he confronted the tradeoffs – between text and context, ex ante and ex post, formal and informal enforcement – head on. He concluded that the economic relationalists will be right in some cases and the socio-relationalists will be right in others.[87] Macaulay then offered an accommodation: choose the approach that best encourages settlements, which approach, he argued (somewhat tentatively), supports socio-relationalism in the courts.

This is not the conclusion I would reach, but that is not important. What is important is that 'The Real and the Paper Deal' challenges two assumptions that underlie the entire debate. The first is that contract law must be unitary. To the contrary, Macaulay states: 'In some situations, more formality and relatively clear default rules may be justified.'[88] One of those contexts is 'when parties are represented by lawyers, the document represents real negotiation and parties and lawyers worried at the outset about the consequences of failures of performance'.[89] Another context where clear rules rather than standards might be preferred is, paradoxically, in consumer transactions where 'clear rules might cut the costs of consumers seeking remedies'.[90] The important point here is that the rules for consumer transactions should be clear, but they would be *different rules.*

The second assumption challenged in 'The Real and the Paper Deal' is that the contract law rules that regulate both sophisticated business transactions and consumer transactions are best made by courts. But why? As noted above, Macneil's vision was quite different: He envisioned a regulatory regime, similar to that which governs union labour contracting, as the mechanism with the expertise to maintain continuing relations, protect against exploitation and preserve relational norms.[91] While 'The Real and the Paper Deal' does not embrace the notion of a regulatory regime for relational contracts, his description of the settlement induced by Judge Teitlebaum's decision in *Alcoa v Essex Group, Inc*[92] hints at just such a supervised administrative mechanism.[93]

[86] Macaulay, 'The Real and the Paper Deal' (n 3).
[87] Macaulay states: 'There will be costs and benefits flowing from focusing on the paper deal and from focusing on the real deal.' ibid 45.
[88] ibid 64.
[89] ibid.
[90] ibid.
[91] See text accompanying nn 56–58 above.
[92] *Alcoa v Essex Group, Inc*, 499 F Supp 53 (Pa App 1980).
[93] Macaulay, 'The Real and the Paper Deal' (n 3) 71–73.

In sum, if 'The Real and the Paper Deal' points the way, then any movement toward a unified theory of relational contract must provide space for both perspectives to function. That requires, at a minimum: (1) a contract law that applies different rules for different contexts; and (2) reliance on 'dispute-resolvers' other than generalist courts. In Part III, I offer some tentative thoughts about the contours of such a regime.

III. TOWARD A UNIFIED RELATIONAL CONTRACT THEORY

A. Different Rules for Different Contexts

The preceding discussion underscores the dilemma: So long as the common law rules of contract are regarded as background rules that apply to all contractual domains, and so long as courts continue to demand that the judicial process that implements these rules must govern all contract disputes, the clash of perspectives between economic relationalists and socio-relationalists will continue unabated.

Thus far, the battle between the two relationalist camps has resulted in something of a standoff. Textualism predominates in the common law of the large majority of jurisdictions, but contextualism rules both the *Uniform Commercial Code* as well the common law of several important commercial jurisdictions.[94] The effects of this conflict are felt in the confusion faced by transactional lawyers trying to design efficient contracts for sophisticated parties as well as in the risk that consumers or other disadvantaged parties may be barred from proving context evidence that rebuts false claims of contractual obligation.

This tension between what contracting parties actually do and how the courts frame doctrine calls out for a new, unified theory of relational contract – one that follows what the parties actually do and makes available to them both textual and contextual interpretive regimes, ex ante and ex post perspectives, and formal and informal enforcement mechanisms. In this Part, I outline a possible path toward unification and tailored contract law and adjudication to fit the very different questions that are raised when interpreting the many dimensions of relational contracts.

First, it is important to separate the question of how to regulate adhesion contracts – whether a particular contract is exploitative and, if so, what terms would be reasonable – from the regulation of commercial contracts between firms.[95] Consumer protection – the scrutiny of transactions in mass-market settings – is an important goal of public policy. But this

[94] See text accompanying nn 71–77 above.

[95] By 'adhesion contracts' I include all contract settings where the terms of the contract are not negotiated between the parties ex ante. These settings vary from pure consumer transactions to franchise relationships and the like.

goal is best achieved by regulation, market by market, of the fairness and efficiency of non-negotiated contract terms. Viewing the general questions of doctrine and scholarship of contract interpretation from the vantage point of the vulnerable consumer is at best a diversion, at worst the source of error and confusion. Consumer transactions, and the equitable issues they present, are better resolved within a regime separate from the contract rules that govern commercial parties. We need to debate whether a particular market adequately supports the fairness and efficiency of non-negotiated contract terms. But this is a debate over whether regulation is required, and what shape the regulation should take, not one over contract interpretation.

Second, a new theory governing relational contracts between commercial parties requires a reframing of the conflict between text and context and between the ex ante and ex post perspectives: The question is not whether a court can have recourse to context ex post, but *who decides* whether and when the court should have recourse to context. Framed this way, a unified theory would allocate to *those parties that the state believes are competent to exercise choice* the power to choose the mix of text and context. Then, a generalist court's role would simply be to follow the parties' instructions. Consider, for example, the choices open to parties in those jurisdictions that follow a hard parol evidence rule and the plain meaning rule, and thus exclude extrinsic evidence in resolving disputes. Sophisticated parties who prefer to have context evidence considered are not disadvantaged by this rule: these parties can (and do) determine the context within which any interpretive inquiry is conducted. They can embed within the formal contract directions for the context within which the contract should be interpreted. A variety of contract clauses perform this function. These include: (a) 'whereas' or 'purpose' clauses that describe the parties' business plan and the transaction;[96] (b) definition clauses that ascribe particular meanings to words and terms that may vary from their plain meaning;[97] and (c) appendices that provide more precise specifications governing performance as well as any memoranda the parties want an interpreting court to consider in interpreting the contract's text.[98] Alternatively, sophisticated parties can elect not to incorporate a merger clause into the agreement so that any and all context evidence will be admissible. Or, they can specify in

[96] See, eg the 'purpose' clause from the Fountain Manufacturing Agreement between Apple Computer, Inc and SCI Systems, Inc (available at contracts.onecle.com/apple/scis.mfg.1996.05.31.shtml).

[97] See, eg Data Management Outsourcing Agreement Between Allstate Insurance Company and Acxiom Corporation, Art 2. Definitions (defining 34 technical or non-standard meanings, including specialised meanings of 'Agreement', 'Confidential Information', 'Data Integrity', 'Current Projects', 'Affiliate', 'End User', 'Material Default', 'Party', 'Person', 'Problem', 'Term', 'Work Order', and 'Work Product') (available at contracts.onecle.com/acxiom/allstate.outsource.1999.03.19.shtml).

[98] See, eg 'Apple/SCI Manufacturing Agreement' (n 96).

the integrated agreement that the meaning of terms should be interpreted according to the customs and usages of the relevant trade or industry. Casual empiricism suggests that all of these strategies are pursued in one degree or another by commercial parties who write customised contracts in textualist jurisdictions. The point is not to exclude context, but to empower sophisticated parties to design their contracts to include text and context.

Contrast the flexibility provided to sophisticated commercial parties to combine text and context under this regime with the alternative of contract design under a pure contextualist regime. If contextualism is the only interpretive style, it necessarily disadvantages all those commercial parties who would have excluded self-guided judicial recourse to context, or would have instrumentally braided text and context as they – and not a reviewing court – thought most efficient. Since contextualist regimes do not allow the parties to limit the court's inquiry into context, the choice of what context matters (and how much) is left to a generalist court with no particular expertise in commercial matters generally, nor particular experience in the subject matter of the contract. At this point, Karl Llewellyn's purpose of coupling a contextualist interpretative regime with a merchant jury becomes much clearer. Although the parties in that regime cannot limit the inquiry into context, the risk of judicial mistake and strategic behaviour in litigation is mitigated by the experience and expertise of the merchant tribunal. By dropping the concept of a merchant jury from the *Uniform Commercial Code* (UCC), Llewellyn ended up with the worst of all possible worlds – mandatory recourse to context with a generalist court and with restrictions on the parties' ability to shape the scope of the inquiry.

The case for a unified theory of relational contract thus rests on the claim that contracting parties and contract relationships are heterogeneous and that different contexts and different parties will call for different approaches to ex ante regulation and ex post review whether by courts or by regulatory processes. That claim requires a framework that first shows how contract law might create a distinct regime for those parties deemed incapable of making autonomous choices about the form of their legal obligations. And, for those parties free to choose the mix of text and context to govern their relationship, the framework requires, in turn, a template showing how those choices are best made. In the following part, I sketch the outlines of such a framework.

B. A Framework for the Interpretation of Relational Contracts

i. A Regulatory Regime for Adhesion Contracts

I have argued above that it is a category mistake to treat the problem of exploitation in adhesion contracts as a question of contract interpretation.

The assumption that only a pure contextualist approach can protect the weak against the powerful underlies the deep resistance of many socio-relationalists to the argument that interpretive styles should be defaults and that sophisticated parties should be permitted to choose the mix of text and context that best achieves their goals. Despite calls by progressives for common law contract rules that equip generalist courts with the tools to police consumer transactions, such an evolution simply has not occurred. One reason, surely, is that courts are peculiarly ill-equipped to the task. In a forthcoming paper, my colleagues Ronald Gilson, Charles Sabel and I argue for a regulatory regime that can draw lines between those transactions in which parties are free to choose their interpretive styles and those where mandatory regulation of terms is required to insure fair treatment.[99]

The emerging regulatory regime in the European Union offers a first step in crafting a regulatory process that separates agreements deserving special scrutiny from contracts between sophisticated parties. To safeguard consumers and to assure the legal certainty on which commerce depends, the EU has chosen to detach contracts with consumers from the larger body of general contract law and to regulate it through several directives harmonising standards of consumer protection. The aim is to establish rules of commercial good conduct in settings in which consumers may be especially vulnerable to exploitation; to ban contract terms that serve only the interests of one party to the transaction; and to do this without affecting the contract law that generally governs agreements between commercial parties.

Thus, for example, the Directive on unfair terms in consumer contracts aims to 'facilitate the establishment of the internal market [and] also to ensure protection for individuals in their capacity as consumers when they purchase goods or services under a contract'.[100] An Annex to the Directive contains a blacklist of terms deemed unfair in all circumstances and a grey list of terms presumed to be unfair. In the same vein, the Doorstep Selling Directive addresses the element of surprise in contracts concluded away from the business premises of the trader, under circumstances where the consumer, not contemplating a purchase, may be caught off-guard.[101]

These two directives have recently been integrated into a Consumer Rights Directive, with the aim of full harmonisation of the legal rules

[99] The following discussion draws on R Gilson, C Sabel and R Scott, 'Text *and* Context: A Unified Theory of Contract Interpretation' (mimeo 2012).

[100] Council Directive 93/13/EEC of 5 April 1993 (available at eur-lex.europa.eu/LexUriServ/LexUriServ.do?uri=CELEX:31993L0013:EN:NOT); compare Opinion by AG Geelhoed, in Case C-478/ 99 *Commission v Sweden* (2002) ECR I-04147, para 23 (available at eur-lex.europa.eu/LexUriServ/LexUriServ.do?uri=CELEX:61999CJ0478:EN:HTML).

[101] Council Directive 85/577/EEC of 20 December 1985 (available at eur-lex.europa.eu/LexUriServ/LexUriServ.do?uri=CELEX:31985L0577:EN:HTML).

within its domain.[102] Harmonisation ensures that the governments of Member States may not impose rules less stringent than those in directives. Importantly, 'full harmonisation' also means that the states may not impose more demanding rules, thus preserving the separation established by the Directive between regulated and unregulated contracts. To take account of the evolution of unfair practices, the EU has established an updating mechanism: under Article 32 of the Directive, terms used in particular contracts that are perceived as potentially unfair by a court may be referred to a standing body of experts. This body decides whether the challenged term is to be added to the black or grey lists. This mechanism enlists courts in the task of updating the register of impermissible terms without empowering the judiciary to routinely question the express meaning of agreements in a way that undercuts party autonomy.

The national courts of the Member States thus play a quasi-administrative function – drawing the attention of the regulators to possibly unfair terms. In turn, the European Court of Justice acts as a judicial backstop, clarifying ambiguities in the protective framework. This preserves a role for a generalist court with regard to grey list items, but much of the tension inherent in a unitary regime of contract law is alleviated. The European Court of Justice acts as a backstop for the regime as a whole, intervening to ensure that national process rules do not undermine the effectiveness of the protective legislation, and that the statutory remedies are not themselves used strategically by vulnerable parties. The overall effect is to protect consumers, and by extension other vulnerable parties, without allowing the protection to unsettle the surrounding body of contract law.

ii. Interpreting Commercial Contracts between Sophisticated Parties

Freed from an overriding concern about exploitation of the weak by the strong, Gilson, Sabel and I turn to the complex question of how courts can best interpret the relational contracts of sophisticated parties. In this Part, I outline the factors that influence how commercial parties determine the mix of text and context that (they believe) courts should use in resolving any future disputes. The central element in this framework is the level of uncertainty associated with a particular obligation to be imposed under the contract: the balance between text and context in contract drafting reflects the impact of uncertainty on the tradeoff between the ex ante (or front end) and the ex post (or back end) costs of contracting.

In terms of the tradeoff between ex ante and ex post contracting costs, the use of a vague standard as opposed to a precise rule necessarily increases ex post contracting costs. It is tempting to suggest, therefore,

[102] Council Directive 2011/83/EU of 25 October 2011 (available at eur-lex.europa.eu/LexUriServ/LexUriServ.do?uri=OJ:L:2011:304:0064:0088:EN:PDF).

that sophisticated parties will always invest ex ante contracting costs in formulating precise terms. But standards also have special utility. Courts assess performance with respect to standards only after the relevant future events have occurred. Thus parties can obtain the advantage of hindsight: at the time for dispute resolution, the court has information that at the time of drafting the contract the parties lacked. In this way, parties can choose their mix of rules and standards to optimise the admissibility of context evidence over two dimensions – *when* the court will look to context and *who* decides what context matters. The choice of who will decide these questions is between the parties at the time of the contract and the court at the later time of litigation. The parties have the comparative advantage at the time of contracting since they share in the benefits of efficient contracting, but the court will have the benefit of hindsight at the time of dispute resolution. The parties can't foresee all contingencies so they can delegate to the court the task of completing the contract ex post by considering relevant context and they can indicate this intention by adopting a general contract term or standard. The standard directs the court to limit its efforts to recovering only that context evidence relevant to the particular obligation embedded in the standard.

a. Low Uncertainty – The Discrete Contract Setting

The driving force in how sophisticated parties choose among different combinations of text and context (or rules and standards) is the impact of uncertainty on this tradeoff between the ex ante and ex post costs of contracting. At low levels of uncertainty – the discrete contract setting, in Macneil's terminology – commercial parties will expend front-end costs in drafting (relatively) complete contracts and will exclude ex post judicial resort to context. In this setting, any gains from adopting vague standards for courts to apply with the benefit of hindsight are outweighed by the increase in litigation costs and the moral hazard risk that such standards create.

That the need for context reduces as uncertainty dissipates helps explain a puzzling pattern in the managerial literature on contracting. As we learned from 'Non-Contractual Relations', reliance on informal enforcement is generally framed as an alternative to formal contract The insight is that learning about a counterparty allows one to go forward in the face of uncertainty based on trust, whether from the expectation of reciprocity or the accumulation of information about the counterparty's character.[103] Thus, rather than relying on formal contractual obligations, contracts can be much less complete since the parties will have the correct incentives to fairly respond to unanticipated changes when they occur.

[103] Gilson, Sabel, and Scott, 'Braiding' (n 36) 1392–95.

On this account, contractual formality and the complexity of the formal contract's terms should *reduce* with experience – learned trust can substitute for detailed drafting as experience grows. The puzzle, however, is that there is empirical evidence that the pattern is exactly the opposite: as experience grows, contracts become more complex rather than less.[104] This phenomenon reflects a reduction in uncertainty both about the subject of the repeated contracts and the counterparty. Experience substitutes for prediction as a means of identifying the relevant contingencies going forward. The result is that formal contracts can become more complete with less need to rely on standards and context to inform dispute resolution. In repeated contracting, therefore, contractual completeness becomes part of an endogenous process: repetition results in a learning process that reduces uncertainty and formal contracts become more complete going forward.

b. Increasing Uncertainty – The Relational Context

The level of uncertainty increases, however, when parties are able to specify their goals but not the steps to be taken to achieve those goals, nor the accommodations that would be required by a change in the commercial environment. Here, resort to standards becomes compelling. For example, contracts may state one party's performance obligation as to make 'commercially reasonable efforts', 'reasonable efforts', or 'reasonable best efforts'.[105] Indeed, commercial contracts often include combinations of both precise rules and general standards, and courts actively interpret and enforce such standards by reference to context evidence. By crafting the reference to context in a fashion that focuses the court's inquiry, whether through the substance of the contract or the clarity of the relevant industry, the parties can capture the benefit of judicial gap filling but with limits on the cost of litigation and the inducement to moral hazard.

The combination of general standards and precise rules, therefore, offers sophisticated contracting parties the ability to braid the text with context evidence that is revealed over the course of contract performance.[106] The

[104] See K Mayer and N Argyres, 'Learning to Contract: Evidence from the Personal Computer Industry' (2004) 15 *Organization Science* 394 (contracts are more complete or detailed when firms have prior alliances, whether with the same firm or other firms); N Argyres, J Berkovits, and K Mayer, 'Complementarity and Evolution of Contractual Provisions: An Empirical Study of IT Service Contracts' (2007) 18 *Organization Science* 3.

[105] See University of Missouri: Contracting & Organizations Research Institute (CORI), *The CORI K-Base*, cori.missouri.edu/pages/ksearch.htm (As of 2010 – Total contracts in CORI database: 24,965. Contracts with 'best efforts' terms: 4,328 (17.34%); contracts with 'reasonable expenses' terms: 2,584 (10.35%); contracts with 'reasonably withheld' terms: 38 (0.0015%); contracts with 'unreasonably withheld' terms: 3,525 (14.12%); contracts with 'reasonable' terms: 13,281 (53.20%).

[106] The options available to the parties are even broader than the stark choice between a rule and a standard. For discussion, see Scott and Triantis, 'Anticipating Litigation' (n 73).

more effectively context can be harnessed to resolve uncertainty in the judicial application of contractual standards, the more attractive the use of standards that take advantage of the court's better information as compared to contractually specified rules that reduce back end costs but at the cost of directing the wrong outcome.

When and to what extent parties will resort to standards depends on a particular form of uncertainty – how effectively context can be used to reduce the risk that a court will misunderstand or misapply the standard. This will depend in the first instance on the subject matter of the contract and the industry, and on the surrounding circumstances. At one end of a continuum, if the subject matter, industry and surrounding circumstances are themselves clear enough to narrow the relevant context for a reviewing court, little more need be done through drafting beyond a reference to 'commercial reasonableness'. Alternatively, at the drafting stage the parties can specify the context that will be relevant – what industry, what kind of products and, when possible, even the relevant proxy the court should use to measure performance under the standard.

The judgment about the extent to which directions to the court concerning the relevant context are incorporated into the formal contract will be heavily influenced by the thickness of the market for the product or service covered by the contract. Where there are a large number of parties engaged in the same type of transaction – when there is 'scale' to the particular commercial activity – parties collectively are able to produce designations of context such as trade association norms, industry codes and form contracts.[107] These efforts endogenise the relevant context and therefore save both front-end drafting and back-end litigation costs and, critically, reduce the likelihood of interpretative error by the courts

In commercial transactions that lack the scale to support collectively created forms and standards, individual contracting parties must choose for themselves the combination of precise terms (taking into account the risk that their specifications will turn out to be wrong ex post) and standards (taking into account the likelihood of judicial error) that optimises total contracting costs. They do this by weighing the cost of agreeing to specifications that might prove erroneous against the cost of drafting a standard that sufficiently captures the benefit of ex post information without incurring too large a risk of judicial error and moral hazard.

[107] As an example of the point in text, the recent past has seen a marked standardisation of industry-specific contract terms. Standardisation has been stimulated in construction contracting, for example, through the offices of key intermediaries such as the American Institute of Architects and the Associated General Contractors. See American Institute of Architects, 'General Conditions of the Contract for Construction' (Doc Nos A101/CM, A201/CM, B141/CM, B801); Associated General Contractors, Standard Form of Agreement Between Owner and Construction Manager, Doc Nos 8a (1977), 8d (1979), 8 (1980), 520 (1980).

c. High Uncertainty – The Example of Collaborative Contracting

As uncertainty becomes pervasive (perhaps owing to technological changes such as the information revolution or globalisation), parties can no longer allocate risks in the normal way. This problem is exemplified by the problem of 'contracting for innovation'.[108] Here, parties are contracting over the creation of something of which the features, and the contributions of each of the parties, are unknowable and will emerge only after many iterations. Moreover, this uncertainty will not be resolved; rather, it is continuous; the product will continue to evolve and new elements of uncertainty will arise as it does so.

When uncertainty is high and continuous, the parties cannot trade off between ex ante and ex post contracting costs. No stable ex post period arises in which standards and resort to context can be used to fill in the uncertainty-driven gaps in an incomplete formal contract. The contracting problem then is to craft a structure which is neither discrete nor standard-based and that (a) induces efficient, transaction-specific investment by both parties; (b) establishes a framework for iterative collaboration and adjustment of the parties' obligations under conditions of *continuing* uncertainty; and (c) limits the risk of opportunism that could undermine the incentive to make relation-specific investments in the first place.[109]

The common challenges facing parties contracting for innovation give rise to solutions with common elements. This common solution is a contract structure that *braids* formal and informal elements in a fashion that is neither discrete nor relational. In general, the formal contract is process rather than outcome oriented; it defines a process of collaboration that substitutes for the ex ante specification of the desired product that high uncertainty renders impossible. Thus, unlike contracting in low or moderate uncertainty environments, the process defines the specification, not the other way around. In each case, the parties make relation-specific investments in learning about their collaborator's capabilities that raise the costs of switching to new partners, and so restrain either party from taking advantage of their mutual dependency. The formal element of a braided contract is thus sharply and distinctively limited in what it aims to accomplish. It supports both parties' efforts to learn about each other's skills and capabilities for collaborative innovation and to develop jointly the routines necessary to working together. The formal contract does not, however, commit either party to develop, supply or purchase any product. That commitment emerges from the informal contract, where the barrier to ex post opportunism results not from the formal enforcement of obligations created by explicit contract, but from increased switching costs generated by the collaboration process itself.

[108] Gilson, Sabel, and Scott, 'Contracting for Innovation' (n 67).
[109] ibid.

The result is a contractual structure in which, despite the high uncertainty, there is no role for context in contract interpretation. The uncertainty exists with respect to whether a product in the end will be developed, whether actual sales will result, and how the parties will continue to interact in the future. But because the uncertainty concerning these matters is so high and continuous, standards informed by context are ineffective. Rather, by building switching costs through process-based learning, and then relying on informal contracting for substance, the parties endogenise context. Put differently, in the face of high and continuous uncertainty, context is too important to allocate to the courts: the parties create their own context through a contractually specified process.

CONCLUSION

Stewart Macaulay's remarkable scholarly career spans the entire period in which relational contract theory has flourished. Although he has long identified himself principally as an empiricist rather than a theorist, his foundational paper in 1963 laid the groundwork for the some of the most important private law scholarship of the past 50 years. Looking back in 2003 on what he had started 40 years earlier, Macaulay offered the promise of an accommodation between the diverse strands of relational theory that developed in the intervening years. I have argued that this accommodation might serve to free the relational enterprise from its current peril: Those who believe that contract law scholarship requires attention to the 'law in action' must concentrate their energies on developing unifying themes that will permit the relational project to be as vibrant and influential in this new century as it has been in the last one. In this chapter, I have offered a proposal, developed in connection with my on-going collaboration with Ronald Gilson and Charles Sabel, that looks to just such a unification. What we need now are the voices of other 'perfectionists', like Macaulay, who will continue to examine the complex environment of contracting and propose legal principles that best maintain and support the ideal of human engagement through co-operative endeavour.

BIBLIOGRAPHY

Argyres, N, Berkovits, J, and Mayer, K, 'Complementarity and Evolution of Contractual Provisions: An Empirical Study of IT Service Contracts' (2007) 18 *Organization Science* 3.

Bar-Gill, O and Bebchuk, L, 'Consent and Exchange' (2010) 39 *Journal of Legal Studies* 375.

Bar-Gill, O and Shahar, OB, 'The Law of Duress and the Economics of Credible Threats' (2004) 33 *Journal of Legal Studies* 391.

Bernstein, L, 'Private Commercial Law in the Cotton Industry: Creating Cooperation Through Rules, Norms, and Institutions' (2001) 99 *Michigan Law Review* 1724.

——, 'Merchant Law in a Merchant Court: Rethinking the Code's Search for Immanent Business Norms' (1996) 144 *University of Pennsylvania Law Review* 1765.

Bohnet, I, Frey, B, and Huck, S, 'More Order with Less Law: On Contract Enforcement, Trust and Crowding' (2001) 95 *American Political Science Review* 131.

Braucher, J, 'Politics and Principle in the Drafting of UCC Consumer Protection Provisions' (1996) 29 *Uniform Commercial Code Law Journal* 68.

——, 'Defining Unfairness: Empathy and Economic Analysis at the Federal Trade Commission' (1988) 68 *Boston University Law Review* 349.

——, 'An Informal Resolution Model of Consumer Product Warranty Law' (1985) 1985 *Wisconsin Law Review* 1405.

Brooks, R and Stremitzer, A, 'Remedies On and Off Contract' (2011) 120 *Yale Law Journal* 690.

Case, MA, 'Perfectionism and Fundamentalism in the Application of the German Abortion Laws' in S Williams (ed), *Constituting Equality: Gender Equality and Comparative Constitutional Law* (Cambridge, Cambridge University Press, 2009).

Charny, D, 'Non-Legal Sanctions in Commercial Relationships' (1990) 104 *Harvard Law Review* 373.

Choi, A and Triantis, G, 'Completing Contracts in the Shadow of Costly Verification' (2008) 37 *Journal of Legal Studies* 503.

Council Directive 2011/83/EU of 25 October 2011.

Council Directive 93/13/EEC of 5 April 1993.

Council Directive 85/577/EEC of 20 December 1985.

Deci, E, Koestner, R, and Ryan, R, 'A Meta-Analytic Review of Experiments Examining the Effects of Extrinsic Rewards on Intrinsic Motivations' (1999) 125 *Psychological Bulletin* 627.

Dilts, D, 'Of Words and Contracts: Arbitration and Lexicology' (May–July 2005) *Dispute Resolution Journal* 40.

Fehr, E and Gachter, S, 'Do Incentive Contracts Crowd Out Voluntary Cooperation?' (2002) Institute for Empirical Research in Economics, University of Zurich Working Paper No 34.

Fehr, E and Schmidt, K, 'Theories of Fairness and Reciprocity – Evidence and Economic Applications' (2001) Institute for Empirical Research in Economics - University of Zurich Working Paper No 75, 2–3.

Fehr, E, Gachter, S, and Kirchsteiger, G, 'Reciprocity as a Contract Enforcement Device: Experimental Evidence' (1997) 65 *Econometrica* 833.

Frank, R, *Passions Within Reasons: The Strategic Role of the Emotions* (New York, Norton, 1988).

Geelhoed, AG, Opinion in Case C-478/ 99 *Commission v Sweden* (2002) ECR I-04147, para 23.

Gilson, R, Sabel, C, and Scott, R, 'Braiding: The Interaction of Formal and Informal Contracting in Theory, Practice, and Doctrine' (2010) 110 *Columbia Law Review* 1377.

——, 'Contracting for Innovation: Vertical Disintegration and Interfirm Collaboration' (2009) 109 *Columbia Law Review* 431.

Goetz, C and Scott, R, 'The Mitigation Principle: Toward a General Theory of Contractual Obligation' (1983) 69 *Virginia Law Review* 967.
——, 'Principles of Relational Contracts' (1981) 67 *Virginia Law Review* 1089.
Goldberg, V, 'Relational Exchange: Economic and Complex Contracts' (1980) 23 *American Behavioral Scientist* 337.
——, 'The Law and Economics of Vertical Restrictions: A Relational Perspective' (1979) 58 *Texas Law Review* 91.
——, 'Regulation and Administered Contracts' (1976) 7 *Bell Journal of Economics* 426.
Hillman, R, 'Court Adjustment of Long-Term Contracts: An Analysis Under Modern Contract Law' (1987) *Duke Law Journal* 1.
Houser, D and others, 'When Punishment Fails: Research on Sanctions, Intentions and Non-Cooperation' (2008) 62 *Games and Economic Behavior* 509.
Kahneman, D, Slovic, P, and Tversky, A, (eds), *Judgment Under Uncertainty: Heuristics and Biases* (Cambridge, Cambridge University Press, 1982).
Kimel, D, *From Promise to Contract: Toward a Liberal Theory of Contract* (Oxford, Hart Publishing, 2003).
Klass, G, 'Three Pictures of Contract: Duty, Power and Compound Rule' (2008) 83 *New York University Law Review* 1726.
Kraus, J, 'The Correspondence of Contract and Promise' (2009) 109 *Columbia Law Review* 1603.
Lazzarini, S, Miller, G, and Zenger, T, 'Order with Some Law: Complementarity versus Substitution of Formal and Informal Arrangements' (2004) 20 *Journal of Law, Economics, and Organization* 261.
Leib, E, 'Contracts and Friendship' (2010) 59 *Emory Law Journal* 649.
LoPucki, L, 'The Unsecured Creditors Bargain' (1994) 80 *Virginia Law Review* 1887.
Macaulay, S, 'Freedom from Contract: Solutions in Search of a Problem?' (2004) 2004 *Wisconsin Law Review* 777.
——, 'The Real and the Paper Deal: Empirical Pictures of Relationships, Complexity and the Urge for Transparent Simple Rules' (2003) 66 *Modern Law Review* 44.
——, 'Relational Contracts Floating on a Sea of Custom? Thoughts About the Ideas of Ian Macneil and Lisa Bernstein' (2000) 94 *Northwestern University Law Review* 775.
——, 'An Empirical View of Contract' (1985) 1985 *Wisconsin Law Review* 465.
——, 'Lawyers and Consumer Protection Laws: An Empirical Study' (1979) 14 *Law & Society Review* 115.
——, 'Private Legislation and the Duty to Read – Business Run by IBM Machine, the Law of Contracts and Credit Cards' (1966) 19 *Vanderbilt Law Review* 1051.
——, 'Changing a Continuing Relationship Between a Large Corporation and Those who Deal with It: Automobile Manufacturers, Their Dealers, and the Legal System, Law and Society' (1965) 1965 Fall *Wisconsin Law Review* 740.
——, 'Non-Contractual Relations in Business: A Preliminary Study' (1963) 28 *American Sociological Review* 55.
Macneil, I, 'Relational Contract Theory: Challenges and Queries' (2000) 94 *Northwestern University Law Review* 877.
——, 'Values in Contract: Internal and External' (1983) 78 *Northwestern University Law Review* 340.

Macneil, I, 'Economic Analysis of Contractual Relations: Its Shortfall and the Need for a "Rich Classificatory Apparatus"' (1981) 75 *Northwestern University Law Review* 1018.
——, *The New Social Contract* (New Haven, Yale University Press, 1980).
Macneil, I, 'Contracts: Adjustment of Long-Term Economic Relations Under Classical, Neoclassical, and Relational Contract Law' (1978) 72 *Northwestern University Law Review* 85.
——, 'The Many Futures of Contracts' (1974) 47 *Southern California Law Review* 1018.
——, 'Restatement (Second) of Contracts and Presentation' (1974) 60 *Virginia Law Review* 589.
Mayer, K and Argyres, N, 'Learning to Contract: Evidence from the Personal Computer Industry' (2004) 15 *Organization Science* 394.
Miller, G, 'Bargaining on the Red-Eye: New Light on Contract Theory' (2008) NYU Law & Economics. Working Papers, No 131.
Pratt, M, 'Contract: Not Promise' (2008) 35 *Florida State University Law Review* 801.
Palay, T, 'A Contract Does not a Contract Make' (1985) 1985 *Wisconsin Law Review* 561.
Rigdon, M, 'Trust and Reciprocity in Incentive Contracting' (2009) 70 *Journal of Economic Behavior and Organization* 93.
Scott, R, '*Hoffman v. Red Owl Stores* and the Limits of the Legal Method' (2010) 61 *Hastings Law Journal* 859.
Scott, R and Triantis, G, 'Anticipating Litigation in Contract Design' (2006) 115 *Yale Law Journal* 814.
Scott, R and Stephan, P, *The Limits of Leviathan: Contract Theory and the Enforcement of International Law* (Cambridge, Cambridge University Press, 2006).
Scott, R, 'A Theory of Self-Enforcing Indefinite Agreements' (2003) 103 *Columbia Law Review* 1641.
——, 'The Limits of Behavioral Theories of Law and Social Norms' (2000) 86 *Virginia Law Review* 1603.
——, 'Chaos Theory and the Justice Paradox' (1993) 35 *William and Mary Law Review* 329.
Schwartz, A, 'Law and Economics Next?' (2011) 105 *Illinois Law Review* 1531.
Schwartz, A and Scott, R, 'Contract Interpretation Redux' (2010) 119 *Yale Law Journal* 926.
——, 'Contract Theory and the Limits of Contract Law' (2003) 113 *Yale Law Journal* 541.
Shapiro, F, 'The Most-Cited Law Review Articles Revisited' (1996) 71 *Chicago-Kent Law Review* 751.
Shiffrin, S, 'The Divergence of Contract and Promise' (2007) 120 *Harvard Law Review* 708.
Speidel, R, 'The Characteristics and Challenges of Relational Contracts' (2000) 94 *Northwestern University Law Review* 823.
——, 'Court-Imposed Price Adjustments Under Long-Term Supply Contracts' (1983) 76 *Northwestern University Law Review* 369.
——, 'The New Spirit of Contract' (1982) 2 *Journal of Law and Commerce* 193.
Sullivan, T, Warren, E, and Westbrook, J, *As We Forgive Our Debtors: Consumer Credit and Bankruptcy in America* (Oxford, Oxford University Press, 1989).

Tomaszewski, J, 'The Pandora's Box of Cyberspace: State Regulation of Digital Signatures and the Dormant Commerce Clause' (1997–98) 33 *Gonzaga Law Review* 417.

Trakman, L, 'Winner Take Some: Loss Sharing and Commercial Impracticability' (1985) 69 *Minnesota Law Review* 471.

University of Missouri: Contracting & Organizations Research Institute (CORI), *The CORI K-Base*.

Warren, E and Bar-Gill, O, 'Making Credit Safer' (2008) 157 *University of Pennsylvania Law Review* 1.

Warren, E, 'Making Policy with Imperfect Information: The Article 9 Full Priority Debates' (1998) 82 *Cornell Law Review* 101.

——, 'A Principled Approach to Consumer Bankruptcy' (1997) 71 *American Bankruptcy Law Journal* 483.

Whitford, W, 'Relational Contracts and the New Formalism' (2004) *Wisconsin Law Review* 631.

——, 'Consumer Protection in Consumer Bankruptcy' (1994) 68 *American Bankruptcy Law Journal* 397.

——, 'The Appropriate Role of Security Interests in Consumer Transactions' (1986) 7 *Cardozo Law Review* 959.

——, 'Ian Macneil's Contribution to Contracts Scholarship' (1985) *Wisconsin Law Review* 545.

——, 'Structuring Consumer Protection Legislation to Maximize Effectiveness' (1981) *Wisconsin Law Review* 1018.

—— 'A Critique of the Consumer Credit Collection System' (1979) *Wisconsin Law Review* 1047.

——, 'Law and the Consumer Transaction: A Case Study of the Automobile Warranty' (1968) 1968 *Wisconsin Law Review* 1006.

Williamson, O, *The Economic Institutions of Capitalism* (New York, Free Press, 1985).

——, 'Transaction Costs Economics: The Governance of Contractual Relations' (1978) 22 *Journal of Law and Economics* 223.

——, *Markets and Hierarchies: Analysis and Antitrust Implications* (New York, Free Press, 1975).

4

Ambition and Humility in Contract Law

JAY M FEINMAN

INTRODUCTION

WHAT ARE THE aims of contract law? How can it achieve those aims? How well does it achieve them?

There are, of course, many ways of thinking about contract law that approach those questions. There are various approaches embodied in high-level scholarship. There are the stories told by contracting parties that are often at a considerable remove from the stated law. But in the law school classroom and mainstream judicial opinions, there is a familiar story about contract law that answers these questions. In this account, contract law aims primarily to support the free market by providing security of transaction for private parties. It does so through a relatively coherent doctrinal system that includes rules, principles, precedents, and policies. Courts are the primary authors and interpreters of this system, with substantial assists from time to time from legislatures and scholars, and they apply the system in the adjudication of disputes. The doctrine shapes the conduct of private actors, as they attend to it to some degree in planning transactions and to an even greater degree when disputes arise. The formulation and application of rules and parties' attention to them is never costless, frictionless, nor fully effective, but for the most part, contract law and the portion of the world it regulates operates in this way.

In a series of articles in the 1960s, Stewart Macaulay addressed these questions in a systematic way.[1] The articles developed an organisation of

[1] S Macaulay, 'Restitution in Context' (1959) 107 *University of Pennsylvania Law Review* 1133; S Macaulay, 'Justice Traynor and the Law of Contracts' (1961) 13 *Stanford Law Review* 812; S Macaulay, 'Private Legislation and the Duty to Read – Business Run by IBM Machine, The Law of Contracts and Credit Cards' (1966) 19 *Vanderbilt Law Review* 1051. See also J Hetherington, 'Trends in Enterprise Liability: Law and the Unauthorized Agent' (1966) 19 *Stanford Law Review* 76, cited in Macaulay, 'Private Legislation' (ibid) 1056 fn 18.

Some four decades later, in an article celebrating his former colleague William Klein, Macaulay explained the origins of his system and provided further explication with a different the fundamental policies underlying contract law, the structures through which contract law acts, and some policies of the legal system that influence the fundamental and structural policies. The organisation provided a system for analysing contract law decisions and regulations according to the aims they served and the means by which they served them. Macaulay applied the system to a variety of topics including developed accounts of the duty-to-read rule and the contracts jurisprudence of Justice Traynor and less-developed suggestions about other issues.

Macaulay's organisation is important because it occupies a central place in the construction and critique of the familiar story about contract law. Not central in the sense that the organisation has been frequently cited; unfortunately although the articles have garnered their share of citations, Macaulay's organisation has not. But central in the sense that the analysis is situated intellectually, and to an extent chronologically, in the middle of that construction and critique. Its origins lie in the social theory of Max Weber and the later Realist jurisprudence of Friedrich Kessler and Malcolm Sharp. The organisation's themes reflect the work of other of Macaulay's colleagues, including notably J Willard Hurst, Lawrence Friedman, Marc Galanter and William Whitford, and those themes resonate through what I have suggested elsewhere might be the Interstate 90 school of contracts scholarship, linking Macaulay at Wisconsin with Ian Macneil and Richard Speidel at Northwestern.[2] It also contributed to critical legal studies' account of private law through its influence on Duncan Kennedy's *Form and Substance In Private Law Adjudication*[3] and other works. Indeed, Macaulay's different attempts at the organisation illustrate these shifts in contract thinking; the early 1960s articles read as an effort to deepen the mainstream story and to ground it in better analysis, while his 2005 account of it emphasises tension and contradiction, reflecting decades of attacks on that story.

This chapter restates Macaulay's organisation, at points expands it, and considers its implications for our understanding of contract law. From a mainstream perspective, the organisation reaffirms that contract law has grand ambitions but must operate with a dash of humility. From perspectives outside the mainstream, it presents a view of contract law that is deeply problematic.

emphasis. S Macaulay, 'Klein and the Contradictions of Corporations Law' (2005) 2 *Berkeley Business Law Journal* 119.

[2] J Feinman, 'The Insurance Relationship as Relational Contract and the "Fairly Debatable" Rule for First-Party Bad Faith' (2009) 46 *San Diego Law Review* 553.

[3] D Kennedy, 'Form and Substance in Private Law Adjudication' (1976) 89 *Harvard Law Review* 1685.

I. MACAULAY'S ORGANISATION

Macaulay presented his organisation of contract and legal system policies in slightly different ways in different articles. In its most developed form, the organisation separates the substantive policies that contract law serves from an admittedly incomplete list of 'goals related to the proper or efficient operation of the legal system'.[4] The substantive policies are primary; the legal system policies operate mostly as limitations on the application of the substantive policies.

The substantive contract policies are of two kinds. The first kind concerns the objectives to be served – whether the law aims to support the private market or to correct market imperfections and serve non-market goals. The second kind of policy is not actually substantive in the same way as the first; it concerns the type of strategy or structure used by the legal system to serve those objectives – whether the courts apply general rules or use a case-by-case approach.[5]

Combining the two types of policies yields a two-by-two matrix with four resulting policy approaches.[6]

	Market goals	**Other than market goals**
Generalising approach ('rules')	market-functioning policy	social (or economic) planning policy
Particularising approach ('case-by-case')	transactional policy	relief-of-hardship policy

Macaulay's organisation of contract policies is in the first instance descriptive. He notes: 'It serves to clarify issues and separates distinct arguments so that they reinforce each other rather than confuse matters. The classification also serves as a checklist to lessen the chance that a relevant argument will be neglected.'[7] But he also used it as a tool of evaluation, concluding, for example, that '[n]one of [Justice Traynor's] transactionally oriented opinions appears to be clearly wrongly decided'.[8]

The realisation of the substantive policies is affected by a set of legal system policies. The threat of pressure on the docket cautions courts against creating rules or precedents that will create a flood of litigation; more cases consume more social resources and, given that adequate social resources are not likely to be forthcoming for the courts, they create delay,

[4] Macaulay, 'Private Legislation' (n 1) 1056.
[5] Macaulay, 'Justice Traynor' (n 1) 813.
[6] Macaulay, 'Private Legislation' (n 1) 1057.
[7] ibid 1064–65.
[8] Macaulay, 'Justice Traynor' (n 1) 862.

which diminishes the value of rights to the extent that parties cannot incur the costs of delay. The need for accurate fact-finding cautions courts about creating rules that present issues difficult of proof, either because of complexity or because of the possibility of perjury – or, less pejoratively, differing recollections as the sole basis of proof. Obeisance to democratic ideals cautions judges about the gap between courts and legislatures and warns about the appropriateness of judges deciding which social values should be effectuated through contract law.[9]

'Efficiency and efficacy' may be the most important of the legal system policies. It raises the question that has permeated much of Macaulay's career: What can be done by the law and at what cost? This operates at two stages. The first relates to the inputs required by the different policies. Case-by-case adjudication 'increases the demands on the fact-finding process'.[10] In addition, different substantive policies place different demands. For example, the transactional policy, designed to effectuate the parties' actual agreement, requires examination of contracting parties' expectations, implicit assumptions and understandings, information that is not easily obtained. The second relates to the outputs; case-by-case adjudication has less impact on parties' planning going forward, but it increases their uncertainty. Rule-based adjudication, on the other hand, at least increases the opportunity for certainty and therefore bargaining with respect to legal rights. If the goal is social planning, however, the court is hampered by the accidental nature of cases brought before it, its limited capacity for fact-finding, and, over the long term, its limited ability to assess the consequences of its decisions.

II. AMBITION

In both its descriptive and normative aspects, Macaulay's structure begins by stating the ambition of contract law as expressing a primary goal of framing the legal structure of the market. 'Our society has strong commitments to freedom in economic affairs and to allocation of resources by the market institution. Contract law, it seems generally agreed, is and ought to be primarily designed to support the market institution.'[11] Contract law provides 'tools to facilitate the operation of a market economy-focusing on the needs of those exchanging goods, services, labor and capital'.[12]

[9] Although Macaulay does not make the point, this would seem to apply to market values as well as non-market values.

[10] Macaulay, 'Private Legislation' (n 1) 1066.

[11] Macaulay, 'Justice Traynor' (n 1) 857.

[12] Macaulay, 'Private Legislation' (n 1) 1057. Contract law supports 'the network of private, unregulated transactions which form[s] the basis of the economic system'. L Friedman, *Contract Law in America: A Social and Economic Case Study* (Madison, University of Wisconsin Press, 1965) 184.

This is familiar stuff. The footnotes establish our society's long-standing commitment to the market as the primary institution of economic welfare, including citations to Hayek, Knight, Hurst and others. Contract law hornbooks and casebooks echo and expand the same commitment.[13] The market requires legal structures, first in the law of property and elsewhere to create exchangeable value and then in the law of contract to facilitate and enforce exchanges of values, particularly in executory contracts.

Macaulay describes two strategies for achieving contract law's support of the market: the application of general rules and a case-by-case approach. (Of course, there are not only two strategies but many, arrayed along a spectrum of which the pure rules or case-by-case approaches are the endpoints.)

Implementation of the market goal through rules produces the market-functioning policy. The ideal is 'rules of general application in relatively specific terms which minimise (but never eliminate) the creative role of judge and jury or administrators'.[14]

The primary advantage of rules is certainty: 'Rules allow a bargainer to take steps to reach the results he desires . . . One is given guidance on when he may back out and when he must perform, and on what he must do, and when, as well.'[15] Rules also have consequences that are not as clearly advantageous in promoting welfare through the market, but can be seen as more or less so, depending on one's perspective. Rules reward those market actors who, being aware of the rules, plan their relationships, rationally assess risks, and are otherwise careful. Viewed positively, this is how the market should work, through rational calculation. Viewed less positively, it gives 'rewards to the crafty'.[16]

> In one view, those who can drive the best bargains, short of gross fraud, are entitled to their winnings . . . This is just good salesmanship. In this view, a bargain is not an exchange of mutual advantage but a game where each party is to maximise his own gains at the expense of the other.[17]

The certainty provided by rules also is advantageous to the operation of bureaucratic organisations. In an economy increasingly dominated by large economic organisations, the ability to plan and the certainty that the

[13] 'The law of contracts is our society's legal mechanism for protecting the expectations that arise from the making of agreements for the future exchange of various types of performance, such as the conveyance of property (tangible and intangible), the performance of services, and the payment of money.' C Knapp, N Crystal, and H Prince, *Problems in Contract Law: Cases and Materials*, 6th edn (New York, Aspen, 2007) 3. 'The economic importance of promise making and promise keeping can hardly be exaggerated . . . The facilitation of economic exchange is a basic policy of commercial law in general and contract law in particular.' I Ayres and R Speidel, *Studies in Contract Law*, 7th edn (New York, Foundation Press, 2008) 3–4.

[14] Macaulay, 'Private Legislation' (n 1) 1057.

[15] Macaulay, 'Justice Traynor' (n 1) 861.

[16] Macaulay, 'Private Legislation' (n 1) 1058.

[17] ibid.

organisation's planning will be effectuated are crucial. Large organisations increase the general economic welfare by producing efficiently. To do so, they require certainty along several dimensions. One important dimension is what contracts teachers sometimes refer to as the 'Lukowitz problem', after the excessively eager franchise salesman in *Hoffman v Red Owl Stores, Inc.*[18] Organisations can only act through their agents, but the agents' goals and actions may imperfectly align with that of the organisation. The written contract that the organisation's customer signs becomes a vehicle of certainty in the face of aggressive or inconsistent statements or promises by the agent. Another dimension is the contract as an internal communication device for the organisation, specifying to all participants the rights and obligations of the organisation.[19]

The second strategy for furthering the market-favouring policy of contract law rejects rules in favour of a case-by-case approach. As a general matter, one might favour a case-by-case approach as a means of best furthering goals in every case. As the example of *Hoffman v Red Owl Stores, Inc* suggests, rules have their costs, the most significant of which is that '[a] rule which leads to good results in many cases may lead to a very poor one in a particular instance'.[20] A poor result would occur if the rule, favouring generality over specificity, fails to account for divergent facts, or if the purpose of the rule or even other purposes cannot be adequately accounted for in the rule. Accordingly, '[a]ny system of flat rules must be tempered by the power to deal with particular cases'.[21]

The application of a case-by-case approach in the transactional policy rests partly on this defect of the rule-based market functioning policy. It also reflects a different approach toward support of the market. In order to support the market,

> the courts ought to take steps to carry out the particular transaction brought before them – they should discover the bargain-in-fact and enforce it with appropriate remedies cut to fit the facts of the case. If this discovery is not possible, the court should work out a result involving the least disruption of plans and causing the least amount of reliance loss in light of the situation at the time of the dispute. In short, courts should seek to implement the 'sense of the transaction'.[22]

Inherent in this approach is a different account of how contract law can provide security of transaction. Security is not provided by the application

[18] *Hoffman v Red Owl Stores*, 133 NW2d 237 (WI 1965). For background, see R Scott, '*Hoffman v. Red Owl Stores* and the Myth of Precontractual Reliance' (2007) 69 *Ohio State Law Journal* 71; W Whitford and S Macaulay, '*Hoffman v. Red Owl Stores*: The Rest of the Story' (2010) 61 *Hastings Law Journal* 801.

[19] Macaulay, 'Private Legislation' (n 1) 1059–60.

[20] Macaulay, 'Justice Traynor' (n 1) 861.

[21] ibid.

[22] Macaulay, 'Private Legislation' (n 1) 1060.

of rules but through the certainty that the substance of the transaction will be validated by the court. This decreases the emphasis on form and assumes that market actors understand the essential nature of their transactions and adjust their conduct accordingly. For large organisations, however, it diminishes the power of formality.

As this point indicates, the choice between the rule-oriented market functioning policy and the case-by-case transactional policy rests in part on assumptions about how the market does and should operate. Macaulay recognises that the relative merits of the two policies as means to support the market also will vary depending on the issue involved. At least with respect to the duty to read rule, the subject of one of his articles about the organisation of policies, he favours 'treating different kinds of situations differently with a decided bias towards transactional policy where it is not clearly outweighed by the other factors'.[23]

III. HUMILITY

Macaulay states that the aim of contract law is 'to support the market institution'[24] by furnishing 'tools to facilitate the operation of a market economy – focusing on the needs of those exchanging goods, services, labor and capital'.[25] But as he also points out, that ambition must be tempered – indeed, it may even be thwarted – by three issues that urge humility. First, there is not a single 'market' that contract law should support. There are many markets, and their variety complicates our understanding of the issues and generates principles that are not always consistent. Second, markets do not always function well, and the fact that they do not do so makes apparent a conflict of goals underlying the law. Third, even to the extent that contract law can identify its subject matter and purposes, it may not be well equipped to achieve its aims through the institutions of the legal system. Macaulay's identification of these issues is crucial to understanding the limits of contract law's ambition, and those limits are even more profound than his articles on the organisation of contract policies develop.

A. Markets

What does it mean to support the market? Indeed, what is the 'market institution' that needs to be supported?

[23] ibid 1069.
[24] Macaulay, 'Justice Traynor' (n 1) 857.
[25] Macaulay, 'Private Legislation' (n 1) 1057.

Macaulay makes clear that the market that contact law aims to support is not the ideal type of a transactional market, with fully informed, steely-eyed parties bargaining for advantage over economic value. Instead, the market which contract law aims to support is a real market, existing in the world.

One fact about markets in the world is that there is not one market that needs to be supported; there are many. This point permeates Macaulay's body of work: Contract is contextual. The market of sophisticated businesses negotiating complex deals is very different than the market of consumer transactions. Nor are all complex deals alike, any more than are all consumer transactions.

Macaulay's recognition that if contract law aims to support the market, it must recognise many contexts, has powerful implications. It first leads us to fragment analysis, to study particular topics and particular markets, as a necessary step in contextualising the inquiry. Macaulay's 'Duty to Read' article is exemplary in this respect. The article introduces the rule that a contracting party must read the terms of the contract it signs or assume the risk of terms it has not read – the so-called 'duty to read rule' – and posits the organisation of contract policies as a means of more clearly understanding the issues involved. But even the relatively limited contract law doctrine of 'duty to read' is of too grand a scope and needs to be fragmented further for proper analysis. Macaulay comments: 'Obviously, the analysis presented to this point does not yield a clear answer to the question of when should a duty to read and understand be imposed . . . Given this imprecision, an example considered in some detail seems called for.'[26] Considered in some detail indeed; the article next spends 52 law review pages – three-quarters of the entire article – analysing the much narrower question of the duty of a credit card holder to read and understand the information provided by the issuer concerning liability for unauthorised use of a stolen card. And that is only one application of the duty-to-read rule.

> An equally lengthy essay would result if one were to look to the operation of the whole cluster of duty to read rules as they apply to the sale of residential real estate, insurance releases, personal injury disclaimers found in instruction manuals to consumer items, and the other areas where documents and actual understanding is alleged to conflict.[27]

But at the same time, contract law could hardly function if every issue demanded this level of analysis and was treated as a 'tub on its own bottom'. Generalisation is needed, too. Some generalisation is obvious; the distinction between business transactions involving sophisticated parties and ordinary consumer transactions is an example. Sale of goods cases are treated differently than non-sales cases through Article 2 of the *Uniform*

[26] Macaulay, 'Private Legislation' (n 1) 1069.
[27] ibid 1121.

Commercial Code. The burgeoning field of employment law suggests that employment contracts are different to other commercial contracts. The coursebook of which Macaulay is co-author segments cases involving contracts in the family for separate treatment. And so on.[28]

The best-known instance of generalisation in the scholarly literature is Ian Macneil's distinction between discrete and relational contracts. Discrete contracts involve short duration, limited-party interactions, and precise measurement of the value of the objects exchanged. Relational exchanges involve significant duration, many facets of the parties' lives, and the exchange of values that cannot easily be quantified.[29] The distinction raises the question about how to support these classes of transactions. Indeed, because relational exchanges are more numerous and more important in our economy, contrary to the idealised market of rational, discrete bargainers, it is particularly important in supporting the market institution to create mechanisms for support of relational contracts.[30]

Generalisation complicates the question of how to support the market as much as does fragmentation. Macneil teaches that supporting the market is not the same as simply supporting value-maximising transactions. His system of contract norms makes clear that values such as trust, co-operation, reciprocity and role integrity are essential to relational contracts and are therefore essential to the proper analysis of contract law. If relational contracts predominate and contracting is about co-operative behaviour, the baseline, at least for relational contracts, is one of obligation, not lack of obligation except where specifically assumed, and contract law needs to reflect that baseline of obligation. How it will do so is complex both because of the depth of empirical analysis and the complexity of the normative structure that are involved.

i Market Corrections

A second fact about markets in the real world is that they do not work perfectly. For these cases, Macaulay articulates a second set of substantive contract policies, which he describes as 'other than market goals', 'non-market goals' or 'social control'.[31] As he defines them, these might be better described initially as 'market-correcting goals'.

[28] Macaulay demonstrates both fragmentation by context and generalisation in his nod to Harold Havighurst's 1934 casebook. H Havighurst, *A Selection of Contract Cases and Related Quasi-contract Cases* (Rochester, NY, Lawyers' Co-op,1934), cited in Macaulay, 'Klein and the Contradictions' (n 1) 127.

[29] J Feinman, 'The Significance of Contract Theory' (1990) 58 *University of Cincinnati Law Review* 1283, 1301.

[30] Macneil's solution was to employ a system of contract norms, some of which are intensified in discrete contracts and relational contracts respectively.

[31] Macaulay, 'Private Legislation' (n 1) 1057.

These goals are market-correcting in two ways. Sometimes the ideal conditions for the functioning of an effective market are absent, either because of factors that are particular to a given transaction or because of endemic defects. These factors include contracting parties who are insufficiently skilled to bargain effectively, necessitous of a contract and therefore unable to bargain on terms, or just plain unlucky.[32] At other times the market 'works' in the sense of producing transactions through a process of bargaining to advantage, but the process is distorted because some bargainers engage in contracting practices that are 'socially undesirable'[33] or worse, or because of the unequal distribution of wealth or ability that precedes the market's products. Then the resulting bargains conflict with social values that are external to the market, values that are 'based not upon considerations of market functioning or protecting actual expectations but upon ethical ideals and emotional reactions to the plight of the underdog, to pressing an advantage too far, to making too much profit, or to inequality of resources'.[34]

As a structural matter, the market can be corrected through contract law by rules, which creates the cell in Macaulay's matrix called 'social planning policy'. Rules can declare certain types of contracts or contract terms to be unenforceable, or they can specify the content of contracts. In either case, the effect must be general and the designation must be specific – prohibiting a disclaimer of liability for personal injury but not prohibiting an unconscionable term, for example. Or it can be corrected on a case-by-case basis by relieving one party of its bargain for non-market reasons but without making rules applicable to classes of cases.

The market deserves support because it respects individual autonomy and promotes economic welfare. But it does not do so everywhere and always, and contract law must be humble in attempting to do so. In defining market-correcting goals, Macaulay occasionally recognises that these goals can be very broad, even extending so far as the redistribution of wealth.[35] He similarly notes that the market is not appropriate as the sole regulator of some classes of contracts because of broader concerns for social welfare, so direct regulation is desirable.

> An important goal in this society is the achievement of the best balance of economic freedom and order. We seek the best proportion of (a) individual and corporate freedom to make choices in the market to (b) governmental action to promote general economic welfare. Clearly, contract is a legal device primarily designed to support the market institution; yet it shows as well the impact of ideas of economic planning and control apart from the market process.[36]

[32] Macaulay, 'Justice Traynor' (n 1) 857.
[33] Macaulay, 'Private Legislation' (n 1) 1057.
[34] ibid 1063.
[35] Macaulay 'Private Legislation' (n 1) 1062.
[36] Macaulay, 'Justice Traynor' (n 1) 813.

In Macaulay's organisation, the non-market goals, however defined, are clearly secondary to the objective of supporting the market. For contract law, the market is the primary social institution, so market goals predominate. Non-market goals are secondary because they are less important – or at least there is less agreement on their importance.[37]

Macaulay's framing of market-promoting goals as primary and market-correcting goals as secondary correctly states the customary objectives of contract law as ambition tempered with humility. That framing also makes apparent why contract law needs to be even more humble in ways Macaulay does not fully develop.

First, the conflicting market and non-market goals need to be balanced, and the measures for doing so are controversial. Even if one accepts that non-market goals are secondary, secondary does not imply absent. In resolving a case or formulating a rule, courts have to balance potentially conflicting goals, and they have to do so in the characterisation of the contextual and generalised market at issue. In his discussion of the liability for loss of a credit card leading to unauthorised use, Macaulay speculates about the incentive effects of imposing liability on either the issuer or cardholder and concludes that knowledge of those effects would be important in formulating a rule. But as he also notes, 'it is easy to talk of spreading losses' by imposing liability on the issuer, a question of 'political philosophy'.[38] Even full knowledge of the incentive effects would not resolve the question of political philosophy – whether we are seeking a result that favours consumers through loss spreading, a Pareto optimal result, a result that favours the innocent, or some other result.

The case law and literature offer a variety of mechanisms for carrying out this balancing. Courts employ different tropes including avoidance by doctrinal formalism, casual policy analysis, and ad hoc paternalism. The *Restatement Second* frequently lists factors to be balanced without specifying the techniques of balancing. Economic analysis aims for efficient results, variously defined and sought. In his later reflections on the systematic presentation of contract law policies, Macaulay recognised the inadequacy of these efforts and the difficulty, perhaps impossibility, of this balancing process. There he entitles the table 'The Contradictions of Contract Law' and comments that contract law 'inconsistently rests on policies that both promote the market and those that attempt to blunt it'.[39]

Second, the hierarchy and separation between market and non-market goals needs to be established in practice. Consider the choice between a rule-oriented market functioning policy and a case-by-case transactional

[37] 'We have at least a rough working agreement in our society on the market philosophy; social control is not as clearly accepted – at least there are important differences on when and how it should come into play.' ibid 858.

[38] Macaulay, 'Private Legislation' (n 1) 1116–17.

[39] Macaulay, 'Klein and the Contradictions' (n 1) 121.

policy. One of the substantive contract policies Macaulay identifies is self-reliance. In the conception of the market as private, individual and self-actuating, self-reliance is crucial.[40] Macaulay writes of promoting self-reliance by encouraging or requiring parties to look out for themselves, in a world in which the law will rigidly enforce apparent bargains they have made, through a market-functioning or transactional policy. In an early version of his organisation, he listed 'the self-reliance policy' as of equal stature with the transactional policy and the functional policy (later the market-functioning policy).[41] In one construction of the matrix, he contrasts the basis of the transactional policy as 'Individual Maximising, Self-reliance, Choice' with the basis of the relief of hardship policy as 'Altruism, Paternalism'.[42]

But implicit in this construction is the illogic of simply promoting the market by promoting self-reliance through a body of contract law that rewards initiative and punishes dependence. Instead, the law can further self-reliance in either of two opposite ways – by creating a minimal body of contract law that puts parties at risk or creating an aggressively interventionist body of law that provides parties with security. A body of contract that provides relief from one's ill-informed or ill-fated promises encourages self-reliant action by assuring that the consequences of action will not be too severe. The risk of intervention or non-intervention in this way protects all economic actors, as all are potentially subject to bad decisions or bad luck, although the weak probably more so than the strong.

Therefore, a combination of the transactional policy and the relief of hardship policy – determining the enforceability of contracts, or not, on a case-by-case basis – may maximise social welfare; whether the social welfare so produced is greater or lesser than that generated by the rule-based market functioning policy ameliorated with social or economic planning policy is an empirical question for which no theoretical answer exists.

Third, as the theoretical conflict about self-reliance illustrates, it is problematic even to attempt to define market and non-market goals as separate. Inherent in the separation is the conception that market goals involve the facilitation of private activity, a process that is distinct from the imposition of public values such as redressing inequality. Private activity is fundamentally individual, whereas public goals are collective. Courts in private law cases are primarily a forum for the adjudication of private disputes; legislatures are the arena in which public goals are primarily enunciated. And so on.

But these dichotomies are exaggerated. There is no institution of the market separate from and preexisting to non-market activity, just as there is no private law not constituted by public values. The exchange of goods

[40] J Feinman, 'Critical Approaches to Contract Law' (1983) 30 *UCLA Law Review* 829, 841.
[41] Macaulay, 'Justice Traynor' (n 1) fig 1.
[42] Macaulay, 'Klein and the Contradictions' (n 1) 122.

may be a private activity, but the exchange of goods that the law has made the subject of property and which exchange is enforceable by law is an essentially public activity. Law constitutes the market for reasons of the public good, so supporting the market through contract law is only another way of advancing the public good, and not a particularly distinct way at that.

Because the market is not distinctively private, the hierarchy of market goals and the need for self-reliance in the service of those goals are not evident. The justification for contract law and its rules must rest elsewhere than on a claim that the market is distinctive and distinctively important. And that is a claim that is assumed but seldom justified in the case law or literature. Part of the power of Macaulay's organisation is the way in which it makes clear the great defects of contract law's ambition.

B. Efficiency and Efficacy

Beyond the problems of defining the market, its goals, and the conflicting non-market goals, Macaulay points out that achieving the goals through the legal system is complex, often ineffective, sometimes even counter-productive. This is a further reason for humility, which he mostly subsumes under efficiency and efficacy. Whatever its goals, contract law has at its disposal only the ordinary tools of the legal system: lawmaking by legislatures and courts and adjudication of cases by courts. Those tools are imperfectly suited to the task of achieving the goals of contract law. Here is raised the question that has permeated much of Macaulay's career: What can be done by the law and at what cost?[43]

The effectiveness of courts in adjudicating cases to achieve policies embodied in rules is particularly problematic with case-by-case approaches. The market-oriented transactional policy 'calls for a careful assessment of expectations created by the entire exchange situation . . . Often one would have to work with tacit assumptions and implicit understandings based on practices in particular industries. This is not easy, and there is a great risk of error.'[44]

The non-market, relief of hardship policy in turn 'calls for a careful weighing of such factors as who can best bear the loss, decisions loaded with implicit value judgments as well as factual issues'.[45] Applying clear rules, on the other hand, presents fewer fact-finding challenges; applying a Willistonian parol evidence rule is easier than engaging in a Corbinesque analysis of the intentions of the parties.

[43] Macaulay also discusses other issues, notably the legitimacy of lawmaking by courts, which I omit here.

[44] Macaulay, 'Private Legislation' (n 1) 1066.

[45] ibid.

But formulating rules is not easier than formulating standards to be applied case by case. One challenge for the courts is that the selection of cases before them limits their ability to assess situations and advance goals. And there is a more fundamental problem.

> Ideally, rational lawmaking requires knowledge of the alternative solutions to the problem, knowledge of the consequences of each solution, and the selection of the alternative with consequences which best attain a desired goal at the least social cost. Yet courts have limited resources for obtaining knowledge of alternatives and consequences. It is not always easy to determine whether a decision which attempts to implement social control will achieve its goal because of the almost necessary vagueness of that goal. Moreover, it is not easy to tell whether or not a position has undesirable side effects that cost more than any gain produced is worth.[46]

Legislatures are at least potentially better equipped to determine and respond to the fullness of social issues, but the potential is not always realised.[47] In 'Duty to Read' Macaulay conducted an extensive examination of the liability of a credit card holder for its unauthorised use. Here he is in full form: exploring the context of the growth of credit cards, examining credit card applications and the cards themselves for the presence or absence of limitations of liability, and surveying customers as they entered gas stations, as well as examining cases and statutes. His conclusion: 'After all of this evaluation, what have we learned about this system policy? First, those decisions that tried to regulate seemed to be shooting in the dark.' Why? 'The judiciary would seem to lack much of the essential inputs for a regulatory decision either favoring issuer or holder . . . I would not suppose that the legislative committee would have heard all that is reported here.'[48]

There is a further problem in lawmaking: the lack of feedback. Once a rule is made and applied, whether the lawmaker will receive accurate and effective feedback on the efficacy of the rule depends on a variety of factors. Those affected by the rule must be sufficiently able and willing to take action to change it, either by further litigation or by legislation. Ability and willingness depend on stakes and resources. Institutional factors are at play, too. Legislatures are not often prone to consider an issue

[46] Macaulay, 'Justice Traynor' (n 1) 859–60.

[47] A few years after the publication of Macaulay's 'Private Legislation and the Duty to Read', Congress enacted the Truth in Lending Act, which limited a cardholder's liability for unauthorised use to $50. 15 USC § 1643(a)(1).

[48] Macaulay, 'Private Legislation' (n 1) 1118. A significant portion of contract law is formulated by the private legislatures, The American Law Institute and the National Conference of Commissioners on Uniform State Laws. Robert Scott's work, among others, demonstrates that they are not better equipped in this respect than public legislatures. See R Scott, 'Contract Theory and the Limits of Contract Law' (2003) 113 *Yale Law Journal* 541, 598; A Schwartz and R Scott, 'The Political Economy of Private Legislatures' (1995) 143 *University of Pennsylvania Law Review* 595.

once dealt with to be settled. Courts depend on the cases that come before them, and may not see enough cases of a certain kind 'to work out a sensible solution to a problem'.[49]

These problems are intensified with non-market goals. Advancing non-market goals even on a case-by-case basis or in modest ways threatens the market goals in ways that are not always apparent. Correcting defects in the bargaining process or providing relief to the disadvantaged or unfortunate comes at the expense of a contracting party who may be innocent of any wrongdoing. That party's plans and expectations will be upset, often with severe collateral consequences on third parties. Where the party is a large organisation, intervention undermines its planning and efficiency, which are essential for a productive economy.[50] And the operation of the system is likely to be erratic. 'But the power to let a party out of his disastrous bargain on a case-by-case basis is an arbitrary one largely turning on the attitudes of the judge or jurors faced with the case. Sometimes it will be used wisely; sometimes not.'[51]

CONCLUSION

Macaulay's organisation of contract law policies clearly and powerfully expresses the underpinnings and operations of the field. Mainstream contract law scholars can use it to tell a story of ambition with only a dash of humility. In this story, analysis in legislation, adjudication, and scholarship are well served by a clear statement of the policies contract law aims to achieve and the means of achieving them. In serving the market, some cases call for rules, others for case-by-case adjudication, for example. The worst that can be said, as Macaulay wrote, is that 'American law is always messy, but we should expect this because Americans want to have their cake and eat it too'.[52] But the key point is that it is possible to tell which is which. Contract law is neither perfect nor complete; the lessons about legal system policies and the need for market correction must be learned. The imperfection makes the project a continuing one, however.

From the same perspective, the continuing nature of the project can be seen at the level of large historical changes and at the level of smaller doctrinal change. In the early nineteenth century, traditional, pre-modern contract law hindered the enforcement of executory, speculative transactions. During the nineteenth-century rise of capitalism, these transactions came into prominence with the rise of national markets and large-scale enterprises. Contract law provided a measure of security in these new

[49] Macaulay, 'Private Legislation' (n 1) 1118–19.
[50] Macaulay, 'Justice Traynor' (n 1) 857–58.
[51] Macaulay, 'Justice Traynor' (n 1) 863.
[52] Macaulay, 'Klein and the Contradictions' (n 1) 133.

markets to encourage entrepreneurs to invest capital and thereby promoted economic growth. Later in the century, the development of a mass markets increasingly required standardisation and predictability, which contract law provided through doctrines such as the objective theory of contract formation and the foreseeability principle in damages. During the twentieth century, rigid, arcane and archaic doctrines that impeded ordinary commercial transaction were modified or swept away, and excesses in bargaining and inequality were redressed through a variety of ameliorative and flexible doctrines. For example, rigid rules of offer, acceptance and consideration were softened in the period between the *First Restatement* and the *Second Restatement* and the *Uniform Commercial Code*. Fortunately for law professors, the process is never complete. Subsequently the rise of the internet created new formation problems with the ubiquity of terms of service and the 'I accept' box. Those formation problems are addressed through market and non-market concerns, rules and exceptions, as in the American Law Institute's *Principles of Software Contracts*.

For those on the fringes of contract law scholarship, however – empiricists, crits, race crits, and the generally curmudgeonly[53] – Macaulay's organisation suggests a different lesson. The organisation demonstrates that contract law is at best badly confused and at worst incoherent and largely ineffective. Nevertheless, because the mainstream story of contract law serves such a powerful ideological function for judges and law professors, it retains an extraordinary vitality. One more statement of critique will not cause the edifice to fall. But the career of Stewart Macaulay demonstrates the continuing virtue of telling truth to power.

BIBLIOGRAPHY

Ayres, I and Speidel, R, *Studies in Contract Law*, 7th edn (New York, Foundation Press, 2008).

Feinman, J, 'The Insurance Relationship as Relational Contract and the "Fairly Debatable" Rule for First-Party Bad Faith' (2009) 46 *San Diego Law Review* 553.

——, 'The Significance of Contract Theory' (1990) 58 *University of Cincinnati Law Review* 1283.

——, 'Critical Approaches to Contract Law' (1983) 30 *UCLA Law Review* 829.

Friedman, L, *Contract Law in America: A Social and Economic Case Study* (Madison, University of Wisconsin Press, 1965).

Havighurst, H, *A Selection of Contract Cases and Related Quasi-contract Cases* (Rochester, NY, Lawyers' Co-op,1934).

Hetherington, J, 'Trends in Enterprise Liability: Law and the Unauthorized Agent' (1966) 19 *Stanford Law Review* 76.

[53] Such as the hard-to-characterise Grant Gilmore.

Kennedy, D, 'Form and Substance in Private Law Adjudication' (1976) 89 *Harvard Law Review* 1685.
Knapp, C, Crystal, N, and Prince, H, *Problems in Contract Law: Cases and Materials*, 6th edn (New York, Aspen, 2007).
Macaulay, S, 'Klein and the Contradictions of Corporations Law' (2005) 2 *Berkeley Business Law Journal* 119.
——, 'Private Legislation and the Duty to Read – Business Run by IBM Machine, The Law of Contracts and Credit Cards' (1966) 19 *Vanderbilt Law Review* 1051.
——, 'Justice Traynor and the Law of Contracts' (1961) 13 *Stanford Law Review* 812.
——, 'Restitution in Context' (1959) 107 *University of Pennsylvania Law Review* 1133.
Schwartz, A and Scott, R, 'The Political Economy of Private Legislatures' (1995) 143 *University of Pennsylvania Law Review* 595.
Scott, R, '*Hoffman v. Red Owl Stores* and the Myth of Precontractual Reliance' (2007) 69 *Ohio State Law Journal* 71.
——, 'Contract Theory and the Limits of Contract Law' (2003) 113 *Yale Law Journal* 541.
Whitford, W and Macaulay, S, '*Hoffman v. Red Owl Stores*: The Rest of the Story' (2010) 61 *Hastings Law Journal* 801.

Part II

Contractual Relations Between Businesses: Law and Behaviour

5

What Do We Mean by the Non-Use of Contract?

DAVID CAMPBELL*

> The reason why Macaulay observes so few litigated cases in business is because markets work well for nonspecific transactions, while recurrent non-standard transactions are governed by bilateral or unified structures.
>
> Oliver Williamson[1]

INTRODUCTION

IN A PAPER written for a conference celebrating Stewart Macaulay's achievement, one can avoid the principal obstacle to giving an accurate assessment of that achievement, which is sparing Macaulay's blushes. Macaulay and his colleagues at Wisconsin[2] have so improved our understanding of exchange and its law that they have altered our very conception of the relationship between the two. The classical law of contract's implicit claim that the formal law of contract closely prescribes the form of exchange has been shown to be wholly inadequate, and this has obliged us to ask fundamental questions about the way that the law of

* I am grateful to Hugh Beale, John Gava, Stewart Macaulay, Peter Vincent-Jones and Bill Whitford for their comments on substance and, in Bill's case, form. In academic debate and private conversation over many years, Hugh Beale has repeatedly told me that he sees neither Macaulay's nor his own work as evidence of non-use. Reflecting on this has been a great help to my formulation of the ideas I am trying to express in this paper. A much earlier version of this paper was presented at a panel discussion of the work of Stewart Macaulay at the Law and Society Association Annual Conference, Humboldt University and The Free University, Berlin, July 2007. In revising this paper, I have relied particularly heavily on Sally Wheeler's paper cited in n 31 below.

[1] O Williamson, 'Transaction Cost Economics: The Governance of Contractual Relations' (1979) 22 *Journal of Law and Economics* 233, 259.

[2] Now including Jean Braucher of the James E Rogers College of Law, University of Arizona, who since 2007 has held a concurrent appointment at Wisconsin which has led to the production of S Macaulay and others, *Contracts: Law in Action*, 3rd edn (New Providence, LexisNexis, 2011).

contract regulates exchange, or even about the extent to which it can regulate it.

Macaulay has reached that pinnacle of scholarly standing at which the significance of his work is demonstrated by it being intimately associated with a universally known position, but a position which misrepresents that work. Macaulay's work is the subject of a myth about contract theory which we might call the 'Gilmore myth'. This is, of course, the myth that has grown up around Gilmore's reference to Macaulay as 'the Lord High Executioner of the Contracts is Dead school'.[3] When I first drafted what has become this paper in order to contribute to a discussion of Macaulay's work at the 2007 Law and Society Association conference, I was at pains to claim that Macaulay did not want to kill the law of contract. I was able to point to many passages in his work in which he extolled the extent and potential value of that law, and to the great achievement of establishing the innovative form of teaching of contracts in Wisconsin,[4] as evidence in support of my claim. There must be a question about how far argument of this sort should ever have been necessary. Macaulay raised clear objections to the Gilmore myth as long ago as, to my knowledge, 1985,[5] and for some years his Wisconsin Law School web page has told us that he 'declined the honour' of being Lord High Executioner and believed 'only that academic contract was dead while the real institution was alive and well'.[6] This message was surely confirmed when, giving a keynote paper at another event in his honour in 2011, the Sixth Annual International Conference on Contracts held at the Stetson University School of Law, Macaulay declared that 'There Is No "Contracts is Dead" Movement'.[7]

Gilmore has, of course, been subject to some pretty severe criticism of the accuracy of his own history of the 'doctrinal disintegration' of contract law,[8] and a number of interesting attempts have been made to disentangle what of Gilmore's is and is not of value in light of such criticism.[9] What I

[3] G Gilmore, *The Death of Contract*, 2nd edn (Columbus, Ohio State University Press, 1995) 1 fn 1.

[4] L Friedman and S Macaulay, 'Contract Law and Contract Teaching: Past, Present and Future' (1967) 1967 *Wisconsin Law Review* 805.

[5] S Macaulay, 'An Empirical View of Contract' (1985) 1985 *Wisconsin Law Review* 465.

[6] University of Wisconsin Law School, 'Stewart Macaulay' (*University of Wisconsin, Madison*, 1 January 2012) www.law.wisc.edu/facstaff/macaulay/.

[7] UW Law News, 'Stewart Macaulay Honored at 6th Annual International Conference on Contracts' (University of Wisconsin Law School, 28 February 2011) law.wisc.edu/newsletter/Articles/Stewart_Macaulay_Honored_at_6th_2011-02-22.

[8] The late Professor Brian Simpson had a very low opinion of Gilmore as a legal historian, describing him as a mere 'amateur' (AWB Simpson, 'Contract: The Twitching Corpse' (1980) 1 *Oxford Journal of Legal Studies* 265, 273), or even as someone 'who never felt inhibited by mere ignorance from writing legal history', whose work 'needs to be treated with extreme caution on matters historical'. AWB Simpson, 'The Beauty of Obscurity: *Raffles v Wichelhaus and Busch* (1864)' in AWB Simpson, *Leading Cases in the Common Law* (Oxford, Oxford University Press, 1995) 135, 162. This did not prevent Simpson from insisting upon the other than historical value of *The Death of Contract*.

[9] eg R Scott, 'The Death of Contract Law' (2004) 54 *University of Toronto Law Journal* 369.

will argue here is that, however little value there is in the idea of the death of contract, it transpires that Gilmore chose his words rather carefully when he said that Macaulay was the Lord High Executioner because, as Gilmore put it, Macaulay had shown 'the irrelevance of traditional contract theory'.[10] This is exactly what Macaulay has done. It is the classical law of contract[11] that Macaulay has done much to falsify,[12] though, of course, to the considerable extent that the classical law still influences 'contract law in practice', then that law remains 'a flawed product'.[13] But this evaluation must be separated from Macaulay's overall positive attitude toward the legal institution of the law of contract, which, he hopes, is not entirely '*perdido* (lost)' and may have a better future.[14]

A myth as powerful as the Gilmore myth must, however, have a basis in fact,[15] and I will argue that the basic concepts of non-use and non-contractual relations introduced in Macaulay's two great 1963 papers – 'The Use and Non-use of Contracts in the Manufacturing Industry'[16] (UNUC) and 'Non-Contractual Relations in Business: A Preliminary Study' (NCRB)[17] – but poorly capture the relationship of economic exchange and legal contract that Macaulay has done so much to reveal to us. It is in an obvious sense foolish to criticise the coining of terms which have given rise to such valuable discussion,[18] but surely one cannot be surprised if these terms sanction effective disregard of the actual law. On their face, they depict

[10] Gilmore, *The Death of Contract* (n 3) 1 fn 1 (emphasis added).

[11] Macneil came to describe modern mainstream US contract scholarship as 'neoclassical' in order to capture the way it is characterised by ad hoc attempts to deal with the failures of the classical law. I Macneil, 'Contracts: Adjustment of Long-Term Economic Relations Under Classical, Neoclassical, and Relational Contract Law' (1977) 72 *Northwestern University Law Review* 854. Macaulay came to adopt this usage, including in his account of the construction of the Johnson Building discussed below. I shall persist in using the term 'classical law'.

[12] D Campbell, 'The Undeath of Contract: A Study in the Degeneration of a Research Programme' (1992) 22 *The Hong Kong Law Journal* 20.

[13] S Macaulay, 'Relational Contracts Floating on a Sea of Custom? Thoughts About the Ideas of Ian Macneil and Lisa Bernstein' (2000) 94 *Northwestern University Law Review* 775, 804.

[14] S Macaulay, 'Contracts, New Legal Realism and Improving the Navigation of The Yellow Submarine' (2006) 80 *Tulane Law Review* 1161, 1194.

[15] Perhaps the passages in Macaulay which are the strongest evidence that he ever maintained that the law of contract is dead are his numerous warm references to L Friedman's *Contract Law in America* (Madison, University of Wisconsin Press, 1965), for Friedman does, in my opinion, take this line, (eg ibid 25, cited above in Macaulay, 'Contracts, New Legal Realism' (n 14) 1192–93). Macaulay has discussed *Contract Law in America* at length in S Macaulay, 'The Death of Contract: Dodos and Unicorns or Sleeping Rattlesnakes' in R Gordon and M Horwitz (eds), *Law, Society and History* (Cambridge, Cambridge University Press, 2011) 193.

[16] S Macaulay, 'The Use and Non-Use of Contracts in the Manufacturing Industry' (1963) 9 *Practical Lawyer* 13.

[17] S Macaulay, 'Non-Contractual Relations in Business: A Preliminary Study' (1963) 28 *American Sociological Review* 55.

[18] More correctly, Macaulay accepted the title suggested for NCRB by the great American sociologist RK Merton; S Macaulay, 'Crime and Custom in Business Society' (1995) 22 *Journal of Law and Society* 248, 251.

the relationship between what we might call the legal, economic and social aspects of contract in a way which invites criticism of the law of contract as such, and, in my opinion, they should no longer be used.

I am by no means the first to question the appositeness of the terms non-use and non-contractual relations.[19] The earliest such questioning of which I am aware was that of Schur in 1967, who told us that Macaulay's findings 'do not refer to the express failure of legal norms but rather to the limitations of legal control and the tendency for non-legal norms to complement legal ones'.[20] I learned of Schur by reading the first British paper attempting to reproduce Macaulay's research, by Beale and Dugdale in 1975, which had, for a paper with that intent, the provocative subtitle 'Planning and the Use of Contractual Remedies'.[21] But, of course, in work as important as Macaulay's, issues of this sort are by no means merely terminological. Macaulay's work expresses the shifts in our general understanding of the regulation of exchange over the period of his professional lifetime. Seeing this helps us to understand Macaulay's thought, and, from that, to orient ourselves to the current problems facing the theory of the law of contract by allowing us more precisely to understand what we mean by the non-use of contract.

I. THE NON-USE OF CONTRACT

As is known by every competent contract scholar, the basic thrust of NCRB and of UNUC is that, though 'legal sanctions, while not an everyday affair, are not unknown in business', 'there is little evidence that . . . today's businessmen would use the courts to settle disputes'.[22] Macaulay's identification of non-use led him to argue that: 'Two questions need to be answered: (a) How can businesses successfully operate exchange relationships with relatively so little attention to detailed planning or to legal sanctions, and (b) Why does business ever use contract in light of its success without it?'[23]

Macaulay's answer to the first question has been the basis of the Gilmore myth. Macaulay described 'a hesitancy to speak of legal rights or to threaten

[19] I am restricting to a footnote a highly interesting reservation about 'non-use' entered by Macaulay himself in 2007: '[NCRB] is a study of when business people use formal processes of law and, more importantly, when they do not. Would it be accurate, however, to say that [NCRB] was a study of the "non-use" of law or would it be more to the point to say it was a study about informal rules, norms and practices – which happen not to coincide with the rules "on the books"?' S Macaulay, L Friedman and E Mertz, *Law in Action: A Socio-Legal Reader* (New York, Foundation Press, 2007) 90.

[20] E Schur, *Law and Society* (New York, Random House, 1967) 131.

[21] H Beale and T Dugdale, 'Contracts Between Businessmen: Planning and the Use of Contractual Remedies' (1975) 2 *British Journal of Law and Society* 45, 46 fn 4.

[22] Macaulay, NCRB (n 17) 62.

[23] ibid 62.

to sue'[24] which arose for three reasons. First, '[i]n most situations contract is not needed' as most failures to perform are relatively clear-cut and easily resolved 'because usually there is little room for honest misunderstandings or good faith differences of opinion' amongst 'experienced professionals who will know the customs of their industry and of those industries with which they deal'.[25] Secondly, 'contract and contract law are often thought unnecessary because there are many effective non-legal sanctions', in particular, 'the most obvious' sanction of preserving an ongoing relationship between 'business units [which] want to deal with each other again' and to enjoy a good 'general business reputation'.[26] Thirdly, the use of 'contract and contract law . . . may have, or may be thought to have, undesirable consequences' such as delay, loss of 'flexibility' in the handling of the exchange relationship, legal and related costs (which are unlikely to be fully recovered even in the event of successful litigation), and the generation of an unhelpful working atmosphere, 'turning a co-operative venture into an antagonistic horse trade'.[27] All this led to the identification of what was described in UNUC as a 'common' 'attitude toward contracts that can best be described as indifferent or even hostile to the whole idea',[28] and to the then startling conclusion that 'many, if not most, exchanges reflect no planning, or only a minimal amount of it, especially concerning legal sanctions and the effect of defective performances'.[29]

The principal conclusion that Macaulay drew from this account of the non-use of contract and of the work done by non-contractual relations was that '[t]o understand the functions of contract the whole system of conducting exchanges must be explored more fully'.[30] This was and is true, and in pursuing its implications Macaulay has made the principal contribution to the 'law in action' approach to the study of the law of contract, producing some of the most interesting studies of specific contracting practices and reviews of our understanding of contracting in general that have ever been written. A now large literature has taken Macaulay's apparent demonstration of non-use in his 1963 papers as its starting point when seeking to describe the non-contractual relations that explain what really happens in law in action. I hope to be the last to deny the interest of this literature, but I do think it has sometimes taken a mistaken tack, in which confusion over the concept of trust has played a large part.[31]

[24] ibid 61.
[25] ibid 62–63.
[26] ibid 63–64.
[27] ibid 64.
[28] Macaulay, UNUC (n 16) 14.
[29] Macaulay, NCRB (n 17) 60.
[30] ibid 67.
[31] S Wheeler, 'Contracts and Corporations' in P Cane and H Kritzer (eds), *The Oxford Handbook of Empirical Legal Research* (Oxford, Oxford University Press, 2010) 125, 147.

In this literature, the unused contract generally falls entirely out of consideration and attention shifts entirely to non-contractual relations. This analysis turns to what is now usually called the 'embeddedness' of exchange in social relations,[32] in which an idea of trust effectively displaces contract in the analysis. Now, as Macaulay rightly tells us, some notion of trust is 'necessary to make any economic system work'.[33] But we must carefully distinguish between two senses of trust:[34] one in which trust makes the market work by channelling self-interest in welfare enhancing directions,[35] and another sort of trust that sets itself against the market. This latter concept of trust is social, not only in the sense that it is grounded in sociological theory, but in the sense that, though it is very amorphous, one can say of it that it is non-economic; perhaps altruistic is the best term to describe it. The role of non-contractual relations of trust is taken to be evidence, not merely of the non-use of contract, but of the non-use of economics. These non-contractual relations are regarded as social in the double sense of being, indeed, social relations, but also social relations which articulate an altruistic orientation of action as opposed the to the self-interest analysed in economics, which is identified with contract. This second sense of social relations turns on the idea that a welfarist[36] organisation of exchange should, to a lesser or greater degree falling short of a complete rejection of the market, replace self-interest with altruism.

There is some flavour of this that we can recognise in Macaulay's work, to which I shall return. But disregard of economics is far from easy to identify in NCRB and UNUC. It will be recalled that Macaulay thought that his findings required us to answer, not only the question: 'How can businesses successfully operate exchange relationships with relatively so little attention to detailed planning or to legal sanctions', but also the

[32] M Granovetter, 'Economic Action and Social Structure: The Problem of Embeddedness' (1985) 91 *American Journal of Sociology* 481.

[33] Macaulay, 'Relational Contracts' (n 13) 804.

[34] S Deakin, C Lane and F Wilkinson, 'Contract Law, Trust Relations and Incentives for Cooperation: A Comparative Study' in S Deakin and J Michie (eds), *Contracts, Cooperation and Competition: Studies in Economics, Management and Law* (Oxford, Oxford University Press, 1997) 105.

[35] D Campbell, 'The Relational Constitution of Contract and the Limits of "Economics": Kenneth Arrow on the Social Background of Markets' in Deakin and Michie, *Contracts* (n 34) 307.

[36] I am using the terms 'welfarism' and 'welfarist' to denote the advocacy in economics, law and social policy of a social market turning on the 'communitarian values . . . which gave birth to the Welfare State' 'of paternalism, fairness and co-operation' as an alternative to the individualist values of the capitalist market. In the discussion of the general principles of the law of contract over, say, the last 30 years, the principal UK exponents of welfarism have been Roger Brownsword and Hugh Collins, though the views of both are now significantly different. The above quotation is taken from the first edition of Collins' contract textbook. H Collins, *The Law of Contract* (London, Weidenfeld & Nicolson, 1986) 15. For a discussion of the concept of welfarism at the point where Brownsword and Collins were clearly moving away from it, see D Campbell, 'Reflexivity and Welfarism in the Modern Law of Contract' (2000) 20 *Oxford Journal of Legal Studies* 477.

question: 'Why does business ever use contract in light of its success without it?'[37] A very considerable part of NCRB addressed the question, 'Why do relatively contractual practices ever exist?'[38] The picture that emerges from NCRB and UNUC is not one of literal non-use but of a complex interplay between the use of legal and non-legal sanctions which Macaulay explains by reference to 'the functions and dysfunctions of using contract to solve exchange problems'.[39] The argument which I wish to put forward is that Macaulay's ability to mount an analysis of 'the functions and dysfunctions of using contract to solve exchange problems' does not turn on the general social embedding of legal issues, although this does of course obtain, but on his conception of the relationship in contract of law to economics and the way contract law facilitates economic exchange.

II. THE ECONOMICS AND LAW OF CONTRACT AND THEIR RELATIONSHIP

A proper understanding of NCRB must begin with its definition of 'contracts' as 'devices for conducting exchanges':

> Contract is not treated as synonymous with an exchange itself, which may or may not be characterised as contractual. Nor is contract used to refer to a writing recording an agreement. Contract, as . . . the term [is used] here, involves two distinct elements: (a) rational planning of the transaction with careful planning for as many future contingencies as can be foreseen, and (b) the existence or use of actual or potential legal sanctions to induce performance of the exchange or to compensate for non-performance.[40]

These 'devices for conducting exchanges', Macaulay goes on to tell us,

> may be used or may exist in greater or lesser degree, so that transactions can be described relatively as involving a more or a less contractual manner (a) of creating an exchange relationship or (b) of solving problems arising during the course of such a relationship.[41]

The great virtue of this definition of contract is that it breaks the complete identification of economic exchange and legal contract, which in effect extinguishes the former, in the classical law's conception of contract. In the first edition of the oldest of the contract textbooks still in general use in England and Wales, that of Sir William Anson first published in 1879, contract is defined 'as a combination of the two ideas of agreement and obligation. It is that form of agreement which directly contemplates

[37] Macaulay, NCRB (n 17) 62.
[38] ibid 65.
[39] ibid 56.
[40] Ibid 56.
[41] ibid 56.

and results in an obligation.'[42] In the twenty-fifth, centenary edition, 'the law of contract' was described as 'that branch of law which determines the circumstances in which a promise shall be legally binding on the person making it'.[43] Approaching contract in this way identifies the contract with legally enforceable promises, and the economic exchange which is its proper foundation does not feature at all. On this basis, it is inevitable that the classical approach to the subject will be 'to analyse the concept of a promise'.[44] A complicated legal doctrine of contract and an elaborate speculative ethics of promising may be erected, but there is nothing to the classical conception of contract other than law, and this is not what is essential. Economic exchange is what is essential.

The reason why parties make promises in the form of contracts cannot naturally emerge from the classical understanding of the subject, and this question has been either entirely ignored, so that the whole thing seemed a sort of abstract legal game as so memorably parodied by Llewellyn,[45] or, especially more recently, as some feeling of disquiet about the purely legal approach has had to be acknowledged by all but the most obdurate, has been discussed as an appendix to the basic concept. In the most recent edition of *Anson's Law of Contract*, a discussion of the economic 'functions of contract'[46] now follows the definition of contract, but this definition remains in all important respects identical to that given in the centenary edition,[47] and so this discussion, though welcome, is a mere addition to what remains a purely legal concept of contract as promise which it cannot theoretically deepen.

In contrast to this entirely legal conception of contract as promise, Macaulay's definition of contract as 'devices for conducting exchanges' has an integral economic component, with the economic exchange being the object and the legal contract a means of achieving that object. Contractual promises are identified as the constituent units of an economic exchange. Now, parties do not have to intend that their promises to exchange will be legally binding, but they may do so in order to obtain security, ultimately backed by the state, against non-performance. If they do intend this, then contract emerges as a unity of economic exchange and legal device for providing security for the exchange.[48] This understanding

[42] W Anson, *Principles of the English Law of Contract* (Oxford, Clarendon Press, 1879) 1.

[43] A Guest, *Anson's Law of Contract*, 25th edn (Oxford, Clarendon Press, 1979) 2.

[44] ibid.

[45] K Llewellyn, 'Our Case Law of Contract: Offer and Acceptance II' (1939) 48 *Yale Law Journal* 779, 785.

[46] J Beatson, A Burrows, and J Cartwright, *Anson's Law of Contract*, 29th edn (Oxford, Oxford University Press, 2010) 2–4. A ritual reference to NCRB made in the course of this discussion completely plays down its significance.

[47] ibid 1–2.

[48] Putting promises to exchange in the form of a contract has other functions than providing security, such as clarifying the intentions of the parties. But it is not essential that such

of the nature of contract lies behind the distinction, clearly drawn in a number of important English cases, between 'primary' and 'secondary' obligations.[49] The former are the parties' promises to exchange. The latter is a legally binding obligation to provide a remedy in the event of breach.[50] This secondary obligation arises at the time of agreement, but remains latent during performance of the primary obligation, crystallising only if a breach is committed, when the defendant must provide a remedy.

There is an immense theoretical benefit to this conception of contract as a unity of economic exchange and legal security which has, in my opinion, underpinned Macaulay's contribution to the subject. Whilst it was perhaps not entirely inevitable, the classical law's purely legal conception of contract was highly likely to lead, and has led, to the core belief that the function of contract should be the literal enforcement of legally binding promises, for if one asks how one should adequately enforce a promise, then literal enforcement is the natural answer. How else could one really enforce a promise? In the famous words of Rolt LJ: 'Contracts ought to be performed. To break them, and to propose compensation for the breach by damages, is not complete justice.'[51] But all we know of the way contract remedies work, especially as understood in the light of what Macaulay has told us,[52] is counter-evidence to this literal belief in *pacta sunt servanda*, which is the fundamental error of the classical law.

Parties enter into an exchange in order to maximise the satisfactions they obtain from their ownership of economic goods. They exchange goods they own prior to the exchange in order to realise a surplus satisfaction from the goods they own after it. It is this surplus that Fuller and Perdue tried to focus on when identifying the expectation interest.[53] This surplus may take a non-pecuniary form or the pecuniary form of profit, on which we shall concentrate. The crucial advantage which the approach used in NCRB enjoys over purely legal classical law is that it generates an integral flexibility in the relationship between economic exchange and the form of the legal security provided by the contract. For, as I have said, the legal contract is not what is essential. It is the exchange, and particularly

clarification take the legal form of agreeing a contract. The provision of security underwritten by the state analytically must have a legal form.

[49] *Photo Productions Ltd v Securicor Ltd* [1980] AC 827, 848–49 (HL).

[50] Or to submit to the legally endorsed methods of discharging the contract in the event of a failure to perform which does not amount to a breach, such as frustration or commercial impracticability.

[51] *Tilley v Thomas* (1867) LR 3 Ch App 61, 72. For a US equivalent, see *Union Pacific Railway Co v Chicago, Rock Island and Pacific Railway Co*, 163 US 564, 600 (1896). For a comprehensive contemporary statement of the thinking, see M Hogg, *Promises and Contract Law* (Cambridge, Cambridge University Press, 2011) 334.

[52] S Macaulay, 'Almost Everything that I Did Want to Know About Contract Litigation: A Comment on Galanter' (2001) 2001 *Wisconsin Law Review* 629, 630.

[53] L Fuller and W Perdue, 'The Reliance Interest in Contract Damages I' (1936) 46 *Yale Law Journal* 52, 54.

the profit, that is essential. The actual performance of the primary obligations is incidental to obtaining that profit, indeed, entering into contractual obligations is a cost of obtaining it. NCRB allows us to see that what really matters is not 'performance' but 'expectation', and to assess the way the contract device conducts the exchange in terms of how well it protects expectation. This is the true function of contract, but it is not something that can coherently emerge from the classical law. Taking this approach allows Macaulay to analyse 'the functions and dysfunctions of using contract to solve exchange problems' and to distinguish cases of the adoption of a 'more or less contractual manner' of solving these problems, depending on the costs and benefits imposed by those functions and dysfunctions. On the basis of the economic argument 'that economic actors will employ the litigation process to settle disputes only to the extent that (1) the present value of continuing relationships is low, and (2) the anticipated return from the litigation process is high',[54] Macaulay has shown us many cases where the litigation process has such costs as to be entirely dysfunctional, and it is to these that we now turn.

III. NON-USE AND THE COMPLEX CONTRACT

The case Macaulay has principally studied is the long-term, initially incompletely specified, contractual relationship between competent commercial parties; the type of contract that the late Ian Macneil used to call relational and which Macaulay himself often calls relational, but which I think it better to call complex, for reasons to which I shall return. Macaulay has shown us that holding the parties to primary obligations which they have agreed under these contracts would often work against or completely defeat the purpose of realising the parties' expectation interests. I cannot here quote at sufficient length to convey the richness of the detail and the degree of understanding in the sociological sense which are the particular merits of these studies, but perhaps these are well enough known. Let me, however, concentrate on the conclusions Macaulay draws from his study of the construction of an Administration Building for SC Johnson and Son Inc by Frank Lloyd Wright.[55] Although what is now known as the Johnson Building is 'an architectural masterpiece', the process of its construction was 'not a smooth one';[56] indeed, it was thought by the Company to be 'a financial and construction nightmare'.[57] The very

[54] Macaulay, 'An Empirical View' (n 5) 509.

[55] S Macaulay, 'Organic Transactions: Contract, Frank Lloyd Wright and the Johnson Building' (1996) 1996 *Wisconsin Law Review* 75. I am putting to one side the general influence on Macaulay's work of his discussions with his father-in-law, John R Ramsey, General Manager of the Johnson Company. ibid, 79 fn 14; Macaulay, 'Crime and Custom' (n 18) 248–49.

[56] Macaulay, 'Organic Transactions' (n 55) 77.

[57] ibid 109.

marked delay and cost overrun made nonsense of any provision for such problems as was made in the contract, and the construction was able to be finished only because the parties 'did not talk about what was originally agreed or threaten to sue' but got on with 'managing a relationship with a shared purpose'.[58]

But to what extent was even this extreme case a case of non-use and non-contractual relations? Macaulay does not claim that 'contract' was entirely irrelevant. First, a contract was needed to get the ball rolling, but, recalling the definition of contract in NCRB, we might put this to one side as a matter 'of creating an exchange relationship'.[59] Secondly, Macaulay's views of the part contract played in this case in 'solving problems arising during the course of such a relationship'[60] must be examined closely. He is prepared to:

> concede that contract litigation might be a potential last resort, contributing an unknown, if not unknowable, measure of trust in some situations. In many, if not most cases, however, it will fail to serve this insurance function . . . My guess is that it operates as a vague threat of turning matters over to lawyers and other form of unpleasantness that should be avoided in all but a few situations. As I argued in 1977: 'The contract litigation process may also maintain a vague sense of threat that keeps everyone reasonably reliable.'[61]

The contract, then, does provide a security which one imagines actually is very important for it does mean that the parties do not have carte blanche to simply walk away. Macaulay is of the view that this security is generally essential to the functioning of the market.[62] But this is undeniably a very vague sense of security and it certainly is the case that the solution to the problems arising out of the Johnson Building contract did not depend on the contract remedies in any detail. Why was this? It was because, as Macaulay so convincingly shows on this and so many other occasions, those remedies, boiling down to (the threat of awarding) compensatory damages after litigation based on disputes about supposedly initially agreed primary obligations, were wholly inappropriate. This inappropriateness meant that the written contract was, not merely of no detailed use, but to a considerable extent a threat to the completion of the project were its remedies ever sought, and it was this inappropriateness that led to non-use and non-legal relationships.[63] In essence, the adversarial spirit embodied in the written contract had to be replaced by the far more co-operative spirit of the non-contractual relations.

[58] ibid 108.
[59] Macaulay, NCRB (n 17) 56.
[60] ibid.
[61] Macaulay, 'Organic Transactions' (n 55) 119 (quoting S Macaulay, 'Elegant Models, Empirical Pictures, and the Complexities of Contract' (1977) 11 *Law and Society Review* 507, 519).
[62] ibid; Macaulay, 'Relational Contracts' (n 13) 804.
[63] Macaulay, 'Organic Transactions' (n 55) 114–15.

The question becomes why did two competent commercial parties agree a contract which stipulated inappropriate remedies? A proper answer to this question has, I believe, four parts, the first two of which I mention only for the sake of completeness. First, it is not the case that the law of contract entirely leaves even competent commercial parties free to agree their remedies, and in the Johnson Building case the refusal of the US courts to specifically enforce a personal service contract was obviously significant.[64] I do not think that many of the limits on what competent parties may agree to be their remedies are in the end defensible (though this one is), but we may put this to one side.

Secondly, although the parties have the legal capacity to devise appropriate remedies, this does not mean that they have the practical possibility of doing so, for their bounded rationality in the face of transaction costs may effectively prevent this. During the construction, it seems to have gradually dawned on the SC Johnson that paying Lloyd Wright a fee calculated as a fixed percentage of costs which were steeply rising in part because of his conduct, was unwise. As I read Macaulay's account of this I imagined that the company might have wished that it had thought to cap Lloyd Wright's fee at the outset rather than having to negotiate for this during the construction as happened.[65] But Macaulay has revealed the remarkable facts that the company subsequently engaged Lloyd Wright to build another building for them; initially took the same line over his fee for that building; had to go through the unpleasant rigmarole of capping his fee when all the same problems cropped up again; and then, to top it all, effectively gave him more than his capped fee after the later building was completed![66]

The necessity for the parties to negotiate appropriate remedies arises, of course, because the inappropriate remedy of compensatory damages after litigation is applied by default. In the section on 'Long-Term Relationships in Commercial Transactions' in the Wisconsin contracts casebook, Macaulay and his colleagues cite this study of the Johnson Building as part of the 'considerable evidence that when a contract is breached, the aggrieved party does not obtain or expect "benefit of the bargain" damages to protect the expectation interest'.[67] Realising this leads us to address the third and fourth parts of an answer to the question why the contract provided inappropriate remedies. Thirdly, then, why, if they realised that the default remedies for breach of contract were inappropriate, did the parties fail to negotiate appropriate ones? Macaulay shows quite a bit of muddled if well-intentioned thinking on the part of the company and a disdain for matters such as these on the part of Lloyd Wright, who, in my

[64] ibid 115.
[65] Macaulay, 'Organic Transactions' (n 55) 105.
[66] ibid 106–107.
[67] Macaulay and others, *Contracts* (n 2) 476.

opinion – which I fear is much less sympathetic to Lloyd Wright than Macaulay's – appears quite like the picture painted of him in *The Fountainhead*, and no doubt these attitudes would have made such negotiations extremely difficult. But I submit that another reason is that the parties had indeed accepted that contract remedies are inevitably based on default compensatory damages (following litigation), and they didn't fully explore the possibilities of negotiating alternatives. Macaulay's account of the construction is itself based on the resultant unproductive opposition between contract and non-use and non-contractual relations, and what I believe is the surprising thing is that he does not fully explore the possibility of breaking down this opposition.

Now, as Macaulay is seeking to explain an empirical situation, it is hardly a criticism of him to say that he accurately describes the lack of contractual acuity in the parties. But, in my opinion, it is not the institution of contract as such that is at fault but the parties' failure to use contract's resources to help, rather than hinder, them in the attempt to conduct their exchange. And the principal reason I would give for this is that the parties and their legal advisors were working within the framework of the classical law of contract, in which the issue is the performance of primary obligations on the supposedly initially agreed terms. When the law of contract is understood in this way, the remedies are ultimately directed at compelling such performance even if the benefits and burdens of the initial allocation of risk bear little relationship to the allocation which would have taken place had the agreement been negotiated at later stages of the performance, and so those remedies come to be perceived as inappropriate and unfair by the parties. As Macaulay has been at the forefront in demonstrating, though the basic point long antedates legal realism,[68] the serious cracks in the classical law initially appeared at the points where it was unable to deal acceptably coherently with the many ways in which parties modified their ostensible primary obligations under the contract in order to preserve an inadequately negotiated exchange, the value of which they still wanted to realise.

The provisions of a modern construction contract essentially seek to provide for modification in the light of the knowledge of the benefits and burdens of the contract which is gained throughout the course of performance.[69] Parallel provisions for such modifications are to be found in other complex contracts governed by specific areas of advanced commercial law which are thought to be quite distinct from the general principles

[68] eg J Ames, 'Two Theories of Consideration' (1899) 12 *Harvard Law Review* 515, 531.

[69] For a detailed and coherent (despite the two qualities often being mutually exclusive in works of this nature) account of the variation provisions in one of the UK's leading standard forms of construction contract, see I Ndekugri and M Rycroft, *The JCT 05 Standard Building Contract* (London, Butterworth Heinemann, 2009) ch 6.

of contract.[70] But so long as the background understanding of the parties to these contracts is based on the classical law, these provisions will tend to appear to be at odds with the basic purpose of contract, which is the literal enforcement of the primary obligation, and will do so for the very good reason that they are indeed at odds with that purpose. This background understanding will, of course, tend to thwart modification provisions by interpreting them in a literal spirit, for, as Don Harris and I have put it elsewhere, 'one cannot create a co-operative attitude by writing it down that such an attitude will be taken to contingencies as they arise'.[71] So long as this is the case, contractual practice must be beset by a schizophrenia between the classical law's promise of performance of primary obligations and the lesson of actual complex contracting, which is that, if it is to be welfare-enhancing, it has to be a matter of compromise and settlement; in essence, co-operation.

Macaulay, a self-proclaimed 'card carrying member of the Macneil party',[72] was extremely generous to Macneil's relational theory in explaining how the Johnson Building ever got built, and this is an instance of the way that Macaulay has made, in his empirical work, a contribution to the relational theory which complements Macneil's concentration on theory. The construction of the Johnson Building is described as a paradigm case of both the failure of what Macneil called 'presentiation'[73] and of the importance of the parties' direct recourse to what Macneil called the relational norms of 'good faith, solidarity, role integrity and mutuality' as the 'overarching obligations' which allowed the project to be completed by making it relatively clear that 'the object of contracting is not primarily to allocate risks, but to signify a commitment to co-operate'.[74]

All this is right, but, with respect, I do not think Macaulay directs attention to that part of Macneil's work which allows us to think of devising

[70] With respect to the law of England and Wales, the clearest expression of this is Sir Roy Goode's magisterial *Commercial Law*, which first appeared in 1982 (Harmondsworth, Penguin, 1982). The extraordinary thing about this book, other than its combination of breadth of learning and practical acuity, is that, of its 989 pages, only 56 are taken up with a conventional account of the general principles of contract. The bulk of the rest of the book is an acute account of the actual security devices used by competent commercial lawyers, which typically appear as exceptions to those general principles! This is a sort of schizophrenia. Nothing much was changed, save a growth in the size of the book to now 1,355 pages, in the two further editions produced by Goode or in the recent 4th edition, edited by Professor Ewan McKendrick (London, Penguin Books, 2010).

[71] D Campell and D Harris, 'Flexibility in Long-term Contractual Relationships: The Role of Co-operation' (1993) 20 *Journal of Law and Society* 166, 173.

[72] Macaulay, 'Relational Contracts' (n 13) 782. Perhaps Macaulay's best single account of Macneil is in S Macaulay, 'Long-term Continuing Relations: The American Experience Regulating Dealerships and Franchises' in C Joerges (ed), *Franchising and the Law* (Baden-Baden, Nomos Verlagsgesellschaft, 2001) 179.

[73] I Macneil, 'Restatement (Second) of Contracts and Presentation' (1974) 60 *Virginia Law Review* 589. Perhaps out of concern for the lyrical quality of his prose, Macaulay avoids this ugly term, which has never caught on.

[74] Macaulay, 'Organic Transactions' (n 55) 110–11.

complex contracts which help, rather than hinder, the parties. What Macaulay says of the contract between Lloyd Wright and the company no doubt applies to the conduct of 'modern business', but the main thing Macaulay has shown us is that such conduct is costly and, in the case of dealing with Lloyd Wright, markedly so. The Johnson Building got built, but do we always have to go through this 'nightmare'? Macaulay hints at an answer to this question when he asks whether 'the story of the Johnson Building [is] one of a failure of contract planning or drafting,' and answers: 'This is not the case'.[75] As I have said, I find this surprising. For though Macaulay is perfectly well aware that there are 'many ways in Mr Wright and the Johnson Company could have structured their transaction that might have minimised the problems they later encountered', he does not think too much of this possibility. Employing these 'elaborate contractual structures', he tells us, 'would have involved high transaction costs' and, much more importantly, would generate a climate of mutual antagonism 'out of control of the parties' which would ruin the co-operative atmosphere and make it 'harder to continue a relationship'.[76]

I am obliged to say I disagree with Macaulay here. What he says is true of the contract that was written but not of the contract that might have been written. There is a relatively little known part of Macneil's work which is, in my opinion, effectively a blueprint for the reform of contracting in the sense of telling us how to write better contracts, including better complex contracts, when faced with the inevitable failure of presentiation. Having identified the shortcomings of presentiation in 'Restatement (Second) of Contracts and Presentiation' in 1974,[77] in 1975 Macneil published what I think is his best paper, 'A Primer of Contract Planning',[78] which showed that the proper contractual response to this failure is to provide for co-operative modification in the original agreement.[79] Macneil insists and Macaulay would, I think, more firmly insist, 'no contract can ever be fully planned',[80] but properly devised contracts could, and to various extents do, provide for necessary co-operation by ousting the classical provisions that militate against them:

> There may be countless reasons why good risk planning calls for explicitness in drafting . . . Among these may be dissatisfaction with the legal allocation, the need for greater explicitness than is provided by the applicable rules of law, costs imposed by use of the legal system that may be avoided or reduced by

[75] ibid 112.

[76] ibid 112–14.

[77] Macneil, 'Restatement' (n 73).

[78] I Macneil, 'A Primer of Contract Planning' (1975) 48 *Southern California Law Review* 627.

[79] Macaulay, 'Organic Transactions' (n 55) 110 n 127. Macneil returned to the theme of adjustment in a number of subsequent fine papers, including the ones to which Macaulay refers here, but in these papers the legal detail drops away and the sociology of the contractual norms comes to the fore in the way typical in Macneil's later work.

[80] Macneil, 'A Primer' (n 78) 668.

> specific planning, ineffectiveness of the techniques supplied by the legal system for implementing its risk allocation, inflexibility of the legal rules, or even such things as a need to have the planning spelled out in contract documents in order to insure ready availability if dispute arises.[81]

Macaulay is, of course, perfectly well aware of all this. It is hardly necessary to mention in this connection that Bill Whitford and he taught from Macneil's second casebook and used it as a sort of template when, with Marc Galanter and the late John Kidwell, they drew up their own,[82] and that 'A Primer of Contract Planning' is the framework of the second part of Macneil's casebook.[83] I am not trying to point to something that has been missed. I am merely, though this is presumptuous enough, asking for a refocus of Macaulay's, and therefore our, attitude to the written contract.[84] In the end, I think Macaulay accepts that the 'real deal' over the Johnson Building could be 'realised' only by departing from the 'paper deal', and that this is a general position even in contracting between competent commercial parties.[85] This is a strong positive position because Macaulay, and others following him, have furnished compelling empirical evidence that he is right. But normatively this is not a strong position, for where do we go with this reliance on truly non-contractual relations? The coherent understanding of what is going on in these contracts requires reference to intentions expressed in the contract as well as to the non-contractual relations that are sorely needed because the contract expresses those intentions so badly. The idea that complex contracting can be ordered by truly non-contractual relations, entirely divorced from the contract, boils down only to the altruism we have noted above.[86] This altruism has an attraction, but it is a superficial one. One can sympathise with the sentiment behind a welfarist rejection of economics, but, for the reasons which Wicksteed has perhaps stated most clearly,[87] this does not make it one jot easier to believe that altruism is a plausible principle of economic allocation.

[81] ibid 670.

[82] Macaulay, 'Relational Contracts' (n 13) 775–76.

[83] I Macneil and P Gudel, *Contracts: Exchange Transactions and Relations*, 3rd edn (New York, Foundation Press, 2001) pt 2.

[84] It is at this point that I should say that I have found works by John Kidwell and William Whitford enormously helpful in guiding my path through the nuances of the Wisconsin approach. In particular, as I have stated previously, D Campbell, 'Breach and Penalty as Contractual Norm and Contractual Anomie' (2001) 2001 *Wisconsin Law Review* 681, 692, I believe my argument about non-use develops the basic thrust of J Kidwell, 'A Caveat' (1985) 1985 *Wisconsin Law Review* 615.

[85] S Macaulay, 'The Real Deal and the Paper Deal: Empirical Pictures of Relationships, Complexity and the Urge for Transparent, Simple Rules' in D Campbell, H Collins, and J Wightman (eds), *The Implicit Dimensions of Contracts* (Oxford, Hart Publishing, 2003) 51.

[86] See text accompanying nn 35–36 above.

[87] P Wicksteed, *The Commonsense of Political Economy*, rev edn (London, Routledge & Kegan Paul, 1933) 170–83.

It is as a way of avoiding this unsatisfactory position that work of Macaulay's stamp has been criticised by the new formalism as unhelpfully loose,[88] as imposing impossible tasks[89] on a fallible court,[90] and as therefore giving no real assistance to the parties.[91] It has been entirely open to Macaulay[92] to respond that the novelty of this formalism has been more an aspiration than an achievement because, as gap-filling simply cannot be avoided, adjudication will always be more open than the new formalism can really embrace and still in any helpful way be regarded as formalist.[93] To me at least, this debate quickly lost its initial interest, and I think that this was because it was never really a debate about adjudicative technique at all but rather a debate about what weight should be given to the sanctity of contract, that is to say, about the values which fundamentally inform adjudication.

A recent exhibition of the differences of opinion at work has been the contrary evaluations Whitford and Macaulay[94] and Scott[95] have given of *Hoffman v Red Owl Stores*.[96] I think Whitford and Macaulay got to the root of the matter when they observe that 'perhaps Scott would not support recovery in *Hoffman* even if he accepted our view of the facts',[97] but only in the sense that I do not think Scott would ever be able to accept their view, not for any crude reason,[98] but because of the complex nature of the judgement that is being attempted here. What we really need to know about *Hoffman* is how far Hoffmann's[99] reliance was reasonable. But no amount of legal archaeological uncovering of what went on in the case will itself determine this, for to say something is reasonable is a synthetic

[88] eg O Ben-Shahar, 'The Tentative Case Against Flexibility in Commercial Law' (1999) 66 *University of Chicago Law Review* 781.

[89] eg E Bernstein, 'The Questionable Basis of Article 2's Incorporation Strategy: A Preliminary Study' (1999) 66 *University of Chicago Law Review* 710.

[90] eg E Posner, 'A Theory of Contract Law Under Conditions of Radical Judicial Error' (2000) 94 *Northwestern University Law Review* 749.

[91] eg R Scott, 'The Case for Formalism in Relational Contract' (2000) 94 *Northwestern University Law Review* 847.

[92] And his colleagues, eg E Mertz, 'An Afterword: Tapping the Promise of Relational Contract Theory – "Real" Legal Language and a New Legal Realism' (2001) 94 *Northwestern University Law Review* 909, and W Whitford, 'Relational Contracts and the New Formalism' (2004) 2004 *Wisconsin Law Review* 631. Kidwell's remarkable comment that I have already mentioned, above n 84, seems to me to anticipate much of what of value emerged from this debate.

[93] Macaulay, 'The Real Deal' (n 85).

[94] W Whitford and S Macaulay, '*Hoffman v Red Owl Stores*: The Rest of the Story' (2010) 61 *Hastings Law Journal* 801.

[95] R Scott, '*Hoffman v Red Owl Stores* and the Limits of the Legal Method' (2010) 61 *Hastings Law Journal* 859.

[96] *Hoffman v Red Owl Stores*, 133 NW 2d 267 (WI 1965).

[97] Whitford and Macaulay, *Hoffman* (n 94) 855 fn 296.

[98] ibid 849; Scott, *Hoffman* (n 95) 865.

[99] On the spelling of Hoffmann's name, see Scott, *Hoffman* (n 95) 861 fn 5.

judgement in which, as I have put it elsewhere, 'the facts *are* values'.[100] Scott is substantially right when he says in his *Hoffman* article that '[t]he shorthand for the differences' between Macaulay and Whitford and himself 'is expressed as the divide between "law and society" and "law and economics"',[101] though I am here trying to show, or perhaps expand, a law and economics dimension to Macaulay's thought.

How far the courts should attempt to give effect to the objective intentions of the parties, or how far they should try to produce what they believe is a better outcome than this by seeking to give effect to what one of the parties really subjectively meant when it has failed to give that meaning an adequate objective statement in the contract, is an issue which is, in Gallie's famous phrase, essentially contested because the values which underpin both positions on this issue have their attractions.[102] As Macaulay penetratingly observed more than 50 years ago, contract turns on the 'problem of proportioning' these values.[103] I want no more than that it be clear that, in an appropriately delimited market sphere, freedom of contract is the paramount – it cannot be the sole – value which should guide us when taking a position on this issue.

I must just say outright that I do not think Macaulay has always maintained this position, and in the earlier draft of what has become this paper that I have mentioned,[104] I criticised what I thought were some instances of an avoidably excessive strain of welfarism in Macaulay's work.[105] I think the degree of his sympathy for Lloyd Wright's disdain for the duties of negotiation over the Johnson Building is one of these instances. These instances no doubt are reflective of the general background sympathy towards welfarism that Anthony Downs has so influentially shown obtained when Macaulay began his professional life.[106] But not only has Macaulay been in advance of the general thinking on this, his clear relinquishment of the title Gilmore bestowed on him now renders such criticism unnecessary. We are dealing with legitimate disagreements about how to realise the function of the law of contract. In my own view, which I believe represents the best development of Macaulay's work, it is not the

[100] D Campbell, 'Truth Claims and Value-freedom in the Treatment of Legitimacy: The Case of Weber' (1986) 13 *Journal of Law and Society* 207, 210.

[101] Scott, 'Hoffman' (n 95) 867.

[102] W Gallie, 'Essentially Contested Concepts' (1956) 56 *Proceedings of the Aristotelian Society* 167.

[103] S Macaulay, 'Justice Traynor and the Law of Contracts' (1961) 13 *Stanford Law Review* 812, 813.

[104] See text accompanying n 3 above.

[105] I must repeat my previously stated opinion, however, that Kennedy's deservedly very influential gloss, particularly on the work of Macaulay, seems to have played a large part in forming this view of Macaulay's position. D Kennedy, 'Distributive and Paternalist Motives in Contract Law, with Special Reference to Compulsory Terms and Unequal Bargaining Power' (1982) 41 *Maryland Law Review* 563, 582.

[106] A Downs, *An Economic Theory of Democracy* (Boston, Addison Wesley, 1957) ch 15.

law of contract as such that is at fault but contracts entered into on the basis of the classical law of contract. Complex contracts do not have to take the classical form which leads to their non-use, and we have to ask why they continue to do so, and why Macaulay himself has not explored the possibility of devising adequate contracts as far as one might expect. An essential preliminary to this is to turn to the other pole of Macneil's spectrum of contracts and study the discrete contract.

IV. NON-USE AND THE DISCRETE CONTRACT

It will be recalled that I believe that a full answer to the question why the parties to the Johnson Building contract in particular, and to complex contracts in general, fail to agree more adequate contracts has four parts, and I have described three. The third part of the answer is the parties' failure to design and agree terms appropriate to their contract. The fourth part is the obverse of this. Why is it necessary to devise such terms? Why are the default remedies for breach of contract so inappropriate to complex contracts? These remedies are, in an important sense, the villain of the piece in Macaulay's account of complex contracting, for it is they that are so costly as to be dysfunctional. We have noted the significance of the US law's refusal to specifically enforce personal service contracts for the Johnson Building contract,[107] and of this Macaulay says: 'Contract law works better in agreements to sell specified quantities of fungible goods than in bargains to hire genius and talent.'[108]

It is at this point that, I believe, Macaulay has halted his criticism of the classical law rather than press home the logic of that criticism. Macaulay pours scorn on the fact that 'Academic contracts celebrates free market capitalism, the few exceptions [allowed serving] to make this institution seem wonderful or at least tolerable',[109] for he shows that there are more than a few exceptions. But, paradoxically, this criticism in substantial part accepts the classical understanding of the basic structure of the law and economics of contract. The default rules of contract are allowed to govern what Macneil called the discrete contract, in which market exchanges are made on relatively narrowly confined and sharply defined terms by effectively anonymous parties. In essence, Macaulay allows that the classical law and its corollary economics to be accurate for the discrete contract, but, of course, there are many occasions on which they do not fit the facts:

[107] See text accompanying n 64 above.

[108] Macaulay, 'Organic Transactions' (n 55) 115.

[109] S Macaulay, 'Bambi Meets Godzilla: Reflections on Contracts Scholarship and Teaching vs. State Unfair Trade Practices and Consumer Protection Statutes' (1989) 26 *Houston Law Review* 575, 576.

> [T]he empirical picture of the contract process in capitalist societies differs sharply from the classical model . . . The classical model of the contract process may fit one-shot transactions, such as those sometimes found in financing and real estate, but the reality of modern business generally involves long-term continuing relationships . . . The classical model of the contract process thus operates only in 'a special and limited case'.[110]

Macaulay's basic achievement rests on the fact that his criticism of the inadequacies of the classical law and its corollary economics to complex contracting has been very powerful. The limitation of this criticism, however, is that it cedes the core ground, where those assumptions can usefully be said to apply, to that law and those economics. I very respectfully suggest that Macaulay's claim that 'much, if not most, significant economic behaviour takes place almost untouched by contract norms or litigation'[111] is only partially correct. The discrete contract is not 'a special and limited case' but, as it embraces the basic sale, is rather the paradigm contract.[112] If the discrete contract is ceded to law and economics, then the relational theory can be marginalised by being said to apply only to an interesting and significant but nevertheless exceptional set of cases, and this is indeed what has happened.[113] Having identified 'the classical model' as one in which 'one-shot transactions are performed largely because of the threat of the sanctions that follow a breach',[114] Macaulay has not given enough attention to discrete contracts because, as he rightly perceives, these contracts are but little attended by the threat of sanction in the way meant in the classical law. But this does not mean that the law of contract does not play an indispensable role in facilitating discrete exchange.

Interpretation of Macneil's relational theory has typically failed to grasp that the essence of that theory is that all contracts, both the discrete and what I have called the complex, are relational. Though he was of that view that he had maintained that all contracts were relational ever since he came fully to appreciate the inadequacy of the classical law,[115] Macneil himself came to acknowledge that he had been insufficiently clear about this, and that inconsistent statements which strongly distinguished relational from discrete contracts were to be found in his work. In his later writings he sought to move away from the confusing use of 'relational' to

[110] Macaulay, 'An Empirical View' (n 5) 509.

[111] Macaulay, 'Elegant Models' (n 61) 523.

[112] There must, as Macaulay is perfectly well aware, also be a question about how far the findings in NCRB and UNUC can be extended to other businesses involved in complex contracting. Macaulay, 'Contracts' (n 14) 1182 fn 94.

[113] This is the thrust of sympathetic mainstream commentary on the relational theory. See M Eisenberg, 'Relational Contracts', in J Beatson and D Friedmann (eds), *Good Faith and Fault in Contract Law* (Oxford, Clarendon Press, 1995) 291; see also E McKendrick, 'The Regulation of Long-term Contracts in English Law' in ibid 305.

[114] Macaulay, 'Elegant Models' (n 61) 523.

[115] I Macneil, *The Relational Theory of Contract* (London, Sweet & Maxwell, 2001) xiii.

mean both all contracts and a class of contracts different to discrete contracts,[116] using 'intertwined' to describe what he had formerly called relational contracts.[117] I myself think 'complex' is a much less confusing term (in this context) than relational and a much more natural term than intertwined. I have argued at length that the relational theory is essential to a proper understanding of, not merely the complex, but of all contracts,[118] including the discrete,[119] for it is possible for economic actors to 'reveal' their preferences by discrete exchange on the market only by recognising the reciprocal rights and duties, underpinned by the state, which constitute that market.[120] I have argued at particular length that the remedies for breach of discrete contracts institutionalise co-operative relations between the parties,[121] and it is on this latter argument that I shall focus here. Given constraints of space, I can give only one example of this argument. For a reason of which I am proud, set out below, this is not as unsatisfactory as it initially appears.

Let us consider the paradigm case of breach of contract, a seller's failure to perform its sale obligation to deliver generic goods. The response of the buyer will be to cover and, if the substitute goods cost more than the contracted goods, the legal position is that the buyer would have its expectation protected by compensatory market damages (perhaps with an additional component to cover incidental costs). Beale and Dugdale's empirical study mentioned above shows that the seller typically pays a sum in effective compensation of this loss without dispute, much less with any involvement of lawyers, in the course of normal business relations.[122] If the parties were competent when agreeing the sale price and

[116] I Macneil, 'Relational Contract Theory: Challenges and Queries' (2000) 94 *Northwestern University Law Review* 877, 894.

[117] I Macneil, 'Relational Contract Theory as Sociology: A Reply to Professors Lindenberg and de Vos' (1987) 143 *Journal of Institutional and Theoretical Economics* 272, 276.

[118] D Campbell, 'Ian Macneil and the Relational Theory of Contract' in Macneil, *Relational Theory* (n 115) 3.

[119] D Campbell, 'The Relational Constitution of the Discrete Contract' in D Campbell and P Vincent-Jones (eds), *Contract and Economic Organisation: Socio-legal Initiatives* (Aldershot, Dartmouth Publishing, 1996) 40; D Campbell and H Collins, 'Discovering the Implicit Dimensions of Contracts' in Campbell and others, *Implicit Dimensions* (n 85) 25.

[120] D Campbell, 'The Relational Constitution of Contractual Agreement' in P Heugens, J Vromen, and H Oosterhout (eds), *The Social Institutions of Capitalism: Evolution and Design of Social Contracts* (Cheltenham, Edward Elgar, 2003) 38.

[121] D Campbell, 'The Relational Constitution of Remedy: Co-operation as the Implicit Second Principle of Remedies for Breach of Contract' (2005) 11 *Texas Wesleyan Law Review* 455; D Campbell, 'A Relational Critique of the Restatement (Third) of Restitution § 39' (2011) 68 *Washington and Lee Law Review* 1063.

[122] Beale and Dugdale, 'Contracts Between Businessmen' (n 21). Though the practice is central to the law of contract, there is no explicit law of cover in the Commonwealth. In the US, White and Summers believe that the dearth of cases on UCC § 2-712 makes it difficult to say with certainty how important it is. J White and R Summers, *Uniform Commercial Code*, 6th edn (St Paul, West, 2010) para 7-4 fn 1. I am suggesting that it is of the first importance, but this is reconcilable with the views of White and Summers because it is a rule which works so well it does not normally lead to disputes.

the market is stable, it is entirely possible that the cover price will not diverge from the sale price, and in these circumstances the buyer will cover and there will be no claim.

This seems like a perfect case of non-use but it is not. It is a case where the contract remedies so align the interests of the parties that they make recourse to the law in the classical sense of threat of legal action redundant. Even successful litigation, if we allow this almost entirely theoretical possibility, could at most yield only market damages, which the claimant would have to use to obtain substitute goods if he wished to realise his expectation under the original contract. These legal rules give a very efficiently working incentive to the parties to reach the optimal outcome themselves.

Nothing could capture the fundamental weakness of the classical law more than the fact that it meets with puzzlement or distaste the positive law of contract's remedial response to a failure to deliver a generic good when contract price and market price are identical. Work on the default rules for breach of contract in the broad tradition of Holmes' choice theory can better come to terms with the actual form of the positive law of remedies, and has done so in the hands of some of the most distinguished contract scholars of the twentieth century. But almost always the Holmes theory is accepted as a sort of regrettable paradox. The positive law is as Holmes says, but the lingering normative atmosphere is that it is a shame that this is so, for here is the bad man at work is costlessly breaching.[123] But in the standard case of cover we are, in fact, dealing with a thoroughly co-operative remedial response. The buyer obtains an adequate substitute, and therefore avoids loss, especially consequential loss, and the seller without dispute pays a sum, representing what he would have to pay in damages, that is quantified in such a way as to keep those damages as low as possible consistent with protection of the buyer's expectation. Indeed, as we have seen, those damages may well be zero. Bounded rationality makes breach an ineluctable feature of the market, and this optimally low-cost way of dealing with it is possible only because the parties effectively co-operate in dealing with the consequences of breach. Far from articulating amoral or immoral self-interest, the structure of the positive law is fundamentally co-operative and works only because it is fundamentally co-operative.

The lessons I have drawn from this paradigm case is that it is simply absurd to claim that the function of contract is to prevent breach and that understanding the structure of the positive law turns on recognising that '*a major function of the law of contract is to allow breach*, but on the right occasions and on the right terms; in essence, on terms which encourage claimants to cover in the knowledge that the defendant will compensate lost

[123] eg J Perillo, 'Misreading Oliver Wendell Holmes on Efficient Breach and Tortious Interference' (2000) 68 *Fordham Law Review* 1085.

net expectation'.[124] Although the brief illustration I have given can hardly itself convince the reader of the truth of this, I find this way of stating that argument less unsatisfactory than it otherwise would be because Macaulay has considered my argument at length,[125] and has been good enough to say it is 'most unorthodox' but '[n]onetheless . . . has great plausibility'.[126] The principal attraction of the argument to Macaulay is that it describes an interplay between the formal legal sanction and the law in action response,[127] and Macaulay's reservations about the argument largely concern, in my opinion, the occasions when this interplay, because of the exercise of unacceptable inequality of bargaining power, does not lead to co-operative but to opportunistic action. I do not want to deny this possibility, far from it, but it is, I believe, a point we can regard as incidental, in a sense about which I now wish to be very clear.

My views on the default remedies for breach of contract are, in fact, a justification of efficient breach, but of a very substantially different sort to the usual justification.[128] By far the most common understanding of efficient breach, brought to great prominence by Posner's popularisations of the concept,[129] is a rationalisation for allowing a breaching party to move to a more profitable contract. This is not a practically significant issue, and one of the reasons for this is that it undermines the trust needed for repeat contracting, as Macaulay's and Macneil's telling criticisms of efficient breach as conventionally understood make clear. But efficient breach in the sense I mean encompasses the normal case of breach of contract, with the efficiency being identified in the minimisation of the costs of breach for both parties. The production of an efficient outcome by effective co-operation is the key to the structure of the law of remedies for breach of contract. We must understand that the occasions when the rules for minimising the cost of breach are not desirable are exceptions to a fundamentally co-operative and immensely successful structure, not illustrations of a fundamentally deficient structure.

[124] Campbell, 'The Relational Constitution' (n 121) 468.

[125] S Macaulay, 'Renegotiations and Settlements: Dr Pangloss' Notes on the Margins of David Campbell's Papers' (2007) 29 *Cardozo Law Review* 261. This was not the first time Macaulay had adopted the stance of Dr Pangloss; see S Macaulay, 'The Impact of Contract Law on the Economy: Less than Meets the Eye?' (unpublished paper, 1994) www.law.wisc.edu/facstaff/macaulay/papers/impact_of_contract_law.pdf.

[126] S Macaulay, 'A New Legal Realism: Elegant Models and Messy Law in Action' in S Macaulay and others (eds), *New Legal Realism* (Cambridge, Cambridge University Press, forthcoming) vol 1.

[127] Macaulay, 'Renegotiations' (n 125) 287.

[128] The nub of these views is set out in Campbell, 'A Relational Critique' (n 121) 1093–96. A longer statement, with references to the relevant views of Macaulay (and Macneil and others), is made in Campbell, 'The Relational Constitution' (n 121) 461–67.

[129] R Posner, *Economic Analysis of Law*, 8th edn (Austin, Wolters Kluwer, 2011) 151. Though I will not describe this development here, Posner's treatment of efficient breach has grown rather more sophisticated over successive editions of his textbook, and it is no longer, in fact, directly open to the criticisms typically made of the early editions.

V. WHY THE PARTIES TO COMPLEX CONTRACTS SOMETIMES DO SO BADLY

We are now in a position clearly to see why the classical law of contact is so unsatisfactory for the governance of the complex contract. Its remedies are intended to work for the discrete contract, and there they do usually lead to very satisfactory outcomes for commercial parties. The main way (there are many relatively minor doctrines to similar effect) they do this is by making literal enforcement an exceptional remedy, and by quantifying compensatory damages on the basis of a doctrine of causation which minimises loss. The rules of causation ensure that the claimant's loss: (1) can be quantified (requirement of certainty); (2) was in reasonable contemplation when the contract was agreed (requirement of proximity); and (3) that the claimant keeps his loss to a minimum (requirement of mitigation).

But the very elements of the doctrine of causation that lead to excellent outcomes in cases of breach of a discrete contract are precisely what make those rules inappropriate to complex contracts. Losses in complex contracts may well not be able to be avoided by cover, and consequential losses may well be uncertain (this is the main problem) and give rise to remoteness and mitigation issues, all of which so limit the claimant's damages that the claimant believes that those damages do not (fully) compensate its loss. Extremely troublesome disputes will arise because a claimant which finds itself confined to nominal or relatively small damages when it believes its loss is substantial will seek to challenge quantum, or even seek literal enforcement so as to avoid damages quantification altogether.

Obviously, what the parties to complex contracts which carry a risk of uncertain loss should do is oust the inappropriate default rules and supply their own.[130] Now, of course, the parties sometimes do this. I have mentioned construction cases in this connection,[131] and that this is what the pursuit of real rather than legal remedies in advanced commercial law is largely about. But it is evident from the prevalence of problems with complex contracting that the parties do not do this sufficiently frequently. I suggest that the reason they do not do so is that they hold to the classical view of contract and fundamentally believe that the remedies for breach will secure the actual performance of primary obligations. Acting in accord with this belief, they do not sufficiently explore the possibilities of planning for co-operative resolution of inevitable disputes. They then find

[130] Or choose a non-market form of economic organisation. See, eg I Macneil, 'Economic Analysis of Contractual Relations: Its Shortfalls and the Need for a "Rich Classificatory Apparatus"' (1981) 75 *Northwestern University Law Review* 1019, 1025–26.

[131] See text accompanying n 69 above.

they have to adopt co-operative strategies in just the way Macaulay has shown us they do, or the contract ends in a bad way, in dispute and (the threat of) litigation. Typically, endings of this sort finally bring home to the parties the inadequacy of their contracting practice, for they do not get what they think vindicates their position but find that they have to settle, settlement being the final confirmation of the inappropriateness of the excessively self-interested attitude they have taken towards their contractual relationships.[132]

VI. THE OUTSIDE POINT OF VIEW AND THE CRITIQUE OF THE CLASSICAL LAW OF CONTRACT

In this paper on the law of contract, I have said little about Macaulay's huge contribution to the general development of the law in action approach to the study of law, which extends beyond its application to the law of contract to law in all its forms. Leaving aside Macaulay's forays into substantive areas of law other than contract, his contribution to the general theory of law in action essentially amounts to a sociologically sophisticated elucidation of the methodological necessity of studying the reciprocal relationship of statements of the law and their effect on empirical action.[133] The implications for this for our approach to contract adjudication and doctrinal or theoretical scholarship in contract are currently being restated as a call for 'new legal realism'.[134]

With regard to the critique of the classical law of contract, I wish to try to add to that part of Macaulay's methodology which insists upon the social scientist, and the legal scholar as social scientist, taking 'the outside point of view'.[135] By this is meant 'looking at legal phenomena from the standpoint of one or more of the social sciences',[136] which analytically requires being at a distance from the 'inside explanation'[137] of those phenomena maintained by '[l]aw professors, lawyers and judges (and often the public)'.[138] Of course, having taken that distance, the social scientist might independently confirm the inside explanation. But this is typically not what has happened in law in action scholarship in general or in Macaulay's work on complex contracting in particular, both of which

[132] H Collins, *Regulating Contracts* (Oxford, Oxford University Press, 1999) ch 14.

[133] Macaulay and others, *Law in Action* (n 19) ch 1.

[134] S Macaulay, 'The New Versus the Old Legal Realism: "Things Ain't What They Used To Be"' (2005) 2005 *Wisconsin Law Review* 365; Macaulay 'Contracts' (n 14); Macaulay, 'A New Legal Realism' (n 126).

[135] Macaulay and others, *Law in Action* (n 19) 1.

[136] ibid.

[137] ibid 6.

[138] ibid 4.

have been, usually justifiably, 'critical of the assumptions of liberal legalism about the role of law in capitalist society'.[139]

Macaulay has shown that, in effect, the legal understanding on which business parties typically contract is wrong in a fundamental way. The contracts on which they purport to conduct their business relationships are drafted on the basis of an essentially classical understanding of the way contract works, and so, whilst such contracts allow the relationships to begin, reference to them could engender an attitude of narrow self-interest towards the resolution of inevitable disputes which is either irrelevant or harmful to those relationships. The inevitable response to this has been apparent non-use and non-contractual relations. This classical understanding must strike some chord in the business parties' own understanding of their relationship, otherwise it would not have such purchase, but the conduct of the economic exchange also generates co-operative attitudes which prevail in the successful complex contract.

I hope to have developed the understanding of the relationship of economic exchange and legal contract that Macaulay has made possible by complementing the ostensible co-operation in complex contracts with an exposure of the co-operation underlying the ostensible self-interest in discrete contracts. This allows us, not to oppose a class of relational contracts articulating co-operation to a class of discrete contracts articulating self-interest, but to say that all contracts are relational, and to redescribe the undoubted differences between discrete and complex contracts in these overall relational terms. The law of contract must be seen as a fundamentally co-operative structure making self-interested exchange possible within legitimate channels. As such, it cannot have the aim of literally ensuring performance, but must have the aim of allowing and regulating breach as a way of co-operatively dealing with the problems of realising profit through exchange.

From the perspective of the classical law, the essential structure of the law of contract based on expectation is either just a complete puzzle or a markedly defective attempt to literally enforce promises. When we pass a judgement on this classical misunderstanding of the law, and its corollary in economics' conception of exchange as the untempered pursuit of self-interest, it seems to me undeniable that we are not merely drawing Macaulay's distinction between the inside and the outside points of view, but we are claiming that the classical understanding is alienated in the sense of expressing an ideological fallacy, the kind of fallacy which Marx made central to critical social theory. Business parties conduct their relationships on the basis of a profoundly mistaken understanding of them, and the consequences of this are, to return to this term, dysfunctional.

[139] S Macaulay, 'Law and the Behavioural Sciences: Is There Any There There?' (1984) 6 *Law and Policy* 149, 181.

Marx's own specific critique of an alienated belief in *Capital* is of what he called the fetishism of commodities.[140] I believe this critique is wrong because of serious shortcomings in Marx's own understanding of the commodity. However, I believe that Marx's way of formulating the critique of an alienated belief is an indispensable part of a correct understanding of the capitalist economy in general and of the law of contract in particular. The difficulties with this approach to social analysis are enormous. The critique of the alienated beliefs of contracting parties requires us to claim that those actually carrying out the practice of contract do not adequately understand what they are doing and that they nevertheless both accomplish their aims in substantial part and reproduce the social structure which makes all of this possible.

Nevertheless, the law of contract is an institution that those who use it systematically misunderstand, the misunderstanding being the basis of the persistence of the denial of contractual co-operation in the classical law. When Macaulay observed that: 'Our economies might be better off . . . if we sought to recognise and legitimate compromise rather than rights vindication as the goal of the legal system',[141] he was profoundly right. But this would require the refutation of the ideology of the classical law and the corollary economics that give rise to the vindication mentality. However, in what I am certain will be regarded as an historically important contribution to contract scholarship in particular and the social sciences in general, Macaulay has done a very great deal to make us see this.

CONCLUSION

I believe that we must either use non-use and non-contractual relations as terms of art which do not bear their obvious meaning or, preferably, stop using them. As Macaulay has explicitly said, but as all his work, including his two great 1963 papers, should lead us to believe, he did not and does not want to be responsible for the death of contract. However, the reform of contract does, I believe, require an execution; the execution of the classical law of contract. Now, this beast is proving very hardy, and this has given rise to quite a cottage industry in the coining of puns to describe classical law's hardiness. My own contribution is 'the undeath of contract',[142] but there are many more, some much funnier and intriguing, such as Macaulay's own 'rattlesnake' which 'only looked dead but . . . could awaken and strike'![143] I think the reason the classical law has proven

[140] K Marx, 'Capital vol 1' in K Marx and F Engels, *Collected Works*, vol 35 (New York, International Publishers, 1996) 81–94.

[141] Macaulay, 'The Impact of Contract Law' (n 125).

[142] Campbell, 'The Undeath of Contract' (n 12).

[143] Macaulay, 'Contracts' (n 14) 1193; see also Macaulay, 'The Death of Contract' (n 15).

so resilient is that there is no adequately worked out alternative theory to which those dissatisfied with the classical law can move. Macneil attempted to state it, but evidently failed. For good reasons which underpin his commitment to a new legal realism, Macaulay is sceptical about the possibility of stating and implementing such a theory.[144] As he has said, he likes 'the present uncertain law plus . . . chaotic law-in-action'[145] far better than I do. But I believe the goal of a superior understanding of contractual action is fundamentally impossible without the new general theory. I have not attempted to argue here that the new theory can be stated because this cannot be argued in any other way than by doing it. But I believe it can be done.

What I have tried to do is to clear away an obstacle to the proper interpretation of Macaulay's work which has, more than any other single contribution, exposed the failings of the classical law, and, I believe, also shows the necessity of stating a rival theory in the way attempted by Macneil. Ultimately, that obstacle has been our understanding of the role of economics in an adequate law of contract. Macaulay's work has tended to be interpreted as a sociology, and so it is. But it is a sociology of a fundamentally economic relationship, whereas the interpretation of it as a sociology has typically taken the line that opposes the social to the economic. But just as the classical law of contract is inadequate law, the analysis of what is mistakenly taken to be purely selfish economic action is inadequate economics, and there is no need to let the Devil keep the best tunes. An adequate law and sociology of exchange and contract shows them to be fundamentally co-operative structures. In Macaulay's work, both sociology and law opposed to economics, and sociology and law in support of a thereby transformed economics, may be found. I believe the latter is the better way forward, and the better interpretation of Macaulay's work overall.

BIBLIOGRAPHY

Ames, J, 'Two Theories of Consideration' (1899) 12 *Harvard Law Review* 515.

Anson, W, *Principles of the English Law of Contract* (Oxford, Clarendon Press, 1879).

Beale, H and Dugdale, T, 'Contracts Between Businessmen: Planning and the Use of Contractual Remedies' (1975) 2 *British Journal of Law and Society* 45.

Beatson, J, Burrows, A and Cartwright, J, *Anson's Law of Contract*, 29th edn (Oxford, Oxford University Press, 2010).

Ben-Shahar, O, 'The Tentative Case Against Flexibility in Commercial Law' (1999) 66 *University of Chicago Law Review* 781.

[144] Macaulay, 'The Real Deal' (n 85) 52 fn 3; Macaulay, 'Contracts' (n 14) 1193–94.

[145] Macaulay, 'Renegotiations and Settlements' (n 125) 263.

Bernstein, E, 'The Questionable Basis of Article 2's Incorporation Strategy: A Preliminary Study' (1999) 66 *University of Chicago Law Review* 710.

Campbell, D, 'A Relational Critique of the Restatement (Third) of Restitution § 39' (2011) 68 *Washington and Lee Law Review* 1063.

——, 'The Relational Constitution of Remedy: Co-operation as the Implicit Second Principle of Remedies for Breach of Contract' (2005) 11 *Texas Wesleyan Law Review* 455.

——, 'The Relational Constitution of Contractual Agreement' in P Heugens, J Vromen, and H Oosterhout (eds), *The Social Institutions of Capitalism: Evolution and Design of Social Contracts* (Cheltenham, Edward Elgar, 2003).

——, 'Breach and Penalty as Contractual Norm and Contractual Anomie' (2001) 2001 *Wisconsin Law Review* 681.

——, 'Ian Macneil and the Relational Theory of Contract' in I Macneil, *The Relational Theory of Contract* (London, Sweet & Maxwell, 2001).

——, 'Reflexivity and Welfarism in the Modern Law of Contract' (2000) 20 *Oxford Journal of Legal Studies* 477.

——, 'The Relational Constitution of Contract and the Limits of "Economics": Kenneth Arrow on the Social Background of Markets' in S Deakin and J Michie (eds), *Contracts, Cooperation and Competition: Studies in Economics, Management and Law* (Oxford, Oxford University Press, 1997).

——, 'The Relational Constitution of the Discrete Contract' in D Campbell and P Vincent-Jones (eds), *Contract and Economic Organisation: Socio-legal Initiatives* (Aldershot, Dartmouth Publishing, 1996).

——, 'The Undeath of Contract: A Study in the Degeneration of a Research Programme' (1992) 22 *The Hong Kong Law Journal* 20.

——, 'Truth Claims and Value-freedom in the Treatment of Legitimacy: The Case of Weber' (1986) 13 *Journal of Law and Society* 207.

Campbell, D and Collins, H, 'Discovering the Implicit Dimensions of Contracts' in D Campbell, H Collins, and J Wightman (eds), *The Implicit Dimensions of Contracts* (Oxford, Hart Publishing, 2003).

Campell, D and Harris, D, 'Flexibility in Long-term Contractual Relationships: The Role of Co-operation' (1993) 20 *Journal of Law and Society* 166.

Collins, H, *Regulating Contracts* (Oxford, Oxford University Press, 1999).

——, *The Law of Contract* (London, Weidenfeld & Nicolson, 1986).

Deakin, S, Lane, C and Wilkinson, F, 'Contract Law, Trust Relations and Incentives for Cooperation: A Comparative Study' in S Deakin and J Michie (eds), *Contracts, Cooperation and Competition: Studies in Economics, Management and Law* (Oxford, Oxford University Press, 1997).

Downs, A, *An Economic Theory of Democracy* (Boston, Addison Wesley, 1957).

Eisenberg, M, 'Relational Contracts', in J Beatson and D Friedmann (eds), *Good Faith and Fault in Contract Law* (Oxford, Clarendon Press, 1995).

Friedman, L and Macaulay, S, 'Contract Law and Contract Teaching: Past, Present and Future' (1967) 1967 *Wisconsin Law Review* 805.

——, *Contract Law in America* (Madison, University of Wisconsin Press, 1965).

Fuller, L and Perdue, W, 'The Reliance Interest in Contract Damages I' (1936) 46 *Yale Law Journal* 52.

Gallie, W, 'Essentially Contested Concepts' (1956) 56 *Proceedings of the Aristotelian Society* 167.

Gilmore, G, *The Death of Contract*, 2nd edn (Columbus, Ohio State University Press, 1995).
Goode, R *Commercial Law* (Harmondsworth, Penguin, 1982).
Goode, R and McKendrick, E (ed) *Goode on Commercial Law*, 4th edn (London, Penguin Books, 2010).
Granovetter, M, 'Economic Action and Social Structure: The Problem of Embeddedness' (1985) 91 *American Journal of Sociology* 481.
Guest, A, *Anson's Law of Contract*, 25th edn (Oxford, Clarendon Press, 1979).
Hogg, M, *Promises and Contracts Law* (Cambridge, Cambridge University Press, 2011).
Kennedy, D, 'Distributive and Paternalist Motives in Contract Law, with Special Reference to Compulsory Terms and Unequal Bargaining Power' (1982) 41 *Maryland Law Review* 563.
Kidwell, J, 'A Caveat' (1985) 1985 *Wisconsin Law Review* 615.
Llewellyn, K, 'Our Case Law of Contract: Offer and Acceptance II' (1939) 48 *Yale Law Journal* 779.
Macaulay, S, 'A New Legal Realism: Elegant Models and Messy Law in Action' in S Macaulay and others (eds), *New Legal Realism* (Cambridge, Cambridge University Press, forthcoming) vol 1.
——, 'The Death of Contract: Dodos and Unicorns or Sleeping Rattlesnakes' in R Gordon and M Horwitz (eds), *Law, Society and History* (Cambridge, Cambridge University Press, 2011).
——, 'Renegotiations and Settlements: Dr Pangloss' Notes on the Margins of David Campbell's Papers' (2007) 29 *Cardozo Law Review* 261.
——, 'Contracts, New Legal Realism and Improving the Navigation of The Yellow Submarine' (2006) 80 *Tulane Law Review* 1161.
——, 'The New Versus the Old Legal Realism: "Things Ain't What They Used To Be"' (2005) 2005 *Wisconsin Law Review* 365.
——, 'The Real Deal and the Paper Deal: Empirical Pictures of Relationships, Complexity and the Urge for Transparent, Simple Rules' in D Campbell, H Collins and J Wightman (eds), *The Implicit Dimensions of Contracts* (Oxford, Hart Publishing, 2003).
——, 'Almost Everything that I Did Want to Know About Contract Litigation: A Comment on Galanter' (2001) 2001 *Wisconsin Law Review* 629.
——, 'Long-term Continuing Relations: The American Experience Regulating Dealerships and Franchises' in C Joerges (ed), *Franchising and the Law* (Baden-Baden, Nomos Verlagsgesellschaft, 2001).
——, 'Relational Contracts Floating on a Sea of Custom? Thoughts About the Ideas of Ian Macneil and Lisa Bernstein' (2000) 94 *Northwestern University Law Review* 775, 804.
——, 'Organic Transactions: Contract, Frank Lloyd Wright and the Johnson Building' (1996) 1996 *Wisconsin Law Review* 75.
——, 'Crime and Custom in Business Society' (1995) 22 *Journal of Law and Society* 248.
——, 'The Impact of Contract Law on the Economy: Less than Meets the Eye?' (unpublished paper, 1994).
——, 'Bambi Meets Godzilla: Reflections on Contracts Scholarship and Teaching vs. State Unfair Trade Practices and Consumer Protection Statutes' (1989) 26 *Houston Law Review* 575.

——, 'An Empirical View of Contract' (1985) 1985 *Wisconsin Law Review* 465.
——, 'Law and the Behavioural Sciences: Is There Any There There?' (1984) 6 *Law and Policy* 149.
——, 'Elegant Models, Empirical Pictures, and the Complexities of Contract' (1977) 11 *Law and Society Review* 507.
——, 'Non-Contractual Relations in Business: A Preliminary Study' (1963) 28 *American Sociological Review* 55.
——, 'The Use and Non-Use of Contracts in the Manufacturing Industry' (1963) 9 *Practical Lawyer* 13.
——, 'Justice Traynor and the Law of Contracts' (1961) 13 *Stanford Law Review* 812.
Macaulay, S, and others, *Contracts: Law in Action*, 3rd edn (New Providence, LexisNexis, 2011).
Macaulay, S, Friedman, L and Mertz, E, *Law in Action: A Socio-Legal Reader* (New York, Foundation Press, 2007).
McKendrick, E, 'The Regulation of Long-term Contracts in English Law' in J Beatson and D Friedmann (eds), *Good Faith and Fault in Contract Law* (Oxford, Clarendon Press, 1995).
Macneil, I, *The Relational Theory of Contract* (London, Sweet & Maxwell, 2001).
Macneil, I, 'Relational Contract Theory: Challenges and Queries' (2000) 94 *Northwestern University Law Review 877*.
——, 'Relational Contract Theory as Sociology: A Reply to Professors Lindenberg and de Vos' (1987) 143 *Journal of Institutional and Theoretical Economics* 272.
——, 'Economic Analysis of Contractual Relations: Its Shortfalls and the Need for a "Rich Classificatory Apparatus"' (1981) 75 *Northwestern University Law Review* 1019.
——, 'Contracts: Adjustment of Long-Term Economic Relations Under Classical, Neoclassical, and Relational Contract Law' (1977) 72 *Northwestern University Law Review* 854.
——, 'A Primer of Contract Planning' (1975) 48 *Southern California Law Review* 627.
——, 'Restatement (Second) of Contracts and Presentation' (1974) 60 *Virginia Law Review* 589.
Macneil, I and Gudel, P, *Contracts: Exchange Transactions and Relations*, 3rd edn (New York, Foundation Press, 2001).
Marx, K, 'Capital vol 1' in K Marx and F Engels, *Collected Works*, vol 35 (New York, International Publishers, 1996).
Mertz, E, 'An Afterword: Tapping the Promise of Relational Contract Theory – "Real" Legal Language and a New Legal Realism' (2001) 94 *Northwestern University Law Review* 909.
Ndekugri, I and Rycroft, M, *The JCT 05 Standard Building Contract* (London, Butterworth Heinemann, 2009).
Perillo, J, 'Misreading Oliver Wendell Holmes on Efficient Breach and Tortious Interference' (2000) 68 *Fordham Law Review* 1085.
Posner, E, 'A Theory of Contract Law Under Conditions of Radical Judicial Error' (2000) 94 *Northwestern University Law Review* 749.
Posner, R, *Economic Analysis of Law*, 8th edn (Austin, Wolters Kluwer, 2011).
Scott, R, '*Hoffman v Red Owl Stores* and the Limits of the Legal Method' (2010) 61 *Hastings Law Journal* 859.
——, 'The Death of Contract Law' (2004) 54 *University of Toronto Law Journal* 369.

Scott, R, 'The Case for Formalism in Relational Contract' (2000) 94 *Northwestern University Law Review* 847.
Schur, E, *Law and Society* (New York, Random House, 1967).
Simpson, AWB, *Leading Cases in the Common Law* (Oxford, Oxford University Press, 1995).
——, 'The Beauty of Obscurity: *Raffles v Wichelhaus and Busch* (1864)' in AWB Simpson, *Leading Cases in the Common Law* (Oxford, Oxford University Press, 1995).
——, 'Contract: The Twitching Corpse' (1980) 1 *Oxford Journal of Legal Studies* 265.
University of Wisconsin Law School, 'Stewart Macaulay' (University of Wisconsin, Madison, 1 January 2012) www.law.wisc.edu/facstaff/macaulay/.
UW Law News, 'Stewart Macaulay Honored at 6th Annual International Conference on Contracts' (University of Wisconsin Law School, 28 February 2011) law.wisc.edu/newsletter/Articles/Stewart_Macaulay_Honored_at_6th_2011-02-22.
Wheeler, S, 'Contracts and Corporations' in P Cane and H Kritzer (eds), *The Oxford Handbook of Empirical Legal Research* (Oxford, Oxford University Press, 2010).
White, J and Summers, R, *Uniform Commercial Code*, 6th edn (St Paul, West, 2010).
Whitford, W, 'Relational Contracts and the New Formalism' (2004) 2004 *Wisconsin Law Review* 631.
Whitford, W and S Macaulay, S, '*Hoffman v Red Owl Stores*: The Rest of the Story' (2010) 61 *Hastings Law Journal* 801.
Wicksteed, P, *The Commonsense of Political Economy*, rev edn (London, Routledge & Kegan Paul, 1933).
Williamson, O, 'Transaction Cost Economics: The Governance of Contractual Relations' (1979) 22 *Journal of Law and Economics* 233.

6

Conflict and Collaboration in Business Organisation: A Preliminary Study

LI-WEN LIN AND JOSH WHITFORD

INTRODUCTION

THIS CHAPTER REPORTS on results in a quantitative study of the dynamics between co-operation and conflict in inter-organisational networks. The study investigates both alliances and litigation among 231 globally-prominent semiconductor companies, examining not only dyads but also triads and regions. The quantitative network analysis used in the study builds upon qualitative work that can be traced to Macaulay's 1963 'Non-Contractual Relations in Business: A Preliminary Study'.[1] We find that firms seldom mix collaborative and conflictual relations at the dyadic level, which is consistent with Macaulay's depictions of socially embedded contractual relations. We also study 'triadic' relations between firms, and the findings show that collaboration and conflict are common in the network writ only slightly larger. This begs investigation. Digging deeper, we show that there are some normative spaces in the industry where the conflicts tend to be minimised. Our findings suggest that collaboration and conflict are not in opposition, but rather have a complex relationship to each other, while indicating also that there may be structural explanations for the use and non-use of alliances and business litigation.

I. BACKGROUND

Macaulay's 1963 article was ahead of its time. The article was published in a prominent place, the *American Sociological Review* (ASR), one of sociology's two flagship journals. Still, citations to the Macaulay article (in the ISI index) were but drips until the mid 1970s, and had grown only to a trickle by the mid 1980s. Then, however, something happened. There was an

[1] S Macaulay, 'Non-Contractual Relations in Business: A Preliminary Study' (1963) 28 *American Sociological Review* 55.

explosion of interest in the article across the social sciences – sociology, business, economics, law and beyond. The trickle of citations grew into a stream, and by the 1990s, a river. Macaulay's article is today among the 20 most cited articles in the history of the ASR. It was recognised by the journal's editor in 2005 as one of its 'greatest hits'.[2] And it was cited more times in 2010 than in any previous year. This did not happen because the article somehow improved with age. While prescient in its considerations, it is not obviously better now than it was in 1963. Rather, at least as things look from our vantage point in sociology, what changed first was the world; scholarship followed (and, probably, became also generative of that change).[3]

The 1970s saw a weakening of the hold of the M-form (or multi-divisional) corporation – which had played a central role in the theories of Oliver Williamson – on the minds of managers the world over.[4] The M–form corporation gave way in the face of market and technological uncertainties that led the vertically integrated corporate behemoths that had dominated the post-war period to turn outward. Businesses increasingly relied on a raft of suppliers and other organisations for help designing, making and selling their products. These changes naturally made relationships between organisations – where contract rather than employment law reigns – far more important than they had been in previous years. Hence the 1980s gave rise to spirited debates over how best to understand this new 'post-Fordist' world. Michael Piore and Charles Sabel published *The Second Industrial Divide*, which criticised Alfred Chandler for supposing that technology might be destiny. Mark Granovetter published an article on the 'embeddedness of economic action' taking to task Williamson for his 'undersociali[s]ed' actors.[5] And, in sociology, a new subdiscipline – the 'new economic

[2] J Jacobs, 'ASR's Greatest Hits' (2005) 70 *American Sociological Review* 1–3.

[3] To clarify: the way businesses are organised has changed, leading in turn to a greater reliance on, and thus salience of, relational contracting. Scholars noticed, but also systematised, and were thus likely generative – since many managers, after all, are trained by those who write scholarly articles; and many management scholars also work as consultants and therefore train incumbent managers.

[4] Oliver Williamson – awarded the Nobel Prize in Economics in 2009 – is by any measure a figure of enormous consequence in the study of organisations. The so-called 'new' economic sociology has for much of its life been in dialogue with Williamson's work. It has been respectful of the attention he has brought the study of alternative governance structures, but has disputed much of his theoretical apparatus. Those disputes run, of course, beyond the scope of this study. The relevant point here is twofold. First, Williamson was wrong in his expectation – developed in his seminal 1975 book, *Markets and Hierarchies* – that the M-Form would outperform firms that operated with other organisational forms. And secondly, economic sociologists (and theorists of relational contracting) were not just cognisant that companies were already rapidly transitioning away from the M-form in the 1970s, but were developing a theoretical apparatus to explain why. (Williamson himself recognises as much in the respect he gives to Macneil as he explains why he had by 1985 accepted that 'hybrid' contracting was more common than he had previously realised. O Williamson, 'Transaction Cost Economics' in R Schmalensee and R Willig (eds), *Handbook of Industrial Organization* (New York, Elsevier, 1990).)

[5] See M Granovetter, 'Economic Action and Social Structure: The Problem of Embeddedness' (1985) 91 *American Journal of Sociology* 481.

sociology' – was organised around the finding that actors' 'embedding' in wider webs of social relations enables them to transact far more successfully than by undertaking an analysis that only looks at characteristics of the transactions themselves.

The new economic sociology took another turn in the work of Walter W Powell, whose taking to task of Oliver Williamson in a 1990 article has significantly marked the sociological debate. Powell chastised Williamson not just for his undersocialised actors, but also for his insistence on treating all transactions as being governed either by markets, hierarchies, or a hybrid of those two classic forms. Echoing Macaulay – who had based his 1963 article on a field study of contracting between organisations, Powell attacked the view that 'network' modes of transactional governance might usefully be seen as a mixed mode or intermediate notion.[6] That view, he wrote, 'is not particularly helpful. It is historically inaccurate, overly static, and it detracts from our ability to explain many forms of collaboration that are viable means of exchange.' And, he therefore argued, it was better to think of about 'networks as a distinctive form of coordinating economic activity', a form with its own distinctive logic that is 'more social – that is, more dependent on relationships, mutual interests and reputation – as well as less guided by a formal structure of authority' than are the logics that govern market and hierarchy.[7]

The attacks prompted Williamson and the transactions-cost economists to respond. They accepted that Williamson had been wrong in his presumption that the distribution of governance forms 'was thick in the tails'[8] and have conceded that hybrid forms are quite common, but have retained their attachment to a conception of the actor that, in the eyes of most sociologists, is still 'undersociali[s]ed'. Sociologists, for their part, certainly respect Williamson's contributions, including especially his success in turning the eyes of social science towards institutions and questions of governance. But there remains a relative consensus in sociology that Granovetter and Powell were essentially right. An enormous number of studies have sought to show that exchange and contract are embedded in social relations and that this embeddedness matters for a variety of outcomes. They have also documented the diffusion and workings of forms of transactional governance characterised by a distinctive 'network' logic of exchange that renders them irreducible either to market or to hierarchy, or to some 'mongrel hybrid'.[9]

[6] W Powell, 'Neither Market nor Hierarchy' (1990) 12 *Reseach in Organizational Behavior* 295, 301. As the intellectual genealogy had it, Powell certainly drew on the ideas of Macaulay; however, he cited Macneil when he wrote of relational contracting as an exemplar of a 'network' form of contracting that was neither market nor hierarchy.

[7] ibid.

[8] O Williamson, *The Economic Institutions of Capitalism: Firms, Markets, Relational Contracting* (New York, Free Press, 1985) 84.

[9] Powell, 'Neither Market' (n 6).

These are advances. The sociological debate, however, in the intervening years has somehow also managed to forget some of the 'lawyerly' considerations that sat naturally in Macaulay's original article, neglecting to recognise – as Macaulay did – the degree to which collaboration and conflict are often *simultaneously* present in the same relationships.[10] This oversight is probably due to the way in which that literature has grown in the wake of Granovetter and Powell's writings. This literature has been fundamentally marked by its dialogue with the work of Williamson, transaction cost economics (TCE), and the presumption that collaboration among self-interested actors will in most cases be relatively fragile. Sociological studies have thus primarily sought to show that collaborative inter-organisational relations are not just feasible but prevalent when transactions are frequent, assets are specific, and outcomes uncertain (that is, under exactly the condition that TCE expects to generate hierarchy). And they have in the process identified a broad range of institutional, social and cultural mechanisms to explain variation in the diffusion and character of network forms of transactional governance.[11] Indeed, the field of inter-organisational relations has become so established that it even has its own handbook from Oxford University Press – published in 2008.[12]

Yet while the existence of that handbook evidences the institutionalisation of the inter-organisational network as a legitimate conceptual entity worthy of sustained investigation, the handbook's content quite plainly evinces a gap. The field, as the handbook editors note, includes the analysis of both collaborative *and* conflictual relations; the studies in the handbook – like most studies in the field – concentrate their attention just on collaboration. This is not to say that sociological studies are *unaware* of conflict, or that they pay no attention to formal contract with its at least implicit (and often explicit) recognition that conflict and competition are the backdrop against which collaboration occurs. There are many studies

[10] What do we mean by 'lawyerly'? Macaulay is responding to a legal literature that focuses on the role of contract as a means to circumvent conflict – a focus that is premised on the recognition that conflicting interests may bubble to the surface at any time. His point was that business people, though aware of that possibility, have also worked out alternative means by which they sometimes manage and circumvent dispute. One of the most evocative quotes in the article, for example, comes from a businessman who says, 'You can settle any dispute if you keep the lawyers out of it. They just do not understand the give-and-take needed in business.' The quotation makes clear both that there is collaboration, and that the party is aware that litigation is potentially in the background – and, in another insight from that article – might be forced on otherwise collaborative parties from elsewhere in their organisations.

[11] See, eg J Whitford, *The New Old Economy* (Oxford, Oxford University Press, 2005); J Lincoln and M Gerlach, *Japan's Network Economy: Structure, Persistence, and Change* (New York, Cambridge University Press, 2004); M Hitt and others, 'The Institutional Effects on Strategic Alliance Partner Selection in Transition Economies: China vs. Russia' (2004) 15 *Organizational Science* 173.

[12] See S Cropper et al (eds) *The Oxford Handbook of Inter-Organizational Relations* (Oxford, Oxford University Press, 2008).

of patterns of formal (contractual) alliances and joint ventures. Especially notable studies include work by Gulati and by Gulati and Gargiulo showing that firms sharing a common partner are likely to form collaborative relations among themselves.[13] There is also a study by Stuart showing that semiconductor firms with a high degree of technological overlap are more likely to form alliances, both in order to avoid duplicating investment and because 'organi[s]ations are better able to evaluate and internalise the know-how of technologically similar firms'.[14] But those studies and others like them have not investigated the ways in which collaboration and conflict may be present across the very same relationships, or may be simultaneously present in the same social milieu. Rather, extant empirical studies on inter-firm relations tend to focus on a single dimension of relation – typically collaboration or its absence – when inter-firm relations tend in reality to be multiplex and dynamic, and to intermingle collaboration, conflict, trust and distrust.[15]

The focus on collaboration to the relative exclusion of conflict is especially notable in light of the fact that business litigation – as a percentage of court cases – increased in the 1970s and early 1980s.[16] This increase, however, does not necessarily show growth in the tendency to litigate, *ceteris paribus*. This change notably occurred simultaneously with the blurring of organisational boundaries, and may be a function of a consequent increase in the sorts of disputes 'ripe' for litigation,[17] making the

[13] R Gulati, 'Social Structure and Alliance Formation Patterns: A Longitudinal Analysis' (1995) 40 *Administrative Science Quarterly* 619; R Gulati and M Gargiulo, 'Where Do Interorganizational Networks Come From?' (1999) 104 *American Journal of Sociology* 1439.

[14] T Stuart, 'Network Positions and Propensities to Collaborate: An Investigation of Strategic Alliance Formation in a High-Technology Industry' (1998) 43 *Administrative Science Quarterly* 668. Trapido uses the idea of 'competitive embeddedness' theorising that competing firms are likely to collaborate due to the mechanisms of 'familiarity and knowledge-based trust, both are greater between competitors'. Trapido finds supportive evidence in investment syndicates in the venture capital industry. D Trapido, 'Competitive Embeddedness and the Emergence of Interfirm Cooperation' (2007) 86 *Social Forces* 165.

[15] K Dirks, R Lewicki, and A Zaheer, 'Repairing Relationships Within and Between Organizations: Building a Conceptual Foundation' (2009) 34 *Academy of Management Review* 68. A prominent example, for instance, is illustrated in the recent relation between Apple and Google – where a once-close relation rapidly devolved into an ugly fight. See B Stone and M Helft, 'Apple's Spat with Google Is Getting Personal' (*New York Times*, 13 March 2010) www.nytimes.com/2010/03/14/technology/14brawl.html?pagewanted=all. The interesting part of the Apple–Google relation is that the close collaboration began in 2006, but as Google entered into the mobile market, their relation became sour. In March 2010, Apple sued Google's smartphone alliance partner (HTC, a Taiwanese company). Although Apple did not directly sue Google, the IT community interpreted the case as the true fight being between Apple and Google.

[16] L Kenworthy, S Macaulay, and J Rogers, '"The More Things Change . . .": Business Litigation and Governance in the Automobile Industry' (1996) 21 *Law and Social Inquiry* 631; T Dunworth and J Rogers, 'Corporations in Court: Big Business Litigation in US Federal Courts, 1971–1991' (1996) 21 *Law and Social Inquiry* 497.

[17] Most scholarship on litigation focuses on the general economic or institutional environment that a firm faces. Legal scholars have suggested that the likelihood of business litigation is a function of the degree of competition and performance pressure in the industry; the direct

decision to downplay conflict puzzling. The rise in litigation along with increased use of alliances raises a series of questions. What are the relationships and dynamics between collaborative relations and conflictual relations? Do pre-existing alliances avoid a subsequent battle? Does a prior fight prevent a subsequent formation of alliance? How does a firm's relation with another firm affect the firm's relation with a third party when the relation is multiplex? To answer these questions, we investigate contractual alliances and lawsuits – the very formal form of collaboration and conflict, among globally important semiconductor companies – and employ a quantitative approach (social network analysis).

We recognise that these may at first blush seem like strange choices, given that we have introduced our research question in terms that highlighted the significance of Macaulay's 1963 study of non-contractual relations in business – which explicitly focused on de-emphasis of the importance of formal contract by business persons, and which was decidedly qualitative and interview-based in its selection of empirical material to analyse. There is, however, a logic to our choice.

The literature that has grown up in sociology around non-contractual relations in business has taken its impetus from studies like that by Macaulay, Granovetter's theorising of embeddedness, and Powell's descriptions of networks that are 'neither market nor hierarchy' – all of which are essentially qualitative and focused on the social embedding of contract. The subsequent development of that literature, however, has sought in many cases to expand those initial insights to populations of firms with the tools of social network analysis. Key studies here include, for example, the aforementioned works by Gulati and by Gulati and Gargiulo showing that firms sharing a common partner are likely to form collaborative relations among themselves.[18] Those and similar studies generally aim to look beyond dyadic relations to understand how a network *context* affects patterns of organisational behaviour. They are thus attentive to what Granovetter refers to as 'structural embeddedness', by which he meant the extent to which a 'dyad's mutual contacts are con-

and non-direct costs of litigation (eg the substitution cost of an existing supplier); the availability of alternative dispute resolution mechanisms (eg arbitration); and the organisation of legal services providers. M Galanter and others, 'The Transformation of American Business Disputing: A Sketch of the Wisconsin Project' (1991) Institute of Legal Studies, University of Wisconsin-Madison Law School, Dispute Process Research Program Working Paper DPRP10-6; Kenworthy and others, 'The More Things Change' (n 16); J Gersen, 'Markets and Corporate Conflict: A Substitute-Cost Approach to Business Litigation' (1999) 24 *Law and Social Inquiry* 589; R Cheit, and J Gersen, 'When Businesses Sue Each Other: An Empirical Study of State Court Litigation' (2000) 25 *Law and Social Inquiry* 789; M Suchman, and M Cahill (eds), 'The Hired Gun as Facilitator: Lawyers and the Suppression of Business Disputes in Sillicon Valley' (1996) 21 *Law and Social Inquiry* 679.

[18] Gulati, 'Social Structure and Alliance Formation Patterns' (n 13); Gulati and Gargiulo, 'Interorganizational Networks' (n 13).

nected to one another'.[19] Network studies often also rely (albeit sometimes only implicitly) on a distinction drawn by Joel Podolny. Podolny, in an important 2001 paper, draws an important distinction between networks as the 'pipes' and the 'prisms' of the market.

These two dimensions are by no means mutually exclusive. Seeing networks as 'pipes', Podolny wrote, references the 'channels or conduits through which "market stuff" flows, where "market stuff" encompasses information about exchange opportunities as well as the actual goods, services, and payments that are transferred between buyer and seller'.[20] Seeing networks as prisms, recognises that ties are often visible to third parties, and that this matters. Podolny explains: 'In this second view . . . the presence (or absence) of a tie between two market actors is an informational cue on which others rely to make inferences about the underlying quality of one or both of the market actors.'[21] These dimensions, when combined, can help to understand patterns of inter-organisational relations. However, in studies to date the 'market' impact examined is generally just the 'good stuff' – the stuff of collaboration; and the ties present (or absent) are generally just the pipes through which that good stuff is flowing.

Our own strategy, given the development of these tools and our desire to bring attention back to the multiplexity of inter-firm relations, is to run in the tack opposite to that taken by Macaulay in his seminal 1963 paper. We have argued that a literature rooted in qualitative analyses has since grown to include more formal analyses. And while much of our own research is qualitative and interpretive,[22] in this case we believe it would be fruitful to move in the opposite direction – that is, to use formal tools to develop questions and hypotheses to be investigated by means of less blunt empirical methodology, including especially interviews and case studies. Our arguments are thus built around a *joint* analysis of collaboration *and* conflict networks – where the former is operationalised as the signing of a formal alliance, the latter as the filing of a lawsuit. These 'markers' of collaboration and conflict are not, of course, coextensive with collaboration and conflict. However, consistent with the imagery of the network as prism, they have the virtue of making co-operation and conflict *visible* to third parties and shape third-parties' perception of the collaboration and conflict structure in the industry.[23] We therefore analyse them at three levels. We look first at the dyadic level, which treats them as

[19] Granovetter (n 5).

[20] J Podolny, 'Networks as the Pipes and Prisms of the Market' (2001) 107 *American Journal of Sociology* 33, 33–34.

[21] ibid 34.

[22] See, eg Whitford, *The New Old Economy* (n 11).

[23] Arbitration is a popular alternative to litigation. However, since arbitration is typically confidential and unobservable to third-parties, the presence or absence of arbitration between two firms would be much less likely to shape third-parties' perception of the collaboration and conflict structure in the industry.

pipes – but allows for good and bad 'stuff' to flow. We turn then to a more prismic triadic and regional level analysis.

II. THE SETTING

Strategic alliances and joint ventures are commonly-examined forms of inter-organisational collaboration. According to extant research, firms engaging in strategic alliances and joint ventures often acquire access to new knowledge and thick information, gain legitimacy and status, and reduce uncertainties and risks.[24] Inter-organisational collaboration is particularly important for firms whose competiveness hinges on innovation ability and adaptability to high uncertainty. High-technology sectors such as computer and biotechnology are generally characterised by a high degree of competition. Unsurprisingly, many important empirical studies take these high-technology industries as attractive empirical testing grounds.[25] Meanwhile, firms in these high-technology industries frequently use litigation, especially intellectual property and antitrust litigation, as a competition strategy to construct market entry barriers for competitors. Litigation is a classical sort of – and measure of – conflictual relationships between companies. The prevalence of strategic alliances and lawsuits in the high-technology industries hence provide fertile ground for a preliminary analysis of the dynamics of collaboration and conflict.

This study investigates a population of internationally important semiconductor companies tracked by IC Insights, an institute specialising in the global semiconductor industry. It includes 231 semiconductor companies, all of which are globally prominent (though mainly concentrated in a small number of countries).[26] The period under examination runs from 2000 to 2010. The strategic alliance data are collected from SDC Platinum Database, which is the most commonly-used database concerning strategic alliances. The litigation data are from the following sources: (1) LexisNexis: it covers all kinds of lawsuits in the jurisdictions of the United States, Canada, the European Union and a number of other jurisdictions;[27] (2) Lex Machina: it is a database originally created by the Stanford Program in Law, Science and

[24] J Podolny and K Page, 'Network Forms of Organization' (1998) 24 *Annual Review of Sociology* 57; Powell, 'Neither Market' (n 6); A Saxenian, *Regional Advantage: Culture and Competition in Silicon Valley and Route 128* (Cambridge, Harvard University Press, 1994).

[25] T Stuart and J Podolny, 'Positional Causes and Correlates of Strategic Alliances in the Semiconductor Industry' (1999) 16 *Research in the Sociology of Organizations* 161; Saxenian, *Regional Advantage* (n 24).

[26] For the nationality distribution of the 231 companies, see Appendix. The US-based companies account for 45% of the sample firms. According to the ranking released by iSuppli, an authoritative source in the industry, about 48% of the top 25 semiconductor companies in the world are US-based companies.

[27] The database covers jurisdictions related to the sample firms including firms in Australia, Canada, EU, Hong Kong, Malaysia and UK.

Technology; Lex Machina focuses on intellectual property rights and anti-trust lawsuits in the United States, the major litigation battlefield of the global semiconductor companies; (3) East Asian jurisdictions: the lawsuits in Taiwan, Japan, and China are collected from specific databases in these jurisdictions.[28] Although there may be lawsuits in other jurisdictions not covered in this study, the omission is unlikely to significantly affect the result because the United States is the main battlefield and 94 per cent of the sample firms are incorporated in the covered jurisdictions.[29]

III. DYADS

Scholars have long been interested in the relationship between contract and collaboration (trust). There is evidence, for example, that contracts – as a form of formal/external control – can impair trust and crowd out more intrinsic reasons for collaboration.[30] In other words, not only is there putative incompatibility between invocation of legal sanction and collaboration, but the actual or even potential use of legal sanctions could impede or at least condition collaboration. As Macaulay showed[31] – and as Bernstein, Cheit and Gersen, and Kenworthy and others have confirmed[32] – firms seldom use legal sanctions as a preferred strategy in solving disputes. In-house counsels are called into the dispute settlements at a relatively late stage when managers cannot solve the disputes themselves through give-and-take negotiations. When a dispute develops into a formal lawsuit, it

[28] For Taiwan, jirs.judicial.gov.tw/Index.htm; for Japan, LexisNexis Japan; for China, vip.chinalawinfo.com/case/. These three countries are the jurisdictions besides the United States in which the sample firms are mainly concentrated.

[29] Note that there are in total only six lawsuits in the jurisdictions of China, Japan and Taiwan. In other words, most legal actions are carried out in the US jurisdiction.

[30] Macaulay, 'Non-Contractual Relations' (n 1); E Deci and R Ryan, *Instrinsic Motivation and Self-Determination in Human Behavior* (New York, Plenum, 1985); E Fehr, and S Gachter, 'Do Incentive Contracts Crowd Out Voluntary Cooperation?' (2001) University of Southern California Center in Law, Economics and Organization Research Papers (CLEO) Research Paper No C01-3 (http://papers.ssrn.com/sol3/papers.cfm?abstract_id=229047); B Frey, 'A Constitution for Knaves Crowds Out Civic Virtues' (1997) 107 *Economic Journal* 1043; M Taylor, *The Possibility of Cooperation* (New York, Cambridge University Press, 1987); M Lubell and J Scholz, 'Cooperation, Reciprocity, and the Collective-Action Heuristic' (2001) 45 *American Journal of Political Science* 160; D Malhotra and J Murnighan, 'The Effects of Contracts on Interpersonal Trust' (2002) 47 *Administrative Science Quarterly* 534; A Tenbrunsel and D Messick, 'Sanctioning Systems, Decision Frames, and Cooperation' (1999) 44 *Administrative Science Quarterly* 684.

Other scholars, however, argue that contracts can help trust formation. For example, Lazzarini, Milller and Zenger argue whether the use of contracts would hurt relationships depends on social uncertainty and exchange value uncertainty. S Lazzarini, G Miller and T Zenger, 'Dealing with the Paradox of Embeddedness: The Role of Contracts and Trust in Facilitating Movement Out of Committed Relationships' (2008) 19 *Organization Science* 709.

[31] Macaulay, 'Non-Contractual Relations' (n 1).

[32] L Bernstein, 'Opting Out of the Legal System: Extralegal Contractual Relations in the Diamond Industry' (1992) 21 *Journal of Legal Studies* 115; Cheit and Gersen, 'When Businesses Sue' (n 17); Kenworthy and others, 'The More Things Change' (n 15).

implies that the firms have failed to work out the problem internally, an indicator of distrust and serious conflict. Thus, in order to preserve trust and collaboration willingness (as well as to avoid the high litigation costs), we might expect alliance partners to be unwilling to initiate litigation against each other.

In our data, there are 671 alliance relations (non-directional) and 206 litigation relations (directional) among the 231 companies. Two companies may have repeated alliance or litigation relations. Each company on average has 5.81 alliance relations and 1.78 litigation relations. Each company on average has 2.98 alliance partners and 1.38 litigation enemies. The findings thus confirm, as expected, that litigation relations are considerably less common than alliance relations. The alliance relations and litigation relations together constitute a network of the 231 companies, as illustrated in Figure 1 below. In Figure 1, a blue tie indicates there is an alliance relation between two companies; a red tie indicates a litigation relation between the companies; and a black tie indicates there are alliance *and* litigation relations between the companies. There are only 13 mixed alliance-and-litigation ties (black ties). In other words, few companies mix alliance and litigation relations with another company. Companies that have litigation relations are unlikely to form alliance relations with each other, while companies having alliance relations are unlikely to engage in litigation against each other.

Figure 1: The Collaboration and Conflict Network of the Global Semiconductor Companies, 2000–2010

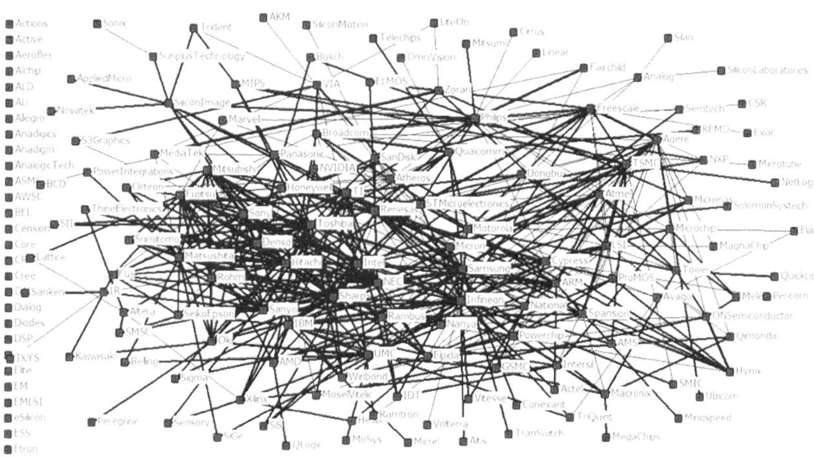

Note: The red (thin) ties indicate litigation relations; the blue ties indicate alliance relations; the black (thick) ties indicate alliance-and-litigation relations. This figure is available in colour at https://sites.google.com/site/liwensite/Home/conflict-and-collaboration-in-business-organization-a-preliminary-study.

Although rare relative to the population, it is nonetheless interesting to analyse the 13 alliance-and-litigation relations (the black ties in Figure 1). Table 1 below shows the details of the 13 alliance-and-litigation relations. Nine of the 13 alliance-and-litigation relations have a sequence pattern in which an alliance relation predates a litigation relation – which naturally raises suspicions of alliances gone bad. However, in fact, all nine litigation cases arose out of legal causes unrelated to the pre-existing alliance relations.

Three of the 13 alliance-and-litigation relations have a pattern in which a litigation relation predates an alliance relation. The Zoran-MediaTek alliance was a settlement of litigation between the two companies. But the other two alliance relations (Freescale-STMicroelectronics and Philips-Fairchild) are unrelated to the pre-existing legal suits. Their rarity, but existence, suggests that perhaps prior conflict – or, the condition that lead to conflict – renders collaboration rare, but does not necessarily preclude the formation of collaborative relations.

The remaining instance is an approximate concurrence of litigation filing and alliance formation between Toshiba and Samsung. The cases are unrelated.

IV. TRIADS AND REGIONS

In our data, alliance is more common than litigation, and the coexistence of alliance and litigation in an inter-organisational relation is uncommon but does occur. These finding are easily squared with extant theory. Most scholarship on network forms of organisation hold that collaboration and litigation are tendentially – but only tendentially – antithetical, and recognise that those relations may be both tense and fluid. There is, for example, evidence that inter-firm collaborative relations (typically measured as joint ventures or strategic alliances) suffer high failure rates.[33] Alliance failures may be attributed to interfirm rivalry, managerial complexity/uncertainty, and to a lesser extent, environmental factors.[34] Many collaborative relations are formed between actual or potential competitors. The presence of actual or potential competition makes the collaborative relation unstable because it increases opportunistic hazards and needs to adopt various forms of formal control to reduce opportunism. In such

[33] B Kogut, 'The Stability of Joint Ventures: Reciprocity and Competitive Rivalry' (1989) 38 *Journal of Industrial Economics* 183; S Park and M Russo, 'When Competition Eclipses Cooperation: A Event History Analysis of Joint Venture Failure' (1996) 42 *Management Science* 875; *Economist*, 'Airline Alliances: Flying in Formation' (*The Economist*, 29 January 1998) www.economist.com/node/111904.

[34] S Park, S and G Ungson, 'Interfirm Rivalry and Managerial Complexity: A Conceptual Framework of Alliance Failure' (2001) 12 *Organization Science* 37; Kogut, 'The Stability of Joint Ventures' (n 33); A Parkhe, '"Messy" Research, Methodological Predisposition, and Theory Development in International Joint Ventures' (1993) 18 *Academy of Management Review* 227.

Table 1: Semiconductor Companies with Alliance-and-Litigation Relations, 2000–2010

Companies in Relation		Litigation Filing Date	Litigation End Date	Alliance Date	Event Sequence	Notes
Broadcom	Qualcom	5/18/2005	4/28/2009	3Q2003	Alliance>>>Litigation	Litigation unrelated to previous alliance (joint product development and marketing)
Philips	Broadcom	12/17/2007	9/18/2009	2/17/2004	Alliance>>>Litigation	Litigation unrelated to previous alliance (joint product development)
LSI	Micronas	4/21/2008	N/A	8/30/2006	Alliance>>>Litigation	Litigation unrelated to previous alliance (joint product development)
Agere	Freescale	4/21/2008	N/A	Jun2002	Alliance>>>Litigation	Litigation unrelated to previous alliance (alliance terminated in June 2006 because both parties lacked interest)
Rambus	Samsung	1/25/2005	N/A	2/24/2003	Alliance>>>Litigation	Litigation unrelated to previous alliance
IBM	Rambus	9/7/2010	N/A	3/17/2006	Alliance>>>Litigation	Litigation unrelated to previous alliance
Motorola	STMicroelectronics	3/4/2003	9/1/2004	2/2/2002	Alliance>>>Litigation	Litigation unrelated to previous alliance

OnSemiconductor	Hynix	10/18/2010	1/5/2011	6/19/2003	Alliance>>>Litigation	Litigation unrelated to previous alliance
Mitsubishi	Toshiba	2010	N/A	2000/2001/2002	Alliance>>>Litigation	Litigation unrelated to previous alliances
Freescale	STMicroelectronics	3/4/2003	9/1/2004	1Q2006	Litigation>>>Alliance	Alliance (joint product development) unrelated to previous litigation
Philips	Fairchild	10/2/2000	1/24/2002	Sep2002	Litigation>>>Alliance	Alliance unrelated to previous litigation (joint marketing)
Zoran	MediaTek	6/29/2004	1/27/2006	1Q2006	Litigation>>>Alliance	Alliance (licensing agreement) as a result of litigation
Toshiba	Samsung	4/26/2002	9/27/2002	5/26/2002	Concurrence?	Alliance unrelated to litigation (litigation due to an alliance since 1993)

competitive collaboration, alliance partners would pursue short-term self-interests over long-term collaborative goals. Alternatively, collaboration may fail due to cultural dissimilarity, communication difficulties and conflict between the parent partner and the alliance may reduce the binding strength or trust in the collaborative relation.[35] When a collaborative relation becomes unstable, it may reduce the need/desire to preserve trust and the co-operative atmosphere between alliance partners. In this case, there would be less hesitation to resort to legal sanctions to govern inter-firm relations.

Our network analysis cannot discern between these multiple causes, at least at a dyadic level. However, it is notable that extant explanations for tensions in, and fluidity of, inter-firm relations turn on claims about the environment in which relations form (or fail to form). Relation formation is not, in short, just an internal process between two firms unaffected by their relations with third parties. Rather, as Gulati and Gargiulo show,[36] alliance partners are likely to share common third-party partners. They do so for a variety of reasons. In part, existing partners can serve as 'trusted informants', allowing firms to leverage their past dealings with a potential partner to reduce search costs as they seek new partners.[37] Moreover, allying with common partners creates 'a reputational lock-in' whereby good behaviour is encouraged and bad behaviour is deterred for the local reputation concern.[38] Such 'collaboration cohesion' can reduce opportunism.

Network effects are understood in terms of highlighting the salience of structural embeddedness (defined, again, as the extent to which a 'dyad's mutual contacts are connected to one another'[39]). To see them, we must move beyond the analysis of dyads to look also at triads and thus to think about those networks not just as 'pipes' but also as 'prisms'.[40] It is here, in short, that we move beyond extant research that has recognised the importance of structural embeddedness, but that has only examined relations in the uniplex setting (that is, collaborative relations). We look simultaneously at multiple relationship dimensions. In particular, we think that an analysis of the structural embedding of both conflict and collaboration can enrich the understanding of relation/network formation by incorporating what is referred to in the networks literature as 'structural balance' and 'structural imbalance'. These concepts treat as analogous on the one side situations that are all 'balanced': (i) the 'friend of my friend is my

[35] Park and Ungson, 'Interfirm Rivalry' (n 34).

[36] Gulati and Gargiulo, 'Interorganizational Networks' (n 13).

[37] Granovetter, 'Economic Action' (n 5) 490.

[38] Gulati and Gargiulo, 'Interorganizational Networks' (n 13) 1447.

[39] M Granovetter, 'Problems of Explanation in Economic Sociology' in N Nohria and R Eccles (eds), *Networks and Organizations: Structure, Form, and Action* (Boston, Harvard Business School Press, 1992) 35.

[40] Podolny, 'Networks' (n 20).

friend'; (ii) the 'enemy of my friend is my enemy'; or (iii) the 'enemy of my enemy is my friend'. Imbalanced situations include social structures in which: (i) the 'enemy of my enemy is my enemy'; (ii) the 'friend of my enemy is my friend'; or (iii) the 'friend of my friend is my enemy'.[41]

Structural balance is generally held to be more stable than structural imbalance. Empirical evidence, however, examined in the interstate not interfirm context, suggests that things may be more complicated when we are speaking of corporate actors. Healy and Stein found that in the period of 1871–1880 the Germany–Austria–Russia triad swung between balance and imbalance but converged towards balance in the late 1870s.[42] However, they did find that structural imbalances are more likely to move towards balance, than balances were to move towards imbalances. McDonald and Rosecrance conversely found that a high percentage of structural imbalances sustained over time and some structural balances became imbalances, concluding that there was no swing to balance in the European system in the late nineteenth century.[43]

More recently, Maoz and others examined the dynamics between alliance and conflict between nation-states in the period of 1816–2001.[44] They found that the allies of a state's enemies and the enemies of a state's allies are likely to become direct enemies of the state, which is consistent with intuition. Meanwhile, they also found that the number of past disputes between two states has a positive effect on the probability of subsequent alliance formation, which is quite counter-intuitive. The findings in the interstate setting are insightful but might not be readily applicable to the interfirm setting. The conflict and collaboration dynamics in business might be different in international politics. There may be more social thickness and interpersonal ties in interfirm relations, which may make structural imbalances uncommon and hard to endure.

To examine structural balance and imbalance in the alliance-litigation network shown in Figure 1, we have parsed relations into ten triangle types. They are shown in Figure 2A-J. They comprise the full set of combinations of alliance, litigation and mixed relations. There are 619 triangles of all types in total.

[41] In social network analysis parlance, there are two types of relation – positive and negative – in structural balance/imbalance. When all the sides of a triad are positive (eg friendship, liking) or when two sides are negative (eg hostility, disliking) and one side is positive, the triad is considered to be in structural balance. But when all the sides of a triad are negative relations or when two sides are positive and one side is negative, the triad is defined as in structural imbalance.

[42] B Healy and A Stein, 'The Balance of Power in International History: Theory and Reality' (1973) 17 *Journal of Conflict Resolution* 33.

[43] H McDonald and R Rosecrance, 'Alliance and Structural Balance in the International System: A Reinterpretation' (1985) 29 *Journal of Conflict Resolution* 57.

[44] Z Maoz and others, 'What Is the Enemy of My Enemy? Causes and Consequences of Inbalanced International Relations, 1816–2001' (2007) 69 *Journal of Politics* 100.

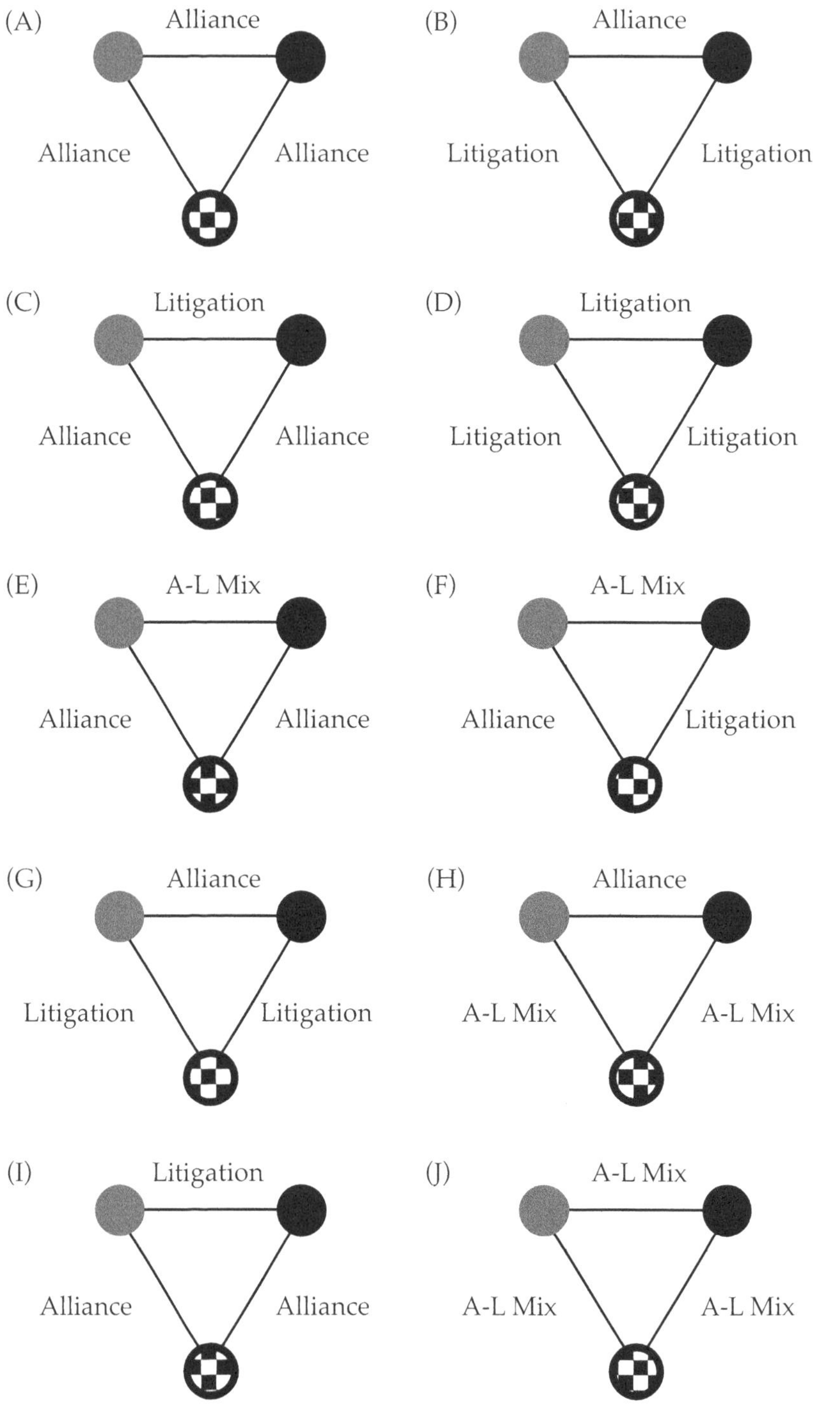

Figure 2: Types of Alliance and Litigation Triangles

Figure 2.A illustrates two companies (solid round nodes) are in an alliance relation and they share a common alliance partner (pattered round node). This type of triangle arises from 'structural embeddedness' as illustrated by Gulati and Gargiulo, which goes to a point made above.[45] We know from past research that existing partners can serve as 'trusted informants', allowing firms to leverage their past dealings with a potential partner to reduce search costs as they seek new partners,[46] and that allying with common partners creates 'a reputational lock-in' whereby good behaviour is encouraged and bad behaviour is deterred for the local reputation concern.[47] But how often – and where – does such 'collaboration cohesion' occur in the semi-conductor industry? That is, how often do we see these cohesive collaborative ties, which can be expected to strengthen the view that participants to alliances are suitable and trustworthy alliance partners (that is, all participants to the triangle have a means to observe that their partner is trustworthy with others as well)? There are 395 such collaboration cohesion triangles, accounting for 64 per cent of all the triangles (and thus the most common type of triangle among these 231 semiconductor companies).

The second most common triangle is a scenario where two firms in an alliance relationship are involved in litigation with a common third party, as shown in Figure 2.B. This is an intuitive situation where friends have a common foe. The two alliance partners not only have internal collaboration cohesion but also external conflict consistency, briefly called *conflict-collaboration consistency*. There are 91 conflict-collaboration-consistency triangles among these 230 semiconductor companies.

The predominance of the collaboration cohesion triangles and conflict-collaboration consistency in our data is, of course, expected. There is considerable structural balance, which aligns consistently with past examinations of similar cases (supporting the accuracy of these findings). But it is not, notably, our only finding. If we look at Figure 2.D, we see the *conflict triangle*, a type of structural imbalance – though the one that seems intuitively most likely (all-out-war). Figure 2.D shows two firms suing each other are also engaged in a litigation relation with a common third party. In other words, it is a situation where foes have a common foe. The conflict triangle suggests the firms may have intense competition against each other in similar technology or market position. Such triangles would intuitively be the most common sort of finding with regard to litigation. Curiously, however, there are just 19 conflict triangles among the 231 semiconductor companies. And when we look at Figure 2.C – where the triad forms a *conflict-collaboration inconsistency* (a firm's friend may collaborate with the firm's enemy), we see instead a surprising high number of cases.

[45] Gulati and Garguilo, 'Interorganizational Networks' (n 13).
[46] Granovetter, 'Economic Action' (n 5) 490.
[47] Gulati and Garguilo, 'Interorganizational Networks' (n 13) 1447.

There are 73 conflict-collaboration-inconsistency triangles, taking up 12 per cent of all the triads. This suggests a possible source of instability in alliance relationships. The collaboration-conflict inconsistency suggests that firms may use formal contracts to govern their collaboration relations in order to guard the possible flow of valuable information or technology to the enemy through the common friend.[48]

Among the 10 types of triangles, conflict-collaboration consistency and conflict-collaboration inconsistency are the most interesting types and deserve more analysis. The conflict-collaboration consistency and inconsistency include subtypes because litigation relations are directional and there is a temporal sequence in the formation of alliance and litigation relations. [Table 3] shows the different patterns of relation formation of conflict-collaboration consistency and inconsistency.

Our findings on conflict-collaboration consistency – the intuitively common but empirically uncommon situation – show that the majority involved a situation where two companies formed an alliance first and were then sued by a third party in the same lawsuit [Table 3(A)]. In other words, alliance partners are sued, together, by a third party. Because of information flows and resource sharing between alliance partners, a third party may sue the alliance partners together in order to effectively protect its interests. The others involved situations where two companies were sued by a third party in the same lawsuit but only subsequently formed an alliance [Table 3(B)], or a situation where the company first created an enemy through litigation and then created an alliance partner with another company and finally the company's enemy sued the company's friend [Table 3(C)]; where the friend of my enemy is my enemy.

In our findings on conflict-collaboration inconsistency, a majority – 57.5 per cent – of these triangle formation sequences involve a situation [Table 3(D)] where a company established alliances with two companies and

[48] The following types of triangle are of less theoretical and empirical importance. Figure 2.E shows two firms having an alliance-litigation-mixed relation share a common alliance partner. There are 17 triangles of such type. This type of triangle fundamentally can be viewed as a combination of the collaboration cohesion triangle in Figure 2.A and the collaboration-conflict inconsistency triangle in Figure 2.C. Figure 2.F shows two firms engaged in an alliance-litigation-mixed relation have opposing relations with a common third party. There are 14 triangles of such type. This type of triangle fundamentally is constituted of a collaboration-conflict-consistency triangle in Figure 2.B and a collaboration-conflict-inconsistency triangle in Figure 2.C. Figure 2.G is a type of triangle where two firms involved in an alliance-litigation-mixed relation sue a common third party. Seven triangles belong to this type. Figure 2.H shows a scenario where two alliance partners both have an alliance-litigation-mixed relation with a common third-party. The two alliance partners have internal coherence and external consistency, like the situation in Figure 2.B. There are only two triangles of this type. Figure 2.I shows a situation where two firms involved in a litigation relation have an alliance-litigation-mixed relation with a common third-party. There is only one triangle of this type. Finally, Figure 2.J shows the three firms have an alliance-litigation-mixed relation with one another. This type of triangle does not occur among these 231 companies, however.

Table 3: Patterns of Relation Formation

<table>
<tr><th>Triangle Type</th><th>No. of Sequence (%)</th><th>Subtypes</th></tr>
<tr><td rowspan="3">
</td><td>67
(73.6%)</td><td>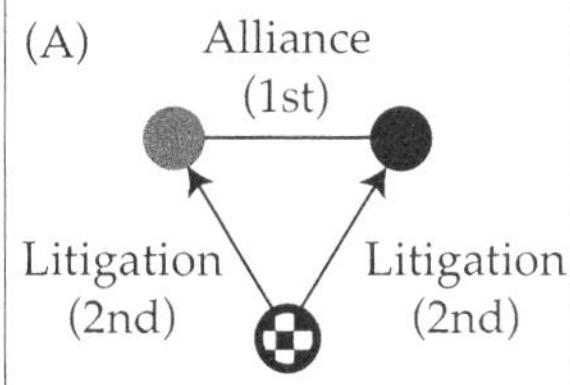
</td></tr>
<tr><td>16
(17.6%)</td><td>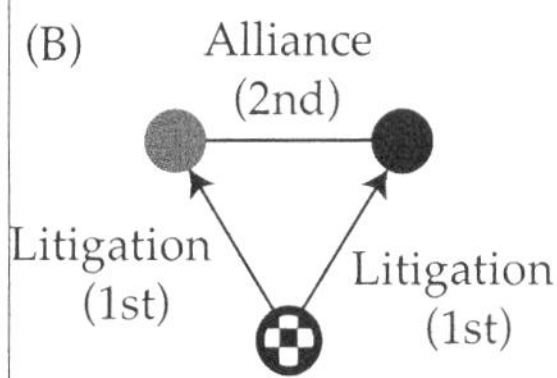
</td></tr>
<tr><td>8
(8.8%)</td><td>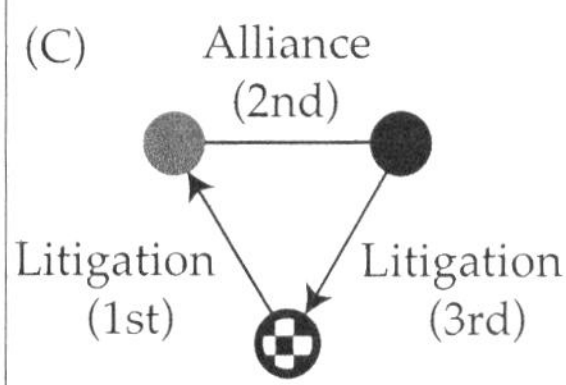
</td></tr>
<tr><td></td><td>91
(100%)</td><td></td></tr>
<tr><td rowspan="3">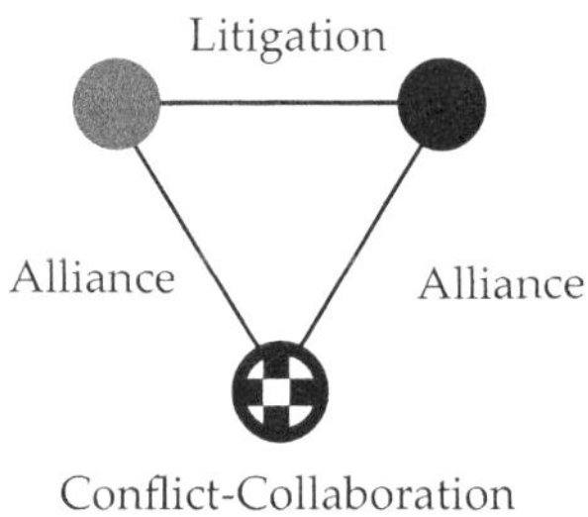
</td><td>42
(57.5%)</td><td>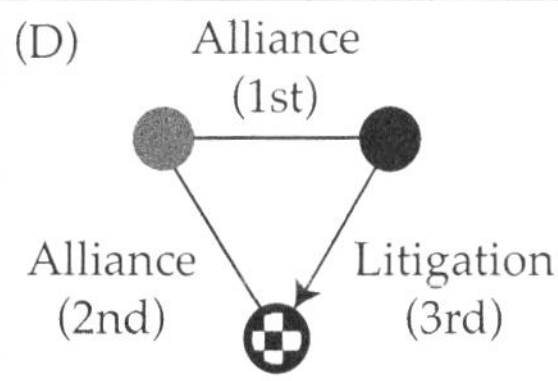
</td></tr>
<tr><td>15
(20.5%)</td><td>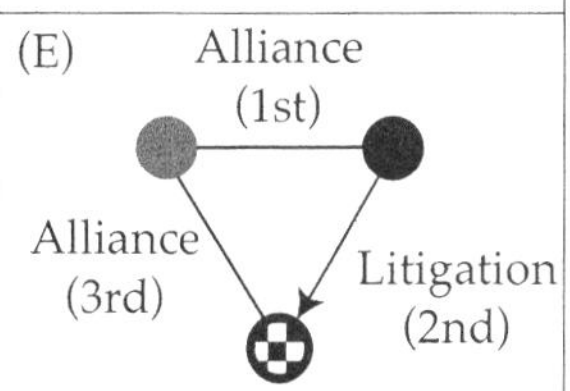
</td></tr>
<tr><td>16
(22%)</td><td>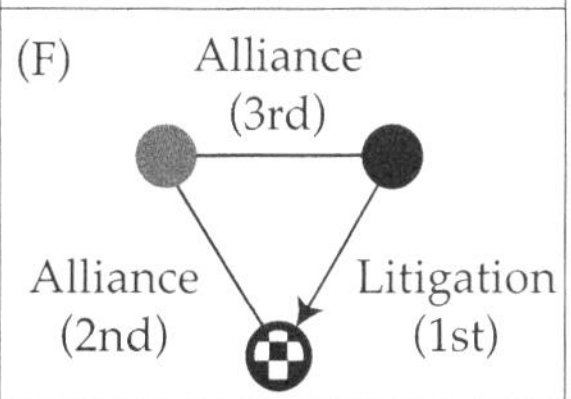
</td></tr>
</table>

then one of the company's alliance partners sued the other. They negate the hypothesis that a firm would avoid litigation against the friend of the firm's friend. The additional cases are comprised of situations where a company's alliance partner sued a third party and later on the third party formed an alliance with the company [Table 3(E)], or where a company (the plaintiff company) sued another company (the defendant company) and the defendant company later on formed an alliance with a third party, and finally the plaintiff company also collaborated with the third party [Table 3(F)]. Both [Table 3(E) and 3(F)] show that a company can collaborate with the friend of the company's enemy.

Overall, the triadic analysis suggests that structural balance is more common than structural imbalance in inter-firm alliance-litigation relations, but there is enough structural imbalance to suggest some interesting avenues for deeper research. If we move beyond triads – which are a very simple conceptual tool – we can identify more such avenues. In reality, after all, a firm often has collaborative or conflictual relations not only with two other firms but with many other firms. There is multiplexity of relations among multiple companies. We therefore also look at the dynamics of alliance and litigation at the regional (subgroup) level. We ask how likely firms in a strong cohesive alliance group are to sue each other. In other words, is there any collaboration space in which conflict is minimised or even excluded? Similarly, are there any conflict spaces in which collaboration does not exist? To answer these questions, this study uses the k-core method in social network analysis. A k-core is a subgraph in each node (that is, each company in this study), adjacent to at least a minimum number, k, of the other nodes in the subgraph.[49] A k-core is formed by recursively pruning the least-connected vertices (firms in this case), up to the number k. It is used to 'disentangle the hierarchical structure of networks by progressively focusing on their central cores'.[50] We examined cores in which the variable k ranged from 10 to 3, as discussed below.

The most straightforward finding from our analysis frames our study of K-cores. There are 206 litigation relations among the 231 companies. Litigation remains minimal in such alliance subgroups. It suggests there are some normative spaces in which litigation is avoided. But what are they? Figure 3 shows the k-core subgraphs of the alliance network. There is a highly cohesive subgroup (a 10-core) in the alliance network. Again, a '10-core' is a restrictive and highly connected subgraph, in which each firm must have alliance relations with at least 10 other firms in the subgroup. The companies in the 10-core are all Japanese companies, as listed

[49] S Wasserman and K Faust, *Social Network Analysis* (Cambridge, Cambridge University Press, 1994).

[50] I Alvarez-Hamelin and others, 'Large Scale Networks Fingerprinting and Visualization Using the K-core Decomposition' in Y Weiss, B Scholkopf and J Platt (eds), *Advances in Neural Information Processing Systems* (Cambridge, MIT Press, 2006).

in Table 4. In fact, this 10-core is also a '10-clique', in which every company is connected with one another in this subgroup. This suggests quite strongly that culture matters in the formation of such highly cohesive subgroups. Business organisation in Japan is well-known as a form of 'alliance capitalism'.[51] Moreover, Japanese society is relatively non-litigious,[52] and there is but one lawsuit (between Toshiba and Mitsubishi) found in this highly cohesive subgroup constituted of Japanese companies.

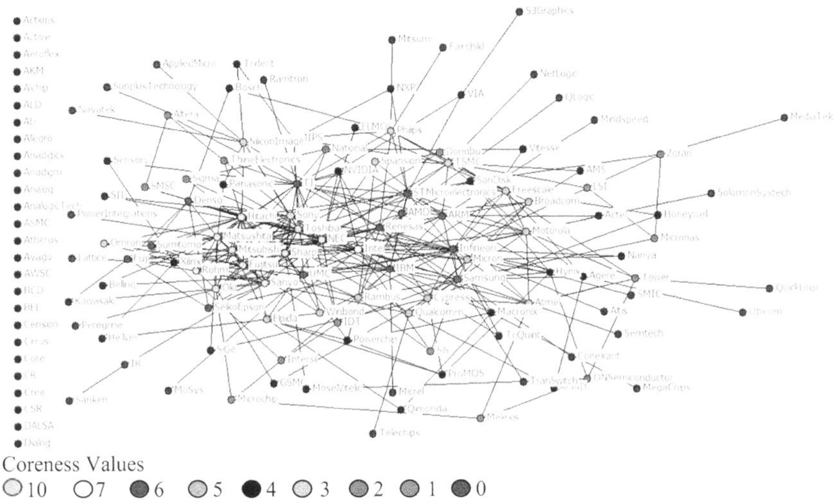

Figure 3: Alliance K-core

This figure is available in colour at https://sites.google.com/site/liwensite/Home/conflict-and-collaboration-in-business-organization-a-preliminary-study.

This tendency to collaboration and to avoid litigation preserves cohesiveness among the Japanese companies. It also raises more general questions about the role of the Japanese companies in cementing the relations in the alliance network, given the fact that Japanese companies account for just 12.5 per cent of all the sample companies but their removal from the network would reduce network density by 50 per cent.[53] We have, therefore, looked at other k-cores to see how and if things change as other nationalities embed in the network core. The second most cohesive subgroups are 7-cores, in which each company has alliance relations with at least seven other companies in the subgroup. There are 12 companies involved in the

[51] M Gerlach, *Alliance Capitalism* (Berkeley, University of California Press, 1997).

[52] Some legal scholars have argued that the cultural preferences are overstated. The low litigation rate in Japan has something to do with the legal institutions in Japan. See, eg T Ginsburg and G Hoetker, 'The Unreluctant Litigant? An Empirical Analysis of Japan's Turn to Litigation' (2006) 35 *Journal of Legal Studies* 31; J Ramseyer and M Nakazato, 'The Rational Litigant: Settlement Amounts and Verdict Rates in Japan' (1989) 18 *Journal of Legal Studies* 263.

[53] In social network analysis, network density is the proportion of all possible ties that are actually present.

Table 4: Companies with the Highest Coreness Values in the Alliance Network

Company Name	Country	Coreness Value
Fujitsu	Japan	10
Hitachi	Japan	10
Matsushita	Japan	10
Mitsubishi	Japan	10
NEC	Japan	10
Oki	Japan	10
Rohm	Japan	10
Sanyo	Japan	10
Sharp	Japan	10
Sony	Japan	10
Toshiba	Japan	10
Intel	USA	7
AMD	USA	6
ARM	UK	6
Denso	Japan	6
Fuji	Japan	6
IBM	USA	6
Infineon	Germany	6
Renesas	Japan	6
Samsung	Korea	6
SeikoEpson	Japan	6
STMicroelectronics	Switzerland	6
Sumitomo	Japan	6
TI	USA	6
UMC	Taiwan	6
Atmel	USA	5
Broadcom	USA	5
Cypress	USA	5
Elpida	Japan	5
Freescale	USA	5
Micron	USA	5
Motorola	USA	5

Company Name	Country	Coreness Value
Omron	Japan	5
Philips	Netherlands	5
Qualcomm	USA	5
Rambus	USA	5
SiliconImage	USA	5
Spansion	USA	5
TSMC	Taiwan	5
Winbond	Taiwan	5
Agere	USA	4
Hynix	Korea	4
Macronix	Taiwan	4
NVIDIA	USA	4
Panasonic	Japan	4
Powerchip	Taiwan	4
ProMOS	Taiwan	4
SanDisk	USA	4
Xilinx	USA	4
Altera	USA	3
Dongbu	Korea	3
IDT	USA	3
Intersil	USA	3
LSI	USA	3
Melexis	Belgium	3
Microchip	USA	3
Micronas	Germany	3
MIPS	USA	3
National	USA	3
ONSemiconductor	USA	3
Sigma	USA	3
SiS	Taiwan	3
SMSC	USA	3
ThineElectronics	Japan	3
Tower	Isreal	3

Table 4: (*cont.*)

Zoran	USA	3
Actel	USA	2
AMS	USA	2
Belling	China	2
Bosch	Germany	2
ELMOS	Germany	2
GSMC	China	2
HeJian	China	2
Honeywell	USA	2
Kawasaki	Japan	2
MoselVitelic	Taiwan	2
Nanya	Taiwan	2
NXP	Netherlands	2
Qimonda	Germany	2
RFMD	USA	2
Sensory	USA	2
SiGe	Canada	2
SII	Japan	2
Trident	USA	2
TriQuint	USA	2
VIA	Taiwan	2
Vitesse	USA	2

7 cores. Intel is the only non-Japanese company, as shown in Table 4. Still, in the 7-cores, there is only one lawsuit (between Toshiba and Mitsubishi) among the 12 companies. The third most cohesive subgroups are 6-cores, involving 25 companies. There is more nationality diversity in the 6-cores, including companies from Japan, the United States, the United Kingdom, Germany, Korea, Switzerland and Taiwan. There are five lawsuits found in the 6-cores.[54] These five lawsuits are either between two Japanese companies or between a Japanese company and a Korean company (Samsung). In other words, the existence of the five lawsuits is not because non-Japanese companies, especially companies coming from litigious societies

[54] The five lawsuits are: between Matsushita and Samsung; between Toshiba and Samsung; between Denso and Mitsubishi; between Samsung and Sharp; and between Toshiba and Mitsubishi.

such as the United States, join the alliance subgroups. This suggests that national culture, although it plays a role, does not determine the rise of litigation in a cohesive group.

Finally, if we look at the k-core subgraphs of the *litigation* network in Figure 4 below, we see that the most interconnected subgroups are 3-cores. The largest coreness value (3) in the litigation network is much smaller than the largest coreness value (10) in the alliance network. There are 31 companies involved in the 3-cores. Table 5 below lists the companies involved in the 3-cores. About 58 per cent of them are US companies and 42 per cent are non-US companies. Unlike the most cohesive alliance subgroups, which are mainly composed of Japanese companies, the most conflictual subgroups mainly include American companies.

DISCUSSION AND CONCLUSION

This is a preliminary study. We first described the development of a literature in sociology that owes a substantial debt to Stewart Macaulay's 1963 article, 'Non-Contractual Relations in Business'.[55] That literature, we argued, drew heavily on the underlying insight in Macaulay's article, which is that there is in fact no bright line between administration and contract. Each is shaped by its embedding in the larger social and institutional context – and scholars ignore that embedding at their peril. We then described the way in which that insight has been integrated into a

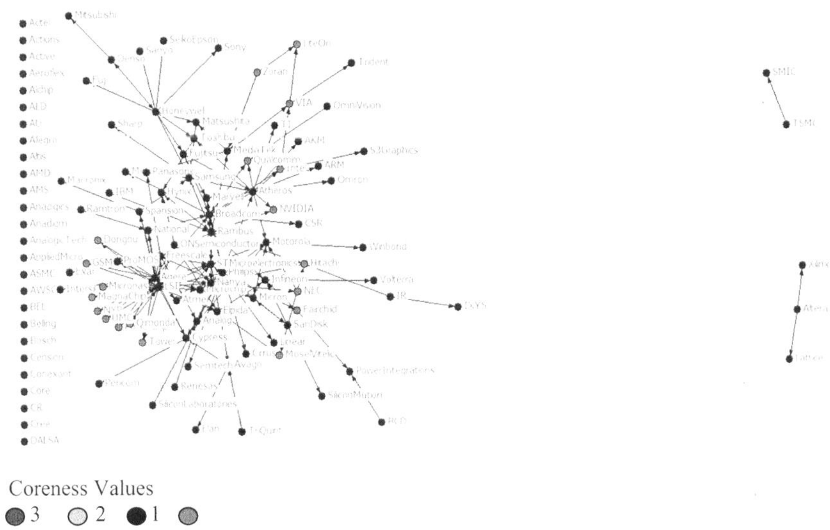

Figure 4: Litigation K-Core

[55] Macaulay, 'Non-Contractual Relations' (n 1).

Table 5: Companies with the Highest Coreness Values in the Litigation Network

Company Name	Country	Coreness Values
Agere	USA	3
Analog	USA	3
Atheros	USA	3
Atmel	USA	3
Broadcom	USA	3
Cypress	USA	3
Elpida	Japan	3
Freescale	USA	3
Fujitsu	Japan	3
Honeywell	USA	3
Hynix	Korea	3
Infineon	Germany	3
LSI	USA	3
Marvell	USA	3
Matsushita	Japan	3
MediaTek	Taiwan	3
Microchip	USA	3
Micron	USA	3
Motorola	USA	3
Nanya	Taiwan	3
National	USA	3
ONSemiconductor	USA	3
Panasonic	Japan	3
Philips	Netherlands	3
ProMOS	Taiwan	3
Rambus	USA	3
Samsung	Korea	3
SanDisk	USA	3
Spansion	USA	3
STMicroelectronics	Switzerland	3
Toshiba	Japan	3

sociological literature that has endeavoured to identify the contours of 'networks' that are neither market nor hierarchy, 'nor some mongrel hybrid, but a distinctly different form'.[56] We explained that the sociological literature has been marked by its positioning against transaction-cost economics, and has thus focused primarily on the perceived need to show that collaborative relations between organisations – 'networks' – are far more distinctive and common than Oliver Williamson presumed. We argued that this positioning has been fruitful in the main, but that it has also generated an inattention to some of the 'lawyerly' considerations that sat naturally in Macaulay's 1963 paper.

The sociological literature has been primarily interested in the blurring of organisational boundaries and an ensuing – and profound – set of transformations in patterns of inter-organisational relations across the last few decades. Many important quantitative empirical studies have relied, either implicitly or explicitly, on the presumption that formal contracts of particular sorts – including especially joint-venture and other alliance contracts – indicate organisational boundaries have somehow been blurred.[57] This only made sense in light of an idea for which sociology is indebted to relational contract theory: contracts are not just documents spelling out what is to be done when various contingencies come to pass; they are also social artifacts.[58] Cognate qualitative examinations of inter-organisational dynamics have shown that particular sorts of contracts do suggest some blurring of organisational boundaries and furthermore the blurring is marked not just by co-operation, but also by conflict.[59] Extant quantitative studies have made little of this additional finding, however.

In our own study, we have sought to bring some of these insights from qualitative work into a social network analysis of inter-organisational alliances in the semi-conductor industry. Just as others in this literature have relied on the formalisation of an alliance as an indicator of collaboration – and thus of some blurring of the organisational boundary – we have turned to litigation as an indicator of formalised conflict. We are, of course,

[56] Powell, 'Neither Market' (n 6) 299.

[57] R Gulati, 'Alliances and Networks' in J Reuer (ed), *Strategic Alliances: Theory and Evidence* (Oxford, Oxford University Press, 2004); G Baker, R Gibbons, and K Murphy, 'Strategic Alliances: Bridges between "Islands of Conscious Power"' (2008) 22 *Journal of Japanese International Economies* 2, 146.

[58] M Suchman, 'The Contract as Social Artifact' (2003) 37 *Law & Society Review* 91.

[59] See, eg Whitford, *The New Old Economy* (n 11); A Schrank and J Whitford, 'The Anatomy of Network Failure' (2011) 29 *Sociological Theory* 151; Dirks and others, 'Repairing Relationships' (n 15); D Ferrin, M Bligh, and J Kohles, 'Can I Trust You to Trust Me? A Theory of Trust, Monitoring, and Cooperation in Interpersonal and Intergroup Relationships' (2007) 32 *Group and Organization Management* 465; R Lewicki, and B Bunker, 'Developing and Maintaining Trust in Work Relationships' in R Kramer and T Tyler (eds), *Trust in Organizations: Frontiers of Theory and Research* (Thousand Oaks, Sage Publications, 1996); K Nakayachi and M Watabe, 'Restoring Trustworthiness After Adverse Events: The Signaling Effects of Voluntary "Hostage Posting" on Trust' (2005) 97 *Organizational Behavior and Human Decision Processes* 1.

well aware that most conflict in the relations that interest us and other sociologists does not culminate in litigation. It is for this reason that we have in our study paid little attention to dyads – analysing them primarily as a sort of 'due diligence' to verify our and others' expectation that alliance and litigation will combine in the same relation only rarely. We have instead focused primarily on 'triads' and 'regions' in an effort to develop insights into the ways in which interactions between alliance and litigation – as co-operation and conflict visible to third parties (that is, network as prism) – might affect norms of co-operation and conflict in network space.

We have also some provocative findings that, we hope, might structure future efforts to understand the multiplexity of relations between firms in those instances where they are marked neither by administration nor contract, but by something in between. Our analysis of dyads, as just noted, confirms the utility of recent scholarly interest in the intermingling of co-operation and conflict in particular relations. Certainly, alliance partners seldom initiate litigation against each other. But rarity is not non-existence and still begs explanation. And, we think, our analysis of triads and regions can help both to structure some of that explanation and to open new questions. We offer, for example, a potential new factor to help explain why firms sue each other against a background of 'non-contractual' relations. Most scholarship on litigation focuses on the general economic or institutional environment that a firm faces. Our study suggests there may be a 'structural' explanatory factor concerning the use or nonuse of business litigation. For instance, the triadic analysis in this study indicates that the use or non-use of litigation can be affected by a firm's relation with a third party. The regional analysis implies that there may be different normative spaces in an industry, with firms embedded in different normative spaces following different sets of norms to govern their behaviour.

In general, we have shown that structural balance, while common, is hardly ubiquitous. The quantitative salience of conflict-collaboration inconsistency deserves future research. Why do firms construct alliances with friends of their litigation enemies? And we have shown, with our analysis of k-cores, that there are spaces in the network in which collaboration is common and litigation rare, and others in which the opposite holds. What structures such spaces? The national origin of particular companies certainly plays some role, but it is not determinative. Does entry into a network 'core' dominated by collaborative firms reduce the propensity to conflict, net of culture? Does it channel that conflict so that it occurs by way of other channels? Such questions can only be answered, of course, with forms of analysis that operate not just at 'forest level' (as with social network analysis), but that include observation also at the level of the 'trees'. We hope, however, that our descriptions of the forest and our preliminary examination of the multiplexity of inter-organisational relations in the semi-conductor industry can help to frame that research, and to underscore that collaboration and conflict are not opposite – one cognate to contract, the other to suit – but part and parcel of the relational ecology of a modern economy.

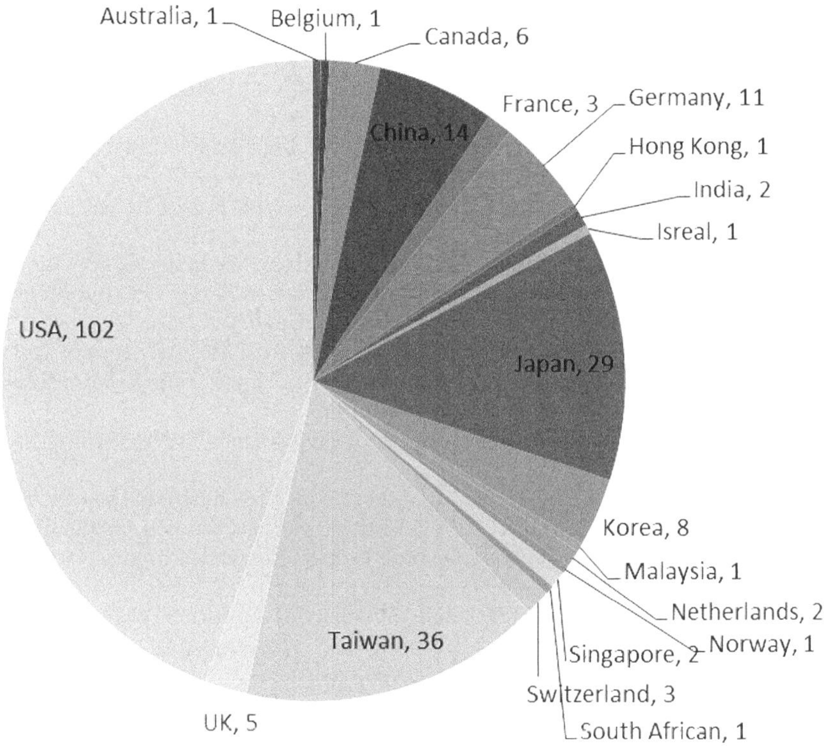

Appendix: Country of Origin of the 231 Semiconductor Companies

BIBLIOGRAPHY

Alvarez-Hamelin, I and others, 'Large Scale Networks Fingerprinting and Visualization Using the K-core Decomposition' in Y Weiss, B Scholkopf and J Platt (eds), *Advances in Neural Information Processing Systems* (Cambridge, MIT Press, 2006) 41–50.

Baker, G, Gibbons, R, and Murphy, K, 'Strategic Alliances: Bridges between "Islands of Conscious Power"' (2008) 22 *Journal of Japanese International Economies* 2, 146.

Bernstein, L, 'Opting Out of the Legal System: Extralegal Contractual Relations in the Diamond Industry' (1992) 21 *Journal of Legal Studies* 115.

Bottom, W and others, 'When Talk is not Cheap: Substantive Penance and Expessions of Intent in Rebuilding Cooperation' (2002) 13 *Organization Science* 497.
Cheit, R and Gersen, J, 'When Businesses Sue Each Other: An Empirical Study of State Court Litigation' (2000) 25 *Law and Social Inquiry* 789.
Cropper, S and others (eds), *The Oxford Handbook of Inter-Organizational Relations* (New York, Oxford University Press, 2008).
Deci, E and Ryan, R, *Instrinsic Motivation and Self-Determination in Human Behavior* (New York, Plenum, 1985).
Dirks, K, Lewicki, R and Zaheer, A, 'Repairing Relationships Within and Between Organizations: Building a Conceptual Foundation' (2009) 34 *Academy of Management Review* 68.
Dunworth, T and Rogers, J, 'Corporations in Court: Big Business Litigation in US Federal Courts, 1971–1991' (1996) 21 *Law and Social Inquiry* 497.
Economist, 'Airline Alliances: Flying in Formation' (*The Economist*, 29 January 1998).
Fehr, E and Gachter, S, 'Do Incentive Contracts Crowd Out Voluntary Cooperation?' (2001) University of Southern California Center in Law, Economics and Organization Research Papers (CLEO) Research Paper No C01-3.
Ferrin, D, Bligh, M and Kohles, J, 'Can I Trust You to Trust Me? A Theory of Trust, Monitoring, and Cooperation in Interpersonal and Intergroup Relationships' (2007) 32 *Group and Organization Management* 465.
Frey, B, 'A Constitution for Knaves Crowds Out Civic Virtues' (1997) 107 *Economic Journal* 1043.
Galanter, M and others, 'The Transformation of American Business Disputing: A Sketch of the Wisconsin Project' (1991) Institute of Legal Studies, University of Wisconsin-Madison Law School, Dispute Process Research Program Working Paper DPRP10-6.
Gerlach, M, *Alliance Capitalism* (Berkeley, University of California Press, 1997).
Gersen, J, 'Markets and Corporate Conflict: A Substitute-Cost Approach to Business Litigation' (1999) 24 *Law and Social Inquiry* 589.
Ginsburg, T and Hoetker, G, 'The Unreluctant Litigant? An Empirical Analysis of Japan's Turn to Litigation' (2006) 35 *Journal of Legal Studies* 31.
Granovetter, M, 'Problems of Explanation in Economic Sociology' in N Nohria and R Eccles (eds), *Networks and Organizations: Structure, Form, and Action* (Boston, Harvard Business School Press, 1992) 25–56.
Granovetter, M, 'Economic Action and Social Structure: The Problem of Embeddedness' (1985) 91 *American Journal of Sociology* 481.
Gulati, R, 'Social Structure and Alliance Formation Patterns: A Longitudinal Analysis' (1995) 40 *Administrative Science Quarterly* 619.
——, 'Alliances and Networks' in J Reuer (ed), *Strategic Alliances: Theory and Evidence* (Oxford, Oxford University Press, 2004) 378–412.
Gulati, R and Gargiulo, M, 'Where Do Interorganizational Networks Come From?' (1999) 104 *American Journal of Sociology* 1439.
Healy, B and Stein, A, 'The Balance of Power in International History: Theory and Reality' (1973) 17 *Journal of Conflict Resolution* 33.
Hitt, M and others, 'The Institutional Effects on Strategic Alliance Partner Selection in Transition Economies: China vs. Russia' (2004) 15 *Organizational Science* 173.
Jacobs, J, 'ASR's Greatest Hits' (2005) 70 *American Sociological Review* 1-3.

Kenworthy, L, Macaulay, S and Rogers, J, '"The More Things Change . . .": Business Litigation and Governance in the Automobile Industry' (1996) 21 *Law and Social Inquiry* 631.

Kogut, B, 'The Stability of Joint Ventures: Reciprocity and Competitive Rivalry' (1989) 38 *Journal of Industrial Economics* 183.

Lazzarini, S, Miller, G, and Zenger, T, 'Dealing with the Paradox of Embeddedness: The Role of Contracts and Trust in Facilitating Movement Out of Committed Relationships' (2008) 19 *Organization Science* 709.

Lewicki, R and Bunker, B, 'Developing and Maintaining Trust in Work Relationships' in R Kramer and T Tyler (eds), *Trust in Organizations: Frontiers of Theory and Research* (Thousand Oaks, Sage Publications, 1996) 114–39.

Lincoln, J and Gerlach, M, *Japan's Network Economy: Structure, Persistence, and Change* (New York, Cambridge University Press, 2004).

Lubell, M and Scholz, J, 'Cooperation, Reciprocity, and the Collective-Action Heuristic' (2001) 45 *American Journal of Political Science* 160.

Macaulay, S, 'Non-Contractual Relations in Business: A Preliminary Study' (1963) 28 *American Sociological Review* 55.

Malhotra, D and Murnighan, J, 'The Effects of Contracts on Interpersonal Trust' (2002) 47 *Administrative Science Quarterly* 534.

Maoz, Z and others, 'What Is the Enemy of My Enemy? Causes and Consequences of Inbalanced International Relations, 1816-2001' (2007) 69 *Journal of Politics* 100.

McDonald, H and Rosecrance, R, 'Alliance and Structural Balance in the International System: A Reinterpretation' (1985) 29 *Journal of Conflict Resolution* 57.

Nakayachi, K and Watabe, M, 'Restoring Trustworthiness After Adverse Events: The Signaling Effects of Voluntary "Hostage Posting" on Trust' (2005) 97 *Organizational Behavior and Human Decision Processes* 1.

Park, S and Ungson, G, 'Interfirm Rivalry and Managerial Complexity: A Conceptual Framework of Alliance Failure' (2001) 12 *Organization Science* 37.

Park, S and Russo, M, 'When Competition Eclipses Cooperation: A Event History Analysis of Joint Venture Failure' (1996) 42 *Management Science* 875.

Parkhe, A, '"Messy" Research, Methodological Predisposition, and Theory Development in International Joint Ventures' (1993) 18 *Academy of Management Review* 227.

Piore, M and Sabel, C, *The Second Industrial Divide* (New York, Basic Books, 1986).

Podolny, J, 'Networks as the Pipes and Prisms of the Market' (2001) 107 *American Journal of Sociology* 33.

Podolny, J and Page, K, 'Network Forms of Organization' (1998) 24 *Annual Review of Sociology* 57.

Powell, W, 'Neither Market nor Hierarchy' (1990) 12 *Reseach in Organizational Behavior* 295.

Ramseyer, J and Nakazato, M, 'The Rational Litigant: Settlement Amounts and Verdict Rates in Japan' (1989) 18 *Journal of Legal Studies* 263.

Saxenian, A, *Regional Advantage: Culture and Competition in Silicon Valley and Route 128* (Cambridge, Harvard University Press, 1994).

Schrank, A and Whitford, J, 'The Anatomy of Network Failure' (2011) 29 *Sociological Theory* 151.

Stone, B and Helft, M, 'Apple's Spat with Google Is Getting Personal' (*New York Times*, 13 March 2010).

Stuart, T, 'Network Positions and Propensities to Collaborate: An Investigation of Strategic Alliance Formation in a High-Technology Industry' (1998) 43 *Administrative Science Quarterly* 668.

Stuart, T and Podolny, J, 'Positional Causes and Correlates of Strategic Alliances in the Semiconductor Industry' (1999) 16 *Research in the Sociology of Organizations* 161.

Suchman, M, 'The Contract as Social Artifact' (2003) 37 *Law & Society Review* 91.

Suchman, M and Cahill, M (eds), 'The Hired Gun as Facilitator: Lawyers and the Suppression of Business Disputes in Sillicon Valley' (1996) 21 *Law and Social Inquiry* 679.

Taylor, M, *The Possibility of Cooperation* (New York, Cambridge University Press, 1987).

Tenbrunsel, A and Messick, D, 'Sanctioning Systems, Decision Frames, and Cooperation' (1999) 44 *Administrative Science Quarterly* 684.

Trapido, D, 'Competitive Embeddedness and the Emergence of Interfirm Cooperation' (2007) 86 *Social Forces* 165.

Wasserman, S and Faust, K, *Social Network Analysis* (Cambridge, Cambridge University Press, 1994).

Whitford, J, *The New Old Economy* (Oxford, Oxford University Press, 2005).

Williamson, O, *Markets and Hierarchies: Analysis and Antitrust Implications* (New York, Free Press, 1975).

Williamson, O, 'Transaction Cost Economics' in R Schmalensee and R Willig (eds), *Handbook of Industrial Organization* (New York, Elsevier, 1990).

——, *The Economic Institutions of Capitalism: Firms, Markets, Relational Contracting* (New York, Free Press, 1985).

Wollschlager, C, 'Historical Trends of Civil Litigation in Japan, Arizona, Sweden, and Germany: Japanese Legal Culture in Light of Judicial Statistics' in H Baum (ed), *Japan: Economic Success and Legal System* (Berlin, Walter de Gruyter, 1997).

7

What Mistakes Do Lawyers Make in Complex Business Contracts, and What Can and Should be Done About Them? Some Preliminary Thoughts

CLAIRE A HILL*

All the time, I would find things weren't clear. Commas all over the place. Complete confusion.[1]

Managing director of a broker-dealer, referring to securitisation documentation

Of course, when the going is good, it's straight onto the next deal. Now, though, sharp-beaked litigators are circling the bloodied corpse of the mortgage securities market, their beady eyes carefully inspecting for food – and law firms may prove the entrée.[2]

The cable read: PARDON. IMPOSSIBLE TO BE SENT TO SIBERIA. In one of his famous 'Believe it or Not' columns, Robert Ripley wrote about that cable, and how a man's life had been spared when some Czarist apparatchik mistakenly placed the period after the first word of it instead of after the second.[3]

* I want to thank Afra Afsharipour, Steven Davidoff, Allan Erbsen, Scott Faga, Mitu Gulati, Kristin Johnson, Brett McDonnell, Paul Lawrence Rubin, Carol Sanger, Dan Schwarcz, Larry Solan, and participants at the Empirical and Lyrical Symposium for Stewart Macaulay at the University of Wisconsin, Madison, and especially Bill Whitford, an editor of the volume in which this paper will appear, for very helpful comments.

[1] Arturo Cifuentes, managing director of broker-dealer RW Pressprich & Co, commenting on securitisation documentation during the boom. R Gera and D Robinson, 'What does the sub-prime mortgage crisis mean for lawyers?' (*Chambers*, 2008 Issue 24) (available at www.chambersmagazine.co.uk/Article/What-does-the-sub-prime-mortgage-crisis-mean-for-lawyers).

[2] ibid.

[3] D Margolick, 'At the Bar; How Three Missing Zeros Brought Red Faces and Cost Millions of Dollars' (*New York Times*, 4 October 1991) (available at www.nytimes.com/1991/10/04/news/bar-three-missing-zeros-brought-red-faces-cost-millions-dollars.html?pagewanted=print&src=pm).

INTRODUCTION

WHEN STEWART MACAULAY'S seminal paper 'Non-Contractual Relations in Business: A Preliminary Study'[4] was published, it didn't influence me very much. (In my defense, I was five years old at the time.) But when I entered academia and started thinking about contracting practices, I came across the paper and immediately felt an enormous sense, intellectually and aesthetically, of 'rightness'. The paper, and Macaulay's later work on the subject,[5] captures elegantly and with profundity a great deal about contracting relationships, and commercial relationships and reputational communities more broadly.

As Macaulay's work makes clear, notwithstanding the prominent place given to contract law in legal scholarship, contracting is importantly also about 'something else'. I have tried to analyse what that 'something else' is in a series of papers on contracting practices, and the role of norms, reputation, and reputational communities, in complex business transactions.

This paper continues my work in this area. It is about the mistakes made in complex business contracts – 'true' mistakes, mistakes that are inadvertent, *not* strategic. What types of 'true' mistakes are made? Why are they made?[6] I provide the beginnings of a taxonomy and analysis, based on interviews with practitioners and my own practice experience. I make no claim to offer 'proof' – indeed, empirical evidence that goes beyond the suggestive would be quite difficult to obtain.

I also consider what can and should be done about contractual mistakes. Ultimately, I think not much (more) can be done about them. One obvious candidate to do more is law firms; they have the opportunity to spend much more time and trouble preventing and detecting mistakes, an opportunity they do not take. Indeed, parties may benefit from leaving defects, including mistakes, in their documents. They are posting a bond that they will not precipitously resort to litigation; the defects may give the other party grounds to (counter) sue them, something the other party may be motivated to do if it is sued.[7]

[4] S Macaulay, 'Non-Contractual Relations in Business: A Preliminary Study' (1963) 28 *American Sociological Review* 1.

[5] See, eg S Macaulay, 'An Empirical View of Contract' (1985) 1985 *Wisconsin Law Review* 465; S Macaulay, 'Relational Contracts Floating on a Sea of Custom? Thoughts About the Ideas of Ian MacNeil and Lisa Bernstein' (2002) 94 *Northwestern Law Review* 775; S Macaulay, 'The Real and the Paper Deal: Empirical Pictures of Relationships, Complexity and the Urge for Transparent Simple Rules' (2003) 66 *Modern Law Review* 44.

[6] In other work, I have considered why law firms and clients do not do more to prevent or catch mistakes. See C Hill, 'Why Contracts are Written in Legalese' (2002) 77 *Chicago-Kent Law Review* 59; C Hill, 'Bargaining in the Shadow of the Lawsuit: A Social Norms Theory of Incomplete Contracts' (2009) 34 *Delaware Journal of Corporate Law* 191.

[7] Hill, 'Bargaining' (n 6).

Another obvious candidate is law and in particular, judicial 'punishments' for contractual mistakes in the form of unfavourable rulings. Again, the mistakes I am concerned with are not attempts by one party to take advantage. Parties are not deliberately forsaking certainty for some other benefit. Thus, it seems hard to imagine how one interpretive convention (for instance, textualism) would appreciably increase the parties' incentives to avoid mistakes over and above the incentive existing with another convention.

I also think a good case can be made that not much *should* be done about it. Whether a mistake in a contract will cause difficulties for the parties (or anyone else, for that matter) turns far more on external factors such as whether the transaction meets the parties' expectations than on defects in drafting. Indeed, once a deal closes, parties might very well not look at the transaction documents unless something goes wrong, in which case they review the documents to see if they have grounds to sue. Many drafting defects might simply go unnoticed – and do no harm.

When a mistake appears to cause appreciable difficulties to 'the public', thus presenting a good case for a 'public' response (such as a change in law), it is unlikely that absent the mistake, the situation would have been much better. Subprime documentation provides a good example. The documents were deeply flawed, but even with perfect documentation, we would still be in a crisis.

I. WHAT TYPES OF MISTAKES ARE MADE?[8]

What types of mistakes do lawyers make in complex business contracts? Mistakes can be divided into four categories: a particular mistake can fit into one or more categories. One type of mistake is a 'mechanical' mistake – a term is not defined, for instance, or is defined two different ways. Typographical errors would fall into this category as well. A second is a technical mistake – a formula does not work. A third is inconsistency. For instance, two different provisions purport to govern some event, but yield different results. This may result from warring 'notwithstanding' clauses – two different clauses, each of which say 'notwithstanding anything else in this agreement [or some other section] to the contrary'. I have elsewhere called these provisions 'band-aids' since they are intended to provide a quick local fix.[9] And it's not just when the parties notice, and try to fix, potential inconsistency and contradiction that it can arise: any two

[8] The examples and some of the text in this Section are adapted from Hill, 'Bargaining' (n 6). An article that discusses some survey evidence on lawyer mistakes is J Coates IV, 'Explaining Variation in Takeover Defenses: Blame the Lawyers' (2001) 89 *California Law Review* 1301, 1313–14.

[9] Hill, 'Legalese' (n 6) 69; Hill, 'Bargaining' (n 6) 194.

provisions could, of course, be inconsistent or contradictory. A fourth type is lack of clarity, where there is more than one reasonable way to read a provision and no straightforward interpretive convention or other rule that dictates which meaning should prevail.

There is a fine line between mistakes, on the one hand, and attempts to capture a complicated point that in hindsight reveal ambiguity. But there are many clear cases, as well, where there was a straightforward way to 'do better', and it is those that my analysis addresses. As noted above, my analysis expressly excludes strategic 'mistakes' – attempts to gain advantage by means of ambiguities, inconsistencies and the like.[10]

The following is an example of a mechanical mistake, as described in a recent blog posting by the 'Deal Professor', Steven Davidoff:

> Finally, for those interested in topping Darden's bid, the termination fee is $39.6 million. If another bidder makes a superior proposal, then under Section 5.02(b) of the merger agreement, RARE cannot terminate the agreement 'unless concurrently with such termination the Company pays to Parent the Termination Fee and the Expenses payable pursuant to Section 6.06(b)'. The only problem? Expenses is used repeatedly throughout the Agreement as a defined term everywhere except 6.06(b) – which makes no references to Expenses or even expenses. In fact, it appears that nowhere does the agreement define Expenses. Transaction expenses can sometimes be 1–2% of additional deal value, a significant amount that any subsequent bidder must account for. So how much should a subsequent bidder budget here? Or to rephrase, what expenses must RARE pay if a higher bid emerges? And how can RARE terminate the deal to enter into an agreement with another bidder if RARE does not know which expenses it is so required to pay? Darden may also want similar certainty as to its reimbursed expenses, if any, in such a paradigm. Lots of questions in this ambiguity. Not the biggest mistake in the world, but Wachtell, attorneys for the buyer, and Alston & Bird, attorneys for the seller [both sophisticated firms, with Wachtell being one of the most prominent law firms in the US and probably the world], both have incentives to fix this one.[11]

An example of a technical mistake (and arguably also of inconsistency and lack of clarity, my third and fourth categories) is discussed in an article on securitisation from *Chambers Magazine*, a UK publication:

[10] Mistakes and 'boilerplate' are related concepts, although some (many?) mistakes are not in boilerplate, and much boilerplate does not contain mistakes. There is voluminous literature on boilerplate; see, eg O Ben-Shahar (ed), '"Boilerplate": Foundations of Market Contracts Symposium' (2006) 104 *Michigan Law Review* 5.

[11] M & A Law Prof Blog, 'Mistakes M&A Lawyers Make' (*M & A Law Prof Blog*, 20 August 2007) (available at lawprofessors.typepad.com/mergers/2007/08/mistakes-ma-law.html) as quoted in Hill, 'Bargaining' (n 6) 198–99. In another recent albeit much less egregious example, the parties used the term 'Requisite Transaction Funds' but provided a definition for 'Required Transaction Funds'. S Davidoff, 'Smoke Gets In Your Eyes' (*New York Times*, 11 September 2008) (available at dealbook.blogs.nytimes.com/2008/09/10/smoke-gets-in-your-eyes/). See Hill, 'Bargaining' (n 6) fn 16.

> Like all bonds, CDO [collateralised debt obligation] agreements contain a range of triggers that classify the CDO as being in default – for example, if a payment to bondholders is missed, or if the ratio of value of the underlying mortgage pool to the outstanding payments drops below a certain level. When this happens, bondholders must decide whether to hang on and hope for recovery, or to cut their losses, 'enforce' the bond and demand full payment, usually meaning a quick sale of the underlying assets.
>
> The problem is that the complex 'waterfall' system of CDOs – which spreads return, and risk, across different 'tranches' – often puts different bondholders at odds. Senior bondholders, will be the first to be paid if the bond is wrapped up. But those holding riskier junior debt have little to gain.
>
> 'Let's say you're the most senior bondholder of a $900 million CDO, and you hold $600 million and there's another $300 million in the tranches below you', explains James Waddington, a partner at Orrick, Herrington & Sutcliffe. 'As long as the fire-sale of the assets recovers $600 million, you're covered. But the guys below you? They get nothing.'
>
> With such differing interests, it's vital that CDOs contain clear guidance on how the decision to enforce should be made – and how the proceeds should be distributed. Unfortunately, when the market is booming and timetables are short, planning for what could go wrong is usually the first corner to be cut. 'Default used to be something that happened once in a blue moon', explains one finance lawyer. Eventually, 'people began to believe assets could only go up. And they stopped paying attention to the plans for after an event of default.'
>
> The result? Confusion. At least $64 billion of CDOs have experienced event of default since mid-October, and many are believed to have guidance for after default which is incomplete, unclear, or contradictory. 'When you look at CDO documents, you find that some of the post-enforcement waterfalls simply don't work, or that it's not always clear how some of the waterfall provisions interact with other substantive provisions in the legal documents', explains Sanjev Warna-Kula-Suriya at Slaughter and May. In several cases, senior bondholders believed the documentation to give them complete control over the decision to enforce, only to find on closer inspection that it wasn't clear.
>
> Without proper instructions in the documentation, trustees face a nightmare. 'The pressure on them is enormous – one side urging them to act quickly, the other to do nothing', explains one finance lawyer. 'They're middle-ranking administrative staff, not highly paid, and suddenly they've got pension funds yelling at them, demanding they get the assets valued for sale, and hedge funds yelling at them, demanding they don't.'[12]

Mistakes of the third and fourth types were arguably at issue in a recent case, *URI v RAM Holdings Inc*.[13] The relevant provisions of the contract documents contain one 'notwithstanding anything to the contrary in this Agreement' clause, two 'in no event' clauses, and one 'nothing in this Section [] shall be deemed to affect [the parties'] rights [. . . under Section []]'

[12] R Gera and D Robinson, 'Sub-prime mortgage crisis' (n 1).

[13] *United Rentals, Inc v RAM Holdings, Inc and RAM Acquisition Corp*, 937 A2d 810 (Del Ch 2007).

clause. Each of these clauses offers the opportunity for inconsistency and contradiction. When the parties use one of these clauses, it means that they have foreseen the possibility of inconsistency and contradiction.[14] They could be sufficiently careful (or simply lucky), and have dealt successfully with the issue. For instance, two provisions that expressly purport to supersede every other provision (or one provision that purports to supersede another) might do so without inconsistency or contradiction. But, in my experience, parties may not be sufficiently careful or lucky: the two 'notwithstandings' may be at war with one another. The *URI v RAM* case provides a good illustration.

The issue in the case was the availability of specific performance. In the case, the judge's ruling for one party (RAM) turned on the judge's application of a well-worn interpretive doctrine: that RAM had communicated to the other party, URI, its view that specific performance was *not* available, so that URI knew of RAM's view, but URI had not communicated to RAM its view that specific performance *was* available. In this case, the 'mistake' was only on RAM's side: URI's decision not to try to reconcile the warring 'notwithstandings' was presumably strategic, and not a 'mistake'. Still, the example illustrates the point. Indeed, in his discussion of John Coates's expert opinion in the *URI v RAM* case, Chancellor Chandler effectively acknowledges my third category of mistake.

Coates opined that:

> One of the ways that the parties commonly economize on time and costs is not to attempt to review every provision of every related agreement every time a new change is made, particularly when documents are in the final stages of negotiation. Rather, they rely on succinct but legal terms of art to achieve what is, in essence, 'editing' of the entirety of a document with minimal change. Among the terms of art customarily relied upon are phrases such as 'subject to' or 'notwithstanding'. These phrases allow the parties to specify that one phrase or provision will take precedence over others, and thus avoid the need to attempt to synthesize every provision of every related agreement that is or may be partly or wholly in conflict with the provision in question.[15]

Chancellor Chandler, ruling on the admissibility of Coates's opinion, said:

> Professor Coates states that the parties, in contravention of basic principles of contract interpretation and drafting, use certain phrases (eg, 'subject to' or 'notwithstanding') so as to avoid the need to attempt to synthesize every provision of every related agreement that is or may be partly or wholly in conflict with the

[14] A contractual mistake of this type could also arise where the clauses were not inserted by these parties, but rather by parties to a prior transaction that used the same 'form' for their transaction documents. Indeed, a mistake could arise just because of inconsistency or contradiction that nobody noticed (and therefore nobody tried to fix).

[15] J Coates, 'Expert Report of Professor John C Coates IV' (*United Rentals, Inc v RAM Holdings, Inc and RAM Acquisition Corp*, 6 December 2007) 10–11 (available at lawprofessors.typepad.com/mergers/files/102xx_expert_report_12062007.pdf).

provision in question' . . . Not surprisingly, disputes often arise precisely because of provisions that are 'partly or wholly in conflict' with each other.[16]

II. WHEN, AND HOW OFTEN, ARE MISTAKES MADE?

Are these four types of mistakes common? And are they more common in cases in which a dispute arises? Again, empirical evidence for these propositions is difficult to obtain. Logic and intuition provide support for dueling conclusions – that these mistakes are more common in cases where litigation is conducted or threatened, and that they are not more common. In support of the latter, parties don't have disputes because their documents are defective. Rather, they have disputes because the transaction disappoints and one party (or both) looks at the documents and finds a way to sue. In support of the former, once a dispute arises, it may be more apt to settle if the documentation is clearer, and to proceed to litigation if it is less clear.[17]

Which conclusion is correct is not important for my account so long as there are appreciable, even if fewer, mistakes in documents where the parties do not move towards litigation. Certainly, the transacting process as it is conducted makes appreciable numbers of mistakes likely. The mistakes start early, before the first draft of the deal documents. Lawyers' starting points in their drafting are documents used in previous transactions – these documents probably have mistakes. In one lawyer's felicitous description: 'Documents are like ships travelling the oceans: they gather barnacles as they go'.[18]

Consider the following account of securitisation documentation from the *Chambers Magazine* article quoted above. Admittedly, it relates to a period in which an especially large number of mistakes can be expected – the period preceding the crisis, in which deal volume rose to massive levels (and deal staffing did not keep pace). But the mechanisms the writer discusses are at issue in even 'normal' times – that is, in normal harried times, since deals are never done at leisure.

> The complex financial instruments – mortgage-backed securities (MBS) and collateralised debt obligations (CDO) – that made the crisis possible were complex legal documents, but were frequently generated at high speed and sometimes with limited care. Those documents could lie at the heart of multimillion-dollar lawsuits, and they – and the lawyers responsible for them – face close scrutiny.

[16] *URI* (n 13) fn 7. See also Letter to Counsel from W Chandler III, Chancellor (13 December 2007) fn 7 (available at lawprofessors.typepad.com/mergers/files/decision_re_coates_report.pdf).

[17] An early exposition of this idea is in G Priest and B Klein, 'The Selection of Disputes for Litigation' (1984) 13 *Journal of Legal Studies* 1.

[18] P Wood, *Life After Lehman: Allen & Overy Analysis of Changes in Market Practice* (London, Allen & Overy, 2009), quoted in M Weidemaier, R Scott and G Gulati, 'Origin Myths, Contracts, and the Hunt for Pari Passu' (2012) 37 *Law & Social Inquiry*.

> . . .
>
> Of course, with some of the professions' best brains documenting these highly complex instruments, you might expect the likelihood of mistakes to be low. Unfortunately not. Legal work on such instruments, once high-end, has become commoditised – and more and more rushed. 'Lawyers were central to the development of securitisation and CDOs, and the first such transactions were carefully structured by the leading lawyers in the profession', explains one finance partner. 'But as the practice has developed, things have been put together more and more quickly.' In the fast-moving world of finance with its famously demanding clients, lawyers have been called upon to produce documents more and more quickly. 'Deals have been closed in time frames that we all knew were insane', admits one city finance lawyer. While a CDO or MBS may take as much as three months to document, the basic structure of the documents can be thrown together literally overnight. 'Once the term sheet is agreed, the bank often wants a first draft overnight or over a weekend.'
>
> To respond to the need for quick document turnaround, the documentation surrounding such instruments – particularly CDOs – has become more and more standardised. 'Errors become compounded in documents, if you are using a bad precedent', explains a securitisation specialist at another London law firm. 'The client needs a deal in one week that should take eight, and they say, why don't you use this form and adapt it? And we tell clients it's deficient, but they say: "It's been signed off on, it's adequate, use it."' Nor is time the only constraint. 'It's also question of budgets – so-called innovations like fixed billing have made it harder and harder to justify doing things right', argues another harassed city finance partner.
>
> The effect of standardisation is to allow errors to spread throughout the system and become common, just as sub-prime exposures spread through the financial markets. The result is that, in one finance partner's words, the 'securitisation market is riddled with documents with errors in them'. Clients confirm the problem. Arturo Cifuentes, managing director of broker-dealer RW Pressprich & Co, despairs of the quality of drafting of many CDOs he reviewed during the boom. 'All the time, I would find things weren't clear. Commas all over the place. Complete confusion.'
>
> Some finance lawyers argue that even the agreed industry standard documentation is deficient. 'The standard document templates have been drafted by consensus between a number of different market players', explains David Shearer of Allen & Overy. 'The resulting documents do contain a number of compromises between the positions of the different players. For the most part, the documents are pretty good, but they can contain ambiguity and a lack of clarity in some areas.'[19]

In what contexts would mistakes be most likely? The following factors are potentially relevant.

— The extent to which documents are customised for a particular transaction and the extent to which transactions in the same general category

[19] Gera and Robinson, 'Sub-prime mortgage crisis' (n 1).

are different. At one end of the continuum is a transaction document that looks very much like the other documents from other deals of the same type – a so-called 'cookie cutter' deal (or, more precisely, a 'cookie' generated by a 'cookie cutter'. See the Northwest leasing example discussed below in Section III). At the other end, documents for each deal of a certain type could be quite customised, on fewer or more dimensions.
— The extent to which the subject matter is tractable. In some types of deals, a general consensus exists as to what needs to be addressed, and the possible ways to address it; negotiations are relatively circumscribed.[20]
— The extent to which subject matter and documents are complex and/or 'technical'.
— The extent to which negotiations are adversarial. For some deals, the process is more about trying to figure out the mechanics than about adversarial negotiation. M & A can be quite adversarial; some financing transactions may be far less so.
— Length of transaction documents (and whether they all have the same parties). In some types of transactions, there are many different documents, and some are signed by all parties whereas others might be signed by A and B, or B and C and so on. One mistake I have seen in early drafts of transaction documents in multi-party deals is what I have called the 'third party burdenficiary' problem – A and B are the parties to a document, which purports to require C, another party involved in the deal but not signatory to the document, to do something.
— Composition and responsibilities of the legal team: Are the documents sufficiently reviewed (or prepared) by knowledgeable lawyers?
— The relative haste in which the transaction is done (since most transactions are done in some sort of haste).

More transaction complexity and less tractability, less review by knowledgeable lawyers, longer document length, and more haste would seem unambiguously to yield more mistake-ridden documents, although the number of mistakes probably does not rise linearly. But the other factors' effects are harder to predict. The more customised a deal is, the more

[20] Sovereign debt is arguably in this category. See M Gulati and R Scott, 'The Three and a Half Minute Transaction: Boilerplate and the Limits of Contract Design' (5 October 2011) (available at papers.ssrn.com/sol3/papers.cfm?abstract_id=1937900). In the paper, the authors quote a senior lawyer as saying: 'These [sovereign debt] contracts are not that complex. Sovereign lending is pretty basic. There are maybe fifteen key terms that one has to understand . . . you know, negative pledge, redemption, dispute resolution, events of default and so on. And one can easily get the basics from that Buchheit book.' Lee Buchheit is the leading sovereign debt lawyer (as recently acknowledged in the *New York Times*, who called him 'the philosopher king of sovereign debt lawyers'. L Thomas, Jr, 'An Architect of a Deal Sees Greece as a Model' *New York Times* (Madrid, 6 March 2012) (available at www.nytimes.com/2012/03/07/business/global/mitu-gulati-an-architect-of-greeces-debt-deal-wants-more.html?_r=1&pagewanted=all)). The book at issue is L Buchheit, *How To Negotiate Eurocurrency Agreements* (London, Euromoney Publications, 2000).

likely one might be to review it carefully. But perhaps the more a transaction is one of a series – say, a 'cookie-cutter' financing rather than a merger – the more opportunities there may be to discover a mistake with the repeated viewings of the similar iterations of the same form. Something more technical might be more difficult to get right. But a lawyer might know he had to check a technical provision more carefully, and perhaps bring in someone else to help. More adversarial negotiation might yield more opportunities for mistakes, as accommodations on particular provisions yielded more 'notwithstanding' clauses that were not assessed for their impact on the deal as a whole. Or it might mean looking at more portions of a document, and especially, looking with a more critical eye for ways the other party might be seeking advantage. Empirical work would be needed to determine which factors contributed more to mistakes; such work should be helpful to efforts to minimise mistakes. But, as I have argued in other work, more could be done even without such knowledge – more systematic attempts could be made to 'clean up' either documents for particular deals or the 'forms' themselves, the precedents from other deals. Efforts along these lines are made; however, further non-heroic steps that can readily be identified are not taken.[21]

III. WHY ARE MISTAKES MADE (AND NOT CAUGHT OR CORRECTED)?

Assume that I am right, that transaction documents contain a fair number of mistakes that lawyers are not fixing. Why would this be the case?

Mistakes occur for many reasons. Document drafters may not work through technical provisions, perhaps because they don't fully understand them. They may unthinkingly perpetuate errors in portions of the 'form' that they don't change, or they may not look closely enough at provisions addressing contingencies they deem unlikely. For instance, and as discussed in the earlier quote on 'waterfalls' in CDOs, in some types of transactions, lawyers (and their clients) may consider bankruptcy (or even default) very unlikely, and thus may not spend much time considering how to deal with those contingencies. An opinion in the bankruptcy case of Northwest Airlines provides a good example:

> It appeared [from the testimony of the lawyers who had negotiated the Trust Indenture Agreement (TIA)] that the documents governing the leveraged leases for the five Avro aircraft, including the TIAs, were 'cloned' virtually word-for-word from the documentation of an earlier transaction . . . the lawyers who drafted the TIAs for all eight Aircraft were tax lawyers, and they testified that while they had extensively negotiated the tax aspects of the TIAs, they had

[21] See Hill, 'Bargaining' (n 6) 204–207.

never discussed [the section at issue in the case, which turned on the meaning of the term 'paid'], and they had never given any thought to the possibility that there might be a bankruptcy default that triggered rights under the TIA. [A footnote said, 'The corporate lawyers, who might have given some thought to the possibility of bankruptcy, were in the next room but were apparently not consulted about the TIAs'.][22]

The reasons for mistakes fall on a continuum reflecting the lawyer's state and extent of knowledge and awareness.

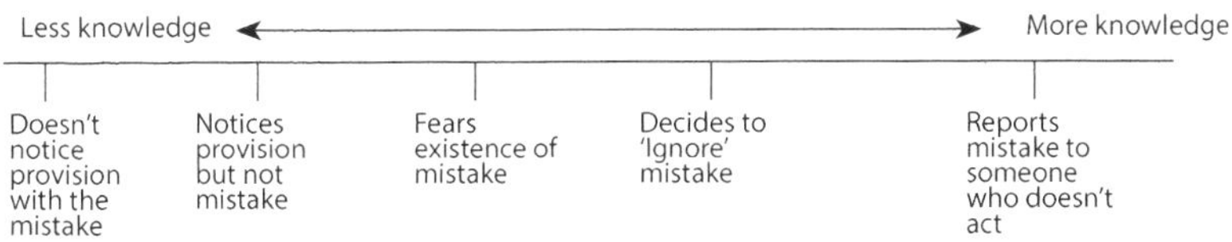

At one end are the mistakes a lawyer may not see or notice – for instance, in portions of a transaction document that were in the 'form' he started with and that are not changed in the course of the deal he is doing. In the middle are mistakes a lawyer suspects but does not investigate, such as the other provisions potentially implicated when he or someone else inserts a 'band-aid' clause. At the other end are mistakes the lawyer knows to be mistakes but decides not to act upon, or is overruled in trying to do so. The explanations at the middle and at the 'knowledge' end of the continuum have ready and (to me) relatively straightforward (and therefore less interesting) answers. The suspicion-not-pursued may reflect the lawyer's fear that checking the rest of the document to see what else needs to be changed may cause the deal to unravel as points deemed concluded are effectively reopened.[23] The knowledge-not-acted-upon, paradigmatically because the mistake was in previous deals, may reflect the lawyer's fear that the senior lawyer will want to shoot the messenger, or the senior lawyer's fear that the predecessor client will want to fire or even sue the

[22] *In Re Northwest Airlines Corp*, 393 BR 337, 346 (SDNY 2008). A famous example of a contract provision supposedly motivated by a party's fear that the other party wasn't reading the contract is one that required a bowl of M&Ms, with no brown ones, in Van Halen's dressing room during the 1982 tour. One account of the provision's purpose was as follows: 'Apparently, beyond the backstage food and drink requirements, tour riders (which are contract provisions) contain very important instructions that affect how smoothly the show will run – for example, electricity or weight requirements for the band's gear. Well, if the promoter at the local venue does not read the rider, it is likely that something will go very wrong at the show. So, Van Halen used the M&M's for signaling purposes: if there were no brown M&M's in the bowl, the band knew that the local promoter read the rider. If the brown M&M's were there, the band knew that the local promoter had not read the rider carefully, and technical and safety requirements might not have been met.' M Miller, 'Another Take on the Van Halen "No Brown M&Ms Rider"' (*Contracts Prof Blog*, 17 August 2009) (available at lawprofessors.typepad.com/contractsprof_blog/2009/08/another-take-on-the-van-halen-no-brown-mms-rider.html).

[23] See Hill, 'Bargaining' (n 6) 204–205, discussing the point and citing and discussing other literature.

law firm.[24] These explanations are scarcely novel. While I suspect that they are accurate, and I suspect too that the phenomenon is not on some plausible metric uncommon, again, empirical evidence would be needed to make any kind of authoritative claim.

What about the less-knowledge end of the continuum? I argued in 'Why Contracts Are Written in Legalese'[25] that the process by which junior lawyers get the experience they need is often a rather tortured one (and sometimes almost literally so, as they are lambasted by senior lawyers for their ignorance). I discussed at length a 'playlet' of a deal from the book *Anatomy of a Merger*. I quote a passage in which a junior associate (Preppie) is being lambasted for his bad job on a first draft. The senior lawyer (Prudent) explains to the junior lawyer what the junior lawyer did wrong, and tells the junior lawyer, Preppie, that he just 'didn't think'. One mistake Preppie made was to write a provision addressing what would happen if the Copyright Act were repealed. I noted that:

> The lesson Prudent is teaching Preppie is much more complex than it appears. Preppie will presumably know, as would just about anyone in Preppie's position, not to have three pages describing consequences of the repeal of the Copyright Act next time he gives Prudent a first draft. He will almost certainly know not to give such a draft to any other senior lawyer. But Prudent wants Preppie to learn a far more general lesson: he wants Preppie to learn not to write in new provisions addressing contingencies *as remote as* the repeal of the Copyright Act. Which contingencies are as remote as repeal of the Copyright Act? How is Preppie to know? The generic instruction 'think' is scarcely much of a guide. But, coupled with a few examples, it may be the best Prudent can do – Preppie will have to look to his imagination and judgment, and, as time goes on, experience, hopefully not so hard-won as in his encounter with Prudent. Prudent speaks as though 'thinking' were a matter of brawn rather than brains – something you could simply do by trying to do it. But Preppie's problem, as Prudent surely would agree, is not lack of effort. After all, Preppie produced this draft quite quickly, in the week that included Christmas Day. Preppie's problem is that he doesn't know what to think *about* – and there may be no good way to tell him. This dynamic extends far beyond determinations about which contingencies to include in a contract. Learning effectively from experience requires generalising to an experience's salient features. There is no formula to determine which features of an experience are salient.[26]

Note that the type of transaction at issue is a comparatively simple merger and acquisition transaction, with issues and accepted resolutions generally agreed upon among members of the relevant community, and the

[24] See the discussion on a closely related point in Gulati and Scott, 'The Three and A Half Minute Transaction' (n 20) 100; see also M Boardman, 'Contra Proferentem: The Allure of Ambiguous Boilerplate' (2005) 104 *Michigan Law Review* 1105.

[25] See Hill, 'Legalese' (n 6); see also J Freund, *Anatomy of a Merger: Strategies and Techniques for Negotiating Corporate Acquisitions* (New York, American Lawyer Media, 1975).

[26] Hill, 'Legalese' (n 6) 65.

senior lawyer, Prudent, the alter ego of the book's author, is looking quite carefully at the transaction documentation. The contract probably won't have any (serious) mistakes. But in many cases the transaction is more complex and more novel, and there is no close analogue to Prudent.[27] The Prudent figure may know less, and may be far less involved. There is almost certainly somebody senior to the very-junior Preppie, but that person may have very little time to review Preppie's work and he may not know that much either. In this regard, consider the example above of the tax lawyer not considering the possibility of bankruptcy. Or the issues with the 'waterfall' provisions in structured finance documents. There was clearly no Prudent reviewing those documents.[28]

Does associate training linearly lead to the Preppies of the world becoming Prudents? Even when it does – and the statistics as to the low proportion of associates who become partners suggest that this isn't frequent – it may take quite a while. There may be a considerable period of deference, when the junior lawyer thinks his job is one of execution rather than one of questioning. As I argued in 'Legalese':

> Preppie accords a rebuttable presumption to provisions in the form. For particular provisions, he weighs whether the presumption has been rebutted. The presumption will not be rebutted for benign provisions (such as the typical boilerplate about references to one gender including the other and captions of provisions not being part of the meaning of the provision); saving trees (or secretarial overtime or shipping charges) will not be a sufficient counterweight. His best guess may be that a provision seems benign, but he's not completely sure: the calculation will favor keeping the provisions. Indeed, Preppie will make as few changes as possible. He will often favor 'band-aids', requiring the least tinkering possible, over a more elegant, structural solution. The paradigm band-aid says 'anything else in this agreement to the contrary notwithstanding' or other words to that effect. Preppie has been told that the form – the contract he's marking up – 'works': that the provisions, in the aggregate, create internally consistent rights and duties, and cover the appropriate universe of events and contingencies. He will worry that any larger changes might make the contract not work.[29]

IV. WHY DON'T LAW FIRMS DO MORE TO DEAL WITH MISTAKES? THE ROLE OF REPUTATION

Why isn't more done to deal with mistakes? To be sure, changing the production process that yields mistakes would be exceedingly costly. The

[27] Lee Buchheit may be an analogue to Prudent for sovereign debt deals.

[28] Gulati and Scott, 'The Three and A Half Minute Transaction' (n 20) includes some remarkable quotes from interviews with associates: 'The firm told us when we got here that we were not to circulate anything that we didn't understand. Talk about a contradiction. Most of what we mark up and send around, we don't understand at all.' ibid 109.

[29] Hill, 'Legalese' (n 6) 68.

problem may be one of co-ordination – no firm may want to be the first mover. A firm might draw undesirable attention to itself if it appreciably changed its production process for this purpose. Perhaps it would even need to 'close up shop' while it cleaned up its forms, something also presumably undesirable. Certainly, a firm would not be eager to advertise its new status – 'now 99% mistake free'. But, critically, mistakes also may be less costly than might appear to be the case – reputation may constrain use of mistakes for strategic advantage.

We cannot know how many contracts contain mistakes. Nor can we know how much litigation there would be if parties were unconstrained by reputation. But it seems safe to conclude that most contracts with mistakes will probably not be litigated (and indeed it follows from the propositions I have argued for here, that most contracts contain mistakes and that most contracts are not litigated); in this regard, it defies logic to believe that the mistakes would in any significant sense cause litigation. Litigation occurs when a transaction does not meet one or both parties' hopes or expectations. Given the many intricacies of the transaction documents, disappointed parties will almost certainly find grounds to sue. A sensible and, I believe, uncontroversial, view is that reputational ties constrain parties from bringing lawsuits,[30] but that the constraint can be overridden if the stakes are high enough (or if the parties are in an end-game and no longer value a continuing relationship). As Stewart Macaulay notes:

> When long-term continuing relationships do collapse, those disadvantaged often turn to contract law and legal action. We have seen litigation prompted by major shocks to the world economic system. OPEC and the energy crises of the 1970s provoked many cases where contracts had rested on relational sanctions and assumptions about the costs of energy. Relational considerations gave way to the large amounts of money that businesses would have lost had they performed their commitments. Westinghouse, for example, promised electric utilities buying its nuclear reactors that it would guarantee the price of fuel. A world cartel sent the price soaring far beyond the price Westinghouse had guaranteed. Westinghouse found a plausible excuse in the Uniform Commercial Code and announced that it would not perform. After elaborate rituals before the courts, the cases were settled. Westinghouse injured its reputation, but the alternative might have been the destruction of a major multinational corporation.[31]

[30] See Hill, 'Bargaining' (n 6). As to the composition of reputational communities, see C Hill, 'A Comment on Language and Norms in Complex Business Contracts' (2002) 77 *Chicago-Kent Law Review* 29.

[31] Macaulay, 'Empirical View' (n 5) 471–72. Steven Davidoff discusses the role of reputation in constraining private equity firms, especially in leading them to complete unprofitable deals, in S Davidoff, 'The Failure of Private Equity' (2009) 82 *Southern California Law Review* 481, 511–13; see also M Cain, S Davidoff and A Macias, 'Broken Promises: Private Equity Bidding Behavior and the Value of Reputation' (March 2012) (available at papers.ssrn.com/sol3/papers.cfm?abstract_id=1540000); Hill, 'Bargaining' (n 6) 217–18.

Indeed, it may be that when many parties in a reputational community are significantly adversely affected, the reputational constraint that prevents parties from acting adversarially towards one another – not just as to lawsuits, but in other respects as well – is not just overridden, but may even disappear, at least in the short term. But when reputational constraints are operative, mistakes in contract documents apparently don't do enough damage, either to the parties or to the lawyers, to prompt sufficient action to prevent or appreciably limit them.

Even when inartful drafting is brought to light, the elite law firms that do complex business transactions do not seem to suffer significant reputational costs. Consider the example discussed in Section I above in which the term 'Expenses' was used but not defined. Consider, too, the observation by Mark Weidemaier, Robert Scott and Mitu Gulati that lawyers at the elite firms that do sovereign bond deals sometimes 'tell stories' that depict them as complicit in sloppy drafting practices;[32] presumably, they do not think they will lose business as a result. Perhaps even the contrary: abiding by standard contracting rituals, including those that predictably and reliably yield mistakes, is one way the contracting community knows and defines its members. Behaving differently in one respect raises the question: what else someone might be doing differently? An excellent, albeit far-flung (and far-fetched), example, from Omri Ben-Shahar and John AE Pottow's work on sticky default rules, makes the point. (There are certainly more straightforward expositions of the point that conventions are sticky because departing from them imparts the information – the negative signal – that one is able, or willing, to do so, but I was unable – unwilling, actually – to resist an example with chocolate.) The authors hypothesise a person trying to buy a wireless router on eBay and finding many choices, all quite similar except that one includes in addition to the router some fancy chocolate as a prize to the successful bidder. The router is worth no more than $50 to the person. They conclude that the prospective buyer might bid less for the router plus chocolate than the router without the chocolate. They argue that:

> While the bundling itself does not provide any direct indication that something might be wrong with the router, the fact that this deviation is so uncommon may raise your suspicion that the seller is trying to trick you, and other potential buyers, into a transaction that you will later regret. The bundling of chocolate into the transaction, being such an unfamiliar practice, may scare you away by raising a host of 'unknown' worries you had not originally perceived. So while there is nothing wrong with such bundling – in fact, it should increase the value of the sale to the buyer – it may never be offered.[33]

[32] Weidermaier and others, 'Origin Myths' (n 18) 41–42 .

[33] See O Ben-Shahar and J Pottow, 'On the Stickiness of Default Rules' (2006) 33 *Florida State Law Review* 651, 681–82.

CONCLUSION

I have argued that complex business contracts have appreciable numbers of mistakes; I have sketched a preliminary taxonomy of those mistakes, and why and when they are made. Law firms could do more to limit mistakes, but they do not. Law itself probably cannot do much to limit mistakes. Certainly, an interpretive convention is unlikely to help. It is hard to envision a real-world interpretive convention that would materially increase the expected costs of contractual mistakes.

The types of mistakes made may be on display in all their glory when litigation occurs. Of course, litigation might occur precisely when contracts have more mistakes. Even if that were so, it seems likely that contracts not litigated also have an appreciable number of mistakes. I would go further, though, and argue that the quantity and severity of mistakes is only loosely related to whether a contract is litigated. A far more important determinant of litigation is a deal that disappoints one or both parties where a party's losses potentially put it in an endgame, or norms within the relevant community allow for litigation in the circumstances at issue. Complex business contracting occurs within a community, and community norms will importantly dictate the parties' behaviour as they consider a contracting relationship, as they negotiate to decide on the terms of that relationship, as they act in the course of that relationship, and as they act should the relationship fail to produce the hoped-for benefits. These benefits are not something that contract documentation by itself can produce. Success – profits for business ventures, repayment as promised – is far more dependent on business decisions and the state of the industry and economy than on the terms in the contract. Nor is a failed transaction a predictable or even likely result of defective contract documentation. In this regard, consider that many contracting mistakes are in provisions specifying what happens when things go wrong; almost by definition, these provisions can't be responsible for making the deal go wrong.

When a deal blows up badly, a lawsuit may follow. Reputational constraints that might otherwise limit such suits may evaporate or be overridden. It will be virtually impossible to prevent parties from being able to impose costs on each other using litigation, even with near-perfect documents.[34] But in less extreme circumstances when things are going well (enough) the documents will stay in the drawer (or perhaps, in a virtual

[34] Textualists might dispute this proposition on grounds that if courts cannot use context, imposition of costs will be greatly minimised. See, eg A Schwartz and R Scott, 'Contract Interpretation Redux' (2010) 119 *Yale Law Journal* 926. But given the extensive costs that can be imposed in discovery and motion practice, and the difficulties in interpreting language on its face even without reference to contextual factors, significantly minimising a party's ability to impose costs does not seem feasible.

drawer on one's computer), not consulted. When things are not going well (enough), the documents will be consulted, but reputation and self-interest will argue against a precipitous resort to litigation.

My ultimate answer is thus that contracting mistakes persist because in ordinary circumstances, they don't do much harm. They may even do some good if they constrain litigation and solidify the community through its common acceptance of (litigation-constraining) norms. Complexity of the transaction documents, and the necessarily highly repeat nature of the players, mean that reputation will win out over opportunistic use of contractual mistakes for a party's advantage except in extreme circumstances.

The financial crisis is an extreme circumstance. Are contractual mistakes a matter of public concern in such a circumstance? Public concern is implicated especially insofar as mistake-making can have considerable externalities; documentation for subprime securities is a recent visceral example. But the bulk of the externalities are caused by the failure of the underlying transaction, not the defects in the documents.[35] Contractual mistakes occur in a broader context – indeed, contracting itself occurs in a broader context, where community norms importantly dictate how parties conduct their relationship.

BIBLIOGRAPHY

Ben-Shahar, O (ed), '"Boilerplate": Foundations of Market Contracts Symposium' (2006) 104 *Michigan Law Review* 5.

Ben-Shahar, O and Pottow, J, 'On the Stickiness of Default Rules' (2006) 33 *Florida State Law Review* 651.

Boardman, M, 'Contra Proferentem: The Allure of Ambiguous Boilerplate' (2005) 104 *Michigan Law Review* 1105.

Buchheit, L, *How To Negotiate Eurocurrency Agreements* (London, Euromoney Publications, 2000).

Cain, M, Davidoff, S and Macias, A, 'Broken Promises: Private Equity Bidding Behavior and the Value of Reputation' (March 2012).

Coates, J, 'Expert Report of Professor John C Coates IV' (*United Rentals, Inc v RAM Holdings, Inc and RAM Acquisition Corp*, 6 December 2007).

——, 'Explaining Variation in Takeover Defenses: Blame the Lawyers' (2001) 89 *California Law Review* 1301.

Davidoff, S, 'The Failure of Private Equity' (2009) 82 *Southern California Law Review* 481.

——, 'Smoke Gets In Your Eyes' (*New York Times*, 11 September 2008).

Freund, J, *Anatomy of a Merger: Strategies and Techniques for Negotiating Corporate Acquisitions* (New York, American Lawyer Media, 1975).

[35] Indeed, in some respects, the documentation problems may be beneficial. Slowing the pace of foreclosures, as is occurring as banks scramble to find an alternative means to demonstrate their rights to foreclose, might be a good thing.

Gera, R and Robinson, D, 'What does the sub-prime mortgage crisis mean for lawyers?' (*Chambers*, 2008 Issue 24).
Gulati, M and Scott, R, 'The Three and a Half Minute Transaction: Boilerplate and the Limits of Contract Design' (5 October 2011).
Hill, C, 'Why Contracts are Written in Legalese' (2002) 77 *Chicago-Kent Law Review* 59.
——, 'Bargaining in the Shadow of the Lawsuit: A Social Norms Theory of Incomplete Contracts' (2009) 34 *Delaware Journal of Corporate Law* 191.
Letter to Counsel from W Chandler III, Chancellor (13 December 2007).
M & A Law Prof Blog, 'Mistakes M&A Lawyers Make' (*M & A Law Prof Blog*, 20 August 2007).
Macaulay, S, 'The Real and the Paper Deal: Empirical Pictures of Relationships, Complexity and the Urge for Transparent Simple Rules' (2003) 66 *Modern Law Review* 44.
——, 'Relational Contracts Floating on a Sea of Custom? Thoughts About the Ideas of Ian MacNeil and Lisa Bernstein' (2002) 94 *Northwestern Law Review* 775.
——, 'An Empirical View of Contract' (1985) 1985 *Wisconsin Law Review* 465.
——, 'Non-Contractual Relations in Business: A Preliminary Study' (1963) 28 *American Sociological Review* 1.
Margolick, D, 'At the Bar; How Three Missing Zeros Brought Red Faces and Cost Millions of Dollars' (*New York Times*, 4 October 1991).
Miller, M, 'Another Take on the Van Halen "No Brown M&Ms Rider"' (*Contracts Prof Blog*, 17 August 2009).
Priest, G and Klein, B, 'The Selection of Disputes for Litigation' (1984) 13 *Journal of Legal Studies* 1.
Schwartz, A and Scott, R, 'Contract Interpretation Redux' (2010) 119 *Yale Law Journal* 926.
Thomas, L, Jr, 'An Architect of a Deal Sees Greece as a Model' (*New York Times*, 6 March 2012).
Weidemaier, M, Scott, R and Gulati, G, 'Origin Myths, Contracts, and the Hunt for Pari Passu' (2012) 37 *Law & Social Inquiry*.
Wood, P, *Life After Lehman: Allen & Overy Analysis of Changes in Market Practice* (London, Allen & Overy, 2009).

8

The Role of Contract: Stewart Macaulay's Lessons from Practice

BRIAN H BIX*

INTRODUCTION

FROM HIS EARLIEST works,[1] Stewart Macaulay's rich and impressive empirical and theoretical work has taught those academics sufficiently open-minded to listen, about 'the limited practical role of what professors call contract law'.[2] This paper will reflect on what this divergence from actual contracting behaviour means for the content of most contract law courses and much of mainstream contract law scholarship.[3]

A second task of this paper is to consider some of the theoretical sources for Macaulay's empirical work, as well as its influence on a wide range of later thinkers. While, in a sense, Macaulay's approach owes something to the American legal realists (in particular, Oliver Wendell Holmes, Jr and Karl Llewellyn), the view of contract law and practice he has developed is much deeper and more well-rounded. His work has inspired parallel yet differing lines of inquiry: including law and society approaches, on one hand, and the social norms sub-field of law and economics, on the other.

* I am grateful for the comments of Jean Braucher, Claire Hill, William Whitford, and other participants at the 'Empirical and Lyrical: Revisiting the Contracts Scholarship of Stewart Macaulay' conference held at the University of Wisconsin (21–22 October 2011).

[1] Most prominently, S Macaulay, 'Non-Contractual Relations in Business: A Preliminary Study' (1963) 28 *American Sociological Review* 55.

[2] S Macaulay, 'An Empirical View of Contract' (1985) 1985 *Wisconsin Law Review* 465.

[3] This is a topic I have discussed in B Bix, 'Some Reflections on Contract Law Theory' (2007) 1 *Problema* 143, available in modified form at papers.ssrn.com/sol3/papers.cfm?abstract_id=892783. For much earlier work on the subject, see, eg L Friedman, *Contract Law in America: A Social and Economic Case Study* (Madison, University of Wisconsin Press, 1965). And for excellent recent work on the same themes, see, eg J Braucher, 'The Sacred and Profane Contracts Machine: The Complex Morality of Contract Law in Action' (2012) 45 *Suffolk University Law Review* 667.

There have also been hybrids of the two approaches, such as the empirical investigations of some economically-minded theorists, including Lisa Bernstein.

This chapter will begin to explore how contract law and theory needs to be re-thought in the light of Macaulay's work, and in the light of the investigations that have followed his path. Section I uses the notion of how one thinks about contracts and contract law to illustrate basic differences among various approaches to contract law and scholarship. Section II focuses on one such approach, law and economics, and examines the way that some empirical and social norms theorists within that school have offered approaches comparable to Macaulay's. Section III examines Macaulay's distinction between 'real deals' and 'paper deals' and considers some of the practical problems of translating a more contextual approach to contract law to judicial decision-making. Section IV examines the dangers of less realistic approaches to law school teaching, before concluding.

I. WHAT SORT OF THING IS 'CONTRACT [LAW]'

Jurisprudence scholars never tire of asking: what is law? Many of the debates within and about law derive from (vastly) different assumptions and starting positions regarding a version of this question: not so much the analytical legal theorist's question, asking about the elements of what makes an entity or system 'law' or not 'law', but rather the slightly more general question, of what sort of thing 'law' is. Let me try to be a bit clearer through example. Much of the debate between the legal positivists and the natural theorists regarding the nature of law seems to come down to the legal positivists viewing law primarily *as a kind of social institution*, and the natural law theorists viewing law primarily *as a facet of practical reasoning*.[4] The disagreement between the two major camps of contemporary jurisprudence can be understood as merely a difference of focus, or of the lens through which the matter is viewed.

One can similarly ask: What sort of thing is 'contract?'[5] To the formalists, contract was a particular sort of logical construct, which followed basic principles, without regard either to moral claims or empirical investigation. Thus, Christopher Columbus Langdell famously argued against the postal acceptance rule: after noting the argument in favour of that rule, that it would lead to fairer or more efficient practice, he responded

[4] See, eg B Bix, 'Theorizing About Law' (2010) *Analisi e Diritto* 271, 273–74.

[5] Here I am *not* trying to invoke Arthur Leff's excellent article with a similar title: A Leff, 'Contract as Thing' (1970) 19 *American University Law Review* 131. Somewhat closer to my own purposes is M Suchman, 'The Contract as Social Artifact' (2003) 37 *Law and Society Review* 91.

that such arguments were irrelevant.[6] Langdell's view was that the answer to when an acceptance occurred was to be derived, in a matter of logical deduction, from the basic premises and concepts of contract law, not from any sort of discussion of practices, policies, or consequences.

'We are all realists now', or so we are told, which is meant to entail that we all deride the sort of formalism associated with Langdell's approach. However, there is a sense in which many of us who teach contract law (especially those of us unwise enough *not* to use the casebook that Macaulay and his colleagues have written[7]) follow modern versions of that same formalism.[8] What we teach sometimes seems more like a logical (or theological) exercise than a set of skills or facts related to an actual practice. We often go on at length about contract law doctrines that we then note have been superseded by federal and state consumer protection statutes (for example, on how advertisements are not offers and do not bind sellers[9]), statutes most of us understand poorly and thus wisely largely ignore.[10] (Of course, if a contract law teacher *were* to spend a lot of time teaching consumer protection statutes, I would likely criticise that professor for not mentioning the reality of such statutes often being made toothless by limiting judicial constructions[11] and by mandatory arbitration provisions that effectively limit rights, send disputes to very partial decision-makers,[12] and circumvent state-law unconscionability claims with the blessings of the federal courts.[13])

[6] C Langdell, *A Summary of the Law of Contract*, 2nd edn (Boston, Little, Brown & Co, 1880) 20–21.

[7] S Macaulay and others, *Contracts: Law in Action*, two vols, 3rd edn (Charlottesville, LexisNexis, 2011).

[8] I recognise the irony (if not hypocrisy) of an armchair theorist joining in criticism of armchair theorising and celebrating the importance of empirical scholarship. However, I never let a risk of irony (or hypocrisy) get in the way of proclaiming a view I consider correct.

[9] But see J Feinman and S Brill, 'Is an Advertisement an Offer? Why It Is, and Why It Matters' (2006) 58 *Hastings Law Journal* 61.

[10] A lesson taught by Macaulay in S Macaulay, 'Bambi Meets Godzilla: Reflections on Contracts Scholarship and Teaching vs. State Unfair and Deceptive Trade Practices and Consumer Protection Statutes' (1989) 26 *Houston Law Review* 575.

[11] ibid 594–99.

[12] While there is some evidence that AAA-certified arbitrators adhere to relatively fair procedures and have outcomes that appear to be fair, see C Drahozal and S Zyontz, 'An Empirical Study of AAA Consumer Arbitrations' (2010) 25 *Ohio State Journal of Dispute Resolution* 843, there is ample evidence of arbitration companies providing something less than a fair resolution of disputes. See, eg C Mayer, 'Win Some, Lose Rarely? Arbitration Forum's Rulings Called One-Sided' *Washington Post* (1 March 2000) (firm hired to do First USA's credit card arbitration decided for First USA 99.6% of the time). See also T Eisenberg, G Miller, and E Sherwin, 'Mandatory Arbitration for Customers but Not for Peers' (2008) 92 *Judicature* 118 (while companies included mandatory arbitration in three-quarters of their contracts with consumers, such terms appeared in only 10% of the contracts those same companies entered with other companies).

[13] See, eg *Stolt-Nielsen SA v AnimalFeeds International*, 130 S Ct 1758 (2010); *Rent-A-Center, West v Jackson*, 130 S Ct 2772 (2010); *AT&T Mobility LLC v Concepcion*, 131 S Ct 1740 (2011).

And when we pass on the diktat of the 7th Circuit Court of Appeals that sales of computer hardware and software are not in fact complete when the purchaser hands over the money or even when the product arrives, but only once the purchaser has the opportunity to read the new terms, and when we add the instructions from the same source that the purchaser can return the product for a full refund if the terms are not agreeable to him or her,[14] have we cleared this with Best Buy or Wal-Mart? At times, one might wonder if taught contract law is becoming like formalist judicial reasoning during the time of the legal realists: a form of 'transcendental nonsense' equally unmoored from facts and from moral reasoning.[15] (The topic of teaching and how it can mislead will be considered further below, in Section IV.)

Secondly, one could view contract law as part of practical/normative reasoning. That one has entered a valid contract with another person would affect one's moral obligations, for example, regarding one's obligation to perform what one has promised as part of the contract. Charles Fried, in his 1981 book, *Contract as Promise*, focused on the way in which contract doctrines mostly did (though occasionally did not) reflect the morality of promising and other basic moral principles.[16] More recently, Seana Shiffrin has sparked a debate among other contract theorists regarding the extent to which contract law is consistent with our obligations to act virtuously regarding our promises and bargains.[17] Within these debates, contract law is treated somewhat abstractly: the focus is often on quite specific doctrines or case decisions, but there is little concern regarding whether or how the rules and doctrines reflect or are reflected in the general behaviour of judges, lawyers or contracting parties.

There are certainly important questions to ask about how contract law can or should reflect the moral obligation to keep promises. And there are also distinct and interesting questions about how the presence of certain legal rules of contract – which may act to either supplement or undermine our general moral obligations relating to promises and transactions – affect our moral reasons for action. The danger, though, for law professors, is that abstract discussions of this sort may deflect attention from different, real-world moral and practical issues that arise where promises and contracts are often not kept and not enforced either.[18] And the pattern

[14] See *Hill v Gateway 2000, Inc*, 105 F3d 1147 (7th Cir 1997); *ProCD, Inc v Zeidenberg*, 86 F3d 1447 (7th Cir 1996).

[15] See F Cohen, 'Transcendental Nonsense and the Functional Response' (1935) 35 *Columbia Law Review* 809.

[16] C Fried, *Contract as Promise* (Cambridge, Harvard University Press, 1981). See also Symposium: '*Contract as Promise* at 30: The Future of Contract Theory' (2012) 45 *Suffolk University Law Review* 601.

[17] See S Shiffrin, 'The Divergence of Contract and Promise' (2007) 120 *Harvard Law Review* 708.

[18] See Braucher, 'The Sacred and Profane Contracts Machine' (n 3).

of non-enforcement tends not to be random: it is not the large corporations or well-represented parties that tend to be harmed by intentional (or 'efficient') breach, doctrinal and contractual limitations on damages, mandatory arbitration, discovery abuse, narrow readings of consumer protection statutes and so on.[19]

Thirdly, one could look at contract law as a series of rules and principles which have (or *may* have) consequences for the actual practices of business people and others. This has arguably been the main message of Macaulay's work,[20] and of the law and society ('law in action') movement generally.[21] It is, simultaneously, a focus of at least parts of the law and economics movement – some members of this school approach questions of consequences in an armchair (or formula-based) sort of way, but others do genuinely empirical work. I will have more to say about Macaulay's approach, below, but will mostly leave the commentary to better situated colleagues whose work appears in this collection. I will have more to say about law and economics in the next Section.

II. LAW AND ECONOMICS

Law and economics is a wide-ranging school or movement, and so there are dangers to making broad claims about it, as any claim will likely not cover every theory self-labeled or labeled by others as law and economics.[22] Nonetheless, some generalisations will be offered here, fully aware of the dangers, and open to modification or denial.

Law and economics examines the incentives and disincentives that affect our behaviour, focusing primarily, though not exclusively, on the way legal rules and processes have that effect in our lives.[23] While non-economic

[19] See ibid; Macaulay, 'Bambi Meets Godzilla' (n 10) 594–99; S Macaulay, 'The Real and the Paper Deal: Empirical Pictures of Relationships, Complexity and the Urge for Transparent Simple Rules' (2003) 66 *Modern Law Review* 44, 49–56.

[20] See, eg Macaulay, 'Non-Contractual Relations in Business' (n 1); S Macaulay, 'The Use and Non-Use of Contracts in the Manufacturing Industry' (1963) 9 *Practical Lawyer* 13; S Macaulay, 'Private Legislation and the Duty to Read – Business Run by IBM Machine, the Law of Contracts and Credit Cards' (1966) 19 *Vanderbilt Law Review* 1051; Macaulay, 'An Empirical View of Contract' (n 2); S Macaulay, 'The New Versus the Old Legal Realism: "Things Ain't What They Used to Be"' (2005) 2005 *Wisconsin Law Review* 365; S Macaulay, 'Contracts, New Legal Realism, and Improving the Navigation of *The Yellow Submarine*' (2006) 80 *Tulane Law Review* 1161.

[21] See, eg S Macaulay and others, *Law in Action: A Socio-Legal Reader* (New York, Foundation Press, 2007).

[22] In particular, I will not be discussing game theory, public choice theory, or social choice theory, and will discuss behavioural law and economics only partially or indirectly. For an overview of the different schools within law and economics, see B Bix, *Jurisprudence: Theory and Context*, 6th edn (London, Sweet & Maxwell, 2012) 205–34.

[23] See, eg R Craswell, 'In That Case, What is the Question? Economics and the Demands of Contract Theory' (2003) 112 *Yale Law Journal* 903; see generally R Posner, *Economic Analysis of Law*, 8th edn (New York, Aspen, 2011).

commentators about contract law often advocate rules that they believe will create the most just outcomes in the resolution of disputes (the view 'ex post'), law and economics tends to argue for rules that will produce the best (most efficient) set of behaviours in the future (the view 'ex ante'). Theorists such as Richard Craswell have worked out, in abstract terms, the way that different rules of damages for breach of contract and liability for pre-contractual reliance can affect our willingness to invest prior to performance, to perform, re-negotiate or breach, and so on.[24]

Like the American legal realists, law and economics theorists (at least in principle, and among its better practitioners) focus more on the way contract actually operates in judicial decision-making and individual decision-making, rather than blithely assuming that rules are always followed, that they are always enforced, or that they always affect judicial or individual decisions in uniform ways.[25]

While classical law and economics (like classical economics generally) focuses on decisions a 'rational actor' makes under different incentives and disincentives, a different set of strands within the law and economic tradition focuses on social norms: how they develop, and the way they influence or compete with legal norms to influence behaviour. One line of development came from Robert Ellickson, who seemingly (re-)discovered what Macaulay had pointed out long before: that individuals and businesses interact on the basis of norms which may have little connection with the norms established by contract, property and tort law.[26]

A different convergence with Macaulay's work can be found in Lisa Bernstein's recent empirical studies. She has examined the way that merchants in certain industries effect a kind of escape from contract law – in particular, from Article 2 of the *Uniform Commercial Code* (UCC): opting out of litigation under those rules, and choosing instead industry arbitration. Substantively, Bernstein's work shows, within the industries she has examined, an antipathy for the contextual, incorporationist standards of the UCC (in which contracts are held to have incorporated understandings from course of performance, course of dealing, and trade usage[27]), in favour of a plain-meaning textualism.[28] She has argued that the incorpora-

[24] See R Craswell, 'Two Economic Theories of Enforcing Promises' in Peter Benson (ed), *The Theory of Contract Law: New Essays* (Cambridge, Cambridge University Press, 2001) 19–44.

[25] Llewellyn's earlier analysis of these phenomena will be discussed in the next Section.

[26] R Ellickson, *Order Without Law: How Neighbors Settle Disputes* (Cambridge, Harvard University Press, 1991). Ellickson cites Macaulay approvingly – see, eg ibid 8, 141, 149, 154, 189–91, 251.

[27] See, eg UCC §§ 2-202, 2-208.

[28] See L Bernstein, 'Private Commercial Law in the Cotton Industry: Creating Cooperation Through Norms, Rules, and Institutions' (2001) 99 *Michigan Law Review* 1724; L Bernstein, 'The Questionable Empirical Basis of Article 2's Incorporation Strategy: A Preliminary Study' (1999) 66 *University of Chicago Law Review* 710; L Bernstein, 'Merchant Law in a Merchant Court: Rethinking the Code's Search for Immanent Business Norms' (1996) 144

tionist approach of UCC Article 2 has at least two basic flaws: that there are few if any of the customs and trade usages that the provisions assume to be present; and that applying course of performance and course of dealing in disputes confuses what parties are willing to do for one another when things are going well (relationship-enhancing norms) with what they will insist upon when things go badly (endgame norms).[29] In many ways, Bernstein's work is very much in the spirit of Macaulay's research,[30] even if Bernstein works nominally under the flag of 'law and economics' rather than within the less powerful jurisdiction of 'law and society'.[31]

III. CONTEXT AND COURTS

Karl Llewellyn observed that there is a fallacy among both practitioners in the legal system and observers of it: the fallacy that legal rules *describe* perfectly the behaviour of citizens and judges, and that they *prescribe* or predict those behaviours without error.[32] It is not that many people assert or defend such claims, but such views seem to act as assumptions that we do not articulate, operating just underneath our beliefs about the world. Lawmakers often do seem to behave as if legislating against some practice ensures its eradication, or that establishing a standard for judicial decision-making on some issue guarantees that judges will in fact make decisions in line with that standard. In any event, the reality is, of course, quite different. In the case of citizens, we are all aware (at least those of us who have recently driven on highways or talked to other people about their payment of taxes) that there are many legal rules that are not followed by all or even most, and there are quite a few legal rules that are almost universally ignored.

The situation with judges, as Llewellyn pointed out, is similar, if also more complex. Not only will some legal rules be ignored by judges (or cited only selectively relative to their potential scope of application); there are also circumstances where a rule is in fact cited by a judge, but we have

University of Pennsylvania Law Review 1765; L Bernstein, 'Opting Out of the Legal System: Extralegal Contractual Relations in the Diamond Industry' (1992) 21 *Journal of Legal Studies* 115.

[29] See Bernstein, 'The Questionable Empirical Basis' (n 28); Bernstein, 'Merchant Law in a Merchant Court' (n 28).

[30] Macaulay expresses his admiration for Bernstein's work in S Macaulay, 'Relational Contracts Floating on a Sea of Custom? Thoughts About the Ideas of Ian Macneil and Lisa Bernstein' (2000) 94 *Northwestern University Law Review* 775; see also Macaulay, 'The Real and the Paper Deal' (n 19) 50–54.

[31] An interesting, if occasionally contentious and partial, discussion of the differences between the two approaches can be found in I Ayres, 'Never Confuse Efficiency with a Liver Complaint' (1997) 1997 *Wisconsin Law Review* 503.

[32] K Llewellyn, 'A Realistic Jurisprudence – The Next Step' (1930) 30 *Columbia Law Review* 431, 438–40, fn 9.

real doubt as to whether the rule in fact influenced the judge's reasoning or decision. Llewellyn referred to this as the difference between 'real rules' and 'paper rules'.[33] Some rules have the effects in the world that we generally want and expect, acting as reasons that affect the behaviour of judges and citizens, but other legal rules have only the surface structure of valid rules, while having little actual role in the practical reasoning of either citizens or judges.

Llewellyn's terminology of 'real rules' and 'paper rules' was echoed in Macaulay's equally useful distinction between the 'real deal' and the 'paper deal'.[34] Macaulay's point, however, was somewhat different from Llewellyn's: instead of Llewellyn's observation about rules that did or did not have effects in the world, Macaulay's insight focused on the fact that the parties' (shared or diverging) subjective understanding of their agreement frequently varies from the written text they have signed.

Parties sign agreements or assent to terms (especially standardised forms and on-line terms) they have not read, and would not understand even if they did read them. They are given oral assurances that vary or are otherwise contrary to written provisions (including, prominently, the integration clause which asserts that *there are no* assurances other than the written terms). Many merchants assume that if problems arise, they will be worked out and accommodations made, and these assumptions are frequently reasonable, based on past dealings between the parties or in that industry and location.[35] This all seems to point to the realist conclusion, that judges should be more attentive to context in resolving the contract disputes that reach them.

Yet, one can concede that context is important to understanding contracting practices, and the role of contract rules and principles in those practices, and still be doubtful that this perspective justifies a significant change in the way contract law disputes are decided by the courts. Two contract law theorists, David Barnhizer and Nathan Oman, have recently offered thoughtful critiques of contextual approaches to regulation and enforcement in contract law.

Barnhizer[36] points out that increasing the factors that courts can consider in the interpretation and application of contracts, especially when those factors are necessarily variable in how they should effect the evaluation, and thus the outcome of a case, gives courts greater discretion and makes

[33] ibid 434–43, 447–53.

[34] Macaulay, 'The Real and the Paper Deal' (n 19).

[35] See, eg Macaulay, 'Non-Contractual Relations in Business' (n 1); Macaulay, 'The Use and Non-Use of Contracts in the Manufacturing Industry' (n 20); Macaulay, 'An Empirical View of Contract' (n 2); Macaulay, 'The Real and the Paper Deal' (n 19).

[36] D Barnhizer, 'Context as Power: Defining the Field of Battle for Advantage in Contractual Interactions' (2010) 45 *Wake Forest Law Review* 607.

case outcomes more unpredictable.[37] Barnhizer also suggests that contextual analysis of this sort has the effect (and perhaps the purpose) of shifting power from repeat players who benefit the most from careful contract drafting – and careful contract reading – to non-repeat players (consumers, but also some franchisees and employees). Perhaps most importantly, Barnhizer argues that the use of contextual analysis tends to be selective – perhaps necessarily so, given the limitation of court resources. However, that can lead to courts assuming that an employee or franchisee is relatively poor and unsophisticated when the party may in fact be neither.[38]

Oman offers a slightly different set of arguments against a second kind of contextual analysis.[39] Oman wants the courts to resist the tendency favoured by legal realist and law and society schools to give different sorts of transactions separate doctrinal rules and principles. He argues that specialised rules for particular transaction types creates a greater risk of capture of the whole area by specialised interests (a risk that would be much smaller if each transaction type simply applied 'general contract principles'), and also creates problems when particular transactions do not meet the (stated or unstated) narrative underlying the legal rules and principles of the area.[40]

From these writers, and others, we might at least learn caution about context and contract law. Even if it is the case that one can only properly understand the contract practice when one understands the quite different contexts – and understandings and expectations and history and power dynamics – of different sorts of transaction types, or different communities, it does not mean that this insight translates easily or well into the reform of doctrinal rules or judicial approaches to decision-making.

As noted, the problems here either exemplify, or are analogous to, the general difficulty Macaulay's works locate: what should the courts do about the obvious and frequent disparity between the agreement as written and the subjective perception the parties had of the agreement?[41] Charles Knapp has also made a similar point about the dilemma courts have in responding to the fact that business people live both in a world where you can rely on writings (and cannot rely on something *until* it is

[37] Unpredictable far in advance, at least. Once a case goes to trial, or on appeal, and the judge(s) deciding the case are known, the outcome might be more predictable, based more on the known inclinations of the judge(s) rather than on the contract and its context.

[38] Barnhizer, 'Context as Power' (n 36) 620–28 (looking at Ninth Circuit unconscionability cases).

[39] N Oman, 'A Pragmatic Defense of Contract Law' (2009) 98 *Georgetown Law Journal* 77.

[40] See also N Oman, 'Bargaining in the Shadow of God's Law: Islamic Mahr Contracts and the Perils of Legal Specialization' (2010) 45 *Wake Forest Law Review* 579. I respond to this article by Oman, on both theoretical and substantive grounds, in B Bix, 'Mahr Agreements: Contracting in the Shadow of Family Law (and Religious Law) – A Comment on Oman's Article' (2011) 1 *Wake Forest Law Review Online* 61 (available at http://wakeforestlawreview.com/2011/05).

[41] Macaulay, 'The Real and the Paper Deal' (n 19) 47–49.

put into writing), *and*, simultaneously, in a world where we trust the oral assurances of our contracting partners offer us even if, or especially if, those assurances deviate from what the writing says.[42]

How should courts respond to these gaps and dilemmas? As Macaulay notes, sometimes they simply ignore the gap, and respond contemptuously to the idea that anything other than the written terms should prevail.[43] Modern commentators offer a more sophisticated (and less dismissive) reason for enforcing the written deal rather than any contrary understandings: for example, that at least with business-to-business transactions, a purely textualist approach (as contrasted with a more contextualist or incorporationist approach) would save money while not creating significantly more errors than alternative approaches.[44]

Macaulay has responded to similar arguments (made by Robert Scott[45]), arguing that while some would prefer certainty and predictability over equity and context, his (Macaulay's) preference is the other way.[46] He has conceded that a textualist approach might be tolerable if confined to negotiated contracts between well-represented parties, though he expressed doubts that judges would be able entirely to shut their eyes to the equities and context of the disputes before them.[47]

IV. TEACHING AND CONSEQUENCES

As Macaulay pointed out long ago,[48] the way that businesses deal with contractual performance and non-performance bears little if any resemblance to all the rules and exceptions one learns (and, for many of us, one teaches[49]) in contract law courses. He wrote: '[A]cademic contract law is not now and never was a descriptively accurate reflection of the institution in operation.'[50] As I have written elsewhere,[51] one might reasonably

[42] C Knapp, 'Rescuing Reliance: The Perils of Promissory Estoppel' (1998) 49 *Hastings Law Journal* 1191, 1322–25.

[43] See, eg *James Baird Co v Gimbel Bros, Inc*, 64 F2d 344, 346 (2nd Cir 1933) ('in commercial transactions it does not in the end promote justice to seek strained interpretations in aid of those who do not protect themselves').

[44] See, eg A Schwartz and R Scott, 'Contract Theory and the Limits of Contract Law' (2003) 113 *Yale Law Journal* 541; see also the works of L Bernstein cited above (n 28).

[45] eg R Scott, 'The Case for Formalism in Relational Contract' (2000) 94 *Northwestern University Law Review* 847.

[46] Macaulay, 'The Real and the Paper Deal' (n 19) 50–52.

[47] ibid 52.

[48] Macaulay, 'Non-Contractual Relations in Business' (n 1).

[49] Many teachers are aware of this discrepancy, but few seem to be as bothered by it as they should be.

[50] Macaulay, 'An Empirical View of Contract' (n 2) 466.

[51] See Bix, 'Some Reflections on Contract Law Theory' (n 3). I expand on the argument in B Bix, *Contract Law: Rules, Theory, and Context* (Cambridge, Cambridge University Press, 2012) 128–62.

be concerned that contract law pedagogy that diverges sharply from contracting practices is not merely a failure to help prospective lawyers as much as one should, but could be causing moral harm by indirectly legitimating unjust rules and practices.

As one looks through contract law casebooks, there are a variety of misleading impressions that teachers give their students through these texts. Students leave these books and our courses believing that most agreements are worked out through back and forth negotiations; that contracts of adhesion are often not enforced as written; that unconscionability, promissory estoppel, and unjust enrichment are claims that commonly prevail; that breaches of contracts generally lead to compensatory damages that approximate the damages caused; and that good faith will usually constrain expressly granted discretion or impose duties of disclosure.[52] Generally, and most damagingly, students learn that the good guys frequently win. It is perhaps only the constraint of trying to teach all of contract law in three or four credits that prevents us from going on to mention the Tooth Fairy and unicorns.[53]

Standardised contracts, rolling contracts (pay now, terms later), mandatory arbitration, and numerous practical barriers for consumers and other less wealthy and less sophisticated parties to enforce their contractual rights: these are not exceptions to the cheery paradigm of contracting practices; these are the present norms of American contracting practice (and I have little reason to believe that matters are significantly different in most other countries).

The casebook I use contains the case *Winternitz v Summit Hills Joint Venture*,[54] in which a sympathetic plaintiff (sympathetic, at least as presented in the court's decision) looked like he was going to suffer significant damages due to a malicious landlord and the technicalities of the Statute of Frauds, but at the last minute (that is, towards the end of the decision), the appellate court finds a way to affirm a jury award based on a 'kitchen sink' claim that the plaintiff had thrown in at trial (intentional interference with contractual relations), and that, apparently, neither party had paid much attention to on appeal. Students love this case: the irrationally technical and formalistic rules of contract law are upheld *and* the good guy wins in the end (due to the creativity of the innovative judge(s)). Probably this sort of thing *does* happen from time to time; I just do not think it happens very often, and, for that reason, I am troubled by anything that encourages the

[52] See *Hill v Jones*, 725 P2d 1115 (Ariz App 1986) (good faith imposes duty on house seller to disclose past termite infestation), excerpted in C Knapp and others, *Problems in Contract Law: Cases and Materials*, 6th edn (New York, Aspen, 2007) 567–73.

[53] Compare Friedman, *Contract Law in America* (n 3) 25 ('the common law approach to law in the schools and in legal literature at its worst can be compared to a zoology course which confined its study to dodos and unicorns').

[54] *Winternitz v Summit Hills Joint Venture*, 532 A2d 1089 (Md App 1987), in Knapp and others, *Problems in Contract Law* (n 52) 314–20.

belief that it does. As it is, students are already too programmed by mainstream movies and television to believe that goodness is rewarded and justice done, often at the last minute.

To be fair, the casebook in question also contains a number of cases where a sympathetically presented party lost due to a combination of doctrine and a court unwilling to read that doctrine broadly or creatively,[55] though I still suspect that the percentage of 'good outcomes' (outcomes that most students would perceive as fair and just, or outcomes where the most sympathetic party prevails) in the casebook is much higher than it is in real life.

The course-book with which Macaulay is identified[56] does better on these concerns than do most contract law course-books. The Introduction emphasises the way in which contract law 'in action' often involves seeing beyond the doctrinal truths to the way that 'the haves come out ahead'.[57] And the book contains many cases in which sympathetic plaintiffs lose (often to unsympathetic corporations). However, even in that fine set of materials, it is quite possible that students will leave with a more optimistic view of contract doctrine and practice than is warranted. For example, the book (following many other contract texts) uses *C & J Fertilizer, Inc v Allied Mutual Insurance Co*[58] to teach the doctrine of reasonable expectations – a doctrine under which some courts have held that, at least with insurance policies, the reasonable expectations of a party will be enforced, even if those expectations are negated by clear language (hidden) somewhere in the policy documents. *C & J Fertilizer* is a case in which this most consumer-friendly version of reasonable expectations was applied, but the book does not note the way in which most courts have expressly or implicitly rejected this strongest form of reasonable expectations (even for insurance policies),[59] and how the Iowa court which decided the case also later came to read that decision narrowly.[60]

I understand why most course-books are written the way that they are, and why the courses are taught the way most of us teach them. A more representative selection of cases and a more realistic discussion of contract-

[55] See, eg *Sherrodd, Inc v Morrison-Knudsen Co*, 815 P2d 1135 (MT 1991) (fraud exception to parol evidence rule read narrowly); *Donahue v Federal Express Corp*, 753 A2d 238 (Pa Sup Ct 2000) (good faith and other limitations on ability to fire at-will employees read narrowly), excerpted in Knapp and others, *Problems in Contract Law* (n 52) 410–15, 480–86.

[56] See Macaulay and others, *Contracts: Law in Action* (n 7).

[57] ibid 26, quoting M Galanter, 'Why the Haves Come Out Ahead: Speculations on the Limits of Legal Change' (1974) 9 *Law and Society Review* 95.

[58] *C & J Fertilizer, Inc v Allied Mutual Insurance Co*, 227 NW2d 169 (IA 1975), excerpted in Macaulay and others, *Contracts: Law in Action* (n 7) 616–24; see also Knapp and others, *Problems in Contract Law* (n 52) 370–82 (excerpting the same case, but with more cautionary notes afterwards).

[59] eg D Schwarcz, 'A Products Liability Theory for the Judicial Regulation of Insurance Policies' (2007) 48 *William & Mary Law Review* 1389, 1427–30.

[60] *Lepic v Iowa Mutual Insurance Co*, 402 NW2d 758, 761 (IA 1987) (reading *C & J Fertilizer* and 'reasonable expectations' doctrine narrowly).

ing practice would probably come across as equally tedious and dire. There would be too many observations about the lack of consent or autonomy in contracting,[61] and the rarity for either quick or adequate recourse for breaches of contract. And almost every course, not just contract law, would have endless, depressing analyses about why the powerful usually prevail over the powerless (regardless of who had moral or legal 'right' on their side).[62] However, when we teach the legal fictions we offer in the name of contract law, we leave law students – and the general population they will later represent and educate – with the belief that law in general and contract law in particular is fair, legitimate, and even efficient, and that is rarely the case. And thus the process of teaching contract law too often ends up (unknowingly) working to legitimate injustice (and inefficiency).

CONCLUSION

Stewart Macaulay's work reminds us contract law teachers and scholars not to lose track of our true subject: the actual practice of transactions and promises among business people and others. We need to remind our students – and ourselves – that contractual terms and doctrines play only a sporadic, uneven and unpredictable role in the transactions they purport to govern, and that the parties' subjective perception of their agreement will likely vary greatly from the terms that appear in writing or that are imposed upon them by the courts. And we need to keep struggling to find a way that contract law doctrines and judicial decision-making could better respond to the real deals that people enter, while also being conscious of (but without overvaluing) the social values of predictability and certainty.

BIBLIOGRAPHY

Ayres, I, 'Never Confuse Efficiency with a Liver Complaint' (1997) 1997 *Wisconsin Law Review* 503.

Barnhizer, D, 'Context as Power: Defining the Field of Battle for Advantage in Contractual Interactions' (2010) 45 *Wake Forest Law Review* 607.

Bix, B, *Contract Law: Rules, Theory, and Context* (Cambridge, Cambridge University Press, 2012).

——, *Jurisprudence: Theory and Context*, 6th edn (London, Sweet & Maxwell, 2012).

——, 'Mahr Agreements: Contracting in the Shadow of Family Law (and Religious Law) – A Comment on Oman's Article' (2011) 1 *Wake Forest Law Review Online* 61.

[61] See B Bix, 'Contracts' in F Miller and A Wertheimer (eds), *The Ethics of Consent: Theory and Practice* (Oxford, Oxford University Press, 2010) 251–79.

[62] Marc Galanter's classic piece remains perhaps the best place to begin on this topic. Galanter, 'Why the Haves Come Out Ahead' (n 57).

Bix, B, 'Contracts' in F Miller and A Wertheimer (eds), *The Ethics of Consent: Theory and Practice* (Oxford, Oxford University Press, 2010) 251–79.
——, 'Theorizing About Law' (2010) *Analisi e Diritto* 271.
——, 'Some Reflections on Contract Law Theory' (2007) 1 *Problema* 143.
Bernstein, L, 'Private Commercial Law in the Cotton Industry: Creating Cooperation Through Norms, Rules, and Institutions' (2001) 99 *Michigan Law Review* 1724.
——, 'The Questionable Empirical Basis of Article 2's Incorporation Strategy: A Preliminary Study' (1999) 66 *University of Chicago Law Review* 710.
——, 'Merchant Law in a Merchant Court: Rethinking the Code's Search for Immanent Business Norms' (1996) 144 *University of Pennsylvania Law Review* 1765.
——, 'Opting Out of the Legal System: Extralegal Contractual Relations in the Diamond Industry' (1992) 21 *Journal of Legal Studies* 115.
Braucher, J, 'The Sacred and Profane Contracts Machine: The Complex Morality of Contract Law in Action' (2012) 45 *Suffolk University Law Review* 667.
Cohen, F, 'Transcendental Nonsense and the Functional Response' (1935) 35 *Columbia Law Review* 809.
'*Contract as Promise* at 30: The Future of Contract Theory' (2012) 45 *Suffolk University Law Review* 601.
Craswell, R, 'In That Case, What is the Question? Economics and the Demands of Contract Theory' (2003) 112 *Yale Law Journal* 903.
——, 'Two Economic Theories of Enforcing Promises' in Peter Benson (ed), *The Theory of Contract Law: New Essays* (Cambridge, Cambridge University Press, 2001).
Drahozal, C and Zyontz, S, 'An Empirical Study of AAA Consumer Arbitrations' (2010) 25 *Ohio State Journal of Dispute Resolution* 843.
Eisenberg, T, Miller, G, and Sherwin, E, 'Mandatory Arbitration for Customers but Not for Peers' (2008) 92 *Judicature* 118.
Ellickson, R, *Order Without Law: How Neighbors Settle Disputes* (Cambridge, MA, Harvard University Press, 1991).
Feinman, J and Brill, S, 'Is an Advertisement an Offer? Why It Is, and Why It Matters' (2006) 58 *Hastings Law Journal* 61.
Fried, C, *Contract as Promise* (Cambridge, Harvard University Press, 1981).
Friedman, L, *Contract Law in America: A Social and Economic Case Study* (Madison, University of Wisconsin Press, 1965).
Galanter, M, 'Why the Haves Come Out Ahead: Speculations on the Limits of Legal Change' (1974) 9 *Law and Society Review* 95.
Knapp, C, 'Rescuing Reliance: The Perils of Promissory Estoppel' (1998) 49 *Hastings Law Journal* 1191.
Knapp, C and others, *Problems in Contract Law: Cases and Materials*, 6th edn (New York, Aspen, 2007).
Langdell, C, *A Summary of the Law of Contract*, 2nd edn (Boston, Little, Brown & Co, 1880).
Leff, A, 'Contract as Thing' (1970) 19 *American University Law Review* 131.
Llewellyn, K, 'A Realistic Jurisprudence – The Next Step' (1930) 30 *Columbia Law Review* 431.
Macaulay, S, 'Contracts, New Legal Realism, and Improving the Navigation of *The Yellow Submarine*' (2006) 80 *Tulane Law Review* 1161.

——, 'The New Versus the Old Legal Realism: "Things Ain't What They Used to Be"' (2005) 2005 *Wisconsin Law Review* 365.
——, 'The Real and the Paper Deal: Empirical Pictures of Relationships, Complexity and the Urge for Transparent Simple Rules' (2003) 66 *Modern Law Review* 44.
——, 'Relational Contracts Floating on a Sea of Custom? Thoughts About the Ideas of Ian Macneil and Lisa Bernstein' (2000) 94 *Northwestern University Law Review* 775.
——, 'Bambi Meets Godzilla: Reflections on Contracts Scholarship and Teaching vs. State Unfair and Deceptive Trade Practices and Consumer Protection Statutes' (1989) 26 *Houston Law Review* 575.
——, 'An Empirical View of Contract' (1985) 1985 *Wisconsin Law Review* 465.
——, 'Private Legislation and the Duty to Read – Business Run by IBM Machine, the Law of Contracts and Credit Cards' (1966) 19 *Vanderbilt Law Review* 1051.
——, 'Non-Contractual Relations in Business: A Preliminary Study' (1963) 28 *American Sociological Review* 55.
——, 'The Use and Non-Use of Contracts in the Manufacturing Industry' (1963) 9 *Practical Lawyer* 13.
Macaulay, S and others, *Contracts: Law in Action*, two vols, 3rd edn (Charlottesville, LexisNexis, 2011).
Macaulay, S and others, *Law in Action: A Socio-Legal Reader* (New York, Foundation Press, 2007).
Mayer, C, 'Win Some, Lose Rarely? Arbitration Forum's Rulings Called One-Sided' *Washington Post* (1 March 2000).
Oman, N, 'Bargaining in the Shadow of God's Law: Islamic Mahr Contracts and the Perils of Legal Specialization' (2010) 45 *Wake Forest Law Review* 579.
——, 'A Pragmatic Defense of Contract Law' (2009) 98 *Georgetown Law Journal* 77.
Posner, R, *Economic Analysis of Law*, 8th edn (New York, Aspen, 2011).
Schwarcz, D, 'A Products Liability Theory for the Judicial Regulation of Insurance Policies' (2007) 48 *William & Mary Law Review* 1389.
Schwartz, A and Scott, R, 'Contract Theory and the Limits of Contract Law' (2003) 113 *Yale Law Journal* 541.
Scott, R, 'The Case for Formalism in Relational Contract' (2000) 94 *Northwestern University Law Review* 847.
Shiffrin, S, 'The Divergence of Contract and Promise' (2007) 120 *Harvard Law Review* 708.
Suchman, M, 'The Contract as Social Artifact' (2003) 37 *Law and Society Review* 91.

Part III

Contractual Relations with Individuals: Law and Behaviour

9

What is the Relational Theory of Consumer Form Contract?

ETHAN J LEIB*

INTRODUCTION

ONE OF THE most puzzling and embarrassing facts about contract law and contracts scholarship in the United States is that neither has found a consistent way to treat the real contracts of our lives: standardised consumer form contracts.[1] We are all consumers and enter form contracts daily, more or less. Yet we teach, apply and reinforce the law of contract in ways that keep it basically unsettled about one of most common contractual practices our own consumers – litigants, clients and students – experience. I have a hard time explaining to my students why the law has not fully reckoned with this most common contractual modality. Scholars have, of course, spilled much ink on the subject as a matter of theory. But when law professors teach the law of form contracting, they can barely keep a straight face as they try to shoehorn the consumer form contract into the texture of doctrine that occupies the course. Every case is an opportunity to reinvent the wheel, using a wide variety of spokes, usually built for different models of bicycle.

* Thanks to University of California–Hastings College of the Law and Fordham Law School for financial support; to Bill Whitford and David Campbell for the invitations to write this essay; to Stewart Macaulay for the years of support and inspiration; to Bill Whitford for early conversations on this topic that helped me become clearer about what I wanted to say; to Aditi Bagchi, Jean Braucher, Tal Kastner, Mark Patterson, Peggy Radin, Todd Rakoff, Dan Schwarcz and Steve Thel for comments on the manuscript; to participants in a conference on Stewart Macaulay's work at the University of Wisconsin Madison; and to Christina Lee for helpful research assistance. I was lucky enough to read a draft of Professor Radin's forthcoming manuscript on my subject right before drafting my essay, so I'm sure the influence of that book on my work here extends beyond the places I have cited and acknowledged it throughout.

[1] I focus here upon *consumer* form contracts rather than form contracts or 'boilerplate' generally. O Ben-Shahar (ed), *Boilerplate: The Foundation of Market Contracts* (Cambridge, Cambridge University Press, 2007). Some 'B2B' (business-to-business) form contracting raises similar concerns – but for the current paper, I am isolating consumer form contracts; I leave to others to analyse when B2B contracts should be treated similarly.

Admittedly, it is possible that we don't need a specialised law of consumer form contracts for the courts to apply. Maybe there is no problem in need of a solution.[2] We have muddled by for centuries with form contracts and we haven't yet rendered doctrinal analysis completely irrelevant – nor have we destroyed our ability to get our consumer needs met, legal uncertainty notwithstanding. Although the variety of tools available to courts for adjudicating disputes about form contracts is hardly systematic, the interaction of the common law, the market, and regulation by legislatures and agencies has produced a world where we perhaps only rarely have truly grotesque contract terms that screw the consumer. Moreover, the consumer probably knows that whatever those unread terms are, only a self-sabotaging company would rely upon them in an age where each consumer has a direct feed to thousands of 'friends' who read her tweets, blog-posts and Facebook updates about her displeasure with companies' customer service.[3] No company can prey any longer on those who don't read Consumer Reports or the Federal and State Reporters because we all see information all the time about company performance on Yelp! and other free comprehensive review fora.[4] Watching the early successes of Elizabeth Warren's work in overseeing form contracts in the financial products area[5] gives us a sense that even if we aren't fully paying attention, someone is actually representing our interests as consumers.

Notwithstanding this plausible story about there being no story to report with respect to consumer form contracts, it is likely that 'e-commerce' has upped the ante from the early days of form contracting. We probably enter more and longer form contracts than we did before complicated terms could be hidden in scroll boxes no one scrolls through or behind links no one clicks. Companies probably have gotten savvier at contracting around regulations, capturing agencies that are supposed to be regulating them, circumventing common law limitations, and choosing their own laws, whether through form contracts that choose governing law or limit who may serve as the adjudicator of any dispute under

[2] eg O Ben-Shahar, 'The Myth of the "Opportunity to Read" in Contract Law' (2009) 5 *European Review Contract Law* 1, 16 (arguing that customers *want* to be exploited through form contracts).

[3] C Gillette, 'Rolling Contracts as an Agency Problem' (2004) 2004 *Wisconsin Law Review* 679; and L Bebchuck and R Posner 'One-Sided Contracts in Competitive Consumer Markets' (2006) 104 *Michigan Law Review* 827 (together suggesting that companies may try to enforce unread terms only against opportunistic consumers who are trying to prey on the goodwill of the sellers or are trying to abuse companies' overly cautious standard practices by seeking favourable treatment they do not 'deserve').

[4] This fact might mitigate subsidisation concerns by democratising access to information about company performance under their contracts, leaving less of a worry that only sophisticates will benefit from better information. eg Ben-Shahar, 'The Myth' (n 2) (arguing that 'it might well be that the advantages secured by [contract] readers would be cross-subsidized by non-readers' by providing consumers with an 'opportunity to read').

[5] E Warren, 'Unsafe at Any Rate' (2007) 5 *Democracy: A Journal of Ideas* 8; O Bar-Gill and E Warren, 'Making Credit Safer' (2009) 157 *University of Pennsylvania Law Review* 1.

the contract. The people who have the resources to shop for terms and/or complain are likely those who are getting better deals under their form contracts, leaving most people worse off and implicating equity and distributional concerns.[6] The progression (or regression) from short term sheets in proverbial 'plain English' that were actually signed to long forms in legalese that one gets in junk-mail folders to box-top licenses, to shrink-wrap 'agreements', to pay now-terms later offerings to click-through 'agreements', to browse-wrap 'notifications' of terms has probably shifted some of the ground, rendering consumers stunningly passive in their reception of terms. There is no 'cautionary' moment[7] as there once was when we got to use our signet rings (or even our fancy ballpoints) to seal a deal. Even though deals have been offered by stronger parties to weaker parties on take-it-or-leave-it bases for a long while, the iterative loss of formalities probably exacerbates notice and consent issues. Clicking 'I agree' is more like clicking a remote control's channel change button than it is a channeling function.[8]

The Supreme Court's recent decision in *AT&T Mobility v Concepcion*[9] reminds us that there are still some pretty disempowering terms that make their way into the forms that purport to bind us as consumers, ones that really do infringe upon one of the most basic rights we have as consumers: the right to turn to a local and public legal system when we feel we have been abused or cheated.[10] To be sure, we have unconscionability limits, clauses that are unenforceable because of 'public policy', and some rules requiring conspicuousness and specific disclosure about particular terms to render them enforceable. But it is hard to resist the urge for a more comprehensive approach – an approach that allows us never to forget that it is a consumer form contract that courts are expounding.[11]

Although the ambition may seem grand, we must keep it in perspective. By now, virtually everyone agrees that courts can only fix bad consumer form contracts in marginal cases where some consumer (or his motivated class action lawyer[12]) really pushes the issue and the form-provider decides

[6] Bar-Gill and Warren, 'Making Credit Safer' (n 5).

[7] L Fuller, 'Consideration as Form' (1941) 41 *Columbia Law Review* 499.

[8] C Knapp, 'Opting Out or Copping Out? An Argument for Strict Scrutiny of Individual Contracts' (2006) 40 *Loyola of Los Angeles Law Review* 96, 117 n 71.

[9] *AT&T v Concepcion*, 131 S Ct 1740 (2011).

[10] One certainly needs to be industry-sensitive before making pronouncements about what sellers do in their forms, since forms seem to vary substantially by industry. D Schwarcz, 'Reevaluating Standardized Insurance Policies' (2011) 78 *University of Chicago Law Review* 1263; see also A Newitz, *Dangerous Terms: A User's Guide to EULAs* (White Paper, Electronic Frontier Foundation, 2005) (available at www.eff.org/wp/dangerous-terms-users-guide-eulas) (highlighting the many 'dangerous' terms that are still often found in consumer form contracts).

[11] R Barnett, 'Consenting to Form Contracts' (2002) 71 *Fordham Law Review* 627, 639.

[12] That lawyer might be motivated for pecuniary or ideological reasons; some legal services providers for indigent consumers don't actually work for the promise of large fees. Suspicion of plaintiffs' lawyers seems to drive at least some of the resistance to regulating form contracts through judicial review.

not to settle for one reason or another, notwithstanding reputational incentives to do so. Many recognise that a systematic legal approach to consumer form contracts probably needs to come from legislatures and administrators, not the common law.[13] As Macaulay has taught us, contract law barely applies to consumers because it has largely been displaced by statutes and regulation.[14] Yet, those laws and regulations will have to be implemented by judges, and, given certain public choice and political economy realities,[15] it remains useful to help judges nudge the common law to confront these contracts of our lives. The feedback from these cases can help the regulators of the future, too.[16] Even those sympathetic to law-and-economics approaches to consumer form contracts can often agree that 'a measure of special legal treatment for standard form contracts is appropriate on economic grounds'.[17]

But should anyone turn to relational contract theory to furnish a judicial approach for this special legal treatment? Let's be frank: relationalism hasn't obviously had huge successes in changing the way judges do their work, at least in the US.[18] Still, some features of relationalism have been vindicated through doctrine and have then been incorporated into prevailing neoclassical contract practice,[19] like generalised good faith obligations and the fragmentation of the scope of contract law, which has parceled off sales, insurance, property and products liability into their own bodies of law. Given that the reigning neoclassical paradigm had something to learn from relationalism's basic prescriptions,[20] it is worth

[13] A Leff, 'Unconscionability and the Crowd – Consumers and the Common Law Tradition' (1970) 31 *University of Pittsburgh Law Review* 349; A Leff, 'Contract as Thing' (1970) 19 *American University Law Review* 131; L Kornhauser, 'Unconscionability in Standard Forms' (1976) 64 *California Law Review* 1151. There is some reason to worry about whether government regulation can dramatically improve the quality of terms in consumer form contracts. A Katz, 'Standard Form Contracts' in P Newman (ed), *New Palgrave Dictionary of Economics and the Law* (Houndmills, Palgrave Macmillan, 1998); I Macneil, 'Bureaucracy and Contracts of Adhesion' (1984) 22 *Osgoode Hall Law Journal* 5, 25 ('The question is always: if the public bureaucrats get in there and mess with this . . . contract of adhesion, can the business still deliver the goods?').

[14] S Macaulay, 'Bambi Meets Godzilla: Reflections on Contracts Scholarship and Teaching vs. State Unfair and Deceptive Trade Practices and Consumer Protection Statutes' (1989) 26 *Houston Law Review* 575.

[15] Macneil, 'Bureaucracy' (n 13) 25.

[16] The likelihood of the US following the European Union's Unfair Terms Directive is, however, infinitesimal. J Winn and M Webber, 'The Impact of EU Unfair Contract Terms Law on US Business-to-Consumer Internet Merchants' (2006) 62 *Business Lawyer* 209; see Council Directive 93/13/EEC of 5 April 1993 (available at eur-lex.europa.eu/LexUriServ/LexUriServ.do?uri=CELEX:31993L0013:EN:NOT).

[17] Katz, 'Standard Form Contracts' (n 13).

[18] For some reasons why Macneil's work had not been absorbed into contract law more substantially, see W Whitford, 'Ian Macneil's Contribution to Contracts Scholarship' (1985) 1985 *Wisconsin Law Review* 545.

[19] J Feinman, 'Relational Contract Theory in Context' (2000) 94 *Northwestern University Law Review* 737.

[20] Relational contract theory's critics can sometimes utter that 'we are all relationalists now'. R Scott, 'The Case for Formalism in Relational Contract' (2000) 94 *Northwestern*

taking a fresh look at relationalism's approach to consumer form contracts to see if contract law might be further fragmented, enabling it to develop a targeted approach to the consumer form contract context. The nature of what that approach might look like hasn't been fully worked out; it is my intention here to mine relationalism to see if we can't find a more comprehensive and systematic judicial approach to these instruments, which embarrass our courses in contracts and our legal doctrines. Doing this now – 45 years after the publication of Stewart Macaulay's early effort to get to the bottom of the consumer form contracting problem from a relationalist perspective[21] and nearly three decades after the publication of Ian Macneil's relationalist inquiry into the problem[22] – seems as urgent as ever.

This essay proceeds as follows: Section I reviews some basics of relational contract theory; Section II explores Stewart Macaulay's and Ian Macneil's efforts to say what the relational law of consumer form contract should be; and Section III offers an argument for why and how an application of the insurance law doctrine of 'reasonable expectations' best captures what the relationalist legal analysis of consumer form contracts should become. Given the many complexities and ambiguities in the doctrine of reasonable expectations, I show how relationalist insights from Macaulay and Macneil can refine our understanding of the proper application of the doctrine in the consumer form contract context. That refined understanding will both help judges develop a useful approach to consumer form contract – and will help relationalist scholars forge a research agenda to support this salutary (albeit incomplete) proposal for the development of the common law of consumer form contract.

I. RESTATEMENT (SECOND) OF RELATIONAL CONTRACT THEORY

In a recent lengthy article, I reconstructed and restated the main thrust of relational contract theory – in as sympathetic a fashion as possible.[23] In this second restatement, I will be much briefer, hoping to capture the main propositions to which relationalists tend to be committed.

The most accepted and uncontroversial relationalist commitment is an empirical one: that many contracts involve long-term and complex relationships, in which social norms constrain party behaviour much more

University Law Review 847, 852; R Barnett, 'Conflicting Visions: A Critique of Ian Macneil's Relational Theory of Contract' (1992) 78 *Virginia Law Review* 1175, 1200. I analyse the limits of that proposition elsewhere. E Leib, 'Contracts and Friendships' (2010) 59 *Emory Law Journal* 649, 653–73.

[21] S Macaulay, 'Private Legislation and the Duty To Read – Business Run by IBM Machine, the Law of Contracts and Credit Cards' (1966) 19 *Vanderbilt Law Review* 1051.

[22] Macneil, 'Bureaucracy' (n 13).

[23] Leib, 'Contracts and Friendships' (n 20) 653–73.

than does the threat of legal action. Informal accommodation of parties' interests by counterparts is commonplace. And although parties might use legal formalities as distancing devices,[24] much more often parties to contracts do not treat one another in purely transactional ways as strangers but instead allow norms from their relationships to guide their behaviour. Their pre-existing and ongoing relationships provide the edifice for appropriate behaviour, not (only) their formal agreement; implicit dimensions of the arrangement[25] and 'real deals' rather than their 'paper deals'[26] drive their performance standards. Of course, the real deal might be to allow only formal paper agreements to control any dispute[27] – but that possibility (one which can materialise between equal and/or heavily 'lawyered' parties) should not always be presumed to be the real deal.[28]

Somewhat more controversial is the relationalists' analytic commitment to change the paradigm of contract law and theory. If they had their druthers, relationalists would not analyse all contracts as discrete transactions but rather evaluate them on a continuum, taking account of their relational dimensions. This form of analysis facilitates a fragmentation of the domain of contract,[29] enabling a deeper contextualism than would be possible for those who want to stay committed to one law of contracts.[30] Relationalists are ultimately pluralistic and think little of the promotion of unity in contract law and theory.[31] Perhaps more importantly, relational-

[24] D Kimel, *From Promise to Contract: Towards a Liberal Theory of Contract* (Oxford, Hart Publishing, 2003).

[25] D Campbell, H Collins and J Wightman (eds), *Implicit Dimensions of Contract: Discrete, Relational, and Network Contracts* (Oxford, Hart Publishing, 2003).

[26] S Macaulay, 'The Real and the Paper Deal: Empirical Pictures of Relationships, Complexity and the Urge for Transparent Simple Rules' in D Campbell, H Collins and J Wightman (eds), *Implicit Dimensions of Contract: Discrete, Relational, and Network Contracts* (Oxford, Hart Publishing, 2003).

[27] As David Campbell reminds us, one of biggest misconceptions about relational contract theory is that 'the virtues of certainty, discreteness, and planning have no value in the relational theory because all [relationalists] like is flexibility'. F Snyder, 'Relational Contracting in a Digital Age: A Panel Discussion with Franklin G Snyder, Ian R Macneil, John Kidwell, David Campbell, and Rachel Arnow-Richman' (2005) 11 *Texas Wesleyan Law Review* 675, 695. This is not the case, however: If the underlying relationship recommends treatment through formalism, relational contract theory would support courts holding parties to formalistic doctrines.

[28] Whether to give legal effect to real deals over paper deals is a controversial normative question that is at the core of the relationalist inquiry; formalists prefer paper deals.

[29] Feinman, 'Relational Contract Theory' (n 19).

[30] Friedrich Kessler explored how courts behaved when they were eager not to allow insurance law to splinter off from the main tenets of contract doctrine. They preserved the unity of contract by using workarounds from tort law to achieve contractual justice. F Kessler, 'Contracts of Adhesion – Some Thoughts About Freedom of Contract' (1943) 43 *Columbia Law Review* 629, 635–36.

[31] This statement is somewhat misleading. There is a large strain in Macneil's work that 'search[es] for and identif[ies] unifying principles – in both contract behavior and contract law of all kinds'. I Macneil, 'Values in Contract: Internal and External' (1983) 78 *Northwestern University Law Review* 340, 382 fn 132. Still, he concedes that he 'consider[s] the search for a *single* central or unifying contract principle to be a will-o'-the-wisp'. ibid 382 fn 132.

ists are especially sceptical about approaching contract law and theory as if contracts exist always and only to ensure co-operation among parties who are essentially suspicious of one another. Although contracts can be used to guarantee trust, relationalists argue that they are commonly built atop trust earned prior to contracting.

Paradigm orientation provides a foundation for institutional and doctrinal design – and the meta-theoretical commitment of 'fitness' recommends building a contract theory and doctrine to match the real-world practice of contracting. This fitness can also serve an ideological function. Consider Bob Gordon:

> Some theorists . . . advance[] a bold hypothesis of a specific historical causal relationship between the fantasy world of political-legal ideological discourse about contracts and the social world of contracting: they contend that encouraging people to deal with one another as strangers progressively erodes the underlying relations of solidarity, reciprocity and trust upon which capitalist economies essentially depend.[32]

Relationalists are eager to make sure that contract theory is oriented in a way that promotes rather than hinders social solidarity.

Aside from the empirical claim and the analytic or meta-theoretical claim, is also a normative claim about how to design contract law. The core of relationalist contract doctrine is to instruct courts to bring the intrinsic norms of the governing relationship to bear when disposing of a legal dispute.[33] This instruction could enable courts to

> soften or reverse the bite of the rigid offer-and-acceptance format of classical contract law, and the corresponding intolerance of classical contract law for indefiniteness, agreements to agree, and agreements to negotiate in good faith[;] . . . impose upon parties . . . a broad obligation to perform in good faith[;] . . . broaden the kinds of changed circumstances . . . that constitute an excuse for nonperformance . . . [;] . . . treat relational contracts like partnerships, in the sense that such contracts involve a mutual enterprise and should be construed in that light[;] . . . impose upon parties . . . a duty to bargain in good faith to make equitable price adjustments when changed circumstances occur[,] and would perhaps even impose upon the advantaged party a duty to accept an equitable adjustment proposed in good faith by the disadvantaged party.[34]

Although courts applying relationalism's doctrinal commitments are not supposed to ignore all legal norms (indeed, parties may very well have

[32] R Gordon, 'Macaulay, Macneil, and the Discovery of Solidarity and Power in Contract Law' (1985) 1985 *Wisconsin Law Review* 565, 578–79.

[33] I Macneil, 'Relational Contract Theory: Challenges and Queries' (2000) 94 *Northwestern University Law Review* 877, 900; R Speidel, 'Article 2 and Relational Contracts' (1993) 26 *Loyola of Los Angeles Law Review* 789, 793.

[34] M Eisenberg, 'Why There Is No Law of Relational Contracts' (2000) 94 *Northwestern University Law Review* 805, 817–18. I have enumerated and explored my differences with Eisenberg on relationalism elsewhere. Leib, 'Contracts and Friendships' (n 20) 663–67.

incorporated legal norms into their relationship through documents and conduct), relationalists urge them to calibrate the application of those rules and standards with internal norms that come from representations, conduct, and reasonable assumptions that emerge from within the parties' relationship. That the relationship is not clearly part of the paper deal is immaterial; the real deal should usually govern the transaction – and that real deal may evolve over time rather than getting locked in at one moment of formation.

To be sure, much of modern contract law takes this lesson to heart: after all, it is routine for courts to consider usages of trade, courses of performance, courses of dealing, and good faith obligations to address questions of formation, performance, modification, interpretation and remedies. But relationalists urge courts to go even deeper, where possible, to mine parties' relationships for implicit understandings, notwithstanding the litigation costs of discovering and arguing about them, evidentiary concerns about a court's ability to ferret those out, and general concerns about the institutional competence of the judiciary.[35]

This isn't the place to defend relationalism against its formalist detractors. But it is worth highlighting two arguments for relationalism that have some importance for what is to follow. First, relationalists urge courts to render contract law in a manner that expresses 'organic solidarity';[36] failing to have our contract law reflect our most basic normative commitments will derogate from law's legitimacy – and could have some impact on individuals' willingness to comply with the law.[37] This means relationalists will apply private law in ways that are sensitive to larger concerns of public policy. Second, relationalists suggest that formalism's doctrines are not especially predictable in courts anyway and that relationalism's doctrinal suggestion is conducive to a different sort of 'calculability' – predictability for parties themselves. The capitalist system can work better, relationalists suggest, if parties can rely on the real deals they know they have entered, not some formalistic jargon they would need lawyers to decipher for them.[38]

[35] Lisa Bernstein's work, of course, suggests that even the limited incorporationist strategy of the UCC (and its relationalism) has been a failure. eg L Bernstein, 'The Questionable Empirical Basis of Article 2's Incorporation Strategy: A Preliminary Study' (1999) 66 *University of Chicago Law Review* 76. For some effort to save relationalism from Bernstein's empirical evidence, see Leib, 'Contracts and Friendships' (n 20), 667–68 and S Macaulay, 'Relational Contracts Floating on a Sea of Custom? Thoughts About the Ideas of Ian Macneil and Lisa Bernstein' (2000) 94 *Northwestern University Law Review* 775, 784–804.

[36] Macaulay, 'Relational Contracts' (n 35) 777–96.

[37] For work suggesting the relationship between compliance and perceived substantive fairness of legal institutions, see J Nadler, 'Flouting the Law' (2005) 83 *Texas Law Review* 1399; P Robinson and J Darley, 'The Utility of Desert' (1997) 91 *Northwestern University Law Review* 453.

[38] H Collins, 'The Research Agenda of Implicit Dimensions of Contract' in D Campbell, H Collins and J Wightman (eds), *Implicit Dimensions of Contract: Discrete, Relational, and Network Contracts* (Oxford, Hart Publishing, 2007).

What, then, does relational contract theory have to offer for an analysis of consumer form contracts? Section II explores Macaulay's and Macneil's early efforts to devise a relationalist account of consumer form contract. Because relational contract theory has been refined in the decades since Macaulay and Macneil initially wrote about this contractual context (and the context itself has changed, too), these preliminary engagements with the problem were not fully developed. In Section III, I offer a modern relationalist doctrinal prescription for consumer form contracts, integrating, updating, and generalising from these earlier efforts to grapple with this pervasive contractual form, which has grown ever more common and more complex.

II. EXTANT RELATIONAL ANALYSIS OF CONSUMER FORM CONTRACTS

Macaulay's (1966) early work laid the groundwork for a relational law of consumer form contract. He argued that courts should decide cases under consumer form contracts 'with a decided bias towards transactional policy' by which he meant that courts should adopt 'case-by-case' adjudication, paying careful attention to the 'bargain-in-fact', implementing the 'sense of the transaction', and honouring the 'reasonable expectations' of the consumer.[39] 'Transactional policy', as Macaulay understands it, has a market-promoting goal – but it prevents corporations from using a 'duty to read' strategically to force consumers to accept terms they could not reasonably have read or understood. Although at the time Macaulay wrote, consumer form contracts were shorter – and therefore it was easier to impute to the consumer constructive notice of terms – the most natural application of his argument emphasises 'reasonable expectations' over letting 'a writing get in [the] way'.[40] His early warning that the 'reasonable expectations of . . . individual[s] have not counted'[41] for enough in courts' analyses of consumer form contracts was prescient; the 'reasonable expectations doctrine' of insurance law wasn't fully on the agenda for another four years.[42] And yet this is the natural direction for the relational theory of consumer form contract to develop: the place Stewart Macaulay was already trying to take us in 1966.

In Ian Macneil's large oeuvre of thousands of pages specifying and developing the relational theory of contract, only about 23 are explicitly devoted to the issues surrounding consumer form contracts, each one of

[39] Macaulay, 'Private Legislation' (n 21) 1060–69.
[40] ibid 1061.
[41] ibid 1080.
[42] R Keeton, 'Insurance Law Rights at Variance with Policy Provisions' (1970) 83 *Harvard Law Review* 961.

which likely builds off of Macaulay's early insights in this area. Although Macneil's work has been cited approximately 1,200 times in legal academic work (as of this writing in the summer of 2011), a mere 31 citations are to his essay 'Bureaucracy and Contracts of Adhesion', the piece most specifically about consumer form contracts.[43] That piece makes a direct effort to apply relational theory to the consumer form contract context – and surprises those who read it because people falsely assume relationalism is inspired by some kind of pro-consumer, pro-state, communitarian project.[44] What Macneil reveals there instead is that relational contract theory can actually supply legitimation for consumer form contracting rather than provide arguments to reject them as unenforceable.[45] Having a contract theory that encourages the legal enforcement of norms from within relationships turns out to bless consumer form contracts generally, as theories of classical consent or promise might not.

So how does Macneil reach the result of general enforceability from a set of principles that seem to focus on a form of 'social solidarity'? He makes several arguments, many of which look familiar from within orthodox law and economics.[46] Macneil first observes that 'no one can honestly say that consumers *ought* to read' consumer form contracts; 'if consumers actually did such a foolish thing', he suggests, 'the modern economy would come to a screeching halt'.[47] He recognises quickly that it makes no sense to impose a 'duty to read', calling it 'a very poor joke'.[48] This orientation dovetails with most of what standard law and economics would tell us.

Yet Macneil emphasises that although general enforceability of consumer form contracts can be justified, it cannot facilely be vindicated

[43] Macneil, 'Bureaucracy' (n 13). If you discount citations by me and the 'Wisconsin school', you are down below 25.

[44] Barnett, 'Conflicting Visions' (n 20).

[45] Macneil, after all, wrote that '[u]nequal bargaining power is one of the great mindless clichés of the day'. Macneil, 'Bureaucracy' (n 13) 27 fn 50. David Campbell has been making efforts (without too much success, alas) to remind scholars that relational contract theory has plenty of room for the view that contracts need not be 'lovely and warm and co-operative'. Snyder, 'Relational Contracting' (n 27) 695.

[46] S Macaulay, 'Freedom From Contract: Solutions in Search of a Problem?' (2004) 2004 *Wisconsin Law Review* 777, 779–80; R Craswell, 'Remedies When Contracts Lack Consent: Autonomy and Institutional Competence' (1995) 33 *Osgoode Hall Law Journal* 209.

[47] Macneil, 'Bureaucracy' (n 13) 5–6. It is worth noting that Macneil probably should have distinguished between form contracts that are very short in length and very easy to read and the more common multi-page document in impenetrable legalese. At the core of Liz Warren's concern about consumer credit contracts is that in the 1980s they were one page – and are now, on average, '30 pages of incomprehensible text'. Warren, 'Unsafe at Any Rate' (n 5) 11. There seems to be an important difference between the unseen pages and pages of unreadable text and a simple half-page document that summarises a transaction, which even if unread could be read and understood by an average consumer without huge transaction costs. But see *Yauger v Skiing Enterprises*, 557 NW2d 60 (WI 1996) (invalidating portions of a half-page form contract).

[48] Macneil, 'Bureaucracy' (n 13) 6–7.

through attenuated notions of consent or assent, as much liberal theory (and some law and economics) prefers. As he argues, 'the fundamental idea of liberal contract is not just to choose to be bound in some undefined way, but to choose with some degree of precision how and to what one is bound, or at least to be reasonably able to do so'. *Pace* Barnett,[49] form contracts need legitimation from somewhere outside traditional notions of liberal consent. That legitimation, for Macneil, comes from an understanding of private bureaucracy and the consumer's role as a bureaucratic functionary.[50]

Macneil argues that consumers participate in the governance of the organisations that offer them products and services in an essential way.[51] Whether it is by using products or services, throwing them away, or gossiping about them, consumers are woven into a *relationship* with the companies that furnish products and advertise to them. That relationship is always planning for future behaviour, the *sine qua non* of bureaucratic organisation. Those plans take many forms: with the use of signals, form contracts, representations, signage, maps, instruction manuals and the conduct related to these multifarious instruments of planning. All of these, taken together, become a mini-constitution – a *private* constitution – for how the bureaucracy is to be run.

What legitimates the mini-constitution that accompanies the bureaucratic relation is not specific assent to precise terms or the content of the bureaucratic planning – but consensual entry into *already legitimate relations*.[52] The idea of 'joining a relation' that is a participatory bureaucracy is the core of Macneil's relationalist defence of the legitimacy of the consumer form contract. Just like we can join a university faculty without knowing in advance all that we may be called upon to do (or the full terms of our agreement), so can we undertake our roles as consumer functionaries 'in spite of large-scale ignorance about the restraints we are accepting'.[53]

Ultimately, then, consent doesn't fully disappear in Macneil's story:[54] Macneil does require actual individual consent to join the relation (usually a requirement that could be met when we click 'I agree' in the modern

[49] Barnett, 'Consenting to Form Contracts' (n 11).

[50] In the article under consideration, there is a very odd digression about how a Zamboni – a machine that freshens ice on a skating rink – is a bureaucracy. Macneil, 'Bureaucracy' (n 13) 14–15. I have never found that characterisation of the Zamboni to be particularly illuminating, I confess. I recently asked Rory Macneil – Ian's son – why his father wrote about the Zamboni. Rory reported that he had tried to get his father interested in ice hockey during the family's time in Ithaca without much success. But something about the Zamboni apparently stuck with him.

[51] ibid 15–17.

[52] ibid 20–21.

[53] ibid 21.

[54] When we realise that even Macneil needs agreement somewhere, we can understand just how robust Kastner's insight is into our cultural need for a view of contract as agreement. T Kastner, 'The Persisting Ideal of Agreement in an Age of Boilerplate' (2010) 35 *Law & Social Inquiry* 793.

transactional environment);[55] and he requires collective consent that blesses that 'kind of relation in question'.[56] Yet these versions of consent are different from the standard liberal consent that provides so much difficulty for those trying to square the circle of consumer form contracts within classical contract theory.[57] Indeed, this formulation of the kind of consent necessary to trigger the validity and enforceability of consumer form contract takes us away from liberal individualism some distance and 'back' to *status*.[58] The ultimate legitimacy of that status – the status we all hold as consumers – is decided collectively: as a society we are committed to the 'consumer-mission, the mission of seeing to it that consumers have, at relatively low prices, vast quantities of the goods and services so dear to most of the denizens of the modern liberal state'.[59] Macneil's view – and requirement for blessing these contracts – is that the mission and the form of the relation are 'thoroughly legitimized by the democratic processes of the state'.[60]

Notwithstanding his embrace of an essentially market-oriented solution to the consumer form contract context,[61] Macneil well understood conventional 'market failure' worries.[62] But, ultimately, he was very cautious before proposing solutions, legislative or otherwise: he worried about capture and holding back business with too much intervention. So in his most direct foray into understanding consumer form contract, he looks very much like Easterbrook in basic result on legitimation, though he is speaking from a very different part of Chicago: 'The consumer vote in the marketplace is a powerful force toward harmony of motivation and mission, but far from all powerful. And to the extent there is disharmony,

[55] One could distinguish 'click-wrap' from 'browse-wrap' here: whereas a consumer knows that a relationship is being entered when she clicks that she agrees (though she has no knowledge of the terms of that relationship), no such entry into relations can be plausibly inferred from reading a webpage with no notice of the relationship. Accord *Specht v Netscape*, 306 F3d 17 (2d Cir 2002). So Macneil's theory can, in principle, bless 'rolling contracts', click-wrap agreements, and other standard form contracts – but not browse-wrap contracting.

[56] Macneil, 'Bureaucracy' (n 13) 21.

[57] The sleight of hand, as it were, in Barnett's argument for consent in the consumer form contract scenario is his analogising the acceptance of unread and unseen terms of a consumer form to a promise to abide by the requests in a sealed envelope handed to an individual *by a good friend*. But it should be obvious that the good friend recipient has very good reasons to trust the specific unseen and unread requests. By contrast, the consumer is likely to be much more suspicious. See generally Barnett, 'Consenting to Form Contracts' (n 11).

[58] Macneil thinks reintroducing status into liberal theory is more radical than it is. He writes, 'There is no room in liberal theory for the idea of status.' Macneil, 'Bureaucracy' (n 13) 22 fn 37. But this is probably false. Liberal society uses status to determine membership as citizens; and friends, family and fiduciaries are all categories of status that are given expression widely throughout liberal law. E Leib, *Friend v. Friend: The Transformation of Friendship – and What the Law Has To Do with It* (New York, Oxford University Press, 2011).

[59] Macneil, 'Bureaucracy' (n 13) 21.

[60] ibid 22.

[61] Macaulay, 'Relational Contracts' (n 35) 800–21.

[62] Macneil, 'Bureaucracy' (n 13) 26.

public intervention must be considered. Considered, mind you, not automatically chosen.'[63]

Macaulay's view is not to the contrary:

> I prefer to see . . . consumers as 'citizens' of a private government. Just as most citizens of Wisconsin have very imperfect ideas of what is buried in the Wisconsin Statutes, most consumers do not and cannot learn in advance about such things as warranty disclaimers and arbitration clauses. In both cases, however, ignorance of the law is seldom an excuse that courts find acceptable.[64]

Let us be clear, then, what this analysis accomplishes – and what it does not. It does seem to highlight that relationalists need not (and, indeed, may not) reject the enforceability of consumer form contracts per se. It furnishes a justification for what has been known since Karl Llewellyn as 'blanket assent':

> Instead of thinking about 'assent' to boilerplate clauses, we can recognize that so far as concerns the specific, there is no assent at all. What has in fact been assented to, specifically, are the few dickered terms, and the broad type of the transaction.[65]

Macneil provides a way of understanding why it is legitimate to treat consumers as being bound to the form of the transaction and the relation, something that has puzzled others who see no consent or assent possible in the consumer's position.[66]

But the specific contours and limitations of the assent thereby provided – and the place of the *documents themselves* in governing the whole of the transaction – are not determined by this theory. Although there is some 'blanket assent' to features of the relation, there is nothing in this theory that necessitates drawing the outlines of that assent as Llewellyn did (or as Barnett subsequently did).[67] Another way to say this is that the account tells us *why* there is a contract between the parties to a consumer form agreement, but it does not fully determine the rules of the relationship because the contract emanates from the relationship rather than only the attached documents.[68]

[63] ibid.

[64] Macaulay, 'Relational Contracts' (n 35) 780.

[65] K Llewellyn, *The Common Law Tradition: Deciding Appeals* (Boston, Little Brown, 1960) 370. But see K Llewellyn (1939), 'Book Review of Otto Prausnitz, *The Standardization of Commercial Contracts in English and Continental Law*,' 52 *Harvard Law Review* 700 (already trying to work out what 'relational thinking' could do to furnish an approach to the consumer standard form contract and approximating a reasonable expectations approach: 'where bargaining is absent in fact, the conditions and clauses to be read into a bargain are not those which happen to be printed on the unread paper, but are those which a sane man might reasonably expect to find on that paper.')

[66] eg T Rakoff, 'Contracts of Adhesion: An Essay in Reconstruction' (1983) 96 *Harvard Law Review* 1194; WD Slawson, 'The New Meaning of Contract: The Transformation of Contracts Law by Standard Forms' (1984) 46 *University of Pittsburgh Law Review* 21.

[67] See, eg Barnett, 'Consenting to Form Contracts' (n 11).

[68] For this reason, Campbell is too quick to conclude that the relational 'solution' to the problem of consumer form contracts was already indicated in Macneil's 1984 article on the subject. Snyder, 'Relational Contracting' (n 27) 702.

So are relationalists apologists for consumer form contracting? Yes and no. Relational contract theory does basically legitimate the practice and provides a way to understand consumers as bound to a deal with the drafter, notwithstanding widespread ignorance about terms. This account is both sociological and justificatory: relationalists have an analytic tool to understand how we keep acting as if they are enforceable and how their enforceability is consistent with our governance norms. But little has been offered by relationalists to explain the *limits* of enforceability and the relevant law that should control.[69] Just because some sense can be made of consumers giving some assent to form contracts, *pace* Rakoff,[70] it doesn't follow that rendering the relationship with drafters as voluntary gives drafters a 'blank cheque'. What does follow is that these transactions flow from actual relationships with ethical parameters of their own; internet and modern consumer form contracting is surely impersonal – but that doesn't mean that they aren't relational contracts of a type, constrained by relational norms.[71]

In 2005, in fact, Macneil explicitly rejected Easterbrook's reasoning in *Hill v Gateway* in a panel discussion, but with only the outlines of an argument for what the law of consumer form contracts should be from a relationalist perspective. This might have been a surprise to readers of his earlier article, if the reader didn't also appreciate the limits of the argument there (as I've identified them here). In 2005, he insisted that 'it's a nutty case. The buyer could not know what the devil he was getting into. To carry consent beyond some reasonable penumbra of actual knowledge is absurd.'[72] He was also further exercised by the failure of the opinion to 'pay any attention at all to the power relationship between Gateway and an individual consumer': 'It is perfectly plain you cannot allow Gateway a free hand to legislate in the relationship, which is exactly what the decision does.'[73]

Yet Macneil provided little guidance to courts about how to both bless consumer form contracts generally as he did in 1984 – and still judicially regulate their content from a relationalist perspective. Campbell, in following up on Macneil's statement at the panel, clarified that relational theory actually provides some basis for enforcement in cases like *Hill* – but also 'points towards the necessity of legislative guidance of what can

[69] See Whitford, 'Ian Macneil' (n 18) 551–52 (noting that Macneil 'rarely indicates how courts should decide particular cases before them or expresses support for reasonably particularistic legislation'); Barnett, 'Consenting to Form Contracts' (n 11) (focusing on Macneil's specific reticence to differentiate the dimensions of relationships that should be deemed legally enforceable and those that should not have legal effect).

[70] Rakoff, 'Contracts of Adhesion' (n 66) 1400.

[71] In support of this argument, see R Mann and T Siebeneicher, 'Just One Click: The Reality of Internet Retail Contracting' (2008) 108 *Columbia Law Review* 984, 1011.

[72] Snyder, 'Relational Contracting' (n 27) 695.

[73] ibid 696.

be put into the terms of the contract'.[74] If democratic processes serve to legitimate consumer form contracting, those processes can also regulate the terms of these relationships and the content of the related contracts. Still, when pressed about what a relationalist court should do absent governmental legislation – I say governmental because the relationalist emphasises that consumer form contracts promulgated by organisations are essentially non-governmental private legislation – Macneil only says that the content of the contract has to be 'reasonable'.[75]

This is unsatisfactory. To be sure, it is conventional to use 'reasonableness' as a baseline in consumer form contracting. This is done in one way or another by Easterbrook (all terms come in unless unconscionable); Llewellyn (all terms are enforceable that are not unreasonable or indecent and do not eviscerate the reasonable meaning of dickered terms); Barnett (all terms are binding so long as they are not radically unexpected); and others using similar formulations. But relational contract theory should be able to do more by way of providing a specific approach for courts to follow. In any event, behind this superficial consensus about reasonableness as a constraint on consumer form contracting is actually a diverse array of applications of reasonableness tests. That which is *radically unexpected* is surely a smaller class of terms than that which is *merely* unreasonable. It seems likely that Llewellyn would have decided *Hill v Gateway* differently from Easterbrook. So can relational contract theory be somewhat more specific in its legal prescriptions? Can it cash out its own version of 'reasonableness' and how it serves to limit the reach of the justification provided by 'joining a relation'?

To conclude this Section where we began, Macaulay was ahead of his time even on this nitty-gritty question, too. In 1966, he understood that one needs to be much more specific about how to divine what is empirically reasonable in context. His effort to dig deep into a transactional constellation to figure out what is reasonable to expect of consumer-drafter relationships furnishes some insight into how well done – but also how difficult – the empirical project of assessing reasonable expectations can be. Others have suggested that empirics are necessary;[76] few have been willing to do the work themselves.[77] Of course, that the work is hard to do does raise institutional competence questions about the relative ability of courts to understand relational context sufficient to regulate optimally

[74] ibid 696–97.

[75] ibid 700.

[76] Craswell, 'Remedies' (n 46).

[77] Hillman also makes some effort to assess empirically the reasonable expectations of consumers to form contracts. R Hillman, 'Rolling Contracts' (2002) 71 *Fordham Law Review* 743, 758–59; R Hillman, 'On-Line Consumer Standard-Form Contracting Practices: A Survey and Discussion of Legal Implications' in J Winn (ed), *Consumer Protection in the Age of the Information Economy* (Burlington, Ashgate, 2006) 283.

and/or fairly[78] – but there is little reason to think legislatures, agencies, or parties themselves are necessarily going to do much better.[79] Indeed, legislatures and agencies themselves may wish to use reasonable expectations as relevant benchmarks in delineating requirements for how to regulate these relationships.[80] In the next Section, I explore what it means to ask courts to pursue consumers' reasonable expectations in enforcing contracts between sellers and their bureaucratic consumers.

III. ANOTHER LOOK AT 'REASONABLE EXPECTATIONS' AS RELATIONAL LAW

If, as I have suggested in Section I, relational theory's core normative claim is that courts should bring the intrinsic norms of relationships to bear on legal disputes, it seems natural for relationalists to embrace some form of the insurance law doctrine of 'reasonable expectations', instructing courts to treat all consumer form contracts as many jurisdictions treat insurance contracts between issuers and lay policyholders. If Macaulay had written 'Private Legislation and the Duty to Read'[81] post-Keeton,[82] that piece might have rooted its prescriptions in a doctrine developed to subject insurance contracts to judicial review. Keeton's formulation is canonical, even if the details and applications cannot be so neatly summarised:[83] 'The objectively reasonable expectations of applicants and intended beneficiaries regarding the terms of insurance contracts will be honored even though painstaking study of the policy provisions would have negated those expectations.'[84] Enthusiasts acknowledge that this doctrine is generally limited to insurance cases,[85] although most concede that there is no 'principled justification for being limited to insurance

[78] Craswell, 'Remedies' (n 46) 224.
[79] Macaulay, 'Private Legislation' (n 21) 1085.
[80] Thanks to Alan White for seeing that reasonable expectations might be relevant to regulation outside of judicial review as well.
[81] Macaulay, 'Private Legislation' (n 21).
[82] Keeton, 'Insurance Law' (n 42).
[83] The version of the doctrine I emphasise here is selective, but it is selected to conform most neatly to what I think relationalist contract law would recommend. For a range of sources on courts' use of the doctrine, see D Schwarcz, 'A Products Liability Theory for the Judicial Regulation of Insurance Policies' (2007) 48 *William & Mary Law Review* 1389; J Thomas, 'An Interdisciplinary Critique of the Reasonable Expectations Doctrine' (1998) 5 *Connecticut Insurance Law Journal* 295; S Popik and C Quackenbos. 'Reasonable Expectations After Thirty Years: A Failed Doctrine' (1998) 5 *Connecticut Insurance Law Journal* 425, 426; M Rahdert, 'Reasonable Expectations Revisited' (1998) 5 *Connecticut Insurance Law Journal* 107; S Ware, 'A Critique of the Reasonable Expectations Doctrine' (1989) 56 *University of Chicago Law Review* 1461; R Henderson, 'The Doctrine of Reasonable Expectation in Insurance Law After Two Decades' (1990) 51 *Ohio State Law Journal* 823.
[84] Keeton, 'Insurance Law' (n 42) 967.
[85] ibid; Slawson, 'The New Meaning of Contract' (n 66).

policies'.[86] Indeed, some argue that: 'Insurance contracts may be viewed as . . . a paradigm of boilerplate.'[87]

The doctrine is traditionally defended in the insurance context because (1) policy provisions are difficult for a lay reader to understand; (2) policies are often issued and made available for inspection only after payment; and (3) policies are issued in a standardised form with no opportunity to bargain over terms.[88] Indeed, in explaining the rationale of the doctrine, Keeton's description focuses on what we would call today the 'rolling contract' nature of the standard insurance transaction: it is a 'pay now, terms later' affair.[89] Moreover, the doctrine specifically seeks to depart – in proper relationalist fashion – from seeing contracts as fixed, seeing them instead as 'ongoing legal relation[s]'.[90] And many of the early cases applying the doctrine focused on the impersonal nature of the transaction, like buying insurance through a vending machine.[91] Accordingly, it seems like a congenial relationalist doctrine for all consumer form contracting, which shares this litany of features with insurance contracts: provisions are routinely unread, standardised, not comprehended (if incomprehensible), often rolling, and quite impersonal, given their prominence in e-commerce. Courts ultimately might not be terribly unsympathetic to an expansion of the reasonable expectations doctrine into this arena because all the basic

[86] Slawson, 'The New Meaning of Contract' (n 66) 52. Applications of the doctrine have crept into relevance in other relational settings (with and without underlying written agreements), though these adoptions aren't quite as formalised as they are in the insurance context. See, eg *Barber v Jacobs*, 58 Conn App 330, 338 (2000) (employment); *Labovitz v Dolan*, 545 NE2d 304 (Ill App 1989) (partnership); *Mangla v Brown University*, 135 F3d 80 (1st Cir 1998) (college-student relationship, using the doctrine to interpret manuals, student handbooks and registration materials); *Goodman v President and Trustees of Bowdoin College*, 135 FSupp2d 40 (D Me 2001) (same); *Stern v Board of Regents, University System of Maryland*, 380 Md 691 (2004) (university-student relationship, using the doctrine to evaluate the propriety of mid-year tuition increases by the university); *Shell Oil Co v Marinello*, 294 A2d 253 (NJ Super 1972) (franchisee-franchisor relationship, respecting reasonable expectations notwithstanding franchise contract terms in variance); *Lippincott v Mississippi Bureau of Narcotics*, 856 So2d 465 (Miss App 2003) (government informant relationship); *State v Alba*, 697 NW2d 295 (Neb App 2005) (plea bargain agreements).

Montana actually appears to utilise the reasonable expectations doctrine for all contracts of adhesion, consistent with relationalist principles. See, eg *Kloss v Edward D Jones & Co*, 54 P3d 1 (MT 2002); *Iwen v US West Direct*, 977 P2d 989 (MT 1999). As far as I can tell, the big sky in Montana has not fallen.

[87] Kastner, 'The Persisting Ideal' (n 54) 811 fn 36.

[88] K Abraham, 'Judge-Made Law and Judge-Made Insurance: Honoring the Reasonable Expectations of the Insured' (1981) 67 *Virginia Law Review* 1151, 1181.

[89] Keeton, 'Insurance Law' (n 42) 968.

[90] 'When courts are motivated to use the reasonable expectations concept . . . they tend to depart from [a] fairly static, private model of contract law to a more dynamic and flexible one that views the provisions of the contract as potentially subordinate to overriding policy and relational concerns.' Rahdert, 'Reasonable Expectations Revisited' (n 83), 115. This helps us see why the concept would be so attractive to the relationalist, something Rahdert appreciates. ibid 148–49.

[91] Abraham, 'Judge-Made Law' (n 88) 1156.

dynamics that led to the reasonable expectations approach in the insurance context are mimicked in many consumer form contract contexts.

Notice, however, that it is really only one party's expectations that are respected through the doctrine: the policyholder's.[92] The issuer's reasonable expectations are routinely (though not universally) ignored by the judicial inquiry in insurance law. Although this asymmetry might be deemed inconsistent with a thorough-going relationalist inquiry into the relational norms of all parties to a contract (and potentially third-party beneficiaries too!), Macneil already furnished a ready-made explanation for why this asymmetry is appropriate: to do any relational analysis, one must 'pay[] attention to the power structure in which [consumer form] contracts are made'.[93] With an acknowledgment of the asymmetric power between form drafter and consumer comes a commitment to focus on the reasonable expectations of the consumer first and foremost.[94] How, then, would this work for consumer form contracts generally, using the insurance law doctrine to apply to many more form contracts?

The reasonable expectations principle extended to consumer form contracts would require courts to inquire in the first instance about what an average consumer could reasonably expect out of a transaction given all the surrounding circumstances.[95] Once that positive and empirical conclusion is drawn, the court must then read out of the contract anything in the standard form document to the contrary, irrespective of whether it is 'decent' – or itself 'reasonable' using other metrics. Although the doctrine has some affinity with late Llewellyn, it isn't coextensive with Llewellyn's proposed treatment of consumer form contracts.[96] For Llewellyn, so long as a term is not unreasonable or indecent, the form's term prevails upon the consumer. The reasonable expectations doctrine in a relationalist rendering, by contrast, requires that a buyer's reasonable expectations cannot be defeated, even if that defeat would be reasonable or decent.[97] What this means is that the 'contract' to which consumers are bound is only

[92] Thomas, 'An Interdisciplinary Critique' (n 83).

[93] Snyder, 'Relational Contracting' (n 27) 696.

[94] Slawson assumes that sellers have no reasonable expectations of their own in the enforcement of their documents; their only reasonable expectations, according to Slawson, are that buyers won't read the forms and that drafters can put anything in them that they please. See, generally Slawson, 'The New Meaning of Contract' (n 66). But drafters may have good faith expectations about what their transactions mean, based on trade usages, aggressive policing of their agents, the conspicuousness of disclosures, and their own reasonable interpretations of their advertisements. One needs a *reason* to prefer only the reasonable expectations of the buyer or consumer. The power relationship is that reason, which relational analysis invites us to consider.

[95] Keeton is pretty clear that an objective standard is to be used. Keeton, 'Insurance Law' (n 42) 968, 974. Slawson would use a subjective standard. Slawson, 'The New Meaning of Contract' (n 66) 43.

[96] Llewellyn, *The Common Law Tradition* (n 65).

[97] Slawson, 'The New Meaning of Contract' (n 66) 36.

partially encapsulated by the form documents.[98] When a consumer clicks 'I agree', that agreement is to what we would call a contract, governed by the general principles of contract law. But the *terms* are not provided exhaustively in the documents: the agreement for the relationalist is to join the relationship. Reasonable expectations control what that relationship entails as a matter of contract law, informed but not wholly determined by the document's terms.

As Slawson appreciates, companies and their advertisements 'provide us with expectations about the kinds of products we might buy long before we buy them. We also gain such expectations from our experiences with products we have used or seen used by others.'[99] All of these baselines provide relevant information for a court in delineating the reasonable expectations of a consumer in a given context.[100] It would thus be virtually incoherent to treat any merger or integration clause in a consumer form contract as having preclusive effects for the purposes of the parol evidence rule (unless the drafter found a way to achieve 'superconsent' to the merger clause specifically). Indeed, Iowa courts acknowledge that reasonable expectations may be established through proof of representations during pre-contractual activity.[101]

For this reason, among others, a relationalist should not be able to stomach the *Restatement (Second)*'s approach to 'standardized agreements' in its § 211. That provision as written (even if not always as applied) virtually assumes that all form agreements are 'integrated' writings.[102] There is a common misconception that the *Restatement (Second)* adopts a meaningful inquiry into reasonable expectations in its § 211.[103] Section 211, by its

[98] To be fair, very few courts in insurance law cases see the doctrine quite this way. Very often, the court starts with the terms in the policy and will apply their version of the reasonable expectations principle 'only if the terms . . . are ambiguous or conflicting, or if the policy contains a hidden trap or pitfall, or if the fine print purports to take away what is written in large print'. *Hallowell v State Farm Mutual Auto Ins Co*, 443 A2d 925, 928 (DE 1982). In a relationalist version of the doctrine, the policy document shouldn't be the core anchor for the 'real deal' of the parties.

[99] Slawson, 'The New Meaning of Contract' (n 66) 25.

[100] Slawson would enforce all pre-contractual expectations created by mass communications – except to the extent that they are reasonably expected to change through the form contract. ibid 26, 34–35. The relationalist would likely have a more fluid conception of the evolution of expectations, which are not set in stone at one moment pre-contract but vary throughout the relationship with the drafter.

[101] *Cairns v Grinnell Mutual Reinsurance Co*, 398 NW2d 821, 825 (IA 1987).

[102] J Murray Jr, 'The Parol Evidence Process and Standardized Agreements Under the *Restatement (Second) of Contracts*' (1975) 123 *University of Pennsylvania Law Review* 1342. Jerry has suggested that § 211 'repudiates the "four-corners" approach to contract interpretation in the standardized agreement setting and in effect approves a doctrine of "reasonable expectations"'. R Jerry, *Understanding Insurance Law* (Albany, Matthew Bender, 1987) 99. But neither of those claims is accurate: the text of § 211 alludes to the parol evidence consequences of all standardised forms (presumably even those without merger clauses) – and, as the remainder of the paragraph tries to show, the text does not embrace a full-bodied commitment to the relationalist reasonable expectations approach.

[103] Hillman, *'Rolling Contracts'* (n 77) 749; Ben-Shahar, 'The Myth' (n 2) 8.

adopted terms, however, makes all terms in a consumer form contracts enforceable, except those in which the drafter 'has reason to believe' that the consumer would not have 'manifest[ed] assent' to the form if the consumer 'knew that the writing contained a particular term'. In such cases, that deal-killing term is not enforceable, though the remainder of the deal remains enforceable without it – controlled by the form.

Notice first that the provision in the *Restatement* is drafted simply to excise terms from the form rather than challenge whether the form is actually the total agreement. More technically, to snip a term out of a term sheet under § 211, a consumer would have to show that she would have walked away from the deal altogether if she had known about the offending term – and that the drafter would have reason to believe that this would be so. Yet that is hardly a proxy for reasonable expectations being the baseline against which the form sheet is read: A consumer could very well have reasonably expected better terms than she got based on representations, advertisements and other relational considerations but still would not have held up the deal overall when learning of an unexpected term. A consumer might have wanted a slightly better price or some other concession without actually walking away from the transaction; or she might have had a reasonable expectation that no court in their right mind would have upheld the provision so there was no reason to hold up the deal. And what the *drafter* has reason to know about the consumer's 'walk-away' threshold isn't of concern to an application of the reasonable expectation doctrine focused on enforcing only the reasonable expectations of the consumer. In short, the § 211 standard doesn't use reasonable expectations as a benchmark, though it is perhaps to be commended for not limiting itself to insurance contracts only.[104] Rather, it uses a very high standard for dropping a term – and it is no wonder that few terms are removed from form contracts under this provision or its corollaries in state law.[105]

With this introduction to the doctrine and its possible extension to the world of all consumer form contracts, it is worth highlighting that nothing about the reasonable expectations doctrine undermines other regulatory

[104] This is notwithstanding comment f's suggestion that consumers 'are not bound to unknown terms which are beyond the range of reasonable expectation'. *Restatement (2d) Contracts* § 211 cmt f. Comment e also focuses on reasonable expectations. Iowa and Arizona, to the extent that they formally embrace § 211 (and few states do) actually try to do more with the reasonable expectations focus of comments e and f – and their Keetonian heritage – than they do with the more restrictive text. Henderson, 'The Doctrine of Reasonable Expectation' (n 83) 850–52. But in various applications of § 211, courts routinely treat reasonable expectations as a mere *exception* to the enforceability of a form contract rather than a starting point, in which the form's terms are taken to be evidence of the actual expectations of a consumer. See *Southwest Pet Prods v Koch Indus*, 32 Fed Appx 213 (9th Cir 2002).

[105] J White, 'Form Contracts Under Revised Article 2' (1997) 75 *Washington University Law Quarterly* 315, 324–35; R Korobkin, 'Bounded Rationality, Standard Form Contracts, and Unconscionability' (2003) 70 *University of Chicago Law Review* 1203, 1271.

devices provided by 'general' contract law. To wit, unconscionability and *contra proferentem* are frequently incorporated into the insurance law reasonable expectations doctrine.[106] But these alternative modes of term invalidation and interpretation are clearly severable from the command to honour reasonable expectations. Still, a relationalist might very well embrace the reasonable expectations principle *instead* of *contra proferentem* in the consumer form contracting context, as more fair to the drafter and consumer alike.[107] The more general unconscionability rule, however, would likely be endorsed by relationalists even in a consumer form contracting world governed by the reasonable expectations doctrine: sometimes there are provisions that must be struck *even if* a consumer reasonably expects that provision because they have been put on careful notice of an offensive, illiberal or irrational term. This escape hatch allows relationalists an answer to the very difficult question of what to do when consumers reasonably expect to be exploited (as many surely do in some industry contexts). Of course, even unconscionability will not be enough to stop drafter abuses altogether for all the reasons Leff already understood in light of the limitations of the 'litigation model'.[108] But if statutes and agencies cannot control the creep of authoritarian private governance in consumer form contracting, judicial review may be all we've got left.

Radin would use tort principles to attack the problem of consumer form contracts judicially (as would Schwarcz, who focuses on products liability law).[109] From the perspective of remedies, this is appealing because it opens up the possibility for punitive damages and other metrics of remuneration that could do a better job of deterring offensive consumer form contracts in the first place. It also provides some congenial doctrine: mandatory warranties and peer-evaluated duties of care are much more common in tort than they are in contract; and 'mass torts' are much more commonplace a doctrinal category than 'mass contracts'.

Still, Radin's conceptualising those who foist boilerplate upon us as 'strangers' is troublesome (and not only from a relationalist perspective). In short, our relationships with our banks, credit card underwriters and mobile phone carriers are intuitively considered voluntary undertakings:

[106] Abraham, 'Judge-Made Law' (n 88); Rahdert, 'Reasonable Expectations' (n 83); Henderson, 'The Doctrine of Reasonable Expectation' (n 83).

[107] Indeed, as Keeton explores, *contra proferentem* could end up being more generous to a consumer: an ambiguity read to favour the consumer might give her more than would be fairly hers under her reasonable expectations. Keeton, 'Insurance Law' (n 42) 969. A relationalist could use *contra proferentem* as a tiebreaker if reasonable expectations cannot be ascertained with clarity (to mitigate power inequalities) – and reasonable expectations could be used as a ceiling on what a consumer can get through the canon of *contra proferentem*.

[108] A Leff, 'Unconscionability and the Code – The Emperor's New Clause' (1967) 115 *University of Pennsylvania Law Review* 485.

[109] M Radin, *Boilerplate: The Fine Print, Vanishing Rights, and the Rule of Law* (Princeton, Princeton University Press, forthcoming 2012) ch 8; Schwarcz, 'A Products Liability Theory' (n 83).

it is precisely our ongoing relationships with them and our ongoing dependence upon them that reinforces the wrong of form contract terms outside our reasonable expectations. With strangers, it is much less reasonable to have any expectations other than expectations of pure exploitation. We ultimately have relationships with the entities that throw contracts at us; they are not indiscriminately carpet-bombing us with weapons or causing accidents.

It also seems unrealistic to contract the domain of contract law so substantially and parcel the real contracts of our lives into tort. We could do that, of course, but then what would be left for contract law is a crumb – and one that continues the ideological project of maintaining a mythical contract law of perfect choice where liberal citizens are supposed to come for their true freedom. By letting contract law get messy with consumer form contracts (appreciating that even business contracts have many form terms with limited consent), we are left with a more realistic and more complex practice, truer to the redistributionist and fairness aspirations that have always intruded into the fictional enterprise of classical liberal contract. It also enables us to reveal that all contract law is a governance project of mediating freedom and unfreedom. We do that less well if we just start calling the vast majority of contracts that we all enter into every day torts-in-the-making.

None of this is to suggest that the reasonable expectations approach – relationally conceived – as applied to consumer form contracting is a panacea. Since Keeton, scholars and courts have piled on the criticism. Given its 'indefinite contours',[110] the doctrine in insurance law hasn't been predictably applied:[111] this has led to the hypothesis that coverage is made more expensive and less available for the very consumers that the doctrine seeks to protect.[112] The costs of error of judicial decisions are borne by the consumers themselves, critics argue, so using a doctrine that is seemingly prone to error may be counter-indicated.[113] Other critics instead focus on the way that the doctrine seems to be a naked wealth transfer from insurer to policyholder and a further tax on insurance activities in a realm that is already heavily regulated by state agencies.[114] Obviously – as

[110] Popik and Quackenbos, 'Reasonable Expectations' (n 83).

[111] Ware, 'A Critique' (n 83) 1466–67.

[112] Popik and Quackenbos, 'Reasonable Expectations' (n 83) 427, 431–32. I have seen no empirical evidence testing this claim. It should be possible to estimate the effect of the doctrine on price and coverage: there are natural experiments available because not every jurisdiction embraces the doctrine (though there is variation in the form of the doctrine adopted by state courts) – and announcements by courts accepting or rejecting the doctrine would likely have an effect on price if insurance companies were actually imposing the cost of the doctrine onto policyholders.

[113] Craswell, 'Remedies' (n 46) 231.

[114] Ware, 'A Critique' (n 83) 1492. That the doctrine more or less thrives notwithstanding regulation highlights how regulation is not a substitute for and does not preempt judicial review.

with other relationalist prescriptions – the reasonable expectations approach gets caught in the cross-fires of the contract culture wars, with formalists and private law purists lining up against the doctrine's subordination of text and the 'four corners' of the document.[115]

In most ways, the reasonable expectations doctrine in insurance law is an easy target. It *is* hugely unpredictable as practiced and the courts that use it do so in wildly different ways: as a stand-in for *contra proferentem* or unconscionability analysis – and as a way of simply rewriting policies they don't like.[116] If we want insurance companies to write better contracts, applying the doctrine in a way that ignores the language of the form contract does not create the right incentives for insurers.[117] But that courts have used it badly in the past hardly tells us whether it couldn't be used better, more broadly and more consistently.

Another core difficulty, however, that remains a major threat to the success of the doctrine in regulating consumer form contracts is that '[t]he opinions speak of expectations without satisfactorily pointing to their source'.[118] Some mistakenly explore expectations about what policy terms in the documents mean[119] – but that is the wrong source for the inquiry because the relevant expectations are derived not merely from the text of the document but from all surrounding circumstances. Still, that only brings us back to a more basic difficulty measuring expectations. As one court opined, 'most insured develop a "reasonable expectation" that every loss will be covered by their policy. Therefore, the reasonable expectation concept must be limited by something more than the fervent hope usually engendered by loss.'[120] Some scholars do not help matters here, maintaining with little empirical support elaborate sets of expectations they assume consumers must have.[121]

One possibility is to shift the relevant inquiry away from 'positive' reasonable expectations – what the average consumer actually expects as a matter of fact – to what might be called 'normative' reasonable expectations – what the average consumer is justified in hoping for from a civilised society. Relationalists might embark on this inquiry too, since

[115] Rahdert, 'Reasonable Expectations' (n 83) 113–15.

[116] ibid 112–14; Henderson, 'The Doctrine of Reasonable Expectation' (n 83). Rahdert traces four disparate uses. There is also a basic dispute about whether a reasonable expectation of coverage is a question of law, see *Christie v Ill Farmers Ins Co*, 580 NW2d 507 (Minn Ct App 1998); *Jarvis v Aetna Cas & Sur Co*, 633 P2d 1359 (AK 1981), or a question of fact, see *Wessman v Mass Mut Life Ins Co*, 929 F2d 402 (8th Cir 1991). My view is that this inquiry is a deeply factual one and thus the doctrine should be developed to pursue the question as one of fact, notwithstanding larger discovery costs in litigation.

[117] M Boardman, '*Contra Proferentem*: The Allure of Ambiguous Boilerplate' in O Ben-Shahar (ed), *Boilerplate: The Foundation of Market Contracts* (Cambridge, Cambridge University Press, 2007) 176.

[118] Abraham, 'Judge-Made Law' (n 88) 1163.

[119] Thomas, 'An Interdisciplinary Critique' (n 83).

[120] *Darner Motor Sales, Inc v Universal Underwriters Ins Co*, 682 P2d 388, 390 (AZ 1984).

[121] Slawson, 'The New Meaning of Contract' (n 66) 72.

Macneil's view of form contracts does seem to contemplate a role for social solidarity, which normative reasonable expectations could support. There is no doubt that the doctrine in insurance law can veer in this direction, too, with courts importing normative assessments of what policyholders are right to hope they have covered. But this is the most controversial and most criticised implementation of the doctrine, the one least likely to gain more widespread acceptance outside the insurance context. If the empirical questions are difficult, the normative questions are even harder to answer – and our current system does try to keep judges out of this business to the extent feasible. It may be, however, that unconscionability law comes close enough to serving this function, critical in dealing with the possibility that at some point all consumers reasonably expect to be exploited by the companies that distribute form contracts.[122]

To be fair, some have tried to explore what consumers' empirical expectations of coverage actually are. For example, citing survey studies from 1989, Thomas found that substantial numbers of homeowner insurance policyholders (15 per cent) simply didn't know that they were covered for liability for injury or property damage; 16 per cent didn't realise they were covered for storms; and 21 per cent didn't realise they were covered for vandalism. Only 18 per cent correctly understood that they *were* covered for damage caused by riots. Policyholder understanding of exclusions was even less impressive: most policyholders assumed incorrectly that the basic policy covered floods, earthquakes and mudslides; a bare majority understood that nuclear accidents were excluded (54 per cent), though about 74 per cent understood that 'wear and tear' is excluded from their policies.[123] Thomas would put a different emphasis here: a full 26 per cent of policyholders mistakenly thought they might be insured for 'wear and tear'! Morons!

Although this survey data is surely of interest in figuring out consumers' objective reasonable expectations, interpreting the results is a tricky matter. Thomas thinks this one survey from 1989 'undermine[s] the assumption that insureds consistently develop specific expectations regarding insurance coverage'.[124] But that is hardly the only way to read the limited data. Quite the reverse could be true: consumers have pretty consistent expectations of coverage – even if consumers get it 'wrong' some of the time. Remember, though, 'wrong' may be the wrong concept here: consumers may have legitimate and reasonable expectations of coverage, even if a careful reading of the policy might negate the coverage. True enough, in some cases – such as nuclear accidents – consumers are

[122] Thanks to Peggy Radin for pushing me on this – and for suggesting the distinction between 'positive' and 'normative' reasonable expectations to me.

[123] Thomas, 'An Interdisciplinary Critique' (n 83) 319–34.

[124] ibid 321.

evenly divided so it is hard to say there is an expectation one way or another. But that there are some cases where there is confusion does not tell us much about whether reasonable expectations cannot otherwise be a reliable guide. Some tiebreaker will be necessary when the average consumer simply has no expectation one way or the other – but the reasonable expectations approach simply runs out in such cases. In such cases, the law probably should just pick the form terms, though one could reasonably argue for a 'penalty default' against the drafter, since, generally speaking, drafters are likely best situated to tilt the consumers' expectations in the direction they prefer, putting consumer cognitive biases to one side.

A potentially more difficult 'finding' within the relevant survey was that 82 per cent of respondents agreed with this statement: 'If you don't look at the fine print when you buy an auto or homeowners insurance policy, you are likely to find you are not covered in an emergency.'[125] It isn't clear what to make of this, however.[126] From one perspective, we might say that consumers by and large expect their insurance companies to try to deny their valid claims that come within their reasonable expectations of coverage. But that would tell us precious little about their reasonable expectations of actual coverage, which, by hypothesis, could be legally enforceable. There is, of course, a way to read this finding to suggest that 82 per cent of policyholders expect to be exploited by their policies – raising the complicated problem of what to do when consumers know full well that they are entering dangerous agreements and expect to be exploited.[127] In such contexts, the reasonable expectations doctrine can't solve any useful problem: we would simply have to rely on unconscionability, perhaps *contra proferentem*, legislation, and regulation.

No approach solves all problems in this domain – and there are many terms that we, as a society, simply don't think anyone can consent to even if he reasonably expected that outcome: a litigant cannot give away her right to hire a lawyer on her own behalf; a consumer cannot sell himself into slavery – or even agree to pay rent to live in uninhabitable conditions (waiving the warranty of habitability); a company cannot attempt to disclaim its liability for its own intentional torts (and even disclaiming liability for its own negligence is controversial); a litigant must be able to call the shots in her relationship with her lawyer; a borrower cannot agree to a usurious interest rate. To the extent we are committed to more limitations on agreement, we are always free to try to move our laws in that direction. Doctrine alone cannot get us there, however; only repeated litigations,

125 ibid 323.

126 In any event, the way the question was asked on this survey was absurd, undermining its value as a barometer of reasonable expectations. The question of coverage in an 'emergency' also seems quite beside the point – and hardly specific enough to derive any sense of whether a policyholder would be entitled to coverage in a scenario in which a dispute is likely to arise.

127 Radin, *Boilerplate* (n 109) ch 5.

common law development and legislative mobilisation will get us those results.

This limited analysis of extant empirical work trying to measure reasonable expectations does, however, help us see how hard it will be to adjudicate cases under the doctrine well. If Macaulay's early article taught us anything, it is that one must actually study expectations in a nuanced manner with sound methodologies – and not assume them or utilise blunt surveys to divine them. What this means is that a principled use of the doctrine to regulate consumer form contracts will be difficult to achieve. But good adjudication – and relationalist adjudication – is never easy. As Slawson understands, '[t]he complications [the reasonable expectations approach] will confront . . . are those that are inherent in ascertaining what . . . reasonable expectations are in the varied and unpredictable course of modern life'.[128] This is an empirical project ultimately – as Macaulay already knew in 1966 – and relationalists ought to undertake further efforts to learn consumers' reasonable expectations in their various form contracting relationships to help judges adjudicate disputes under these contracts better. Instead of merely conceding the institutional competence challenge, relationalists should be producing reliable empirical evaluations of contractual context themselves, helping to alleviate the considerable difficulties courts will have in applying the doctrine. Those studies will also be good starting points for regulators focused on the task of constraining the choices available to drafters.

Ultimately, when relationalists fragment consumer form contracts into its own sphere for treatment with the reasonable expectations approach, relationalist empirical work will need to be even further fragmented to be useful to courts and regulators. Google may create its own expectations in its customers with its 'don't be evil' ethos (and Gmail users may have different expectations from AdSense subscribers); Facebook may have created its own reasonable expectations with recent kerfuffles associated with its privacy practices; airlines may have successfully created expectations that ticketholders must buy insurance to switch flights freely because of a popular checkout system which routinely asks buyers to opt-out of travel insurance during the payment process.[129] This is the work ahead for

[128] Slawson, 'The New Meaning of Contract' (n 66) 74.

[129] This strategy is not unlike Macaulay's discussion of when credit card companies clearly made available insurance plans to protect against (the limited liability of the customer for) unauthorised use. Macaulay, 'Private Legislation' (n 21) 1105. We might call this, with Calo, 'visceral notice'. M Calo, 'Against Notice Skepticism' (2012) 87 *Notre Dame Law Review* 1027. As Zev Eigen has recently shown, giving a consumer the sense that she 'participated' in choosing the terms of the contract can lead consumers to feel more inclined to comply with chosen terms; perhaps participation changes the reasonable expectations of consumers and their consequent sense of obligation under the form's terms. Z Eigen, 'When and Why Individuals Obey Form-Adhesive Contracts: Experimental Evidence of Consent, Compliance, Promise and Performance' *Journal of Legal Studies* (forthcoming) (available at ssrn.com/abstract=1640245).

relationalists that want to make a distinctive contribution to the development of the law of consumer form contract.

CONCLUSION

The tide has turned against recommending more and more disclosure as a solution to the problem of consumer form contract.[130] But relationalists can make a contribution to the development of the law in this area by getting behind the reasonable expectations doctrine as an approach to the judicial review of these contracts. As I've argued here, this legal approach flows naturally from relationalists' theoretical commitments. Moreover, relationalists' methodological commitments to empirical assessments of contractual context and implicit dimensions of contract suggest a research agenda for the future to further support the development of this relationalist doctrine and regulatory strategy. Citizens of private governments or bureaucratic consumers can have legally enforceable reasonable expectations of their agreements that depart from the text of their organising documents drafted by organisations. This insight is consistent with the view in public law that citizens may have reasonable and enforceable constitutional expectations that might depart from the text of the Constitution.[131] All the debate to come will – quite reasonably – be about exactly what counts as a reasonable expectation.

BIBLIOGRAPHY

Abraham, K, 'Judge-Made Law and Judge-Made Insurance: Honoring the Reasonable Expectations of the Insured' (1981) 67 *Virginia Law Review* 1151.
Bar-Gill, O and Warren, W, 'Making Credit Safer' (2009) 157 *University of Pennsylvania Law Review* 1.
Barnett, R, 'Consenting to Form Contracts' (2002) 71 *Fordham Law Review* 627.
Barnett, R, 'Conflicting Visions: A Critique of Ian Macneil's Relational Theory of Contract' (1992) 78 *Virginia Law Review* 1175.
Bebchuck, L and Posner, R, 'One-Sided Contracts in Competitive Consumer Markets' (2006) 104 *Michigan Law Review* 827.
Ben-Shahar, O, 'The Myth of the "Opportunity to Read" in Contract Law' (2009) 5 *European Review Contract Law* 1.
—— (ed), *Boilerplate: The Foundation of Market Contracts* (Cambridge, Cambridge University Press, 2007).

[130] eg R Mann, '"Contracting" for Credit' (2006) 104 *Michigan Law Review* 899, 924; O Ben-Shahar and C Schneider, 'The Failure of Mandated Disclosure' (2011) 159 *University of Pennsylvania Law Review* 647.

[131] E Leib, 'The Perpetual Anxiety of Living Constitutionalism' (2007) 24 *Constitutional Commentary* 353; R Primus, 'Constitutional Expectations' (2010) 109 *Michigan Law Review* 91.

Ben-Shahar, O and Schneider, C, 'The Failure of Mandated Disclosure' (2011) 159 *University of Pennsylvania Law Review* 647.

Bernstein, L, 'The Questionable Empirical Basis of Article 2's Incorporation Strategy: A Preliminary Study' (1999) 66 *University of Chicago Law Review* 76.

Boardman, M, '*Contra Proferentem*: The Allure of Ambiguous Boilerplate' in O Ben-Shahar (ed), *Boilerplate: The Foundation of Market Contracts* (Cambridge, Cambridge University Press, 2007) 176.

Calo, M, 'Against Notice Skepticism' (2012) 87 *Notre Dame Law Review* 1027.

Campbell, D, Collins, H and Wightman, J (eds), *Implicit Dimensions of Contract: Discrete, Relational, and Network Contracts* (Oxford, Hart Publishing, 2003).

Collins, H, 'The Research Agenda of Implicit Dimensions of Contract' in D Campbell, H Collins and J Wightman (eds), *Implicit Dimensions of Contract: Discrete, Relational, and Network Contracts* (Oxford, Hart Publishing, 2007) 1.

Craswell, R, 'Remedies When Contracts Lack Consent: Autonomy and Institutional Competence' (1995) 33 *Osgoode Hall Law Journal* 209.

Eigen, Z, 'When and Why Individuals Obey Form-Adhesive Contracts: Experimental Evidence of Consent, Compliance, Promise and Performance' *Journal of Legal Studies* (forthcoming).

Eisenberg, M, 'Why There Is No Law of Relational Contracts' (2000) 94 *Northwestern University Law Review* 805.

Feinman, J, 'Relational Contract Theory in Context' (2000) 94 *Northwestern University Law Review* 737.

Fuller, L, 'Consideration as Form' (1941) 41 *Columbia Law Review* 499.

Gillette, C, 'Rolling Contracts as an Agency Problem' (2004) 2004 *Wisconsin Law Review* 679.

Gordon, R, 'Macaulay, Macneil, and the Discovery of Solidarity and Power in Contract Law' (1985) 1985 *Wisconsin Law Review* 565.

Henderson, R, 'The Doctrine of Reasonable Expectation in Insurance Law After Two Decades' (1990) 51 *Ohio State Law Journal* 823.

Hillman, R, 'On-Line Consumer Standard-Form Contracting Practices: A Survey and Discussion of Legal Implications' in J Winn (ed), *Consumer Protection in the Age of the Information Economy* (Burlington, Ashgate, 2006) 283.

——, 'Rolling Contracts' (2002) 71 *Fordham Law Review* 743.

Jerry, R, *Understanding Insurance Law* (Albany, Matthew Bender, 1987).

Kastner, T, 'The Persisting Ideal of Agreement in an Age of Boilerplate' (2010) 35 *Law & Social Inquiry* 793 (reviewing Ben-Shahar 2007).

Katz, A, 'Standard Form Contracts' in P Newman (ed), *New Palgrave Dictionary of Economics and the Law* (Houndmills, Palgrave Macmillan, 1998) 502.

Keeton, R, 'Insurance Law Rights at Variance with Policy Provisions' (1970) 83 *Harvard Law Review* 961.

Kessler, F, 'Contracts of Adhesion – Some Thoughts About Freedom of Contract' (1943) 43 *Columbia Law Review* 629.

Kimel, D, *From Promise to Contract: Towards a Liberal Theory of Contract* (Oxford, Hart Publishing, 2003).

Knapp, C, 'Opting Out or Copping Out? An Argument for Strict Scrutiny of Individual Contracts' (2006) 40 *Loyola of Los Angeles Law Review* 96.

Kornhauser, L, 'Unconscionability in Standard Forms' (1976) 64 *California Law Review* 1151.

Korobkin, R, 'Bounded Rationality, Standard Form Contracts, and Unconscionability' (2003) 70 *University Chicago Law Review* 1203.

Leff, A, 'Unconscionability and the Crowd – Consumers and the Common Law Tradition' (1970) 31 *University of Pittsburgh Law Review* 349.

——, 'Contract as Thing' (1970) 19 *American University Law Review* 131.

——, 'Unconscionability and the Code – The Emperor's New Clause' (1967) 115 *University of Pennsylvania Law Review* 485.

Leib, E, *Friend v. Friend: The Transformation of Friendship – and What the Law Has To Do with It* (New York, Oxford University Press, 2011).

——, 'Contracts and Friendships' (2010) 59 *Emory Law Journal* 649.

——, 'The Perpetual Anxiety of Living Constitutionalism' (2007) 24 *Constitutional Commentary* 353.

Llewellyn, K, *The Common Law Tradition: Deciding Appeals* (Boston, Little Brown, 1960).

——, Book Review of O Prausnitz, 'The Standardization of Commercial Contracts in English and Continental Law' (1939) 52 *Harvard Law Review* 700.

Mann, R, '"Contracting" for Credit' (2006) 104 *Michigan Law Review* 899.

Mann, R and Siebeneicher, T, 'Just One Click: The Reality of Internet Retail Contracting' (2008) 108 *Columbia Law Review* 984.

Macaulay, S, 'Freedom From Contract: Solutions in Search of a Problem?' (2004) 2004 *Wisconsin Law Review* 777.

——, 'The Real and the Paper Deal: Empirical Pictures of Relationships, Complexity and the Urge for Transparent Simple Rules' in D Campbell, H Collins and J Wightman (eds), *Implicit Dimensions of Contract: Discrete, Relational, and Network Contracts* (Oxford, Hart Publishing, 2003).

——, 'Relational Contracts Floating on a Sea of Custom? Thoughts About the Ideas of Ian Macneil and Lisa Bernstein' (2000) 94 *Northwestern University Law Review* 775.

——, 'Bambi Meets Godzilla: Reflections on Contracts Scholarship and Teaching vs. State Unfair and Deceptive Trade Practices and Consumer Protection Statutes' (1989) 26 *Houston Law Review* 575.

——, 'Private Legislation and the Duty To Read   Business Run by IBM Machine, the Law of Contracts and Credit Cards' (1966) 19 *Vanderbilt Law Review* 1051.

Macneil, I, 'Relational Contract Theory: Challenges and Queries' (2000) 94 *Northwestern University Law Review* 877.

——, 'Bureaucracy and Contracts of Adhesion' (1984) 22 *Osgoode Hall Law Journal* 5.

——, 'Values in Contract: Internal and External' (1983) 78 *Northwestern University Law Review* 340.

Murray Jr, J, 'The Parol Evidence Process and Standardized Agreements Under the *Restatement (Second) of Contracts*' (1975) 123 *University of Pennsylvania Law Review* 1342.

Nadler, J, 'Flouting the Law' (2005) 83 *Texas Law Review* 1399.

Newitz, A, Electric Frontier Foundation, *Dangerous Terms: A User's Guide to EULAs* (White Paper, 2005).

Popik, S and Quackenbos, C, 'Reasonable Expectations After Thirty Years: A Failed Doctrine' (1998) 5 *Connecticut Insurance Law Journal* 425.

Primus, R, 'Constitutional Expectations' (2010) 109 *Michigan Law Review* 91.

Radin, M, *Boilerplate: The Fine Print, Vanishing Rights, and the Rule of Law* (Princeton, Princeton University Press, forthcoming 2012).
Rahdert, M, 'Reasonable Expectations Revisited' (1998) 5 *Connecticut Insurance Law Journal* 107.
Rakoff, T, 'Contracts of Adhesion: An Essay in Reconstruction' (1983) 96 *Harvard Law Review* 1194.
Robinson, P and Darley, J, 'The Utility of Desert' (1997) 91 *Northwestern University Law Review* 453.
Schwarcz, D, 'Reevaluating Standardized Insurance Policies' (2011) 78 *University of Chicago Law Review* 1263.
——, 'A Products Liability Theory for the Judicial Regulation of Insurance Policies' (2007) 48 *William & Mary Law Review* 1389.
Scott, R, 'The Case for Formalism in Relational Contract' (2000) 94 *Northwestern University Law Review* 847.
Slawson, WD, 'The New Meaning of Contract: The Transformation of Contracts Law by Standard Forms' (1984) 46 *University of Pittsburgh Law Review* 21.
Slawson, WD, 'Standard Form Contracts and the Democratic Control of Lawmaking Power' (1971) 84 *Harvard Law Review* 529.
Snyder, F, 'Relational Contracting in a Digital Age: A Panel Discussion with Franklin G Snyder, Ian R Macneil, John Kidwell, David Campbell, and Rachel Arnow-Richman' (2005) 11 *Texas Wesleyan Law Review* 675.
Speidel, R, 'Article 2 and Relational Contracts' (1993) 26 *Loyola of Los Angeles Law Review* 789.
Thomas, J, 'An Interdisciplinary Critique of the Reasonable Expectations Doctrine' (1998) 5 *Connecticut Insurance Law Journal* 295.
Ware, S, 'A Critique of the Reasonable Expectations Doctrine' (1989) 56 *University of Chicago Law Review* 1461.
Warren, E, 'Unsafe at Any Rate' (2007) 5 *Democracy: A Journal of Ideas* 8.
White, J, 'Form Contracts Under Revised Article 2' (1997) 75 *Washington University Law Quarterly* 315.
Whitford, W, 'Ian Macneil's Contribution to Contracts Scholarship' (1985) 1985 *Wisconsin Law Review* 545.
Winn, J and Webber, M, 'The Impact of EU Unfair Contract Terms Law on US Business-to-Consumer Internet Merchants' (2006) 62 *Business Lawyer* 209.

10

Acquiring Children Contractually: Relational Contracts at Work at Home

CAROL SANGER*

INTRODUCTION

MY TOPIC IS the use of contract in family formation. More specifically, I want to look at how contract is now used by parents in the process of acquiring children, and as we shall see, also as a means of retaining interests in those same children under the developing regime of open adoption. In thinking about the contractual acquisition of relatives, the more familiar example is probably marriage. We know that historically, marriages – particularly among the propertied – commonly resulted from bargaining between families, and sometimes between ministers of state when diplomatic or dynastic concerns were at stake. Over time individual men and women began to contract with one another for marriage. By the nineteenth century, couples were regarded as contractually bound to one another by virtue of their engagement alone; thus the lively nineteenth-century cause of action for breach of the promise to marry.[1] There were also less congenial examples of the contractual acquisition (and deacquistion) of spouses. Both in England and in the colonies, husbands could sell their wives, and some did.[2]

* I am indebted to Joy Ziegeweid, Columbia Law School, Class of 2012, for her excellent research and for our on-going discussions about the problem of class in American family law. Please do not cite this chapter without permission from the author.

[1] M Grossberg, *Governing the Hearth: Law and the Family in Nineteenth-Century America* (Chapel Hill, University of North Carolina Press, 1985); S Lettmaier, *Broken Engagements: The Action for Breach of Promise of Marriage and the Feminine Ideal, 1800–1940* (Oxford, Oxford University Press, 2009).

[2] See C Dayton, 'Divorce: The Limits of a Puritan Remedy' in *Women Before the Bar: Gender, Law, and Society in Connecticut* (Chapel Hill, University of North Carolina Press, 1995) 104–56; see also J Suk, 'The Moral and Legal Consequences of Wife-Selling in The Mayor of Casterbridge' (Cardozo Legal Studies Research Paper No 327, 2011) (available at papers.ssrn.com/sol3/papers.cfm?abstract_id=1777555); P Leesony, P Boettke and J Lemke, 'Wife Sales' (available at papers.ssrn.com/sol3/papers.cfm?abstract_id=1859387) (claiming that the wife sales show how well the marriage market works).

Of course, things have changed over the last few centuries. While money still changes hands to bring about marriages in certain parts of the world, for the most part brides are no longer bartered.[3] Similarly, although arranged marriages still exist, the modern practice increasingly takes the form of parental *brokering*, with ultimate approval for the match residing in the couple.[4] Consent of the parties is now accepted not only as a desirable social practice but also as a legal prerequisite to marriage under both domestic law and human rights regimes.

Of course, aspects of private contracting still surround and sometimes structure a marriage even if contract no longer *creates* it. Prenuptial agreements are a good example. The assurance of a background regime of enforceable contracts is understood to bring about marriages that might otherwise not have been entered. In 1990, the Pennsylvania Supreme Court upheld a prenuptial agreement between a 24-year-old unemployed nurse and a 39-year-old neuro-surgeon, observing that '[p]arties would not have entered such agreements, and, *indeed, might not have entered their marriages*, if they did not expect their agreements to be strictly enforced'.[5] More recently, in the 2010 case of *Radmacher v Granatino*, the Supreme Court of the United Kingdom recognised that an important factor in the enforceability of prenuptial agreements is 'whether the marriage would have gone ahead without an agreement, or without the terms which had been agreed'.[6]

This paper focuses on the use of contract not to acquire a spouse, but in the process of obtaining a child. As with wives, children were certainly acquired contractually in the past. In the United States, enslaved children were sold outright, and the custody of free children was also regularly subject to contractual transfer. During the colonial and republican periods, poor children were often indentured and children in general often were 'placed out' by their parents as apprentices or domestics with other families.[7] These arrangements were highly contractual, the terms of obligation set out on both sides.[8] Actions for breach of contract were brought by apprentices against masters for failing to teach them the promised

[3] Significant exceptions include parts of India, Pakistan, Afghanistan, and a number of African countries. The practice is not specifically prohibited by Convention on the Elimination of Discriminination Against Women (CEDAW).

[4] See P Gagoomal, 'A "Margin of Appreciation" for "Marriages of Appreciation": Reconciling South Asian Adult Arranged Marriages With the Matrimonial Consent Requirement in International Human Rights Law' (2009) 97 *Georgetown Law Journal* 589, 596–97.

[5] *Simeone v Simeone*, 581 A 2d 162, 166 (PA 1990) (emphasis added) (observing that a rule 'invoking inquiries into reasonableness' severely undermines the 'functioning and reliability of prenuptial agreements').

[6] *Radmacher v Granatino*, [2010] UKSC 42, All ER(D) 186 (Oct) [72] (available at www.supremecourt.gov.uk/decided-cases/docs/UKSC_2009_0031_Judgment.pdf).

[7] See, generally R Bremmer, *Children and Youth in America*, vol 1 (Cambridge, Harvard University Press, 1970) 103.

[8] J Demos, *A Little Commonwealth: Family Life in Plymouth Colony* (Oxford, Oxford University Press, 1970) 71; MA Mason, *From Father's Property to Children's Rights* (New York, Columbia University Press, 1994) 39.

craft, and by masters against parents for harbouring runaway apprentices (their own children). Masters may have agreed to certain parent-like obligations – feeding, housing and moral education in the case of apprentices. They did not, however, understand themselves to be acquiring a *relation* but rather an employee (in the case of indenture) or a trainee (in the case of apprenticeship). While such arrangements sometimes resulted in 'family-like ties', the child did not by virtue of the agreement become a member of the master's legal family.[9] The transfer of custody was temporary and largely for vocational purposes.

In this paper, I consider the *modern* use of contract to transfer the custody of children, not for educational or training purposes, but rather to create the legal relationship of parent and child. In so doing, I move us out of the early nineteenth century and into the early twenty-first, where the use of contract to create and acquire children is ever more familiar as adults contract to buy both gestational services and genetic material (eggs, sperm or embryos). And not all contracting for children involves reproductive technology. Foster parents, for example, contract with the state to raise children, and special 'fost-adopt' programmes aside, their parental duties are time-bound, a contractual form of temporary parenting.

Here, however, I investigate the use of contracts for *permanent* parenting. I focus on adoption and, within that context, on a new category of contract, the postadoption visitation agreement. I have chosen this topic in part because I teach both contracts *and* family law and so connections between the two – private ordering in the quasi-public realm – have become part of my world view. There is no telling what intimates will get up to with one another when you put the possibility of a deal in front of them.

But there is another reason that I have taken this occasion to think harder about the use of contract to form families, or what I have called 'relational contracts at work at home'. When turning to Stewart Macaulay's webpage to look again (and, as always, with awe) at his scholarship, I discovered an entry I had not expected. This was a link to the webpage of *Jackie* Macaulay.[10] Her webpage provides a lovely photograph and a condensed biography: 'Born: Aug. 2, 1932, Racine, Wisconsin; Married: March 20, 1954. (To Stewart Macaulay); Died: January 2, 2000, Madison, Wisconsin. Children: Monica; John; Philip; Laura.' The site also lists Jackie Macaulay's publications, and one in particular drew my attention. This was 'Adoption for Black Children: A Case Study of Expert Discretion' written in 1978 by Jackie and her husband Stewart, five years before Jackie got her law degree at the University of Wisconsin Law School.[11] The article seeks to understand the structural,

[9] Grossberg, *Governing the Hearth* (n 1) 259.

[10] See www.law.wisc.edu/facstaff/macaulay/jmacaulay.html.

[11] J Macaulay and S Macaulay, 'Adoption for Black Children: A Case Study of Expert Discretion' in *Research in Law and Sociology: An Annual Compilation of Research* (Greenwich, JAI Press, 1978).

ideological, and particularly the *institutional* reasons, why and how in the early 1970s trans-racial adoption became a disfavoured mode of family formation.

Although I did not know Jackie Macaulay, I am grateful for the introduction through her work. I took the Macaulays' article on race and adoption as the occasion to think about a topic I had been puzzling over. This is the use of contract in the process of creating, and as we shall see, simultaneously *preserving* parent–child relationships through adoption. As with the adoption practices of the 1970s (and as with much else in the US), here too race places a hand. So too, it turns out, does the opinion of experts, although like the Macaulays in the 1970s, we may again want to challenge the accuracy of that designation. From his earliest work, Stewart Macaulay has taught us that in order to assess any legal regime, it must be placed in the context of social values and practices, both of which evolve over time. As we shall see, this is certainly the case with regard to adoption.

I. ADOPTION TRANSFORMED

To understand how contract has made its way into adoption, it helps to understand how adoption practices in the United States have evolved in the last few decades from a regime of closed and confidential proceedings into the more transparent process known as open adoption. In a traditional closed adoption, the unmarried birth mother surrendered her parental rights (and where known, the birth father his) to the state or to a licensed private adoption agency.[12] The *agency* then selected an appropriate married couple from its applicant pool to become the infant's new parents. Following a satisfactory home study, the family or probate court then issued an order declaring the adoption to be in the baby's best interest. The childless couple was thereby transformed into legal parents with a baby of their very own.

The combination of termination of the birth mother's parental rights ('the complete severance of the legal relationship, with all its rights and responsibilities, between the child and his parent or parents')[13] and the final adoption decree ('all rights, duties and other legal consequences of the genetic relation of parent and child shall hereafter exist between the adopted person and the adopting parent') created a new legal family and obliterated the old.[14] The birth mother would have no idea where her child had gone or who the adoptive parents were, and they in turn knew

[12] Some states also permit private adoptions brokered through attorneys. States also sometimes permit adoption by single people. See, generally J Hollinger, *Adoption Law and Practice* (New York, Matthew Bender, 1997).

[13] Connecticut General Statutes §§ 45–61b (2011).

[14] Connecticut General Statutes §§ 45–64a (2011).

very little about her. Indeed, the baby's original birth certificate was sealed and a new one issued with the adoptive parents' names filled in as the parents from the date of birth. Under prevailing mid-century ideology, this process was understood as a domestic trifecta. The birth mother could move on with her own life free from the burdens and stigma of unwed motherhood. The adoptive parents could proceed with a facsimile (legal and often physiological) of biological parenthood, their reproductive secrets safe and their domestic privacy protected. And the child himself could be raised by loving and enthusiastic parents whose dominion over their child was as complete as any natural parent.

Beginning in the 1970s, the logic of this system of secrecy began to unravel as adult adoptees, acting individually and through fledgling organisations such as the Adoptees Liberty Movement Association (ALMA), began to challenge the view that they were better off not knowing anything about their birth families.[15] The adoptees were supported in their efforts by research findings identifying 'genealogical bewilderment' and 'identity lacunae' in adopted children, particularly during adolescence.[16] There was already an uncanny cultural phenomenon: the widespread popularity of Alex Haley's *Roots*. Both the book and the subsequent television series sparked great interest in the pursuit of one's origins; *Roots* 'diminished [adoptees'] sense of marginality' in seeking *their* roots.[17] Best-selling confessional books such as Betty Jean Lifton's *Twice Born: Memoirs of an Adopted Daughter* added to the interest in the lot of adopted people and contributed to a cultural rethinking of closed adoption.[18] Adoptee rights campaigns were not entirely successful as a matter of law; courts rejected constitutional claims that confidentiality provisions violated an adoptee's fundamental right to personhood.[19] Nonetheless, legislatures began to authorise states to collect and adult adoptees to retrieve at least non-identifying information about birth parents – such things as ethnicity and medical histories.

At about the same time, women who had placed children for adoption in the past also began to step forward and to identify themselves, at least to

[15] ALMA has since been joined by the more radical Bastard Nation; see www.bastards.org/activism/access.htm.

[16] See A Baran and R Pannor, 'Perspectives on Open Adoption' (1983) Spring *Future of Children* 119, 120 (noting that adopted children 'live the knowledge that an essential part of their personal history lies on the other side of the adoption barrier'). Against, see W Carp, *Family Matters: Secrecy and Disclosure in the History of Adoption* (Cambridge, Harvard University Press, 2000) 219 (noting that both 'open and closed adoption advocates marshaled pseudoscience to advance their positions').

[17] J Modell, *A Sealed and Secret Kinship: The Culture of Policies and Practices in American Adoption* (New York, Berghahn Books, 2002) 35. See also Carp, *Family Matters: Secrecy and Disclosure* (n 17).

[18] See generally Carp, *Family Matters: Secrecy and Disclosure* (n 17) 138–66; Betty Jean Lifton, *Twice Born: Memoirs of an Adopted Daughter* (New York, McGraw Hill, 1975).

[19] See, eg *In re Roger B*, 418 NE 2d 751 (IL 1981) (upholding confidentiality state against constitutional challenge).

one another. As a social group, birth mothers have been a largely invisible category of mother. As birth mother Jan Waldron observed: 'There are millions of birthmothers in this country, yet most people will tell you they've never met one.'[20] In the pre-internet days of the 1980s, when support groups of any kind were hard to identify and mobilise, birth mothers who wanted to talk about their feelings – whether loss or guilt, regret or relief – began to meet in living rooms and church basements under the auspices of local discussion groups such as Concerned United Birthmothers (CUB). Such support groups offered a welcome forum for birth mothers dissatisfied with their treatment in law. CUB founder Lee Campbell acknowledged a debt: '[W]e're grateful to you Adoptees for waking us up. If you hadn't come out of the closet, we birth mothers would be in pain forever'.[21] As with adult adoptees, birth mothers rarely prevailed in court in their efforts to open sealed adoption records.[22] Yet states began to create official registries where birth parents and adult children could inquire about one another and, if both agreed, there was the possibility of reunion.[23]

These early forms of adoption activism by adoptees and birth mothers took place against a perfect demographic storm regarding the availability of eligible newborns. The decriminalisation of abortion in 1973, the advent of the contraceptive pill in the 1960s, and the greater social and legal acceptability of unwed motherhood resulted in a significant decrease in the number of infants placed for adoption. As the National Committee for Adoption stated in 1989, '[m]ore than a million couples are chasing the 30,000 white infants available in the country each year'.[24] In consequence, the market power of birth mothers increased and adoption agencies began to pay serious attention to what it would take to get them to place their newborns for adoption.

The answer was understood to be greater control by birth mothers over the adoption process. This power manifested itself in two ways. The first concerned the selection of the adoptive parents, which within a relatively short period of time moved from agency social workers to birth mothers themselves. Agencies began to act more as brokers, compiling and presenting the carefully drafted letters and resumes received from their child-

[20] J Waldron, *Giving Away Simone* (New York, Times Books, 1995) xvii.

[21] Carp, *Family Matters: Secrecy and Disclosure* (n 17) 204.

[22] See, eg *In re Christine*, 397 A2d 511, 513 (RI 1979) (noting the 'heavy burden' birth mothers must bear to establish a claim for access to sealed records). Birth mothers also failed in later efforts to keep adoption records secret retroactively; *Does v Oregon*, 993 P 2d 822 (OR 1999).

[23] See, eg the New Jersey Adoption Registry at www.nj.gov/njfosteradopt/adoption/registry/; Texas Central Adoption Registry at www.dshs.state.tx.us/vs/reqproc/adoptionregistry.shtm.

[24] C Crossen, 'In Today's Adoptions, the Biological Parents are Calling the Shots' *The Wall Street Journal* (12 September 1989) A1; See also 'It's a Seller's Market' *Life* (September 1988) 80 (noting that 100 couples vie for each healthy Caucasian infant).

less clients to pregnant women and girls considering adoption.[25] As birth mothers increasingly knew the identity, background and location of the adoptive parents – after all, they had chosen them – the confidentiality and secrecy of adoption records became relics in a collapsing regime.

II. EARLY POSTADOPTION AGREEMENTS

In addition to giving birth mothers primary control in choosing the adoptive parents, the second incentive was the possibility of on-going communication and even contact between birth mothers and adoptive families. That is, birth mothers wanted to know not only where and with whom the child was placed, but how he or she was doing over time. With the help of agency social workers, birth parents and adoptive families began to negotiate about the extent and form that post-adoption contact might take. The resulting agreements typically included the promise of photographs and progress reports to the birth mother, and sometimes even scheduled visits between the birth mother and the adopted child.

And the legal status of such agreements? The question arose most often when the adoptive parents decided that the arrangement was not working and discontinued visitation. In such cases, the birth mother would sue to have the agreement specifically enforced. The earliest cases seeking birth mother visitation in the days of closed adoption were quite clear about the outcome: nothing doing. Because adoption is a legal status completely created by statute, parties could not by agreement add to or detract from whatever rights and duties the state had fixed. Recall that closed adoption statutes provided for the comprehensive and mandatory substitution of adoptive parent for birth parent.[26] As the Oregon Supreme Court explained in the early 1950s:

> When the adoption took place, a new status in the life of the child was created; its care, nurture, well-being, and all the incidents of parenthood . . . devolved upon the adoptive parents. Old ties were severed and it was off with the old, and on with the new, so to speak.[27]

The policies behind this total severance sought to advance the well-being of adoptive children, as it was then conceptualised, as well as the authority of adoptive parents. A 1937 Maryland decision explained that adoption statutes do not contemplate that 'an adoptive infant would be subject . . . to the conflicting authority or custody of the natural and adoptive parents'.[28]

[25] See L Caplan, *An Open Adoption* (Boston, Houghton Mifflin, 1990).

[26] For an account of 'outlaw' open adoption in the days of closed adoption, see B Yngvesson, 'Negotiating Motherhood: Identity and Difference in "Open" Adoptions' (1997) 31 *Law & Society Review* 31.

[27] *Whetmore v Fratello*, 252 P 2d 1083 (OR 1953).

[28] *Spencer v Franks*, 195 A 306 (MD 1937).

In the 1980s, however, courts began to take account of developing shifts in law and in sentiment regarding open adoption, and they began to reassess the nonenforceability of visitation agreements. Most of the cases from the period involved mothers who had existing relationships with their children prior to the adoption; the adopted children were children, not newborns, who had lived with their birth mothers for some time. A 1983 Maryland decision upheld a written agreement between the natural mother (Sally) and her former husband and his new wife (Shirley). Sally had consented to Shirley's adoption of the children on the understanding that 'Sally's right to visitation is an integral part of this Agreement'.[29] When Shirley later withheld visitation, Sally sought to have the arrangement enforced. Characterising the agreement as 'unusual', the court noted that '[b]eing unusual . . . does not make it illegal, against public policy, or contrary to the best interests of the child'.[30] Nothing in Maryland's adoption statute 'purport[s] to mandate that the adoptive parents and the natural parents may not under any circumstance agree to visitation privileges by the natural parents'.[31]

A Connecticut court reached the same conclusion in 1988, upholding a visitation agreement between a natural mother and her four-year-old son.[32] The court found that the agreement had been 'openly and lovingly negotiated, in good faith, in order to promote the best interest of the child' and that the child herself thought the agreement between her mother and her soon-to-be adoptive parents would be 'the best world that she could imagine'.[33] Noting that Connecticut had a general statute authorising third party visitation when in the best interests of a child, the court concluded that: 'It would be elevating form over substance to allow the plaintiff to obtain visitation rights by filing an appropriate "application" in the Superior Court, but to deny her the opportunity to seek such rights under a contractual umbrella.'[34] And in *Groves v Clark*, the Montana Supreme Court made clear that 'natural parents and prospective adoptive parents may contract for post-adoption visitation' and that when in the best interests of the adopted child, such agreements 'should be enforced'.[35] In that case, Debbie Groves had consented to the adoption of her four-year-old daughter Laci by Lonn and Loralee Clark upon the express condition that the Clarks sign a visitation agreement. This they did: 'We, Lon and Loralee Clark, are willing to honor Debbie Groves' wishes regarding her requests for contact with Laci Lee Groves.'[36] When the Clarks cut off visitation,

[29] *Weinschel v Strople*, 56 Md App 252, 257 (1983).
[30] ibid 261–62.
[31] ibid 263.
[32] *Michaud v Wawruck*, 551 A 2d 738, 742 (CT 1988).
[33] ibid.
[34] ibid 741.
[35] *Groves v Clark*, 920 P 2d 981, 985 (MT 1996).
[36] ibid 982.

Debbie sought enforcement. In remanding the case for a best interests determination, the Court carefully underscored the nature of Debbie's claim. It was not premised on 'an ongoing *genetic* relationship that somehow survives a termination of parental rights and an adoption', but rather on a continued *contractual* right to visit a child with whom she had an ongoing relationship.[37]

Such decisions took a broader, more contemporary view of the best interests of adopted children and of the nature of American families. The Connecticut Supreme Court observed that it was 'not prepared to assume that the welfare of children is best served by a narrow definition of those whom we permit to continue to manifest their deep concern for the child's growth and development'.[38] Courts further acknowledged a relationship between postadoption visitation and a birth mother's decision to place her child in the first place: visitation agreements do 'not appear to run counter to public policy inasmuch as [they] will not ordinarily impede adoptions, but might even foster them in cases where the natural parent and adoptive parent are known to each other and the natural parent is reluctant to yield all contact with his or her child'.[39]

Open adoption has also had implications for inter-racial adoption, the subject of the Macaulays' article. In 1992, two-year-old FH, an Indian child, was adopted by the Hartleys, a non-Indian couple. FH's birth mother had voluntarily relinquished her parental rights to the Hartleys upon the condition that she and the birth family retain contact and visitation rights with FH. Although the birth mother supported adoption by the Hartleys, the Native Village of Noatak, a registered Indian tribe, sought to have the adoption set aside as a violation of the Indian Child Welfare Act (ICWA). The ICWA provides a hierarchy of placement preferences for Indian adopted children, starting with members of the child's extended family, then with other members of the child's tribe, and finally with any other Indian family.[40] Nonetheless, the trial court found that on these facts there was good cause to deviate from the ICWA placement preferences. Not only was there an established bond between the Hartleys and FH, but also because the adoption was open in character, the arrangement gave the birth mother access to FH, thereby 'possibly giving FH exposure to her Native American heritage'.[41]

Yet not all courts were convinced about enforcing visitation agreements. In 2000, the Rhode Island Supreme Court determined that a postadoption visitation agreement ('one visit a year with the mom') was *not* specifically

[37] ibid 985.
[38] *Michaud* (n 32) 742.
[39] *Weinschel* (n 29) 262.
[40] Indian Child Welfare Act, 25 USC § 1915 (1988).
[41] *In re Adoption of FH*, 851 P 2d 1361, 1363 (AK 1993); see also *In re Vito*, 728 NE 2d 292 (MA 2000).

enforceable. Because open adoption legislation had been enacted shortly after the adoption in question, the court agreed that such agreements were 'not necessarily repugnant to public policy'.[42] Nonetheless, the Court concluded that because the new legislation was unambiguously non-retroactive in application, 'all the respondent's parental rights were obliterated and any alleged agreement vanished'.[43] The New Jersey Supreme Court similarly declined to uphold a visitation agreement, finding that the agreement was intended only to 'enable' the birth mother to be a part of the baby's life, but it did not *require* an ongoing relationship between the two.[44] In so holding, the Court observed that the New Jersey legislature had recently declined to enact a postadoption visitation statute, noting further that: 'Courts have differed with respect to the clarity and strength of public policy on the issue of "open adoptions" under their respective statutory schemes.'[45]

III. POSTADOPTION VISITATION STATUTES

In the last 20 years, states have significantly revised their statutory schemes regarding open adoption in general and postadoption visitation in particular. By 2009, 24 states had enacted laws providing for some form of enforceable agreement between birth parents and adoptive parents.[46] While the statutes differ in interesting ways, each provides that postadoption visitation agreements are legal so long as the agreement is in writing and approved by the court, most often by being incorporated into the final order of adoption. The statutes also specify the type of contact that may be agreed to. These include actual visitation, the sharing of information (identifying or non-identifying), and other forms of communication such as letters and photographs; the parties may exchange information directly or through an adoption agency.

The statutes also clarify who may seek visitation with an adopted child. All include the birth parents, but several include other birth relatives, such as siblings and grandparents, aunts and uncles; Minnesota permits visitation by foster parents. When the adopted child is an Indian child, three states – California, Minnesota and Oklahoma – provide that members of the child's *tribe* may seek visitation. States also specify which *children* can be the subject of a postadoption visitation agreement. While most statutes apply to *any* adopted child, Connecticut and Nebraska permit

[42] *In re Alicia S*, 763 A2d 643, 646 (RI 2000).
[43] ibid 647.
[44] *Adoption of Child by DH and SH*, 641 A2d 235 (NJ 1994).
[45] ibid 244.
[46] For an overview, see 'Postadoption Contact Agreements Between Birth and Adoptive Families: Summary of State Laws' (*Child Welfare Information Gateway* May 2011) www.childwelfare.gov/systemwide/laws_policies/statutes/cooperative.cfm.

visitation only with children adopted from foster care; Indiana limits coverage to foster children who are two and over. In this way, some states distinguish between older children who are more likely to have known their birth families and newborns who are not.

Anticipating that visitation may not always go smoothly, a number of postadoption visitation statutes require the parties to participate in mediation before they may seek specific performance in court. Importantly, at the time enforcement is sought, the court must determine whether visitation is in the child's best interests,[47] and a few provide that the court may consider the wishes of older children, if 12 years or older (Arizona and Louisiana); in New Hampshire, Oregon and Virginia, if over 14 years.

A 2010 Louisiana case highlights how this is all supposed to work. The postadoption visitation agreement 'clearly and unambiguously' stated that the grandparents were granted permanent care and custody of the children subject to 'reasonable supervised visitation by the birth parents, to be supervised by the court should the parties be unable to agree to the visitation schedule'.[48] Noting that '[w]hen the words of a contract are clear and explicit and lead to no absurd consequences, the intent of the parties is to be determined by the words of the contract', the court ordered that the provisions of the consent judgment be enforced according to its terms. The new contractual arrangements reflect new family structures. For example, in *Adoption of SKLH*, an Alaska teenager agreed to the adoption of her new baby by the teen's own father and her stepmother, having bargained with them for liberal postadoption visitation.[49] In upholding the adoption, the Court noted that 'the child's living situation will tend to foster the kind of open adoption that must have been contemplated: (1) the parties live in a small community; (2) the child will be raised by her biological grandparents; . . . and (4) Donna will be the child's adoptive sister as well as biological mother'.[50] The court noted that in this case, the adoptive parents were keeping two baby books for the child, one reflecting the child's biological parents and the other, its adoptive family.

The fairly widespread enactment of these statutes, the variety of contracts entered under their auspices, and the developing case law make clear that open adoption is now a familiar and expected part of adoption practice and culture. It is the subject of workshops and continuing education programs put on by lawyers who specialise in the area, and it is a

[47] See, eg *In the Interest of CS*, 49 So 3d 38 (La App 2010) (holding that '[w]hen the words of a contract are clear and explicit and lead to no absurd consequences, the intent of the parties is to be determined by the words of the contract' and that 'therefore the provisions of the consent judgment should be enforced according to its terms'; ibid at 43); see also *In the Matter of Heidi E*, 889 NYS2d 762 (NY App Div 2009) (remanding the case to the Family Court for a determination on whether or not an annual visit was detrimental to the child).

[48] *In the Interest of CS* (n 47) 43.

[49] *Adoption of SKLH*, 24 P3d 320 (AK 2009).

[50] ibid 333.

ubiquitous feature on adoption agency websites.[51] Indeed, most adoptions in the US are now open in some respect. Details from a set of actual agreements give the individualised flavour of the bargains: 'The Adopting Parents . . . shall provide the Maternal Aunt with a "letter of update" two times year describing the minor's adjustment, developmental progress and any significant achievements'; the parties 'shall utilize "Skype" as a method of contact every other month for the first seven (7) years of the Child's life'; 'Birth Mother agrees to not put any photos, now or forever, on Facebook or other public website without the written permission of the Adoptive Parents'.[52]

Postadoption visitation agreements provide a way to formally secure the interests and preferences of birth mothers and of adoptive parents. The birth mother, in most cases unmarried, recognises that the demands of motherhood are too much for her at this stage in her life. At the same time, she doesn't want to abort (or perhaps it is too late to do so legally). Adoption presents itself as a possibility that is at once sensible, maternal (doing what is best for the baby), and altruistic (making the adoptive couple very happy). Even so, 'giving away one's baby' may still be unsettling, especially when keeping a non-marital child has in recent years become acceptable as a social matter. To reject motherhood, become a 'legal stranger' to one's child, knowing that the child is out there somewhere, is for some women a hard bargain indeed.

Open adoption softens the situation. With a postadoption visitation agreement in place, the birth mother may no longer be the child's legal mother, but neither is she a stranger at law. She can do what she herself acknowledges as the right thing by providing her child with loving and able parents while preserving a bond for herself that is no longer legally parental, but is still meaningful. Even so, her decision is understood as difficult and she herself is understood to be doing something close to heroic. This sense of valour is emphasised on adoption agency websites. As one birth mother testimonial on the Catholic Charities adoption website states: 'Giving up my little angel for adoption was the hardest thing I've ever done.'[53]

Adoptive parents are also understood to benefit. As already noted, open adoption appears to make placing one's newborn significantly more attractive than keeping it, so that the practice secures, or at least contributes to, an on-going supply of desirable newborns. From a developmental

[51] See, eg M Goldstein, 'Post-Adoption Contact Agreements Can Lead to Shorter Time in Foster Care' (Healing Connections conference by the New York State Citizens' Coalition for Children, Albany, May 2011) (available at nysccc.org/conference/2011conference/2011-workshop-handouts/).

[52] Four redacted contracts are available at nysccc.org/conference/2011conference/2011-workshop-handouts/ as PAC Examples A, B, C and D.

[53] Catholic Charities, 'Pregnant?' (*Adoption – Catholic Charities USA*, 2011) www.catholiccharitiesusa.org/page.aspx?pid=1667.

viewpoint, open adoption benefits the adoptive parents and their child. The parents accept, as evidenced by their willingness to choose a birth mother seeking open adoption, that transparency about origins is good for their soon-to-be child and that it will not threaten their own status as legal parents.[54] Finally, open adoption provides the adoptive parents with a keen understanding of the birth mother's regard for her child. After watching the birth mother of his adoptive son 'crumple into a ball sobbing' when adoptive father Dan Savage and his partner left the hospital with their new baby, Savage explains 'the logic of open adoption, its absolute necessity':

> In a closed adoption, we wouldn't have witnessed the moment our son's mother gave him up . . . Because of open adoption, we'll be able to sit him down and tell him about this one day. We'll be able to describe the moment Melissa gave him to us, and how hard it was for her. We won't have to guess at what it was like or tell him that we're sure his mother loved him. We know she loved him; we saw it.[55]

The law too is fairly satisfied. Postadoption visitation agreement statutes accommodate both private and public interests by facilitating the preferences of birth parents and adoptive parents while retaining the court's traditional supervisory role over the welfare of the child. To return to the idea of acquiring children, the agreements both create and preserve parent–child relationships. Indeed, the preservation appears to be what makes the creation possible. Postadoption visitation agreement statutes provide the background law against which the mother's voluntary relinquishment and her assurance of contact take place.[56] One might say that the agreements are to adoption what prenuptial agreements are to marriage. They are a species of contract that facilitate the primary relationship – whether wedlock or parenthood – and that make the acquisition of relatives – whether spouses or children – possible. If the adoptive parents renege, the birth mother can seek specific performance, unless of course the court finds visitation is not in the child's best interest. This all sounds very good, very promising.

Yet, things are seldom what they seem. Postadoption contact agreements may not be skimmed milk but neither, on closer inspection, are they always cream. That is because it turns out that unwed pregnant girls who are not quite ready for motherhood – young women regarded sympathetically,

[54] C Macaskill, *Safe Contact?: Children in Permanent Placement and Their Birth Relatives* (Lyme Regis, Russell House, 2002).

[55] D Savage, *The Kid: What Happened After My Boyfriend and I Decided to Go Get Pregnant* (New York, Plume, 2000) 215–16. For a fictional account of the problems created when the adoptive parents have nothing to tell their child, see E Gasco, *Can You Wave Bye, Bye, Baby?* (Toronto, McClelland & Stewart, 1999).

[56] For a discussion of the role of contract law attempting to stabilise the market in the case of children acquired through reproductive surrogacy, see C Sanger, 'Developing Markets in Baby-Making: *In the Matter of Baby M*' (2007) 30 *Harvard Journal of Law and Gender* 67, 80.

even perhaps gratefully – are not the *only* women who enter into post-adoption visitation agreements. This is where our story becomes more complicated and my celebration of contract as the special relational glue that only law can provide becomes somewhat messier.

IV. A HARDER LOOK

Although the imagined poster girl for open adoption may be the white, unwed, college-bound student who struggles with her decision but ultimately does the right thing by her baby, it turns out that many of the cases seeking enforcement of postadoption visitation agreements are brought by women with a very different profile. These are women who never wanted to relinquish their children for adoption in the first place, but whose children have been removed by the state on account of abuse or neglect. These are women whose parental rights the state seeks to terminate *involuntarily*.

And here a shadow set of legal rules surface and come into play. The first and crucial rule is this: involuntary termination *permanently* and comprehensively severs the legal parent–child relationship. However, if a negligent or abusive mother agrees to terminate her parental rights *voluntarily*, then she too can bargain for some form of contact under the postadoption visitation statutes. Indeed, it turns out that many mothers facing involuntary termination are advised by their social workers or attorneys to do exactly that. In her study of parental termination cases over a 10 year period in St Joseph's County, Indiana, law professor Hillary Baldwin concludes that 'knowing that a termination petition is imminent, and feeling as if they probably will not win', many parents decide to give up their children for adoption rather than have them taken away. 'Voluntary termination gives the parent his only chance to work out a postadoption visitation agreement. If the termination proceeds involuntarily, the parents risks never seeing the child again.'[57] In Baldwin's study, in only three of 303 termination cases brought by the state did the parent retain his or her child. Baldwin observes that: 'If statistically a parent's chance is less than one per cent that the court will dismiss an open termination case, word will get around.'[58] (I will return to the question of why so few mothers prevail in their attempts to keep their children.)

As might be expected in these more complicated cases – more complicated if only because there is a longer familial history – visitation does not always work out as planned, and adoptive parents may cut off or suspend

[57] H Baldwin, 'Termination of Parental Rights: Statistical Study and Proposed Solutions' (2002) 28 *Journal of Legislation* 239, 274.

[58] ibid 274.

visitation. Reasons have included on-going maternal drug problems,[59] missed visitation,[60] or simply that visitation is no longer thought to be in the child's best interests. In a 2006 Massachusetts case, a court found that because 'unexpectedly (and happily)' an adoptive home had been found for the children and they were adjusting well to the adoptive home and parents, it was not in their best interests to continue visitation with their biological mother.[61]

The remedy these disappointed mothers tend to seek, however, is not specific enforcement of the visitation agreement but rescission of the entire deal. They want to revoke their consent to the entire adoption and have their own parental rights restored. This makes some sense in that these mothers never wanted to have their children adopted in the first place; voluntary termination was a means of avoiding the dire consequences of involuntary termination. Their argument is that the voluntary termination of those rights was expressly conditioned on ongoing visitation and absent that, the entire arrangement is off. The case is put clearly in *Re Joe*, a 2005 California case: The natural mother 'claims she is entitled to reversal of the order terminating parental rights because she did not get what she bargained for, namely [an enforceable] postadoption contact agreement'.[62] The mother argued that she 'forfeited her right to a contested hearing as to whether the court should terminate her parental rights in return for a valid and enforceable postadoption contact agreement'.[63]

Here the formation process – the exact circumstances under which the postadoption visitation agreement was entered – becomes key. Under state adoption laws, once an adoption is final, the only grounds for the revocation of parental consent are the traditional equitable defences of fraud, mistake, undue influence and misrepresentation. As we shall see, these defences are seldom successful. But their success seems to depend in part on just what kind of mother is seeking to overturn the adoption. We see this in a comparison of two Texas cases, the first involving a good girl gone temporarily wrong; the second involving a mother who failed her protect her baby from abuse.

In *Vela v Marywood*, the 19-year-old, unmarried birth mother Corina sought to rescind her consent to the surrender of her infant.[64] While pregnant, Corina had gone to Marywood, a licensed adoption agency, to learn about adoption. Her Marywood 'maternity counselor' explained that in an open adoption, Corina would 'always be the child's birth mother'; that

[59] *In re Judicial Surrender of Daijuanna Priscilla M*, 735 NYS 2d 544 (NY App Div 2002).
[60] *Adoption of Mya VP*, 913 NYS 2d 477 (NY App Div 2010).
[61] *Adoption of Edgar*, 853 NE 2d 1068, 1074 (Mass App 2006).
[62] *In re Joe C*, No F047570, 2005 WL 2008461, at *2 (Cal Ct App Aug 22, 2005).
[63] ibid.
[64] *Vela v Marywood*, 17 SW3d 750 (Tex App 2000).

she would 'always have a relationship with her [child]'; that the baby would have 'two mothers', 'both of whom would have input into his life'; and that that the birth family would be 'like the child's extended family'.[65] Corina and her mother testified that these representations were 'the only reason' she signed the relinquishment affidavit surrendering her parental rights. The Court held that as a matter of law, Marywood's 'statements and omissions to Corina constituted misrepresentation, fraud, or overreaching'.[66] This was so in part because Marywood's close counseling relationship with Corina created a fiduciary relationship. Marywood was therefore bound 'in equity and good conscience' to act in good faith and to fully disclose that the 'shared parenting plan' had no legal effect at all.[67] Throughout the decision, the Court radiates sympathy, even fondness, for Corina and her family. She is introduced in the second line as 'an exemplary young woman who made a mistake', and a paragraph is devoted to her record of community service, her strong and supportive parents, and testimony characterising Corina as 'the envy of all the mothers in the neighborhood'.[68]

But not all birth mothers are regarded so warmly and it is worth figuring out why and where the boundaries are set. With that in mind, I return to a 2009 Texas case, *In the Interests of DEH*.[69] DEH was six months old when she was removed from her unmarried parents on grounds of abuse: the baby had been beaten by her father and suffered two fractures to each femur, four fractures to each tibia, multiple rib fractures, a liver contusion, and a spleen laceration. DEH was placed in foster care, and the Texas Department of Family and Protective Services moved to terminate the parental rights of the father and of the baby's mother, EL. The father's rights were involuntarily terminated, but following a mediation with her attorney and the baby's pre-adoptive foster parents, EL agreed to relinquish her parental rights and entered into a post-termination agreement with the foster parents. A month later, EL sought to have her consent withdrawn on the grounds of fraud, duress and coercion. Her claim was that she had been told that if the termination case against her went to trial, 'the likely outcome was that she would never see [her child] again' and that her only other option was to sign the affidavit of relinquishment and enter into an agreement for limited visitation.[70] As EL put it, she had 'no way out'.[71]

[65] ibid 755.
[66] ibid 763.
[67] ibid 761.
[68] ibid 753; see also *Jones v Texas Dept of Protective and Regulatory Services*, 85 SW 3d 483 (Tex App 2002).
[69] *In the Interest of DEH*, 301 SW 3d 825 (Tex App 2009).
[70] ibid 830.
[71] ibid 831.

Each of these defences proved a loser. After reviewing the evidence, the Court concluded that EL 'failed to demonstrate by a preponderance of the evidence that signing the affidavit in exchange for an allegedly legally unenforceable promise resulted from fraud, duress, or coercion'.[72] Coercion, the Court explained, 'occurs if someone is compelled to perform an act by threat or force'; duress occurs when 'a person is incapable of exercising her free will'; fraud has five elements, which the court then listed. But as the court detailed, EL had legal counsel, took advice from her family, and had been told that the visitation agreement was not 'a contract that we could take to court'.[73] The process was not rushed; as EL's attorney, testified: 'The judge spoke . . . Spanish, so . . . we would kind of back off and say, we would kind of rest for a little while and the family would talk. It went really slowly.' The affidavit of relinquishment was translated and read to EL at least twice before she signed it. It stated: 'I REALIZE THAT I SHOULD NOT SIGN THIS AFFIDAVIT OF RELINQUISHMENT IF THERE IS ANY THOUGHT IN MY MIND THAT I MIGHT SOMEDAY SEEK TO CHANGE MY MIND . . . BECAUSE I REALIZE HOW IMPORTANT THIS DECISION IS FOR THE FUTURE OF MY CHILD, I HAVE PUT MY INITIALS BESIDE EVERY LINE OF THIS PARAGRAPH SO THAT IT WILL ALWAYS BE UNDERSTOOD THAT I HAVE READ THIS AFFIDAVIT OF RELINQUISHMENT, UNDERSTAND IT, AND DESIRE TO SIGN IT.' Although witnesses testified as to EL's anguish and fear at the possibility of losing all contact with her child, EL's own attorney testified that the pressure on her was not 'undue'; it was 'just a very emotional time'.[74]

Other attempts in other cases to prove duress, fraud, misrepresentation or coercion have been similarly unsuccessful.[75] In a 2009 case, the birth mother argued her consent should be set aside on the ground of mutual mistake.[76] Her child had been removed by the state on grounds of neglect; when he was eight, the mother agreed to his adoption by her aunt and uncle. The parties had agreed that 'should' the adoption with the aunt and uncle be finalised, the mother would have continuing contact rights, but the agreement had not been incorporated into the formal relinquishment signed by the mother. (The mother had signed and faxed the agreement to the aunt and uncle who never returned it.) When the adoption fell

[72] *DEH* (n 69) 832.

[73] ibid.

[74] ibid 831.

[75] See *In re Daijvanna Priscilla*, 290 AD 2d 298 (NY App Div 2002). (No fraud because no evidence that adoptive mother never intended to permit visitation by natural mother and so entered agreement in bad faith; rather, adoptive mother withdrew consent to visitation due to natural mother's 'undisclosed drug abuse'); *In re Termination of Parent-Child Relationship of KV v IDCS*, 946 NE2d 655 (Ind App 2011) (although evidence showed that all parties 'contemplated that post-adoption visitation between Mother and KV might be a possibility', postadoption privileges were never guaranteed and mother's consent was not obtained under duress nor was her free will overcome at the time she signed the consent).

[76] *In re Christopher G*, 984 A 2d 1111 (Con App 2009).

though, the mother sought to set aside the termination of her parental rights on the grounds that she would never have agreed to terminate had she known that an open adoption with her aunt and uncle would not follow. The court rejected the claim on the ground that her decision was 'voluntary and free from force or threat' and that she 'understood her consent could not be withdrawn' once accepted by the court. The court also held that there was no evidence that any mistake regarding the conditional nature of the agreement to terminate was mutual; although the parties may have *anticipated* an adoption by the aunt and uncle, the record did not support the argument that the mother's consent was conditional on the existence of open adoption with them.[77]

Claims of fraud based on the failure (of someone) to properly file the postadoption visitation agreement arise with some regularity. In a 2011 California case, *Carla M v Susan E*, the birth mother (Carla) brought an action in fraud to rescind her consent to the adoption and to reestablish her own parental rights. Carla explained that the adoptive parents had failed to file the visitation agreement with the court, as required by California law. Carla argued that she would not have relinquished the baby without the assurance of visitation, which she thought she had secured by *signing* the agreement.[78] (The agreement, signed by both parties, stated, 'We all understand that [this] is not a legally binding document, except . . . when filed with the court at the time of the finalization of the adoption.'[79]) The court upheld the trial court's finding that there had been no fraud: there was no evidence that the adoptive parents had reason to believe that birth mother expected them to file the agreement or that it was important to her.[80] In addition, stated the court, because the adoptive parents were not in a fiduciary relationship with the birth mother, they had no duty to file the agreement.

Yet a closer look at the facts suggests why in this most relational of agreements- – the creation of a new family and the dismantling of an existing one – a birth mother might well have plausible, if unactionable, expectations about the bargain she has entered. In *Carla M v Susan E*, Carla contacted the adoptive mother Susan only after she had read Susan's 'Dear Birth Mother' letter at the adoption agency. The letter stated: 'We admire your courage and love in considering open adoption. If you choose to do this, you will be part of our lives forever.'[81] The parties then

[77] ibid1115.

[78] *Carla M v Susan E*, WL 2739649 (Cal App 2011).

[79] The specific contact agreed was the provision of photographs to the birth mother twice a year, an annual visit between birth parents and the child, and that both birth parents and adoptive parents could initiate phone contact with the other.

[80] See also *In re Termination of Parent-Child Relationship of KV* (n 75) (although mother was told that if she voluntarily relinquished rights, she would get visitation, the court found no fraud when she did not).

[81] *Carla M* (n 78) *1.

met and over the next two months, developed a close friendship, were in near daily contact with one another, and were even filmed for a programme on open adoption for the Discovery Health Channel. At the same time as all this familiarity was shaping up, however, Susan notified the adoption agency that she and her husband would not sign any visitation agreement that was legally binding and would not go through with the adoption if required to do so. The agency's adoption counselor then told Susan that if they signed a Preliminary Agreement, they would not have to file the official form. It is not hard to imagine that Carla might have misunderstood the importance of formal filing, especially against the background of the encouraging promise in Susan's 'Dear Birth Mother' letter.

A 2002 Nevada case similarly turned on the issue of filing.[82] Here too, the birth mother relinquished her parental rights, having entered into a 'communication agreement' with the adoptive parents drafted by their adoption agency. When the birth mother sought to overturn the adoption, the adoptive parents then denied all contact. The birth mother then sued for specific performance of the agreement. The district court granted the adoptive parents motion to dismiss on the grounds that state law (at the time) did not provide for agreements regarding visitation or contact to be enforced independently as contracts. Unless such an agreement was incorporated into the final adoption decree (this one was not), 'a natural parent has no rights to the child'.[83] Yet while holding that the birth mother had no basis for relief, the Court paused to note that:

> This decision leads to an unsatisfactory result in that natural parents may consent to an adoption because, pursuant to an agreement, they believe they have a right to post-adoption contact with the child. However, what they natural parents fail to realize is that, if the agreement is not incorporated in the adoption decree, their rights as to the child are terminated upon adoption and any contact with the child may be had only upon the adoptive parents' permission, regardless of the agreement.[84]

[82] *Birth Mother v Adoptive Parents*, 59 P 3d 1233 (NV 2002); see also *Fast v Moore*, 135 P 3d 387 (Or App 2006) (visitation agreement found unenforceable because it wasn't court-approved at time of adoption).

[83] Whether a postadoption visitation agreement is incorporated into the final decree of adoption also has constitutional significance, should the adoptive parents relocate from one state to another. In a North Carolina case, the birth mother and adoptive parents entered into an agreement in Florida that was not incorporated in the Florida final decree. *Quets v Needham*, 682 SE2d 214 (NC 2009). The birth mother sought to have the agreement enforced in North Carolina, where the adoptive parents had moved, on the grounds that North Carolina was required to give Full Faith and Credit to the Florida adoption decree. However, since the agreement was not part of the decree, it was regarded merely a private contract entered into in another state and therefore entitled to specific enforcement by a North Carolina court only as a matter of comity. Because postadoption visitation agreements were then unenforceable in North Carolina, comity was not required. ibid 223.

[84] *Birth Mother* (n 82) 1235–36.

The dissent put the case even more forcefully. Declaring the result to be 'patently unfair', Judge Rose observed that: 'The enforcement of the adoption agreement without also recognizing the contract provision leaves the biological parent with an adoption she or he never would have agreed to otherwise. We should not permit birth parents to be so misled.'[85]

Some of the problem – the problem of mothers not grasping the significance of the incorporation of their agreement with adoptive parents into the final adoption decree – may stem from the somewhat confusing and opaque structure of the entire arrangement. Open adoption is not one transaction, but several, each with a distinct (though interrelated) significance. There is the relinquishment of the natural mother's parental rights to the state or licensed agency; there is the agreement between the natural mother and the adoptive parents; there is final decree issued by the court, and into which the private agreement must be properly folded. Certainly the first two of these are often executed at or around the same time, though each has its own requirements and protocols. For example, the relinquishment must contain clear and conspicuous language of its irrevocability, often to be separately acknowledged by the mother through her initials or signature. Yet it is not hard to understand how a birth mother might think that the irrevocability that has been so pointedly brought to her attention applies to the obligations undertaken by *all* parties to the transaction. She has foresworn her parental rights forever, but the adoptive parents have also made what might seem a binding promise. Civilians, which is to say, most of us most of the time, do not dwell on the technical aspects of our legal decisions, though divorce and custody matters aside, I suspect we rarely face the circumstance of severing ties permanently with a child. In agreeing to terminate her parental rights, the birth mother may have done the hardest thing imaginable, and not understand that there is more to secure or supervise, and that her consent to termination is really the only thing that will stick.

VI. AN APTER ANALOGY

In light of all this, I want to make a substitution in my earlier analogy. I suggested at the outset that postadoption visitation agreements were rather like prenuptial agreements. Both contracts made the desired, underlying endeavour – marriage and parenthood – possible by fleshing out and settling terms of particular importance to the parties. Having looked more closely at the case law and roughed out the edges of how this all works in practice, I now think that the more accurate analogy, certainly in the subset of cases involving mothers facing termination of their parental rights, is not

[85] ibid 1236–37.

between postadoption visitation agreements and prenups, but rather between postadoption visitation agreements and *plea bargains*.[86]

Like plea bargains, voluntary relinquishments, are necessarily hard decisions made under hard circumstances. As one mother testified in her unsuccessful attempt to rescind her consent:

> I thought I was . . . actually, I don't know exactly what I was doing. All I know is that I wanted to see [AY], and that I'm continuing to see . . . I was told if I . . . if I didn't sign them and [the trial court] took my rights, I would never see her, and if I did sign them I could. This . . . I wasn't really . . . I don't know. I wasn't thinking right. I just wanted her to be happy, and I wanted her to be with me.[87]

Like prisoners rolling the dice with regard to their liberty, mothers who are about to lose their children have a very small range in which to operate, and their odds are even worse. As in the Indiana county studied by Professor Baldwin, three out of 300 mothers prevailed in preventing the involuntarily termination of their parental rights in actions brought by the state. Mothers understand the odds, and know they will either lose all contact with their children forever under an involuntary termination, or they can negotiate some form of contact or communication under a voluntary relinquishment and hope that nothing ever happens that is found to be contrary to the child's best interest that might cause the part of the deal they care about to be set aside.

Plea bargaining and voluntary relinquishment share another crucial feature in common: each implicates due process concerns. In the criminal context, the defendant agrees to waive his right to a jury trial in exchange for the prosecutor's promise of an agreed upon sentencing recommendation to the court.[88] In the family context, the mother who relinquishes her parental rights has waived the hearing that is otherwise required if the state seeks to terminate those same rights involuntarily.[89] (Indeed, in enacting its postadoption visitation statute, the State of Maryland noted that avoiding termination hearings through voluntary relinquishment might result in 'significant savings in the cost of litigation related to adoption cases . . . For illustrative purposes only, based on the average cost of a

[86] Indeed, voluntary termination has aspects of charge bargaining (the state withdraws its involuntarily termination petition) and sentence bargaining (in exchange for her consent, the mother gets some limited contact instead of none), and even of a recommendation plea in that the departments of social services seem to recommend to the adoptive parents that the agreement become part of the order, and recommend to the court that the order be granted as in the child's best interest.

[87] *Youngblood v Jefferson County Division of Family and Children*, 838 NE2d 1164 (Ind App 2006).

[88] For an expanded contractual analysis, see R Scott and W Stuntz, 'Plea Bargaining as Contract' (1992) 101 *Yale Law Journal* 1909. For the view that the contractual analysis is small potatoes, see S Schulhofer, 'Plea Bargaining as Disaster' (1992) 101 *Yale Law Journal* 1981.

[89] *Stanley v Illinois*, 405 US 645, 651 (1972); *MLB v SLJ*, 519 US 102, 104 (1996) ('parental status termination is irretrievably destructive of the most fundamental family relationship').

permanent placement for a child of $600 per month, if 100 children achieved placement six months earlier than otherwise would have occurred under current law, the Judiciary could achieve savings of $360,000 annually.'[90] Of course, the fiscal consequence of maternal waivers is but an incidental benefit to the state.)

Our concern here is the process by which the waiver is obtained, a concern raised by the dissent in the Texas *DEH* case. Recall that unlike the sympathetic Corina, the most unsympathetic EL was not able to unwind her relinquishment. But as dissenting Justice Terrie Livingston stated, the involuntary termination of parental rights is a decision of constitutional significance. The evidence regarding the knowing and voluntary nature of the consent should therefore be 'clear and convincing'. Justice Livingston noted that in *DEH*, EL's Spanish speaking therapist testified that EL 'signed the agreement because she thought it was irrevocable and that it would ensure her lifetime visitation'.[91] There were also indications that the Department of Family and Protective Services (DFPS) was less than forthcoming in its role in the process and about who said what when. For example, the DFPS attorney testified that 'EL was not misled into believing any promises were given to her by the Department at any time. We were not part of any of the mediations proceedings in that we were not in the room with her.'[92]

Attempting to rescind the relinquishment of one's parental rights is akin to attempts to withdraw a plea bargain after the deal is done. There are a few cases where guilty pleas have been withdrawn. In *State v Nichols*, for example, the court held that

> where the responsible arms of the judicial and law enforcement establishment, together with defendant's own counsel, have misinformed him as to a material element of a plea negotiation, which the defendant has relied thereon in entering his plea, as we conclude was here the case, it would be manifestly unjust to hold the defendant to his plea.[93]

More typical, however, is *Allen v State*.[94] There the Delaware Supreme Court held that a defendant who sought to withdraw his guilty plea because both his public defender and the trial court judge misinformed him about the range of punishment he should expect if convicted at trial (they told him three to 30 years when the range was three to 15 years) had 'failed to demonstrate prejudice amounting to manifest injustice'.[95] So too

[90] Maryland General Assembly Fiscal and Policy Note, SB 710, at 5 (2005).

[91] *DEH* (n 69) 835.

[92] ibid 835–36.

[93] *State v Nichols*, 365 A2d 467 (NJ 1976); see also the US Supreme Court's recent decision in *Missouri v Frye*, 131 S Ct 856 (2011) (holding to meet the standard of effective assistance of counsel, defence counsel must at least inform their clients of any formal offers from the prosecution to accept a plea on terms and conditions that may be favourable to the accused).

[94] *Allen v State*, 509 A2d 87 (DE 1986); see, generally R Scott and W, 'Plea Bargaining as Contract' (1992) 101 *Yale Law Journal* 1909.

[95] *Allen* (n 94) 88.

with parental relinquishment. There are a few cases in which courts have acknowledged the constitutional dimension of postadoption visitation. In *TB v Indiana Department of Child Services*, for example, the state moved for termination of the mother's visitation on grounds of children's best interests, but the mother did not receive notice of the hearing.[96] The Court held this amounted to a denial of her due process rights and remanded the case for a hearing on the merits.

There is one final piece in this picture to consider, and this returns us to a central concern of the 1978 Macaulay article on the role of expert discretion in interracial adoptions. The Macaulays laid out a history of adoption over the twentieth century, focusing particularly on where decision-making authority over interracial adoptions was systemically placed. They conclude that the real authority was not located in the judiciary, but in social workers, who became embedded in the adoption process in the 1920s, first as volunteers with charities and over time as professionals working for newly licenced agencies. As 'best interests of the child' became the industry standard for adoption approval, judges came to rely increasingly on the expertise of social workers as to what that meant in any particular case. The Macaulays argued – and relatively early in the policy debate about the desirability of interracial adoption – that the formal opposition by the National Association of Black Social Workers in the late 1960s was a grave misuse of their professional authority that operated to the detriment of black children in foster care. The Macaulays' objection was not that social workers were unable to evaluate children's best interests, but rather that in this circumstance, the criteria they used were not scientific but ideological.

Expert opinion – or opinion, in any case – also plays an important role in creating the background conditions against which relinquishment decisions are made and postadoption visitation agreements entered. Recall that the reason mothers agree to relinquish their children is that their chances of succeeding at a termination hearing are worse than dismal. Why is this? Part of the answer concerns judicial reliance on the expert opinion of social workers, or more precisely, on the opinions of court appointed guardians ad litem (GALs) or court appointed special advocates (CASAs). But as Hilary Baldwin and others have pointed out, the problem is that these guardians and CASAs are often community volunteers, with little or no training in child development.[97] Their job is to

[96] *TB v Indiana Dept of Child Services*, 921 NE 2d 494 (IN 2009).

[97] G Russ, 'The Child's Right to Be Heard' (1998) 5 *Georgetown Journal on Fighting Poverty* 305, 308 ('[I]n most jurisdictions these individuals are typically not attorneys, they do not have adequate training, and they often do not have any idea what children are all about or how to deal with them.'); H Peterson, 'In Search of the Best Interests of the Child: The Efficacy of the Court Appointed Special Advocate Model of Guardian ad Litem Representation' (2005–06) 13 *George Mason Law Review* 1083, 1083 ('[M]any guardians ad litem have very little training or education in children and families, receive little compensation for their work, and often are reported to provide substandard representation to their child clients').

represent the interests of the child, but as Baldwin shows, their assessments are often based on personal opinion or prejudice.[98] Moreover, studies have shown that many GALs do not even meet with the children whose interests they purport to represent. A 2000 study of Colorado GALs indicated that in 41 per cent of cases, the GAL did not meet with the child; a 2007 study of Ohio GALs, showed that while 90 per cent of attorneys indicated that they nearly always met with the children face-to-face, only 63 per cent of them documented these meetings. Even fewer attorneys observed the child interacting with his or her parents: 82 per cent reported they did so, but only 41 per cent documented these observations.[99] In addition, because the CASAs are regarded as neutral evaluators, rather than as witnesses for the state, they are not subject to cross-examination by the mother's counsel, and their views are most often accepted by judges as the final word on what is best for any particular child.[100] Thus the recommendations of layfolk, well intentioned as they may be, have set the statistical stage – the one per cent success rate reported by Baldwin – that make voluntary relinquishment by mothers facing termination something less than a foolhardy choice.

CONCLUSION

My focus has been on the circumstances under which postadoption visitation agreements are entered and the circumstances under which they are enforced. Whether an analogy to plea bargains or to prenuptial agreements is more apt may be a matter of maternal circumstance. In cases where adoption is actively, even if reluctantly, *sought* by the mother – the heroic birth mother doing the best for everyone – the logic of open adoption is clear. In contrast, in cases where a mother's children have already been removed and termination looms, open adoption and the promise of visitation scan quite differently.

Of course, the cases do not fall so neatly into two distinct piles; there are certainly cases where advantage seems to be taken even of heroic mothers. Although 'good mothers' appear more regularly in infant adoption (and certainly in the marketing literature that now surrounds it), and bad ones appear more regularly in terminations involving older children, the cases are a mix of both. And while coercion seems apparent in the termi-

[98] Baldwin, *Termination of Parental Rights* (n 57) 281–89.

[99] B Glesner Fines, 'Pressures Toward Mediocrity in the Representation of Children' (2008) 37 *Capital University Law Review* 411, 428.

[100] R Lidman and B Hollingsworth, 'The Guardian ad Litem in Child Custody Cases: The Contours of Our Judicial System Stretched Beyond Recognition' (1998) 6 *George Mason Law Review* 255, 257–58 (noting that attorneys warn clients to co-operate with GALs because their recommendations carry such weight with the court).

nation cases, pressure, if not full-out coercion, is often at play in infant adoption too. Yet, it seems clear that there are important differences in how postadoption visitation agreements are used and regarded depending where in the tricky constellation of motherhood the birth mother finds herself. These bargains look one way when sought by birth mothers who have considered their options and are satisfied with the slice of relational association that visitation or progress reports provide. They look quite another for mothers for whom open adoption is simply the least worst choice.

BIBLIOGRAPHY

Baldwin, H, 'Termination of Parental Rights: Statistical Study and Proposed Solutions' (2002) 28 *Journal of Legislation* 239.

Baran, A and Pannor, R, 'Perspectives on Open Adoption' (1983) Spring *Future of Children* 119.

Bremmer, R, *Children and Youth in America*, vol 1 (Cambridge, Harvard University Press, 1970).

Caplan, L, *An Open Adoption* (Boston, Houghton Mifflin, 1990).

Carp, W, *Family Matters: Secrecy and Disclosure in the History of Adoption* (Cambridge, Harvard University Press, 2000).

Catholic Charities, 'Pregnant?' (*Adoption – Catholic Charities USA*, 2011) www.catholiccharitiesusa.org/page.aspx?pid=1667.

Crossen, C, 'In Today's Adoptions, the Biological Parents are Calling the Shots' *The Wall Street Journal* (12 September 1989) A1.

Dayton, C, 'Divorce: The Limits of a Puritan Remedy' in *Women Before the Bar: Gender, Law, and Society in Connecticut* (Chapel Hill, University of North Carolina Press, 1995).

Demos, J, *A Little Commonwealth: Family Life in Plymouth Colony* (Oxford, Oxford University Press, 1970).

Gagoomal, P, 'A "Margin of Appreciation" for "Marriages of Appreciation": Reconciling South Asian Adult Arranged Marriages With the Matrimonial Consent Requirement in International Human Rights Law' (2009) 97 *Georgetown Law Journal* 589.

Gasco, E, *Can You Wave Bye, Bye, Baby?* (Toronto, McClelland & Stewart, 1999).

Glesner Fines, B, 'Pressures Toward Mediocrity in the Representation of Children' (2008) 37 *Capital University Law Review* 411.

Goldstein, M, 'Post-Adoption Contact Agreements Can Lead to Shorter Time in Foster Care' (2011: Healing Connections conference by the New York State Citizens' Coalition for Children, Albany, May 2011).

Grossberg, M, *Governing the Hearth: Law and the Family in Nineteenth-Century America* (Chapel Hill, University of North Carolina Press, 1985).

Hollinger, J, *Adoption Law and Practice* (New York, Matthew Bender, 1997).

'It's a Seller's Market' *Life* (September 1988) 80.

Leesony, P, Boettke, P and Lemke, J, 'Wife Sales' (available at papers.ssrn.com/sol3/papers.cfm?abstract_id=1859387).

Lettmaier, S, *Broken Engagements: The Action for Breach of Promise of Marriage and the Feminine Ideal, 1800–1940* (Oxford, Oxford University Press, 2009).
Lidman, R and Hollingsworth, B, 'The Guardian ad Litem in Child Custody Cases: The Contours of Our Judicial System Stretched Beyond Recognition' (1998) 6 *George Mason Law Review* 255.
Macaskill, C, *Safe Contact?: Children in Permanent Placement and Their Birth Relatives* (Lyme Regis, Russell House, 2002).
Macaulay, J and Macaulay, S, 'Adoption for Black Children: A Case Study of Expert Discretion'in *Research in Law and Sociology: An Annual Compilation of Research* (Greenwich, JAI Press, 1978).
Mason, MA, *From Father's Property to Children's Rights* (New York, Columbia University Press, 1994).
Modell, J, *A Sealed and Secret Kinship: The Culture of Policies and Practices in American Adoption* (New York, Berghahn Books, 2002).
Peterson, H, 'In Search of the Best Interests of the Child: The Efficacy of the Court Appointed Special Advocate Model of Guardian ad Litem Representation' (2005–06) 13 *George Mason Law Review* 1083.
'Postadoption Contact Agreements Between Birth and Adoptive Families: Summary of State Laws' (*Child Welfare Information Gateway* May 2011).
Russ, G, 'The Child's Right to Be Heard' (1998) 5 *Georgetown Journal on Fighting Poverty* 305.
Sanger, C, 'Developing Markets in Baby-Making: *In the Matter of Baby M*' (2007) 30 *Harvard Journal of Law and Gender* 67.
Savage, D, *The Kid: What Happened After My Boyfriend and I Decided to Go Get Pregnant* (New York, Plume, 2000).
Schulhofer, S, 'Plea Bargaining as Disaster' (1992) 101 *Yale Law Journal* 1981.
Scott, R and Stuntz, W, 'Plea Bargaining as Contract' (1992) 101 *Yale Law Journal* 1909.
Suk, J, 'The Moral and Legal Consequences of Wife-Selling in The Mayor of Casterbridge' (Cardozo Legal Studies Research Paper No 327, 2011).
Waldron, J, *Giving Away Simone* (New York, Times Books, 1995).
Yngvesson, B, 'Negotiating Motherhood: Identity and Difference in "Open" Adoptions' (1997) 31 *Law & Society Review* 31.

11

Is There a 'Duty to Read'?

CHARLES L KNAPP

> It is the policy of the law to protect the unwary and foolish as well as the vigilant from the wiles and artifices of evil-doers and negligence in trusting a representation will not, according to the greater weight of authority, excuse a positive willful fraud . . . The party perpetrating the fraud should not be permitted to say that he should not have been believed or trusted.[1]

> How could you believe me when I said I loved you when you know I've been a liar all my life?[2]

INTRODUCTION

THE NOTION THAT there is in general contract law a 'duty to read' persists in the decisions of American courts. That was certainly true in 1966, when Stewart Macaulay wrote his classic article on that subject.[3] In his piece Stewart explored both theoretically and empirically how that principle of a 'duty to read' might be applied, in a particular commercial setting. But it is equally true today, as a rapid run through the last few years of Westlaw reports will quickly demonstrate. In this article, I will explore the question of what it may mean today to say that there is a 'duty to read', and suggest what role (if any) that doctrine should play in our present-day law of contract.

I. STATEMENTS OF THE RULE

The duty to read principle is commonly expressed in American jurisprudence in two ways: as a 'duty', and as a 'presumption'. Although the end

[1] *Rowen Petroleum Properties, LLC v Hollywood Tanning Systems, Inc*, 2009 WL 1085737, *5 (DN), quoting *Peter W Kero, Inc v Terminal Constr Corp*, 78 A 2d 814, 818 (NJ Dist 1951).

[2] AJ Lerner, 'How Could You Believe Me?', *Royal Wedding* (MGM, 1951).

[3] S Macaulay, 'Private Legislation and the Duty to Read – Business Run by IBM Machine, the Law of Contracts and Credit Cards' (1966) 19 *Vanderbilt Law Review* 1051.

result in practice is in most cases likely to be substantially the same, the difference in articulation may nevertheless affect how the legal community thinks about this principle. In this section, I will compare and contrast these two modes of expression.

A. An Implicit Contractual Duty

The 'duty to read', although regarded as a part of contract law, is not a 'duty' imposed *by* contract, but rather a statement about how parties should behave during the contract-making process. Here are some examples of that statement:

> It is beyond cavil that a party accepting an offer has an absolute duty to read and understand the terms of an offer, and failure to do so will not diminish the force and effect of the resulting contract.[4]
>
> A person signing an agreement has a duty to read it and, absent a showing of fraud, if the person is capable of reading and understanding the contract then he is charged with the knowledge of what the contract says . . . He cannot avoid the consequences of what he signed by simply saying that he did not know what he signed.[5]

To consider the implications of such a principle, it is useful to compare the 'duty to read' (DTR) with two other contractual 'duties' that in some ways resemble it: the duty to bargain in good faith; and the duty to mitigate damages.

i. The Duty to Bargain in Good Faith

When it comes to regulating the bargaining process, the common law of contract is traditionally loath to interfere. Certain kinds of conduct are understood as being outside the sphere of acceptable bargaining: duress, misrepresentation and wrongful nondisclosure, undue influence, and the like. These proscriptions are not unique to the common law, as many of them are spelled out or particularised in various kinds of regulatory statutes. Nor are they unique to the law of contract, since the same kind of conduct is liable to render the actor liable in tort. But collectively they represent a set of Marquis of Queensbury rules for bargainers; they locate the belt below which hitting is forbidden. Above the belt, however, anything goes, and the job of contract law traditionally is merely to referee the bout.

The duty to bargain in good faith also applies to the bargaining process, but it is quite a different proposition. At least under the common law of contracts, there is no implied duty to bargain in good faith. Such a duty

[4] *66 VMD Assoc, LLC v Melick-Tully & Assoc*, 2011 WL 3503160, *5 (NJ Super Ct 2010).
[5] *Nunn v CC Midwest*, 151 SW 3d 388, 402 (Mo Ct App 2004).

might be imposed by statute, regulating some sphere of economic activity. But otherwise it arises, if at all, only from the agreement of the parties, either as part of an earlier transaction between them, or – implicitly or explicitly – from their words and actions in the course of working toward a new contractual agreement. Whether it has been breached in a given case may be particularly hard to determine, since bargainers who see themselves as bound by such a duty may be at some pains to create at least the appearance of having bargained in good faith; the remedy for failure to live up to its demands may also be difficult to assess. But in the small proportion of cases in which it does apply, the duty to bargain in good faith typically binds both parties equally, to negotiate in a candid, honest and co-operative manner.

The DTR, on the other hand, is not a creature of the parties' agreement, past or present, implicitly or explicitly. It is a creature of contract law itself. And although in theory it could apply to both parties, the effect of its application will nearly always be to demand a certain standard of conduct from one who assents to – in most cases, literally 'signs on to' – an agreement the terms of which have been prepared and presented by the other. Conceivably the DTR could be seen as a manifestation of a more general obligation to bargain in good faith, imposed not on the drafter but on the adhering party, although this is an interpretation that would strike some as marginal, not to say perverse.

ii. The Duty to Mitigate the Damages Flowing from Breach of Contract

Some first-year law students encountering the general topic of contract remedies may be surprised by the notion that the victim of a breach of contract should have an 'obligation' to the breaching party to mitigate, or 'minimise', the injurious effects of the latter's breach. But they come to understand that this is merely a reflection of the broader principle that contract remedies are designed to compensate one party, not to punish the other, and that – for the sake of both parties, and the system as well – even the completely innocent victim of a truly wilful breach is expected to take reasonable measures to limit or reduce her damages.

There are many characteristics that the duty to read and the duty to mitigate have in common. Most fundamentally, both are articulated as a 'duty', but in fact (with a few exceptions, some of which are discussed in the notes below), neither doctrine imposes a 'duty' in the Hohfeldian sense: neither imposes upon one party an obligation of performance for which a remedy would be available to the other if that duty were not to be performed. Although phrased in terms of 'duty', both principles are really limitations on what might otherwise be rights: Both require a party to be treated *as if she had* behaved in a certain way, *whether or not* she has actually done so. And both can be seen as expressing a policy preference for the virtue of self-reliance, by providing that even if one party has been (or is likely to be) injured by the actions of another in some way that might otherwise merit relief, such relief will nevertheless be denied to the extent that the injured party might with prudent actions have reasonably avoided or minimised the harm resulting from that conduct.

Although significant and substantial, the 'duty to mitigate' is not an absolute one. See, for example, the statement of that rule in the *Restatement (Second) of Contracts* §350,[6] which is phrased in term of 'avoidability'. If a reasonable effort to mitigate is actually made, but unsuccessfully, the injured party won't be penalised for that failure; indeed, the expense incurred in attempting to mitigate, if reasonable (and reasonably foreseeable), will be added to her recoverable damages. Furthermore, the plaintiff doesn't have to endure 'undue risk, burden or humiliation' in attempting to meet her burden of mitigation. Those various limitations on the 'duty to mitigate' suggest an analogous approach to the 'duty to read'. If the DTR were seen as an obligation to act 'reasonably', but *only* that, then there could well be instances in which a party is seen as having made a reasonable effort to carry out that 'duty'. And indeed there are; this will be explored further below.

Despite the ways in which they are similar, the two 'duty' rules operate in quite different circumstances: the 'duty to mitigate' applies in a situation where the 'wrong' has already occurred, and the issue is one of remedies. Whether the plaintiff adequately attempts to mitigate or not after a breach has occurred has no effect on whether the defendant's conduct was or was not a breach of an enforceable duty. In the case of the 'duty to read', however, the 'failure' to read typically takes place in the making of the contract. If the DTR rule applies, then the only existing contract between the parties is the one expressed in the writing that the non-drafting party signs. Presumably this is a contract that the drafter is willing to perform, but that the signer in some respect does not want to perform. If the DTR rule is applied against the signer, then if she does not perform her duties as provided in the writing, she may well be the one and only party in breach. Note that this further undercuts the notion that this doctrine literally imposes a contractual 'duty' to read. In the ordinary case, the signer's failure to read comes at a time before she has any duties at all to the other party; the 'breach' for which she might become liable is her failure to perform as required by the written contract, not her initial failure to read and understand it.

[6] *Restatement (Second) of Contracts* (St Paul, ALI, 1981) § 350.

B. A Conclusive Presumption

Often courts, instead of or in addition to phrasing the principle as a 'duty to read', will characterise it as a 'conclusive presumption'. '[A] party who signs a written contract is conclusively presumed to know its contents and assent to them.'[7]

This could be seen as a somewhat stronger statement of the principle. It seems, potentially at least, to make its application inescapable – if a person has signed an agreement, then she is necessarily going to be treated as though she had read and completely understood the writing she signed, without regard to whether she did or not, and also without regard to other factors in the case.

In law, there is a significant difference between a mere 'presumption' and a 'conclusive' presumption. The ordinary presumption is merely a device for relieving one party of the burden of pleading and/or proving a (potentially) material fact, a burden which that party would otherwise bear under substantive and procedural rules. The existence (or not) of that fact may be central to a determination of the parties' rights, and the party having the burden of establishing it may even ultimately continue to bear the burden of proof on that issue, but if the fact is initially presumed to exist, then the initial burden of showing its *non*existence will be on the other party. But ordinarily there is at least a possibility of doing that, because ordinarily a presumption will be rebuttable: if the other party produces evidence to show that the presumed fact truly did not exist, then the effect of the presumption is dispelled, and the party with the burden is required to produce actual evidence of its own.

The 'conclusive' presumption, however, is another matter. It does not merely shift the burden of pleading or proof from one party to the other; it has the effect of treating the fact in issue as having been established beyond contravention. In that sense, the 'conclusive presumption' is in effect another name for 'legal fiction' – the law's decision, for reasons of policy, to regard as true a fact which may not be true, and may indeed in a given case be demonstrably false.[8]

II. DEFENCES AGAINST THE RULE

Whether stated as a 'duty' or as a 'presumption' (conclusive or otherwise), the DTR rule is a strong one. However, in practice, the presumption created by signing an agreement is not regarded as truly conclusive, nor is

[7] *Bibbs v House of Blues New Orleans Restaurant Corp*, 2011 WL 1838783, *5 (ED La).

[8] See the discussion of the common law's traditional conclusive presumption of legitimacy for an in-wedlock child in *Michael H v Gerald D*, 491 US 110, 124 (1989).

the duty absolute. The rule may still be countered (or avoided) in various ways. Possible defences against its application include the following:

A. Interpretation

This is actually an avoidance of the DTR, rather than a direct defence against it. Even though one party may be generally presumed to have read and understood the writing that she signed, if that writing is ambiguous or otherwise in need of interpretation, the mere act of signing on does not signify assent to any and all unfavourable interpretations, merely to the existence of an ambiguous contract. Indeed, where one party was clearly the drafter, this could mean that the other party is given the benefit of the doubt on disputed issues of interpretation, by application of the familiar maxim of construction *contra proferentem* – against the drafter.

B. Lack of Assent

The party resisting enforcement of a written agreement may claim that she didn't actually sign or manifest effective assent to the agreement at issue. This can take a number of forms:

1. Forgery: she didn't sign the agreement at all.
2. Lack of authority: the person purporting to sign as her agent did not have the authority to do so. This could have the same effect as forgery, and both could present difficult factual questions, but the situation is apt to be very different.
3. Duress: either actual physical duress, or economic duress. If established, either defence will relieve the signing party, but the factual issues may be difficult, and particularly in the area of economic duress, often problematic for courts.

C. Mistake

As a contract law doctrine, this comes in two principal varieties, mutual and unilateral. Equally important to the analysis is the nature of the mistaken fact – what are the parties mistaken *about*?

i. Mistake as to What the Writing Says

If both parties share the same mistaken belief about the contents of the writing – perhaps the traditional 'scrivener's error' has occurred, or a printer has garbled the text – and this is convincingly proven, the court may view this as a 'mutual' mistake for which equitable relief should be available, and reform the contract to read the way they both apparently intended it to read. Of course, when this happens, the theory at least is not that one party's interpretation or expectation prevails over the other; it's rather that at the time of contracting, they both shared the same intent, which was inaccurately reflected in the writing. If, however, the drafting party knows full well what the writing says but the other party does not, can the latter claim this 'unilateral' mistake as a defence to enforcement? This may depend on whether the drafting party knows of the other's mistake, and has done anything to conceal the true effect of the writing, or to mislead the signer. If so, it could be more usefully be analysed as fraud, or at least as 'wrongful nondisclosure', the legal equivalent of active fraud, discussed below. In the absence of any wrongful conduct by the drafter, however, the defence is likely to founder on the rock of the DTR.

ii. Other Forms of Mutual Mistake

Where the parties are mutually mistaken about some fact extrinsic to the writing, which has a material effect on their exchange, this can sometimes be a basis for relief in the form of rescission and avoidance. Relief may be denied, however, if the adversely affected party has manifested agreement to a writing that has a provision that the court interprets as waiving such a defence to enforcement.[9] So the DTR may play a role here.

iii. Other forms of unilateral mistake

Here again, a mistake about some extrinsic material fact can sometimes be a basis for avoidance, although the rule here is less lenient to the adversely affected party. Again, contract language might be asserted as a bar to such a claim.

D. Fraud or Misrepresentation

The signing party can assert this in a number of different situations; the following are illustrative but not exhaustive.

[9] eg *Lenawee County Bd of Health v Messerly*, 331 NW2d 203 (1982) ('as is' clause in sale of real property).

i. 'Fraud in the Factum', also called 'Essential Fraud'[10]

Most courts appear to regard this as a potentially effective defence. Where one party has misrepresented to the other the nature of the thing she is signing, this may provide basis for resisting enforcement. If the signing party's story is credible, it undercuts the rationale for the DTR rule, and it makes the other party appear particularly unsympathetic.[11] If the signer knows that what she signs is intended to have contractual effect, the defence becomes more problematic, and the signer is more likely to be bound to whatever its contents may be, even if those were misrepresented to her. But active misrepresentation about the nature or contents of a writing if convincingly made in a conducive setting will in some cases overcome the drafter's assertion of the DTR.

ii. 'Fraud in the Inducement'

'Fraud in the inducement' refers to the intentional making of false statements which are intended to, or at least have the effect of, inducing the other party to sign on to an agreement. If the signing party indeed knows that what she is signing is intended to be a contract, then this defence is likely to be unsuccessful.[12] Even though the fraudulent party is still (or should be) regarded unsympathetically (assuming one were to believe the signer's story, that is), courts will routinely declare that a successful claim of fraud depends on, inter alia, reasonable reliance by the defrauded party, and that as a matter of law one cannot *reasonably* rely on oral statements that are directly contradicted by a writing that one is signing (and is therefore 'conclusively presumed' to have read).

iii. 'Innocent Misrepresentation'[13]

This is a misstatement of fact *not* fraudulently made. It's difficult to imagine an innocent instance of 'fraud in the factum', so as a practical matter it's going to be an innocently-made statement that induces the signing. If there is no guilt attached to the other party, then this is even less likely than 'fraud in the inducement' to succeed as a defence for the signing party, if the statement is contradicted by the terms of the writing, or the writing generally excludes any representations and so on not contained in the writing itself.

[10] *Restatement (Second) of Contracts* (n 6) § 163 cmt a.

[11] Compare 'fraud in the factum' as a 'real defence' to the enforcement of a negotiable instrument under UCC § 3-305(a)(1).

[12] *Restatement (Second) of Contracts* (n 6) § 164.

[13] ibid. The *Restatement (Second)* provides that both a fraudulent and an innocent misrepresentation may be grounds for avoidance, the latter only if also material.

E. Other Defensive Doctrines

Besides the defences enumerated above, there are two doctrines which can be invoked to counter the effect of DTR rule, by providing relief from enforcement of all or at least some of a written agreement.

i. The Doctrine of 'Reasonable Expectations'

In its strongest form, this doctrine goes beyond merely resolving ambiguity against the drafter to actually give one party the benefit of her reasonable expectations as to the effect of the contract, even though 'close reading [of that document] would contradict that'. In this form, this can potentially override the literal terms of a written agreement, DTR or not. Its most likely application is in the area of insurance contracts, however, where traditionally contracting parties are not expected actually to read and understand the terms of their policies. Even there it may represent a minority view, at least in its strongest form. (A weaker version of the 'reasonable expectations' principle seems to be just another way of stating the maxim of 'construing against the drafter'.) Although logically this doctrine might be employed in any case involving a consumer and a standardised form, such cases appear to be rare.

ii. The Doctrine of 'Unconscionability'

At least since the mid twentieth century, American courts have generally been understood to possess the residual power to refuse to enforce a contract all or some of whose terms are extremely and unfairly one-sided. The *Uniform Commercial Code* so provides, in Article 2,[14] and the common law (as reflected both in judicial decisions and in the *Restatement (Second) of Contracts*) agrees.[15] Successful assertions of this principle nearly always involve not only a demonstration that the contract or clause in question is extremely and egregiously unfair to the adhering party ('substantive unconscionability') but also usually that there is something in the circumstances that impairs the quality of that party's consent ('procedural unconscionability', or 'absence of meaningful choice'). In the usual case where this doctrine is successfully advanced, the contract (whether or not expressed in a standardised form) was at least memorialised in some form of writing, drafted by one party and adhered to by the other, so in such a case the DTR is necessarily implicated and overcome.

[14] UCC § 2-302.

[15] *Restatement (Second) of Contracts* (n 6) § 208.

III. OTHER JUSTIFICATIONS FOR THE EXISTENCE OF A 'DUTY TO READ'

The above formulations of the DTR rule may seem to be merely conclusory statements of a result, but they can be supported by substantial policy arguments.

A. Defending the Document

The law's willingness to enforce the terms of a writing even in the teeth of possibly persuasive evidence of active fraud by the other party suggests that the true reason for the DTR rule – whether phrased as a 'duty' or a 'conclusive presumption' – is the law's desire to insulate a written contract from later claims that it does not truly represent the complete and final contract of the parties. If the written agreement is assumed to be complete and accurate, then later attempts to undermine its legitimacy deprive the other party of the benefits of that agreement, to which she is legitimately entitled. (Obviously a rule imposing the 'duty to read' must envision some form of writing or at least a 'record'; to speak of the 'duty to read' an oral agreement seems meaningless.) Viewed this way, the DTR seems to be simply a more sweeping version of the parol evidence rule (PER) – or at least, to function as its complement. Together they express a policy judgment that when a person signs onto a more-or-less formal writing (that is, one which that person knows is intended to create or modify a legal relation), then:

(a) she ought to be bound by all the terms of that writing, whether she read or understood it or not;
(b) she should have no ability to add to, subtract from, or contradict that writing on the basis of evidence of other agreements or statements, no matter how convincing that evidence might be; and
(c) this is an appropriate general policy for the law to effectuate, even at the cost of discouraging or denying redress to persons who may have genuine, good-faith claims that they were mistaken or even actively misled, because it is 'efficient'.

The efficiency basis of the DTR rule is often very explicit: '[To do otherwise] . . . would absolutely destroy the value of all contracts.'[16] It is grounded at least in part on the obviously true observation that the commercial world today (and indeed for the last century or so) has completely embraced the notion of using standardised forms not merely as a means

[16] *Busching v Griffin*, 542 So2d 860, 865 (MO 1989).

of gathering, storing and transmitting information about contractual agreements, but as the conventional way of expressing and memorialising such agreements for the purpose of contract formation. Of course, this is particularly the case where one party is a 'repeat player', entering into multiple versions of what is essentially the same transaction with many different contracting parties. However, it goes beyond those incontrovertible propositions to assert that, as a general matter, agreements expressed in writings to which parties have apparently assented should generally be immune from later challenge on the basis that one of the parties did not read, did not understand, or perhaps was even actively misled, about the contents or effect of the writing. Although often expressed in cases where standardised forms have been utilised, this position is not limited to standardised forms, but extends to written contracts generally.

Although sometimes the DTR will be trumped by a successful application of one or more of the defensive doctrines enumerated above, a strong DTR rule explicitly contemplates the possibility that genuine instances of mistake and misrepresentation will from time to time occur, but will be tolerated and not corrected. The justification for this attitude of tolerance appears to rest on one or more of the following assumptions, explicit or tacit:

1. Genuine claims of mistake or fraud are relatively few; most parties who advance such claims in cases like these are (possibly at the instigation of unscrupulous attorneys) attempting to commit a fraud on the court, or to pressure the other party into settling.
2. The public good (or at least the functioning of the commercial marketplace) is better served by a policy that makes it difficult or impossible to later challenge a written contract merely on the basis that it was not read or understood, because the costs of making contracts universally understandable (if not actually understood) at the time of their making would be literally unbearable – if indeed that goal could even be accomplished.
3. Often a written agreement contains declarations that the persons signing onto it have read the agreement, do in fact understand it, and are not relying on any promises or representations not expressed in that writing. In such cases, each party is necessarily going to rely on the truth of that statement, and both parties should therefore be estopped later from denying its truth.

B. Estoppel to Challenge the Writing

The last point above leads to another justification sometimes put forward for the DTR rule, the possibility of *reliance*. Under this approach, the signer of a contractual document should be estopped to later claim that she is not bound by the agreement set forth in that document.

> [I]f, without being the victim of fraud [a person] fails to read the contract or otherwise learn its contents, he signs the same at his peril and is estopped to deny his obligation, will be conclusively presumed to know the contents of his contract, and must suffer the consequences of his own negligence.[17]

An argument for estoppel might run something like this:

1. Traditionally, an estoppel can arise in law when one party makes a statement (or a promise) on which the other party can reasonably rely, and that party does rely by materially changing his position, so that injustice will result if the first party is thereafter allowed to deny the truth of her earlier statement (or to repudiate her promise). How could an estoppel argument be used to justify enforcing a DTR rule?
   (a) When one party signs onto a written agreement, this is a general manifestation by that party of her intention to be bound by the terms of that agreement. This is particularly the case where the writing includes a statement that the signer has read and understood the terms of the contract, contains a merger clause (designed to invoke the PER), and/or states that the signer is not relying on any promises or representations not contained in the writing. The writing could also have a disclaimer of agent-authority to vary the terms-as-written. Even without any of those terms, the writing might well be protected by the DTR rule, if the signer knows (or should have known) that it was intended to have legal effect; however, if it does contain any or (as is often the case) all of them, the argument for an estoppel is considerably stronger.
   (b) On the strength of that manifestation of agreement, the other party will proceed to prepare for and then to perform the obligations imposed on it by that agreement. This is a change of position that the law should recognise. And because such reliance is likely, and likely to begin immediately, and may sometimes take place in ways that are hard to prove, the law in order to encourage prompt and reasonable reliance should protect the drafter from the time the contract is signed against later challenges by the signer.
   (c) Such change(s) of position on the drafter's part can be seen as both reasonable on his part, and reasonably foreseeable to the other party, the signer. Anyone who signs what she knows or should know is intended to have legal consequences should also know that the other party may rely, immediately and substantially, on her manifestation of assent to that agreement.

[17] *Brubaker v Barrett*, 2011 WL 2749611, *6 (ED Tenn).

(d) Will injustice result if the drafter's reliance is not protected by enforcement of the writing? Proponents would claim that both fairness and efficiency are best served when marketplace reliance is protected by a strong DTR rule, and that these two policy goals represent the kind of justice that contract law should strive to achieve.

2. As thus stated, the estoppel justification seems to depend on a tacit assumption that the drafting party can necessarily rely in good faith on the signer's expression of apparent assent. This will not always be the case, however:

   (a) Where the signer's assertion is simply that she failed to read or understand the terms of the document she was signing, but she admits knowing it was intended to have contractual effect, the drafter's reliance argument seems strongest, assuming the absence of any drafter-misconduct. (Whether the law might still allow the signer a reasonable time to become aware of her mistake and attempt to rescind could remain an open question.) The doctrines of reasonable expectations and unconscionability should remain available to the signing party in any event, if the facts of the case justify their application, but as a general matter the signer could appropriately be estopped to repudiate her expression of agreement.
   (b) Where the signer failed to read or understand the terms of the writing she signed because she thought it was something other than a contractual document, the case for protecting the drafter's reliance on her signing may be a weaker one. The argument in favour of estoppel in this case might depend on whether it was reasonable for the signer to have that (mistaken) belief, and whether the drafter knew or reasonably should have known of her mistake. If the answers to both questions are yes, then the drafter's claim of reliance on the signer's apparent assent may be regarded as being in bad faith. And further, if the signer's mistake occurred because she was lied to by the drafter about the nature of the writing ('essential fraud'), then obviously the drafter cannot in good faith have relied on her expression of assent.
   (c) Where the signer admits she knew she was signing a contractual document, but alleges that she was lied to, not about the nature or contents of the writing, but about other, extrinsic matters, to induce her to assent, the drafter's conduct is merely fraud 'in the inducement', not 'in the factum'. It does not go to the fundamental issue of consent to be bound. Still, if the signer's story is true, the drafter again cannot in good faith rely on such fraudulently induced assent.

3. So the estoppel case for the DTR rule is not necessarily a persuasive one; its strength depends on the good faith of the drafter, which in many

cases is controverted by the allegations of the signer. To say that the signer should be estopped from showing the truth of her allegations because of the drafter's good faith reliance on her apparent assent is obviously circular reasoning, where the fact of the drafter's good faith is called into question. If that proof is precluded by some asserted 'duty to read', this can't be justified on an estoppel basis. It must depend on some other underlying policy claim.

(a) Contract law (or perhaps, here, 'commercial law') is less worried about individual injustice than about overall market efficiency. The needs of the marketplace demand that written contracts – even those of 'adhesion' – be generally enforceable, whether or not they were read or understood by the adhering party at the time of her signing.
(b) In many cases the court disbelieves the plaintiff's claim, and wants to relieve the drafter of the burden of litigating that issue on the merits, even if that litigation would eventually be resolved in the drafter's favour.
(c) Even if the plaintiff's claim is credible, the law – or at least, the judge – often finds her to be unworthy of protection. For years the law has tolerated untruthful salestalk, deeming it to be mere 'puffing', which a reasonable buyer should be able to discount and ignore. That tolerance may have declined somewhat,[18] but the principle remains that contracting parties will often be held to a 'reasonable' level of self-protection.[19]

C. Signing as Consent to Be Bound

There is another type of argument that might be advanced in favour of a vigorous DTR rule: Even though both parties to an agreement may know that one of them has not read all or perhaps any of the document, never-

[18] See *Restatement (Second) of Contracts* (n 6) §§ 168, 169.

[19] A corollary of the estoppel/reliance argument is the possibility that the rights of third parties will be adversely affected if signers are permitted to withdraw from their contract or assert claims at variance from the writing. Compare *Restatement (Second) of Contracts* (n 6) § 166(b) (reformation may be denied if rights of innocent third parties as good faith purchasers would be adversely affected). This is the issue that is addressed by the negotiable instrument rules of UCC Art 3, protecting the holder in due course of a negotiable instrument against many 'personal' defences. UCC § 3-305. The same issue can also arise with the assignment of an ordinary contract. In many cases the assignee of a written contract would be able to claim with justification that it has changed its position in actual and reasonable reliance on the apparent consent of the signer to the terms of that contract, so that it [the assignee] should not be subject to any claim that the signer may later make to be relieved of, or modify, her obligation. This should not necessarily end the matter, however, since the assignee might have a claim back against the assignor if the assigned rights should prove to be unenforceable.

theless, by signing it, that party is manifesting her intention to be legally bound to the contents of the writing, whatever they may be. From Llewellyn[20] to Barnett,[21] commentators have suggested the possibility that one party in signing a writing with contents unknown to her may nevertheless be manifesting truly her *consent to be bound* to whatever may in fact be the contents of that writing, provided those do not exceed the bounds of what might be legitimately expected in light of what the signer *does* know. That consent is thus not without limits, but those limits are found in the context, not inherent in the act of manifesting apparent consent.

This expanded notion of consent obviously has potential application to the paradigmatic 'duty to read' case, where a complete and detailed writing exists at the time of signing, is presented by one party to the other, and signed by her. However, it could also be applied in the following situations:

1. To justify holding one party to the terms of a writing which she knows is intended by the other party to be a contract, and to whose terms she can be seen as having consented, even if she does not literally 'sign' that document at any point. This could thus encompass the so-called 'rolling contract', 'terms-to-be-added-later' or 'terms-in-the-box' contract. These are typically cases in which the signer knew (or arguably should have known) of the writing's existence; (probably) had access to it before signing; and if not, had (at least in theory) an opportunity thereafter to review the writing and withdraw, an opportunity which she failed to take.
2. To justify holding one party to the terms of a writing that she did see (or at least could have seen) on a computer screen, at or before her manifestation of consent to those terms by clicking on 'Submit', or 'I agree', or some such. Such 'clickwrap' contracts are becoming steadily more commonplace, and their efficacy is less and less open to challenge.[22]
3. To justify holding one party to the terms of whatever modified or additional terms that the other party might in the future propose, because the terms of the original agreement expressly gave it that power, particularly if either the original agreement or the new modification provided some mechanism for the adhering party to escape from the relationship if she did not find those new or revised terms to be acceptable. This expanded notion of 'consent to be bound' goes considerably beyond the traditional DTR, which focuses on the ability of the signing party to see and review the terms of the proposed agreement *at or before* the time of her expression of assent. When the original contract gives the drafting party the power later to unilaterally add to or modify the agreement,

[20] K Llewellyn, *The Common Law Tradition – Deciding Appeals* (Buffalo, Hein & Co, 1960) 370.

[21] R Barnett, 'Consenting to Form Contracts' (2002) 71 *Fordham Law Review* 627, 635.

[22] eg *Feldman v Google, Inc*, 513 F Supp 2d 229 (ED Pa 2007).

> the adhering party's 'agreement' in this case might well be characterised not as assent to any particular term or collection of terms, but to the existence of a *relationship*, in which one party voluntarily subjects herself to the power of the other party to set whatever terms it pleases for that relationship, limited only by whatever overarching supervision the law might choose to maintain. Because the power-imbalance in this relationship is so extreme, it seems appropriate to characterise the adhering party's action as one not of 'assent', but of 'submission'. To speak of this arrangement in terms of the traditional DTR principle strains that principle to the breaking point.[23]

IV. APPLICATIONS OF THE DUTY TO READ

Even if confined to the last few years, an on-line search for 'duty to read' decisions will yield dozens if not hundreds of cases. Here is a selection of cases none earlier than 2006, grouped by subject matter, which discuss the DTR, relying on it in some cases but not in others.

A. Insurance

It is not surprising that the DTR principle figures prominently in disputes involving insurance coverage. In nearly every litigated dispute of this type, the loss of which the plaintiff insured is complaining has already occurred, and there is no way for her to mitigate by purchasing better coverage, from the defendant insurer or anybody else. The only way for the plaintiff to be compensated for her loss is thus to show either that the insurer itself should be liable on the policy, or that an insurance agent acting for the plaintiff should be liable to her for failing to procure the disputed coverage. Except for the possibility of the plaintiff's bringing a bad faith claim against the company, or in extreme cases a disciplinary action against the plaintiff's attorney, neither side has much to lose by digging in its heels. And if the insurer or agent is relying on language in the policy that supports its claim of non-coverage, the plaintiff will have to confront the general principle of DTR.

In *City Blueprint & Supply Co v Boggio*,[24] the insured business sued its insurer and insurance agent in the aftermath of Hurricane Katrina, for failure to provide flood coverage. Neither the two owners of the insured nor their agent ever read their policy, which had been in force for many years, and contained a flood damage exclusion. Plaintiffs claimed they

[23] See generally D Horton, 'The Shadow Terms: Contract Procedure and Unilateral Amendments' (2010) 57 *University of California, Los Angeles Law Review* 605.

[24] *City Blueprint & Supply Co v Boggio*, 3 So 3d 62 (La Ct App 2008).

had believed, and had been assured by their agent, that they had 'full coverage'. The trial court's denial of recovery was affirmed; neither the company nor the agent had been shown ever to have promised flood coverage, and plaintiffs had never specifically requested it. Whether or not the agent ever said they were 'fully covered', the plaintiffs could not have reasonably believed that they would have flood coverage, because their policy contained 'a straightforward, uncomplicated exclusion against damage caused by flood', which 'a simple review of the policy' would have disclosed. 'An insured is responsible for reading his policy and is presumed to know its terms.'[25] But see *C's Discount Pharmacy v Pacific Insurance Co*,[26] where a long-standing relationship and a seven-months' delay before delivery of the policy enabled the insured to avoid summary judgment for the insurer.

Some cases state as a general rule that the insured cannot rely on possible fraud by agents of the company or of the insured to overcome lack of stated coverage in the policy.

> Fraud cannot be perpetrated upon one who has full knowledge to the contrary of a representation . . . An insured party is presumed to have read the terms of his insurance policy . . . Therefore, if the insured has made a statement which clearly conflicts with the terms of the policy, an insured cannot argue that he reasonably relied upon it.[27]

Similarly, in *Guideone Mutual Insurance Co v Rock*,[28] the insurer sued for a declaration that the policy was void and that the insureds' fire losses (their house and its contents, plus two automobiles) were not covered by their homeowners and auto insurance policies. (The insurer also claimed that the insureds were guilty of fraud and that the fire was not accidental.) The insureds' fraud claim was held to be precluded by the DTR: 'A signatory to an insurance policy has no right to rely on misrepresentations by the agent that are contrary to the terms of the contract.'[29]

However, some jurisdictions have in insurance cases a weaker version of the rule, which permits a plaintiff to show, and the jury to find, that the defendant insurer was in fact guilty of fraud, and that the insured was not unreasonable in failing to read the policy and discover the falsity of the agent's representation. For example: '[U]nder Pennsylvania law, there is no general duty to read the policy; rather, the insured may be justified in relying on oral representations made to him at the time he applied for the policy'.[30]

[25] ibid 67.
[26] *C's Discount Pharmacy v Pacific Ins Co*, 31 So 3d 1103 (La Ct App 2010).
[27] *Burger v Allstate Ins Co*, 667 F Supp 2d 738, 746 (ED Mich 2009) (interior quotation marks omitted).
[28] *Guideone Mutual Ins Co v Rock*, 2009 WL 2195047 (ND Miss).
[29] ibid *3.
[30] *Scarpato v Allstate Ins Co*, 2007 WL 172341, *4 (ED Pa) (interior quotation marks omitted).

In states with this more lenient rule, the insured may show the company or its agents made misrepresentations about the policy, and will not necessarily be deemed negligent for failure to discover the discrepancy between statements made and the terms of the policy. The question will be for the jury.[31]

Other possible means of circumventing the DTR rule in insurance cases include ambiguity in the fine print of the policy,[32] and the insurer's failure to make the terms of the policy reasonably available.[33]

B. Pre-injury Releases

Like the insurance cases, these present a situation where the plaintiff has already been injured at the time of her claim, and may have no alternative means of obtaining compensation. Here the suit will probably be a tort claim against the proprietor of the premises where the plaintiff was injured (although it could also be for breach of contract), and the defence will be a release that she signed before the injury. Two recent Pennsylvania cases fall into this category. One involves the plaintiff's participation in a paintball game, where he lost the sight of one eye because the goggles he was furnished by the proprietor were defective.[34] In the other the plaintiff was injured in helping friends remove a transmission from a car in the defendant's car scrapyard, without adequate tools because he had been assured defendant's employees would perform the necessary work.[35] Both plaintiffs were Spanish-speaking, and could read little or nothing of the written releases they were presented with, but both signed anyway. The traditional DTR rule makes no exception for signers who cannot read the language of the writing they are signing, and in both cases the release was held binding. Martinez, the paintball player, was permitted to proceed on a product liability or strict liability basis, because the language of the release was strictly construed in his favour, to apply only to ordinary negligence. The defendant scrapyard proprietor in *Arce* was held entitled to summary judgment, however, both because of the release that plaintiff had signed and because he had failed to show actionable negligence. A similar case to *Martinez* is *Oelze v Score Sports Venture, LLC*,[36] where the plaintiff was injured while playing tennis in the defendant's club; she was

[31] *Williams v Hilb, Rogal & Hobbs Ins Services, Inc*, 98 Cal Rptr 3d 910 (Cal Ct App 2009); *Nolan v Conseco Health Ins Co*, 2008 WL 2609659 (Ohio Ct App).

[32] *Blumenthal v New York Life Ins Co*, 2009 WL 498961 (WD Okla).

[33] *Citizens Property Ins Corp v European Woodcraft & Mica Design, Inc*, 49 So3d 774 (Fla Dist Ct App 2010).

[34] *Martinez v Skirmish, USA, Inc*, 2009 WL 1676144 (ED Pa).

[35] *Arce v U-Pull-It Auto Parts, Inc*, 2008 WL 375159 (ED Pa).

[36] *Oelze v Score Sports Venture, LLC*, 927 NE 2d 137 (Ill Ct App 2010).

held to be precluded by her signed release from pursuing a claim of ordinary negligence, but not one for gross negligence.

C. Real Property

This is an area where one might expect relatively strict adherence to the 'duty to read' principle, in light of the need for land titles to be not easily overturned by evidence outside the written record. Two decisions illustrate the traditional position of strict application of the rule despite potentially mitigating factors. In *Guzman v Inter National Bank,*[37] the purchaser of a house and land made a number of claims based on the seller's failure to disclose to her an existing mechanic's lien on the property, which eventually caused her to default on her mortgage loan, after which the mortgage lender purchased the property at the foreclosure sale. The plaintiff could not read or speak English, had no legal counsel or prior experience with institutional lenders, and asserted that she relied on an employee of the seller for counsel. The court held that because no fiduciary duty existed, there was no duty to disclose on the bank's part, and plaintiff's claims must fail. In *Ballard v Commercial Bank of DeKalb,*[38] the defendant bank was permitted to proceed with foreclosure despite the debtor's claim of fraud in connection with the execution of a deed of trust. To the extent that there was fraud, however, it appeared to have been committed by the debtor's grandson, rather than the lender bank, in order to obtain his grandfather's guarantee on outstanding debts of the grandson, secured by the deeded property. The defendant debtor was elderly, but apparently competent and experienced in business; the case is notable for the quotation attributed to him: '[W]ho reads all the fine print and all junk? [Sic] Nobody. I never did.'[39]

Another case illustrates one of the possible counters to the DTR rule, a claim for reformation based on mutual mistake. In *Chandler v Charleston Volunteer Fire Dept,*[40] the lessors claimed that their lease agreement with the local volunteer fire department did not give the lessee the right to renew its lease for another 20-year term, the renewal option being expressly vested by the words of the lease in the 'Lessor'. The court granted reformation of the lease so at to provide that the right to renew was instead with the 'Lessee', pointing out that since the rental was only a dollar a year, it made little sense to give the option to renew to the landlord. The provision was clearly a 'scrivener's error', the result of mutual

[37] *Guzman v Inter National Bank,* 2008 WL 739828 (Tex Ct App).
[38] *Ballard v Commercial Bank of DeKalb,* 991 So 2d 1201 (MS 2008).
[39] ibid 1207.
[40] *Chandler v Charleston Volunteer Fire Dept,* 2011 WL 4026844 (Tenn Ct App).

mistake, and reformation was appropriate, even more so because the fire department had already spent over $70,000 in improving the property.[41]

Another possible way to overcome an assertion of the DTR principle is the doctrine of unconscionability. *Mattingly v Palmer Ridge Homes LLC*[42] involved a home warranty scheme that has generated litigation in several states in recent years.[43] Plaintiff home buyers sued the builder of their assertedly defective newly built home, as well as the company that purported to have contracted to provide a home warranty in lieu of the builder's warranties under the construction contract. The plaintiffs' failure to read the terms of the booklet describing and limiting the warranty was not fatal to their claims, despite the fact that they signed a document which said that they had read it and that they agreed to be bound by it, where they did not actually receive a copy until several months later. The court found procedural unconscionability (as had other courts in similar cases involving the same programme),[44] and permitted some of plaintiffs' claims to proceed.

Finally, in *Rowen Petroleum Properties, LLC v Hollywood Tanning Systems, Inc*[45] the plaintiff landlord asserted that after he had orally agreed to permit the defendant commercial tenant to assign its lease to an entity which had been shown to have adequate financial resources, the defendant substituted for the plaintiff's signature a document granting approval for assignment to a different entity, a 'shell' with no financial resources. The plaintiff signed in the belief that no change had been made from the earlier version. The defendants argued that because plaintiff was a 'savvy businessman' he should have read the document he signed, and therefore could not assert fraud.[46] The court felt otherwise, using the language quoted at the beginning of this chapter; even a negligent failure to read, it held, is not necessarily a bar to the assertion of active fraud.

D. Sale of Goods

Two cases of this type illustrate contrasting approaches and results. In *Fitzsimmons v Fleet Truck Sales, Inc*,[47] the plaintiff purchased a used truck from the defendant to use in his trucking business. The contract called for a 2005 vehicle of a designated make and type, but the vehicle actually delivered was a 2006. Instead of making the vehicle slightly more valuable (although it might have done that, too), the error made it unsaleable,

[41] ibid *4, 6.
[42] *Mattingly v Palmer Ridge Homes LLC*, 238 P 3d 505 (Wash Ct App 2010).
[43] eg *Burch v State ex rel Washoe County*, 49 P 3d 647 (NV 2002).
[44] ibid.
[45] *Rowen Petroleum Properties, LLC v Hollywood Tanning Systems, Inc*, 2009 WL 1085737 (DNJ).
[46] ibid *3.
[47] *Fitzsimmons v Fleet Truck Sales, Inc*, 2010 WL 5030117 (Conn Super Ct).

unregisterable and uninsurable, once the mistake was discovered. The defendant seller at first claimed the plaintiff was responsible for the mistake, but eventually admitted responsibility, and supplied the vehicle originally contracted for. The plaintiff sued for a variety of types of damage, including lost revenue as a result of the first truck being inoperable, and various payments made on that vehicle (maintenance, storage costs, taxes) while it was out of service. The 'Purchase Order' used by the seller was a two-page form, only one page of which, apparently (the facts were disputed), the plaintiff had received. The first page of that document had a reference to 'Terms and Conditions' listed on page two; among the terms on the latter page was a disclaimer of liability for consequential damages. Although the plaintiff did not see the second page at the time, the reference to its contents was enough for the court to find that the disclaimer bound the plaintiff. As a result some (though not all) of his claimed damages were disallowed as being consequential.

In contrast, the buyer in *Woodruff v Bretz, Inc*,[48] was a consumer, buying a used motor home from defendant dealer for a price of $135,000. The purchase took place in Montana, in March; when the weather warmed up, the home began to smell. It was found to be heavily contaminated (all the carpet as well as some of the walls) with cat urine. The plaintiff hired a restoration service to make the home liveable, at a cost of over $17,000; the service informed her that the defendant had contacted them in January with questions about how to clean carpeting contaminated with animal urine. The issue for decision at this stage of plaintiff's suit for damages was only the question whether an arbitration clause in the contract bound the plaintiff. A sharply divided (4–2) Montana Supreme Court held that the clause was not part of the parties' contract. The greater part of the warring opinions was devoted to the question whether the sale contract was or was not a contract of adhesion. Finding the agreement to be a standard-form, take-it-or-leave it consumer contract, the majority held that the clause was indeed a contract of adhesion, and that the arbitration clause was not within the reasonable expectations of the buyer.[49] The dissent disputed all of those conclusions, contending that plaintiff had failed to establish her inability to negotiate better terms with the seller, and took the majority to task for sweeping aside 'a basic tenet of contract law', the duty to read. However 'incorrigible' and 'egregious' the defendant's actions may have been, the dissent maintained, the issue was simply whether the plaintiff should be bound to arbitrate her claims.[50] The dissent may well be right that the majority in *Woodruff* allowed its feelings about the merits of plaintiff's case to control their decision on this procedural issue; here is the majority's penultimate paragraph:

48 *Woodruff v Bretz, Inc*, 218 P 3d 486 (MT 2009).
49 ibid 494.
50 ibid.

> In conclusion, the record reflects that Bretz contacted a restoration and janitorial service in January 2006 with questions of how best to clean carpeting contaminated with animal urine. Two months later, Bretz sold Woodruff a motor home that was heavily contaminated with animal urine such that parts of the motor home were non-salvageable. Woodruff then had to spend some $17,000 to refurbish the motor home before she could use it. We are not even remotely persuaded that an ordinary consumer in Woodruff's position and with her relative level of sophistication regarding arbitration clauses would reasonably expect that she is giving up her valuable right to present such facts to a jury and seek reasonable damages in the courts of this state. Indeed, Woodruff would not have agreed to forgo her right to bring this action had Bretz's salesperson told her before she signed the purchase contract: 'By the way, the motor home you are purchasing may be heavily contaminated with animal urine, and when the weather warms up it will smell so bad that you will not be able to use it. But if you spend $15,000 to $20,000, you can probably fix it up.' Rather, Woodruff most likely would have moved on to another dealer. Consumers do not reasonably expect to be treated as Woodruff was here. More to the point, they do not reasonably expect to give up their right to go to court when they are treated as Woodruff was here.[51]

So the dissent in *Woodruff* probably has a point. On the other hand, if unconscionability is just another word for something that the court simply cannot stomach,[52] a coach-full of cat urine is probably near the top of any judge's list.

E. Attorney Misconduct

A few reported cases have involved parties who at the time of their contracting were represented by attorneys, the quality of whose service appears questionable. Plaintiff's reliance on the advice of another person will not necessarily excuse her 'duty to read', as we have seen, and this is likely to be true even where that person is an attorney engaged for the purpose of advising her with respect to the contract she is about to enter into. In *Stokes v Lusker*,[53] the would-be buyer of a co-op apartment unit sued various parties on the seller's side, as well as his own attorney, for the failure of the proposed purchase, a failure that caused the plaintiff to forfeit a $250,000 deposit. The plaintiff claimed that everybody involved had known that the plaintiff's ability to finance the purchase turned on his ability to sublease the apartment for commercial purposes, but that nobody – including his own attorney – advised him that such a sublease was legally

[51] *Woodruff* (n 47).

[52] Or, as Professor Leff put it, something that causes one's gorge to rise. A Leff, 'Unconscionability and the Code – The Emperor's New Clause' (1967) 115 *University of Pennsylvania Law Review* 485, 555.

[53] *Stokes v Lusker*, 2009 WL 612336 (SDNY).

impossible, even though they knew that to be the case. Applying New York's strong DTR rule, the court dismissed all the claims against the seller-related parties, even though the plaintiff had alleged fraud and wrongful nondisclosure on their part. Because the plaintiff could have discovered the restrictions on the apartment's use before committing himself to the purchase, the court held: 'He cannot blame his own recklessness on the acts of others by crying fraud.'[54] On other hand, plaintiff's claim against his own attorney was allowed to proceed, despite the argument that the plaintiff had assumed the risk by signing the purchase documents. Assuming the accuracy of the plaintiff's pleadings, the court held, the defendant attorney knew or should have known that the plaintiff was relying on him to read the documents and advise him accordingly.[55]

As to the signer's ability to sue her own attorney for negligence in failing to advise her of the effect of the document she was signing, the *Stokes* court seems clearly right in its decision to allow such a suit to proceed. A similar recent decision on this point is *Meyers v Sudfeld*,[56] involving claims of legal malpractice stretching over several years. In that case, the court noted that although there might be ways in which a client could be deemed contributorily negligent (such as withholding information from her attorney, or disregarding his advice), a client cannot be so faulted merely for signing documents without reading them, when she has relied on her attorney's advice and representation in so doing. In contrast, in *Marion Partners, LLC v Weatherspoon & Voltz, LLP*,[57] the court appears to have taken the position that even if an attorney has been charged with the responsibility of advising the plaintiff about a proposed contract, the plaintiff's signing of that contract means he cannot complain of his attorney's failure to warn him of any risk that he might have discovered by reading it himself.[58] If that is really what the court in that case means to say, it seems an indefensible, not to say inexplicable, conclusion.

F. Credit Cards

In two cases, credit card issuers were sued by persons claiming to have been hurt by the defendants' dissemination of inaccurate information about their credit standing. In *Heiges v JP Morgan Chase Bk*,[59] the plaintiff was an employee of a corporation that had opened a credit card account with the defendant issuer. The defendant also issued a card to the plaintiff,

[54] ibid *6.
[55] ibid *11.
[56] *Meyers v Sudfeld*, 2007 WL 419182 (ED Pa).
[57] *Marion Partners, LLC v Weatherspoon & Voltz, LLP*, 2011 WL 3904113 (NC Ct App).
[58] *Marion Partners* (n 56) *3–4.
[59] *Heiges v JP Morgan Chase Bk*, 521 F Supp 2d 641 (ND Ohio 2007).

in his own name. The plaintiff's employer was later dissolved, at a time when it owed over $6,000 to the defendant, and the defendant reported the plaintiff as a delinquent debtor to credit agencies, asserting that he was personally liable for his employer's debt on its account, because of language to that effect in the credit agreement. The defendant responded to the plaintiff's suit with a motion to compel arbitration, based on its asserted amendment of the credit agreement by modifications sent with the monthly statements. (The original agreement did not contain an arbitration clause, but it did contain provisions for future amendment.) To the plaintiff's assertions that he never saw a copy of the underlying agreement (which also contained language making personally liable any person in whose name a card was issued), the court responded:

> As to any claim of not seeing a copy of the agreement, Heiges does not dispute receiving monthly statements, including the statements that came with amendments to the Agreement. Regardless, these statements included telephone numbers that he could have called to obtain a copy of the Agreement. If he called that number, he could have learned that the language of the Agreement subjected him to personal liability for the charges placed on the card.[60]

The cardholder fared better in *Kortum-Managhan v Herbergers NBGL*.[61] Here also the plaintiff asserted that the defendant card issuer had disseminated inaccurate information about her credit standing to credit reporting agencies, and sued on a variety of statutory theories. The defendant responded by moving to compel arbitration on the basis of a clause in the original agreement permitting it to 'change any term of this agreement' by notice to the account holder followed by the latter's continued use of her card. The court held that the addition of an arbitration clause was not merely a 'change' in the agreement, but a new addition, and agreed with the plaintiff's characterisation of the defendant's attempt to add the provision via an ambiguous and misleading 'bill-stuffer' as 'sneaky and unfair'.[62] The defendant, the court asserted, had buried the notice in 'copious piles of junk mail'.[63] In this case, as in *Woodruff*, the other Montana decision discussed above, there was a vigorous dissent arguing that the plaintiff should have been bound by the arbitration clause.[64]

[60] ibid 649. As a college classmate of mine used to say, 'If your grandmother had wheels, she'd have been a trolley'.

[61] *Kortum-Managhan v Herbergers NBGL*, 204 P 3d 693 (MT 2009).

[62] ibid 700.

[63] *Kortum-Managhan* (n 60) 696.

[64] ibid 701.

CONCLUSIONS

What kind of conclusions can be drawn from the above analysis? This discussion is written primarily for an audience with some interest in, as well as knowledge of, legal affairs, and its success will depend on the extent to which its observations seem to that audience to be generally well-taken. But its subject is the present and future state of one particular facet of contract law, and the potential readers with most power to affect the future development of that area of law are judges – in particular, judges whose duties at least occasionally include hearing and deciding contract disputes. Based on the observations made above, how might one recommend that they deal with the 'duty to read' as a rule of contract law?

A. Do Not Call It a 'Duty'

This is not only technically incorrect, it encourages judges (and others as well) to moralise or be condescending to persons who don't read everything they sign. Nobody does that, and in fact nobody is expected to. In standardised-form contracting, it is not only *not* encouraged, it is essentially *dis*couraged. Contract recitations that say 'I have read all of this contract' are patently false, and are known to be false – to the party who presents a written contract for signature as well as to the party who signs it. All those words really convey to the signer is this: 'Although we know you haven't read much or any of this contract, and probably wouldn't understand its importance if you had, we expect to hold you to it.' Like a merger clause, it is essentially a message, not to the other party, but to a future court.

If twenty-first century judges want to make better sense of this area of law, they could start by understanding and admitting that:

— *nobody* reads everything she signs;
— nobody *is able* to read everything she signs; and
— nobody *wants* her to read everything she signs.

What drafters *do* want is to be able to treat her as if she *had* read everything. They don't care if in fact she hasn't – and, indeed, in many cases would prefer that she didn't.

So don't call it a 'duty'. This just adds insult to injury.

B. Do Not Call It a 'Conclusive Presumption'

As we have seen, a conclusive presumption is essentially a legal fiction. If there is anything that's a fiction here, it's the notion that anyone does – or even could – read everything they sign. Whatever the merits of such a device might be in other legal contexts, in this area it is clearly an inaccurate description of how people actually behave, as well as an inaccurate statement of how the DTR rule is applied in practice. There are countless court decisions that accept as a fact the proposition that a contracting party has *not* read what she signed, and go on to give that party some relief based on that fact. On the other hand, calling it a *rebuttable* presumption seems not so problematic. When one person has done an act (which is usually signing, but it might be something else – clicking a 'Submit' button, perhaps) that on the face of it seems to express unqualified assent to a bargain proposed by another, it could be useful, at least as a point of departure, for the law to say that this creates a rebuttable 'presumption of knowing assent'. (PKA.) This is admittedly still a misdescription of reality, but it does have the virtue of putting the burden on the signer to overcome the fact of her apparent assent, while at the same time making clear that it is permissible and potentially possible for her to do so.

C. Do Not Replicate the Parol Evidence Rule

Whether the American legal system really needs the PER is certainly open to question. Other functioning legal systems appear to manage quite well without one. And ours is so full of exceptions and anomalies that except possibly for teachers of contract law (whose students can be challenged, to put it mildly, by this body of doctrine) it is hard to see why we tolerate it. In some situations, of course, it does have a certain logic. Parties who have carefully negotiated (probably through their attorneys) an elaborate written contract to which they then express assent should expect to find it difficult or impossible later to claim that they did not intend to have their contractual relationship governed by the terms of that writing. The PER does achieve this result, although in a complicated and arcane way.

In any event, whether or not we need the PER that we have, we certainly don't need *another* one. A modernised PKA rule should be based not on a patently false assumption that of course the parties have all read and understood the written contract, but on the candid admission that in many cases it is necessary and appropriate as a matter of policy to hold a person to a contract to which she has manifested a form of assent without having understood or even read its terms.

D. Do Not Allow the Presumption of Knowing Assent to be a Shield for Wrongdoing

If the PKA is not a conclusive one, then necessarily it can be rebutted. If one party (call her P, for convenience) asserts that she was the victim of a fraud practiced upon her by the other (D), those allegations are *issues of fact*. P's ability to have her story heard by a trier of fact should not be trumped by any 'presumption' that it is necessarily false, unless a judge finds that as a matter of law no reasonable person could believe her story. The test at this point should not be whether in the view of the judge P behaved imprudently or 'unreasonably', but simply whether her story is potentially credible. This should be the case whether the fraud complained of is 'fraud in the factum', 'fraud in the inducement', or fraud in the form of active concealment or wrongful nondisclosure, because the crux here is *misconduct by D*. Carelessness or imprudence on P's part may be 'venial faults', to use Cardozo's phrase,[65] but they are *only* that. Active wrongdoing is something more. The PER has traditionally had an exception for fraud,[66] although in some jurisdictions it has been cabined and to some extent neutralised.[67] Whatever one might say about that version of the PER, the same should not be true of the PKA. If P's allegations of fraud are believed, then in applying the substantive law of fraud the court may need to consider whether P in fact relied on the D's fraudulent representations, and whether, if she did, such reliance was 'reasonable'. But those issues should not turn on whether P signed a document provided by D containing self-serving declarations intended to head P off at the courthouse door.

E. Do Not Let the Presumption of Knowing Assent Preclude Relief for Mistake

Courts have been willing to let parties show the existence of a 'mutual mistake' of the 'scrivener's error' type, even though doing so denies the validity of an apparently agreed-to writing. In such a case, the writing is 'reformed' to become, in legal contemplation, the writing the parties actually intended. Other types of mutual mistake may result in avoidance, not reformation, but the PKA should not necessarily preclude their establishment as a basis for relief. Where one party claims 'unilateral mistake', the availability of relief should depend again – as in the case of relief for fraud, above – on the substantive rules governing such relief, not on any

[65] J Cardozo in *Jacob & Youngs v Kent*, 129 NE 889, 891 (NY 1929).
[66] *Restatement (Second) of Contracts* (n 6) § 214(d).
[67] eg *Danann Realty Corp v Harris*, 157 NE2d 597 (NY 1959).

presumption that the signer of a contract knowingly assented to things of which in fact she was ignorant or mistaken.

F. Do Not Let the Presumption of Knowing Assent Preclude the Application of Other Protective Doctrines

The doctrines of 'reasonable expectations' and 'unconscionability' are legal devices fashioned to protect parties who in some way are vulnerable to over-reaching from the injurious consequences of their vulnerability. Both doctrines contemplate the possibility that in order to achieve justice, a court may have to go beyond the literal wording of a contract in order to enforce the agreement that one party reasonably believed she was making, or to relieve a party from the effects of a contract she should not be held to. Whether the vulnerable party did in fact read and understand the agreement to which she apparently assented can be germane to those issues, perhaps in some cases even determinative, but the application of those other doctrines should not be in principle be precluded by the application of a PKA rule.

G. Do Not Let the Presumption of Knowing Assent Preclude Scrutiny of Adhesion Contracts

To a large extent this point has been dealt with in the preceding discussion. To the extent that a contract of adhesion runs afoul of the principle of unconscionability or reasonable expectations, that has been already addressed. Courts and commentators are generally vocally insistent that a contract cannot be overturned or avoided merely because it is a contract of adhesion. If a contract is indeed one of 'adhesion', that should in the view of many provide a basis for finding it to be 'procedurally unconscionable', but that conclusion typically only opens the door to an examination of the contract for possible 'substantive unconscionability' as well. Even if one imposes a rule of 'strict scrutiny' or even 'presumptive nonenforcement' for contracts of adhesion, that doesn't make them per se unenforceable.[68] In any event, a PKA rule should not deter a court's finding that a given agreement is in fact a contract of adhesion, whatever may be the legal results of that conclusion.

[68] See, generally C Knapp, 'Opting Out or Copping Out? An Argument for Strict Scrutiny of Individual Contracts' (2006) 40 *Loyola of Los Angeles Law Review* 95.

H. What Remains?

Sherlock Holmes famously declared: 'When you have eliminated the impossible, whatever remains, however improbable, must be the truth.'[69] When one has eliminated the various defences to contract enforcement that are not – or at least *should* not – be necessarily barred by the application of a PKA, then what remains? When will that principle be decisive in protecting a written agreement from attack of one kind or another?

Assuming the continued existence of the PER, a PKA as envisioned above seems to have very little work of its own to do. Assuming we trust judges here as elsewhere to perform responsibly and fairly the task of deciding when 'reasonable people' would have to find the facts in one and only one way, and assuming farther that we are willing to trust juries to behave responsibly when assigned a fact-finding task of their own, all that a PKA would accomplish is to state authoritatively a probably non-controversial proposition:

> One who knowingly and voluntarily assents to a contract whose terms are contained in a given writing should be held legally responsible for her actions by being held to those terms, in the absence of fraud, mistake, or other excusing cause.

BIBLIOGRAPHY

Barnett, R, 'Consenting to Form Contracts' (2002) 71 *Fordham Law Review* 627.

Doyle, AC, *Sign of the Four* (London, Spencer, Blackett, 1890).

Horton, D, 'The Shadow Terms: Contract Procedure and Unilateral Amendments' (2010) 57 *University of California, Los Angeles Law Review* 605.

Knapp, C, 'Opting Out or Copping Out? An Argument for Strict Scrutiny of Individual Contracts' (2006) 40 *Loyola of Los Angeles Law Review* 95.

Leff, A, 'Unconscionability and the Code – The Emperor's New Clause' (1967) 115 *University of Pennsylvania Law Review* 485.

Lerner, AJ, 'How Could You Believe Me?', *Royal Wedding* (MGM, 1951).

Llewellyn, K, *The Common Law Tradition – Deciding Appeals* (Buffalo, Hein & Co, 1960).

Macaulay, S, 'Private Legislation and the Duty to Read – Business Run by IBM Machine, the Law of Contracts and Credit Cards' (1966) 19 *Vanderbilt Law Review* 1051.

[69] AC Doyle, *Sign of the Four* (London, Spencer, Blackett, 1890) ch 6.

Part IV

Relational Critiques of Contract Doctrine

12

Restitution Without Context: An Examination of the Losing Contract Problem in the Restatement (Third) of Restitution

WILLIAM J WOODWARD, JR*

INTRODUCTION

IN HIS 1959 article 'Restitution in Context',[1] Stewart Macaulay reviewed a casebook on restitution and wondered whether the subject *could* be considered by itself, outside of the far broader context in which restitution cases usually arise. Thus began a long career of considering legal phenomena within their broader settings: without context, one might well lose nuance essential to understanding a subject.

In 2011, restitution was once again isolated as a subject, this time by the American Law Institute, which gave final approval to a *Restatement (Third) of Restitution of Restitution and Unjust Enrichment* (hereinafter *R3RUE*). Thus culminated a very long project of identifying a field for 'restating', reviewing the cases and commentary about the field, drafting black letter and commentary, and securing approval for the project from the membership of the American Law Institute.[2]

This *Restatement* project offers an opportunity to revisit the insights about the importance of context that Macaulay made in 1959. The focus here will be on a particularly difficult contract remedies problem where

* Many thanks go to Alice Abreu, Rick Greenstein, Greg Mandel and Amy Sinden for their comments on an earlier draft and to the late John Kidwell for his extensive support and editing help with earlier drafts. The author also thanks Temple University for research support.

[1] S Macaulay, 'Restitution in Context' (1959) 107 *University of Pennsylvania Law Review* 1133–48.

[2] The process of creating a *Restatement* is described in M Shapo, 'In Search of the Law of Products Liability: The ALI Restatement Project' (1995) 48 *Vanderbilt Law Review* 631.

contract law and restitution historically have been thought to overlap – the losing contract problem. Simply stated, can a person who has made a losing contract (contracting to give more than he will get) recover damages for breach that disregard a loss on the bargain, the risk of which the non-breacher implicitly agreed to when he made the contract. *R3RUE* treats that problem very differently from the treatment given to the same problem by the *Restatement (Second) of Contracts*. My contention is that if we examine this same problem through a variety of contexts – real, experimental, theoretical, and practical – the solution proposed by the new *Restatement* may lack normative support, but it will, nonetheless, be very hard to predict whether it will appeal to the judiciary, which is, after all, the audience to whom a *Restatement* provision is primarily directed.

Section I will introduce the *R3RUE* project, lay out the losing contract problem using a simple hypothetical, and then briefly outline different approaches to it, including the complex solution proposed in the new *Restatement of Restitution*. Section II will then consider the problem in the wider contexts of actual, observed contracting behaviour pioneered by Stewart Macaulay and of newer work that examines how experimental subjects regard contract obligation and breach. Both of these contexts reveal a 'reciprocity norm' that may animate the behaviour of those who make and perform contracts. When used as a starting point in a normative instrumental analysis of the problem, the reciprocity norm can produce outcomes at odds with a conventional parallel analysis that does not take that norm into account.

Section III will situate this problem within a different context: contract doctrine itself. *R3RUE* regards the losing contract problem as having a 'contract solution' and proceeds to define that solution using a particular vision of contract law. This conception is sharply distinguished from the broad idea of restitution that otherwise animates *R3RUE*, and this particular vision takes scant account of the reciprocity that is endemic to all but a narrow range of contracts. Section III will conclude by showing that this particular vision of contract law contributes strongly to the solution to the losing contract problem found in *R3RUE* and that a different vision, one that takes greater account of reciprocity, may well account for the different treatment given to the same problem in the *Restatement (Second) of Contracts*.

Having suggested that our views about contract law may have changed during the 30 years between these restatement projects and that those views may well contribute to the different solutions to the same problem that we find in those two restatement projects, we come to the uneasy conclusion in Section III that the 'right' solution as a normative matter may depend on how one looks at the problem and, in particular, on the extent to which we believe that the reciprocity norm is an important one in contract law.

Finally, Section IV will consider how the new rule might be received in the world of the courts as well as whether it might have effects outside the litigation system. Here it will be suggested that the rule may *actually* operate differently from the rule supported by most of the supporting commentary in *R3RUE*. This will result in substantial uncertainty that could in turn have the unintended effect (if it has any effects at all) of motivating the parties to modify their ongoing contracts rather than face the uncertainties of litigation. In this respect, the 'success' of the new rule will be in the eye of the beholder.

I. THE LOSING CONTRACT PROBLEMAND *R3RUE'S* PROPOSED SOLUTION

At its Annual Meeting in 2010 the American Law Institute (ALI) approved *R3RUE*, a project led by its reporter professor Andrew Kull. Both the ALI and Professor Kull have reason to be proud of their ambitious 10-year effort to synthesise a wide and unruly field.

By its very nature, a *Restatement* isolates a legal field for 'restating' a narrowing activity that, as Macaulay observed in 1959, carries with it the potential to distort by removing context. The project recognised that restitution and contract often overlap where courts have purported to create a 'quasi contract' or 'restitution' solution to a problem involving a contract that failed. In an important subdivision of the *Restatement*, the project considers the use of restitution in such contract settings.[3] It is here one finds a section addressing restitution for services provided when the provider and recipient disagree whether the contract requires them,[4] restitution of profits from a breacher who has committed an 'opportunistic breach'[5] and the extent to which a person in a losing contract can get restitution of benefits conferred on the breacher without regard to a potential loss on the bargain.[6]

This last is surely one of the most difficult problems addressed by the project and may well be most revealing of the project's underlying assumptions and ideas. The traditional rule, as set out in *Restatement (Second) of Contracts* § 373, permits the plaintiff who has made a losing contract to recover from the breacher the reasonable value of the benefits conferred on the breacher without regard to the bargain loss implicit in the original bargain.[7] The rule was controversial when the *Restatement*

[3] *Restatement (Third) of Restitution & Unjust Enrichment* (St Paul, ALI, 2011) (hereinafter *R3RUE*) ch 4 §§ 31–39 (entitled 'Restitution and Contract').

[4] *R3RUE* § 35.

[5] *R3RUE* § 39.

[6] *R3RUE* § 38.

[7] *Restatement (Second) of Contracts* (St Paul, ALI, 1981) § 373(1) and cmt a.

was drafted,[8] but the ALI elected then to follow the majority rule in the case law. While the case law had not changed appreciably in the interim,[9] *R3RUE* changed this rule[10] to one where the losing party will always absorb in a damages award some of the loss on the original bargain. Though there was scant support for change in the case law, the change was consistent with newly-dominant scholarly commentary supporting some form of reversal of the rule.[11] But it remains to be seen whether the change is a sound one as a matter of policy and, perhaps more practically, whether courts, mired in context as they usually are, will recognise it. While its latest incarnation is in the *Restatement (Third) of Restitution*, the losing contract rule raises questions that lie near the core of *contract* law and offers an opportunity to consider the methodology and underlying assumptions we bring to thinking about contracts.[12]

The easiest way to dig into the question is through a simple problem. Suppose Dimwitted Contractor contracts to build Owner a house for the price of $150,000. Whether desperate for work in the recession, overly optimistic about his own costs, or just plain stupid, Contractor has seriously underpriced the construction. The value of what the contractor has agreed to do and what other contractors would charge for the same job is $200,000 and it will cost the contractor that much to do the work. Owner knows she drove a hard bargain and is getting a great deal (a $200,000 job for $150,000 or a gain of $50,000). Even better from owner's perspective, she has negotiated a payment schedule that requires her to pay half the price ($75,000) when the job is 80 per cent complete and the other half when it is completed. When Contractor has done precisely 80 per cent of work (at a cost of $160,000), Owner refuses to pay anything at all and ejects him from the job, asserting a substantial breach by Contractor as the reason. This act, in fact, constitutes *Owner's* substantial breach of the contract and we can assume a court would so hold. How should we measure the contractor's recovery?

This question has puzzled courts and commentators for more than a century. Were we to award the contractor's 'expectation damages', we would put the contractor into the position he would have been in if the contract were fully performed.[13] In an 80 per cent completed contract like

[8] See *56th ALI Proceedings* (1979) 406–12.

[9] Recent cases are collected in G Palmer and L Kaplan, *Law of Restitution* (2011 Cum Supp) (Wolters Kluwer) § 4.4(a), n 7a.

[10] The issue was settled in 2003.

[11] See authorities cited in *R3RUE* § 38 Reporter's Note d.

[12] The Reporter has gathered much of the scholarly commentary on the rule in *R3RUE* § 38 Reporter's Note d. To the Reporter's list, one must add, at least, the excellent article supporting the traditional approach by B Gegan, 'In Defense Of Restitution: A Comment on Mather, Restitution as a Remedy for Breach of Contract: The Case Of The Partially Performing Seller' (1984) 57 *Southern California Law Review* 723.

[13] *Restatement (Second) of Contracts* § 344 cmt b.

this, it would mean we would award the amount the owner did not pay, $150,000 minus the contractor's 'loss avoided' ($40,000), or $110,000[14] for the $160,000 worth of work completed.[15] An 'expectation damages' award would preserve the integrity of the original bargain, since the contractor should be seen as having bargained at the outset to lose $50,000 if he completed the entire job. One who asserted the sanctity and primacy of the contract that was negotiated would take this approach.[16]

An alternative way of looking at it is to consider the owner's substantial breach to be the equivalent of the end of the bargain. Why, one might ask, should a breacher be effectively entitled to her profit when she induced the contractor's work by making her own promise but then did not then earn her own profit by fully performing the contract? Promises were, of course, exchanged. But in a contract setting, the promisor did not make a promise 'to' herself but made it 'to' another person in the context of a bargain. Each promise was conditional on, and made in anticipation of – in reliance on – *actually receiving* what the other side promised. Indeed, a fair reading in nearly any case is that the parties were bargaining for the *performances* the promises represented, not simply for the substitutional relief value that a later trier of fact might place on the promises; an award of expectation damages is but one of many ways to measure that loss of the anticipated performance.[17] On this view, by destroying the reciprocal context in which the promise was made, a substantial breach has destroyed the only reason to use the bargain as a point of reference for damages. Having removed the implications of the bargain, this view continues, what remains to be done is to assess damages for the owner's breach. Since the expectation measure is itself but an approximation of real damages, there is no essential reason to use expectation as a limit on what the loser might obtain. And since the winner actually received some of the performance contemplated, the reasonable value of which would be easy for the winner to estimate and factor in at the making of the bargain,[18] there is little danger of throwing onto the winner an unknowable risk that might have produced the loser's bad bargain if that 'reasonable value' were used. Under those circumstances, awarding the value of the work done is an acceptable solution.

[14] Our contractor avoided 20% of the $200,000 worth of work due to the owner's breach, so under the expectation measure he should get the contract price, $150,000 minus (0.2 x $200,000) = $110,000 as a final payment for the work done.

[15] eg, *Restatement (Second) Contracts* § 347; compare *Restatement (Second) Contracts* § 373.

[16] This 'full expectation' treatment was advocated in H Mather, 'Restitution as a Remedy for Breach of Contract: The Case of the Partially Performing Seller' (1982) 92 *Yale Law Journal* 14.

[17] Professor Corbin saw the remedy not as a remedy for unjust enrichment but rather as a simple alternative way to measure injury. See A Corbin, *Corbin On Contracts*, vol 5 (St Paul, West Publishing, 1950) § 1106.

[18] Certainly it would be easier for the winner to estimate this figure than it is to estimate the consequential damages that might result from the winner's breaching the contract.

This 'reasonable value' approach (however we might articulate its theory) would give the contractor $160,000, effectively erasing the implications of the bad bargain he made. At the same time, it does *not* preserve the benefit of the bargain for a party who, after all, did not earn that benefit through full performance. This approach, adopted by most courts in the twentieth century but questioned by many commentators, was, after strong debate,[19] enshrined in the *Restatement (Second) of Contracts*.[20] There are also two solutions that might be regarded as compromises, somewhere between 'expectation damages' and 'reasonable value'. One approach would award 'reasonable value' but would limit the owner's liability to the total price she agreed to – here, $150,000.[21]

R3RUE takes a different mid-way approach, creating the 'contract rate rule', an approach recognised by a few nineteenth-century courts (and, in sales of goods cases, by Article 2 of the *Uniform Commercial Code*).[22] In the simple example above, *R3RUE* would provide that plaintiff contractor should be paid at the contract *rate*. Here, that would give the contractor 80 per cent of the contract price – 0.8 x $150,000, or $120,000.[23] This preserves *some* of the contract's profit/loss allocation, but only that portion that 'accrued' during the actual performance of the contract; the owner earns her pro rata profit up to the time she breaches but not afterward. This solution was found in a couple of well-known nineteenth-century cases that were not widely followed in the twentieth century.[24]

In rejecting the conventional judicial solution to this problem, *R3RUE* bends to a chorus of modern academic commentators that viewed the 'reasonable value' solution as 'unjustly enriching' the *contractor*[25] (mostly because it ignored the contractor's loss on the bargain) and rejects the

[19] *ALI Proceedings* (n 8).

[20] *Restatement (Second) Contracts* § 373. The new *Restatement of Restitution* does preserve in § 37 one variation of the *Restatement of Contracts* solution: If a buyer of goods or services has prepaid on a losing contract and the supplier has failed to deliver any performance, the buyer can get his money back without any deduction for having made a bad bargain. This result follows *Bush v Canfield*, 2 Conn 485 (CT 1818), a well-known case reaching that result. *R3RUE* preserves this particular outcome by introducing 'rescission', a remedy that simply reverses the transaction (and therefore gives the buyer restitution of the down payment without any deduction for loss on the bargain). Rescission is not available once values need to be established for a part performance – where the court cannot 'unscramble the egg'. A Kull, 'Rescission and Restitution' (2006) 61 *Business Lawyer* 569, 577. *R3RUE*'s narrow rescission remedy would thus not be available in the example discussed in the text.

[21] See *Johnson v Bovee*, 574 P2d 513 (Colo Ct App 1978); *Wuchter v Fitzgerald*, 163 P 819 (OR 1917).

[22] *Uniform Commercial Code* § 2-607(1). A 'contract rate' approach is also sometimes used in employment contract cases; see G Palmer, *Law of Restitution*, vol 1, § 4.4 (Wolters Kluwer) 394.

[23] *R3RUE* § 38(2)(b).

[24] The main cases supporting illustrations in the *Restatement*'s new rule include *Kehoe v Rutherford*, 27 A 912 (NJ 1893), *Doolittle & Chamberlain v McCullough*, 12 Ohio St 369 (OH 1861), and *Noyes v Pugin*, 27 P 548 (WA 1891).

[25] *R3RUE* § 38 cmt d.

views of earlier contracts scholars such as Corbin and Fuller and restitution scholar Palmer. It also rejects the 'expectation damages' solution, one that preserves the full expectancy of both breacher and non-breacher and is, perhaps, most logically in accord with what one might view as the parties' initial bargain.

Perhaps because it is a compromise, there is something intuitively appealing about the Restatement's 'contract rate' solution to the problem. After all, these parties *did* make a bargain and, assuming no invalidity on account of duress, mistake, or unconscionability, it is perhaps safe to assume that the values they may have placed on their commitments ought to survive anyone's breach. On the other hand, allowing the breacher to preserve the whole benefit of that bargain with little or no performance seems wrong. The contractor bargained for an actual, full performance, not a partial one; and he certainly wasn't simply making a bet.[26]

That the new *Restatement* has rejected what seemed to be the reasonably settled majority view of the courts during the bulk of the twentieth century and replaced it with a very innovative, but not widely followed compromise position reflected in a few nineteenth-century cases is itself interesting. In the process, the 'situation sense',[27] or context,[28] that twentieth-century courts may have brought to the problem has been displaced by judicial visions of contract law from an earlier era and by academic commentary of a century later. If the Restatement's solution has replaced one reached within rich factual contexts with one reached through detached theory, it is one that Macaulay has taught us could be suspect.

II. INSTRUMENTAL ANALYSES OF THE PROBLEM

This Section considers the losing contract problem in the context of empirical research into the behaviour of those who make and perform contracts. It does so by taking findings from an area of that research and inserting them into an instrumental analysis of the kind used to support the new losing contract rule formulated by the Restatement. Instrumental analysis in legal discourse is ubiquitous; it may be no coincidence that it has also proven to be extraordinarily malleable. As one might expect, an instrumental analysis that is begun with different premises or assumptions is likely to produce different outcomes.

[26] See Corbin, *Corbin On Contracts* (n 17).

[27] See K Llewellyn, *The Common Law Tradition: Deciding Appeals* (Boston, Little, Brown & Co, 1960) 121–57.

[28] S Macaulay, 'Restitution in Context' (1959) 107 *University of Pennsylvania Law Review* 1133.

A. Instrumental Analysis and Assumed Party Behaviour

At the core of the instrumental analysis condemning the old 'reasonable value rule' is a prediction about how contractors will behave under it. The instrumental analysis starts with assumed contractor behaviour, proceeds to the conclusion that the traditional rule is 'inefficient' and that, in turn, leads to a normative conclusion that the rule ought to be changed. We consider here the validity of that initial behavioural prediction within the wider context of empirical work of the kind pioneered by Macaulay together with newer experimental work that extends Macaulay's empirical work.

In the context of our hypothetical problem, the instrumental analysis begins with the premise that our dimwitted Contractor, stuck in the midst of performing a losing contract, will react to his situation by responding solely to economic incentives and behave strategically by finding a way to induce the other side to breach.[29] He will do this under the current rules allowing restitution for breach because he will then recover more in the ensuing litigation: the 'reasonable value' of his performance rather than a recovery limited in some way by the breacher's less generous promise. What is worse, the 'reasonable value rule', it is said, encourages this kind of strategic behaviour and is inefficient because the parties will expend resources trying to enhance their litigation position rather than finding an appropriate contract modification.[30] And since, it is said, the parties would not choose such a rule at the outset,[31] setting the 'reasonable value rule' as a default rule would be inefficient because it would require the parties to negotiate a change in this inefficient rule, or be stuck with it, in their contracts.

This abstract analysis is demonstrably malleable. For example, a similar kind of abstract 'efficiency' analysis that could support the opposite normative conclusion (that is, support the current majority rule) would simply denominate the losing contract rule a 'penalty default rule.' To illustrate, let us assume that the parties would respond predictably to strict economic incentives and, therefore, would predictably engage in strategic behaviour. The prescient parties to the contract would know that undesirable remedial incentives would develop during performance. This knowledge would encourage them to negotiate around this 'bad' rule at the outset and thereby avoid the undesirable (and inefficient) judicial

[29] A Kull, 'Restitution as a Remedy for Breach of Contract' (1994) 67 *Southern California Law Review* 1465, 1472; M Gergen, 'Restitution and Contract: Comments on the Third Restatement' (2005) 13 *Restitution Law Review* 224, 237; compare D Laycock, *Modern American Remedies*, 4th edn (New York, Aspen Publishing, 2010) 693 fn 4.

[30] Kull, 'Restitution as a Remedy' (n 29) 1472.

[31] ibid 1517.

intervention about remedy at the litigation stage of their relationship.[32] A party-crafted solution, the argument would go, is inevitably superior to (that is, more efficient than) any general rule developed by the legal system. The parties' knowledge of and desire to avoid the government-imposed default rule would encourage them to develop a more efficient, individualised solution.

Because this kind of instrumental analysis is so easily manipulated, it is ultimately indeterminate as a normative matter. However, even if it were less indeterminate, abstract instrumental analysis begs the question whether it can offer much guidance at all in this complex setting. Unlike those provided by, say, a tax rule (for example, charitable contributions are deductible), the incentives imagined here are required to operate within highly-variable, unique, rich relational contexts where even if the incentives were accurately imagined, they compete with other incentives operating on the parties, such as the contractor's concern for business reputation, the availability of other options for the owner, the delay occasioned by a breakdown in the contract and so on.[33] Moreover, the analysis ignores the substantial transaction costs of the litigation alternative, as well as the potential for consequential damages, and assumes that the expectancy will be 'the same' whether it is delivered through a profitable performance by the losing contractor or through contract damages awarded to the winning owner in the win or lose litigation. Such assumptions are, of course, extremely unrealistic. The relational forces one can expect to operate in this context, and the transaction costs of litigation (not to mention the other unrecoverable losses implicated in a failed contract) may well dwarf other values that might be in play and, if taken into account, suggest that, whatever the rule, it may have little effect on the behaviour of the parties within the troubled contract.[34] Except where the bargain is very large and extremely unbalanced in the winner's favour, the 'winner' will likely be economically better off with (and motivated towards) a successful negotiation regardless of the rule.

But even if one downplays the substantial noise produced by the complicated set of forces operating on the parties when a relational contract is in trouble, the incentives produced within that context by the current losing contract rule might well generate collaborative rather than self-interested responses. If the incentives produced by the losing contract rule

[32] See generally I Ayres and R Gertner, 'Filling Gaps in Incomplete Contracts: An Economic Theory of Default Rules' (1989) 99 *Yale Law Journal* 87.

[33] Compare K Llewellyn, 'What Price Contract' (1931) 40 *Yale Law Journal* 704; S Macaulay, 'The Use and Non-Use of Contracts in the Manufacturing Industry' (1963) 9 *Practical Lawyer* 14.

[34] R Woodward and W Woodward, 'Exemptions as an Incentive to Voluntary Bankruptcy: An Empirical Study' (1983) 57 *American Bankruptcy Law Journal* 53 (finding that the predicted incentive effects on the rate of consumer bankruptcy filings from high and low state exemption provisions were not sustained by the data).

work differently than imagined, the acontextual analysis that proceeds from it (whatever it may be worth) may be faulty.

At the core of the 'noise-free' normative economic analysis described is the implicit empirical assertion that people actually behave in the way the abstract model assumes. An implication is that reform through a different (more efficient) rule will prompt people to behave differently (and, one must assume, more efficiently). Someone following Macaulay and searching for real-world context might well ask: 'Is that *really* how someone performing a losing contract will behave?' If initial assumptions about human behaviour control the ultimate normative prescription, and if the goal is *actually* achieving efficient results in the real world, then we ought to get more valid prescriptions from an analysis that is better grounded in *actual* human behaviour. Actual human behaviour is, obviously, responsive to context; it will respond to whatever incentives the losing contract rule actually provides *within the context* of relatively long-term, relational contracts. Those contracts tend to be personal, unique and complex, on the other end of the contractual spectrum from swaps and other contracts that are *only* about shifting risks.

While one must be extremely sceptical that any rule will have real incentive effects on the parties within this context, a slight variation in initial assumptions tends to press in favour of the 'reasonable value rule'. Consider a different contractor stuck in the same losing contract, but this time with just a little more context added in. Once this contractor discovered he was operating at a loss, he might approach the owner to begin a negotiation. One could imagine many reasons for what has evolved into a losing contract for the contractor – post-contract component price increases, weather problems, labour problems – that many would consider good reasons to open a negotiation aimed at a price adjustment (advantage-taking at the formation stage must be eliminated since this modeling assumes that both parties are fully knowledgeable, have equal bargaining power and so on). Many (if not most) owners, when faced with such a contractor, would in a real construction contract find it in their best interests to reach an accommodation. No owner wants to live with a construction job delivered by an unhappy or angry contractor – there are too many undetectable ways for a contractor to skimp on quality or otherwise frustrate the value of its performance. Put differently, if trust between the parties to a relational contract is broken, even if the owner gets some kind of performance, he might well not receive a reliable product.

If one imagined that the contractor's first move would be to approach the owner for a concession, rather than cutting corners, simply walking away, or strategically inducing the owner into breaching, then perhaps the situation would call for a rule that would encourage a collaborative adjustment of the losing contract in order to avoid its collapse. This would, at minimum, avoid the deadweight costs of non-consensual, governmental dispute resolution.[35] If one begins a rational actor analysis in a slightly different place, one might well come to an entirely different normative outcome.

We can test the available ways to address the losing contract problem by considering the likelihood of a consensual contract price modification when initiated by the losing contractor in the midst of performance of the contract in order to avoid a breakdown of the contract. Assuming that rules could produce *some* effect on the behaviour of the parties in this context, what incentive effects might be imagined from the current rules embodied in the *Restatement (Second) of Contracts*? Under those rules, the winner-owner obtains the gain on the bargain if the loser-contractor has materially breached[36] but loses that gain (and the contractor avoids that loss) if the winner-owner has materially breached.[37] These rules may actually have the effect of motivating an adjustment in order to avoid collapse of the contract, once the loser opens negotiations. These traditional rules create a downside for each of the parties should the litigation go the wrong way for them, a corresponding upside if the litigation goes right, and substantial uncertainty about which it will eventually be. Because of the uncertainty implicit in these rules, both parties will be motivated to reach a modification in order to avoid a breakdown of the contract and the hard-to-consensually-resolve dispute that will follow. And while both parties may have some reason to strategise in this setting, this motivation pales in comparison with their motivation to keep the contract going and avoid the uncertainties of litigation.

Again, recognising that whatever incentive effects the rules might produce are likely to be overwhelmed by the 'noise' of the situation, the full expectancy rule as embodied in *Restatement (Second) of Contracts* §§ 347–48 (where the gain or loss on the bargain was fully allocated at contract formation and did not vary at all depending on who breached) would seem to produce less reason to consensually modify the ongoing contract. Under this rule, the winner 'wins' her expectation regardless of who breached or where in the performance the contract broke down. In this hypothetically 'noise-free' environment, the 'winner' has little downside

[35] See, eg I Macneil, 'Efficient Breach of Contract: Circles in the Sky' (1982) 68 *Virginia Law Review* 947. Professor Macneil argued that an individualistic, non-relational perspective produces 'inefficient' outcomes. In critiquing simple law and economics reasoning epitomised by efficient breach analysis, he wrote: 'The bias against cooperation demonstrated by the simple-efficient-breach theory should surprise no one familiar with the neoclassical model. Such a bias is not limited to this particular fallacy, but is one towards which the neoclassical model inevitably and always tends. That model postulates individuals acting as if the relations in which those individuals exist have no effect on their behavior. Cooperative behavior postulates relations. A model assuming away relations slips with the greatest of ease at any stage into favoring uncooperative and – ironically enough – highly inefficient human behavior.' ibid 969.

[36] *Restatement (Second) Contracts* §§ 347, 349.

[37] ibid § 373.

to holding out – she gets the same expectancy, either through actual performance if the loser sticks it out, through contract damages if the winner wins on the breach question, and through a deduction of that same expectation amount from the loser's damages if she loses on the breach question. If the contract breaks down and a dispute ensues, it will be relatively easy (less costly) to resolve since nothing would depend on who breached first. This is consistent with the view that the contract defines all obligations at the point of contract formation and that post-formation flexibility is either beside the point or undesirable. Professor Henry Mather advanced this view based not on economic analysis (which he viewed as inconclusive) but on a libertarian idea that the law should strive towards minimal coercion and that liability should follow only from consent.[38]

R3RUE's new 'contract rate rule', a hybrid of the two extremes, would at first blush seem to lie somewhere between the two in its tendency to promote a contract adjustment, since it ultimately produces a sliding scale of economic incentive. Like the 'reasonable value rule', its operation, too, depends on who is ultimately identified as the 'first material breacher'. If the loser is the breacher, the economic result is the same as it is under the *Restatement of Contracts*: reliance damages minus the victim-winner's full expectation under the contract.[39] But if the winner is the breacher, the rule is more complicated than the traditional rule. Under the 'contract rate rule', the winner would secure a fraction of her profit (that part represented by the percentage of the contract that is complete) if she were found to be the breacher.[40] So, while material breach continues to be central to triggering that rule, the stakes that ride on the question become smaller the further along the contract proceeds in performance.

If the contract is 90 per cent complete at the time it breaks down, for example, the winner will recover 90 per cent of her expectancy if she is found to be the breacher and 100 per cent if the loser has breached. This gives the winning owner less economic reason to agree to a price adjustment the further along in performance the contract is. The tendency of the new *R3RUE* rule to motivate consensual modification depends on the performance progress of each contract under consideration.

The 'reasonable value rule' also produces a sliding scale of economic motivation but in the opposite direction: as the losing contract progresses, the gap between the winner's expectation recovery and the loser's 'reasonable value' recovery widens. If the size of the gap motivates action, then there is more motivation as the contract progresses towards full completion than there is at the start of the contract. This could supply more

[38] Mather, 'Restitution as a Remedy' (n 16) 30.

[39] *Restatement (Second) Contracts* § 349; *R3RUE* § 38(2)(a).

[40] *R3RUE* § 38(2)(b). The recovery is to be one 'not exceeding the *price* of *such performance* as determined by reference to the parties' agreement' (emphasis added). See also *R3RUE* § 38(2)(b) cmt c.

motivation for strategic action,[41] or, as developed in the text, more motivation to adjust the contract rather than face the uncertainties of a breakdown followed by a dispute resolution process. Which incentives a given rule actually supplies to real people in these settings is ultimately an empirical question that, given the 'noise' of the situation, is not likely to be resolvable.

Relational contracts gather inertia as performance advances and the parties sink tangible and intangible investments into its performance. If a rule can add anything at all to the pre-existing incentives of the parties in these complicated settings, then arguably a rule that increased incentives to keep the contract together as it gathers inertia would seem preferable to one that did the opposite.

R3RUE recognises that it may not be possible to apply the 'contract rate rule' in all cases and, importantly, what the rule should be if that is not possible. Comment d provides, in part:

> By capping the damage calculation at the contract rate *(where it can be determined)*, § 38(2) prevents these plaintiffs as well from electing performance-based damages as a means of escape from an unfavorable bargain. (emphasis added)

This, of course, contributes substantial uncertainty to the rule's application.

The new approach has undoubtedly added complexity to the analysis (in a real dispute, would the parties *ever* fail to contest what portion of the total work was actually completed?); if projected uncertainty in dispute resolution will motivate a contract adjustment to keep the contract together, the *R3RUE* approach might, ironically, supply the best motivation of all the rules.

It should be obvious that a rational actor analysis is highly indeterminate in this setting, not only because of the complexity of the relational contexts in which the parties will likely find themselves but also because the rational actor analysis itself depends on initial speculation about how people will actually behave in a given environment. Rational actor analysis of the kind described here typically assumes a rigorously self-interested actor on whom economic incentives alone operate in a context-free environment. As suggested above, one can imagine a rational actor behaving in different ways in response to economic stimuli and, of course, the behaviour selected can control the ensuing analysis. The alternate rational actor just imagined responds to economic stimulation with co-operation rather than entirely self-interested strategising.

[41] See Kull, 'Rescission and Restitution' (n 20) 1472.

B. Adding Empirical Observations to an Instrumental Analysis

Is there any support beyond pure intuition for recasting the rational actor in the way just described? Following Macaulay, one might ask: 'What would contracting parties *actually* do in this relational contract environment?'

We might be helped in this inquiry by behavioural economics, the discipline within the broad empirical tradition that Macaulay championed over 50 years ago that seeks answers to just these sorts of behavioural questions. Many studies conducted by these scholars have established that human beings do not respond to economic stimuli in the way an exclusive focus on self-interest (indeterminate as that focus may be) might suggest.[42]

The older behavioural scholarship has attacked traditional economic analysis in its most basic assumptions. Shown either to be wrong or to be sufficiently inaccurate as to distort analysis are the assumptions that those making contracts can take into account enough factors to maximise their own utility, that they are realistic in their forecasts of the future, or that they are capable of using the available data to make decisions.[43] While the empirical data supporting these attacks come largely from experimental studies of human behaviour, field observations made much earlier by Macaulay and others about the behaviour of those in business that use contracts in their work tend to corroborate more recent work.[44]

This scholarship has been remarkably provocative, but, like Macaulay's, has not generally produced a positive normative agenda: if analysis begins with the proposition that people are not very rational, are not good planners, or are careless with their communications and commitments, it is hard to see what sorts of rules one might develop to serve them better. Put more specifically, the older researchers could convince us that our losing contractor might be 'irrational' (in a narrow rational actor sense), but could give little guidance into how (other than 'irrationally', in that same narrow sense) he might behave – or what might influence that behaviour – when embroiled in a contract that was losing money. The newer work may have more promise.

[42] It would be great overstatement to suggest that the new research has done much to dampen the continued dogged outpouring of scholarship employing (now) old-fashioned Chicago School economic analysis. The persistence of traditional law and economics analysis might, ironically, be a function of the self-interest of those who practice it. See J Hanson and D Yosifon, 'The Situation: An Introduction to the Situational Character, Critical Realism, Power Economics, and Deep Capture' (2003) 152 *University of Pennsylvania Law Review* 129.

[43] A succinct summary of the then-extant literature is in M Eisenberg, 'Why There is No Law of Relational Contracts' (2000) 94 *Northwestern University Law Review* 405. See also A White, 'Behavior and Contract' (2009) 27 *Minnesota Journal of Law and Inequality* 135.

[44] A recent contribution is C Hill, 'Bargaining in the Shadow of the Lawsuit: A Social Norms Theory of Incomplete Contracts' (2009) 34 *Delaware Journal of Corporate Law* 191.

By designing experiments to test specific assumptions and rules in the law of contracts, the newer empirical researchers have gone beyond simply challenging economic 'rationality' itself to focusing on how real people actually behave when faced with contract problems. That research has identified a strong reciprocity norm affecting the behaviour of those who deal with one another,[45] a norm whose effect is largely missing from the rational actor analysis so pervasive in the literature. Professor Dan Kahan has defined this in the context of public choice this way:

> The reciprocity theory holds that individuals in collective action settings behave not like rational wealth maximizers but rather like moral and emotional reciprocators. When they perceive that other individuals are voluntarily contributing to public goods, most individuals are moved by honor, generosity, and like dispositions to do the same. When, in contrast, they perceive that others are shirking or otherwise taking advantage of them, individuals are moved by resentment and pride to withhold their own contributions and even to retaliate if possible. The reciprocity theory implies that because individuals behave in this fashion, the most effective means to promote cooperative behavior in collective action settings is to promote trust – the shared belief that others can in fact be counted on to contribute their fair share to public goods, whether or not doing so is in their material self-interest. Indeed, the reciprocity theory warns that incentives can often backfire by implying that most individuals are not inclined to contribute to collective goods voluntarily.[46]

This observation is closely related to Robert Axelrod's experiments showing that a 'tit for tat' strategy that began with co-operation was the most successful and 'profitable' strategy for addressing the prisoner's dilemma over the long run. The reciprocity norm, at its core, is relational and co-operative rather than individualist and self-interested.[47] One can also see it as corroborating many of Macaulay's and Macneil's observations.

In one very provocative recent study,[48] researchers examined how the reciprocity norm operated in the context of breach of contract. Their focus was on whether real persons care what the reason for a breach is and, if they do, how much they care and why. The researchers demonstrated that if the breach were the result of the breacher deliberately taking advantage of a better opportunity,[49] the subjects would award higher damages than

[45] In the context of public choice, see, generally D Kahan, 'The Logic of Reciprocity: Trust, Collective Action, and Law' (2003) 102 *Michigan Law Review* 71.

[46] D Kahan, 'Signaling or Reciprocating: A Response to Eric Posner's Law and Social Norms' (2002) 36 *University of Richmond Law Review* 367.

[47] See, generally R Axelrod, *The Evolution of Cooperation* (New York, Basic Books, 1984). Axelrod described his experiments as 'tit for tat', where a cooperative move by the first actor would be met by a cooperative move by the second, whereas an uncooperative or destructive move by the first would trigger a correspondingly uncooperative or destructive move by the second actor.

[48] D Hoffman and T Wilkinson-Ryan, 'Breach is for Suckers' (2010) 63 *Vanderbilt Law Review* 1003.

[49] This, of course, would be a so-called 'efficient breach'.

they would in a case where the breach were for reasons outside the breacher's control. These findings are corroborated by others observing the behaviour of contracting parties in the field.

The researchers inferred from this behaviour that real people who had brought the reciprocity norm to contracting feel 'suckered', and seek to retaliate when that norm is violated by their contracting partner. The authors concede that the findings, while statistically significant, are preliminary.[50] But the implications of the effects of an empirically observed reciprocity norm on contracting behaviour should be deeply disturbing to theorists who assume that no such value, dynamic, or motivation exists. For example, this empirically observed behaviour has the potential to undercut a core assumption of much economic analysis about contracts, that contracting parties are indifferent to whether they receive actual performance or expectation damages.[51] This assumption is behind the largely discredited[52] – but still widely discussed[53] – efficient breach paradigm and is a starting point for scores of articles that analyse contract damage rules through an instrumentalist analysis.

These newer findings may also have the potential for anchoring a less destructive, more positive normative effort at shaping rules to match the behaviour of those subject to them. Our hypothetical case here may be an example: if one took seriously the presence of a reciprocity norm within a relational contract, one might have empirical support for the proposition that our loser, when faced with performing a losing contract, would actually begin with an effort to negotiate, rather than with behaviour that was less relational and more self-centred and strategic. It might also support the proposition that, rather than rebuff such an encounter, the winner might well – and should – entertain it. Indeed, Axelrod's findings on player strategies for addressing the iterated prisoner's dilemma,[54] suggests that this contractor's strategy – initial co-operation rather than 'defection' in addressing the pricing within the contact – and the owner's co-operation, is also the most effective in the long run. Researchers – even those working at the hypothetical level without rich factual context – who began with this different set of initial moves could understand the instrumental dynamics differently and, perhaps, begin a normative analysis that resonates better with observed contracting behaviour.

[50] Hoffman and Wilkinson-Ryan, 'Breach is for Suckers' (n 48) 1036.

[51] Oliver Wendell Homes is usually credited with promulgating the idea. OW Holmes, Jr, *The Common Law* (Boston, Little, Brown & Co, 1881). This idea has been under siege for many years but until recently the attackers have not had empirical data to back up their challenges.

[52] The best of the critiques remains Macneil's; Macneil, 'Efficient Breach of Contract' (n 35).

[53] See, eg M Jiminez, 'The Value of a Promise: A Utilitarian Approach to Contract Law Remedies' (2008) 56 *UCLA Law Review* 59.

[54] Axelrod, *The Evolution of Cooperation* (n 47).

But while different initial assumptions might lead to different normative prescriptions, a main point of the foregoing discussion was to suggest that any prescriptive instrumental analysis of the incentives that might operate within a relational contract is fraught with problems. In the relational contract context particularly, it is very unlikely that instrumental analysis (whatever its initial assumptions about human behaviour) can point to any reliable policy prescriptions, even if one agreed that the goal was simply to produce an 'efficient' rule.

Where does this inconclusiveness lead one as a normative matter? It might well suggest that the wisest course for *R3RUE* would have been to defer (as did the *Restatement (Second) of Contracts*) to the wisdom of the courts, situated as they have been in the thick context of these problems. Certainly the dominant case law and an accepted view of the goals of a 'restatement' project[55] could have justified leaving the *Restatement (Second) of Contracts* rule undisturbed.

III. THE IDEOLOGICAL CONTEXT FOR THE NEW RULE

While the reciprocity norm has enormous implications for contract theory, the complexity of a relational contract context makes an instrumental analysis that emphasises the reciprocity norm subject to the same criticism as an instrumental analysis that emphasises purely self-interested behaviour. The result of such inconclusiveness would suggest deference to the status quo in most instances.

In this Section we consider the losing contract problem from a different perspective. While assumptions about human behaviour can animate an instrumental analysis that can buttress one's normative views about the losing contract rule, one's views about the nature of contract law can also determine how one conceives of the problem and its solution. Here, again, reciprocity has powerful explanatory potential: it may help explain what may have happened between the restatement of the traditional rule in the *Restatement (Second) of Contracts* in 1981 and the 'restatement' of the new rule in *R3RUE* in 2011.[56]

Embedded in *R3RUE*'s approach to the losing contract problem lies an adherence to a particular theory of contract law that leads to its sharp separation from the conception of restitution that animates the new *Restatement*. The two systems are conceived of as entirely separate *and* contract law is dominant.[57]

[55] See Shapo, 'In Search of the Law' (n 2) 634–35.

[56] Some of what follows owes its genesis to the discussion of contract in M Sandel, *Justice: What's the Right Thing to Do?* (New York, Farrar, Straus, and Giroux, 2009) and the lectures that preceded the book.

[57] This same 'system separation' animated attacks on the tort of interference with contract which in many respects, it was contended, was inconsistent with the teaching of 'efficient

R3RUE § 2 Comment c makes this clear:

> Contract is superior to restitution as a means of regulating voluntary transfers because it eliminates, or minimizes, the fundamental difficulty of valuation. Considerations of both justice and efficiency require that private transfers be made pursuant to contract whenever reasonably possible and that the parties' own definition of their respective obligations–assuming the validity of their agreement by all pertinent tests–take precedence over the obligations that the law would impose in the absence of agreement. Restitution is accordingly subordinate to contract as an organizing principle of private relationships, and the terms of an enforceable agreement normally displace any claim of unjust enrichment within their reach.[58]

This means that if a situation involves an enforceable contract, then it *must* have a solution grounded in contract, and only in contract.

That particular conception of 'contract law' that supplies a 'contract' answer to any problem involving an enforceable contract is itself a particular one that sees the field as coextensive with 'promise'[59] or, alternatively, 'consent'.[60] Once the problem is defined as having an enforceable contractual underpinning, then liability should not go beyond the 'promise' made by the breacher or beyond her consent to liability as represented by the promise. Harm to the plaintiff, if it goes beyond the promisor's commitment, might be important but is subordinate to the higher principle of limiting the promisor's liability to the value of the promise. In this way, a promise may serve primarily as a limit to the individual promisor's liability rather than as a reciprocal commitment to one's contracting partner. And expectation damages, being ultimately based on the value of the promise (rather than harm done through breach), becomes a cardinal component in this vision. In the losing contract setting, giving the loser-plaintiff a remedy that exceeds the value one calculates based on the breacher's promise would, it is said, 'unjustly enrich' the plaintiff, presumably by giving the loser plaintiff more than he bargained for,[61] or exposing the promisor to more liability than she assumed.[62] This view of

breach'. Ultimately those attacks, too, conceived of contract law as separate and 'dominant', but this time over tort law. The attacks are described and discussed in W Woodward, Jr, 'Contractarians, Community, and the Tort of Interference with Contract' (1996) 80 *Minnesota Law Review* 1103. The 'citadel' of privity – that is, the dominance of contract – also lies behind the peculiar development of products liability law in the United States. See generally W Prosser, 'Assault Upon the Citadel' (1960) 69 *Yale Law Journal* 1099.

[58] See, generally C Saiman, 'Restating Restitution: A Case of Contemporary Common Law Conceptualism' (2007) 52 *Villanova Law Review* 487. See also M Gergen, 'Restitution as a Bridge over Troubled Contractual Waters' (2002) 71 *Fordham Law Review* 709, 739.

[59] C Fried, *Contract as Promise: A Theory of Contractual Obligation* (Cambridge, Harvard University Press, 1981).

[60] See R Barnett, 'A Consent Theory of Contract' (1986) 86 *Columbia Law Review* 269; compare Mather, 'Restitution as a Remedy' (n 16).

[61] *R3RUE*, § 38 cmt d.

[62] See generally Mather, 'Restitution as a Remedy' (n 16).

contract accords great respect to personal autonomy and freedom, both to make contracts and, importantly in this context, from liability not voluntarily assumed. It tends to regard contract almost solely as a mechanism to shift risk rather than as a mechanism to shift risk *and* accomplish something through joint effort. Reciprocity, and the context that reciprocity gives to the act of making a commitment, has relatively little to do with it.

But there is, and probably always has been, a competing normative vision of the institution of contract, one based on the relational bond formed in many contracts, empirically observed by Macaulay and scores of others.[63] In this view, once a contract is made, the contracting parties owe one another 'more' than the quantifiable measure of their respective promises. One can express that 'more' in a number of ways: the trust formed in the relationship,[64] the sense of mutual reliance the contract represents, 'organic solidarity',[65] 'morality',[66] or (in the language of contemporary researchers) the obligation inferred from the 'reciprocity norm'. The importance of reciprocity in contracting has been described by philosophers[67] and, as briefly developed above, has been identified empirically in contemporary studies of co-operative and contract behaviour.[68]

By definition, reciprocity adds to the act of promising the context in which each individual promise is made; the norm tends towards a 'compensatory' rather than a 'promissory' view of contract remedies, one that would seek to compensate for harm done to the promissee unless competing policies suggested limitations. Expectation damages, in this view, serve not as a bulwark against expanded promisor liability and essential to one's vision of the institution of contract, but as an efficient surrogate for compensating for the harm that one's breach causes another, one that encourages business and credit as well. This was, of course, a theory advanced by Fuller and Perdue in their famous 1936 article.[69]

[63] This vision obviously has no application to bets, derivatives and other kinds of contracts where there is no actual performance contemplated by either side (other than the payoff). If one begins with *this* kind of contract as a paradigm, one will naturally develop a promissory vision of the institution. Compare Kull, 'Restitution as a Remedy' (n 29) 1484, quoted below in text accompanying n 74. While no-one would begin with bets as their touchstone for thinking about contracts, it is likely as an empirical matter that the vision one has of what 'typical' contracts are (lawyered, large transactions; consumer transactions; small-town, informal business transactions; etc) has a lot to do with one's vision of the institution itself.

[64] See, generally O Williamson, 'Transaction Cost Economics: The Governance of Contractual Relations' (1979) 22 *Journal of Law and Economics* 233.

[65] The term is, of course, Ian Macneil's. See generally R Gordon, 'Macaulay, Macneil, and the Discovery of Solidarity and Power in Contract Law' (1985) 1985 *Wisconsin Law Review* 565, 568–70.

[66] See R Hyland, 'Pacta Sunt Servanda: A Meditation' (1994) 34 *Virginia Journal of International Law* 405.

[67] eg Sandel, *Justice* (n 56) 147–51.

[68] See notes and accompanying text beginning at n 44 above.

[69] L Fuller and W Perdue, Jr, 'The Reliance Interest in Contract Damages, Parts 1 and 2' (1936) 46 *Yale Law Journal* 52, 62.

These different views of the rationale for the expectation measure of damages in turn can lead to a difference in one's view of the importance of the original bargain once it has been broken. If one's promise serves also as a core principle of limited liability, then breach should never expand that liability beyond the value we place on that promise. Thus, promise is not an act that can, if breached, inflict harm that must be compensated but, rather, it is an assumption of limited liability. A more reciprocal view of the institution places promissory harm nearer to the centre[70] and might downgrade the breacher's original promise as having much limiting value once she has breached that promise. At least in relational contract settings, perhaps one surrenders one's right to the benefit of the bargain when one breaches that bargain.

One can get a good sense of the contrasting perspectives on the connection between breach and the original bargain in *R3RUE*'s commentary about *Bush v Canfield*,[71] a well-known restitution case where the loser had made a down payment of $5,000 in a goods contract where the contract price was $14,000 and the goods turned out to be worth only $11,000. The seller breached by non-delivery and subsequently resisted the loser's claim for the $5,000 down payment, maintaining that the loser's loss on the bargain should be deducted leaving the buyer's refund claim at $2,000. The court rejected this proposition. This outcome seems very intuitive and nearly self-evident. But how one explains it can reflect powerfully the vision one has for contract law.

R3RUE would follow precedent and permit Bush to get his $5,000 back, undiminished by the consequences of his bad bargain. It does so through its remedy in Section 37 called 'rescission'. But it seems to be a grudging acceptance of this universally followed precedent, embraced by the Article 2 of the *Uniform Commercial Code* since its inception.[72] Comment b to *R3RUE* § 37 explains:

> In theory, and on rare occasions in practice, rescission pursuant to § 37 permits a plaintiff who has paid in advance for a defaulted performance to recover an amount exceeding *compensatory* damages. *See* Illustrations 1–2 [Illustration 2 uses the essential facts of *Bush v Canfield*]. Such outcomes are rare, because a prepaid seller will almost never forfeit a profit that might be earned, at the seller's option, by performing the contract or simply releasing the buyer. The *striking* results of Illustrations 1–2 are the fortuitous consequence of the law's adherence to a simple rule rather than a complex one. The simple rule is that a

[70] Harm done through promising is directly compensated through promissory estoppel even if the promisor did not intend to make a binding commitment. See, eg *Ricketts v Scothorn*, 77 NW 2d 365 (NE 1898).

[71] *Bush v Canfield*, 2 Conn 485 (CT 1818).

[72] The specific facts of *Bush* would today be controlled by Art 2 of the *Uniform Commercial Code*. UCC § 2-711(1) permits a buyer in all cases of seller breach to recover 'so much of the price as has been paid'.

> plaintiff who seeks only the return of a prepaid price, or return of property in specie, will not (for reasons of both fairness and economy) be put to the burden of proving damages from the defendant's breach. There is no comparable *windfall* to the plaintiff if the sequence of performance is reversed because rescission is not available as a remedy for a payment default.[73]

Note the underlying assumptions: that expectation damages (derived from the original bargain) are compensatory; that allowing the plaintiff to recover in excess of the bargain is 'striking'; and that damages in excess of expectation are a 'windfall'.

In this vision, the contract once struck has permanently shifted the risk, survives intact, and is independent of performance; breach – and the violation of the reciprocity norm that breach may represent – has little or no role to play. Indeed, but for the administrative convenience that produced *Bush v Canfield*'s 'striking windfall', one would imagine a policy view that would hard-wire the deal Bush and Canfield stuck and return to Bush only the $2,000 that was left after deducting his self-inflicted loss on the bargain.

One holding such a strong view of the significance of the original – but breached – bargain might also question or reject the proposition suggested earlier that, were the loser to approach the winner in the midst of performance for a concession, the best outcome would be an adjusted contract. Having played the game at contract formation, for all intents and purposes, the game is over. Having legitimately 'won' at the outset by making a good bargain, the winner should have little reason to make a concession to the loser.

Apart from the convenience of remedy, should the fact of breach itself matter in *Bush v Canfield*? A sharply contrasting vision of *Bush* can be seen in the work of Professor George Palmer, a well-known and dominant voice in restitution in the mid to late twentieth century, who wrote a full-throated defence of the traditional losing contract rule eventually embraced by *Restatement (Second) of Contracts* § 373:

> Certainly on those facts it is difficult to see the justice of allowing the seller to retain $3,000 of the amount received from the buyer, on the plea that the buyer would have lost this amount if the seller had performed a contract which in fact he did not perform. The seller gave nothing in exchange for the $3,000 except a broken promise and the principle of unjust enrichment surely is applicable. If the buyer had made no payment and had been the party who repudiated the contract, the seller could have recovered $3,000 damages for loss of his bargain. It would be curious indeed for the seller to obtain the same advantage when he is the one guilty of breach.[74]

[73] *R3RUE* § 37 cmt b (emphasis added).

[74] G Palmer, 'The Contract Price as a Limit on Restitution for a Defendant's Breach' (1959) 20 *Ohio State Law Review* 264, 267.

Significantly, the Reporter's view, compared to Professor Palmer's, is quite different:

> In reality, however, the seller 'gave' the essence of what he undertook to give: He made himself liable for flour for future delivery, at a fixed price, giving the buyer an enforceable right to any profit that might be produced by a market advance. In exchange, the seller obtained the mirror-image to the buyer's contractual position: an enforceable right to any profit produced by a market decline. Because the seller's risk was the price of the seller's potential profit, it can hardly be said that the seller, having borne the risk, is unjustly enriched if he obtains the reward.[75]

Contract, in this latter view, is a matter of individual risk-taking and risk-fixing that occurs at contract formation. The parties are each betting against one another rather than trying to accomplish something through collective effort. The values set at this point are largely immutable and expectation damages are the full equivalent of a contract performed rather than breached. This view may be sound with respect to bets or swaps where there is no performance contemplated other than the payoff; it becomes increasingly implausible as contracts proceed from bets to highly relational contracts such as construction contracts.

In Palmer's vision of contract remedies, breach matters; a promise that is breached is different from a promise that has not been breached. If one views the return of the full prepayment as 'extra' compensation, or as 'supracompensatory' to the party who has made a losing bargain,[76] perhaps this is in implicit recognition (and a form of quantification) of the reciprocity norm that was violated by the defendant. It should matter little whether the loser gave cash or services prior to the winner's breach. And, since the losing plaintiff seeks only the value of what the defendant received, not necessarily his entire reliance expenditure, the winner is protected against the unlimited and unascertainable risk that a reliance-damages-without-deduction rule would supply. In giving strong lip service to the contract-as-liability-limit position, the thrust of the commentary to *R3RUE*'s rules gives a primacy to contract law,[77] tends to enshrine the original bargain of the parties (and the limitations to liability that the bargain might provide), and tends to reduce the significance of breach in *actually* altering the economic exchange created when the parties struck their contract. In that respect, *R3RUE* echoes the sentiments of modern scholars who lean heavily on law and economics analysis and who are inclined toward a non-reciprocal, contract-as-promise vision of contract law.

[75] Kull, 'Restitution as a Remedy' (n 29) 1484.
[76] See Wilkinson-Ryan and Hoffman, 'Breach is for Suckers' (n 48) 1143.
[77] *R3RUE* Introductory Note 2 to § 37; see also *R3RUE* § 38 cmt a.

Beginning with the free market economic theories championed principally by the University of Chicago (and marketed by its most vociferous spokesperson, Milton Friedman), the related political rhetoric of Margaret Thatcher and Ronald Reagan, and the relentless outpouring of judicial opinions and academic writing by Richard Posner, those views have been promoted on many fronts, have gained considerable ground since the mid 1970s, and may well dominate contemporary contract scholarship. The less individualist, more reciprocal way that earlier scholars thought and wrote about contract problems provided a context for the *Restatement (Second) of Contracts*; the work of later scholars provided a context for *R3RUE*. To even the casual observer, the context against which we think about contract law has changed dramatically during the last 25 years and it would be surprising if *this* context did not affect how contract law is perceived. While this cannot offer normative support for the new losing contract rule, it certainly contributes to our understanding of how it came to be.

IV. HOW MIGHT THE NEW RULE FARE IN THE COURTS?

The driving forces behind the new losing contract rule appear to have been instrumental analyses suggesting that the pre-existing rule was inefficient and a view of contract law that saw the breacher's promise (as quantified by the expectation damages system) as providing limitations on the liability that a breacher should shoulder for breaching a contract. Section II suggested that the instrumental effect of contract rules depends on the contractual context, that their operation as incentives in relational contract settings may range from non-existent to extremely small, and in both cases are likely drowned out by other forces. That Section also suggested that instrumental analysis in this context is, in any event, extremely malleable and critically depends on assumptions about complex human behaviour for its predictive power. Actual, empirically-based human behaviour may well be different than (or in some cases, perhaps opposite to) that assumed by those supporting a change in the traditional rule and might well support the older rule itself. That Section concluded by suggesting that an instrumental analysis in this highly-relational context was sufficiently inconclusive as to actually suggest support for the old rule, developed as it was by courts working in the complex contexts that are assumed away in the process of creating a normative instrumental analysis.

Section III argued that a particular vision of contract law and of its primacy over overlapping systems (here, the restitution system) may have driven the rule change, despite case law that remained essentially unchanged. But views of what contract law 'is' change, with a 'contract-as-promise' view dominating the late nineteenth century into the early twentieth,[78] a far fuzzier view ushered in by the legal realists that included (thanks to Ian Macneil and Stewart Macaulay among others) a recognition of 'contract as relation' that gained many adherents during the twentieth century, and a re-awakened 'contract-as-promise' view gathering momentum in the 1980s. It may not be easy to form an apolitical normative judgment about the losing contract rule when that judgment is inevitably and perhaps imperceptibly affected by our ideological beliefs about what contract law (which turns out, to the surprise of many, to be extremely value-laden) should do.

This Section considers the question of whether the new rule will be embraced by the courts in the kinds of cases where it will arise. It will also briefly consider whether the new rule might have effects outside the litigation system.

The 'contract rate rule' proposed in *R3RUE* has been around for a very long time, is intuitively satisfying, and is probably quite well known. But nonetheless it has been widely rejected by twentieth-century courts.[79] The staying power in the courts of the traditional 'reasonable value rule' is its central puzzle. If *R3RUE*'s solution will prove unattractive to judges deciding complex cases, the 'contract rate rule' may ultimately fail to gain judicial adherents and thereby become dead letter. This may be particularly true where there is ample precedent in the case law and support in the *Restatement (Second) of Contracts* for the older approach. In our system, the pressure of work provides strong incentives to judges to follow precedent rather than attempt to explain why a new rule is better.

Despite the primacy-of-contract rhetoric in *R3RUE*'s commentary,[80] as developed earlier, the 'contract rate rule' proposed in § 38 actually *does* take breach (and some of Professor Palmer's view)[81] into account, albeit in a complex way. Section 38(2)(b) provides that a plaintiff may recover for breach of contract:

> (b) the market value of the plaintiff's uncompensated contractual performance, not exceeding the *price of such performance* as determined by reference to the parties' agreement.[82]

When the plaintiff sues for reasonable value conferred, this provision limits the plaintiff to the proportion of the total price represented by the amount of work actually done under the contract. To the extent the loser

[78] This was, of course, the 'contract' that Grant Gilmore declared 'dead' in G Gilmore, *The Death of Contract* (Columbus, Ohio State University Press, 1974).

[79] See Palmer, *Law of Restitution* (n 22).

[80] The logic of that rhetoric would bring us a rule that deducted the loser's *entire* loss from a recovery of the benefit conferred on the breaching winner. See Mather, 'Restitution as a Remedy' (n 16) 48. As developed here, that logic does not lead either to the contract rate rule stated in § 38 or to the price cap rule that may in many cases substitute for it.

[81] Professor Palmer is quoted in the body text, above p 367; compare *R3RUE*'s commentary that captures some of Professor Palmer's view, below n 83 and accompanying text.

[82] *R3RUE* § 38(2)(b) (emphasis added).

had perverse incentives to induce the winner to breach – so he could get a better recovery than would be the case if he were found to be the breacher – those remain incentives under the new rule (since the recovery still depends on who is held to be the breacher), but to a lesser extent.

In amplifying this compromise rule, the commentary explains:

> If the rule were otherwise (so that . . . the whole of the plaintiff's expected loss from performance were deducted from the value of his interrupted performance), the defendant would be in the position of imposing a unilateral modification or novation, on the terms most favorable to himself, and of doing so, moreover, by breach rather than by negotiation.[83]

While this compromise position may be intuitively appealing and the rule is found in Article 2 of the *Uniform Commercial Code* for goods contracts, nearly all of which are easily divisible,[84] the context in which these cases are likely to come up suggest serious problems with the apportionment required to apply the new rule. Indeed, it seems quite likely that the new rule cannot easily be applied at all in the relational settings where it will be called on to perform.

Even in those construction contract cases where some unit rate is stated, a real-world context would suggest that the parties did not intend to apportion their actual performances in the way the stated rate might suggest. In making this point, Professor Palmer wrote:

> Almost without exception such contracts are treated as entire . . . This is true even though the whole contract price is based on a price for each unit of work done and the units are capable of precise measurement, for example, so much for each running foot of street graded or each yard of earth excavated. It is evident that this recognizes the realities of the business arrangement – it is not likely, for example, that a contractor would arrange his working schedules and marshal his labor force and equipment at the site to grade one hundred feet of street at the unit price agreed on for more than four thousand feet.[85]

While the *R3RUE* rule may be intuitively satisfying, apportioning the contract price when the parties' agreement does not lend itself to divisability seems both intrusive and a violation of the parties' intent. Their contract was for an entire performance for an entire price, not the fraction of either. Perhaps this can partially explain why *Kehoe v Rutherford*,[86] a very well-known case[87] that used a percentage rule, and on which the *R3RUE* rule is based, was not widely followed in the twentieth century. In complex

[83] *R3RUE* § 38 cmt d.
[84] UCC § 2-607(1) (buyer pays for goods accepted at the 'contract rate').
[85] Palmer, *Law of Restitution* (n 8) § 4.4 pp 404–405.
[86] *Kehoe v Rutherford*, 27 A 912 (NJ 1893).
[87] The case appears in many Contracts casebooks including (of course) S Macaulay and others, *Contracts: Law in Action*, vol 1, 3rd edn (Charlottesville, Lexis, 2011) 185.

cases, the apportionment approach will be very difficult to implement[88] and will likely be no truer to the parties supposed intent than is the traditional rule that simply awards reasonable value. The commentary to the new rule seems to recognise this and suggests that, when apportionment is not possible, courts should simply cap the reasonable value recovery with the contract price.[89]

This may suggest that the *real* rule that will be available in the complex environments that gave rise to the traditional rule is the contract 'price-cap rule', *not* the more intuitively-satisfying 'contract rate rule' supported by the commentary to *R3RUE* § 38(2)(b). This 'price-cap rule' rests on the normative proposition that the winner should *never* be required to pay more than was explicitly agreed to in the contract.

But capping a reasonable value award by the contract price is even less true to the parties' supposed intent. Indeed, allowing reasonable value up to the contract price, while true to a policy of protecting the winner from paying more than she explicitly promised for the whole performance, may be otherwise incoherent. The big-loser plaintiff who has conferred a small part of the bargained-for benefit receives the same recovery (the contract price) as the small-loser plaintiff who has conferred a much larger part of the work. While one cannot know why an intuitively satisfying *Kehoe* rule was not widely embraced by the courts, one reason may be that, when faced with the complexities of litigation involving partially-performed contracts, the *Kehoe* rule was simply unworkable and the alternative of capping a reasonable value award with the contract price seemed an even less satisfying judicial response to the winner's breach of contract than the traditional, uncapped, alternative.

While the inertia of the past (and precedent) might suggest that modern courts, too, might reject the new rule, it is hazardous to project twenty-first century judicial receptivity from twentieth-century decisions. Section 38 will give modern courts some secondary authority to cap a recovery at the contract price, though the main explanation for the rule is the far more satisfying (to some) contract-rate rule. And while the price-cap outcome is (perhaps) the least coherent approach when measured against likely party intent, it may be appealing to courts who would view contract as a liability-limiting device. Our courts are also a product of our modern times and might well be more receptive to a contract-as-promise view of the situation than were earlier courts that considered expectation damages as simply one of many ways the legal system might legitimately respond to a breach of contract.

What about the effects of the new rule those who perform contracts? It seems extremely unlikely that the parties to the kinds of contracts involved

[88] In most relational contract settings, both the question whether apportionment is appropriate and what the correct apportionment is will (and should) be hotly contested issues.

[89] See the illustrations to *R3RUE* § 38, in particular Illustrations 14 and 15.

here will know of the new rule, at least until the first case is litigated and the new rule implemented within it. But even if they were to know of the new rule, and even if the new rule's incentive effects (whatever they may be) were not overwhelmed by the other motivational forces operating in the context of these complex contracts, the parties' strategic decision-making within their contract has actually been further complicated by the new rule. As before, it will be extraordinarily difficult for the parties to an ongoing relational contract to predict who the court will hold to be the first material breacher (and under the new rule, it will still matter). With the announced new rule, it will also be very difficult to predict which rule ('reasonable value rule', 'price-capped rule', or 'contract rate rule') the court will use once it decides the material breach question. The added uncertainty may have the paradoxical effect of keeping relational contracts together by making what will happen if either party withdraws even more unpredictable.[90] While it would not be a welcome conclusion for those who laboured hard to find the 'right' solution to the losing contract problem, on this basis one might perhaps proclaim the rule 'a success'.

For the contract system more generally, 'success' will be in the eye of the beholder. Quite clearly the new rule further enshrines a particular view of contract law and, in the process, contributes to the marketing of that view. Those who already hold that view will applaud this affirmation of their view, and those now being educated will see additional evidence that it is *the* way to think about contract law.

But the fascination of this subject is that there always are, and always have been, more ways than one to look at it. In concluding this Section, it is worth recalling a famous passage from Grant Gilmore's *The Death of Contract*:

> We have become used to the idea that, in literature and the arts, there are alternating rhythms of classicism and romanticism. During classical periods, which are, typically, of brief duration, everything is neat, tidy and logical; theorists and critics reign supreme; formal rules of structure and composition are stated to the general acclaim . . . But the classical aesthetic, once it has been formulated, regularly breaks down in a protracted romantic agony. The romantics spurn the exquisitely stated rules of the preceding period; they experiment, they improvise; they deny the existence of any rules; they churn around in an ecstacy of self-expression. At the height of a romantic period, everything is confused, sprawling, formless and chaotic – as well as, frequently, extremely interesting. Then, the romantic energy having spent itself, there is a new classical reformulation – and so the rhythms continue.[91]

[90] If, by chance, the parties knew about the uncertainty that would follow if one or the other breached the contract, they might well liquidate damages or limit liability at the outset, an outcome that would be seen by many as the best alternative.

[91] Gilmore, *The Death of Contract* (n 78) 111–12.

We have probably been in another 'classical period' since the 1980s, but we now have a new generation of researchers, following Macaulay's lead, who are challenging theoretical conclusions with real-world observations. There will be, no doubt, many candidates in the new generation of empirical scholars for the title 'Lord High Executioner of the Contract is Dead Movement' that Gilmore conferred on Macaulay at the start of his book.[92] It will only be a matter of time before they work their magic.

CONCLUSION

Stewart Macaulay began his long career with a 1959 article that wondered whether the law of restitution could be understood without its context. From that first effort, he proceeded to a career – and helped begin a tradition – of empirical examination of the many contexts in which the law is used. His many studies might well be described as unsettling: repeatedly, they suggest that real parties in real situations do not behave as the 'rational' people we might hope, imagine or hypothesise them to be. Reading Macaulay would make one sceptical that theory could ever accurately capture or describe a coherent picture, or that rules could have reliably predictable effects on those they aim to affect.

This examination of the losing contract rules – the traditional one found in the *Restatement (Second) of Contracts* and the new one found in the new *Restatement (Third) of Restitution* – extends Macaulay's call for 'context' in an effort both to better understand why the rule changed, and to predict whether it will be a successful change. It has suggested that the normative case for the new rule is, ultimately, contingent on behavioural predictions that may be false, and on an idea of contract law that is debatable and perhaps ideological. On this basis, one could argue that the proponents of change have not met their normative burden, and that the courts who have worked in the thicket of relational contracts are more likely to have got it 'right' than have the theorists.

The new complexity that the added rules contribute to predicting legal outcomes may have the effect of dampening party enthusiasm for ending their contracts and, instead, prompting them to work things out rather than resort to litigation. However one views *that* as an outcome, it may mean that we will not know for a long time whether the new rule will be well-received or rejected in the courts.[93] And given the cyclical nature of our views of contract law and of the expanding work of Macaulay-

[92] ibid fn 1.

[93] Actually, given the replacement of much contract litigation with arbitration, we may never know. See C Knapp, 'Taking Contracts Private: The Quiet Revolution in Contract Law' (2002) 71 *Fordam Law Review* 761.

inspired empiricists, the 'contract law' that has been the predicate and context for the *R3RUE* rule may be 'dead' before we find out.

BIBLIOGRAPHY

Axelrod, R, *The Evolution of Cooperation* (New York, Basic Books, 1984).

Ayres, I and Gertner, R, 'Filling Gaps in Incomplete Contracts: An Economic Theory of Default Rules' (1989) 99 *Yale Law Journal* 87.

Barnett, R, 'A Consent Theory of Contract' (1986) 86 *Columbia Law Review* 269.

Corbin,A, *Corbin On Contracts*, vol 5 (St Paul, West Publishing, 1950).

Eisenberg, M, 'Why There is No Law of Relational Contracts' (2000) 94 *Northwestern University Law Review* 405.

Fried, C, *Contract as Promise: A Theory of Contractual Obligation* (Cambridge, Harvard University Press, 1981).

Fuller, L and Perdue, Jr, W, 'The Reliance Interest in Contract Damages, Parts 1 and 2' (1936) 46 *Yale Law Journal* 52.

Gegan, B, 'In Defense of Restitution: A Comment on Mather, Restitution as a Remedy for Breach of Contract: The Case of the Partially Performing Seller' (1984) 57 *Southern California Law Review* 723.

Gergen, M, 'Restitution and Contract: Comments on the Third Restatement' (2005) 13 *Restitution Law Review* 224.

——, 'Restitution as a Bridge over Troubled Contractual Waters' (2002) 71 *Fordham Law Review* 709.

Gilmore, G, *The Death of Contract* (Columbus, Ohio State University Press, 1974).

Gordon, R, 'Macaulay, Macneil, and the Discovery of Solidarity and Power in Contract Law' (1985) 1985 *Wisconsin Law Review* 565.

Hanson, J and Yosifon, D, 'The Situation: An Introduction to the Situational Character, Critical Realism, Power Economics, and Deep Capture' (2003) 152 *University of Pennsylvania Law Review* 129.

Hill, C, 'Bargaining in the Shadow of the Lawsuit: A Social Norms Theory of Incomplete Contracts' (2009) 34 *Delaware Journal of Corporate Law* 191.

Hoffman, D and Wilkinson-Ryan, T, 'Breach is for Suckers' (2010) 63 *Vanderbilt Law Review* 1003.

Holmes, Jr, OW, *The Common Law* (Boston, Little, Brown & Co, 1881).

Hyland, R, 'Pacta Sunt Servanda: A Meditation' (1994) 34 *Virginia Journal of International Law* 405.

Jiminez, M, 'The Value of a Promise: A Utilitarian Approach to Contract Law Remedies' (2008) 56 *UCLA Law Review* 59.

Kahan, D, 'The Logic of Reciprocity: Trust, Collective Action, and Law' (2003) 102 *Michigan Law Review* 71.

——, 'Signaling or Reciprocating: A Response to Eric Posner's Law and Social Norms' (2002) 36 *University of Richmond Law Review* 367.

Knapp, C, 'Taking Contracts Private: The Quiet Revolution in Contract Law' (2002) 71 *Fordam Law Review* 761.

Kull, A, 'Rescission and Restitution' (2006) 61 *Business Lawyer* 569.

——, 'Restitution as a Remedy for Breach of Contract' (1994) 67 *Southern California Law Review* 1465.

Laycock, D, *Modern American Remedies*, 4th edn (New York, Aspen Publishing, 2010).
Llewellyn, K, *The Common Law Tradition: Deciding Appeals* (Boston, Little, Brown & Co, 1960).
——, 'What Price Contract' (1931) 40 *Yale Law Journal* 704.
Macaulay, S, 'The Use and Non-Use of Contracts in the Manufacturing Industry' (1963) 9 *Practical Lawyer* 14.
——, 'Restitution in Context' (1959) 107 *University of Pennsylvania Law Review* 1133.
Macaulay, S and others, *Contracts: Law in Action*, vol 1, 3rd edn (Charlottesville, Lexis, 2011).
Macneil, I, 'Efficient Breach of Contract: Circles in the Sky' (1982) 68 *Virginia Law Review* 947.
Mather, H, 'Restitution as a Remedy for Breach of Contract: The Case of the Partially Performing Seller' (1982) 92 *Yale Law Journal* 14.
Palmer, G, *Law of Restitution* (Alphen aan den Rijn, Wolters Kluwer).
——, 'The Contract Price as a Limit on Restitution for a Defendant's Breach' (1959) 20 *Ohio State Law Review* 264.
Palmer, G and Kaplan, L, *Law of Restitution* (2011 Cum Supp) (Alphen aan den Rijn, Wolters Kluwer).
Prosser, W, 'Assault Upon the Citadel' (1960) 69 *Yale Law Journal* 1099.
Saiman, C, 'Restating Restitution: A Case of Contemporary Common Law Conceptualism' (2007) 52 *Villanova Law Review* 487.
Sandel, M, *Justice: What's the Right Thing to Do?* (New York, Farrar, Straus, and Giroux, 2009).
Shapo, M, 'In Search of the Law of Products Liability: The ALI Restatement Project' (1995) 48 *Vanderbilt Law Review* 631.
White, A, 'Behavior and Contract' (2009) 27 *Minnesota Journal of Law and Inequality* 135.
Williamson, O, 'Transaction Cost Economics: The Governance of Contractual Relations' (1979) 22 *Journal of Law and Economics* 233.
Woodward, R and Woodward, W, 'Exemptions as an Incentive to Voluntary Bankruptcy: An Empirical Study' (1983) 57 *American Bankruptcy Law Journal* 53.
Woodward, Jr, W, 'Contractarians, Community, and the Tort of Interference with Contract' (1996) 80 *Minnesota Law Review* 1103.

13

Contract in a Pre-Realist World: Professor Macaulay, Lord Hoffmann and the Rise of Context in the English Law of Contract

JOHN WIGHTMAN

INTRODUCTION

REFLECTING ON SOME of the themes of Stewart Macaulay's work from the 1960s and subsequently, it has struck me that, seen from the point of view of English contract law, some of those themes take on a somewhat paradoxical aspect. The classic 1963 paper 'Non-Contractual Relations in Business – A Preliminary Study'[1] became very well known among contract scholars and teachers in the UK, becoming perhaps the American article on contract which is best known here;[2] a significant (though not large) body of empirical work in my country has built on those insights about the operational relevance of contract law.[3] Alongside this, though, there has been little tradition – at least until the last decade – of scholarly debate in the UK about the role of context in the business of interpreting or enforcing contracts,[4] and this, in turn, has reflected the relatively slight emphasis which issues of context have traditionally had – at least

[1] S Macaulay, 'Non-Contractual Relations in Business – A Preliminary Study' (1963) 28 *American Sociological Review* 55.

[2] At least part of the reason the article became widely known was that it was published in the reader by V Aubert (ed), *Sociology of Law* (London, Penguin Books, 1969), and was the model for another widely known piece which contained extensive references to it (H Beale and T Dugdale, 'Contracts Between Businessmen: Planning and the Use of Contractual Remedies' (1975) 2 *British Journal of Law and Society* 45).

[3] See, especially the essays in the second part of D Campbell and PV Jones (eds), *Contract and Economic Organisation* (Aldershot, Ashgate, 1996), and also S Deakin and J Michie (eds), *Contracts, Co-operation, and Competition* (Oxford, Oxford University Press, 1997).

[4] See, especially two collections published in 2003 that responded to the changes of the late 1990s: D Campbell, H Collins, and J Wightman (eds), *Implicit Dimensions of Contract* (Oxford, Hart Publishing, 2003); S Worthington (ed), *Commercial Law and Commercial Practice* (Oxford, Hart Publishing, 2003).

explicitly – in English law. However, starting in the late 1990s with cases on the role of context in the interpretation of express terms, the issue of context has been addressed more explicitly in the law.

Compared with the roots of contextualism in American law, this stirring of an expanded contextual dimension is striking: it was entirely judicially led, with no recourse to pre-existing extra-judicial sources of the kind exemplified by the *Restatement (Second) of Contracts*, or the *Uniform Commercial Code* (UCC). However, although the comparatively rich understanding of context that has emerged was not (as far as one can tell) directly influenced by the work of American scholars such as Macaulay, the use of commercial context as a source of obligations which can disrupt apparently established principles (and in ways contested by some orthodox lawyers), chimes with some of the themes of that work.[5]

It is this emergence of a more explicit role for context in the law that I will explore here. The sense in which I am using context is capacious: it includes everything that could affect or give meaning to the transaction beyond the express words of the contract. It covers the shared knowledge, expectations, customs and norms that prevail in the market in which the parties are engaged, and also the commercial purpose of both the particular contract in question, and of contracts undertaken in the relevant market sector. The focus is on the new ways in which English law *expresses* or *registers* context as a source for determining a legal dispute.[6] I will argue that, in major House of Lords cases since the late 1990s on interpretation of contract and the scope of liability for damages, a new approach has been fashioned which enlarges the role of context in issues where it has already had some relevance (the interpretation cases), and introduces context as a prime consideration in issues where it has previously not been drawn upon (the damages cases); and that the framing of the principle underlying these changes contains the potential to spread the explicit reference to context yet further.

The principle judicial author of this development is Lord Hoffmann,[7] and he has explained the enlarged role for context as being underpinned

[5] See, eg S Macaulay 'Justice Traynor and the Law of Contracts' (1961) 13 *Stanford Law Review* 813, 819–27, discussing an approach to interpretation with some resemblances to that discussed below. Also, Macaulay's paper 'The Real Deal and the Paper Deal, Empirical Pictures of Relationships, and the Urge for Simple Transparent Rules', published in the *Modern Law Review* as well as in *Implicit Dimensions of Contract* (n 4), has provoked discussion of contextualism and neoformalism; see especially C Mitchell, 'Contracts and Contract Law: Challenging the Distinction Between the "Real Deal" and the "Paper Deal"' (2009) 27 *Oxford Journal of Legal Studies* 675.

[6] It is not novel for English contract law to draw on some elements of context. In some areas of doctrine, reference to context or background was established, examples including cases of ambiguity in construction, and implied terms based on the principle of 'business efficacy'. *The Moorcock* (1889) 14 PD 64.

[7] Lord Hoffmann was a judge in the High Court 1986–92, the Court of Appeal 1992–95, and the House of Lords 1995–2009.

by an objective approach to contract. Whilst this underpinning offers what some may see as a reassuringly familiar grounding, I will argue that this is not quite what it may seem: it amounts to a major extension of the objective approach as it has been understood in English law hitherto. At one level, the use of an extended objective approach to gain access to contextual norms which reflect commercial understandings looks like a typical example of neoclassical law, in that it is using a concept with classical origins to adapt the law to cope better with commercial realities. Whilst this has some truth, I will argue that the extended objective approach has the potential to fundamentally shift the balance from the documents, and other orthodox indicia of agreement, drawing more explicitly on the parties' context as a source of the norms that govern their relationship. In the process, the objective approach can become completely detached from the idea of consent or shared intention, and can operate effectively as a mirror of contextual norms.

This contextual 'turn' in English law is striking when it is compared with the more explicit ways in which context is expressed in American law. English law lacks any equivalent of the general provisions of the UCC on course of performance, course of dealing, and usage of trade (Article 1-303), and good faith (Article 1-304). It has been less hospitable to contextual readings and understandings in the law of contract, and I will argue that this is partly traceable to the 'pre-realist' tradition of the English law of contract.

In the Section I, I provide a short account of what I mean by describing English contract law as 'pre-realist'. This section looks at the intellectual context – both judicial and scholarly – in which these developments have occurred, and pinpoints what seem to me some key differences in the substance and infrastructure of English and American law; as will become clear, however, 'pre-realist' is only a partial characterisation. In Section II, I examine the resurgence of context in the case law, focusing especially on four leading cases in the House of Lords. In Section III, I focus on what is distinctive about the extended objective approach, and the arguably different theory of contract that underlies it, despite its expression in neoclassical terms.

I. A PRE-REALIST LAW OF CONTRACT?

American and English contract law have strong and well-known affinities which stem from the common law method, their shared pre-modern history, and strong continuing resemblances in their conceptual frameworks. English courts will, on occasion, refer to American case law, and the scholarly writing about contract in American law reviews has been a source of great enrichment of the study of contract law in the UK, especially work on more general theoretical issues, which often can be read as though written about English law. That said, I want here to highlight some key differences, which I think help to shed light on how English contract law has come to embrace a form of contextualism over the last 15 years. In general, I will argue that the rise of context in English law has, compared with American law, been a 'bootstraps' process, by which I mean it has relied more on developing ideas internal to the law and judicial process.

Taken together, these differences form a cluster that I have called 'pre-realist'. I have used this term because most (although not all) of the elements are part of a legal tradition in which judicial decisions have been regarded as self-sufficient and relatively uninfluenced by academic commentary, and where the mainstream of academic commentary has been concerned with the internal coherence of doctrine rather than external factors and external critique.[8] The features identified here are relatively well recognised: for present purposes, their significance lies in their combination.

First is the simple point that the English common law of contract consists of a single body of law, which has been developed within a hierarchical system of courts applying the principle of precedent; the Supreme Court (formerly the House of Lords) is therefore able to conclusively decide a matter of common law, and other courts will follow it.[9] The authority of the Supreme Court over the common law is preserved because of the sharp distinction between common law and legislation.[10] In relation to contracts, legislative reform has been piecemeal, and has carefully modified the common law only in specific ways. In contract, legislative principles that are intended to apply generally are very rare, and so legislation is not a source of principle that can underpin or shape common law development. In fact, legislation has, in some cases, had the opposite effect: by substituting a set of inert detailed rules for pre-existing principles, the common law can become cauterised at that point, and no longer able to craft or borrow a solution to the issues addressed by the legislation.[11] This contrasts markedly with the situation in America where states

[8] For a discussion of a pre-realist discourse in relation to restitution in Commonwealth jurisdictions, see C Saiman, 'Restitution in America: Why the US Refuses to Join the Global Restitution Party' (2008) 28 *Oxford Journal of Legal Studies* 99. There is also evidence of a pre- (or anti-) realist movement in tort; of particular note are A Beever, *Rediscovering the Law of Negligence* (Oxford, Hart Publishing, 2007), and R Stevens, *Torts and Rights* (Oxford, Oxford University Press, 2007).

[9] The almost total removal of juries from civil cases in England since 1945 has reinforced judicial control, arguably creating the need for less law; see W Whitford, 'The Role of the Jury (and the Fact/Law Distinction) in the Interpretation of Written Contracts' (2001) 2001 *Wisconsin Law Review* 931.

[10] On this, see J Beatson, 'Has the Common Law a Future?' (1997) 56 *Cambridge Law Journal* 291.

[11] A good example is the way that judicial attempts to address unfair terms in consumer contracts were effectively terminated by the enactment of the Unfair Contract Terms Act 1977, which implemented a Law Commission report on the matter. One result is that the

which have adopted articles of the UCC that contain general principles shaping the application of the common law of contract.[12]

As well as a lack of general principle in legislation, English contract law has not had the option of drawing on a source of principles like the *Restatement (Second) of Contracts*: apart from the fact that academic commentators have not traditionally had the status to command respect for such a project, the unitary hierarchal system of the courts which apply the common law leaves little space for such an optional source.[13] The status of the Supreme Court at the apex of a unitary system has also meant that some leading judges have come to have a more dominant influence than appears to be the case in American law. There have been a number who reached the House of Lords whose judgments in contract cases have been held in exceptionally high regard, and whose views have heavily shaped the law.[14] In the development of the role of context, Lord Hoffmann in particular has been pre-eminent; the emergence of context in the modern case law is mainly his doing, and his standing has contributed to its becoming embedded in the law.

The English tradition of less respect for the academic role[15] has resulted not just in less notice being taken of academic writing, but may have contributed also to a tendency in traditional mainstream commentary to be somewhat more deferential to courts, resulting in critique which is

general common law rule that people are bound when they sign a standard form contracts remains good law in those situations not specifically dealt with by the legislation, with the result that the development of an alternative counter principle has not happened; see J Wightman, *Contract: A Critical Commentary* (London, Pluto Press, 1996) 4–7. Also, as well as managing without a general conception of good faith, English law does not recognise promissory estoppel as a cause of action, and the doctrine of unconscionability is relatively underdeveloped.

[12] William Whitford identified the structural differences that flow from the contrast between federal and unitary systems, in particular the difficulty of progressing legislative reform of contract, as a reason for greater judicial activism and discretion in American law. W Whitford, 'A Comparison of British and American Attitudes Towards the Exercise of Judicial Attitudes to Discretion in Contract Law' in Campbell and others, *Implicit Dimensions of Contract* (n 4).

[13] The closest is the *Principles of European Contract Law*; first published in 1995, these were drafted by a group of academics to express the core ideas across different European systems. They may be incorporated by the parties but have no other legal status. Whilst they have been the subjects of keen academic debate, Westlaw indicates they have been mentioned in only around 10 English cases. See Commission on European Contract Law, O Lando, and H Beale, *The Principles of European Contract Law, Parts I and II* (Hague, Kluwer Law International, 1999).

[14] In contract and commercial law, the outstanding figures in the House of Lords in recent decades have been Lord Reid (1948–75), Lord Wilberforce (1964–82), Lord Diplock (1968–85), Lord Goff (1986–98), Lord Hoffmann (1995–2009) and Lord Steyn (1995–2005). Lord Hoffmann and Lord Wilberforce were referred to as 'demi-gods' by Munby J in *Beazer Homes Ltd v Stroude* [2005] EWCA Civ 265, para 29 (a case on the interpretation of a contract).

[15] For an account of the clear differences in the traditional roles of academia, see PS Atiyah and RS Summers, *Form and Substance in Anglo-American Law* (Oxford, Oxford University Press, 1987) 398–407.

primarily internal, with the dominant focus on doctrinal coherence.[16] This tradition has meant that mainstream commentary on contract has not been through the kind of intellectual ferment which in the American context has been expressed in the debates around realism, law and economics, law and society approaches, relational contract theory, critical legal studies, consent theory, neo-formalism, and so forth.[17] Although some work on the significance and operation of contract law in practice has built on the approach of Macaulay's 1963 paper on non-contractual relations,[18] the analysis of the relationship between contract law and reality offered by law and economics studies of contracting has not put down significant roots in UK academic commentary. A consequence is that the analysis of rules in terms of the incentive structure they create ex ante, so familiar in much American work, is relatively rare in commentary on English law, and is something I cannot recall coming across at all in English case law.

Although I am arguing that English contract law exhibits some key pre-realist features, I am not suggesting that it is in some sense stuck in a stage of development which is the equivalent of pre-realist contract law in America. Viewed from the point of view of English law, American law on contracts seems to offer a much clearer pattern of periodisation. Macneil's analysis in terms of classical and neoclassical contract is a notably developed account of this periodisation, with neoclassical contract law being seen as superseding classical law in the second half of the twentieth century; while retaining individual autonomy at its core, it has adapted where the classical law account of contracting departed most obtrusively from the reality of contracting practice. Both classical and neoclassical law were tied to landmarks in contract scholarship, with the classical law associated with Williston's treatise (first edition 1920–22) and the first *Restatement of Contracts* (1932), while neoclassical is associated with Corbin's treatise (first edition 1950), the second *Restatement* (1962–79), and the UCC (1952–). English law lacks equivalent landmarks that can be said to crystallise a different approach, and arguably provides a more jumbled picture in terms of general principles that express both classical and neoclassical ideas.

An important reason why these pre-realist features do not mean that English contract law is some formalist, or classical, backwater is that many of the leading judges have espoused what may be called 'commercial

[16] This is perhaps most visible in the contributions to the *Law Quarterly Review* (1885–), the oldest English academic law journal. The more recent *Journal of Contract Law* (1987–), the only specialist contract journal, based in Australia, also has a predominantly doctrinal focus.

[17] The emphasis here is on mainstream commentary: there have of course been a number of contract scholars from the UK who have engaged with the American contract literature over the last two decades – most notably the major contributions of David Campbell and Hugh Collins.

[18] See n 3 references above.

realism'. A number of them have been at pains to explain – indeed celebrate – the ability of the law to take account of business realities by seeing that the law complies with the reasonable expectations of commercial parties;[19] there are many quotations that amply show that this is a recurrent theme.[20] This sense of commercial realism may well be reinforced by the perception that English commercial law, especially contract, has an international significance because of its use as the proper law of many international contracts.[21] This commercial realism on the part of the judges may have fulfilled part of the function of the academic neoclassical reshaping of American law, with the result that the accommodation of commercial 'reality' has been driven by a judicial pragmatism that has not been underpinned by an academic contribution to the refashioning of principle. For better or worse, this pragmatism seems to have been more concerned to achieve what are regarded as sensible outcomes, than to reformulate principle.[22]

The emergence of a greater explicit reference to context in these circumstances, and in a way that seems more than just an adjustment on separate doctrinal issues, is thus of some note. Lord Hoffmann, despite the recourse to the objective approach, appears to have eschewed simple pragmatism and attempted the development of principle, and the result may be to move the law, at least in some respects, closer to a relational contract law.

II. THE RISE OF CONTEXT IN THE ENGLISH LAW OF CONTRACT

The modern focus on context within the law of contract can be seen to have two strains. First chronologically, and much the larger in terms of its

[19] See, eg P Devlin, 'The Relation Between Commercial Law and Commercial Practice' (1951) 14 *Modern Law Review* 249; R Goff, 'Commercial Contracts and the Commercial Court' (1984) *Lloyd's Maritime and Commercial Law Quarterly* 382; J Steyn, 'Contract Law: Fulfilling the Reasonable Expectations of Honest Men' (1997) 113 *Law Quarterly Review* 433, and also judicial pronouncements of K Diplock (eg, *Antaios Cia Naviera SA v Salen Rederierna AB* [1985] AC 191, 201) and Lord Wilberforce (eg *New Zealand Shipping Co Ltd v AM Satterthwaite* [1975] AC 154,167); see also R Brownsword, *Contract Law: Themes for the Twenty-First Century* (Oxford, Oxford University Press, 2006) 124–43.

[20] Diplock: '[I]f detailed semantic and syntactical analysis of words in a commercial contract is going to lead to a conclusion that flouts business commonsense, it must be made to yield to business commonsense.' *Antaios Compania Naviera SA v Salen Rederierna AB* [1985] AC 191, 201.

[21] This sentiment was expressed with notable confidence by the Lord Chancellor, Lord Falconer in a speech to a European Contract Law conference in 2005: '[T]he English common law of contract is now a world wide commodity. It has become so because it is a system that people like. It provides predictability of outcome, legal certainty, and fairness. It is clear and built upon well-founded principles, such as the ability to require exact performance and the absence of any duty of good faith'; quoted in C Mitchell, *Interpretation of Contracts* (London, Routledge Cavendish, 2007) 60.

[22] Whilst this is a statement about contract law in particular, the overall common law picture is mixed; thus the development of the law of restitution over the last two decades has seen the development of principle that has been significantly influenced by academic commentary. See Saiman, 'Restitution in America' (n 8).

impact in case law, is the emphasis on context in relation to the construction of express terms. The key case was *Investors Compensation Scheme Ltd v West Bromwich Building Society*[23] where Lord Hoffmann's judgment has become the classic statement of the modern approach to construction. The second strain is the use of references to the commercial setting of the contract as a source to define the limits of claims for damages; here too, it was Lord Hoffmann who delivered the key judgments that reoriented the law.[24] This second strain provides a different role for context. In the interpretation cases, the development has seen a significant extension of the circumstances where context will be drawn upon to construe the express terms of contract. In the cases on damages, however, the contractual context is drawn upon not as an aid to interpretation of express terms, but as a way to determine the extent of a liability for damages, with a notable shift from basing the limits on ideas of reasonable foresight and probability under the remoteness rules, to grounding those limits in the practices and expectations which prevail in the commercial sector in which the case is set. There is an important thread of continuity between the two strains of context. This lies not just in the same leading protagonist – Lord Hoffmann – but also in the use of informal practices and expectations as sources to shape the obligations of the parties.

A. The Impact of the Investors Decision

The significance of the *Investors* decision was not that it marked a sea change from some previous state in which literalism held sway. Although a literal approach had been espoused in some of the earlier case law,[25] there were cases before *Investors* where reference to context was seen as necessary, most notably in cases of ambiguity. In *Prenn v Simmonds*, Lord Wilberforce had said 'the time has long past when agreements, even those under seal, were isolated from the matrix of facts in which they were set and interpreted purely on internal linguistic considerations'.[26] Arguably, what was significant about Lord Hoffmann's statement in *Investors* was that context is not just relevant in exceptional cases where the literal meaning for some reason does not work: contractual interpretation is inherently contextual.

The issue in *Investors* concerned an express term which only had one 'literal' meaning, in that the syntax of the relevant clause could not made to mean what one of the litigants – ultimately successfully – contended

[23] *Investors Compensation Scheme Ltd v West Bromwich Building Society* [1998] 1 WLR 896.

[24] *South Australia Asset Management Corporation v York Montague* [1997] AC 191; *Transfield Shipping of Panama Ltd v Mercator Shipping (The Achilleas)* [2008] UKHL 48.

[25] eg *Lovell and Christmas Ltd v Wall* (1911) 104 LT 85.

[26] *Prenn v Simmonds* [1971] 1 WLR 1381, 1883.

that it meant. The term in question concerned an assignment of claims to the Investors Compensation Scheme (ICS), a body created as part of as system of investor protection.[27] The ICS paid out compensation to an investor in return for the investor assigning their rights against the potential defendants (in this case a building society) to ICS. However, the standard form used in this contract provided that some rights were excluded from the assignment to ICS, and retained by the investor. The dispute turned on the width of this exclusion, with the defendants, the West Bromwich Building Society, arguing that the claim against it by ICS failed because it was based on rights that had not been assigned.

It was accepted by all the judges, including those eventually favouring the narrower meaning, that the wider meaning contended by the Building Society was the only meaning that the syntax of the clause could accommodate. This was the end of the matter for the Court of Appeal, which applied the wider meaning. However, in the House of Lords, Lord Hoffmann, preferring the contrary view of the judge at first instance,[28] considered something had clearly 'gone wrong' with the drafting, in that the syntactically correct reading was 'commercial nonsense'.[29] Looking at the purpose of the compensation scheme, the wider meaning would undermine it because it would obstruct claims against the key solvent defendants, and it would have meant that claims for the same loss could have been brought on different grounds by both the investor and the ICS.

Lord Hoffmann's approach involved assessing the commercial sense of the alternative meanings by examining them against the background of the contract. He explained this as follows:

> I do not think that the fundamental change that has overtaken this branch of the law, particularly as a result of the speeches of Lord Wilberforce in *Prenn v Simmonds*[30] and *Reardon Smith Line Ltd v Yngvar Hansen-Tangen*,[31] is always sufficiently appreciated. The result has been, subject to one important exception, to assimilate the way in which such documents are interpreted by judges to the common sense principles by which any serious utterance would be interpreted

[27] It was intended to provide compensation where investors had unmet legal claims against entities that had been licensed under the Financial Services Act 1986 to carry out investment business. The cases in this litigation concerned mainly retired people who had borrowed money on the security of their home, which was then used to buy equity-linked bonds. Adverse changes in house prices and interest rates caused the owners to suffer significant losses, and many owners would have had claims in negligence against their financial advisors, the building societies and solicitors.

[28] This had been rejected below: 'In the Court of Appeal, Leggatt LJ said, on the authority of *Through the Looking-Glass*, that the judge's interpretation was "not an available meaning of the words". "Any claim (whether sounding in rescission for undue influence or otherwise)" could not mean "any claim sounding in rescission (whether for undue influence or otherwise)" and that was that. He was unimpressed by the alleged commercial nonsense of the alternative construction.' Lord Hoffmann in *Investors* (n 25) 914.

[29] See n 23.

[30] *Prenn* (n 26) 1384–86.

[31] *Reardon Smith Line Ltd v Yngvar Hansen-Tangen*, [1976] 1 WLR 989.

> in ordinary life. Almost all the old intellectual baggage of 'legal' interpretation has been discarded. The principles may be summarised as follows.
>
> Interpretation is the ascertainment of the meaning that the document would convey to a reasonable person having all the background knowledge that would reasonably have been available to the parties in the situation in which they were at the time of the contract.
>
> The background was famously referred to by Lord Wilberforce as the 'matrix of fact', but this phrase is, if anything, an understated description of what the background may include. Subject to the requirement that it should have been reasonably available to the parties and to the exception to be mentioned next,[32] it includes absolutely anything which would have affected the way in which the language of the document would have been understood by a reasonable man . . .
>
> The meaning that a document (or any other utterance) would convey to a reasonable man is not the same thing as the meaning of its words. The meaning of words is a matter of dictionaries and grammars; the meaning of the document is what the parties using those words against the relevant background would reasonably have been understood to mean. The background may not merely enable the reasonable man to choose between the possible meanings of words which are ambiguous but even (as occasionally happens in ordinary life) to conclude that the parties must, for whatever reason, have used the wrong words or syntax.
>
> The 'rule' that words should be given their 'natural and ordinary meaning' reflects the common sense proposition that we do not easily accept that people have made linguistic mistakes, particularly in formal documents. On the other hand, if one would nevertheless conclude from the background that something must have gone wrong with the language, the law does not require judges to attribute to the parties an intention that they plainly could not have had.[33]

This statement has become the classic starting point in cases on construction of contract terms, and has stimulated an extensive literature. However, the mere invocation of context was not novel, as demonstrated by Lord Hoffmann's reference to statements by Lord Wilberforce from the 1970s.[34] Lord Hoffmann went considerably further than Lord Wilberforce in grounding the resort to context in a theory of meaning which treated context as a necessary part of all interpretation, not just an exceptional case like ambiguity. This is not only visible in the extract from his judgment, but also in a slightly earlier case *Mannai Investment Co Ltd v Eagle*

[32] The exceptions are that pre-contractual negotiations and contractual performance cannot be adduced as evidence; see discussion of *Chartbrook Ltd v Persimmon Homes Ltd,* nn 38–41 below and accompanying text.

[33] *Prenn* (n 26) 913.

[34] 'But it does not follow that . . . one must be confined within the four corners of the document. No contracts are made in a vacuum: there is always a setting in which they have to be placed. The nature of what is legitimate to have regard to is usually described as "the surrounding circumstances" but this phrase is imprecise: . . . [W]hat the court must do must be to place itself in thought in the same factual matrix as that in which the parties were.' *Reardon Smith Line Ltd v Hansen–Tangen* [1976] 1 WLR 989, 995.

Star Life Assurance Co Ltd,[35] and in a lecture – given a few months after the judgment in *Investors* – in which he addressed the issue of meaning in contracts.[36] In essence, his claim is that the meaning of terms is to be found in how a reasonable person would understand them, having in mind the background of the transaction. This results in an extended objective approach, which is not the same thing as an objective interpretation of the intent of the party responsible for the utterance or other communication. It is different because it depersonalises the parties and sees them possessing the characteristic of a reasonable person – the reasonable seller, buyer and so on. Under this approach – referred to as 'committed contextualism' by Hugh Collins[37] – the focus is shifted from the promisor's intent to how a reasonable promisee would construe the utterance or text against the background.

The influence of Lord Hoffmann's statement of the extended role of context was clear in the later House of Lords case of *Chartbrook Ltd v Persimmon Homes Ltd*.[38] This examined the long-standing rules that, even in cases of ambiguity, two types of evidence could not be used as evidence – pre-contractual negotiations, and the performance of the contract. A number of commentators had expected the primacy accorded to context in *Investors* to result in the overturning of at least the prior negotiations rule.[39] However, in the event, the influence of the *Investors* approach lay not in abolishing these exclusionary rules, but in the conclusion that it was not now necessary to allow such evidence in: the new contextual approach meant that contract terms could now be given a satisfactory interpretation without access to this kind of evidence.

Chartbrook concerned a dispute over the selling price of land that the vendor was owed by a developer who was buying the land to develop flats and shops. A formula for determining this was included in the contract, but the parties had different views of what it meant: the vendor claimed that the amount due was just over £9 million, while the developer's figure was just over £5.5 million. The issue turned on how three elements were to be combined to make up a part of the price. It was accepted on all sides that the syntax of the clause defining the payment could not be twisted to mean what the developer claimed it meant. The developer argued that, as in *Investors*, something had obviously 'gone wrong' in drafting, which should lead the court to arrive at a contextual meaning. The developers also argued

[35] *Mannai Investment Co Ltd v Eagle Star Life Assurance Co Ltd* [1997] AC 749, 775.

[36] L Hoffmann, 'The Intolerable Wrestle With Words and Meanings' (1997) 114 *South African Law Journal* 656.

[37] H Collins, 'Objectivity and Committed Contextualism in Interpretation' in S Worthington (ed) *Commercial Law and Commercial Practice* (n 4).

[38] *Chartbrook Ltd v Persimmon Homes Ltd* [2009] UKHL 38.

[39] D McLauchlan, 'Contract Interpretation: What is it About?' (2009) 5 *Sydney Law Review* 5; D Nicholls, 'My Kingdom for a Horse: The Meaning of Words' (2005) 121 *Law Quarterly Review* 577.

that they should be allowed to adduce evidence of the pre-contractual negotiations to clarify this meaning: letters had passed between the parties which showed, it was claimed, that the vendor had clearly envisaged the formula working in the way the developer claimed.

The House of Lords considered at some length whether to overrule the settled rule that evidence of negotiations was inadmissible as evidence of the true construction of a contract. Lord Hoffmann considered such evidence to risk being 'drenched in subjectivity',[40] and would rarely be relevant to the question of how a reasonable person would have interpreted the terms:

> They may be inadmissible simply because they are irrelevant to the question which the court has to decide, namely, what the parties would reasonably be taken to have meant by the language which they finally adopted to express their agreement . . . that will usually be the case.[41]

Although such evidence could – exceptionally – be of assistance in ascertaining what the parties could reasonably be taken to have meant, it was concluded that, given the significant additional litigation costs that could be incurred, the case for overturning the rule was not made out. However, despite the specific evidence in the negotiations that the developer found so helpful being inadmissible, the House of Lords, when construing the clause against the background, unhesitatingly preferred the developer's construction. This view was arrived at by examining the commercial background in order to discern the purpose and commercial logic of the formula. The contending interpretations of the formula were tested under different selling price assumptions, which resulted in some payments reached under the vendor's interpretation being described as 'commercial nonsense'.[42]

The exclusionary rule was thus retained at least in part because Lord Hoffmann's contextual approach meant that the kind of evidence which it had kept out was now largely unnecessary in the majority of cases. The rest of the background could be fully explored in order to establish what the parties could be reasonably taken to have meant. Somewhat paradoxically, although the contextual approach had been argued as the reason for doing away with the rule excluding prior negotiations, in the end it was the strengthening of the contextual approach which gave the court the room to confirm the rule: allowing such evidence would now rarely make any difference.

What is the significance of the *Investors* approach from the point of view of allowing context to shape the obligations of the parties? In terms of a practical impact in cases being decided differently, it is the cases of draft-

[40] *Chartbrook* (n 38) para 38.
[41] ibid para 33.
[42] ibid para 89.

ing errors, with no syntactical ambiguity, where outcomes are most likely to be different. These are cases where the written contract has simply failed to provide a meaning that makes sense, or in Lord Hoffmann's words they are cases where 'something must have gone wrong'. The elasticity of this formulation means that the approach of judges to this key question may well vary,[43] and some commentators have concluded that the process of interpretation in the cases of alleged drafting error continues to involve striking a balance between applying a literal and a contextual approach.[44]

At the level of principle, however, Lord Hoffmann's statement contains the potential to exert a gravitational pull on the shaping of parts of the law where it does not make an immediate practical difference. The claim that contractual interpretation is inherently contextual is an explicit recognition that the context within which the parties operate can be an important source that shapes the content of the parties' obligations. The full implications of this approach have yet to be worked through, but it has already arguably borne fruit in the form of a new approach to the rules determining the scope of liability for breach of contract.

B. Context and Recent Case Law on Damages

The second group of cases in which the role of context or background is invoked do not engage context as an aid to the interpretation of express terms; context is used as resource for qualifying rules that are regarded as imposed by law. Recent case law on damages for breach of contract has seen the House of Lords finally address an issue which, in English contract law, has never been properly resolved since the emergence of the remoteness principles in *Hadley v Baxendale*.[45] This is the situation where a loss is clearly caused by the defendant's breach (in the sense that the plaintiff is worse off than if the contract had been performed), is not excluded by the general limiting doctrines of mitigation and remoteness, yet it is strongly felt that, because of other features of the case, the defendant should not be liable. The classic classroom illustration is where, through the negligence of the taxi (cab) driver, the customer misses a flight, and as a result fails to clinch a highly lucrative deal – and the taxi

[43] 'It is, I am afraid, not unusual that an interpretation which does not strike one person as sufficiently irrational to justify a conclusion that there has been a linguistic mistake will seem commercially absurd to another.' Lord Hoffmann, *Chartbrook* (n 38) para 15.

[44] Mitchell, *Interpretation of Contracts* (n 21); G McMeel, *Construction of Contracts: Interpretation, Implication and Rectification* (Oxford, Oxford University Press, 2007); E Mckendrick, 'The Interpretation of Contracts: Lord Hoffmann's Restatement' in S Worthington (ed), *Commercial Law and Commercial Practice* (n 4); D McLauchlan, 'Plain Meaning and Commercial Construction: Has Australia Adopted the ICS Principles' (2009) 25 *Journal of Contract Law* 7.

[45] *Hadley v Baxendale* (1854) 9 Ex 341.

firm was fully aware of the likely loss when the taxi was booked. Before the case law discussed below, English law struggled to explain why the driver was not liable, since the resulting loss appears to meet the requirement that it was foreseeable, at the time of entering the contract, as a probable result of the breach. In essence, the new case law means that it is no longer sufficient for the loss to have been foreseeable in this way. Context is deployed to reframe the scope of the remoteness doctrine in a way that contains the potential to transcend remoteness as an approach to the availability of damages for breach of contract.

In the first case, *South Australia Asset Management Corporation v York Montague* (*SAAMCO*),[46] the reference to context, although not extensive, is significant because it was built upon by Lord Hoffmann in the second case, *Transfield Shipping of Panama Ltd v Mercator Shipping*.[47] The plaintiff in *SAAMCO* lent money to a purchaser on the security of an office building after receiving a valuation report from the defendant valuer. When the borrower was unable to pay what was due, the plaintiff sought to realise the security. However, when the land was sold it did not cover the outstanding loan. This was partly because the valuer had negligently overvalued the security, but partly because the value of commercial property generally had dropped between the time of the valuation and the borrower's default. The liability of the valuer for the shortfall due to the negligent over-valuation was clear; the issue was whether the valuer was also liable for the shortfall that was attributable to the market fall.

A unanimous Court of Appeal overturned the first instance judge and held the defendant was liable for the loss attributable to the market fall. The approach adopted by Lord Bingham was to apply the principle in *Robinson v Harman*[48] that the aim of damages was to put the plaintiff in the position they would have been but for the breach of duty, and in this case it was found that, had the defendant provided a non-negligent valuation, the plaintiff would not have lent the money to the borrower. In that case, the plaintiff would not have suffered any of the loss, including that flowing from the market fall, and on this basis the plaintiff succeeded. With respect to remoteness of damage, it was accepted that the loss due to market fall was clearly foreseeable by the parties at the time of the contract.

The House of Lords allowed the appeal and held that the defendant was not liable for the element of the loss attributable to the market fall. Lord Hoffmann, giving the only substantive judgment, said that the *Robinson v Harman* principle was the wrong starting point:

[46] *South Australia Asset Management Corporation v York Montague* [1997] AC 191.

[47] *Transfield Shipping of Panama Ltd v Mercator Shipping (The Achilleas)* [2008] UKHL 48.

[48] *Robinson v Harman* (1848) 1 Ex Rep 850.

> Before one can consider the principle on which one should calculate the damages to which a plaintiff is entitled as compensation for loss, it is necessary to decide for what kind of loss he is entitled to compensation.[49]

He then used the concept of the 'scope of a duty' to determine for what losses the defendant was liable. Lord Hoffmann explained how the scope of the duty was to be approached:

> How is the scope of the duty determined? . . . In the case of an implied contractual duty, the nature and extent of the liability is defined by the term that the law implies. As in the case of any implied term, the process is one of construction of the agreement as a whole in its commercial setting. The contractual duty to provide a valuation and the known purpose of that valuation compel the conclusion that the contract includes a duty of care. The scope of the duty, in the sense of the consequences for which the valuer is responsible, is that which the law regards as best giving effect to the express obligations assumed by the valuer: neither cutting them down so that the lender obtains less than he was reasonably entitled to expect, nor extending them so as to impose on the valuer a liability greater than he could reasonably have thought he was undertaking.[50]

On this view, the extent of the defendant's responsibility is defined by the scope of the duty as an implied term of the contract, the content of which is obtained by construing the agreement in its overall commercial setting. This is not, of course, the same thing as the construction of express terms: it is not about the meaning of identifiable words, but about elucidating what term will best reflect the overall objects of the contract, in its commercial context. Here, Lord Hoffmann decided that the responsibility of the defendant was limited to the consequences of the information being wrong; this meant there was no liability for consequences that that would have occurred if the actual information given had been correct. In this case, if the land had been worth the value that the valuer placed on it, then the loss due to market fall would have been suffered in the same way.[51]

What is striking about this approach is that the court has inserted the additional concept of scope of duty, thereby sidestepping the liability for foreseeable loss that would have been the result of applying the traditional remoteness rule. 'Scope of duty' here does not mean the content of the primary duty – that is, what the defendant is obliged to do (in this case, take reasonable care in the valuation); it delimits the consequences of the breach of the primary duty for which the defendant may be liable. Invoking the scope of duty in case of breach of contract seems to have been novel: the usage to which Lord Hoffmann referred was in the scope

[49] ibid 211.

[50] ibid 212.

[51] For further elaboration of the approach, see J Wightman, 'Negligent Valuations and a Drop in the Property Market: The Limits of the Expectation Loss Principle' (1998) 61 *Modern Law Review* 68.

of the duty of care for economic loss in the tort of negligence.[52] It is a distinct approach from remoteness, because the contract remoteness rule selects from among those losses caused by the defendant's breach the ones which meet the general tests of foreseeability and likelihood. The scope of duty test is point blank – is the defendant liable for this kind of loss? This is answered by the 'construction of the agreement as a whole in its commercial setting',[53] an approach which may import limits on the scope of liability which are drawn from the elucidation of features of the context in which the contract is set.

This approach consisted of expressing the extent of the liability of the defendant as depending upon what they should, in the context, be treated as having assumed, and it was applied in the second case to reformulate the remoteness rule. In *Transfield Shipping Inc v Mercator Shipping Inc*,[54] Lord Hoffmann addressed the remoteness rule head on, and proposed an important modification to the principle in *Hadley v Baxendale*. *Transfield* was an action by the owners of the ship *Achilleas*, which was returned late by the defendant charterer. The owners had fixed a follow-on charter with a third party, and, as a result of the ship being returned a matter of days late, the third party, now entitled to cancel, renegotiated a lower daily rate for the charter. Because there had been a sharp fall in rates, the third party was able to renegotiate at a much lower market rate, which saved $1.3 million over the period of the charter. The owners claimed this amount from the defendant, who argued that they were only liable for the difference between the market rate and the charter rate for the nine days they were deprived of the use of the ship; this came to $158,000.

The plaintiffs succeeded before arbitrators, the High Court, and the Court of Appeal. The reasoning was that the loss was clearly within the *Robinson v Harman* principle, and was not too remote: although the defendants were not told of the specific rate of the new fixture, the loss lay squarely within the first limb of *Hadley v Baxendale* – it was the kind of loss which would arise naturally from the breach, and was not an unlikely result of the breach. This conclusion was reached *despite* the arbitrators accepting that the prevailing view among contractors in this market that damages were based on the difference between the charter rate and the market rate only for the days when the ship was unavailable, not for the whole duration of the charter.

This case – at least for Lord Hoffmann – raised in stark form the problem of a loss which is foreseeable and likely, yet should not result in liability. He approached the issue by posing this question:

> The case therefore raises a fundamental point of principle in the law of contractual damages: is the rule that a party may recover losses which were foreseeable

[52] *Caparo v Dickman* [1990] 2 AC 605.
[53] See n 50 and accompanying text.
[54] ibid.

> ('not unlikely') an external rule of law, imposed upon the parties to every contract in default of express provision to the contrary, or is it a prima facie assumption about what the parties may be taken to have intended, no doubt applicable in the great majority of cases but capable of rebuttal in cases in which the context, surrounding circumstances or general understanding in the relevant market shows that a party would not reasonably have been regarded as assuming responsibility for such losses?[55]

Lord Hoffmann concluded that the *Hadley* principle should be treated as a presumption that can be rebutted by evidence:

> If, therefore, one considers what these parties, contracting against the background of market expectations found by the arbitrators, would reasonably have considered the extent of the liability they were undertaking, I think it is clear that they would have considered losses arising from the loss of the following fixture a type or kind of loss for which the charterer was not assuming responsibility.[56]

Although all five law lords agreed on the outcome, two adopted more orthodox reasoning. Lord Rodger and Lord Walker were content to apply the *Hadley v Baxendale* principles; their difference with Lord Hoffmann was that they were prepared to treat foreseeability and probability as applying to the extent of a loss as well as its type, whereas Lord Hoffmann did not feel this path was open in the light of the pre-existing law.[57]

Whilst acknowledging that foreseeability had been used to confine liability in a very flexible way, Lord Hoffmann regarded its use here as an 'intellectual sleight of hand'. This description was contained in a subsequent lecture on the case,[58] and in it he likens the *Hadley* approach to Newtonian physics, in that, while it works in most situations, there are cases it does not explain. The 'broader principle' he develops in the lecture poses the issue as one of clarifying the parties' obligations, and sees the key question as 'what obligation to make compensation for breach of contract would a reasonable observer understand the contracting party to have undertaken'.[59] The Newtonian analogy is striking, and conveys the notion that the explanation of the cases that do not fit the established rule can also be seen as a more convincing explanation of the cases which,

[55] *Robinson* (n 48) para 9.

[56] ibid para 23.

[57] See especially *Jackson v Royal Bank of Scotland* [2005] UKHL 3; Lord Hope agreed with Lord Hoffmann, while the fifth judge, Baroness Hale, had doubts about the outcome but preferred the reasoning of Lord Rodger regarding Lord Hoffmann's use of the scope of duty approach as a *deus ex machina*, which had not been explored in argument.

[58] L Hoffmann, '*The Achilleas*: Custom and Practice of Foreseeability?' (2010) 14 *Edinburgh Law Review* 47, 54.

[59] He saw this principle explaining the generally more restrictive use of *Hadley* in carrier cases, although recognised that it threw into question *Koufos v Czarnikow Ltd (The Heron II)* [1969] 1 AC 350, the leading modern authority on remoteness, where the House of Lords had held a carrier liable for the lost market value of a cargo of sugar when it was delivered late and the market price had fallen.

hitherto, had been seen to follow from the established rule. The established rule becomes an approximation, which is, in Lord Hoffmann's terms, no more than a prima facie assumption about what was intended; and this presumption can be rebutted, by reference to 'context, surrounding circumstances or general understanding in the relevant market'.[60]

This wider scope of Lord Hoffmann's broader principle in *Transfield* means that its implications are more fundamental than a gloss on rules on remoteness. Quite simply, if the scope of a defendant's liability for damages is to be determined by contextual norms, this becomes an issue not just in cases presenting questions about remoteness of damage, but also potentially in *any* situation where the scope of liability for damages is in issue. Whilst it will often be the case that applying a contextual norm would protect the same interest as applying the orthodox contract rules, in principle it is an open issue that could, on Lord Hoffmann's broader principle, be determined by evidence of the practices of the contracting community in question. This contrasts with the orthodox position, which treats the remedial protection of the expectation interest as *logically* derived from the definition of the performance obligation.[61] Crucially, the definition of the claimant's protected interest would no longer be defined by a general rule that applies to all contracts; it is potentially qualified by the expectations and practices in particular contracting contexts. An intriguing consequence of this is that an empirical investigation of contracting practice – of the kind pioneered by Stewart Macaulay – now becomes potentially relevant as evidence in court about those practices and expectations. More generally, it could be illuminating to conduct such empirical research into contracting contexts where the 'logic' of recovery for foreseeable expectation losses may not necessarily reflect the context; examples could include the scope of the liability of private individuals in some types of consumer, employment and residential tenancy contracts.

Conversely, there are areas in the law of damages that have developed ad hoc rules that do not sit easily with the logic of the expectation loss principle. Examples that do not have entirely stable solutions include the

[60] *Robinson* (n 48) para 9. As well as following the scope of duty idea expressed in *SAAMCO*, this approach also draws on case law from the nineteenth century, long regarded as superseded, which based the remoteness test on a theory of tacit agreement, most notably *British Columbia Saw Mill Co Ltd v Nettleship* [1868] LR 3 CP 499. For an excellent analysis of this case law, see A Kramer, 'An Agreement-Centred Approach to Remoteness and Contract Damages' in N Cohen and E McKendrick (eds), *Comparative Remedies for Breach of Contract* (Oxford, Hart Publishing, 2006).

[61] See, especially D Friedmann, 'The Performance Interest in Contract Damages' (1995) 111 *Law Quarterly Review* 628, an influential article setting out a principled justification for protecting the claimant's full expectation under the contract; the reasoning is primarily internal to the law, and seen as a logical implication of the basic idea that contracts are about the enforcement of promises.

availability of damages for mental distress,[62] the liability of a surveyor carrying out a negligent pre-purchase survey of domestic property for the cost of repairs,[63] and the liability of a builder for failure to build to the precise specification.[64] The principle in *Transfield* has the potential to develop an approach in these situations that is more explicitly sensitive to the particularities of context.

III. CONTEXT AND THE EXTENDED OBJECTIVE APPROACH

Although these developments in the interpretation of contracts and the remoteness rule have occasioned considerable debate, the focus has tended to be on the discrete developments, and not on the connections between them. My claim is that there is a clear common thread which Lord Hoffmann's broader principle shares with both the *SAAMCO* scope of duty approach and the contextual approach to interpretation. This is the combination of two elements: the insistence that the exercise is one of understanding the obligations which the parties can be taken to have assumed, and the use of the contextual background to derive the content of those obligations; I refer to this common thread as *the extended objective approach*. Further, the dual elements in this approach are in tension: whilst the idea that contractual obligation is derived from an assumption of responsibility connects that responsibility with the exercise of individual autonomy, the reference to the commercial context as a source of norms imports a social dimension to the responsibility, in that the norm or practice has evolved through the interactions between multiple actors in a contracting community.

Arguably, this dual character of the extended objective approach fits with the pre-realist nature of English contract law, in that, lacking the more explicit reference to contextual resources of the American law of contract, it is using the reference to what the parties can be assumed to have agreed as a gateway to accessing the contextual norms. The fact that context has emerged under the umbrella of the objective approach to contract, with its traditional affinity with a focus on the parties' intention, could lead some to argue that this is not even new wine in old bottles, but mainly old wine in old bottles – that, effectively, little has changed. My claim, however, is that the appearance of a more explicit reference to context has the potential for norms and practices of contracting communities to shape more directly the obligations to which the parties are subject.

[62] Liability currently depends on whether the contract is one to provide enjoyment of freedom from distress; see *Farley v Skinner* [2001] UKHL 49.

[63] There is generally no liability for this; *Watts v Morrow* [1991] 1 WLR 1421.

[64] Damages for the cost of reinstatement will only be available if the cost is not disproportionate to the benefit obtained, and the basis of 'mental distress' damages as an alternative is unclear. *Ruxley Electronics v Forsyth* [1996] AC 344.

This potential stems from a key feature of the extended objective approach – a greater detachment from intention than that which features in more established uses of the objective approach. The objective approach to establishing the existence and meaning of an enforceable contract has been part of the fabric of the common law of contract for at least two centuries,[65] and, while the idea of the objective approach does not have a single determinate meaning,[66] its core meaning lies in the idea that what matters in determining the existence of a contract, or the meaning of its terms, is not the subjective intention of the parties, but rather how that intent would be construed by a reasonable person. Much of the case law in which the objective approach was developed and deployed concerned situations where it was used to resolve cases of the parties being at cross purposes, most famously in *Smith v Hughes*,[67] where the defendant thought the oats he was buying were old, when in fact the oats in the sample were new.[68] Typically, these cases shared the feature that the disputed element was focused upon prior to the contract, with the result that each party had formulated a specific but contrasting intent about the matter in dispute. Cases on the interpretation of terms are not typically like this. They concern issues that the parties did not have at the forefront of their minds when entering the contract, and often had not even considered. In the cross-purposes cases, there are actual subjective intentions, and the role of the objective approach is generally to determine which one to prefer. However, where the choice is between different contentions at trial about what the contract 'means', the idea of an objective approach is rendered more abstract: it is about the interpretation of meaning in circumstances where there may have been no prior subjective intent at all. The move from a choice between different intentions that were actually formed, to a decision on what meaning should be conferred on terms where such prior crystallised intent is lacking, opens the way for an objective approach which may be more detached from the actual intentions of the parties than in the cross-purposes cases.

The move to using context not just in cases of ambiguity, but also where (as in *Investors*) the effect of the clear syntactical meaning suggests 'something must has gone wrong', gives an important impetus to the detachment from intention. Using context to resolve ambiguity retains a strong

[65] JM Perillo, 'The Origins of the Objective Theory of Contract Formation and Interpretation' (2000) 69 *Fordham Law Review* 427 (arguing that the objective approach is much older and that the subjective phase identified by some authors in the early nineteenth century hardly existed).

[66] ibid 431.

[67] *Smith v Hughes* (1871) LR 6 QB 597.

[68] Lord Blackburn provided what became the leading statement: 'If, whatever a man's real intention may be, he so conducts himself that a reasonable man would believe that he was assenting to the terms proposed by the other party, and that other party upon that belief enters into the contract with him, the man thus conducting himself would be equally bound as if he had intended to agree to the other party's terms.' ibid 607.

role for the express term in question as the touchstone: the resort to context is confined to informing the choice between the alternative meanings which are derived from the express term. But once clear syntactical meaning is set aside because it does not appear to make commercial sense, the process is even further removed from the elucidation of meaning with which the parties invested the written contract at the outset.[69]

This focus on how a reasonable promisee would construe the terms in context also facilitates the further extension of the objective approach to situations where the issue is not about the interpretation of the meaning of express terms at all. The broader principle identified by Lord Hoffmann in his lecture on *Transfield* does not refer to the meaning of an utterance, but to what obligation a reasonable observer would have understood the other party to have undertaken.[70] At one level this is a different category of question: it is not about what meaning resides in documents, construed in their context, but about what obligation a party is to be under. However, the broader principle is congruent with the *Investors* approach because both depend on what inferences a reasonable promisee would have made about the obligation that was being undertaken.

The more explicit recourse to contextual norms has thus been clothed in the traditional objective approach, which has an impeccable pedigree in the history of the law of contract. In one sense, refracting the role of context through the objective approach to agreement could be said to exemplify Macneil's idea of neoclassical contract law, which adapts concepts to meet the exigencies of contracting practice, but within a framework of concepts that are structured by the ideas of intention and agreement. Both Lord Hoffmann's own analysis, and that of some commentators, has emphasised the grounding of the enlarged reference to context in what the parties may be assumed to have agreed. For example, Adam Kramer, whose article on damages and the scope of duty was the leading piece cited by Lord Hoffmann in *Transfield*, saw the changes derived from these cases as based on an agreement – centred approach.[71] Similarly, Brian Coote, one of the most highly regarded of contract scholars, saw *Transfield* as based on assumption of obligation.[72] This reference back to intent, which is entailed by the notion of assumption of responsibility, means that is not implausible to treat this approach as neoclassical, as it remains tethered in a formal sense to the idea of agreement as the basis of contractual obligation. However, although there is a formal reference to agreement, the *effect* of

[69] For elaboration of the point that *Investors* detaches the enquiry from the intentions of the parties, see Collins, 'Objectivity' (n 37).

[70] Lord Hoffmann, '*The Achilleas*' (n 58) 58.

[71] A Kramer, 'The New Test of Remoteness in Contract' (2009) 125 *Law Review Quarterly* 408; A Kramer, 'An Agreement-Centred Approach to Remoteness and Contract Damages' in Cohen and McKendrick, *Comparative Remedies* (n 60) 249–86.

[72] B Coote, 'Contract as Assumption and Remoteness of Damage' (2010) 26 *Journal of Contract Law* 211.

the reference to context is to derive the content of what is 'assumed' from the norms and practices of the context within which the parties transact. The references to assumption of responsibility, or the written agreement, that the extended objective approach includes, are wholly vestigial. Intention and agreement do not provide either the content of the obligations, or – arguably – their normative basis.

This aspect of the new approach to context was not always recognised in some of the criticism that the *Transfield* position has drawn. One response has been that Lord Hoffmann's test asks questions which cannot be answered, in that it is asking what parties would have thought, which is unknowable.[73] Although this is a fair point if one is concerned with construing what would actually have been intended, that is to mistake the nature of the extended objective approach. The focus at this point is on the reasonable promisee, and this is detached from an enquiry about what the actual parties had in mind. In the result, the perspective of the reasonable promisee becomes like a mirror in which is reflected back all the relevant elements of context and background alongside the undertakings in the contract. Although the context could be observed directly, the adoption of the perspective of the reasonable promisee is a device that means that the contextual norms are apparently clothed in the more familiar garb of the parties' intent, reasonably construed. Arguably, however, the upshot is that, although due obeisance is done to the idea of agreement, the substance of the parties' obligations, where it is drawn from context, is relational rather than neoclassical in that it is generated by the social processes of the market, specifically the practices and expectations which have emerged and which prevail in particular business sectors.

CONCLUSION

In summary, I have argued that English law has registered a more explicit embrace of contextual norms in the resolution of contract disputes. It has done so by adapting its traditional objective approach, using the device of the perspective of the reasonable promisee. However, the traditional application of the objective approach has been turned outwards, so that it can become a channel for contextual norms. Further, I have suggested that the resort to the objective approach can be understood as a response to the pre-realist character of English contract law, specifically the absence of other more direct ways of accessing contextual norms such as are provided in American law – in particular, the UCC.

The access to context, which the extended objective approach has facilitated, can be seen as creating more space between two large domains of

[73] See, eg A Robertson, 'The Basis of the Remoteness Rule in Contract' (2008) 28 *Legal Studies* 172; see also E Peel, 'Remoteness Re-visited' (2009) 125 *Law Quarterly Review* 6.

contractual obligation. On the one hand are the documented expressions of the parties' agreement; on the other are the imposed terms that are seen as deriving from the operation of the law, in the absence of express agreement. The incorporation of context through the extended objective approach expands the third domain, which consists of expectations and norms which derive from specific contexts, and which are neither derivable from the parties actual agreement in isolation, nor from the generic imposed rules of the law of contract.

The significance of the enlargement of the third domain is that it provides a way of qualifying both imposed law and documented terms, but *without* recourse to the agreement or intentions of the parties of the contract. To be sure, there are issues about the capacity of context to generate determinate norms, even in the hands of a Lord Hoffmann. But the partial pre-realist character of much of English law has meant it was starting from much further back, and this wider emergence of context should at least enable English courts to develop techniques for the effective use of contextual norms in resolving contract cases.

BIBLIOGRAPHY

Atiyah, PS and Summers, RS, *Form and Substance in Anglo-American Law* (Oxford, Oxford University Press, 1987).

Aubert, V (ed), *Sociology of Law* (London, Penguin Books, 1969).

Beale, H and Dugdale, T, 'Contracts Between Businessmen: Planning and the Use of Contractual Remedies' (1975) 2 *British Journal of Law and Society* 45.

Beatson, J, 'Has the Common Law a Future?' (1997) 56 *Cambridge Law Journal* 291.

Beever, A, *Rediscovering the Law of Negligence* (Oxford, Hart Publishing, 2007).

Brownsword, R, *Contract Law: Themes for the Twenty-First Century* (Oxford, Oxford University Press, 2006).

Campbell, D and Jones, PV (eds), *Contract and Economic Organisation* (Aldershot, Ashgate, 1996).

Campbell, D, Collins, H and Wightman, J (eds), *Implicit Dimensions of Contract* (Oxford, Hart Publishing, 2003).

Collins, H, 'Objectivity and Committed Contextualism in Interpretation' in S Worthington (ed), *Commercial Law and Commercial Practice* (Oxford, Hart Publishing, 2003).

Commission on European Contract Law, Lando, O and Beale, H, *The Principles of European Contract Law, Parts I and II* (Hague, Kluwer Law International, 1999).

Coote, B, 'Contract as Assumption and Remoteness of Damage' (2010) 26 *Journal of Contract Law* 211.

Deakin, S and Michie, J (eds), *Contracts, Co-operation, and Competition* (Oxford, Oxford University Press, 1997).

Devlin, P, 'The Relation Between Commercial Law and Commercial Practice' (1951) 14 *Modern Law Review* 249.

Friedmann, D, 'The Performance Interest in Contract Damages' (1995) 111 *Law Quarterly Review* 628.

Goff, R, 'Commercial Contracts and the Commercial Court' (1984) *Lloyd's Maritime and Commercial Law Quarterly* 382.

Hoffmann, L, 'The Intolerable Wrestle With Words and Meanings' (1997) 114 *South African Law Journal* 656.

——, '*The Achilleas*: Custom and Practice of Foreseeability?' (2010) 14 *Edinburgh Law Review* 47.

Kramer, A, 'An Agreement-Centred Approach to Remoteness and Contract Damages' in N Cohen and E McKendrick (eds), *Comparative Remedies for Breach of Contract* (Oxford, Hart Publishing, 2006).

——, 'The New Test of Remoteness in Contract' (2009) 125 *Law Review Quarterly* 408.

Macaulay, S, 'Justice Traynor and the Law of Contracts' (1961) 13 *Stanford Law Review* 813.

——, 'Non-Contractual Relations in Business – A Preliminary Study' (1963) 28 *American Sociological Review* 55.

——, 'The Real and the Paper Deal: Empirical Pictures of Relationships, Complexity and the Urge for Transparent Simple Rules' (2003) 66 *Modern Law Review* 44 (also included in D Campbell, H Collins and J Wightman (eds), *Implicit Dimensions of Contract: Discrete, Relational & Network Contracts* (Oxford, Hart Publishing, 2003)).

Mckendrick, E, 'The Interpretation of Contracts: Lord Hoffmann's Restatement' in S Worthington (ed), *Commercial Law and Commercial Practice* (Oxford, Hart Publishing, 2003).

McLauchlan, D, 'Contract Interpretation: What is it About?' (2009) 5 *Sydney Law Review* 5.

——, 'Plain Meaning and Commercial Construction: Has Australia Adopted the ICS Principles' (2009) 25 *Journal of Contract Law* 7.

McMeel, G, *Construction of Contracts: Interpretation, Implication and Rectification* (Oxford, Oxford University Press, 2007).

Mitchell, C, *Interpretation of Contracts* (London, Routledge Cavendish, 2007).

——, 'Contracts and Contract Law: Challenging the Distinction Between the "Real Deal" and the "Paper Deal"' (2009) 27 *Oxford Journal of Legal Studies* 675.

Nicholls, D, 'My Kingdom for a Horse: The Meaning of Words' (2005) 121 *Law Quarterly Review* 577.

Peel, E, 'Remoteness Re-visited' (2009) 125 *Law Quarterly Review* 6.

Perillo, JM, 'The Origins of the Objective Theory of Contract Formation and Interpretation' (2000) 69 *Fordham Law Review* 427.

Robertson, A, 'The Basis of the Remoteness Rule in Contract' (2008) *28 Legal Studies* 172.

Saiman, C, 'Restitution in America: Why the US Refuses to Join the Global Restitution Party' (2008) 28 *Oxford Journal of Legal Studies* 99.

Stevens, R, *Torts and Rights* (Oxford, Oxford University Press, 2007).

Steyn, J, 'Contract Law: Fulfilling the Reasonable Expectations of Honest Men' (1997) 113 *Law Quarterly Review* 433.

Whitford, W, 'The Role of the Jury (and the Fact/Law Distinction) in the Interpretation of Written Contracts' (2001) 2001 *Wisconsin Law Review* 931.

——, 'A Comparison of British and American Attitudes Towards the Exercise of Judicial Attitudes to Discretion in Contract Law' in D Campbell, H Collins, H and J Wightman (eds), *Implicit Dimensions of Contract* (Oxford, Hart Publishing, 2003).

Wightman, J, *Contract: A Critical Commentary* (London, Pluto Press, 1996).

Wightman, J, 'Negligent Valuations and a Drop in the Property Market: The Limits of the Expectation Loss Principle' (1998) 61 *Modern Law Review* 68.

Worthington, S (ed), *Commercial Law and Commercial Practice* (Oxford, Hart Publishing, 2003).

14

The Deregulatory Effects of Seventh Circuit Jurisprudence

DEBORAH WAIRE POST

INTRODUCTION

STEWART MACAULAY IS variously described as an expert on relational contract law, a pioneer in the study of law and culture, and an advocate for empirical research in the field of law.[1] He has spent his career writing and doing the kind of legal research that examines the way individuals and organisations enter into contractual relationships, as well as the relevance, or often the irrelevance, of formal contract doctrine to these arrangements and/or the settlement of contract disputes.[2] More recently he has argued in his scholarship for a return to legal realism in contract scholarship, encouraging us to take a bottom-up rather than a top-down look at economic relationships.[3] Whether we are looking more closely at the work of trial courts, the facts behind the cases or the operation of 'alternative institutions or systems or private ordering', these sorts of studies are part of what he calls 'new legal realism'.[4]

Professor Macaulay is not advocating empiricism for its own sake, but because he believes such research is a prerequisite to understanding and action. The metaphor he chose to use in one essay, a submarine operating in uncharted waters, suggests the nature of the inquiry he proposes. What intrigued me more than the metaphor was the ultimate question any well-

[1] 'Culture was brought to the center stage of the contract process by Stewart Macaulay and Ian McNeil.' M Mautner, 'Contract, Culture, Compulsion, or: So What is So Problematic in the Application of Objective Standards in Contract' (2002) 3 *Theoretical Inquiries in Law* 545, 547.

[2] S Macaulay, 'Law, Private Governance and Continuing Relationships: An Empirical View of Contract' (1985) 1985 *Wisconsin Law Review* 465.

[3] S Macaulay, 'Contracts, New Legal Realism, and Improving the Navigation of The Yellow Submarine' (2006) 80 *Tulane Law Review* 1161.

[4] ibid 1175, noting that when we have done 'enough contextual work, we might find patterns emerging that that will be important when we debate what kind of contract law we need and for what purpose'.

prepared explorer might ask before he sets out on a journey. Macaulay asks, 'What kind of contract law do we need?'[5] I think he already knows the answer: 'One that is fair and just.'

This advocate for a living law, or law in action, is concerned about the cost of litigation, the inadequacy of damages for breach of contract, and the strategic and coercive use of legal rules. He rejects an 'extreme' law and economics approach that utilises assumptions that have no basis in fact or oversimplifies the complexity of human relationships. More generally, his critique is directed at 'elegant models of contracting' that invite behaviour he characterises variously as a 'scam', 'scorched earth tactics' in litigation, or conduct 'on the border of fraud'.[6] In contrast, what Macaulay embraces and advocates is a 'transactional approach', one that focuses on the particular facts in a case. A fair and just legal system would have judges like Roger Traynor, whom Macaulay wrote about early in his career.[7] Justice Traynor decided cases in a way that ensured that the legitimate expectations of the parties were not thwarted by legal rules that 'run counter to common behavior'.[8] His jurisprudence was grounded in reality.

Macaulay's criticism of law often turns to particular obstacles to a just legal system. He recognises the relationship between contract doctrine and political theory – and the instrumental role that 'captive intellectuals', 'busy fashioning theories useful to the powerful',[9] can play in instantiating inequality. Professor Macaulay also makes note of the role of judges in this process. He once wrote of the remarkable work of Justice Traynor, that the 'innovations of a famous judge tend to influence the development of the law far beyond the boundaries of his own state'.[10] Macaulay admires the work of Traynor, but he is much less admiring of the innovations of some contemporary judges.[11] Perhaps Macaulay's understanding of the work that judges have done, or could do, to produce a just society and a just law of contracts fuels his impatience with judges. At the heart of his discontent is his recognition that neither justice nor fairness can be achieved as

[5] ibid 1164–65.

[6] S Macaulay, 'Relational Contract Theory: Unanswered Questions A Symposium in Honor of Ian R Macneil: Relational Contracts Floating on a Sea of Custom? Thoughts About the Ideas of Ian Macneil and Lisa Bernstein' (2000) 94 *Northwestern University Law Review* 775.

[7] S Macaulay, 'Justice Traynor and the Law of Contracts' (1961) 13 *Stanford Law Review* 812.

[8] ibid 831 (referring to the disconnection between the parol evidence rule and the behaviour of business persons who often do not reduce their agreements to writing).

[9] Macaulay, 'Empirical View of Contract' (n 2) 479.

[10] Macaulay, 'Justice Traynor' (n 7) 812.

[11] Macaulay, 'Yellow Submarine' (n 3) 1165–66, 1168 fn 30 (remarking that he, Macaulay, is among those who no longer think that the world can be made a 'better place' by appellate judges and noting in a subsequent footnote that 'after a revolution led by actors such as Karl Llewelyn and Roger Traynor, we have been going through a counter revolution in the last two decades').

long as a legal system fails to correct for disparities in power, for dependence and domination. Of judges he has written: 'Sometimes our judges confuse the loveable con man of fiction and film with a Fortune 500 company.'[12] Courts 'enforce . . . standardized documents to aid deception and fraud . . . or to help bureaucracies control their street-level personnel'.[13]

Macaulay believes law is just when it vindicates the parties' reasonable expectations, and when it does not reward those who use their superior resources to game the system. This is, as Macaulay notes, an ethical ideal.[14] Of course, a legal system or structure devoid of ethical considerations may still facilitate planning by participants in the market. The rules may be clear and the results that derive from their application may be predictable. In a regime governed by formal rules not grounded in ethical ideals, however, the party with superior power will be able to dictate terms that frustrate the reasonable expectations of trading partners. The absence of meaningful choice or the defeat of reasonable expectations fuels social unrest, resentment, and, ultimately, economic instability.[15] There is also in Macaulay's work an acknowledgement of the power of symbols. Symbols can constrain or enhance the use of power if the sentiments expressed by those symbols have a hold on the hearts and the minds of the participants in a process. In one article he mused that symbols, rhetorical but powerful, might have as their referent a belief that contracts are or should be bargains that validate the principle of free choice.[16] Those with power may choose to 'channel their actions into the forms of contract to gain the symbolism of bargain and free choice'.[17]

In his more recent work, Macaulay might be considered less temperate in his remarks. Intemperate or not, I am in absolute agreement when Macaulay characterises the decision by Judge Easterbrook in *Hill v Gateway 2000*[18] as 'an opinion that tells us that misrepresentation is the oil that lubricates capitalism'.[19] I share his view that: 'In an impossibly just world, measured by my preferences, this doctrine (reasonable expectations) would apply to all form contracts . . . I suspect that the impact would be largely symbolic, but I like symbolising that fraud from fancy

[12] Macaulay, 'Empirical View of Contract' (n 2) 474 fn 50.

[13] ibid 474.

[14] Ethical ideals, Macaulay notes, are implicated when there is inequality of resources, when a powerful party uses power in a way that is illegitimate, 'pressing an advantage too far' or 'making undue profit'. S Macaulay, 'Justice Traynor' (n 7) 815.

[15] The labour movement was fueled by harsh working conditions and unfair terms that were validated by courts as an example of 'freedom of contract'. Today the Occupy Wall Street movement is concerned more generally with disparities in power and wealth.

[16] Macaulay, 'Empirical View of Contract' (n 2) 478.

[17] ibid.

[18] *Hill v Gateway 2000*, 105 F 3d 1147 (7th Cir 1997).

[19] Email from S Macaulay to Contracts Listserv, published in 'Common Sense and Contracts Symposium: The Gateway Thread – AALS Contracts Listserv' (Summer 2000) 16 *Touro Law Review* 1147, 1148–49.

offices is a bad thing.'[20] The only point of disagreement I have with Macaulay is the suggestion that his vision of a just world is simply a personal preference. Rather, Macaulay's vision of a just world is a shared vision and the new legal realism is a description of a shared effort in a political and cultural contest.

This essay takes as its starting point the particular historical moment in which we find ourselves. We have listened to numerous explanations that have been offered for this last speculative bubble, so much larger and more devastating than those that came before, so much more serious than the label 'irrational exuberance'[21] would suggest. When Richard Posner wrote his book, *A Failure of Capitalism: The Crisis of '08 and the Descent into Depression*,[22] he apportioned blame for the economic collapse, faulting the private sector, regulators and economists.[23] No blame is apportioned to the judiciary by Judge Posner.[24] Perhaps the oversight can be attributed to the fact that an earlier understanding of the regulatory role of courts, the doctrines employed to enforce what Corbin referred to as the 'mores' of the market,[25] have receded in memory and virtually disappeared from the cultural scripts employed by judges who embrace a deregulatory ideology .

It is the basic premise of this article that blame should be shared by all three branches of government, including the judiciary. If the current crisis was caused by reckless behaviour, a compulsion or insatiable desire for ever greater profits, the law of contracts and contract theory must have played some part in the excesses that occurred. If Washington DC is the epicentre of the deregulatory impulse that caused capitalism to fail, the Seventh Circuit and a particular brand of law and economic theory has to be the epicentre of the deregulatory impulse in contract theory. Their intellectual prowess and commitment to law and economic theory have made Richard Posner and Frank Easterbrook the two most influential judges on the Seventh Circuit.

[20] ibid.

[21] 'How do we know when irrational exuberance has unduly escalated asset values, which then become subject to unexpected and prolonged contractions as they have in Japan over the past decade?' A Greenspan, 'The Challenge of Central Banking in a Democratic Society' (Speech, Annual Dinner and Francis Boyer Lecture of The American Enterprise Institute for Public Policy Research, Washington DC, December 5, 1996) (available at www.federalreserve.gov/boarddocs/speeches/1996/19961205.htm).

[22] R Posner, *A Failure of Capitalism, the Crisis of '08 and the Descent into Depression* (Cambridge, Harvard University Press, 2009).

[23] Excessive deregulation is responsible for the current depression and if the government was at fault, it was 'abetted by the political and ideological commitments of mainstream economists'. ibid 260.

[24] ibid 269–87.

[25] The treatise by Corbin is replete with references to mores. See, eg 'The keeping of promise is in the folkways and mores of mankind; and in the vast majority of cases they are kept and performed without thought of reach or necessity of enforcement.' A Corbin, *Corbin on Contracts: A Comprehensive Treatise on the Working Rules of Contract*, vol 1A (St Paul, West Publishing Co, 1963) § 240 'Formality and Mystery in Contract Law – Seals'.

I. REVIVING THE FREE WAY OUT – FLEXIBILITY, EFFICIENCY AND RISK

One of the precipitating causes of the current economic crisis was inadequate appreciation of the attendant risks in the creation and marketing of collateralised debt obligations or asset backed securities. There was also a freewheeling, no holds barred, approach to selling both securities and mortgages, in which the desire for profits banished all concern for honesty or caution. A good idea, one that brought more money into the mortgage markets, ostensibly to extend the benefits of homeownership to a wider segment of society, went horribly awry.

There are risks in every innovation; risks in the commitments that are made in market transactions. In retrospect, as we examine the continuing economic crisis, one question that might be asked is when and why a willingness to take some risks became a propensity for recklessness. When there are no consequences for misjudgments or for misconduct, an appreciation of risk disappears. The Seventh Circuit has played a role in altering perceptions of risk, or at least it condoned the use of terms that allow the more powerful party to limit liability or risk of loss and to shift risk contractually.

There is an ideological divide between those who wish to limit the liability of the breaching party in contract and those who believe that a major shortcoming in contract law is the failure to completely compensate the party injured by a breach of contract. The stated ideal, at least as expressed in Article 2 of the *Uniform Commercial Code* (UCC) is to put the 'aggrieved party in as good a position as if the other party had fully performed'.[26] This ideal is seldom achieved, for, as Macaulay has noted, courts operate in a manner that reflects a 'fear of awarding too much', despite the fact that this practice of limiting remedies frequently works to the advantage of the repeat player and more powerful party that fails to perform a contract.[27]

Macaulay's criticism of a contract jurisprudence that defeats the reasonable expectations of the parties to a contract, particularly when it comes to the recovery of consequential damages, stands in opposition to those who believe, despite persuasive arguments to the contrary, that economic growth is facilitated by liability-limiting rules. Often the arguments made in favour of rules that limit liability speak in terms of incentives that minimise risk. Liability-limiting rules do not minimise risk. Liability-limiting rules shift risk and in the process incentivise breach rather than performance. The breaching party can be fairly certain that if the rule is applied,

[26] UCC § 2-106.
[27] S Macaulay, 'Law, Private Governance' (n 2) 469.

some of the loss will be borne by the injured party.[28] This idea of loss sharing, dating back to the mid-nineteenth-century decision in *Hadley v Baxendale*,[29] is antithetical to the UCC's goal of vindicating the reasonable expectation of the parties.

Almost 30 years ago, Judge Posner was at work critiquing, and sometimes rewriting through a process of interpretation, Article 2 of the UCC. Posner's decision in *Western Industries Inc v Newcor Canada Ltd*[30] reiterated his economic analysis of consequential damages.[31] In this case, Judge Posner was explicit in his rejection of what he believed was an attempt by the drafters of the UCC to 'liberalise' the liability-limiting rule in *Hadley v Baxendale*.[32]

Western Industries was a case involving a global transaction. A Canadian company, Newcor, manufactured custom machinery for a US company, Western Industries, which built and sold parts to a Japanese manufacturer of microwave ovens, Sharp. The issue on appeal was the trial court's exclusion of evidence which the trial judge thought insufficient to prove trade usage. In his decision, Judge Posner ventured far beyond the question of admissibility of evidence into the realm of risk allocation and the merits of a provision in Article 2 of the UCC.

When I first read *Western Industries*, I was disturbed by an interpretation of UCC section 2-207. In a battle of forms, rather than a first shot or last shot rule, section 2-207 works best when the contest between buyer and seller ends in a draw and the default terms in the statute fill the gaps. Section 2-715, the provision on consequential damages, fills the gap when there is no common term in the contract documents that addresses the issue of consequential damages.

The contract in *Western Industries* was formed by a process which included a telephone call and the exchange of at least three documents as well as a visit to Newcor's factory. If the parties exchanged forms with conflicting terms, as Judge Cudahy succinctly put it in his concurring opinion, 'the conflicting terms fall out under 2-207(2) or 2-207(3)'.[33] The elimination of both terms meant that UCC section 2-715 would fill the gap and the buyer would be entitled to consequential damages if the seller 'had reason to know of the buyer's general or particular requirements at

[28] M Eisenberg, 'The Principle of *Hadley v. Baxendale*' (1992) 80 *California Law Review* 563, 569.

[29] *Hadley v Baxendale*, 156 Eng Rep 145 (Ex Ch 1854). See also argument by counsel for the defendant in *Hadley v Baxendale* in Eisenberg, 'The Principle of *Hadley v. Baxendale*' (n 28) 569.

[30] *Western Industries Inc v Newcor Canada Ltd*, 739 F 2d 1198 (7th Cir 1984).

[31] See discussion of photographer hypothetical from Posner's 'Economic Analysis of Law' in Eisenberg, 'The Principle of *Hadley v. Baxendale*' (n 28) 582–84. Although Eisenberg cites to the 1986 edition of Posner's book, the first edition was published in 1973, long before this case arrived at the 7th Circuit.

[32] *Western Industries* (n 30) 1203 (noting that the UCC adopted an 'especially liberal standard' for consequential damages).

[33] ibid 1207.

the time of contracting'. Posner took the position, however, that the existence of a trade usage is the 'substantial ground' that the seller would need 'for claiming preference for its disclaimer'.[34] He wrote that trade usage could 'override' the provisions in the UCC.

After a recitation of most of the facts, Judge Posner began his opinion with a discussion of trade usage and contractual allocation of risk, referring to the damage that would be done to the business of the buyer if the seller breached. It soon becomes clear to the reader that his real concern was the risk that consequential damages pose to a seller. The business of a buyer might be ruined, but for the seller 'only the sky would be the limit to the amount of consequential damages that manufacturers of machinery indispensable to their customers' businesses might run up'.[35] Posner criticised UCC section 2-715 for making the manufacturer an 'insurer' against the losses of the buyer unless consequential damages are expressly disclaimed.[36]

Even though the issue before Posner was not the sufficiency of the evidence on the issue of trade usage, but its admissibility, he took it upon himself to construct an argument that would support a finding that the evidence was sufficient. Judge Posner constructed a hypothetical bargain in which buyers know the 'perils of custom design', that anything custom designed won't be delivered on time, and it probably won't work.[37] Posner also argued that 'Western made a serious mistake by agreeing with Sharp (rather casually as it appears) to build microwave oven cavities by projection welding, a process which it turned out, American safety standards made infeasible'.[38] According to Posner, the possibility of recovering consequential damages made Western careless in its negotiations with Sharp. Posner does not explain why the party in the business of designing and manufacturing custom-made goods should not bear the risk of its failure; why the seller, Newcor, could not have consulted with the Japanese firm (Sharp) that already had used the technology in question. In Posner's analysis, the seller was not careless in agreeing 'to design and build a type of welding machine with which it was unfamiliar'.[39]

The methodology Posner used to 'prove' the existence of a trade usage in this case was consistent with a law and economic analysis, involving theoretical speculation about the relationship between risk allocation, efficiency and presumptive choices by rational economic actors. Occasional and selective forays into some of the facts surrounding this particular

[34] ibid 1206.

[35] ibid 1204.

[36] The UCC 'relaxes the rule' of *Hadley v Baxendale* and adopts as a foreseeability standard 'whether or not there was evidence that the promisor had undertaken to insure the promise' for consequential damages. ibid 1203.

[37] ibid.

[38] *Western Industries* (n 30) 1204.

[39] ibid.

exchange by Judge Posner provided no support for a conclusion that a trade, however that trade ultimately would be defined, had adopted a rule that consequential damages could not be recovered. There was only evidence that the seller had witnesses who would testify to the existence of such a trade usage and the fact that a form contract had been adopted by a sellers' trade association.[40]

As Macaulay reminds us, under section 1-205(2) of the UCC, custom must be proved as a matter of fact and those facts must show a 'regularity of observance in a place, vocation or trade'. Empirical evidence may suggest that 'more often than we would have thought, a party will not be able to carry its burden of proving the existence and content of a usage'.[41] It certainly is not sufficient to speculate that the risks attendant to a particular exchange, including the relationship between the particular machinery ordered and safety regulations in the United States, would be sufficient to establish a particular practice and agreement with respect to consequential damages.

Custom and usage is considered 'immanent' in the sense that it is fair to assume that the parties agreed to it. This assumption should be examined critically. A sociologist, Baudouin Dupret, has offered a critique of legal pluralism that has some relevance here.[42] Whether a custom exists is an empirical question, and as such it requires rigorous attention to the 'situated practices' of 'actual people in actual settings'.[43]

The more difficult issue in this case is the role of trade usage as a default term when the parties' forms contain conflicting or different terms. When trade usage limits liability, the spectre of unfair terms or unequal bargaining power should make a court particularly vigilant in adhering to UCC methodology, however sceptical we might be about a court's ability to do so. Hybridity – not within a legal system, but within a statute – may promote fluidity and forestall obsolescence.[44] It does not eliminate, and it might actually exacerbate, issues of distributive justice.[45] In my view the trial court was justified in its concern that the trade usage might be 'unilateral'.[46]

[40] ibid.

[41] Macaulay, 'Relational Contract Theory' (n 6) 788 ('Lisa Bernstein's empirical findings raise questions of evidence rather than challenge the entire approach of the UCC. Why isn't it enough to say that one who wants to rely on usage must prove it?').

[42] B Dupret, 'Legal Pluralism, Plurality of Laws, and Legal Practices: Theories, Critiques, and Praxiological Re-specification' (2007) 1 *Journal of European Legal Studies* 20.

[43] S Macaulay, 'Relational Contract Theory' (n 6).

[44] 'This Act . . . will provide its own machinery for expansion of commercial practices. It is intended to make it possible for the law embodied in this Act to be developed by the courts in the light of unforeseen and new circumstances and practices.' UCC § 1-102 cmt 1.

[45] D Snyder, 'Contract Regulation, With and Without the State: Rumination on Rules and Their Sources, A Comment on Jurgen Basedow' (2008) 56 *The American Journal of Comparative Law* 723.

[46] *Western Industries* (n 30) 1202.

This is not, as Lisa Bernstein has suggested, an argument that the UCC is unsuccessful as a realist project.[47] The approach is not wrong. However, when issues of distributive justice are implicated, some consideration should be given to the behaviour of a party who signals dissent or opposition to a purported trade usage. Trade usage, especially after *Western Industries*, could be used inappropriately, strategically and in bad faith. An ostensible trade usage, like a contract of adhesion where no consent exists, ought to invite some consideration of the appropriateness of displacing the general rule of expectation damages with one that limits liability.

Judge Posner's activism in *Western Industries* is noteworthy. There is nothing that can compare, though, in terms of judicial complicity in the use of contract to protect a seller from liability, to Judge Easterbrook's refashioning of the common law to make a vendor master of the offer in *Hill v Gateway 2000*.[48] A consumer class action suit against Gateway must have seemed ludicrous to Judge Easterbrook, particularly when the penalty would be treble damages under a statute.[49] The solution the lawyers for Gateway created ex ante, an arbitration clause, would have been objectionable even if buyers had been given notice in advance of purchase.

Buyers, who initiated the transaction, received a copy of the warranty and the arbitration provision when the computer was shipped to them. Initially the arbitration provision specified that the arbitration would be governed by the Rules of Conciliation and Arbitration of the International Chamber of Commerce, which was located in France.[50] Those rules required a plaintiff to pay an advance fee of $4,000, and $2,000 of that amount was non-refundable.[51] The fee to arbitrate was more than the cost of a new computer. Macaulay calls it a 'scam'[52] and certainly a strategy that absolves a manufacturer of all responsibility for the quality of the goods it manufactures and sends out into the market raises questions about the integrity of the company and its management.

Gateway made many mistakes, including many 'questionable management decisions'[53] but it survived complaints about the absence of quality control, false advertising and finally a securities fraud claim, until it was

[47] L Bernstein, 'Formalism in Commercial Law: The Questionable Empirical Basis of Article 2's Incorporation Strategy: A Preliminary Study' (1999) 66 *University of Chicago Law Review* 710.

[48] *Hill v Gateway 2000*, 105 F 3d 1147 (7th Cir 1997).

[49] The statute was the Racketeer Influenced and Corrupt Organizations Act, 18 USC §§ 1961–1968 (1970).

[50] Subsequent versions substituted the American Arbitration Association. See *Brower v Gateway 2000*, 676 NYS 2d 569 (NY App Div 1998).

[51] These facts are not disclosed in *Hill v Gateway* but appear in *Brower v Gateway 2000*, (n 50), where plaintiffs alleged the arbitration agreement was unconscionable.

[52] Macaulay, 'Relational Contract Theory' (n 6) 780 fn 29.

[53] The history of Gateway can be found at Gateway, Inc, www.fundinguniverse.com/company-histories/gateway-Inc-Company-History.html.

acquired by another company.[54] We cannot know what would have happened to Gateway if it had acknowledged its missteps and adopted a policy that gave its customers some recompense for its faulty performance. But repeated lawsuits, especially when the public perception is that the company is using unfair tactics to avoid liability, damage the reputation of a company far more publicly and thoroughly than an apology and compensation to customers.

The rhetoric of responsibility, a preoccupation with moral hazard, is seldom applied when courts and lawyers create doctrines or contract terms that incentivise irresponsible or reckless behaviour.[55] Eliminating accountability, or at least direct financial responsibility, is the objective of elite lawyers in big firms who draft contracts precisely for that purpose. Their success in achieving their objectives depends in large part on the validation of those strategies by judges.

In 2000, I was a visitor at DePaul Law School and I had the pleasure of attending the swearing in ceremony for Judge Ann Williams as the guest of my Dean at Touro Law Center and her former teacher at Notre Dame, Howard Glickstein. One of the speakers, a partner at a major Chicago law firm, inappropriately began his remarks with a homage to Judge Easterbrook, lauding his courage on the bench. Although Judge Easterbrook had been heavily criticised by the public interest lawyers in Chicago for his arrogance,[56] it is more likely that the lawyer was referring to the firestorm of criticism that began with Easterbrook's opinion in *ProCD v Zeidenberg*[57] and continued after he decided *Hill v Gateway 2000* the very next year.[58] It was a rare moment, a public acknowledgment of the role that judges play in legitimising boilerplate terms such as the arbitration provision in Gateway and the licence in ProCD. Lawyers have developed a cottage industry crafting agreements in a way that makes it easy for courts to construct a narrative about freedom, choice or negligence to justify decisions that defeat the reasonable expectations of less powerful participants in the market.[59]

[54] The company acquired e-machines, moved to California from North Sioux City, South Dakota, and ultimately was acquired by Acer, a Taiwanese company. See, also J Dean and C Lawton, 'Acer Buys Gateway, Bulks Up for Global Fight' *Wall Street Journal* (28 August 2007) online.wsj.com/article/SB118820817365109596.html.

[55] The asymmetry in the application of the principle was noted in the news recently. S Dewan, 'Moral Hazard: A Tempest Tossed Idea' *New York Times* (25 February 2012) query.nytimes.com/gst/fullpage.html?res=9903E1D61131F935A15751C0A9649D8B63&pagewanted=all.

[56] Chicago Council of Lawyers, 'Evaluation of the United States Court of Appeals for the Seventh Circuit' (1994) 43 *DePaul Law Review* 673, 760.

[57] *ProCD v Zeidenberg*, 86 F 3d 1447 (7th Cir 1996).

[58] For an elucidating example of the debate over Easterbrook's decision in Gateway see 'The Gateway Thread', (n 19). See also E Posner, '*ProCD v Zeidenberg* and Cognitive Overload in Contractual Bargaining' (2010) 77 *University of Chicago Law Review* 1181 (defending Easterbrook's decision against allegations that Easterbrook ignored the law).

[59] E Zacks, 'Contracting Blame' (2012) 15 *University of Pennsylvania Journal of Business Law* (forthcoming) (narrative created by use of boilerplate terms in consumer contracts reveals

II. RISK, SELF-RELIANCE AND INTEGRITY

Values are said to 'regulate' the effect of structure,[60] and structure, in its turn, can be said to 'organise experience'.[61] Norms are contextual, and structure is part of that context. Legal rules can and do restructure relationships, vindicate one or more competing values and announce emergent norms. The relationship between consumers and retailers or manufacturers has been restructured by the validation by courts of boilerplate mandatory arbitration provisions. The judicial imprimatur on these terms facilitates the creation of new revenue streams, including the imposition of additional small fees charged to millions of subscribers, depositors or purchasers of merchandise. In the worst-case scenario, these payments are obtained through fraud or deception and the small fraud committed against a large number of people is not remediable under state consumer protection laws because of class action waivers and contractual arbitration clauses.[62] While this change did not begin with *Hill v Gateway*, the decision in that case and others decided in the Seventh Circuit by Easterbrook and Posner encourage the use of boilerplate terms limiting liability for fraud or misrepresentation. Rules that vindicate honesty and fairness or constrain predation have been eclipsed by those that punish a lack of vigilance or self-reliance.

When I am reading contract cases, I have on occasion considered John Cheever's tongue-in-cheek description of the small town ethos, where the residents tolerated something less than upright behaviour by the merchants with whom they did business. The representations of writers and artists often reveal truths and sentiments that go unremarked in everyday life. Cheever has captured a truth, if not *the* truth, in his description of the local mortician and owner of a furniture store, Emmet Cavis:

> In his dealings with bewildered families he had, in the exchange of furniture and property for his services, been guilty now and then of sharp and dishonest practice; but it is the custom of that country to regard craft and dishonesty with respect. His cunning made him seem formidable and intelligent and like any good Yankee he had never trimmed the bereaved without remarking on The Uncertainty of All Earthly Things.[63]

In two sentences Cheever captures the complex relationship between deception, financial success and admiration in our understanding of mar-

understanding of cognitive bias and attributional theories) (available at ssrn.com/abstract=2018406).

[60] L Pearlin, 'Social Structure and Social Values: The Regulation of Structural Effects' in R O'Gorman (ed), *Surveying Social Life, Papers in Honor of Herbert H Hyman* (Middletown, Wesleyan University Press, 1988) 252–64.

[61] ibid 253.

[62] *AT&T v Concepcion*, 131 S Ct 1740 (2010).

[63] J Cheever, *The Wapshot Chronicle* (New York, Harper Perennial, 1984).

ket transactions. Macaulay too has a clearer eye for human nature and for cultural preferences than most. He has remarked on this same tendency, noting that a person who is able to draft a contract with terms highly favourable to himself might be 'praised for his skill rather than censured'.[64] Doing business is not about 'an exchange of mutual advantage but a game where each party is to maximize his own gains at the expense of the other'.[65] Admiration for the quick and the cunning has a dark side – an impatience or intolerance for those who are thought to be slower and less astute. At its most extreme, a preoccupation with self-reliance becomes disdain for human frailty in the form of gullibility, inattention, ignorance or incaution.

I am not sure what it means for a society when those who are charged with responsibility for administering justice tell us that a 'no reliance' clause has the same function as 'a truthful statement', which is Judge Easterbrook's pronouncement in *Rissman v Rissman*.[66] The strict enforcement of a no reliance clause is judicial sleight of hand. While we are distracted by the incompetence or negligence of a victim, dishonesty is disguised or concealed. Culpability no longer attaches to the person guilty of anti-social behaviour, but to the person who has been insufficiently self-reliant; the person who imprudently believes oral promises or statements of fact on which the writing clearly says he should not or has not relied.

Rissman v Rissman is a securities fraud case involving the sale of stock by one brother to another. Arnold Rissman claimed that he was cheated out of his share of the value of a family business by his brother Randall.[67] The buyer, Randall,[68] was found not liable because of representations and warranties in the contract, attributed to the seller, Arnold, which included a no reliance clause. This written avowal, as far as Easterbrook is concerned, made Arnold the breaker of promises when he sued his brother Randall.[69]

Judge Easterbrook claims to know what happened in this fight between brothers because the written contract tells him what happened. The writing says the brother Arnold entered into an agreement voluntarily, a characterisation that immediately arouses my suspicion. Voluntariness is usually invoked, I find, when there is a relationship that involves domination and subordination, which is how I read the relationship between

[64] S Macaulay, 'Private Legislation and the Duty to Read – Business Run by IBM Machine, the Law of Contracts and Credit Cards' (1966) 19 *Vanderbilt Law Review* 1051, 1058.

[65] ibid.

[66] *Rissman v Rissman and Robert Dunn Glick*, 213 F 3d 381, 384 (7th Cir 2000).

[67] ibid.

[68] While Randall was a party to the contract with his brother for the sale of the stock, the stock was sold to a trust Randall set up for the benefit of his children. *Rissman* (n 66) 588.

[69] ibid. Randall sued Arnold to recover attorney fees incurred in his defence in the earlier suit.

Randall and Arnold. For those of us who teach corporate law, the facts are typical of a classic 'freeze out' – the defendant brother and controlling shareholder, Randall, altered the by-laws or corporate charter to prevent Arnold from electing anyone to the board of directors, threatened to terminate his brother's employment and to reduce any dividends paid on the stock, and then sued Arnold because Arnold asked for access to the books and records of the corporation.[70]

It is received wisdom that progress entails a movement from status to contract.[71] Not true. Status is everywhere present in contract.[72] Courts may be wary of delving too deeply into the particulars of identity, but status is implicated in a variety of different doctrines and in the application of particular legal rules. Courts have separated out the least well off, members of vulnerable populations, and protected them.[73] Another broader and more inclusive category, 'sophisticated party', signals the application of norms associated with formalism in contract law.[74] The expectation is that sophisticated parties will understand the terms of a deal and that they are, or should be, self-reliant. That idea is expressed in a variety of ways in Easterbrook's analysis of all the things that Arnold Rissman could have done, but did not do, to counter Randall's aggressive tactics as majority shareholder.

If status implicates a duty of self-reliance, that duty should vary with social position. 'Brother' is a social status and a relationship. The subject position that seems to concern Judge Easterbrook is not kinship, the fact that the parties are brothers, but the fact that Arnold had a subordinate position in the company and that he could afford a lawyer.[75] We are told that Arnold, a mere salesman, is nonetheless a sophisticated party because he is represented by counsel.[76] There is a certain paradox in Judge Easterbrook's use of Arnold's representation by counsel to exclude evidence of misrepresentations by his brother while enumerating all the strategies a better lawyer might have used to protect Arnold. According to Easterbrook, the methods used by Randall in the freeze out could have been neutralised through legal action and different terms could have been included in the contract for the sale of Arnold's stock which would have allowed him to share in the value realised when the company was finally sold to a third party.[77]

[70] *Rissman* (n 66) 386.

[71] A Kastely, DW Post, and N Ota, *Contracting Law*, vol 5 (Durham, Carolina Academic Press, 2006) (quoting Sir Henry Maine, *Ancient Law*).

[72] S Ball and others, 'Status in Markets' (2001) 116 *The Quarterly Journal of Economics* 161 (the ability of higher status side of the market to capture a great share of surplus supported by results in a laboratory experiment).

[73] A Kronman, 'Paternalism and the Law of Contracts' (1983) 92 *Yale Law Journal* 783.

[74] M Miller, 'Contract Law, Party Sophistication and the New Formalism' (2010) 75 *Missouri Law Review* 493.

[75] ibid 386.

[76] ibid.

[77] ibid 384–85.

The decision announces that boilerplate no reliance clauses will be enforced in the Seventh Circuit. Prudent people protect themselves with the written word because there are people out there who will 'shade the truth'.[78] Decisions in the First Circuit and the DC Circuit court validating no reliance clauses were said to 'fit Arnold's claim like a glove'.[79] It is only when the reader reaches Judge Rovner's concurring opinion that she learns the decision in the First Circuit which Easterbrook cites placed qualifications on the enforceability of no reliance clauses.[80] These qualifications require an examination of the context in which the contract was signed and a consideration of the relationship between the parties, including the existence of a fiduciary or a 'long standing business or personal relationship'.[81] In my judgment, a duty of self-protection should not apply when one brother exploits the weakness of the other.

Boilerplate is used when parties find that it 'serves their ends', but that does not obviate a need to examine the substance and the operative effect of a term. Judge Easterbrook works hard to show the benefit of a no reliance clause to individuals in Arnold's position. The position to which he refers is *not* that of brother. Easterbrook claims that without an assurance that no claim will be made, the price paid to sellers of stock would be lower.[82] Arnold received one-sixth the amount that he would have received for his stock if he had not been forced out of the company or that he might have recovered if he had the opportunity to prove that his brother lied to him or coerced him into the settlement.

Disloyalty and opportunistic behaviour are so predictable in closely held corporations that judges and legislatures both have addressed the problem of oppression.[83] The public policy explicit in legislation and in the common law governing closely held corporations, 'incorporated partnerships',[84] surely should have been enough to prevent a court from dismissing a claim of fraud on a motion for summary judgment. Judge Easterbrook disagrees with this public policy. He has argued elsewhere that fiduciary duties impose costs 'that make it inappropriate to imply such terms as a rule'.[85] Easterbrook is concerned that if the majority gives the minority interest 'too many rights', these rights might be exercised in 'an opportunistic fashion to divert returns'.[86]

[78] ibid 384.

[79] *Jackvony v RIHT Financial Corp*, 873 F2d 411 (1st Cir 1989); *One–o-One Enterprises Inc v Richard E Caruso, et al*, 848 F2d 1283, 1286 (DC Cir 1988).

[80] *Rissman* (n 66) 388.

[81] ibid.

[82] ibid.

[83] See, eg *Galler v Galler*, 32 Ill 2d 16 (IL 1965).

[84] *Donahue v Rodd Electrotype*, 328 NE2d 505 (MA 1975) (noting the fundamental resemblance of closely held corporation to partnership).

[85] F Easterbrook and D Fischel, *The Economic Structure of Corporate Law* (Cambridge, Harvard University Press, 1991) 238.

[86] ibid.

III. VERACITY, RESPONSIBILITY AND THE INTEGRITY OF THE MARKET

Movitz v First National Bank of Chicago[87] does not involve a no reliance clause but it does invite a consideration of the relationship between legal rules, structure and particular values or ideals. The victim in *Movitz*, if we disregard the corporate entity through which he operated, was Dr Jawad Mahmoud Hashim, who shortly before a market collapse had invested in Houston commercial real estate on the advice of the defendant Bank. Movitz, a trustee in bankruptcy, sued the Bank on behalf of Hashim's corporation and its creditors but failed to recover any damages.

Judge Posner conceded in his opinion that the defendant Bank had breached its fiduciary duty and had failed to disclose material facts to Hashim about the condition of the real estate that he purchased. Apparently, as reported in the *Chicago Tribune*, the Bank also violated banking regulations and engaged in 'questionable investment practices' before the oil and real estate bubble burst in Houston in 1984.[88] A jury verdict against the Bank was reversed by Posner; the Bank's misrepresentation and breach of fiduciary duty did not cause the injury that Hashim's company had sustained.

The opinion distinguishes between 'but for' causation, loss causation and transaction causation. In the process, Judge Posner notes sardonically the various 'causes' of Mr Hashim's loss. Hashim (actually the trustee in bankruptcy who sought to recover assets for the benefit of the creditors of Hashim's corporation), blamed First National Bank of Chicago, which brokered the sale and then managed the building, for its failure to disclose, or perhaps even to find, various structural defects in the building that Hashim had purchased. Judge Posner wrote that *the blame might just as well have been placed on* 'Santa Ana, Sam Houston, or Columbus' or, he continues, 'Hashim's parents, or OPEC, which brought about the increase in oil prices that fueled Houston's real estate boom in the 1970s, a boom that made investing in real estate seem so attractive a prospect in 1980'.[89] All, in Posner's reasoning, were necessary preconditions to Hashim's loss.

Further on in his discussion of legal rules, Judge Posner addresses the problem of 'over-deterrence', the point most salient to a discussion of regulation, responsibility and market failure.[90] According to Judge Posner, the intervening cause of the loss sustained by the plaintiff was a market crash in Houston real estate values.[91] The imposition of liability on the Bank

[87] *Movitz v First National Bank of Chicago*, 148 F3d 760 (7th Cir 1998).

[88] J Schmeltzer, 'First Chicago Ordered to Pay Over '80s Deal' *Chicago Tribune* (29 March 1997).

[89] *Movitz* (n 87) 760.

[90] ibid.

[91] See also *Andrew J Maxwell v KPMG LLP*, 520 F 3d 713 (7th Cir 2008) (accounting firms negligence in reviewing financial statements not responsible for collapse of the dot.com market).

would incentivise those who have been injured in market disasters to 'cast about' for someone to blame and to seize upon what was merely a 'technical breach of duty'.[92] Moreover, the law does not take a 'very hard line' with respect to those who fail to tell the truth – in this case, negligently misrepresenting the revenue stream of the office building and failing to disclose the structural and mechanical defects in the building. The reason the law does not do it is that it is 'unrealistic' to assume that a bank would have control over its employees and agents.[93] This is a 'too big to know' defence as opposed to its current analogue, the 'too big to fail' phenomenon.

There is reason not to be sympathetic to Hashim (and therefore his bankruptcy trustee). Mr Hashim's creditor was the Arab Monetary Fund out of Abu Dahbi (AMF), an organisation formed in 1976 by treaty among Islamic states, including Palestine, which was meant to be 'the foundation of Arab economic integration' and the engine of economic development in the region.[94] A British court awarded AMF $50 million in its suit against Mr Hashim for embezzlement. Mr Hashim, an Iraqi citizen, was President and Director General of AMF for five years between 1977 and 1982.[95] He had also been advisor to Saddam Hussein. Mr Hashim claimed that Hussein misappropriated the funds.

Whether you like Mr Hashim or not, whether you like AMF and its owners, whether you think that the behaviour all around was reprehensible and that no-one deserved to get a penny out of this lawsuit as they were all culpable, the blanket absolution given the Bank and the general statements made about right and wrong in this case are disturbing. It suggests that carelessness with the truth and recklessness in the service of profit have nothing to do with market failure.

Judge Posner's decision disregards what Sissela Bok calls the 'veracity principle'.[96] She explains this principle in the following way:

> Were all statements randomly truthful or deceptive, action and choice would be undermined from the onset. There must be a minimal degree of trust in communication for language and action to be more than stabs in the dark. This is why some level of truthfulness has always been seen as essential in human society, no matter how deficient the observance of other moral principles.[97]

Lying, she tells us, has negative consequences for the liar, the person to whom the lie is told, and to 'social trust'.[98]

[92] *Movitz* (n 87) 763.
[93] ibid.
[94] *Arab Monetary Fund v Hashim (Re Hashim)*, 213 F 3d 1169, 1170 (9th Cir 2000).
[95] ibid. The Bank secretly paid AMF $13.5 million in a private settlement before Judge Posner ruled that the trustee in bankruptcy could not recover against the Bank. Schmeltzer, 'First Chicago' (n 88).
[96] S Bok, *Lying: Moral Choice in Public and Private Life* (New York, Vintage Books, 1999) 18.
[97] ibid.
[98] ibid 50.

It is not clear from this decision who Posner thinks should be responsible for monitoring the moral character or competence of employees. The real estate bubble in Houston was localised, but the causes were not that dissimilar from the current housing bubble, or perhaps all forms of 'irrational exuberance' or speculative hysteria. If so, then what rule will work to incentivise less risky behaviour by banking institutions? A systemic problem must be addressed by systemic reforms, on that much Judge Posner and I agree. It would be best if market participants scrutinised more carefully the basis for valuations. While the irrational aspects of valuation may not be obvious until after the fact, there is no justification for overlooking or ignoring obvious defects in goods or real estate. A rule that dismisses the requirement of due care or honesty does nothing to curb such excesses; it may actually incentivise risky behaviour by the party who is made to understand that there is less downside risk for misconduct of the kind in this case. Posner's reasoning suggests that as long as disregard for the truth is pervasive, the risk of loss lies with the investor, not those whose representations invited or facilitated the investment.

Eight years later, Judge Posner returns to his critique of the legal rules and goes even further in limiting claims of misrepresentation. In *Extra Equipamentos E Exportacao Ltda v Case Corporation*,[99] Judge Posner declares that an exception to the parol evidence rule that allows admission of evidence of oral misrepresentations is a 'loophole' in contract law. The term 'loophole' suggests that this exception was inadvertent or a mistake, some oversight that interferes with the proper functioning of the rule. The exception to the parol evidence rule for extrinsic evidence of fraud or misrepresentation is not a 'loophole', but a rule that recognises the importance of accurate information in market transactions, as important a policy as certainty, finality and predictability. Under Judge Posner's approach the party drafting the document is secure in the knowledge that she or it will not be held accountable for lies or half-truths. Again, the purpose and function of a rule is re-characterised in a way that ignores history, tradition or the purpose and intent of particular rules.[100]

The defendant, Case, is a manufacturer of farming equipment and the plaintiff, Extra, is a distributor of that equipment, contracting with the Brazilian subsidiary of Case. When Judge Posner notes that 'in the trade' a no reliance clause is called a 'big boy' clause, this is the signal that we are about to take a minor excursion into the realm of status. The reference to the 'trade' by Judge Posner had nothing to do with the manufacture or

[99] *Extra Equipamentos E Exportacao Ltda v Case Corporation*, 541 F 3d 719 (7th Cir 2008).

[100] In the original treatise by Arthur Corbin, he states: 'Whether they are such as to make the contract void or voidable, it is in no case denied that oral testimony is admissible to prove fraud, illegality, accident or mistake. This is so, even though the testimony contradicts the terms of a complete integration in writing.' A Corbin, *Corbin On Contracts*, vol 3 (n 25) para 580.

sale of farming equipment. It is a reference to the cottage industry that exists in the legal profession for the creation of standard form or boilerplate terms that provide protection to clients.[101] This invites a consideration of the new cultural script that has been written. Big boys don't cry? Big boys can suck it up? Big boys don't need the protection of the courts? This is a bare-fisted struggle for dominance and apparently women are not invited. The court is not an umpire applying the rules and remaining neutral. There is no umpire.

It we were to apply the label 'big boy' to someone, it might be Extra. Extra had New York lawyers and Brazilian lawyers at the time its agents signed a settlement agreement with a no reliance clause and the apparent abundance of legal advice might explain Posner's reference to 'the trade'. The facts of the case suggest that Extra had some leverage in its negotiations with Case because the government of Brazil and the Brazilian courts were significant players in the conflict between these parties. All of this supports the conclusion that the complaining party was sophisticated and should be held to the terms of the writing.

Still, there are structural issues in this case. Relationships between distributors and manufacturers are seldom equal. Brazil is an emerging nation, one that is experiencing rapid economic growth it is true, but still part of the global South. We do not know what will become of the Brazilian subsidiary that Case used to conduct business, whether it has assets with which to satisfy a judgment if one were awarded to the plaintiff in this case. I say this simply to acknowledge how difficult it is to understand what motivated the parties to enter into this settlement agreement.

The most perplexing part of the case may be the assumption that a judge can decide the facts in a motion for summary judgment when one party claims that lies were told as an inducement to enter into a settlement. A legal fiction makes corporations people, but it is the motives of the people who run them that matter. In the corporate setting, ethics and honesty sometimes get lost when ambition and profits are foremost in the minds of its agents.

IV. FAIR DEALING, COMMERCIAL REASONABLENESS AND TRUST

While it would be impossible and unfair to try to suggest a direct causal relationship between the jurisprudence of the Seventh Circuit and the current economic crisis, it is fair to say that the Seventh Circuit, and Judges Easterbrook and Posner in particular, have championed the use

[101] See, eg R Lofgren, 'Protecting your Business with "Boiler Plate" or "Standard Business Terms"' (*The Entrepreneur's Legal Resource, Counsel to Business Leaders*) available at www.elr-law.com/Business_Update_-__Protecting_Your_Business_.pdf; 'Boilerplate Provisions in Contracts' (*AllBusiness*) available at www.allbusiness.com/pring/1291-1-9a0bs.html.

of boilerplate terms that protect participants in the market from certain risks, including the consequences that flow from their own misjudgments or misbehaviour. While both have affirmed the legitimacy of boilerplate, even when it seems to protect fraud or negligence, Judge Easterbrook has further engaged with the issue of morality in the marketplace in his criticism of the implied duty of good faith. Easterbrook appears to consider this implied obligation to act in the marketplace in a way that is honest, fair or reasonable a duty that potentially puts the very institution of contract in jeopardy.

Judge Easterbrook assures us in *Jordon v Duff & Phelps*, that good faith is not 'a version of the Golden Rule, to regard the interests of one's contracting partner the same way you regard your own. An employer may be thoughtless, nasty and mistaken.'[102] We are also told that '[a]vowedly opportunistic conduct has been treated differently'.[103] This might seem reassuring. Good faith may be a standard of behaviour that restrains those with power, if we only knew what Judge Easterbrook considered 'avowedly opportunistic'.

Two years earlier, in *Kham & Nate's Shoes No 2 Inc v First Bank of Whiting*,[104] Judge Easterbrook was emphatic that: 'Firms that have negotiated contracts are entitled to enforce them to the letter, even to the great discomfort of trading partners, without being mulcted for lack of "good faith".'[105] There is so often in the decisions of Judge Easterbrook a tone of derision. In *Kham and Nate's Shoes* the use of the term 'mulcted' makes the Bank a victim. Easterbrook's terminology may express his assessment of the character of the owners, Khamolaw Beard and Nathaniel Parker, their extravagance (head office in a 'snazzy building' on Michigan Avenue), the fact that the company had been in bankruptcy for six years, and/or the fact that they were emerging from bankruptcy still holding all the equity in the company.

Kham and Nate negotiated with the Bank for additional loans to their company and the Bank insisted that it had to be made secure. The parties discussed a bankruptcy petition and an order by the bankruptcy court giving post petition loans superpriority.[106] The Bank would recover even before the administrative costs of bankruptcy would be paid. The Bank promised a $300,000 line of credit to the company if it received this superpriority. But five weeks later, after the company had drawn down $75,000, the Bank terminated the line of credit. The Bankruptcy Judge terminated

[102] *Jordan v Duff and Phelps, Inc*, 815 F 2d 429, 438 (7th Cir 1987) (Judge Easterbrook stating this even as he found in favour of a former employee and shareholder in a closely held corporation in a securities fraud case).
[103] ibid.
[104] *Kham & Nate's Shoes No 2 Inc v First Bank of Whiting*, 908 F 2d 1351 (7th Cir 1990).
[105] ibid 1357.
[106] ibid 1353.

the Bank's superpriority, acting under a section of the Bankruptcy Code allowing equitable subordination of security interests.[107] The Bankruptcy judge found that the Bank's abrupt termination of the line of credit 'unfair' and 'inequitable' given the consequences to the debtor and its suppliers. Equitable subordination left the Bank an unsecured creditor in the ensuing bankruptcy with respect to the amounts advanced under the line of credit. Judge Easterbrook found the attempt to limit the recovery by the Bank problematic. The Bank had a contractual right to terminate the line of credit, on five days notice, at any time (that is, at will).

In the wake of various and sundry exposes of greed, corruption and dishonesty in corporate America, and particularly in the savings and loan and banking business, it seems appropriate to contemplate the motives that might persuade a bank to extend further credit to someone with a failing business. The two men and their company certainly were a bad risk. It might make you wonder why the Bank bothered to negotiate with them at all. If you are deeply suspicious of banks, you might see the Bank's behaviour as strategic and, therefore, inequitable. The bankruptcy judge might have inferred from the alacrity with which it terminated the loan that the Bank never really intended to lend $300,000 to the bankrupt company.

Of greater consequence is the use of the decision in this case as a staging ground for general statements about good faith that have far reaching effects. For instance, Judge Easterbrook announced that in 'commercial life' there must be 'breach *plus* some advantage taking' before behaviour can be condemned – using examples drawn from what we would classify as economic duress, a classic 'hold up' such as a refusal to perform that is used to extract an agreement to modify a contract.[108] In defence of commercial certainty, Easterbrook insists that '[f]irms that have negotiated contracts are entitled to enforce them to the letter' even when 'literal enforcement means some mismatch between the parties' expectation and the outcome'.[109] Enforcement of those expectations is derided as the implication of a 'duty of kindness in performance'.[110] A party to a contract may exercise its rights under a contract 'for any reason satisfactory to itself'.[111]

The statement that good faith does not impose a general duty of 'kindness' diminishes and trivialises the duty of good faith. Nor is it appropriate to suggest that self-interested behaviour, when it is strategic and counter to the expectations of both parties who negotiated the deal, would make the bank an 'eleemonsynary institution'.[112]

[107] 11 USC § 510(c).
[108] ibid 1357.
[109] ibid.
[110] ibid.
[111] ibid.
[112] ibid 1158.

To the extent Judge Easterbrook explicitly acknowledges the potential for exploitation and its relationship to the duty of good faith, it is with reference to the relationship between employer and employee.

> Employment creates occasions for opportunism. A firm may fire an employee the day before his pension vests, or a salesman the day before a large commission becomes payable. Cases of this sort may present difficult questions about the reasons for the decision (was it opportunism, or was it a decline in the employee's performance?). The difficulties of separating opportunistic conduct from honest differences of opinion about an employee's performance on the job may lead firms and their employees to transact on terms that keep such disputes out of court – which employment at will usually does. But no one, not even Professor Epstein, doubts that an avowedly opportunistic discharge is a breach of contract although the employment is at will.[113]

Whether it is the power to fire an at-will employee, terminate a contract or call a note, the exercise of power in a way that is opportunistic, arbitrary or retaliatory should be a violation of good faith.

In *Dan Beraha, MD v Baxter Health Care Corporation*,[114] another panel of Seventh Circuit judges tried to reconcile the obvious inconsistencies in the Circuit's cases dealing with good faith, or the lack of it and employment agreements did not fare well. The court distinguished employment agreements from other contractual relationships. Good faith limits discretion of one of the parties in other kinds of agreements, but an employment relationship is constructed by the courts as 'at will'. An at will employee, the court reminds us, has no reasonable expectation of continued employment.

Over time, however, courts have come to treat any contract with a termination clause like an 'at will' contract. At the same time, the definition of opportunistic behaviour is ever more narrowly defined. Defining bad faith as opportunistic behaviour focuses attention on the economic gain or advantage to one side and not the potential loss to the other. Termination for any reason or no reason at all imposes a huge cost on the party who has had to make the greater investment in the relationship. If the nature and extent of that investment is known or demanded, the apparent symmetry of a termination clause is illusory. One party would not walk away from a contract before it had an opportunity to recoup its investment while the other party could use the termination clause if a better deal were presented.

The judicial construction of bad faith as 'avowedly opportunistic behavior' is flawed because it is too narrow, ignoring both motive and many forms of injury. Nor is it likely that an employment relationship is the only one where exploitation is possible. Exploitation is possible in any

[113] *Jordan* (n 102) 438. Many of us might take issue with the assumption that employees prefer at will employment.

[114] *Dan Beraha, MD v Baxter Health Care Corporation*, 956 F.2d 1436,1445 (7 Cir 1992).

human relationship where there is a differential in power. As Macaulay has pointed out 'long term, continuing relationships which carry a thick coat of relational norms and sanctions' can be 'engines of cooperation for mutual benefit' but they can also involve 'domination of those who cannot easily get out.'[115]

CONCLUSION

No discussion of contract law should be acontextual, whether we are analysing the contract jurisprudence of a particular court or the body of work of Professor Stewart Macaulay. Professor Macaulay has been described by one anthropologist as a contract scholar, who along with Ian Macneil, brought culture onto the centre stage in analysing and theorising the process of contracting.[116] This essay is about culture; about the sentiments and general ethos that propelled the market in the general direction of economic collapse. It is also about the relationship between the recent economic collapse and a jurisprudential approach that ignores the 'reasonable expectation of the parties'. Reasonableness is a word that always brings you back to a collective sensibility. There is room for deviation and accommodation of outliers in a culture, but judges should be careful about abandoning the values that make it possible for people to live and work and engage in commerce with one another.

More than ten years ago, in 2000, *Touro Law Review* published 'The Gateway Thread'. I posted a problem on the contracts listserv and immediately Professor Macaulay responded with a very thoughtful post that provoked a variety of responses. He suggested that we have a right to live in world based on trust. Professor Frank Snyder wrote back that 'we inhabit a legal system that permits people to be wildly negligent with respect to truth and falsehood without legal penalty'.[117] Some time later he dismissed Professor Macaulay's ideas, noting that 'trust is an emotion, and it seems troublesome to say that I have a right to have you conduct yourself in such a way that I can subjectively enjoy a particular emotion'.[118]

This is my answer, 11 years later, to the question about the significance of trust. One anthropologist has stated that there are three 'keywords' these days: transparency, accountability and trust.[119] Each of these reflects our desire for a world that is 'less opaque in its complexity'.[120] Trust, like accountability and transparency is about behaviour. It is not an emotion

[115] Macaulay, 'Yellow Submarine' (n 3) 1170.
[116] Mautner, 'Contract, Culture, Compulsion' (n 1).
[117] 'The Gateway Thread' (n 19) 1152.
[118] ibid 1171.
[119] U Hannerz, *Anthropology's World: Life in a Twenty-First-Century Discipline* (London, Pluto Press, 2010) 90.
[120] ibid.

but an act, behaviour that is possible only in the presence of a certain constellation of beliefs. We believe that people will do the right thing, that they will not be predatory, greedy or grossly negligent in the operation of their business or in their dealings with us. We believe that they will not act in ways that will injure or damage not only themselves but also those with whom they have an immediate economic relationship, and ultimately the vast web of interconnected economic relationships that the financial crisis in the United States has revealed. We believe that there will be access to justice and that the judgments of courts will affirm our most basic beliefs about honesty and decency.

BIBLIOGRAPHY

Ball, S and others, 'Status in Markets' (2001) 116 *The Quarterly Journal of Economics* 161.

Bok, S, *Lying: Moral Choice in Public and Private Life* (New York, Vintage Books, 1999).

Bernstein, L, 'Formalism in Commercial Law: The Questionable Empirical Basis of Article 2's Incorporation Strategy: A Preliminary Study' (1999) 66 *University of Chicago Law Review* 710.

Cheever, J, *The Wapshot Chronicle* (New York, Harper Perennial, 1984).

Chicago Council of Lawyers, 'Evaluation of the United States Court of Appeals for the Seventh Circuit' (1994) 43 *DePaul Law Review* 673, 760.

'Common Sense and Contracts Symposium: The Gateway Thread – AALS Contracts Listserv' (Summer 2000) 16 *Touro Law Review* 1147.

Corbin, A, *Corbin on Contracts: A Comprehensive Treatise on the Working Rules of Contract*, vol 1A (St Paul, West Publishing Co, 1960).

Dean, J and Lawton, C, 'Acer Buys Gateway, Bulks Up for Global Fight' *Wall Street Journal* (28 August 2007).

Dewan, S, 'Moral Hazard: A Tempest Tossed Idea' *New York Times* (25 February 2012).

Dupret, B, 'Legal Pluralism, Plurality of Laws, and Legal Practices: Theories, Critiques, and Praxiological Re-specification' (2007) 1 *Journal of European Legal Studies* 20.

Easterbrook, F and Fischel, D, *The Economic Structure of Corporate Law* (Cambridge, Harvard University Press, 1991).

Eisenberg, M, 'The Principle of *Hadley v Baxendale*' (1992) 80 *California Law Review* 563.

Greenspan, A, 'The Challenge of Central Banking in a Democratic Society' (Speech, Annual Dinner and Francis Boyer Lecture of The American Enterprise Institute for Public Policy Research, Washington DC, December 5, 1996).

Hannerz, U, *Anthropology's World: Life in a Twenty-First-Century Discipline* (London, Pluto Press, 2010).

Kastely, A, Post, DW and Ota, N, *Contracting Law*, vol 5 (Durham, Carolina Academic Press, 2006).

Kronman, A, 'Paternalism and the Law of Contracts' (1983) 92 *Yale Law Journal* 783.

Macaulay, S, 'Contracts, New Legal Realism, and Improving the Navigation of The Yellow Submarine' (2006) 80 *Tulane Law Review* 1161.

——, 'Relational Contract Theory: Unanswered Questions A Symposium in Honor of Ian R Macneil: Relational Contracts Floating on a Sea of Custom? Thoughts About the Ideas of Ian Macneil and Lisa Bernstein' (2000) 94 *Northwestern University Law Review* 775.

——, 'Law, Private Governance and Continuing Relationships: An Empirical View of Contract' (1985) 1985 *Wisconsin Law Review* 465.

——, 'Private Legislation and the Duty to Read – Business Run by IBM Machine, the Law of Contracts and Credit Cards' (1966) 19 *Vanderbilt Law Review* 1051.

——, 'Justice Traynor and the Law of Contracts' (1961) 13 *Stanford Law Review* 812.

Mautner, M, 'Contract, Culture, Compulsion, or: So What is So Problematic in the Application of Objective Standards in Contract' (2002) 3 *Theoretical Inquiries in Law* 545.

Miller, M, 'Contract Law, Party Sophistication and the New Formalism' (2010) 75 *Missouri Law Review* 493.

Pearlin, L, 'Social Structure and Social Values: The Regulation of Structural Effects' in R O'Gorman (ed), *Surveying Social Life, Papers in Honor of Herbert H Hyman* (Middletown, Wesleyan University Press, 1988).

Posner, E, '*ProCD v Zeidenberg* and Cognitive Overload in Contractual Bargaining' (2010) 77 *University of Chicago Law Review* 1181.

Posner, R, *A Failure of Capitalism, the Crisis of '08 and the Descent into Depression* (Cambridge, Harvard University Press, 2009).

Economic Analysis of Law (Boston, Little Brown & Company, 1986).

Schmeltzer, J, 'First Chicago Ordered to Pay Over '80s Deal' *Chicago Tribune* (29 March 1997).

Snyder, D, 'Contract Regulation, With and Without the State: Rumination on Rules and Their Sources, A Comment on Jurgen Basedow' (2008) 56 *The American Journal of Comparative Law* 723.

Zacks, E, 'Contracting Blame' (2012) 15 *University of Pennsylvania Journal of Business Law* (forthcoming).

15

Doctrines of Last Resort

D GORDON SMITH*

INTRODUCTION

STEWART MACAULAY BEGAN his famous study, 'Non-Contractual Relations in Business', with the question, 'What good is contract law?'[1] The traditional answer to this question is that contract law facilitates mutually beneficial exchanges,[2] but Macaulay found little evidence of contract law in the business relationships he examined in the early 1960s. While he observed that 'many business exchanges reflect a high degree of planning' through formal contracts,[3] he also found that 'many, if not most, exchanges reflect no planning, or only a minimal amount of it, especially concerning legal sanctions and the effect of defective performances'.[4] If problems arose, Macaulay noted, the parties often negotiated a solution without relying explicitly on the written contracts or threats of legal sanctions.[5]

Businesses today rely more heavily on contracts than the manufacturing firms studied by Macaulay,[6] but the core insight of 'Non-Contractual Relations in Business' – that '[l]egal doctrine and legal recourse often matter very little . . . since most transactions are governed, in practice, by informal community norms, enforced by informal social sanctions'[7] – is widely accepted and remains relevant.[8]

* Thanks to Jordan Lee, Sheetal Shah, and Shiela Sullivan for excellent research assistance.

1 See S Macaulay, 'Non-Contractual Relations in Business: A Preliminary Study' (1963) 28 *American Sociological Review* 55, 55.

2 See D Markovits, 'Contact and Collaboration' (2004) 113 *Yale Law Journal* 1417, 1419.

3 Macaulay, 'Non-Contractual Relations' (n 1) 60.

4 ibid.

5 ibid 61.

6 See J Esser, 'Institutionalizing Industry: The Changing Forms of Contract' (1996) 21 *Law & Social Inquiry* 593, 626 (1996); see also G Hadfield and I Božović, 'Scaffolding: Using Formal Contracts to Build Informal Relations to Support Innovation' (2012) USC Law and Economics Research Papers Series No C12-3/USC Legal Studies Research Papers Series No 12-6, available at papers.ssrn.com/sol3/papers.cfm?abstract_id=1984915.

7 M Suchman, 'The Contract as Social Artifact' (2003) 37 *Law & Society Review* 91, 96.

8 DG Smith and B King, 'Contracts as Organizations' (2009) 51 *Arizona Law Review* 1, 7–12.

However, a number of prominent scholars over the past two decades have emphasised the importance of contract law, particularly the rules relating to contract interpretation, for those parts of contractual relationships in which parties prefer legal enforcement to self-enforcement.[9] Responding to these scholars, Macaulay wrote 'The Real and the Paper Deal',[10] which makes a case for flexible standards of contract interpretation. This essay connects these two lines of Macaulay's thought, arguing that the informal social sanctions Macaulay observed in 'Non-Contractual Relations in Business' are a natural outgrowth of the inevitable disjunction between expressions and expectations that he explored in 'The Real and the Paper Deal'. That disjunction not only provokes conflicts among contracting parties, but also ensures that the legal system will be incapable of resolving many of those conflicts in a satisfactory manner.[11] Nevertheless, as Macaulay noted in 'The Real and the Paper Deal', 'doctrine can matter.'[12] In this essay, I focus on a collection of legal doctrines, which I call the 'doctrines of last resort,' that facilitate contract formation.

The doctrines of good faith and fair dealing, fiduciary duty, and unjust enrichment are doctrines of last resort because they are activated only when all other potentially applicable commands from constitutions, statutes, regulations, ordinances, common law decisions and contracts have been exhausted. In these circumstances – where positive law and private ordering are otherwise incomplete[13] – contracting parties rely heavily on informal social sanctions to protect against opportunism, but the doctrines of last resort reinforce these social sanctions. Rather than regulating all of the deviations and adjustments that are common in contractual relationships, doctrines of last resort constrain extreme deviations from social norms, reinforcing agreements precisely in those contexts where informal social sanctions are weakest.

I. INCOMPLETE CONTRACTS

'Contracts are always more than the contract document,' Macaulay wrote in 'The Real and the Paper Deal'.[14] He attributes the disjunction of

[9] See, eg A Schwartz and R Scott, 'Contract Theory and the Limits of Contract Law' (2003) 113 *Yale Law Journal* 541; R Scott, 'The Case for Formalism in Relational Contract' (2000) 94 *Northwestern University Law Review* 847.

[10] See S Macaulay, 'The Real and Paper Deal: Empirical Pictures of Relationships, Complexity and the Urge for Transparent Rules' (2003) 66 *Modern Law Review* 44, 45.

[11] Compare R Danzig, *The Capability Problem in Contract Law* (Mineola, Foundation Press, 1978).

[12] Macaulay, 'The Real and Paper Deal' (n 10) 67.

[13] K Pistor and C Xu, 'Incomplete Law' (2003) 35 *New York University Journal of International Law and Policy* 931.

[14] Macaulay, 'The Real and Paper Deal' (n 10) 45.

expressions and expectations to myriad familiar causes: limitations of language,[15] inability to predict the future,[16] lack of time and energy for bargaining,[17] impediments to co-ordination in business organisations,[18] and negotiation strategy.[19] For all of these reasons, according to Macaulay, most contracts have 'text between the lines'.[20]

Economists have long recognised that contracts are incomplete in the manner described by Macaulay.[21] A source of incompleteness is 'bounded rationality',[22] a somewhat malleable term that includes an inability to negotiate future plans because parties 'have to find a common language to describe states of the world and actions with respect to which prior experience may not provide much of a guide'.[23] Thus, bounded rationality might include an inability to write contracts in such a way that they can be enforced by a third party.[24]

The degree to which contracts are incomplete depends in part on the trade-off between the anticipated hazards of ex post opportunism and the costs of ex ante design. If contracting were costless, 'it would be possible in principle to design arrangements complete enough to circumscribe all surplus-eroding redistributive tactics and intricate enough to mitigate investment distortions'.[25] In other words, one reason we so often observe substantial gaps between real deals and paper deals is that contracting is expensive.

[15] ibid 45–46. ('Words do not have a fixed meaning that every speaker of the language will translate the same way. We create the meaning of written language by bringing to the words some measure of context, background assumptions, our experiences, and, too often, our bias, ignorance and stupidities.')

[16] ibid 46. ('The world changes and surprises us: Wars break out in places where we do not expect them; or our contract may have dealt with a war but left open what happens when the indirect effect of a major terrorist attack makes performance much more costly; OPEC drives up energy costs unexpectedly; new technologies, often involving computers, change things so that an older contract no longer makes sense.')

[17] ibid ('[T]here are limits on the time that we can or should spend on trying to provide for all contingencies in our contracts').

[18] ibid ('[W]e must remember that business corporations are collections of people and their activities are seldom tightly coordinated').

[19] Ibid. ('If I want a clause that says If event X takes place, then consequence Y will follow, you may demand something in exchange that I do not want to give you. When I anticipate this, it may be better to avoid raising the issue in negotiations and hope that the matter can be resolved if event X ever takes place.')

[20] ibid 47.

[21] See H Simon, 'A Formal Theory of the Employment Relationship' (1951) 19 *Econometrica* 293.

[22] See H Simon, 'A Behavioral Model of Rational Choice' (1955) 69 *The Quarterly Journal of Economics* 99; H Simon, 'Rationality as Process and as Product of Thought' (1978) 68 *The American Economic Review* 1, 10; H Simon, 'Theories of Decision-Making in Economics and Behavioral Science' (1959) 49 *The American Economic Review* 253.

[23] O Hart, *Firms, Contracts & Financial Structure* (Oxford, Oxford University Press, 1995) 23.

[24] ibid 23.

[25] K Crocker and K Reynolds, 'The Efficiency of Incomplete Contracts: An Empirical Analysis of Air Force Engine Procurement' (1993) 24 *Rand Journal of Economics* 126, 127.

Under incomplete contract theory, the most important consequence of incomplete contracting is the potential for 'holdup'.[26] Holdup occurs when one contracting party threatens another with economic harm unless concessions are granted by the threatened party. Anticipation of holdup is said to motivate the structure of contractual relationships.[27] In particular, the potential for holdup is said to encourage contracting parties to enter into long-term relationships or vertically integrate.

Transactional responses to the potential for holdup can serve as important checks, but private ordering does not reduce the potential for holdup completely. Lawyers often assume that the domain of law is to mitigate this residual potential for holdup. Macaulay, contemplating this challenge, asked: 'How does or should contract law respond to any gap between the paper deal and the real deal?'[28] The answer he provided is that contract law has two options: (1) deny the problem by assuming that the 'plain meaning' of the paper deal is the real deal;[29] or (2) acknowledge the problem by adopting flexible rules of interpretation,[30] which yield indeterminate results.[31] In either case, the possibility that the results achieved through litigation will differ from the contracting parties' actual expectations is very high. As a result, taking a contract dispute to court will often seem unattractive to the contracting parties, and the disjunction of expressions and expectations is usually resolved through informal social sanctions.

II. BOUNDARY ENFORCEMENT

Although Macaulay observed that contracting parties enforce their deals primarily through informal social sanctions, he has acknowledged the possibility that public enforcement of contract may play an important role in encouraging transactions. Business people may 'tacitly rely on the law to fill gaps and provide sanctions,' and the 'contract litigation process may . . . maintain a vague sense of threat that keeps everyone reasonably reliable'.[32] In other words, if law erects boundaries around the pursuit of self-interest, business people may be emboldened to transact.

[26] See B Klein, R Crawford and A Alchian,'Vertical Integration, Appropriable Rents, and the Competitive Contracting Process' (1978) 21 *Journal of Law & Economics* 297. See also R Coase, 'The Conduct of Economics: The Example of Fisher Body General Motors' (2006) 15 *Journal of Economics & Management Strategy* 255, 255.

[27] See, eg DG Smith, 'Team Production in Venture Capital Investing' (1999) 24 *Journal of Corporate Law* 949.

[28] Macaulay, 'The Real and Paper Deal' (n 10) 47.

[29] ibid 47.

[30] ibid 48–49.

[31] ibid 50–51.

[32] S Macaulay, 'Elegant Models, Empirical Pictures, and The Complexities of Contract' (1977) 11 *Law & Society Review* 508, 519.

A similar sentiment is expressed in the works of Max Weber,[33] Douglass North,[34] Hernando De Soto,[35] Rule of Law scholars,[36] authors developing Legal Origins Theory[37] and others[38] who write about the connection between contract law and economic development. In *Law and the Conditions of Freedom*, Willard Hurst argued that contract law provided a stabilising influence that allowed private actors to plan for the future.[39] Within a 'framework of reasonably predictable consequences,' Hurst surmised, private actors were 'likely to cultivate boldness and energy in action.'[40]

The doctrines of last resort play an important role in these accounts of economic development by placing boundaries around the pursuit of self-interest. While each of these doctrines occupies a distinct domain, their jurisdictions sometimes overlap. For example, the same behaviour might trigger claims of bad faith, disloyalty and unjust enrichment.[41] The doctrines of last resort are united by a similar objective: the establishment of boundaries on self-interested behaviour to mitigate opportunism.[42]

III. OPPORTUNISM

The term 'opportunism' has a relatively short provenance, at least in comparison with the doctrines of last resort. The first entry for 'opportunism' or 'opportunistic' in the Corpus of Historical American English (COHA) is in 1898. The *Oxford English Dictionary* suggests that the term was introduced into the English language in the late 1800s via a translation of the Italian word *opportunismo* and the French word *opportunisme*.[43] In both languages, the word emerged in political contexts to connote compro-

[33] M Weber, G Ross and C Wittich (eds), *Economy and Society*, vol 2 (Berkeley, University of California Press, 1978 reissue; originally published 1914) 641–900.

[34] D North, *Institutions, Institutional Change and Economic Performance* (Cambridge, Cambridge University Press, 1990).

[35] H De Soto, *The Mystery of Capital: Why Capitalism Triumphs in the West and Fails Everywhere Else* (New York, Basic Books, 2000).

[36] J Ohnesorge, 'The Rule of Law' (2007) 3 *Annual Review of Law and Social Science* 99.

[37] R La Porta, F Lopez-de-Silanes and A Shleifer, 'The Economic Consequences of Legal Origins' (2008) 46 *Journal of Economic Literature* 285.

[38] See, eg W Nelson, *The Common Law in Colonial America – Volume I, The Chesapeake and New England, 1607–1660* (Oxford, Oxford University Press, 2008); G Kolko, *The Triumph of Conservatism: A Reinterpretation of American History, 1900-1916* (New York, The Free Press, 1963) 179.

[39] JW Hurst, *Law and the Conditions of Freedom in the Nineteenth Century United States* (Madison, University of Wisconsin Press, 1956) 10–11.

[40] ibid 22.

[41] See, eg *Macomber v Travelers Property & Cas Corp*, 804 A2d 180 (CT 2002); *MIC Life Ins Co v Hicks*, 825 So2d 616 (MO 2002).

[42] See DG Smith, 'The Critical Resource Theory of Fiduciary Duty' (2002) 55 *Vanderbilt Law Review* 1399, 1487–91.

[43] *Oxford English Dictionary* (Oxford, Clarendon Press, 1970).

mise, as opposed to 'rigid adherence to party principles'.[44] In this usage, 'opportunism' might be favourably interpreted as something akin to 'adaptability'. It is a short step from this favourable view of opportunism as adaptability to a negative view in which opportunism is viewed as expedience, or in modern parlance, as 'advantage taking'.

When 'opportunism' first appears in American judicial opinions in the early 1900s, its meaning is variegated, but it seems in every instance to carry with it a judgment about the fairness of institutions rather than the morality of individuals. For example, the first case to use the word involved a forced sale of land, in which 'opportunism' was used to describe the structure of the proposed sale, rather than of the individual participants in the transaction.[45] In another case, a court suggests that corporations are not regulated according to 'opportunism', but instead by 'general rules of law'.[46] Finally, in a third early case, also involving a forced sale of land, the court contrasted 'justice' – conceptualised as the principled application of common law rules – with 'opportunism'.[47] In all three of these early cases, therefore, opportunism carries a negative connotation that is tied to the unfairness of institutions, not individuals.

The identification of opportunism with individual immorality, at least in law, was achieved at the hands of Benjamin Cardozo. In *The Nature of the Judicial Process*, Cardozo wrote:

> The principles of the Constitution must be preserved at all hazards, in all their pristine vigor and purity, and the language in which they are expressed given its plain and obvious meaning and true intent, uninfluenced by any spirit of expediency or opportunism.[48]

Cardozo places opportunism in contradistinction to the rule of law. Unlike the earlier cases, however, it is not the institutions of law (in this instance, the Constitution) that are portrayed as opportunistic, but rather those who would manipulate those institutions, presumably for self-gain. From this point forward, with the exception of occasional references to 'opportunistic diseases',[49] most judicial opinions in which 'opportunism' appears to associate the word with a moral failing of an individual.

These early references to opportunism contain the seeds of a theory of the role of legal regulation. Like entropy in nature, opportunism in human relations threatens to create chaos. Legal rules establish order, and the

[44] ibid.

[45] *Mallon v Buster & Allin*, 89 SW 257 (Ky App 1905).

[46] *Maurice H Cook v American Tubing & Webbing Company*, 65 A 641, 644 (RI 1906).

[47] *State ex rel Hartley v Innes*, 118 SW 1168 (Mo App 1909); see also *Holddsworth v Shannon*, 21 SW 85 (Mo 1893).

[48] B Cardozo, *The Nature of the Judicial Process* (New Haven, Yale University Press, 1921) 92–93.

[49] See, eg *Chevron USA v Echazabel*, 122 S Ct 2045, 2052 fn 5 (2002); *Doe v County of Centre, PA*, 242 F 3d 437, 441–42 (3d Cir 2001).

institutions of law – most importantly, the courts, which interpret constitutions, statutes, prior judicial opinions, and various products of private lawmaking (including contracts and corporate charters) – must remain faithful to those legal rules if the forces of opportunism are to be defeated.

Unfortunately, this theory of legal regulation is burdened by the taint of tautology as well as a prickly practical problem. The tautology is subtle and rests on the fact that our conception of 'law' has changed since the time of Cardozo. If 'law' were separate from the decisions of judges, then a conception of opportunism that depended on adherence to law might make sense. On the other hand, if every judicial decision *created* law, adherence to law would follow inevitably from the decision.

Even if one does not embrace this radical notion of the interpretive process, one might observe this conceptual hurdle in areas where an understanding of opportunism is most important, that is, in the standards of last resort. For example, when a court is asked to decide whether someone has acted in good faith, measuring adherence to an established duty is notoriously difficult. In many cases, the 'law' governing the case is unclear, and defining that law effectively decides the case. In these circumstances, the judge must import evidence about what constitutes good faith.

III. FLEXIBLE STANDARDS

While some boundaries on self-interest are susceptible to detailed specification ex ante,[50] Macaulay endorsed 'a contact law with strong elements of flexibility and qualitative norms'.[51] The doctrines of last resort are examples of this sort of flexibility.

Over the past few decades, legal discourse has been greatly influenced by economic thought, particularly the work of transaction cost economists, who embrace the concept of opportunism. The most quoted definition of opportunism belongs to Oliver Williamson, who characterised it as 'a condition of self-interest seeking with guile'.[52] The distinctive feature of this definition is the notion of 'guile', which Williamson describes as 'lying, stealing, cheating, and calculated efforts to mislead, distort, disguise, obfuscate, or otherwise confuse'.[53] In the more recent economic literature, opportunism is typically condensed into 'shirking' and 'cheating'.[54]

[50] R Scott, 'The Rise and Fall of Article 2' (2002) 62 *Louisiana Law Review* 1009, 1021 fn 32.

[51] Macaulay, 'The Real and Paper Deal' (n 10) 63–64.

[52] O Williamson, *Markets and Hierarchies: Analysis and Antitrust Implications* (New York, The Free Press, 1975) 6.

[53] O Williamson, *The Economic Institutions of Capitalism* (New York, The Free Press, 1985) 47.

[54] See D Nagin and others, 'Monitoring, Motivation and Management: The Determinants of Opportunistic Behavior in a Field Experiment' (2002) 92 *The American Economic Review* 850, 852.

For the lawyer, 'shirking' and 'cheating' appear as conclusions that imply the existence of some baseline of comparison. A person whose actions deviate from the actions required in a contract, statute, or regulation, therefore, may be shirking or cheating, and we have no trouble imposing liability on such a person. The more difficult – and more interesting – questions arise in contexts where the baseline is unclear. Behaviours not prohibited by applicable contracts, statutes and regulations may nevertheless be opportunistic. Ambiguity is not a license to act capriciously. Instead, we demand 'good faith', 'loyalty' and 'justice.' In drawing lines for these marginal cases we perceive the structure and intent of the law to regulate self-interested behaviour, and, although the doctrines of last resort allow for contextual contract interpretation, the results are still more or less 'reckonable'.[55]

CONCLUSION

What good is contract law? Much of the law governing contractual relationships is animated by the desire to distinguish the appropriate pursuit of self-interest from the inappropriate pursuit of self-interest. In the absence of statutes, regulations or other publicly enacted laws, courts prefer to leave the definition of that boundary to the contracting parties, and self-interested behaviour is often constrained by the express terms of a deal. But the ultimate issue in many litigated cases is whether self-interest may be checked in the absence of such terms. In these cases, courts often determine the boundaries of the appropriate pursuit of self-interest by using the doctrines of last resort.

Although contract law is not well equipped to regulate the give and take that typifies most contractual relationships, standards such as the duty of good faith and fair dealing, fiduciary duty and unjust enrichment, can facilitate transacting by establishing the boundaries of opportunism. These doctrines are most helpful in circumstances when social sanctions are least effective, namely, when the potential for gain from deviating from expectations is greatest.

BIBLIOGRAPHY

Cardozo, B, *The Nature of the Judicial Process* (New Haven, Yale University Press, 1921).

Coase, R, 'The Conduct of Economics: The Example of Fisher Body General Motors' (2006) 15 *Journal of Economics & Management Strategy* 255.

[55] K Llewellyn, *The Common Law Tradition: Deciding Appeals* (Boston, Little Brown & Co, 1960) 4.

Crocker, K and Reynolds, K, 'The Efficiency of Incomplete Contracts: An Empirical Analysis of Air Force Engine Procurement' (1993) 24 *Rand Journal of Economics* 126.

Danzig, R, *The Capability Problem in Contract Law* (Mineola, Foundation Press, 1978).

De Soto, H, *The Mystery of Capital: Why Capitalism Triumphs in the West and Fails Everywhere Else* (New York, Basic Books, 2000).

Esser, J, 'Institutionalizing Industry: The Changing Forms of Contract' (1996) 21 *Law & Social Inquiry* 593 (1996).

Hadfield, G and Božović, I, 'Scaffolding: Using Formal Contracts to Build Informal Relations to Support Innovation' (2012) USC Law and Economics Research Papers Series No C12-3/USC Legal Studies Research Papers Series No 12-6.

Hart, O, *Firms, Contracts & Financial Structure* (Oxford, Oxford University Press, 1995).

Hurst, JW, *Law and the Conditions of Freedom in the Nineteenth Century United States* (Madison, University of Wisconsin Press, 1956).

Klein, B, Crawford, R and Alchian, A, 'Vertical Integration, Appropriable Rents, and the Competitive Contracting Process' (1978) *21 Journal of Law & Economics* 297.

Kolko, G, *The Triumph of Conservatism: A Reinterpretation of American History, 1900–1916* (New York, The Free Press, 1963).

La Porta, R, Lopez-de-Silanes, F and Shleifer, A, 'The Economic Consequences of Legal Origins' (2008) 46 *Journal of Economic Literature* 285.

Llewellyn, K, *The Common Law Tradition: Deciding Appeals* (Boston, Little Brown & Co, 1960).

Macaulay, S, 'The Real and Paper Deal: Empirical Pictures of Relationships, Complexity and the Urge for Transparent Rules' (2003) 66 *Modern Law Review* 44.

——, 'Elegant Models, Empirical Pictures, and The Complexities of Contract' (1977) 11 *Law & Society Review* 508.

——, 'Non-Contractual Relations in Business: A Preliminary Study' (1963) 28 *American Sociological Review* 55.

Markovits, D, 'Contact and Collaboration' (2004) 113 *Yale Law Journal* 1417.

Nagin, D and others, 'Monitoring, Motivation and Management: The Determinants of Opportunistic Behavior in a Field Experiment' (2002) 92 *The American Economic Review* 850.

Nelson, W, *The Common Law in Colonial America – Volume I, The Chesapeake and New England, 1607–1660* (Oxford, Oxford University Press, 2008).

North, D, *Institutions, Institutional Change and Economic Performance* (Cambridge, Cambridge University Press, 1990).

Ohnesorge, J, 'The Rule of Law' (2007) 3 *Annual Review of Law and Social Science* 99.

Oxford English Dictionary (Oxford, Clarendon Press, 1970).

Pistor, K and Xu, C, 'Incomplete Law' (2003) 35 *New York University Journal of International Law and Policy* 931.

Scott, R, 'The Rise and Fall of Article 2' (2002) 62 *Louisiana Law Review* 1009.

——, 'The Case for Formalism in Relational Contract' (2000) 94 *Northwestern University Law Review* 847.

Schwartz, A and Scott, R, 'Contract Theory and the Limits of Contract Law' (2003) 113 *Yale Law Journal* 541.

Simon, H, 'Rationality as Process and as Product of Thought' (1978) 68 *The American Economic Review* 1.

——, 'Theories of Decision-Making in Economics and Behavioral Science' (1959) 49 *The American Economic Review* 253.

——, 'A Behavioral Model of Rational Choice' (1955) 69 *The Quarterly Journal of Economics* 99.

——, 'A Formal Theory of the Employment Relationship' (1951) 19 *Econometrica* 293.

Smith, DG, 'The Critical Resource Theory of Fiduciary Duty' (2002) 55 *Vanderbilt Law Review* 1399.

Smith, DG, 'Team Production in Venture Capital Investing' (1999) 24 *Journal of Corporate Law* 949.

Smith, DG and King, B, 'Contracts as Organizations' (2009) 51 *Arizona Law Review* 1.

Suchman, M, 'The Contract as Social Artifact' (2003) 37 *Law & Society Review* 91.

Weber, M, Ross,G and Wittich, C (eds), *Economy and Society*, vol 2 (Berkeley, University of California Press, 1978 reissue; originally published 1914).

Williamson, O, *Markets and Hierarchies: Analysis and Antitrust Implications* (New York, The Free Press, 1975).

Williamson, O, *The Economic Institutions of Capitalism* (New York, The Free Press, 1985).

Index